INTERNATIONAL LESSON COMMENTARY

The Standard in Biblical Exposition

Based on the
International Sunday
School Lessons (ISSL)

Victor®
The Bible Teacher's Teacher

COOK COMMUNICATIONS MINISTRIES
Colorado Springs, Colorado • Paris, Ontario
KINGSWAY COMMUNICATIONS LTD
Eastbourne, England

Victor® is an imprint of
Cook Communications Ministries, Colorado Springs, CO 80918
Cook Communications, Paris, Ontario
Kingsway Communications, Eastbourne, England

THE NIV INTERNATIONAL BIBLE LESSON COMMENTARY

© 2007 Cook Communications Ministries

First printing, 2007
Printed in U.S.A.
1 2 3 4 5 6 7 8 9 10   Printing/Year   10 09 08 07

Editor: Daniel Lioy, Ph.D.
Editorial Manager: Doug Schmidt
Cover Design: Ray Moore/Two Moore Design
Cover Photo: © 2000-2006 PhotoSpin, Inc.

ISBN: 0781445035

God Created a People

God's Call to the Christian Community

God, the People, and the Covenant

Images of Christ

A Word to the Teacher

In Paul's farewell address to the Ephesian elders, he said he had not hesitated to proclaim to them "the whole will of God" (Acts 20:27). Expressed differently, though the apostle used tact and discernment, he never tried to conceal any of the truths associated with the Gospel. This especially included the Father's redemptive purpose and plan through His Son, the Lord Jesus Christ.

As a Sunday school teacher, it is also your privilege to teach the whole counsel of God's Word. Sometimes you will discuss a positive topic, such as the promises the Lord made to His people. On other occasions, you will present a less pleasant theme, such as the judgment of God on the rebellious.

Regardless of the subject matter being taught, your job as a Sunday school teacher is eternally relevant. After all, you are not just giving the students important biblical information. God is also using you to be an agent of change in their lives. This is an awesome responsibility, and one that I know you take seriously.

As you purpose to teach God's Word to your students, take a few moments to think about what He has done and is doing through you. Pray that your students will discover that the Scriptures are as relevant today as they were thousands of years ago. Then, watch in fascination as they discover that the Lord is both merciful and just. May God richly bless you as you share the riches of His truth with your students!

Your fellow learner at the feet of the Master Teacher,
Dan Lioy

Use *The NIV International Bible Lesson Commentary* with Materials from These Publishers

Sunday school materials from the following denominations and publishers follow International Sunday School Lesson outlines (sometimes known as Uniform Series). Because *The NIV International Bible Lesson Commentary* (formerly *Peloubet's*) follows the same outlines, you can use *The NIV International Bible Lesson Commentary* as an excellent teacher resource to supplement the materials from these publishing houses.

NONDENOMINATIONAL:

Standard Publishing: *Adult*

Urban Ministries

Echoes Teacher's Commentary (*Cook Communications Ministries*) : *Adult*

DENOMINATIONAL:

Advent Christian General Conference: *Adult*

American Baptist *(Judson Press): Adult*

United Holy Church of America: *Adult*

Church of God in Christ *(Church of God in Christ Publishing House): Adult*

Church of Christ Holiness: *Adult*

Church of God *(Warner Press): Adult*

Church of God by Faith: *Adult*

National Baptist Convention of America *(Boyd): All ages*

National Primitive Baptist Convention: *Adult*

Progressive National Baptist Convention: *Adult*

Presbyterian Church *(U.S.A.) (Bible Discovery Series—Presbyterian Publishing House or P.R.E.M.): Adult*

Union Gospel Press: *All ages*

United Holy Church of America: *Adult*

United Methodist *(Cokesbury): All ages*

God Created the Heavens and the Earth

DEVOTIONAL READING

Psalm 8

DAILY BIBLE READINGS

Monday August 27
Psalm 8 God the Creator

Tuesday August 28
Genesis 1:1-5 The First Day

Wednesday August 29
Genesis 1:6-8 The Sky

Thursday August 30
Genesis 1:9-13 The First Harvest

Friday August 31
Genesis 1:14-19 The Sun and Moon

Saturday September 1
Genesis 1:20-23 The Birds and Sea Creatures

Sunday September 2
Genesis 1:24-25 The Animals

Scripture

Background Scripture: *Genesis 1:1-25*
Scripture Lesson: *Genesis 1:1-6, 8, 10, 12-15, 19-20, 22-23, 25*
Key Verses: *In the beginning God created the heavens and the earth. Now the earth was formless and empty, darkness was over the surface of the deep, and the Spirit of God was hovering over the waters.* Genesis 1:1-2.
Scripture Lesson for Children: *Genesis 1:1-6, 8-11, 13, 16, 19, 21, 23*
Key Verse for Children: *God saw that it was good.* Genesis 1:10.

Lesson Aim

To explore the implications of believing in God as the Creator of all things.

Lesson Setting

Time: *The dawn of human history*
Place: *Earth*

Lesson Outline

God Created the Heavens and the Earth

    I. Forming the Creation: Genesis 1:1-6, 8

        A. *The Primordial Earth: vss. 1-2*

        B. *The First Creation Day: vss. 3-5*

        C. *The Second Creation Day: vss. 6*

        D. *The Third Creation Day: vss.*

    II. Filling the Creation: Genesis 22-23, 25

        A. *The Fourth Creation D*

        B. *The Fifth Creation D*

        C. *The Sixth Creation*

7

Introduction for Adults

Topic: *How Is Creation Possible?*

With fantastic precision and intricacy, our world, as it has for millennia, carries on its macro and micro functions, as we live, love, work, and die here; but what does it all mean? If we have come to believe that the world and its contents are the result of mere chance, then there is no reason to consider its meaning at all. Life exists for no particular reason—it just is, period.

If, however, we have determined that there must be a Creator who purposed to make our world and who put us in it, suddenly there are issues of significance and meaning to consider; and if we believe that the God of the Bible is that Creator, then we can understand, at least in part, His heart and mind concerning His purpose for creation as well as His desire for its eternal future.

Introduction for Youth

Topic: *Starting Line*

"Why did God make that?" The look on his face matched the wonder in his voice. "That" was the largest, ugliest spider ever encountered by my then-four-year-old son.

The spider had taken up residency in our yard that summer, moving its mammoth web from place to place. My son kept a keen eye out for it. Although the web was a marvel to look at when the sun glinted on its intricately woven threads, the spider creeping across it was nightmare material.

God, like our backyard guest, has spun an intricate web; but God's weaving of creation is a true marvel. His web still stands, a testimony to the One who made ~~ᵃ~~ verification that both it and He are "very good" (Gen. 1:31). Unlike our scary ~~~~ God does not stand ready to devour prey. He waits to embrace His chil-

~~~~ildren

~~~~e World

~~~~ted the heavens and the earth because He loves us.

~~~~d did anything, He said what He would create.

~~~~ of each day of creation, God said that what He had done was good.

~~~~d His goodness on all He created.

~~~~ God for His goodness to us.

Lesson Commentary

I. FORMING THE CREATION: GENESIS 1:1-6, 8, 10, 12-13

A. The Primordial Earth: vss. 1-2

In the beginning God created the heavens and the earth. Now the earth was formless and empty, darkness was over the surface of the deep, and the Spirit of God was hovering over the waters.

The Bible begins with God and His creative activity. Genesis, like the rest of the Bible, does not try to prove God's existence; it assumes that He exists. Genesis, after all, was written for a people who already believed in God. Other ancient cultures had their own creation stories involving their many gods. Genesis tells about the creation of all things by the one true God.

Three Hebrew terms are used in the Genesis account to speak of God's creative work. The word used in 1:1 means to make something new. There it refers to the creation of the universe from nothing (sometimes referred to by the Latin phrase *ex nihilo*). A different Hebrew term described the creative action in verse 25. This word means "to fashion." Unlike the previous term, this one indicates the shaping of something that already existed. God first brought the universe into being and then used this material to fashion His creatures. A third term for God's creative work is used in verse 24, which says that the land would "produce" living creatures according to their kinds. In the original, it literally means "to cause to come forth."

The Hebrew word for "God" in Genesis 1:1 is *Elohim*, a widely used plural form emphasizing God's majesty and power. The word allows for the Trinity without falling into the trap of polytheism (belief in many gods). We are not told when the triune God began His work, just that it was "in the beginning." God has always existed (Ps. 90:2). The heavens and the earth, however, had a definite beginning point in time.

In Hebrew speech, pairs of opposites were often used to express totality. In Psalm 139:2, for example, David's phrase "You know when I sit and when I rise" means God knew everything about David. Similarly, the phrase "the heavens and the earth" in Genesis 1:1 means that God created all things—spiritual beings, physical beings, matter, energy, time, and space.

In the Genesis account, it's helpful to remember that God is involved in but distinct from His creation. People have often made the mistake of worshiping parts of creation rather than the Creator Himself. We shouldn't try to appreciate a great painting without considering the painter, and neither should we fail to recognize God as the master designer of the universe.

Verse 2 reveals that in its early stage, the earth was "formless and empty," a phrase that translates the rhyming Hebrew words *tohu wabohu*. The idea is that the earth was chaotic, not ordered; and because the earth was barren, God would spend the days of Creation forming and filling it.

According to a view called the gap theory, an extended period of time passed between the events of verse 1 and those of verse 2. First, God created the heavens and the earth. Later, as a byproduct of Satan's rebellion against God, the earth was converted to a formless state. Then God re-created it. Those who reject the gap theory declare that the temporarily formless state of the earth need not be considered in negative terms. God simply chose to create by beginning with formless matter and then giving it form. Thus, there was only one creation.

Verse 2 refers to the water on the surface of the earth. Water is shapeless; it is the same all over. Water suggests the formlessness of the earth in its early stage. Moreover, "darkness was over the surface of the deep." This was so because, according to the events of Creation week, God had not yet brought the sun and the other celestial lights into existence. Meanwhile, the Spirit of God was "hovering" over the waters of the earth. The Spirit was like a mother bird brooding over her eggs. Here we see that God was about to bring forth life on His new world.

The same Hebrew term rendered "was hovering" in verse 2 is used in Deuteronomy 32:11 to speak of an eagle that "hovers" over the nest when it stirs up the young. The picture Scripture paints is not one in which God sets the universe in motion and passively allows natural forces to operate, but one in which He is directly involved in every aspect of Creation.

B. The First Creation Day: vss. 3-5

And God said, "Let there be light," and there was light. God saw that the light was good, and he separated the light from the darkness. God called the light "day," and the darkness he called "night." And there was evening, and there was morning—the first day.

The biblical account reveals that the universe has not always existed and that it did not come into existence through natural and impersonal forces; instead, God created the heavens and the earth in a miraculous way. For instance, Genesis 1:3 indicates that the one true and living God simply issued His command—"Let there be light"—and it was so. Since it was not until the fourth day of creation that God brought the sun into existence (vss. 14–19), the light present during the first three days did not correspond to what is presently known.

The "light" mentioned in verse 3 contrasts sharply with the "darkness" noted in verse 2. God's provision of light is the first step in the process of bringing order out of chaos and making the earth hospitable for humans. Indeed, during the third day of creation, as God reflected on the light He had commanded into existence, He concluded that it was "good" (Gen. 1:4). In this case, the light served God's benevolent purposes, especially in enabling humanity to fulfill its divinely ordained role in the world. From a broader biblical perspective, light is conducive for life— especially in terms of promoting, enhancing, or producing such—and thus meets with God's approval.

The divine is so sovereign in His rule that He even makes the darkness conform to His will (Ps. 104:19-26). For example, in the creation account, He "separated the light from the darkness" (Gen. 1:4). In this context, light and darkness, while distinct from one another, coexist together in harmony. In later biblical usage, they become mutually exclusive and incompatible entities (see John 1:5; 1 John 1:5-7).

According to Genesis 1:5, God identified the light as "day" and the darkness as "night." Also, the first day of creation was marked by the passage of "evening" and "morning." In fact, six of the seven days are closed out in this way and parallel the Hebrew manner of reckoning time. The idea is that night (which is between evening and morning) ends the day. Then, with the appearance of dawn's first light, a new day begins, along with the new creative possibilities it brings.

There are differing views regarding how literally or figuratively the creation days should be understood. Some conjecture that the days of creation refer to prolonged epochs or ages of time; but the ordering of the week in Exodus 20:8-11 undermines this view. Others think the Creation days should be taken as literal, sequential, 24-hour time periods. After all, God's creation of the universe involved the immediate appearance of complex physical entities.

In recent years, experts have noted that the days of creation form a rhythmical structure around which the Genesis narrative is arranged. When the text is read in a straightforward manner, one senses that the narrative has a dramatic and poetic literary quality. Here one finds that Moses neither described *all* that happened nor explained *how* it happened; instead, he unambiguously stated *what* happened, and he did so with an awareness of God's sovereignty over time as Creator.

C. The Second Creation Day: vss. 6, 8

And God said, "Let there be an expanse between the waters to separate water from water." . . . God called the expanse "sky." And there was evening, and there was morning—the second day.

God's next royal decree resulted in an "expanse" (Gen. 1:6) being created. The Hebrew term denotes an inanimate piece of metal that has been hammered flat. From the perspective of people on earth, such an expanse may have appeared as a hard and shiny barrier that could not be permeated. This vault in the sky was so solidly constructed that it ably separated the waters residing above (which fell from the clouds as rain) from the rivers, seas, and subterranean waters (the last of which came up from the earth).

The Creator-King's act of separating the waters above from the waters below was an act of imposing order upon them; indeed, what God commanded occurred just as He had intended (vs. 7). Then He called the dome-like expanse "sky" (vs. 8). God's naming activity drew attention to His dominion over this aspect of the cosmos and brought an end to the second day in the creation sequence.

D. The Third Creation Day: vss. 10, 12-13

God called the dry ground "land," and the gathered waters he called "seas." And God saw that it was good. . . . The land produced vegetation: plants bearing seed according to their kinds and trees bearing fruit with seed in it according to their kinds. And God saw that it was good. And there was evening, and there was morning—the third day.

At first water covered the entire planet; but then on the third day of creation God separated dry ground and surface water, resulting in land and seas (Gen. 1:9). The dry land was like an island surrounded by and floating upon water. Also, lakes and rivers on the land flowed back into the seas. God called the dry ground "land" (vs. 10; literally, "earth"), and the waters that were gathered together He called "seas." These series of developments were "good" in His eyes because they were conducive to life.

After God decreed the dry land into existence, He commanded the land to produce "vegetation" (vs. 11) in abundance. This included grass and seed-bearing plants as well as trees characterized by seed-bearing fruit. The seeds from each of these, in turn, would produce the appropriate kinds of seeds and plants. All of this occurred as God intended. The Creator-King regarded the fertility of the planet's vegetation to be "good" (vs. 12) because it produced and enhanced life, especially in providing food for air and land creatures, most notably humans (see vss. 29-30). Thus ended the third day of creation (vs. 13).

II. FILLING THE CREATION: GENESIS 1:14-15, 19-20, 22-23, 25

A. The Fourth Creation Day: vss. 14-15, 19

And God said, "Let there be lights in the expanse of the sky to separate the day from the night, and let them serve as signs to mark seasons and days and years, and let them be lights in the expanse of the sky to give light on the earth." And it was so. . . . And there was evening, and there was morning— the fourth day.

On the fourth day of creation, God decreed that there be bright lights in the expanse of the sky to create a separation of the day from the night. Throughout the ancient Near East, people worshiped and feared a pantheon of deities. Among these, the sun and moon would have been foremost in the constellation.

In contrast, the Genesis account reveals that the luminaries were to serve as signs to mark off the seasons, days, and years (Gen. 1:14). It is also possible that the sun and moon serve as visual reminders of the power and majesty of God. Moreover, both functions would help people of faith as they worshiped the one true God during their regularly occurring religious celebrations and festivals.

In verse 15, Moses depicted the luminaries as entities that the great King of creation used for His bidding (see Isa. 40:26). Furthermore, in Genesis 1:16, Moses did not even name these entities, instead indirectly referring to them as "two great lights." In particular, the "greater light" (the sun) illumined the planet during the daytime, while the "lesser light" (the moon) illumined the globe at night.

In ancient Near Eastern beliefs, these sorts of duties were assigned to pagan deities, but in the Genesis account, Israel's one God remained firmly in control when He issued His decrees. We learn that He sovereignly assigned the sun, moon, and stars to their respective roles, as His subordinates, to give light to the inhabitants of the planet (Gen. 1:17), to mark off the seasons of the calendar, and to separate the light from the darkness (vs. 18). What God enjoined on the fourth day of creation met with His approval. It was "good," for it promoted life. Thus ended the fourth day of creation (vs. 19).

This separation of responsibilities can be seen in the remaining portions of the days of creation. For instance, just as the luminaries governed the day and night (Ps. 136:7–9), so too the birds and fish ruled over the sky and sea (respectively). Correspondingly, animals and humans exercised control over the land and its vegetation. Above all, people had responsibility for the entire planet.

B. The Fifth Creation Day: vss. 20, 22-23

And God said, "Let the water teem with living creatures, and let birds fly above the earth across the expanse of the sky." . . . God blessed them and said, "Be fruitful and increase in number and fill the water in the seas, and let the birds increase on the earth." And there was evening, and there was morning—the fifth day.

At the start of the fifth creation day, God focused His attention on water and sky (created on the second day). He decreed that the sea bring forth swarms of aquatic creatures (both fish and other forms of life), while the expanse of the sky was to be filled with flying creatures of every kind (Gen. 1:20). The emphasis is on the rapid increase of these creatures. Fertility and fruitfulness characterized their existence.

As verse 21 reveals, God created the great sea creatures and subjected them to His unchallengeable rule. He also created all the living creatures that swarmed in the ocean and every kind of bird that filled the sky. When God reflected on what He had brought into existence, He determined that it was beneficial for enabling life on earth to flourish.

Accordingly, God "blessed" (vs. 22) all these creatures. The Hebrew term conveys the idea of endowing something with productivity or fruitfulness. In this case, God gave the sea and air creatures the ability to reproduce for the purpose of ruling over their respective realms. In fact, His declaration of blessing ensured their success. Thus with that the fifth day of creation ended (vs. 23).

C. The Sixth Creation Day: vs. 25

God made the wild animals according to their kinds, the livestock according to their kinds, and all the creatures that move along the ground according to their kinds. And God saw that it was good.

At the beginning of the sixth day, God populated the land, seas, and vegetation (created on the third day) with land animals and humans (Gen. 1:24). The narrative, based on the information appearing in the fifth and sixth days of creation, divided the animal world into three categories—sky, water, and land creatures. They in turn governed the realms they populated—sky, water, and land. Fittingly, the priests of Israel would later use these same categories to make a distinction between clean and unclean animals (Lev. 11:1–19).

All the assorted species mentioned in Genesis 1:25, regardless of kind or size, were the work of God's hand and He declared them to be "good." Although His work was not yet finished, what He had created so far was perfect. In addition, He provided for and sustained this vast array of creatures in such a way that they were able to flourish.

Discussion Questions

1. What was the Spirit of God doing at the dawn of time?
2. How is the power of God evident in commanding the light and darkness into existence?
3. In what sense was the sky, water, and land that God brought into existence good?
4. What categories of creatures were brought into existence after the earth was formed?
5. What purpose do the air, land, and sea creatures serve in God's creation?

Contemporary Application

I vividly recall the night when, as an adult, I experienced the most wonderful sense of God's creativity I had enjoyed since early childhood. Strangely enough, it happened on the hood of a 1974 Pontiac Catalina. It was an early August night, and the stars were already standing out from a deep black background. I decided to while away an hour or two just lying on my car hood, watching the sky.

Suddenly, a ball of light streaked across the sky from right to left, high above me; and then another did the same thing. Soon the sky was filled with shooting yellow-red balls of light that seemed impossibly close. I held my breath, my eyes wide open with amazement. "Thank you, Father," I said over and over.

The next day I learned that I had witnessed the annual Perseid meteor shower, named for the constellation Perseus, which is in the area of the sky where the shooting stars appear. According to one expert, Perseus is a beautiful group of stars in the Milky Way galaxy. I cannot speak for the constellation, but its meteor off-spring are breathtaking.

Amazingly, we do not have to look to the sky to see God's handiwork in nature. Our world is a living testament to the goodness in creation, imperfect though it has become due to the Fall. Whether we are digging dirt, wading in surf, or listening to bird songs, every day brings countless reminders of God's incredible creativity. When the Lord Himself stepped back and saw all that He had made, He declared it to be very good (Gen. 1:31). No one should doubt for a moment that it is.

When we truly understand that God created the universe, we feel deeply awed by His power and greatness; and when we realize that He has given us a special place in His created order—a place of distinction and close relationship with Him—we can feel deeply honored and loved.

God Created Humankind

Scripture

Background Scripture: *Genesis 1:26—2:3*

Scripture Lesson: *Genesis 1:26-31*

Key Verse: *Then God said, "Let us make man in our image, in our likeness, and let them rule over . . . over all the creatures that move along the ground."* Genesis 1:26.

Scripture Lesson for Children: *Genesis 1:24-31; 2:2*

Key Verse for Children: *God created man in his own image . . . male and female he created them.* Genesis 1:27.

Lesson Aim

To recognize that God, the all-powerful Creator, cares for His most valuable creation—people.

Lesson Setting

Time: *The dawn of human history*

Place: *Earth*

Lesson Outline

God Created Humankind

   I. The Creation of Humankind: Genesis 1:26-27
      A. *The Divine Decree: vs. 26*
      B. *The Divine Act: vs. 27*
  II. The Blessing of Humankind: Genesis 1:28-31
      A. *The Divine Command: vs. 28*
      B. *The Divine Provision: vss. 29-30*
      C. *The Divine Assessment: vs. 31*

Introduction for Adults

Topic: *Why Are We Here?*

The world has a way of dominating our time, and it tries to shape our desires and values; but as Christians, we are wise to step back and ask why God made us. What does He desire of us? Also, how can we strengthen our faith in Him and not be stunted by the world's values? Meditating on God our Creator is a step in the right direction in recognizing the true reason for our being special in His eyes.

As each generation does this, they discover new wealth in God's creation and just how special humankind is to be overseers of it. These discoveries show how prolific are the mighty acts of God; but each discovery brings new challenges and responsibilities. The more God gives to us as His beloved creatures, the greater our responsibility to exercise wise stewardship according to His commands recorded in Scripture.

Introduction for Youth

Topic: *In Whose Image?*

Advertisers pandering to youth outdo themselves to make their products more attractive than their competitors'. For example, when we consider teen fashions, we can see how important it is for adolescents to stand out in a crowd; yet no matter how impressive our clothes, computers, and cars might be, they are nothing compared to the magnificence of God's creation. We need to be careful, lest we lose sight of God's glory in the welter of things that are supposed to make us happy.

Our greatest failure seems to be our lack of gratitude. Simply put, we take God's gifts for granted. Many times we do not even acknowledge His daily provision of our needs. This is sad, for we could not survive long without the air we breathe, the food we eat, or the water we drink, all of which come from God. Even the essence of what makes us human comes from God, who created us to be like Himself.

In addition to Genesis 1:26-31, Psalm 8 reminds us that God is supremely praiseworthy. Wherever we look, we find reasons to praise Him. Most of all, when we consider what He has done for us in Christ, we should submit to Him as our Lord. After all, He's the Author of life, whether physical or spiritual in nature.

Concepts for Children

Topic: *God Created People*

1. God created people to be like Himself.
2. God told the man and woman He created to take care of the earth.
3. God's creation of the man and woman was the high point of what He had done.
4. God said that everything He had created was very good.
5. God wants us to remember that it is because of Him that we have life.

Lesson Commentary

I. THE CREATION OF HUMANKIND: GENESIS 1:26-27

A. The Divine Decree: vs. 26

Then God said, "Let us make man in our image, in our likeness, and let them rule over the fish of the sea and the birds of the air, over the livestock, over all the earth, and over all the creatures that move along the ground."

Bringing humankind into existence was the final and climactic act of God. Genesis 1:26 begins with the Creator-King decreeing, "Let us make." There are various explanations for the use of the plural here. Some consider this to be a hint of the Trinity, namely, a plurality within the divine unity of the Father, Son, and Spirit. Another possibility is that the Hebrew signifies either a plural of majesty (for example, the royal "we") or a situation in which God addresses the statement to Himself.

A third group proposes that God and His heavenly angelic court are in view (see Isa. 6:8). In this case, while the latter are included in the statement, it is God who actually brings humankind into existence. It is not clear, however, in what sense the cosmic attendants possess the divine "image" and participate in God's creation activity. Some conjecture that the assembly of heavenly beings governs the world and communicates with humanity under God's royal authority.

The broader context of verses 26 and 27 makes it clear that the Hebrew noun *adam* (translated "man") refers to the male and female genders of the species. Additionally, only human beings are created in the divine image. For that reason they are distinguished from the rest of the creatures God brings into existence. Accordingly, all members of the human race bear the "image" (vs. 26; Hebrew, *selem*) and "likeness" (Hebrew, *demut*) of God (who Himself has no gender; see John 4:24). *Selem* is typically used in reference to such replicas as models, statues, and images; and *demut* is derived word that means "to be like" or "to resemble." In Genesis 1:26, the two terms seem virtually synonymous in meaning.

God gave humans the capacity and authority to govern creation as His ruling representatives. Their jurisdiction extended to the fish in the sea, the birds in the sky, and animals on the land (whether small or large, wild or domesticated). The mandate for people to govern the world as benevolent vice-regents of the true and living God is a reflection of His image in them (see Gen. 9:2; Ps. 8:5-8; Heb. 2:5-9). By ruling over the rest of creation in a responsible fashion, people bear witness to the divine likeness placed within humanity. Also, as they mediate God's presence, they make His will a reality on earth.

These statements should not be taken as permission to exploit and ravage either the environment or its inhabitants, including other humans. After all, people are not the owners of creation, but rather stewards who are accountable to their divine Owner. While they have jurisdiction over animals and plants (Gen. 1:28-29), they exercise no authority over cosmic entities and forces (Eph. 6:10-12). Moreover, because all people bear the image of God, they have sanctity and innate worth. Correspondingly, they are to be treated with dignity and respect.

B. The Divine Act: vs. 27

So God created man in his own image, in the image of God he created him; male and female he created them.

What God decreed in Genesis 1:26, He enacted in verse 27. As the sovereign King and Lord, He had the authority and ability to create human beings—both males and females—in His own image. Down through the centuries, people have debated what this means, with the varieties of views stressing either the nature or function of human life. Put another way, the divine likeness is either a special character (or quality) given to humans or a role (or task) entrusted to them.

Perhaps a combination of both views should be affirmed, especially that people somehow and in some way bear the image of God in both the material and immaterial aspects of their existence. This surely includes temporal (physical) life and for believers eternal life. Indeed, only the redeemed enjoy fellowship with the Lord as the object of His special love. The discussion about the divine likeness in humanity has also focused on the ability of people to reason, make ethical decisions, and exercise dominion. Possessing high mental abilities and behaving morally concern the nature of human life, while governing the rest of creation deals with the function of human life.

From a New Testament perspective, the spiritual character of the redeemed cannot be ignored. In short, becoming increasingly more like the Messiah is closely connected with bearing the image of God (Rom. 8:29; 2 Cor. 3:18; Eph. 4:22-24; Col. 3:9-10). Even within fallen humanity, though the image of God has been defaced through sin, people still bear the divine likeness to some degree (Gen. 5:1; 9:6; Jas. 3:9), and this sets them apart from the rest of earth's creatures.

Genesis 2 records a parallel account of God's creation of humankind; but unlike the first one, it focuses narrowly on the first humans and the special place the Lord prepared for them. Verse 7 says that God formed a man from the dust of the ground. The Hebrew term rendered "formed" was commonly used of a potter's work (for example, see Isa. 45:9). In a sense, the Lord was like a potter, and the first man was like a pot made of clay. The Hebrew noun translated "man" is *adam*. Here and in verse 20 the word could be translated either as "man" or as the name *Adam*. Also, there is a pun in verse 7, since the Hebrew for "man" (*adam*) sounds like and may be related to the Hebrew for "ground" (*adamah*).

In regard to his earthly body, Adam was much like the animals. Both he and they were formed out of the ground (compare 2:7 and 19). Likewise, the man had the breath of life in him just like the animals (compare 1:30 and 2:7). Adam became a "living being" (2:7) just as the animals were "living creatures" (1:20, 24)—the same words in Hebrew; yet Adam was also different from the animals because he was made in the image of God (1:27).

God had lovingly prepared a home for Adam. This was a garden occupying part of a place called "Eden" (2:8) in Mesopotamia. The name *Eden* means either "delight" or "a plain" (perhaps both). Moses clearly meant his readers to understand Eden as a real place, since he provided many geographical details. He named the rivers that flowed from Eden's river, along with lands watered by those rivers. He even mentioned some of the natural resources of those lands (vss. 10-14). Some of the names can no longer be linked with known geographic features, but we can guess that they were known at the time Genesis was written.

The Garden of Eden was a lovely place with abundant food; but Adam's stay there was no vacation. He was expected to tend the garden and care for it (vs. 15). Of course, the Lord never planned for Adam to be a loner, the only one of his kind (vs. 18). All along God intended to make a woman for Adam. Likewise, from the start marriage and the family were part of God's plan.

What Adam needed was a "helper suitable for him," and none could be found among the existing creatures God had made. The phrase rendered "suitable helper" (vs. 20) more literally means "a help as opposite him." This could only be a woman, not an animal. The man and the woman would correspond to one another. Expressed differently, they would complement and complete each other.

Verse 21 says that God caused a deep sleep to come over Adam, like anesthetic for an operation. The woman was not created from the dust as Adam had been. She was formed from a part of the man himself (vs. 22). Sharing the same life as Adam, the woman was fully a part of the human race the Lord had started. The woman, like the man, bore the image of God (1:27).

When Adam woke after his operation, God led the woman to him. Genesis 2:23 reveals that Adam was overjoyed to see her. The man recognized that here, finally, was his suitable life partner. In Hebrew, the noun rendered "woman" (*ishshah*) is as similar to the word for "man" (*ish*) that's found here as in English. Thus, it reflects the basic similarity between the first two humans.

Because men and women are made for each other, a man will leave his parents and be united to his wife and be physically intimate with her (vs. 24). Adam and Eve, the first members of the human race, were husband and wife from their initial moment together and remained united for life. Their marriage set a pattern for the marriages of their descendants.

II. THE BLESSING OF HUMANKIND: GENESIS 1:28-31

A. The Divine Command: vs. 28

God blessed them and said to them, "Be fruitful and increase in number; fill the earth and subdue it. Rule over the fish of the sea and the birds of the air and over every living creature that moves on the ground."

Creation stories that date to before the time of Abraham have been found inscribed on tablets in the ruins of Mesopotamian cities such as Babylon and

Nippur. Some scholars have especially noted the similarities between the Genesis account of Creation and one of these stories, known as the *Enuma Elish*, and concluded that the Genesis account is simply a retelling of this Babylonian story; however, when these two are closely studied, the uniqueness of the biblical account is apparent.

In the Babylonian tale, the god of creation is only one among many rival gods. Moreover, the creative activity of the god Marduk, the hero of the *Enuma Elish*, plays a relatively minor role in the story. The Genesis account, on the other hand, focuses on Creation to underscore the reality of God's sovereignty and the unique place that humanity holds in the created order. When the biblical account is compared with the *Enuma Elish* and the other creation myths written in Babylonia and Mesopotamia, the simplicity and monotheism of the Genesis description are unmatched; and there is no conclusive evidence to show that the Genesis account is actually a later story, instead of being the original account from which these others (though possibly recorded earlier) may have come.

Moses noted in Genesis 1:28 that God "blessed" the first man and woman, which means He endowed them (and their descendants) with the ability to flourish and be successful in serving as His vice-regents. Humanity's populating the world and bringing it under their control in a responsible fashion would be a testimony to God's blessing on their lives. In the time period of Moses, the focus would have been primarily agricultural. Such endeavors as domesticating animals, using trees to build homes, cultivating fields, and extracting mineral resources from the land would all be involved. Even today, as people use the resources of the environment in a sensible fashion, they are fulfilling God's original command to subdue the earth (see Ps. 8:5–8).

B.   The Divine Provision: vss. 29-30

Then God said, "I give you every seed-bearing plant on the face of the whole earth and every tree that has fruit with seed in it. They will be yours for food. And to all the beasts of the earth and all the birds of the air and all the creatures that move on the ground—everything that has the breath of life in it— I give every green plant for food." And it was so.

God permitted human beings to eat as food every seed-bearing plant on the earth's surface as well as every tree with seed in its fruit (Gen. 1:29). In addition, God allowed all the animals and birds to eat every green plant (whether grasses or grains) for food (vs. 30). These verses appear to say that only plants are good to eat, and that all animals were once exclusively plant eaters. (Some go so far as to say that birds, animals, and people originally were frugivores, namely, eating only the seeds of plants and trees.) When these verses are coupled with 9:3, in which God told Noah that all plants and animals were good to eat, some have concluded that until the time of Noah, all people were vegetarians.

Those verses, however, should not be pressed too far. All of what God made is later shown in Scripture to be good to eat (1 Tim. 4:3-5). While the Israelites at one time were given lists of animals to eat and not to eat (Lev. 11), in the New Testament Peter's vision showed him that nothing God has made should be declared unclean and not to be eaten (Acts 10:9-15).

C. The Divine Assessment: vs. 31

God saw all that he had made, and it was very good. And there was evening, and there was morning—the sixth day.

At several points during the creation week, God saw that His work was "good" (Gen. 1:4, 10, 12, 18, 21, 25). Then at the end God reflected upon what He had brought into existence and concluded that it was "very good" (vs. 31). In short, all that was necessary for life—in the totality of its rich array and diversity—to flourish was now in place. With that the sixth day of creation ended.

The earth was originally uninhabitable, being unformed and void (1:2). By the end of the creation week, God had made the planet a most hospitable place to live. In fact, as 2:1 states, the Creator-King had perfectly executed His will by bringing order and harmony to the universe—the heavens, the earth, and everything they contained, including the animate and inanimate entities populating the world.

It is fitting that on the seventh day of the creation week, God "rested" (vs. 2). The Hebrew verb is *sabat*, the root from which some maintain the noun *sabbat* (transliterated, "Sabbath") derives. *Sabat* conveys the idea of ceasing from one's work. In connection with the days of Creation, these establish the rhythms in which all of life exists.

With respect to God, He rested (in a manner of speaking) not because He was physically tired, but because there was nothing left that that needed to be created. The heavens and the earth did not need to be revamped or patched up to correct some deficiency. All that God had brought into existence by His royal decrees was flawless in every way. Thus it was fitting for Him to be enthroned in His place of rest as the sovereign Ruler of the universe.

According to verse 3, "God blessed the seventh day and made it holy" (vs. 3). Connected with this are Exodus 20:8-11, which focuses on God's creation of the world, and Deuteronomy 5:12-15, which focuses on the Lord's redemption of the Israelites out of slavery in Egypt. Both passages summon the people of God to imitate the pattern of work and rest established by the Lord of the universe. In this way, people of faith affirm God's rulership over all creation and the promise of rest—both temporal and eternal—for the redeemed.

Israel's entrance into Canaan was one major step in that process, though it did not completely fulfill God's promise (Josh. 1:13, 15; 21:43-45; 22:4). Also, the first advent of the Messiah affords believers the ongoing opportunity to partake of His salvation rest (Matt. 11:28-30). He can make this offer to them because He is Lord of the Sabbath (12:8).

Finally, at the Messiah's second advent, He will bring complete and final rest to all who have trusted in Him (Heb. 3:7—4:11). Even now they are the recipients of eternal life (John 3:16). Nevertheless, at the Messiah's return, they will enjoy unending physical life and more intimate fellowship with the triune God (John 17:3; Rev. 21:3-4).

Discussion Questions

1. Why is it important to see ourselves as being created in the image of God?
2. How should humans treat the animals of creation, over which people have dominion?
3. What are some ways that God's blessing is evident in the lives of His people?
4. How can people be wise stewards of the vegetation of the earth, over which they have responsibility?
5. What are some of the good things of God's creation for which we can praise Him?

Contemporary Application

The first man and woman were uniquely distinguished from the rest of the earth's creatures. They were created, in a fashion, to reflect God's image, to manage the new place He had made, to have the power to make moral choices, and especially to have a close relationship with Him. God's purpose for creation is met when we examine His handiwork and conclude, as He did when He created it, that it is good; and so He, too, must be good.

Louis XIV of France was the monarch who pompously called himself "Louis the Great" and made the famous statement "I am the state!" In his eyes, he had created something grand and glorious and deserved to be exalted. At the time of his death in 1715, his court was the most magnificent in Europe.

To dramatize his greatness, Louis XIV had given orders prior to his death that at the funeral, the cathedral was to be lit by a single candle set above his coffin. When that eventful day arrived, thousands of people packed into the cathedral. At the front lay Louis XIV's body in a golden coffin; and, per his instructions, a single candle had been placed above the coffin. The congregation sat in hushed silence. Then Bishop Massilon stood and began to speak. Slowly reaching down, he snuffed out the candle and said, "Only God is great!"

Massilon recognized that even the greatest human accomplishments are insignificant when compared to the actions of the infinite Creator of the universe. Measured against God's glory, majesty, and greatness, no human can lay claim to greatness. Louis XIV had built a government, but God had created the entire universe!

Abraham, Sarah, and Isaac

DEVOTIONAL READING
Isaiah 51:1-5

DAILY BIBLE READINGS

Monday September 10
Isaiah 51:1-5 Listen!

Tuesday September 11
Genesis 15:1-6 Abraham Believed

Wednesday September 12
Genesis 17:15-22 Abraham Doubted

Thursday September 13
Genesis 18:1-8 Abraham the Host

Friday September 14
Genesis 18:9-15 Sarah's Laughter

Saturday September 15
Genesis 21:1-8 Sarah's Joy

Sunday September 16
Hebrews 11:8-12 The Faith of Abraham

Scripture

Background Scripture: *Genesis 15:1-6; 18:1-15; 21:1-8*
Scripture Lesson: *Genesis 15:5-6; 18:11-14; 21:1-8*
Key Verse: *"Is anything too hard for the LORD?"*
Genesis 18:14.
Scripture Lesson for Children: *Genesis 18:1-8, 10-14; 21:1-3*
Key Verse for Children: *Sarah . . . bore a son to Abraham.*
Genesis 21:2.

Lesson Aim
To learn that God can do what we consider impossible.

Lesson Setting
Time: *Between 2081–2080 and 2067–2066 B.C.*
Place: *Canaan*

Lesson Outline
Abraham, Sarah, and Isaac
    I. The Divine Declaration: Genesis 15:5-6
        A. *God's Pledge: vs. 5*
        B. *Abram's Faith: vs. 6*
   II. The Divine Word of Assurance: Genesis 18:11-14
        A. *Sarah's Skepticism: vss. 11-12*
        B. *God's Promise: vss. 13-14*
  III. The Divine Fulfillment: Genesis 21:1-8
        A. *The Birth of Isaac: vss. 1-2*
        B. *The Naming of Isaac: vs. 3*
        C. *The Circumcision of Isaac: vs. 4*
        D. *The Advanced Age of Isaac's Parents: vss. 5-6*
        E. *The Weaning of Isaac: vss. 7-8*

Introduction for Adults

Topic: *Our Place in the Family!*

A number of Christian organizations report that the tendency of individuals in the West toward independence is a threat to the traditional family structure. These agencies report that it is difficult for us to place our lives and our future in the hands of anyone else. Within our control, the outcome might not be an incredible success, but at least it will be predictable and safe; however, our God desires that we instead step into a wonderful world of adventure with Him at the controls.

How can we entrust our existence to God, especially when it seems impossible at times? Nonetheless, the record of Scripture and of our own experiences in following the Lord tell us that He seems to love the word "impossible." He most often does not work through our agenda, and we do not always see Him working in ways we understand; but He asks us to learn to trust His heart. Indeed, this is the first step in becoming a part of His spiritual family.

Introduction for Youth

Topic: *Child of Promise*

God stretched the faith of Abraham in many ways. God told Abraham that he would have a son. Moving to an unknown country was a risk, but the promise of having children as an old, childless couple was physically impossible. Even Abraham thought God needed help here. Rather than resting in God's promise, Abraham began to create his own plan.

Are we any different than Abraham? God is stretching our faith, for example, when He asks us to watch a family member suffer with cancer or to forgive someone who has terribly wronged us. These become opportunities for us to trust God to cause all things to work together for our eternal good (Rom. 8:28).

Concepts for Children

Topic: *God Gave Abraham and Sarah a Baby*

1. Abraham recognized the presence of God when three visitors appeared at his tent.
2. Sarah laughed when she overheard one of the visitors say she would have a baby.
3. Abraham and Sarah knew that through them and their son, Isaac, God promised to create a special people.
4. Abraham believed God, even when God's promises seemed unlikely.
5. This account teaches us that God keeps promises.

Lesson Commentary

I. THE DIVINE DECLARATION: GENESIS 15:5-6

A. God's Pledge: vs. 5

He took him outside and said, "Look up at the heavens and count the stars—if indeed you can count them." Then he said to him, "So shall your offspring be."

Genesis 11:10-26 records a genealogy from Shem, the son of Noah, to Abram (Abraham). We learn that Terah was the father of Abram, Nahor, and Haran (vs. 26). Haran, who was the father of Lot (vs. 27), died while the family was still living in Ur of the Chaldeans (vs. 28). According to verse 30, Abram's wife, Sarai, was unable to conceive. In the culture of that day, being childless was considered a social disgrace. This circumstance did not change, even when Terah, Abram, Sarai, and Lot left Ur to go to Canaan (vs. 31). After traveling 600 miles north along the Fertile Crescent trade route, the group arrived in Haran, where they stayed for a time, accumulating possessions and servants (12:5). It was also there that Terah died (11:32).

God next called Abram to leave his country, his people, and his father's household, and go to a land he did not know (Gen. 12:1; 15:7; Neh. 9:7; Acts 7:2-3); in other words, a 75-year-old man was to be lifted out of the familiar and placed in the unfamiliar (Gen. 12:4). In return, God promised to bless him in an unprecedented way. Though Abram was childless, God promised to make him a great nation with many descendants. The Lord promised to give Abram honor and make him a source of blessing to others. Through Abram's descendants, God would pour out great blessings for all humanity (vss. 2-3).

The patriarch stepped out in faith and obeyed the divine summons (Gen. 12:4-5; see Heb. 11:8). When he arrived in Canaan, the land was thinly populated by a variety of peoples who had descended from Canaan, the grandson of Noah (10:1, 6). Nomadic tribesmen moved through the hill country and valleys. Some urbanization had begun to take place at fortified cities. Generally, the area was far behind the standard of civilization Abram had left behind in Ur.

While the patriarch was at Shechem (Gen. 12:6), the Lord appeared to him and promised to give the land of Canaan to his descendants (vs. 7). God next appeared to Abram while he was in the Negev (13:1). The Lord repeated His promise that Abram's descendants would one day possess the whole of Canaan (vss. 14-15). God also assured the patriarch that his offspring would be like the dust of the earth in number (vs. 16).

During the next 10 years, Abram got involved in regional politics (chap. 14). He may have begun to wonder whether he would survive much longer and have offspring, as God had promised. Around the time the patriarch was 85, the Lord came to him in a vision at night and told him not to be afraid. Moreover, God pledged to protect him and to reward him in great abundance (15:1).

Abram, however, wondered about the value of such blessings when he remained childless. In that day, the desire to have children—especially sons—was great. With no clear understanding of immortality, people believed that children provided the opportunity for a kind of earthly immorality. A son could carry on his father's name and take over the family's possessions. Abram concluded that he would have to leave his estate to a favored servant, Eliezer of Damascus, rather than to a son of his own (vss. 2-3).

God did not go along with Abram's plan to make Eliezer his heir; instead, the Lord affirmed that a son of Abram's not yet born would become the patriarch's heir (vs. 4). Furthermore, while Abram looked ahead just one generation, God saw the whole future and knew about the multitude of people who would call Abram father. Thus, in a dramatic move, the Lord led the patriarch out of his tent and directed him to look upward at the Palestinian sky.

Abram lived in a time before the invention of electric lights. On a clear night, the stars shone brilliantly against the backdrop of space. Thousands upon thousands of points of light were visible in the heavens. This was the context in which God said to the childless patriarch, "So shall your offspring be" (vs. 5). The idea was that his descendants would be too many to count.

B. Abram's Faith: vs. 6

Abram believed the LORD, and he credited it to him as righteousness.

Upon hearing the Lord's statement, something happened in the heart of Abram. Before he had been doubtful about having a child. Now he finally believed God's promise (Gen. 15:6). An examination of the original indicates that the patriarch considered the Lord's pledge as being reliable and dependable. Indeed, the patriarch was confident that God was fully capable of bringing about what He had promised.

The text says that Abram's faith was "credited . . . to him as righteousness." Expressed differently, the Lord considered the patriarch's response of faith as proof of his genuine commitment and evidence of his steadfast loyalty. Paul referred to this verse in Romans 4:3 to stress that an upright standing before God comes through faith, not by means of obedience to the law (see Gal. 3:6). As Abram's life illustrated, God forgives the believing sinner on the basis of Jesus' atoning sacrifice (Rom. 3:25-26).

God's covenant with Abram had two main provisions: descendants and land. With the matter of the heir settled, the Lord reminded Abram of His promise of the land to which God had called the patriarch. The people as numerous as the stars would need a place to live, and that place would be Canaan (Gen. 15:7).

When Abram asked how he could be sure he would receive the land (vs. 8), the Lord graciously gave the patriarch the reassurance he sought. God chose to copy a common practice of that time used to confirm special agreements (vss. 9-17). In human covenants, both parties to the transaction usually passed between the dead animals; but in this case only the Lord did so. Since the fulfillment of the promise depended on God alone, Abram was merely a spectator.

God defined the extent of the land He would give. It lay between the river of Egypt (probably one of the seasonal rivers in the Negev) in the south to the Euphrates River in the north. At that time, this land was occupied by at least 10 different people groups (vss. 18-21).

II. THE DIVINE WORD OF ASSURANCE: GENESIS 18:11-14

A. Sarah's Skepticism: vss. 11-12

Abraham and Sarah were already old and well advanced in years, and Sarah was past the age of child-bearing. So Sarah laughed to herself as she thought, "After I am worn out and my master is old, will I now have this pleasure?"

When Abram was 99 years old, the Lord again appeared to him (17:1). The patriarch still did not have the son God promised to him, and that's why the Lord reaffirmed His intention to confirm His covenant between Himself and Abram. This included giving him a multitude of descendants (vs. 2). Because the patriarch was destined to become the "father of many nations" (vs. 4) through his yet-to-be-born son, the Lord changed his name from *Abram* (which means "exalted father") to *Abraham* (which means "father of many"; vs. 5).

The patriarch was not the only one to get a name change. The Lord also changed his wife's name from *Sarai*, which means "my princess" or "my queen," to *Sarah*, which means "a princess" or "a queen" (vs. 15). The change emphasizes Sarah's role as the ancestress of royal figures. She would become the "mother of nations" (vs. 16), and kings of countries would come from her.

In response to all the Lord revealed, Abraham had himself and all the males in his household circumcised (vss. 23-27). Not long after that incident, the patriarch had three unexpected visitors (18:1). Though they looked like men, two of them were angels, while the third was called "the Lord" (vs. 13). This third figure may have been God in human form, or may have been an angel who in some special sense represented God.

The three figures arrived at midday, when people traditionally rested and waited for the sun to go down. Perhaps the Lord chose this time for the arrival to test Abraham's willingness to welcome guests, even though they had come at an inconvenient time. Hospitality was (and still is) a much-prized virtue in the Near East. If the timing of the visit was a test, the patriarch acquitted himself admirably. Despite the heat, he hurried to meet his guests' needs, and made sure his wife and servants hurried too (vss. 2-7).

The meal prepared by Abraham's household was served outside, beneath a tree (vs. 8). In keeping with the tradition at that time, the woman of the household, Sarah, kept out of sight. She stayed inside the tent, but was able to hear the conversation outside (vs. 9). One of the visitors—the chief representative—stated that he would assuredly return about the same time the following year (possibly referring to springtime), and when he did, Sarah would already have a son (vs. 10).

Verse 11 notes that Abraham and Sarah were old and advancing in years, and Sarah had long since passed menopause. Thus, when Sarah heard the prediction, she laughed to herself. She found it hard to believe that a worn-out woman such as herself would have the pleasure of becoming pregnant and bearing a son (vs. 12).

B. God's Promise: vss. 13-14

Then the LORD said to Abraham, "Why did Sarah laugh and say, 'Will I really have a child, now that I am old?' Is anything too hard for the LORD? I will return to you at the appointed time next year and Sarah will have a son."

Either Abraham had not told Sarah yet about the birth God had promised, or else Sarah had not believed her husband. Apparently, Sarah kept her laughter and her thoughts to herself. Those outside the tent heard nothing from her; yet the Lord revealed that He knew what was going on in Sarah's mind. Thus He let out another clue to His divine nature (Gen. 18:13).

Sarah had long ago given up hope of having a child. The idea of it seemed impossible; but with the Lord, all things are possible. He repeated His prediction that within a year Sarah would give birth (vs. 14). For Sarah, there was no longer a point in hiding. The Lord knew she was there. Afraid of him, she lied about laughing; but the Lord insisted on the truth, as He always does (vs. 15).

This was not the end of the visit the Lord and the two angels made to earth. They had accomplished one of the purposes of their visit: to renew God's promise of a son to Abraham and Sarah; but they had one other purpose, involving a judgment on some wicked cities.

III. THE DIVINE FULFILLMENT: GENESIS 21:1-8

A. The Birth of Isaac: vss. 1-2

Now the LORD was gracious to Sarah as he had said, and the LORD did for Sarah what he had promised. Sarah became pregnant and bore a son to Abraham in his old age, at the very time God had promised him.

Genesis 21:1 literally says that "the Lord visited Sarah." Depending on the context, the Hebrew verb translated "visited" can be used for divine blessing or judgment. In the case of Sodom and Gomorrah, God destroyed those cities (Gen. 19). With respect to Sarah, the Lord manifested His grace on her by doing what He had promised (21:1). Though Sarah was now 90 years old, this did not prevent God from enabling her to become pregnant and bear a son to Abraham in his old age (vs. 2). Indeed, she and her husband regarded the One who had given the promise of a child to be trustworthy (Heb. 11:11). The birth took place at the divinely appointed time in accordance with the word of the Lord (Gen. 21:2).

B. The Naming of Isaac: vs. 3

Abraham gave the name Isaac to the son Sarah bore him.

Genesis 21:3 says that Abraham named his newborn son "Isaac," which means "he laughs." Sarah wasn't the only person who had previously laughed in disbelief upon initially hearing the divine promise (18:12). According to 17:17, Abraham also laughed. While the patriarch believed that God would give him offspring, he did not think at the time the descendants would come through a son borne by Sarah. The name of Isaac would be a reminder of how the Lord had proved His faithfulness to the aged parents of their newborn.

C. The Circumcision of Isaac: vs. 4

When his son Isaac was eight days old, Abraham circumcised him, as God commanded him.

When Abraham was 99 years old (Gen. 17:1), God decreed that circumcision would be the sign of the covenant. Both the patriarch and all the males in his household were to be circumcised. This practice was to be repeated on all Abraham's male descendants as well as others in the covenant community (vss. 9-14). Circumcision was not unknown at that time. In fact, anthropologists tell us that tribes in America, Africa, and Australia practiced circumcision from earliest times.

In Abraham's day, some Egyptians and perhaps others in the Near East practiced circumcision; but in the patriarch's household, circumcision was new and represented the covenant. The oath connected with this practice could be paraphrased as follows: "May I be cut off like my foreskin if I am untrue to the covenant." In fact, the cutting of circumcision reflected the literal meaning of the phrase "to make a covenant," which is "to cut a covenant." This background information explains why Abraham had his newborn son Isaac circumcised when he was eight days old. The patriarch was heeding the command of God (21:4).

D. The Advanced Age of Isaac's Parents: vss. 5-6

Abraham was a hundred years old when his son Isaac was born to him. Sarah said, "God has brought me laughter, and everyone who hears about this will laugh with me."

The Lord had been faithful to Abraham for many years, and now that the patriarch was a century old, he would remain unwavering in his trust in God (Gen. 21:5). Sarah drew attention to the Lord's faithfulness by noting that He, through the birth of Isaac, had brought her the joy of laughter. Moreover, all those who heard the good news of Isaac's birth would signal their joy over the fulfillment of the divine promise (vs. 6).

E. The Weaning of Isaac: vss. 7-8

And she added, "Who would have said to Abraham that Sarah would nurse children? Yet I have borne him a son in his old age." The child grew and was weaned, and on the day Isaac was weaned Abraham held a great feast.

Many years before, no one could have foretold that Sarah, a seemingly barren and aging woman, would ever be able to nurse children; but against all humanly conceivable odds, she had given birth to a male infant, whom Sarah and her husband would enjoy in their old age (Gen. 21:7). This wasn't a make-believe child. Isaac physically grew and eventually was weaned (vs. 8).

In ancient times, infant mortality was high. By the time a child reached the age of two or three, there was a stronger likelihood he or she would survive. Thus, it was reasonable for children to be weaned at this time. In the case of Isaac, such a milestone called for a great feast, which Abraham gladly held. It was the least he could do to celebrate the maturing of a child the patriarch and his wife had waited so long to have.

Discussion Questions

1. How many descendants did God say Abraham would have?
2. What was Abraham's response to God's declaration regarding his descendants?
3. Why did Sarah initially doubt God's promise of a child?
4. From whom did Sarah receive the ability to conceive?
5. What characterized Sarah's laughter at the birth of Isaac?

Contemporary Application

When Pam chose to become a teacher, she knew she wanted to touch children's lives, just as her mother, who was also a schoolteacher, had done. What Pam had not counted on was the fact that some children would seem so untouchable. I recall her saying to me, "I had a student whom I'll call Gary who I can only describe as obnoxious and obstinate. He was so much trouble, I thought I was being specially punished when I had to teach him for both sixth and seventh grade.

Pam had little real faith that Gary would ever change. Pam said, "But he surprised me. To my amazement, he changed when he discerned I was truly trying to care for him, that I was trying to like him as a person. That realization made a genuine difference for our relationship and for him as a person. After he graduated, I saw him at a mall, and he called out to me. We chatted for a while, and I was just floored. I would have sworn he would be one of the kids who would walk the other way if he saw me coming."

Many of us live with Garys every day—people we are sure will never change; and we see situations that look hopeless or impossible. We may know that God is powerful enough to change any life, or any situation, but it is something else altogether to expect such changes. This week's lesson offers a memorable glimpse into the joy that comes when God's people learn to move from knowledge to faith. It can be hard to believe that God can do all things and is working even when we cannot see Him operating. Even when we do not always see Him working in ways we understand, He asks us to learn to trust His heart.

Abraham, Hagar, and Ishmael

Scripture

Background Scripture: *Genesis 21:9-21*
Scripture Lesson: *Genesis 21:9-21*
Key Verse: *[God said to Abraham,] "I will make the son of the maidservant into a nation also, because he is your off-spring."* Genesis 21:13.
Scripture Lesson for Children: *Genesis 21:9-21*
Key Verse for Children: *[God said,] Lift the boy up . . . , for I will make him into a great nation."* Genesis 21:18.

Lesson Aim

To stress the importance of depending on the Lord in life's most trying moments.

Lesson Setting

Time: *2066 B.C.*
Place: *Canaan*

Lesson Outline

Abraham, Hagar, and Ishmael

   I. Strained Relations: Genesis 21:9-13
      A. *A Troubling Circumstance: vs. 9*
      B. *Sarah's Demand: vs. 10*
      C. *God's Reassurance: vss. 11-13*
  II. Sovereign Intervention: Genesis 21:14-21
      A. *Meager Provisions: vs. 14*
      B. *A Dire Situation: vss. 15-16*
      C. *God's Promise and Provision: vss. 17-19*
      D. *A Brighter Future: vss. 20-21*

Introduction for Adults

Topic: *Dealing with Dissension in Family!*

Scripture does not promise that believers will avoid all forms of conflicts, even with family members; but the Bible does teach that no trouble can destroy our relationship with God or render His power inoperative. Each step we take, each breath we breathe, we can know that God is with us and that we are under His care.

This affirmation of faith rests on what we know about the Lord. God the Creator is aware of every detail of our lives. The Protector's assurance is that He will continue to guide us, regardless of whatever threats might emerge against us in the future. Of course, harm might arise from enemies at home and abroad, or even from within our own families; but because we are people of faith, we have put our trust in God's all-knowing, all-loving care.

Introduction for Youth

Topic: *A Great Nation*

Timing is often extremely important, whether it concerns building a great nation or a young life destined for greatness. When a batter swings just a little too late, he misses the ball. When a driver brakes a few seconds late, she crashes into another car. When travelers arrive at the gate a minute or two late, they get to see their plane departing without them. In instances like these, once the time has passed, the intended result cannot be reclaimed.

The God we trust and serve never misses a deadline. His timing is always perfect, even when we think otherwise. God does not work on our timetables but on His own. As our Shepherd, He faithfully watches over us. In fact, He has assumed this responsibility of taking care of us in the best way possible.

Concepts for Children

Topic: *God Promised to Care for Ishmael*

1. Sarah wanted Hagar and Ishmael to be sent away.
2. Abraham was upset by Sarah's demand.
3. Hagar was concerned about the well-being of her son.
4. God cared for both Ishmael and Hagar.
5. God also loves and cares for us.

Lesson Commentary

I. STRAINED RELATIONS: GENESIS 21:9-13

A. A Troubling Circumstance: vs. 9

But Sarah saw that the son whom Hagar the Egyptian had borne to Abraham was mocking.

We ended last week's lesson by noting that Abraham prepared a large feast to commemorate the weaning of Isaac (Gen. 21:8). Up to this point Moses did not mention Hagar and Ishmael; but in verse 9 the limelight suddenly shifts to them, bringing about a dramatic change in events.

The mother and her son are first mentioned in chapter 16, when Abraham was 86 years old (vs. 16). Over a decade had passed since God had initially declared to the patriarch that his wife, Sarah, would bear him a son. Her continued inability to conceive was a social embarrassment for her. Thus, she recommended that Abraham be physically intimate with Sarah's Egyptian servant named Hagar (vss. 1-2). It may be that the patriarch acquired this slave during his stay in Egypt (see 12:10-20). Sarah's plan was for Hagar to become pregnant and bear Abraham a son, whom the patriarch could then adopt and make the heir of his estate.

Abraham agreed to his wife's plan. The patriarch had sexual relations with Hagar, who in turn conceived (16:2-4). Sarah's plan, however, backfired when her Egyptian servant began to despise her for being barren. The Hebrew verb means "to treat lightly" or "to treat with contempt." In the eyes of society, Hagar's ability to produce an heir for Abraham elevated her status as his wife. Indeed, in Hagar's mind her mistress had been demoted. This unforeseen turn of events could have jeopardized God's plans for Abraham and Sarah.

Sarah blamed her husband for her being made to feel upstaged and worthless by Hagar. Moreover, Sarah believed she would be vindicated by the Lord in this matter (vs. 5). Abraham passively responded by stating that because Sarah's servant was under her authority, it was for her to decide what course of action she thought was best to take. As a result, Sarah mistreated Hagar, who in turn fled from her mistress (vs. 6).

The Lord's angel found Hagar near a spring in the desert that was beside the road to Shur (vs. 7). This was an arid region in the northwest part of the Sinai peninsula near the Egyptian border. The road itself might have been a caravan route between southern Canaan and Egypt. The heavenly messenger promised Hagar that the Lord would give her many descendants through the son in her womb. She in turn was to go back to her mistress and submit to her (vss. 8-10).

The emissary from God reassured Hagar that the Lord had heard her painful cries. Accordingly, she was to name her son "Ishmael" (vs. 11), which means "God hears" or "may God hear." Hagar's son would not only survive but also thrive (vs. 15). The Lord's angel declared that Ishmael would be as free-roaming and untamed as a wild donkey. Furthermore, his solitary, unconventional lifestyle would put him in conflict with his extended family and even the rest of society (vs. 12).

Hagar's encounter with the Lord's angel indicates that He cares deeply about the welfare of the oppressed. The Egyptian servant commemorated the incident by naming the place "Beer Lahai Roi" (vs. 14), which means either "the well of the Living One who sees me" or "the well of the One who sees me and who lives." The name emphasized the fact that Hagar had a direct encounter with God (through His angel) and lived to tell about it (vs. 13). This was significant, for it was believed that such contact with God would result in death (see Gen. 32:30; Exod. 33:20).

Hagar and Ishmael return to the limelight in Genesis 21. Verse 9 states that the festive occasion of Isaac's weaning was shattered when Sarah noticed Ishmael mocking Isaac malevolently. There are two views concerning what Hagar's son was doing. Some think Ishmael was treating Isaac with disdain, while others maintain that Hagar's son was playing with Sarah's son as if the two males were on equal footing. In either case, Sarah regarded Hagar's actions as being sinister and a potential threat to Isaac's inheritance.

B. Sarah's Demand: vs. 10

And she said to Abraham, "Get rid of that slave woman and her son, for that slave woman's son will never share in the inheritance with my son Isaac."

While the exact nature of Ishmael's offense is debated, it's clear that it resulted in him being permanently alienated from God's covenant promises. As a mother concerned for the welfare of her son, Sarah demanded that Abraham banish Hagar and Ishmael. Sarah's contempt was so great that she refused to address the Egyptian servant and her son by name. Moreover, Abraham's wife was determined to prevent Ishmael from being a co-heir with Isaac in the family inheritance (Gen. 21:10).

In Galatians 4:21-31, Paul referred to the episode involving Sarah and Hagar. The apostle was dealing with a circumstance in which his readers seemed eager to take upon themselves the burden of keeping the law. Thus Paul determined that an argument based on passages in books of the law would help bring them around to his side (vs. 21).

The apostle was combating a group of legalists called Judaizers. They taught that faith in the Messiah was not adequate to be declared righteous by God. Supposedly, obedience to the Old Testament law, or at least parts of it, was also necessary. It seems the legalists used historical and geographical features from the Genesis account in an allegory to support their own position.

The apostle began with the same historical incidents that the legalists presumably began with (vss. 22-23). Paul noted that Abraham had two sons, one by the slave woman (Hagar) and the other by the free woman (Sarah). The apostle stated that Ishmael was born as the result of human effort. In contrast, Isaac was born as the result of a divine promise.

When Paul stated that he was speaking figuratively, he was not implying that the Genesis account was an allegory; rather, he was using this historical episode as the basis for his own allegorical construction (vs. 24). Expressed differently, he saw in the historically accurate ancient writings a theological meaning that went beyond the narrative itself.

During the Israelites' wanderings in the wilderness, they stopped at Mount Sinai in Arabia (Exod. 19). There God entered into a covenant with them and gave them the law. It was this law that Paul's opponents tried to enforce on the Galatians. The apostle regarded Hagar's literal slavery to be symbolic of the spiritual slavery caused by the law given at Mount Sinai (Gal. 4:24).

Paul noted that Hagar also corresponded to the Jerusalem of the apostle's day. The reason is that Jerusalem was the center of the Jewish religion and the hometown of the Judaizers. Paul personified the city of Jerusalem and said she was enslaved with her children, meaning the nonbelieving Jews. They were still in bondage to the law because they had not found freedom through faith in the Messiah (vs. 25; see Rom. 9:30-33).

In contrast, the followers of Jesus are the children of another mother, namely, the Jerusalem that is from above (Gal. 4:26), where the Savior reigns (Heb. 12:22; Rev. 21:2) and where believers have their citizenship (Phil. 3:20; Col. 3:1-3). In Galatians 4:27, Paul quoted from Isaiah 54:1 to show how this heavenly Jerusalem can be said to be the mother of all Christians. Isaiah prophesied of the enslavement of the people of Jerusalem and Judah in Babylon. During that time, Jerusalem would be "barren" (that is, largely empty of people), as Sarah was literally barren before conceiving Isaac.

Furthermore, Isaiah prophesied of a later time when Jerusalem would have many children (that is, would once again have inhabitants). In the same way, the Jerusalem above would have many children; in other words, many people would trust in the Messiah for salvation. This is similar to God's promise to give Abraham many descendants. Gentile and Jewish Christians are the fulfillment of this prophecy. Consequently, the Galatians were like Isaac (namely, the children of promise) and the Judaizers were like Ishmael (Gal. 4:28).

Paul stated in verse 29 that the son born by human effort persecuted the son born by the power of the Spirit (see Gen. 21:9). Likewise, those whom the Spirit had spiritually regenerated were being persecuted by the legalists of the apostle's day (see Acts 13:44-45; 14:2, 19-20). In doing so, the Judaizers violated the will of God. They also failed to see that once the Son of promise had come—namely, Jesus the Messiah—the Mosaic law and covenant were obsolete, outdated, and replaced by the new covenant (Jer. 31:31-34; Heb. 8:7-13).

When Sarah saw Ishmael persecuting her son, she urged Abraham to eject Hagar and Ishmael (Gen. 21:10; Gal. 4:30). When the patriarch hesitated, God implied that it would be all right for him to let the mother and adolescent go (Gen. 21:12). Paul wanted his Christian readers to see this as an assurance of them having the authority to expel the Judaizers from their congregation.

Galatians 4:31 contains the apostle's main point in developing the allegory.

While the Judaizers may have taught that the Galatians were children of the slave woman unless they obeyed the law, Paul insisted that his readers were already children of the free woman. By God's grace, all who trust in the Messiah are free.

C. God's Reassurance: vss. 11-13

The matter distressed Abraham greatly because it concerned his son. But God said to him, "Do not be so distressed about the boy and your maidservant. Listen to whatever Sarah tells you, because it is through Isaac that your offspring will be reckoned. I will make the son of the maidservant into a nation also, because he is your offspring."

According to the social conventions of the day, a mistress could not arbitrarily expel a female servant and her children. Perhaps this was one reason the matter involving Hagar and Ishmael displeased Abraham so much. In all probability, he thought Sarah's demand was legally improper and ethically wrong. It's also likely that the patriarch was anguished by the possibility that Hagar and Ishmael might not survive on their own in the harsh wilderness (Gen. 21:11).

God told Abraham (perhaps in a dream) not to be upset about the situation involving his slave wife and her son. It was the divine will for the patriarch to do what Sarah demanded, even though it seemed harsh and inconsiderate. The Lord explained that His covenantal promises would be fulfilled through Isaac, not Ishmael (vs. 12).

This verse factored into Paul's argument recorded in Romans 9:6-8. There the apostle stated that the divine promise had not failed just because many Jews of that day had rejected Jesus as the Messiah. Paul noted that not all of the people of Israel are the true people of God. Indeed, when the Lord originally made His promises to Abraham, God meant that only the patriarch's descendants by his son Isaac were heirs of the covenant (see Heb. 11:18).

In Genesis 21:13, God revealed His intent to make a nation out of the descendants of Hagar's son, for he too was one of Abraham's offspring. Scripture records that Ishmael did leave behind many descendants, including the 12 rulers God promised (17:20), who formed several nations (25:12-18). Many Arabs today trace their lineage back to Ishmael. Thus, in a sense, the struggle between Ishmael and Isaac continues today in the Arab-Israeli tensions.

II. SOVEREIGN INTERVENTION: GENESIS 21:14-21

A. Meager Provisions: vs. 14

Early the next morning Abraham took some food and a skin of water and gave them to Hagar. He set them on her shoulders and then sent her off with the boy. She went on her way and wandered in the desert of Beersheba.

Abraham, having been reassured by God, arose early the next morning and prepared some food (literally, "bread"). He gave this to Hagar as well as strapped an animal skin filled with water (containing about three gallons) on her shoulders.

Then the patriarch sent her away with her son. One has to wonder how long Abraham thought these provisions would last as the mother and her adolescent son wandered aimlessly through the wilderness of Beersheba (Gen. 21:14).

Beersheba was located at the southern end of the land of Canaan. It was there that Abraham and Abimelech (the king of Gerar) made a peace treaty, in recognition of the patriarch's special status and material wealth. The two also swore an oath of mutual assistance (vss. 22-31). In fact, the name "Beersheba" means either "well of the seven" or "well of the oath."

B. A Dire Situation: vss. 15-16

When the water in the skin was gone, she put the boy under one of the bushes. Then she went off and sat down nearby, about a bowshot away, for she thought, "I cannot watch the boy die." And as she sat there nearby, she began to sob.

Eventually the container of water ran out. Hagar, being filled with despair over the deplorable situation facing her and her son, shoved the adolescent under one of the nearby shrubs (possibly a tamarisk, which thrived in that arid region; Gen. 21:15). By this time both of them were weak from dehydration and facing death. Hagar decided to abandon her son, for she could not bear to see him expire. As she sat across from him about a bowshot (that is, around 100 yards) away, she began to sob uncontrollably (vs. 16). Likewise, Ishmael started to cry.

C. God's Promise and Provision: vss. 17-19

God heard the boy crying, and the angel of God called to Hagar from heaven and said to her, "What is the matter, Hagar? Do not be afraid; God has heard the boy crying as he lies there. Lift the boy up and take him by the hand, for I will make him into a great nation." Then God opened her eyes and she saw a well of water. So she went and filled the skin with water and gave the boy a drink.

God, being fully aware of the circumstance, had His angel from heaven call to Hagar and ask what was upsetting her. The Lord's messenger then told her not to be afraid any longer, for God had heard the sound of Ishmael's crying (Gen. 21:17). The mother was commanded to stand up, help the adolescent to his feet, and take him by the hand. They would not expire that day, for God intended Hagar's son not only to live but also to become a great nation (vs. 18). At that moment, God enabled the mother to see a well of water. In turn, she went over to it, filled her container, and gave Ishmael a drink (vs. 19).

D. A Brighter Future: vss. 20-21

God was with the boy as he grew up. He lived in the desert and became an archer. While he was living in the Desert of Paran, his mother got a wife for him from Egypt.

God's favor rested on Ishmael, the son of Abraham through Hagar. Ishmael lived in the wilderness and became an archer (Gen. 21:20). This implies that he learned to survive by the expert use of his weapons. Ishmael eventually settled in the Desert of Paran. This arid region was located in the east central part of the Sinai peninsula. The somewhat ill-defined area was flanked on its eastern border by the Arabah and the Gulf of Aqaba. According to the custom of the day, Ishmael's mother found a wife for him from her native land of Egypt (vs. 21).

Discussion Questions

1. In what way was Ishmael mistreating Isaac?
2. How did Abraham respond to Sarah's demand for him to expel Hagar and Ishmael?
3. What future did God have in store for Ishmael?
4. How did Abraham prepare Hagar and Ishmael for their departure?
5. How did God intervene in the lives of the mother and her son?

Contemporary Application

The account involving Abraham, Hagar, and Ishmael is about God graciously intervening in fractured human relationships. Sarah, the patriarch's wife, felt increasingly anxious about her unchanging childless condition. Thus, she took matters into her own hands, rather than trusting God to bring about His will. The short and long term results were turmoil and anguish, especially for Hagar and Ishmael.

Before Ishmael was born, his pregnant mother found herself fleeing from from Sarah. In the midst of Hagar's frightening situation, the Lord intervened with words of assurance and hope. The young mother learned that God would watch over her and her unborn son, enabling them not only to survive but also thrive. From that encounter with the the Lord, Hagar learned that God sees and cares for the disadvantaged and the disenfranchised.

Years later, family tensions again erupted between Sarah, Hagar, and their respective sons. Unlike before, though, it ended in the permanent banishment of Hagar and Ishmael from the family of Abraham. As the incident unfolded, it proved to be quite traumatic for the expelled mother and her son. As their meager supplies ran out, Hagar and Ishmael weeped at the prospect of perishing in the wilderness.

Again, the Lord intervened in this desperate situation. He directed the mother and son to a supply of water. God also enabled them to pull through that dark moment and move forward with their lives. The Lord proved to be faithful to them, just as He had promised. The two would have a future, one filled with hope.

There are times when we will feel afflicted and anguished by life circumstances. Regardless of the cause of these hardships, the Lord invites us to depend on Him. He can give us the strength to endure the trials we face. He also can fill us with peace and hope that defies comprehension. It all comes down to our willingness to trust Him completely and wholeheartedly.

Isaac and Rebekah

Scripture

Background Scripture: *Genesis 24*

Scripture Lesson: *Genesis 24:34-40, 42-45, 48*

Key Verse: *"And I bowed down and worshiped the LORD. I praised the LORD, the God of my master Abraham, who had led me on the right road to get the granddaughter of my master's brother for his son."* Genesis 24:48.

Scripture Lesson for Children: *Genesis 24:34-40, 42-45, 48*

Key Verse for Children: *Isaac . . . married Rebekah. So she became his wife, and he loved her.* Genesis 24:67.

Lesson Aim

To emphasize that God hears our prayers.

Lesson Setting

Time: *2026 B.C.*

Place: *Canaan*

Lesson Outline

Isaac and Rebekah

 I. The Dispatching of Abraham's Servant: Genesis 24:34-40
   A. *The Servant's Identity: vs. 34*
   B. *The Wealth of Abraham: vs. 35*
   C. *The Servant's Assigned Task: vss. 36-38*
   D. *The Reassurance Given by Abraham: vss. 39-40*

 II. The Servant's Successful Mission: Genesis 24:42-45, 48
   A. *The Servant's Desire for a Prosperous Journey: vs. 42*
   B. *The Specifics of the Servant's Request: vss. 43-44*
   C. *The Arrival of Rebekah: vs. 45*
   D. *The Servant's Grateful Response: vs. 48*

Introduction for Adults

Topic: *Recognizing the Right Woman*

Undoubtedly, Abraham's servant learned many lessons from him. One important lesson was that of humbly asking God to work on behalf of His people to bring the servant to the right woman for Isaac to marry. When we reflect on the life of Abraham—including the testimony of his servant recorded in Genesis 24—the trust that resulted from a life of communion and communication with God is evident.

At times when life feels confusing and out of control, we may wonder how God is able to understand our prayers. If we read the teachings of the New Testament, we will discover that God knows our petitions better than we do ourselves. Even when we are not sure what the right prayers should be or the best method of prayer to use, God actively searches our hearts; and He is able to see the motive of our requests and respond in kind. Indeed, the Spirit intercedes on our behalf in accordance with the Father's will (Rom. 8:26-27).

Introduction for Youth

Topic: *Here Comes the Bride*

In this week's lesson text, the chief servant of Abraham is a good model of how we depend on God and pray to Him concerning every issue in our lives—whether it is choosing a mate or selecting a career path. Perhaps the most important virtue the servant displayed was a view of an awesome God who would work on behalf of anyone who was willing to petition the Lord with their requests—in this case, finding a suitable bride for Isaac.

The consistent testimony of Scripture is that prayers based upon God's Word and will are petitions that especially please the Lord. Moreover, it seems as if the prayers that God delights most in answering are the ones that begin with an acknowledgment of who He is, are filled with humble cries for help, and end with an affirmation of trust that God will always do what is right.

Concepts for Children

Topic: *God Prepares to Bring Isaac and Rebekah Together*

1. Abraham wanted Isaac to marry a woman from among their relatives.
2. Abraham sent his servant to a place called Haran to find a wife for Isaac.
3. Out of devotion to Abraham, the servant took an oath to do what his master wanted.
4. Both Abraham and his servant trusted God to guide them in all that happened.
5. God is pleased when we trust Him with every detail of our lives.

Lesson Commentary

I. THE DISPATCHING OF ABRAHAM'S SERVANT: GENESIS 24:34-40

A. The Servant's Identity: vs. 34

So he said, "I am Abraham's servant."

After the death of Sarah (Gen. 23:1-2), Abraham was concerned about who Isaac would take for a wife. The plan Abraham devised involved the senior servant of his household (24:34), the person who had oversight of all the patriarch owned (vs. 2). Abraham summoned and commissioned this individual to go to the patriarch's relatives and find a wife for Isaac.

Despite the pivotal role this senior member of Abraham's staff played, Moses did not identify him. Some think the servant was Eliezer of Damascus, whom the patriarch had earlier sought to adopt as his heir (see 15:2). If so, we can see why Abraham regarded Eliezer so highly. In the course of his assignment, this servant displayed good discernment and trust in God.

B. The Wealth of Abraham: vs. 35

"The LORD has blessed my master abundantly, and he has become wealthy. He has given him sheep and cattle, silver and gold, menservants and maidservants, and camels and donkeys."

Genesis 24:1 reveals that the Lord had blessed Abraham in every conceivable way. Many years earlier, God had pledged to do just that (12:2); and by the time Abraham journeyed from Egypt to the Negev, he had become very wealthy in livestock and precious metals (13:1-2). Apparently, his material holdings continued to increase in the years that followed. The statement made by the chief servant in 24:35 indicates that Abraham's estate included sheep and cattle, silver and gold, male and female servants, and camels and donkeys.

The patriarch's trust in God was even more noteworthy. Indeed, despite Abraham's faults, the New Testament writers held him up as a model of genuine faith. For instance, the writer of Hebrews emphasized that Abraham believed in God despite the seeming impossibility of having an heir through Sarah (Heb. 11:11). Also, Paul said that all believers, both Jews and Gentiles, are Abraham's spiritual children because they, too, come to God through faith. It was by faith that the sinners came to know God, not through their good works, their heritage, or their obedience to a prescribed set of rules (such as the Jewish law; Gal. 3:6-14).

C. The Servant's Assigned Task: vss. 36-38

"My master's wife Sarah has borne him a son in her old age, and he has given him everything he owns. And my master made me swear an oath, and said, 'You must not get a wife for my son from the daughters of the Canaanites, in whose land I live, but go to my father's family and to my own clan, and get a wife for my son.'"

The senior servant noted that Sarah, the wife of Abraham, bore the patriarch a son when she was old (Gen. 24:36). Sarah died at the age of 127 at Kiriath Arba (namely, Hebron) in Canaan (23:1-2). The rest of chapter 23 records the arrangements Abraham made to secure the burial of his wife in the promised land. The patriarch negotiated the purchase of the cave of Machpelah and the field that went with it. This property represented his first possession of the land in Canaan.

Isaac now remained the only living link between Abraham and his beloved, deceased wife. In the years preceding Isaac's birth, Abraham wondered who would inherit his estate. For a while, it seemed as if Lot would be the heir, but that option was eliminated when Lot moved away from the patriarch and pitched his tents near Sodom (chap. 13).

Eliezer of Damascus became the next likely candidate to inherit Abraham's great wealth; but despite Eliezer's admirable qualities, the Lord declared to Abraham that his senior servant would not be the heir to the patriarch's estate (15:2-4). The birth of Ishmael through Sarah's Egyptian servant (chap. 16) meant that he was next in line to receive the family blessing; but he was never a candidate in God's eyes, for the Lord had already designated Isaac as the recipient of the covenant promises and Abraham's estate (17:18-21).

In light of the preceding information, we can understand more clearly why Abraham had given Isaac everything the patriarch owned (24:36). In an earlier episode, Abraham was willing to sacrifice this son whom he deeply loved (22:2). Most likely, Isaac was in his late teens or early twenties when Abraham took him to be offered on Mount Moriah (especially since Isaac was able to carry the wood by himself to the appointed place).

From all appearances, Isaac quietly and willingly went along with the sacrifice. His obedience to his father, especially as Abraham prepared for the sacrifice, reveals Isaac's confidence in God. Like his father, Isaac believed that the Lord's promises would be fulfilled through him regardless of what happened. Some regard this incident as Isaac's finest hour.

Before Abraham's chief servant left on his mission, the patriarch made him swear an oath. The servant pledged not to acquire a wife for Isaac from among the Canaanites (24:3, 37). The Canaanites were divided into city-states in which the kings had wide powers to raise an army, control lands, impose taxes, and compel subjects to take part in public projects. The Canaanites worshiped their gods with sexual orgies and drunken feasts. Their worst pagan practice consisted of offering children as burnt sacrifices to idols. In later biblical history, the Israelites were forbidden to intermarry with the Canaanites (Deut. 7:1-4).

This information helps explain why Abraham insisted that his chief servant travel to the extended family of the patriarch's father, Terah (Gen. 11:27), and find a wife for Isaac among these relatives (24:4, 38). Because of the length of the journey ahead for the servant, Abraham realized that he might die before the servant returned. The patriarch wanted to guarantee that his instructions would be followed, no matter what happened to him.

To take the oath, the chief servant put his hand under the thigh of Abraham (24:2, 9), possibly near the male organ of procreation. As Abraham faced death, he wanted to ensure the future posterity of his beloved son Isaac. Thus, the patriarch went through a customary practice with his servant that was designed to guard any act of disloyalty. It was a solemn way of saying that if the promise was violated, the person taking the oath called sterility or loss of children upon himself. Moreover, the descendants of Abraham would have the right (and possibly obligation) to avenge the broken vow.

D. The Reassurance Given by Abraham: vss. 39-40

"Then I asked my master, 'What if the woman will not come back with me?' He replied, 'The LORD, before whom I have walked, will send his angel with you and make your journey a success, so that you can get a wife for my son from my own clan and from my father's family.'"

Abraham's chief servant worried that the selected woman would not want to travel so far with him to meet Isaac (Gen. 24:39). In that case, the servant wondered whether his master preferred that his son be returned to the land from which Abraham came (vs. 5). The patriarch, however, insisted that the latter not be done (vs. 6). Abraham explained that the Lord, the God of heaven, had taken him from his father's household and his native land to establish him in Canaan. The Lord also pledged with a solemn oath to give the promised land to the patriarch's offspring (vs. 7). Thus, it was in Canaan that Isaac was to remain.

Many years before, Abraham believed God's promise of a son through Sarah (15:6); and the patriarch was willing to serve the Lord faithfully and live a blameless life, because Abraham knew Him to be the all-powerful God (17:1). As the patriarch's life drew to a close, he could honestly say to his servant that he had faithfully served the Lord (24:40).

Because God Almighty had been so trustworthy and dependable to the patriarch, he could affirm with certainty that the Lord would be with the chief servant on his mission. God would send His angel before the servant to protect and guide him (vs. 7) as well as ensure that the journey was a success (24:40). The servant's ability to find a wife for Isaac from among Abraham's relatives and his father's family would be a testament to God's blessing on the venture.

In the event that the woman refused to travel back to Canaan with Abraham's servant, he would be freed from the oath (vss. 8, 41). The patriarch's words gave the chief servant the reassurance he needed to set out on his mission with a caravan of 10 camels bearing all sorts of gifts for the future bride (vs. 10). The servant journeyed 450 miles to Aram Naharaim (that is, northwest Mesopotamia), and specifically to the town of Nahor. The latter was either Haran or another city nearby.

II. THE SERVANT'S SUCCESSFUL MISSION: GENESIS 24:42-45, 48

A. The Servant's Desire for a Prosperous Journey: vs. 42

"When I came to the spring today, I said, 'O LORD, God of my master Abraham, if you will, please grant success to the journey on which I have come.'"

Once the chief servant arrived at the place where Abraham's relatives lived, he had the camels kneel down by the well outside the city. By then it was evening, and the local women were coming out to draw water (Gen. 24:11). Wells were an important feature of ancient life. By evening a town's well became a busy, sociable place. They were often also the subject of disputes (26:19-22). Some wells were wide holes dug down to the water table and encircled with stone steps, which allowed access to the water. This seems to have been the kind of well Rebekah used (24:16).

The deep faith of the servant is evident in the account. He trusted the Lord and looked to Him for guidance in completing his mission. Abraham's trust in God had profoundly influenced the chief servant, who asked that the sovereign Lord make his journey successful (vs. 42). In so doing, God would be showing His unfailing covenantal love to Abraham (vs. 12).

B. The Specifics of the Servant's Request: vss. 43-44

"'See, I am standing beside this spring; if a maiden comes out to draw water and I say to her, "Please let me drink a little water from your jar," and if she says to me, "Drink, and I'll draw water for your camels too," let her be the one the LORD has chosen for my master's son.'"

In his prayer, the chief servant described the conditions he hoped God would fulfill. The servant did not want to make a mistake. That is why he looked to the Lord to identify just the right woman for Isaac. In this case, the servant noted in his prayer that he was standing beside the local spring where the young women of the village came to draw water (Gen. 24:13).

The sign from God requested by the servant involved asking one of the girls for a drink of water from her jug (vs. 43). The servant wanted the young woman whom God had chosen for Isaac not only to agree to lowering her jar so that the servant could drink, but also to water his master's camels (vs. 44). If this was the way the encounter unfolded, the servant would know that the Lord had been faithful to Abraham (vs. 14). The faith of the servant tells us that Abraham practiced what he believed before his household.

C. The Arrival of Rebekah: vs. 45

"Before I finished praying in my heart, Rebekah came out, with her jar on her shoulder. She went down to the spring and drew water, and I said to her, 'Please give me a drink.'"

The Lord anticipated the prayer of Abraham's servant. Before the emissary had finished making his request for a woman to offer water for him and his master's camels, Rebekah was already approaching the well with her jug on her shoulder.

Genesis 24:15 notes that she was the daughter of Bethuel, the son of Milcah. Milcah was the wife of Abraham's brother, Nahor (see also vss. 24, 47).

This young woman was both strikingly beautiful and a virgin (vs. 16). The emphasis on her sexual purity implies she was well suited to become the wife of Abraham's son and the future mother of the covenant community. Rebekah was also willing to do manual labor. She performed her tasks quickly, even at a run; and she did not shrink from doing extra work for a visitor. Such industry was a desirable quality in a bride at the time (see Prov. 31:10-31).

Abraham's servant had planned to ask for a young woman to get water for him (Gen. 24:14); but Rebekah was too quick for him. Before he could address her, she went down into the walk-in well and filled her jar of her own accord. When she came back with the jug on her head or shoulder, the servant met her and asked for a drink (vss. 17, 45). She gave it to him and volunteered to fill the nearby water trough for his master's camels (vss. 18-20, 46). Since a thirsty camel needs about five gallons of water, and the servant had 10 camels with him, Rebekah must have made many trips to the well!

D. The Servant's Grateful Response: vs. 48

"And I bowed down and worshiped the LORD. I praised the LORD, the God of my master Abraham, who had led me on the right road to get the granddaughter of my master's brother for his son."

While Rebekah was busy performing her tasks, Abraham's chief servant silently watched her, wondering whether she was the person the Lord intended the servant to meet (Gen. 24:21). It probably did not take him long to discern that God had made his journey successful. When the camels had finished drinking, the servant brought out expensive jewelry. He gave Rebekah a gold ring for her nose and two large gold bracelets for her wrists (vss. 22, 47).

The nose ring weighed a beka (about one-fifth ounce), and the bracelets weighed 10 shekels (about four ounces total). The gift of jewelry was to thank Rebekah and to pay for both the lodging the servant and his companions needed as well as for the feed their animals required. Although Rebekah didn't know it at the time, the gift was also a down payment on her bride price.

The servant asked about the identity of Rebekah's family and whether her father had any room to lodge the servant and his caravan (vs. 23). Rebekah's response indicated that she was a near relative of Abraham (vs. 24). She also added that her family had plenty of straw and feed as well as room for the caravan to spend the night (vs. 25).

In the ancient Near East, hospitality was taken seriously. A guest—whether a friend or a stranger—was treated with the utmost courtesy. When a person came to another's home, the following traditions were usually observed. First, the host would show respect by bowing to the guest, perhaps even falling at the guest's feet. Then the host would wish his guest peace, and the guest would respond with the same wish. The two would kiss one another's cheeks. Next, the host would invite the guest to remove his shoes and have the dust washed from his feet. Sometimes the host would anoint the guest's head with olive oil, possibly mixed with spices. Finally, the host would offer the guest a drink of water and prepare a meal for him.

The servant's hopes must have risen high that he had already found a bride for Isaac. The servant bowed his head in worship to the Lord (vs. 26) and praised the God of Abraham for the kindness and faithfulness He has shown the patriarch. The servant was especially grateful that the Lord had led him on his long journey to the house of one of the patriarch's relatives (vs. 27). Indeed, God had enabled the servant to meet Rebekah, who was the granddaughter of Nahor, Abraham's brother (vs. 48).

Discussion Questions

1. What kinds of material wealth did Abraham possess?
2. Why did Abraham insist that his son not marry a Canaanite woman?
3. Where was Abraham's servant directed to find a wife for Isaac?
4. What was the nature of the servant's request to the Lord?
5. How had the Lord led the servant of Abraham on his mission?

Contemporary Application

When a local community church felt the time was right to move ahead on a building project, the congregation's leaders made plans to develop a monthly prayer calendar for the parish. It was God's faithful answers to prayer that had made the project possible. The church had no desire to move forward without making prayer a priority.

Sometimes it seems that our prayers reach no higher than the ceiling. Also, sometimes we may fear that there really is no one on the other end; but Scripture assures us that God hears our prayers. He understands our deepest needs—even those we cannot bring ourselves to voice.

In Philippians 4:6-7, Paul told his friends not to worry about any self-centered concerns. Such anxiety can become all-consuming. It takes our minds off what is important to God and focuses attention on ourselves. We can become self-absorbed, unable to rejoice during hard times and to be gentle with friends and foes alike.

When we turn to God and surrender our anxieties to Him, God's peace can reach our innermost parts. Paul did not imply that our burdens will vanish, nor was he talking about a state of mind. In fact, it is an inner peace that can come only from God and is beyond our comprehension.

God's faithfulness to hear our petitions is why many local churches list prayer concerns in their weekly bulletins. It is why every congregational meeting can begin and end in prayer; and it is why some church members believe there is no sweeter sound than someone saying, "I will remember you in my prayers."

Esau and Jacob as Rivals

DEVOTIONAL READING

1 Corinthians 1:26-31

DAILY BIBLE READINGS

Monday October 1
1 Corinthians 1:26-31 God Chose the Least

Tuesday October 2
Genesis 24:50-61 Rebekah Agrees to Marry Isaac

Wednesday October 3
Genesis 24:62-67 Isaac Takes Rebekah as His Wife

Thursday October 4
Genesis 25:19-23 Rebekah's Twins Struggle in the Womb

Friday October 5
Genesis 25:24-28 The Birth of Jacob and Esau

Saturday October 6
Genesis 25:29-34 Esau Sells His Birthright

Sunday October 7
Genesis 27:30-40 Esau's Lost Blessing

Scripture

Background Scripture: *Genesis 25:19-34*
Scripture Lesson: *Genesis 25:19-34*
Key Verse: *The LORD said to her, "Two nations are in your womb, and two peoples from within you will be separated; one people will be stronger than the other, and the older will serve the younger."* Genesis 25:23.
Scripture Lesson for Children: *Genesis 25:20-34*
Key Verse for Children: *[Esau sold] his birthright to Jacob.* Genesis 25:33.

Lesson Aim

To highlight the importance of making the things of God, not the things of the world, our highest priority.

Lesson Setting

Time: *2006 B.C.*
Place: *Canaan*

Lesson Outline

Esau and Jacob as Rivals

  I. The Birth of Esau and Jacob: Genesis 25:19-26
    A. *Isaac's Family Line: vss. 19-20*
    B. *Isaac's Prayer On Behalf of Rebekah: vs. 21*
    C. *God's Revelation Concerning Rebekah's Twins: vss. 22-23*
    D. *Esau and Jacob's Names: vss. 24-26*
  II. The Selling of the Birthright: Genesis 25:27-34
    A. *Esau and Jacob's Distinct Personalities: vss. 27-28*
    B. *Esau's Demand: vss. 29-30*
    C. *Esau's Disdain of the Birthright: vss. 31-34*

Introduction for Adults

Topic: *Sibling Rivalry!*

In the April 30, 2004 edition of the *San Jose State University Spartan Daily,* John Myers reported being asked at the last minute to fill in as a judge at the eighth annual Perpetratin' lip-sync/dance competition. What impressed Myers the most were the "steps and strolls" of the African-American fraternities. By this he meant the performance of synchronized line dancing punctuated by stomping and clapping.

Myers recalled the routine completed by the Kappa Alpha Psi fraternity. It's members marched in fluid dance steps down the aisle of the auditorium. During this complex routine, they incorporated the use of a cane. "The cane becomes part of the steps," said Alpha English, vice president of Kappa Alpha Psi. "It's a sign of prestige." The steps and strolls unite the chapters, said Ignacio Rios, a member of Sigma Lambda Beta.

Imagine how united the members of a church could become if they cooperated just as much in the work of the Lord. There would be no evidence spiritual "sibling rivalry"!

Introduction for Youth

Topic: *Costly Stew*

The episode involving the costly stew is a sobering reminder that no one can serve two masters. We will either devote ourselves to the Lord or the things of the world (Matt. 6:24). The devil knows this and works through the allures of the world (1 John 5:19) to draw us away from fellowship with God into fellowship with the world. Thus, we must not be ignorant of the devil's schemes (2 Cor. 2:11), for he uses selfishness, greed, and vain status-seeking to appeal to our sinful natures and seduce us from fellowship with the Father and His Son.

Regrettably, some saved teens desperately try to follow the Lord while embracing the very system that despises Him and everything for which He stands. While believers are permitted to use the things in the world (see 1 Cor. 7:31), none of these things must ever take God's place in their affections or interfere with God's will and plan for their lives.

Concepts for Children

Topic: *Jacob Played a Trick on Esau*

1. Rebekah learned from the Lord that two nations would come from her sons.
2. As Esau and Jacob got older, they competed more and more with each other.
3. Isaac favored Esau, while Rebekah favored Jacob.
4. Esau saw little value in his special place as Isaac's firstborn son.
5. God wants us to value our relationship with Him as members of His family.

Lesson Commentary

I. THE BIRTH OF ESAU AND JACOB: GENESIS 25:19-26

A. Isaac's Family Line: vss. 19-20

This is the account of Abraham's son Isaac. Abraham became the father of Isaac, and Isaac was forty years old when he married Rebekah daughter of Bethuel the Aramean from Paddan Aram and sister of Laban the Aramean.

As Genesis 25:19 and 20 state, Abraham was the father of Isaac, who was 40 years old when he married Rebekah. Genesis 24 (the longest chapter in the book) records how Abraham's chief servant found Rebekah as a wife for Isaac. As the daughter of Bethuel, Rebekah was a near relative of Abraham's family. The text says that Bethuel was an Aramean from Paddan Aram (see Deut. 26:5), which means "Plain of Aram" or "Field of Aram." This is another name for Aram Naharaim (Gen. 24:10), which literally means "Aram of the two rivers." The reference is to the Euphrates and Tigris rivers in northwest Mesopotamia.

The land of Aram extended from the Lebanon mountain range (on the east) to the Euphrates River (on the west) and from the Taurus mountain range (on the north) to Damascus (on the south). As early as the second millennium B.C., the Arameans began settling what is now called Syria and some parts of Babylon. Eventually, the Arameans formed a loose confederation of encampments and towns.

A comparison of 25:7 and 20 indicates that Isaac married 35 years before Abraham died. Also, a comparison of verses 20 and 26 reveals that Isaac had to wait 20 years—from the time he was 40, when he married Rebekah, until he was 60— before Rebekah gave birth to Esau and Jacob. Moreover, Abraham would have been alive to see the fraternal twins begin to grow up and reach early adolescence.

According to verse 20, Rebekah was the sister of Laban the Aramean. He is first introduced 24:29-31, where the text relates that he went out to meet the chief servant of Abraham and invited the visitor to lodge at the family home. Laban also played a prominent role in the rest of the account recorded in the chapter. For instance, after the servant rehearsed his encounter with Rebekah, Laban and Bethuel affirmed that the Lord had brought the servant to the area and that God had chosen Rebekah to become Isaac's wife (vss. 50-51). Also, it was Laban and his mother who suggested that Rebekah stay at least 10 days before leaving her family to marry Isaac (vs. 55). Years later, Rebekah had Jacob flee to his uncle Laban as a way to escape from Esau, who threatened to kill his twin brother for stealing the family blessing from him (27:43-45).

B. Isaac's Prayer On Behalf of Rebekah: vs. 21

Isaac prayed to the LORD on behalf of his wife, because she was barren. The LORD answered his prayer, and his wife Rebekah became pregnant.

Like Sarah (Gen. 11:30), Rebekah was childless, and her inability to conceive and bear a son placed the fulfillment of the covenantal promises in jeopardy. A superficial reading of 25:21 might leave the impression that Isaac prayed once or twice and then God answered the patriarch's request; but as was previously noted, two decades passed before the Lord enabled Rebekah to become pregnant (compare verses 20 and 26). From this we see that it was God's grace that enabled Isaac's wife to conceive.

Perhaps in the interim, as time wore on, Isaac became more and more concerned about his lack of children. Undoubtedly, the Lord was testing Isaac's faith, as He had previously tested Abraham's faith. Indeed, many years earlier the patriarch had waited patiently for Isaac's birth. God knew all along what He would do, but He waited to do it in cooperation with the prayers of such individuals as Isaac and Abraham.

It was by faith that Abraham and Sarah were enabled to become parents at a late age (Heb. 11:11). God's promise to Abraham was that his descendants would be "as numerous as the stars in the sky and as countless as the sand on the seashore" (Heb. 11:12; compare Gen. 22:17); and yet Abraham (at age 99) and Sarah (at age 89) were well past the normal parenting age when their son, Isaac, was conceived. Thus, for a long time, the hope of God's promise actually being fulfilled must have looked dim; but Abraham kept faith in God and His promise, and eventually that promise was realized.

C. God's Revelation Concerning Rebekah's Twins: vss. 22-23

The babies jostled each other within her, and she said, "Why is this happening to me?" So she went to inquire of the LORD. The LORD said to her, "Two nations are in your womb, and two peoples from within you will be separated; one people will be stronger than the other, and the older will serve the younger."

The Lord gave Isaac not one son but two. Prior to their birth, the "babies jostled each other" (Gen. 25:22) within Rebekah. The Hebrew verb rendered "jostled" suggests an extraordinarily vigorous struggle between the twins. The activity within Rebekah's womb concerned her so much that she wondered why it was happening to her. There also seems to be a hint of discouragement in her question as she despaired over what the jostling could mean for the future of her babies.

Understandably, Rebekah decided to ask the Lord for clarification. There is no explanation given as to how Rebekah made her inquiry. One possibility is that she went to a nearby place of worship and consulted some sort of oracle, such as a patriarchal altar (see 12:6-7). First Samuel 9:9 states that in later Israelite history, God's people would go to a seer or prophet to seek the Lord's will.

In any case, Rebekah learned that she was pregnant with fraternal twins and that their future would be far from mundane. The Lord revealed that two nations and groups of people (Edom and Israel) would arise from the two children. Esau and Jacob would struggle with each other and so would the nations arising from them. Contrary to custom, however, the descendants of Jacob (the younger twin) would grow stronger than and dominate the descendants of Esau (the older twin; Gen. 25:23). In short, the younger son would receive the blessings of the covenant. This turn of events reflected the Lord's will. Thus, in the final analysis, it was unnecessary for Jacob to use trickery and deceit to gain the upper hand over Esau.

The importance of God's statement cannot be overemphasized. In Romans 9, Paul noted that the Lord made His choice regarding the promised line even before the twins were born and before they had done anything good or bad (vss. 10-11). Some experts stress that God's choice of Jacob over Esau was not based on the works either offspring would do; rather, God simply made a sovereign decision. That choice involved not only the promised line, but also the fact that the "older," Esau, would serve the "younger," Jacob (vs. 12).

In contrast, other experts say that instead of a sovereign election, God looked into the future and saw Jacob's eventual willingness to obey Him and chose him on that basis. Although it would be many years before Jacob displayed maturity in his relationship with God, the characters of Esau and Jacob would eventually confirm the wisdom of the Lord's decision. Indeed, while Jacob takes his place in the honor roll of faith in Hebrews 11, Jacob's brother Esau became a classic case of godlessness. Esau was a prototype of the secular person, for he failed to value what God accorded a high price tag. Esau bartered away his birthright.

Perhaps the most difficult sentence to understand is found in Romans 9:13: "Just as it is written: Jacob I loved, but Esau I hated" (see Mal. 1:2-3). Paul was not talking about an emotional or temperamental hatred. This hatred was not absolute, but was relative to a higher choice. Used in this way, the word "hated" (Rom. 9:13) can carry the meaning "loved less."

Experts also tell us that in ancient days the word "hate" was often used figuratively. In the present context in regard to the promised line, the phrase "Jacob I loved, but Esau I hated" carries the meaning "Jacob I chose, but Esau I rejected." The fact that God did not emotionally "hate" Esau is clear from the fact that the Lord bestowed many temporal blessings on Esau, his family, and his descendants.

D. Esau and Jacob's Names: vss. 24-26

When the time came for her to give birth, there were twin boys in her womb. The first to come out was red, and his whole body was like a hairy garment; so they named him Esau. After this, his brother came out, with his hand grasping Esau's heel; so he was named Jacob. Isaac was sixty years old when Rebekah gave birth to them.

Eventually the time arrived for Rebekah to give birth to the fraternal twins in her womb (Gen. 25:24). The first infant to emerge was reddish all over his body. Also, he was covered with so much hair that it appeared as if he was wearing an animal skin (vs. 25). The baby's appearance was a sign of things to come. For instance, "red" translates the Hebrew word *'admoni*, which is a wordplay on the Edomites, the descendants of Esau. Also, "hairy" renders the Hebrew word *se'ar*, which is a word play on Mount Seir, where the Edomites later lived (36:8, 20). Finally, the name

"Esau" (24:25) may also mean "hairy."

A short time later, the other twin emerged from Rebekah's womb with his hand clutching the heel of Esau (vs. 26). The name given the second twin—"Jacob"—is a play on the Hebrew word for "heel." The name, which is a verb in the original, means "to follow closely," "to guard," and "to protect." One might imagine a rearguard of soldiers dogging the steps of those in front to secure the flank of a military formation. Based on this information, some suggest "Jacob" means "may God protect (him)" or "God has protected."

In 27:36, Esau gave a negative connotation to Jacob's name (see Jer. 9:4; Hos. 12:3). The older twin, being angry over Jacob's theft of the family blessing, focused on a related meaning for the younger brother's name—"one who takes by the heel." This was a Hebrew idiom for "one who supplants," "one who takes advantage of," or "one who deceives."

Later in Jacob's life, God renamed him "Israel" (which may mean "one who struggles with God," "one who perseveres with God," or "one whom God has justified") as a sign of his spiritual struggle (Gen. 32:28; 35:10). This is the same name that Jacob's descendants eventually adopted as their political and religious title. Although Jacob was characterized by deceitfulness in his earlier days, by the time he reached the end of his life, he was a person of genuine faith and integrity (Heb. 11:21).

II. THE SELLING OF THE BIRTHRIGHT: GENESIS 25:27-34

A. Esau and Jacob's Distinct Personalities: vss. 27-28

The boys grew up, and Esau became a skillful hunter, a man of the open country, while Jacob was a quiet man, staying among the tents. Isaac, who had a taste for wild game, loved Esau, but Rebekah loved Jacob.

By the time the fraternal twins reached adulthood, Esau had become a cunning hunter who enjoyed roaming the open fields in search of game. This lifestyle suited his extroverted, rough-and-ready personality. In contrast, Jacob was more introverted, calculating, and domesticated. He was also calm and even-tempered, preferring to live in tents (Gen. 25:27). Because Isaac enjoyed eating wild game, he loved Esau. On the other hand, Rebekah favored Jacob (vs. 28).

The displays of favoritism by the parents caused great problems in the home. It deepened the rivalry between the brothers, and eventually broke apart the family. The sad results of the partiality in Isaac's family serve as a warning to parents today. Human nature has not changed since the time of Isaac and Rebekah. It is easy to play favorites with children, and the resulting strife from such actions still occurs today. Favoritism is almost a guarantee of trouble.

B. Esau's Demand: vss. 29-30

Once when Jacob was cooking some stew, Esau came in from the open country, famished. He said to Jacob, "Quick, let me have some of that red stew! I'm famished!" (That is why he was also called Edom.)

The narrative spotlights one incident in the lives of the fraternal twins. Jacob had been cooking some stew when Esau returned from the open fields exhausted and hungry (Gen. 25:29). Apparently, his efforts that day to hunt wild game had failed. When he spotted some of the red stew Jacob had made, Esau demanded some of it (vs. 30). Just as the stew was red in color, so too Esau's descendants would be called "Edom," which means "red." This designation was appropriate, for the place where they eventually settled was characterized by reddish hills.

This episode depicts Esau as an impulsive and insistent person. Because he felt as if his hunger would not wait, he presumed that Jacob would immediately satisfy his request for a ready-to-eat meal. Esau may have also lived for the moment, given the fact that he loved to be outdoors hunting game. The irony is that he came on the scene like a hungry animal, only to be entrapped by his more civilized and quiet brother.

C. Esau's Disdain of the Birthright: vss. 31-34

Jacob replied, "First sell me your birthright." "Look, I am about to die," Esau said. "What good is the birthright to me?" But Jacob said, "Swear to me first." So he swore an oath to him, selling his birthright to Jacob. Then Jacob gave Esau some bread and some lentil stew. He ate and drank, and then got up and left. So Esau despised his birthright.

In Bible times it was customary for the firstborn son (whether the child of a legal wife or a concubine) to inherit the rights, or privileges, of the family. This typically included receiving the family name and titles. It also included becoming the leader of the family and the one through whom the line was continued. Further, because a child was the firstborn, he usually inherited a double portion of the family estate. Archaeologists have discovered that these customs were not absolutely observed by people in the ancient Near East, and the Bible gives evidence of that as well. A father could ignore the rights of the firstborn and give the inheritance to a younger son (Gen. 48:13-20). A father could also disregard the firstborn son of a concubine in favor of a son he had later through a legal wife (21:10).

In addition to the birthright, there was also the family blessing. This consisted of the father orally conveying his authority and possessions to his children sometime before his death. The father usually followed an informal ceremony in which he first prayed that God's favor would rest upon one of his descendants (most often the firstborn). The father then would divide his power and property among his children. Once the family blessing was conferred, it was considered irrevocable.

Genesis 27:1-40 relates how Jacob stole the family blessing from Esau, while 25:29-34 explains how Esau sold his birthright to Jacob. In the latter incident, Jacob said he was willing to give his brother some stew, but only if Esau would accept it as the price for his family inheritance (vs. 31). Perhaps Jacob recalled the prophecy made at his birth that "the older will serve the younger" (vs. 23). If so, he was ready to do his part in making the prediction come true by securing the birthright. In Isaac's family, this included the promises of the covenant God had made with Abraham.

Esau exclaimed that he was dying of starvation. From his shortsighted perspective, the birthright had little immediate value (vs. 32). Like a skilled hunter who was ready to pounce on his weakened prey, Jacob insisted that Esau swear an oath that he was transferring his inheritance rights (vs. 33). When Esau agreed to the exchange, Jacob gave his older brother some bread and lentil stew, which Esau promptly consumed before getting up and leaving. In this way, he despised his birthright. Expressed differently, he treated the family inheritance with contempt.

If Esau had valued the great covenant blessings given to Abraham and Isaac, he would not have considered selling his birthright under any circumstances. Although there were material benefits to the covenant, the promises revolved mainly around God's redemptive program. We can assume that Jacob wanted to be a part of that. He desired a place in God's plan to bless the whole world. In contrast, Esau had little regard for God's redemptive work.

Discussion Questions

1. How did Jacob respond to Rebekah's childless condition?
2. Why did Rebekah inquire of the Lord concerning her pregnancy?
3. What was the name given to Rebekah's firstborn son?
4. What was the name given to Rebekah's secondborn son?
5. In what way did Esau treat his birthright with disdain?

Contemporary Application

"Profane," "secular," and "godless" are terms that aptly describe the character of Esau. Sadly, he serves as a fitting prototype of many in our day. The impression is of people who care little, if at all, about the things of God. They are irreligious and indifferent to eternal, spiritual realities, as if the here-and-now is all that matters.

The incident of Esau and Jacob gives us an opportunity to examine our values. Are we driven by our appetites or does the prospect of knowing God in a closer and more personal way motivate our hearts and lives? We need to take to heart what James 4:4 declares about friendship with the world. The result of such is enmity against God. Indeed, all who drink heavily from the cesspool of the pagan world system are the Lord's enemies.

At first, such a pronouncement might seem harsh and feel excessive; but before we dismiss what has just been said, consider 1 John 2:15-17. There the apostle encouraged believers to take the high road mandated by their divine calling. He commanded his readers not to love the world or anything in it.

At every turn this ungodly, humanistic system opposes God and actively seeks to subvert His plan of salvation for humankind. For this reason, John wanted it understood that one cannot love that world and all that it has to offer and love God at the same time. A clear choice has to be made—love God and hate the world or love the world and hate God. The two options are mutually exclusive.

Jacob's Dream at Bethel

DEVOTIONAL READING

Psalm 105:1-11

DAILY BIBLE READINGS

Monday October 8
Psalm 105:1-6 Remember God's Works

Tuesday October 9
Psalm 105:7-11 An Everlasting Covenant

Wednesday October 10
Genesis 27:41-45 The Conflict Deepens

Thursday October 11
Genesis 27:46—28:5 To Seek a Wife

Friday October 12
Genesis 28:6-9 Esau Takes Another Wife

Saturday October 13
Genesis 28:10-17 God's Covenant with Jacob

Sunday October 14
Genesis 28:18-22 The Place Named Bethel

Scripture

Background Scripture: *Genesis 27:41—28:22*

Scripture Lesson: *Genesis 28:10-22*

Key Verse: *[The LORD said,] "I am with you and will watch over you wherever you go, and I will bring you back to this land. I will not leave you until I have done what I have promised you."* Genesis 28:15.

Scripture Lesson for Children: *Genesis 27:41-43; 28:10-13, 15-18, 20-21*

Key Verse for Children: *[The LORD said,] "I am with you and will watch over you wherever you go."* Genesis 28:15.

Lesson Aim

To emphasize that God is always with us, even in life's seemingly darkest, fear-inducing moments.

Lesson Setting

Time: *1929 B.C.*

Place: *Beersheba and Luz (Bethel)*

Lesson Outline

Jacob's Dream at Bethel

   I. A Remarkable Dream: Genesis 28:10-15

      A. *Jacob's Departure: vs. 10*

      B. *Jacob's Decision to Rest: vs. 11*

      C. *A Stairway Reaching to Heaven: vs. 12*

      D. *God's Promise to Jacob: vss. 13-15*

   II. A Solemn Vow: Genesis 28:16-22

      A. *Jacob's Exclamation: vss. 16-17*

      B. *Jacob's Commemoration of the Encounter: vss. 18-19*

      C. *Jacob's Pledge: vss. 20-22*

Introduction for Adults

Topic: *Understanding Our Dreams!*

"There is a specialness to this place that you can feel. With all the history here, I just wanted to be a part it." The statement came from a Portsmouth, Ohio, man who had taken a day off from work and had driven seven hours to Gettysburg, Pennsylvania, in order to witness the burial of an unknown Civil War soldier whose body had been exposed by the rains and who was finally laid to rest on July 1, 1997.

Jacob might have felt the same way after having a dream in which he encountered God. There was now a specialness to the place where the incident occurred. Perhaps we can look back to times when we sensed the Lord's presence in an unusual way. Even though it may not have involved experiencing a dream as vivid's as Jacob's, the experience can be a special moment for us from which we draw encouragement and strength to face new challenges in our lives.

Introduction for Youth

Topic: *A Dream and a Promise*

A large teaching hospital's newborn section had a problem. The crying babies kept each other awake. The newborns needed quiet and sleep, but the distraught staff couldn't seem to find a way of reducing the sound level. Soundproofing the walls and ceiling didn't help calm the infants. Finally, a staff member experimented with recording the heartbeat of each baby's mother and playing that recording beside the baby's bassinet. The effect was astonishing. The sound that each little one heard even before birth provided the security and comfort that brought calm.

Jacob had not thought much about the Lord until the young man had a strange dream while fleeing to Haran. Unsettled about the past and frightened about the future, he received the message, "I am with you and will watch over you wherever you go" (Gen. 28:15). Like the heartbeat of God, this message brought calm and a sense of relief to the fugitive Jacob. Regardless of our age, we too can draw similar comfort from God's promises to us.

Concepts for Children

Topic: *Jacob Had a Dream*

1. The hatred between Esau and Jacob reached the point where Esau planned to kill Jacob.
2. In order to save Jacob's life, Rebekah and Isaac sent Jacob to a place called Haran.
3. While on the way, Jacob had a dream in which he saw angels going to and from heaven.
4. When Jacob awoke from his dream, he praised God for His presence.
5. Jacob set up a stone to remember his experience with God.

Lesson Commentary

I. A REMARKABLE DREAM: GENESIS 28:10-15

A. Jacob's Departure: vs. 10

Jacob left Beersheba and set out for Haran.

We learned last week how Esau bartered away his inheritance rights to Jacob (Gen. 25:29-34). Sometime later, Jacob used blackmail and deceit to take Esau's blessing from him (27:1-40). Officially, Jacob was now the more prominent of the two brothers, and Esau detested Jacob for it. Esau's grudge was so intense that he wanted to kill Jacob.

Esau knew he could never profit from murdering his fraternal twin while their father still lived. Esau guessed that Isaac would soon die (vs. 2). In ancient times, it would be customary for the entire family to gather together to grieve the loss of their loved one. Esau concluded that such a situation would be a perfect time for him to get rid of his younger brother (vs. 41).

When Rebekah heard about Esau's murderous plot, the mother took it seriously. She feared that she might lose both sons, perhaps reasoning that if Esau killed Jacob, another member of the clan would avenge the death by murdering Esau. Thus, Rebekah warned her favorite son. The mother's advice was for Jacob to hide out among her relatives until Esau's anger cooled (vss. 42-45).

It would be better if Jacob were to leave home with his father's permission, rather than to desert the family suddenly and without warning. Consequently, Rebekah approached Isaac on Jacob's behalf. The mother chose not to tell her husband about Esau's plan of murder, perhaps because Isaac would not have believed such a tale about his favorite son; instead, Rebekah slyly hinted at another reason for Jacob to leave.

Many years earlier, when Isaac himself had been ready to marry, his father had carefully sought a wife for Isaac from among their relatives (chap. 24). Until this point, however, Isaac had neglected to do the same for his sons. As a result, Esau had married women from among the Hittites (26:34). Jacob, at the age of 77, had not yet taken a wife. According to the custom of the time, Rebekah undoubtedly worked on household chores with the other women of her extended family. She told her husband that their daughters-in-law, the Hittites wives of Esau, were making her life unbearable. Rebekah surmised that things would only get worse if Jacob also married a Hittite woman (27:46; see 26:35).

Isaac took the hint. He ordered Jacob not to marry a Canaanite woman (28:1); instead, he was to leave immediately for Paddan Aram (that is, northwestern Mesopotamia) and journey to the household of his grandfather Bethuel. Jacob was to find and marry one of his cousins on his mother's side of the family, particularly, one of his uncle Laban's daughters (vs. 2).

Isaac also repeated the family blessing on Jacob. In the previous episode (27:27-

29), Isaac prayed that God would always give Jacob plenty of dew for healthy crops and abundant harvests of grain and wine. Isaac also foretold that many nations would one day become the servants of Jacob's descendants and that he would rule over his extended family members.

In 28:3-4, Isaac again prayed for God's richest blessings on Jacob. It was Isaac's desire that almighty God would give Jacob many descendants, who in turn would become a great assembly of nations. Isaac foretold that the land of Canaan, where he and his father lived as foreigners, would one day become the possession of Jacob's descendants. Jacob received these blessings of the Abrahamic covenant because God wanted him to have them, not because of his trickery. Probably for the first time in Jacob's life, he left Beersheba (vs. 5) and set out on his 450-mile trip for Haran (vs. 10).

B. Jacob's Decision to Rest: vs. 11

When he reached a certain place, he stopped for the night because the sun had set. Taking one of the stones there, he put it under his head and lay down to sleep.

One of Jacob's stops along the way was at a place near the town of Luz (Gen. 28:11; see vs. 19). It is doubtful that he made it there on the first day of his journey. Ordinarily, it would have taken three or four days to travel the 70 miles from Beersheba to Luz; but some have suggested that since Jacob was fleeing from Esau, the younger brother might have traveled that far before stopping.

In any case, Jacob chose Luz for his night's stopover because darkness overtook him there. Many years earlier, Jacob's grandfather, Abraham, had built an altar near there and worshiped the Lord through prayer and sacrifice (12:8). We do not know whether Jacob recognized the significance of his campsite, but Bethel would become a holy place for Jacob as it had been for Abraham.

Jacob, being weary from his journey, decided to lay down to sleep. He took one of the nearby stones and placed it under his head before drifting off. His use of a stone to support his head may seem strange to us, but in ancient times, stones and even pieces of metal were commonly used as headrests. Others have noted that many ancient cultures viewed certain types of stones as being magical or sacred. Perhaps Jacob felt the stone he used as a pillow contained some spiritual power. In a short while, what looked like an ordinary object would be transformed into a sanctuary, for Jacob would come to regard it as the residence of God (vs. 22).

C. A Stairway Reaching to Heaven: vs. 12

He had a dream in which he saw a stairway resting on the earth, with its top reaching to heaven, and the angels of God were ascending and descending on it.

Hebrews 1:1-2 notes that during the era of the Old Testament, God spoke to His people through His prophets on a number of occasions, and He did so in various portions and in a variety of ways. This included riddles, visions, and dreams, such as the one Jacob experienced while at Bethel (Gen. 28:12). Dreams in Scripture represent a series of thoughts, images, or emotions that occur during sleep, at which time divine revelation is communicated.

Dreams and visions are often regarded as distinct. Dreams are usually associated with experiences of the night while a person is resting. Visions are thought of as occurring while a person is either awake or in a trance state. In Scripture, however, the terms "dream" and "vision" are often used interchangeably or together to describe the same experience (see Dan. 2:19, 28; 7:1-2). When God spoke through dreams and visions, the time of day or whether a person was asleep or awake was of little importance. What was important was the divine message itself.

In Jacob's dream, he saw a stairway that reached from earth to heaven (Gen. 28:12). Some mistakenly envision this to be a wooden ladder with rungs. In actuality, Jacob's stairway resembled a large stone ramp with steps that mounted the sloping side of a Mesopotamian temple-tower called a ziggurat. Such a structure was square at its base and pyramid-like in shape. At the apex of this massive, lofty, and solid-brick edifice was a small shrine that supposedly served as the gateway between heaven and earth (see 11:4). Sometimes the shrine was covered with blue enamel so that it would more easily blend in with the sky, the reputed celestial home of the gods.

Jacob saw angels of God going up and coming down the other-worldly ramp (28:12). Scripture reveals that angels are spirits (Heb. 1:14) who are in heaven (Matt. 22:30) sent to earth as messengers by God. They are mighty (Ps. 103:20) and powerful (2 Thess. 1:7) and possess great wisdom (2 Sam. 14:20). Ordinarily they are invisible to us (2 Kings 6:17), though they have appeared as people (Luke 24:4).

Contrary to popular belief and artistic portrayal, few angels in the Bible are explicitly stated to have wings. In fact, Isaiah 6:2 may be the sole instance. On the other hand, angels are said to have the ability to fly (Dan. 9:21). Among their duties are serving God by serving us (Heb. 1:14), providing us protection (Dan. 6:22), guarding us (Ps. 91:11), guiding us (Acts 8:26), and helping us (Dan. 10:13). In addition to the elect angels who worship and serve the purposes of God (I Tim. 5:21; Heb. 1:6), there are also fallen angels who serve the purposes of Satan (Rev. 12:7-9).

The activity of angels in the spot where Jacob slept indicates that the locale was sacred, representing the meeting point between the human sphere and the heavenly realm (Gen. 28:19). Bethel, as the "house of God," foreshadowed the Lord Jesus (see John 1:51). As the Mediator between God and people (John 14:6; 1 Tim. 2:5), the Redeemer enables believers to be at peace with God (Rom. 5:1). The Messiah is also the believers' great High Priest who enables them to go before the throne of their gracious God to receive His mercy and help in their time of need (Heb. 4:14-16).

D. God's Promise to Jacob: vss. 13-15

There above it stood the LORD, and he said: "I am the LORD, the God of your father Abraham and the God of Isaac. I will give you and your descendants the land on which you are lying. Your descendants will be like the dust of the earth, and you will spread out to the west and to the east, to the north and to the south. All peoples on earth will be blessed through you and your offspring. I am with you and will watch over you wherever you go, and I will bring you back to this land. I will not leave you until I have done what I have promised you."

As Jacob slept, he saw God standing at the top of the stairway or ramp. It's also possible Jacob experienced the divine presence either beside or directly over him. The Lord spoke to Jacob, identifying Himself as Yahweh, the God of Abraham and Isaac. The ever-living, all powerful God was making Jacob the recipient of the same covenant promises bestowed on his grandfather and father. In particular, Jacob and his descendants would inherit Canaan (Gen. 28:13). Moreover, Jacob's offspring would become as numerous as the dust of the earth. Indeed, they would cover the promised land from east to west and from north to south.

Furthermore, all the families of the earth would be blessed through Jacob and his descendants (vs. 14). The idea is that the patriarch and his offspring would become a channel or source of blessing for others. It's also possible this verse is declaring that others would regard Jacob as an noteworthy example of divine blessing. In this case, they would use his name and that of his descendants as they pronounced blessings on one another (see Gen. 48:20; Ruth 4:11).

When Jacob first began his trip to Haran, he must have been wondering about many things. What would become of him? Would he ever see his home again? Was he really in line to receive the covenant blessings? In the dream, the Lord addressed Jacob's concerns. God was not like pagan deities, whom people of the day believed protected them only within specific regions. The Lord promised to be with Jacob and sustain him wherever he traveled. Moreover, God pledged to bring Jacob back to Canaan, the promised land. In fact, the Lord would be with Jacob constantly, ensuring that all the covenant promises were fulfilled (Gen. 28:15).

II. A SOLEMN VOW: GENESIS 28:16-22

A.   Jacob's Exclamation: vss. 16-17

When Jacob awoke from his sleep, he thought, "Surely the LORD is in this place, and I was not aware of it." He was afraid and said, "How awesome is this place! This is none other than the house of God; this is the gate of heaven."

When Jacob woke up, he realized that the Lord was in the place where he had been resting and Jacob had not even been aware of it (Gen. 28:16). Given the solemnity of the occasion, Jacob was understandably afraid. The emotion was most likely a mixture of terror, reverence, and adoration. He reasoned that the spot where he lodged for the night was especially holy. The locale was awesome, being none other than the dwelling place (or house) of God, the gateway to heaven (vs. 17).

"LORD" (vs. 16) renders the Hebrew noun *Yahweh*. It was a deeply personal name that carried implications of the covenant relationship between God and the people of Israel. Exodus 3:14 is the only place in the Old Testament where the significance of the name is touched on. The name "I am" comes from the Hebrew verb *hayah*, which means "to exist" or "to be." In essence, the name *Yahweh* signifies that God is pure being. He is the self-existent one.

B. Jacob's Commemoration of the Encounter: vss. 18-19

Early the next morning Jacob took the stone he had placed under his head and set it up as a pillar and poured oil on top of it. He called that place Bethel, though the city used to be called Luz.

Jacob got up early the next morning, took the stone he had used as a headrest and set it upright as a pillar. In ancient times, such a stone could be used as a shrine (as in this case), a burial object, or a boundary marker. The stone would serve as a memorial of the vision Jacob had seen at the campsite. The sacred object would also be a reminder of the ramp that stretched from earth to heaven and on which the Lord stood. Jacob consecrated (or set apart) the stone by pouring olive oil over it (Gen. 28:18), which was a common practice in ancient times (see Exod. 30:25-29). The oil also stained the stone so that others who came along later could properly identify it.

Next, Jacob called the place "Bethel" (Gen. 25:19), which means "house of God" in Hebrew. Prior to this episode, the town had been called "Luz," which means "almond tree." Bethel was located in the hill country of Canaan, about 12 miles north of Jebus (later Jerusalem) and close to Ai. By Jacob's day, the bare mountaintop near Bethel had served as a center of worship for hundreds of years. "Bethel" may have been the name of the mountaintop sanctuary, while "Luz" referred to the town nearby. Verse 19 seems to refer to Bethel as a place and Luz as a town. Early Hebrew manuscripts of Joshua 16:2 indicate that Bethel and Luz were separate but close localities.

C. Jacob's Pledge: vss. 20-22

Then Jacob made a vow, saying, "If God will be with me and will watch over me on this journey I am taking and will give me food to eat and clothes to wear so that I return safely to my father's house, then the LORD will be my God and this stone that I have set up as a pillar will be God's house, and of all that you give me I will give you a tenth."

The Lord's promise to always be with Jacob was so meaningful to him that he vowed to make Yahweh his God. Jacob did not ask the Lord for either fame or riches. In a sense, Jacob was establishing a personal relationship with God. Jacob was taking the Lord at His word concerning His promises (Gen. 28:15). The patriarch translated the general promises God had made into specifics relating to his situation. Jacob would trust the Lord to remain with him, protect him on his journey, give him food and clothing, and one day bring him safely back to Canaan (vss. 20-21). By reiterating the covenantal promises, Jacob claimed them as his own.

Jacob then designated the rough stone column as "God's house" (vs. 22); in other words, the pillar would serve as a memorial and place for worshiping the Lord. Jacob also pledged to give the Lord one-tenth of his possessions. By this act (evidently a one-time gift), the patriarch expressed his gratitude to God, acknowledged the Lord as his God and King, and declared his willingness to commit everything to the Lord in wholehearted trust. Exactly who Jacob paid his tithe to is not specified in Scripture.

In ancient times, tithing was the practice of giving a tenth of one's income, whether in material goods or money, to God. That it was done by both Abraham (14:18-20) and Jacob (28:22) shows that it was an ancient practice established before the law of Moses prescribed it (Lev. 27:30-33). Throughout Israel's history, the tithe was used to support the priesthood. Also, every third year a special contribution was made for the poor either out of the tithe or in addition to it (Num. 18:21; Deut. 26:12).

Jacob's experience at Bethel had a profound effect on his life. Years after his first visit to this locale, when he fled from Laban, his father-in-law, Jacob received another divine revelation from the God of Bethel (Gen. 31:13). Jacob eventually returned to Bethel when he came back to the promised land (35:1-14). It was there that God changed Jacob's name to Israel, which permanently linked the city that grew there to him and his future descendants (vs. 10).

Discussion Questions

1. What are the details of the ladder, or stairway, that Jacob saw?
2. What promise did the Lord make to Jacob concerning the land?
3. What pledge did God make to Jacob with respect to his future descendants?
4. What did Jacob realize when he awoke from his dream?
5. What did Jacob pledge to do if the Lord watched over him on his journey?

Contemporary Application

While Jacob was in flight, fearing for his life, God spoke to him in a dream. He promised Jacob that He would always be with him, even assuring him that He would look after his descendants. At times most of us doubt God's presence when something unwelcome occurs in our lives; yet the Lord does not get angry or leave us because our faith wavers. Instead, He indicates to us in many ways that He is always close to us.

It's easy to tell someone not to be afraid when everything seems to be going well, but when a friend comes down with a serious illness, that's a different matter. Automatically, it seems, fear kicks in. Fear has positive value when it keeps us from taking risky chances; however, fear has negative value when it begins to undermine our faith.

In life's darkest, fear-inducing moments, the truth that God is our Shepherd and Guide can be reassuring. Just as shepherds provide lush meadows for their sheep to graze and peaceful streams for them to drink from, so the Lord will provide for the needs of His people. God has surely proven Himself to be trustworthy in meeting our needs in the past, and He can be trusted to provide our needs in the future.

Jacob and Rachel

Scripture

Background Scripture: *Genesis 29*

Scripture Lesson: *Genesis 29:21-35*

Key Verse: *So Jacob served seven years to get Rachel, but they seemed like only a few days to him because of his love for her.* Genesis 29:20.

Scripture Lesson for Children: *Genesis 29:1-6, 9-14, 18-20*

Key Verse for Children: *Jacob was in love with Rachel.* Genesis 29:18.

Lesson Aim

To note that deceit can destroy relationships.

Lesson Setting

Time: *1929 B.C.*
Place: *Nahor*

Lesson Outline

Jacob and Rachel

I. Jacob's Marriage to Leah and Rachel: Genesis 29:20-30
    A. *Jacob's Years of Service for Rachel: vs. 20*
    B. *Laban's Trickery: vs. 21-24*
    C. *Laban's Explanation: vs. 25-27*
    D. *Jacob's Additional Years of Service: vss. 28-30*
II. Jacob's Children: Genesis 29:31-35
    A. *The Birth of Reuben: vss. 31-32*
    B. *The Birth of Simeon: vs. 33*
    C. *The Birth of Levi: vs. 34*
    D. *The Birth of Judah: vs. 35*

Introduction for Adults

Topic: *Dashed Hopes and Fond Wishes!*

A relative of mine saw a layer of lies created when his daughter was in the third grade. Because she wanted the attention of her classmates, she told them that her mother had been in a serious car accident and that her arm was broken. The child's teacher caught wind of the student's fictional story and instructed the entire class to write get-well cards to the "injured" parent.

The scheme came crashing down on the girl when her mother happened to go into the garbage to search for a bill she had misplaced. The parent discovered those cards and realized that her daughter was tangled in a web of lies. The mother took her daughter to school to confess and apologize to the girl's teacher and classmates. That confession produced a flood of tears.

The mother actually felt more sorry for her daughter than upset with her. It was a painful lesson for the third grader; but she and her peers learned that lies are like flies. They breed quickly and menace both the person who lied and the people who were lied to, leading to many dashed hopes and unfulfilled expectations.

Introduction for Youth

Topic: *Date and Switch*

Brad was given one dollar by his parents when his family went to the flea market. Walking the aisles, he finally decided on buying a whoopee cushion, convinced of the fun that he would have later with his relatives. The salesman's pitch was persuasive as he promised the 11-year-old the lowest price on Cape Cod. Brad accepted the adult's word and bought the novelty with his dollar.

That evening, while Brad and his mother shopped, Brad saw his whoopee cushion at the store for 69 cents. Brad was infuriated, claiming that he had been ripped off. If Brad could feel so cheated at something that cost so little, imagine how Jacob felt when he was tricked by Laban. Jacob's dream of marrying Rachel was foiled, at least for the moment. Jacob would have to give Laban an additional seven years of labor to see the goal of marrying Rachel brought to pass.

Concepts for Children

Topic: *Jacob Loved Rachel*

1. Jacob came to the land of the eastern peoples.
2. Jacob met Rachel by a well of water.
3. Jacob then met Rachel's father, Laban.
4. After seven years had passed, Jacob planned to marry Rachel.
5. Jacob's love for Rachel reminds us of how much God loves us.

Lesson Commentary

I. Jacob's Marriage to Leah and Rachel: Genesis 29:20-30

A. Jacob's Years of Service for Rachel: vs. 20

So Jacob served seven years to get Rachel, but they seemed like only a few days to him because of his love for her.

After Jacob's encounter with God at Bethel (Gen. 28:10-22), he resumed his journey to the land of the east, which lay between Canaan and Mesopotamia (29:1). Jacob came upon three flocks of sheep lying in an open field beside a well and waiting to be watered (vs. 2). It was the custom for all the flocks to arrive before such a stone was removed. Then, once all the animals had been watered, the stone was rolled back over the mouth of the well (vs. 3). Jacob learned from shepherds (an occupation shared by both men and women in that culture) that they lived in Haran and that they knew a man named Laban, who was the grandson of Nahor (vss. 4-5). Jacob also found out that Laban was faring well. In fact, one of his daughters, Rachel, had just arrived with some of Laban's sheep (vs. 6).

Jacob advised the shepherds to water their flocks and allow the animals to graze some more (vs. 7); but they explained that they were in the habit of waiting for all the flocks to be assembled before the stone was rolled off the mouth of the well so that the sheep could be watered (vs. 8). While the conversation continued, Rachel arrived with her father's sheep, for she was tending them (vs. 9). Jacob, perhaps being energized by the sight of his beautiful cousin, used his own hands to remove the large stone covering the well. This demonstrated his strength to Rachel and enabled Jacob to be of service by watering his uncle's sheep (29:10).

The patriarch not only gave his cousin a customary kiss of greeting, but also wept aloud for joy (vs. 11). Clearly, this encounter was an emotional one for Jacob. Then, he explained to Rachel that he was a relative of her father and the son of Rebekah. In response, Rachel ran to tell her father. The young woman seems to have been well out in front of him. When Rachel finally reached Laban, she told him about Jacob (vs. 12). Upon hearing the news, Laban rushed out to meet Jacob, warmly embraced him, gave him a kiss of greeting, and brought him to his house (vs. 13).

Jacob took the opportunity to relate his situation to his uncle. Upon hearing his nephew's story, Laban openly acknowledged Jacob as being his own "flesh and blood" (vs. 14). The traveler had found a new home, where he lodged for the next month; but Jacob didn't lounge around in ease. He quickly began to participate in the routines of Laban's family. The uncle raised the issue of Jacob's wages. Thus far, Laban had not paid anything to his nephew. Laban realized he could not expect Jacob to work for room and board indefinitely, so the uncle asked his nephew how much he wanted to be paid for his labor (vs. 15).

It seems as if Laban viewed his relationship with Jacob primarily in economic terms and treated his nephew as a laborer under contract (see 31:38-42). Laban also treated his two daughters like animals to be bartered in trade. The older daughter was named Leah (which means "cow"), while the younger one was named Rachel (which means "ewe"; vs. 16). Leah lacked the kind of beauty people of that day seemed to prize, but the meaning of the Hebrew in verse 17 is uncertain. Views differ as to whether Leah's eyes were plain and dull or tender and delicate. While they may have been appealing in some way, she did not have the exceptional beauty of Rachel, who was gorgeous in both form and appearance.

Because Jacob had fallen in love with Rachel, he offered to serve Laban seven years in exchange for the privilege of marrying his younger daughter (vs. 18). A person could create a lot of wealth in that period of time. Perhaps Jacob made such a generous offer because he had no dowry (or bride price) to give for Rachel. Laban was not so foolish as to reject such an offer, so he agreed to Jacob's terms (vs. 19).

Accordingly, Laban's nephew worked for seven years to acquire Rachel; and because Jacob's love for his cousin was so strong, the time seemed like only a few days to him (vs. 20). Perhaps Jacob felt as if the dowry was rather insignificant in comparison to what he was getting in return—Rachel's hand in marriage. Also, the lengthy engagement gave Jacob and Rachel time to develop their relationship so that they could be as ready as possible for marriage.

B. Laban's Trickery: vs. 21-24

Then Jacob said to Laban, "Give me my wife. My time is completed, and I want to lie with her." So Laban brought together all the people of the place and gave a feast. But when evening came, he took his daughter Leah and gave her to Jacob, and Jacob lay with her. And Laban gave his servant girl Zilpah to his daughter as her maidservant.

At the end of seven years, Jacob told Laban that their contractual agreement had been satisfied. Thus, Jacob wanted to consummate his marriage to Rachel (Gen. 29:21). In response, Laban invited all the people in the area to celebrate with Jacob at a wedding feast (vs. 22). Earlier, in verse 19, Laban had responded ambiguously to Jacob. This was a shrewd decision on Laban's part, for he had not explicitly promised to give Rachel to Jacob in marriage; and to Jacob's chagrin, he was not astute enough to discern the vagueness in his uncle's reply.

When evening came, Laban brought his older, veiled daughter (see 24:65), Leah, to Jacob, and he had marital relations with her (29:23). Perhaps the older daughter said little or nothing that night, so that Jacob would not recognize her voice. According to the custom of the time, Laban gave his female servant, Zilpah, to Leah as her maid (vs. 24). Years earlier, Jacob had capitalized on the blindness of his father, Isaac, in order to deceive him and get the family blessing. Now Laban trumped that feat by using the cover of darkness to pull a fast one over his nephew. In this way, he gave the former trickster a large dose of his own toxic medicine.

We can only guess Rachel's feelings as she found out her father's plan. All her hopes and dreams were being cruelly disrupted by Laban's deceptive scheme. Perhaps he felt compelled to concoct it because he regarded Jacob as a worker who was too valuable to lose. Beyond question, the nephew had enabled Laban's flocks to increase steadily. With respect to Leah, she may have been forced to cooperate reluctantly with her father's plan. Without a doubt, God was using this episode to spiritually prune and mature Jacob.

C. Laban's Explanation: vs. 25-27

When morning came, there was Leah! So Jacob said to Laban, "What is this you have done to me? I served you for Rachel, didn't I? Why have you deceived me?" Laban replied, "It is not our custom here to give the younger daughter in marriage before the older one. Finish this daughter's bridal week; then we will give you the younger one also, in return for another seven years of work."

When Jacob woke up in the morning, he discovered that it was Leah, not Rachel, who was beside him. Understandably, Jacob was incensed by his uncle's shameless act of deception. Thus, the nephew confronted Laban. Jacob thought they had agreed he would work seven years for Rachel, but this did not prevent Laban from disregarding their contractual arrangement (Gen. 29:25). Interestingly, the Hebrew verb rendered "deceived" is lexically related to the noun translated "came deceitfully" appearing in 27:35. The latter term is used in relation to Jacob's deception of Esau. In this case, the adage fits, "what goes around, comes around."

Laban deftly avoided the ethical issue of his actions by referring to what his clan routinely did. The uncle claimed that it was the custom for the firstborn to be married off before any younger daughters (vs. 26). We don't know whether Laban was truly concerned about the local practice of marrying the older daughter first; but even if he was, that did not justify his underhanded tactics. If the uncle wanted, he could have told his nephew about the tradition before the wedding.

In an attempt to mollify Jacob's anger, Laban encouraged his nephew to complete Leah's bridal week. (In those days, a marriage ceremony included an entire week of festivities; see Judg. 14:12.) Then the father would give his younger daughter, Rachel, to Jacob in marriage. Of course, Laban expected seven more years of work out of Jacob in exchange for the younger daughter (vs. 27).

Throughout the transaction, Laban operated in a cunning and calculating fashion; and there was nothing Jacob could do about it. Because his love for Rachel was real and deep, he did not dare jeopardize his chance to consummate his marriage to her. Thus, in this contest of wits, Jacob was forced to comply with Laban's stipulations, which probably turned the nephew's marriage into an occasion for community-wide jesting.

D. Jacob's Additional Years of Service: vss. 28-30

And Jacob did so. He finished the week with Leah, and then Laban gave him his daughter Rachel to be his wife. Laban gave his servant girl Bilhah to his daughter Rachel as her maidservant. Jacob lay with Rachel also, and he loved Rachel more than Leah. And he worked for Laban another seven years.

Jacob agreed to work seven more years and completed Leah's bridal week (Gen. 29:28). In the ancient Near East, the wedding ceremony usually took place after dark at the bride's house. Prior to the wedding ceremony, the groom and his friends would form a procession and walk to the home of the bride. After the couple was officially married, the procession would return to the home of the groom or his father.

As the procession journeyed along a planned route, friends of the groom would join the group and participate in singing, playing musical instruments, and dancing. The bride would wear an ornate dress, expensive jewelry (if she could afford it), and a veil over her face. The groom typically hung a garland of flowers around his neck. Once the procession arrived at its destination, a lavish feast, lasting up to seven days, would begin. Friends would sing love ballads for the couple and share stories about them. Everyone would consume food and drink in generous quantities. At the end of the first day's festivities, the bride and groom would be escorted to their private wedding chamber.

It was only at the end of Jacob's bridal week with Leah that the patriarch was officially married to Rachel. Also, according to the custom of the time, Laban gave his female servant, Bilhah, to Rachel as her maid (vs. 29). Jacob, by having marital relations with Rachel, consummated his union with her; and though the patriarch had been tricked by his uncle, he willingly put in seven additional years of service as a dowry (of sorts) for Rachel. Verse 30 says that Jacob loved Rachel more than Leah. The irony is that God allowed Leah to give birth to Judah, from whom the future Messiah of Israel would come.

Since the discovery of the clay tablets at Nuzi containing ancient legal records, some commentators have regarded the contractual dealings between Laban and Jacob as the uncle's formal adoption of his nephew. The absence of any mention of Laban's sons in the account of Jacob's arrival may indicate that they were not yet born; and if that was the case, then Laban would certainly have been concerned about having a male heir.

According to the Nuzi tablets, one man could adopt another in order to gain him as an heir. One ancient tablet records an instance in which an adopted son received the father's daughter in marriage. According to the slab, if sons were born to the father after the adoption, then the inheritance would change, with some of the laws of the firstborn coming into play. If Laban's sons were born after his agreement with Jacob, that would help to explain the later change in the relationship between the uncle and his nephew (see 31:1-2).

II. JACOB'S CHILDREN: GENESIS 29:31-35

A. The Birth of Reuben: vss. 31-32

When the LORD saw that Leah was not loved, he opened her womb, but Rachel was barren. Leah became pregnant and gave birth to a son. She named him Reuben, for she said, "It is because the LORD has seen my misery. Surely my husband will love me now."

Scripture reveals that God is genuinely concerned with the plight of the those who are deprived and disadvantaged. By way of example, when Hagar fled into the wilderness after being mistreated by Sarah, the Lord's angel ministered to the young Egyptian mother (Gen. 16:6-14). Later, when Abraham sent away Hagar and Ishmael with little more than scant provisions, God's angel again intervened on behalf of the mother and her son with words of assurance and a needed supply of water (21:14-19).

In the case of Leah, the Lord took note of the fact that she was unloved. In the original, the verb rendered "not loved" (29:31) is more literally translated "hated." In the culture of that day, this circumstance put Leah at a distinct disadvantage with respect to Rachel, who was the primary object of Jacob's affection. God intervened by enabling Leah to become pregnant. Meanwhile, Rachel remained childless (29:31). Leah named her firstborn "Reuben" (vs. 32), which means "look, a son." It sounds like the Hebrew for "he has seen my misery." In this case, Leah sensed that the Lord had taken pity on her oppressed condition. The mother hoped that the birth of Reuben would incline Jacob to respond to her in love (vs. 33).

B. The Birth of Simeon: vs. 33

She conceived again, and when she gave birth to a son she said, "Because the LORD heard that I am not loved, he gave me this one too." So she named him Simeon.

The Lord enabled Leah to become pregnant a second time, and again she gave birth to a son. Perhaps the young mother had cried out to God in prayer and interpreted the births as an indication of His positive response to her unloved status. The name Leah gave to her second-born, "Simeon," is derived from a verb that means "to hear." In turn, the name probably means "one who hears," which underscores that the Lord had heard about Leah's forlorn situation and intervened accordingly.

C. The Birth of Levi: vs. 34

Again she conceived, and when she gave birth to a son she said, "Now at last my husband will become attached to me, because I have borne him three sons." So he was named Levi.

For the third time, the Lord enabled Leah to conceive and give birth to a son. The phrase rendered "my husband will become attached to me" (Gen. 29:34) implies that Leah hoped this most recent childbirth would spur Jacob to bond more closely in affection to Leah. Experts are uncertain about the exact meaning of the name "Levi," which Leah gave to the third of her three sons. It sounds like the Hebrew verb *lavah*, which means "to join" or "to attach," making the name an appropriate one under the circumstances.

D. The Birth of Judah: vs. 35

She conceived again, and when she gave birth to a son she said, "This time I will praise the LORD." So she named him Judah. Then she stopped having children.

For a fourth time, the Lord enabled Leah to become pregnant and give birth to a son. By this time she was overjoyed at God's favorable response to her cry for help. Indeed, it was an occasion for her to give praise to the Lord. This is the reason why she named her fourth son "Judah" (Gen. 29:35), which means "he will be praised." It sounds like and may be derived from a Hebrew verb that means "to praise." At this point, Leah stopped having children. Chapter 30 continues the account of the birth of Jacob's sons. By the time of the Exodus, Scripture says the patriarch's extended family had over 600,000 men, not counting women and children (Exod. 12:37).

Discussion Questions

1. How did Jacob feel about serving Laban seven years for the privilege of marrying Rachel?
2. In what way did Laban deceive Jacob?
3. How did Jacob feel concerning what Laban had done to him?
4. What did Laban say Jacob had to do in order to secure Rachel's hand in marriage?
5. At first why was Leah and not Rachel able to conceive and bear children?

Contemporary Application

One of the guiding principles of modern business is this: "Fool me once, shame on you. Fool me twice, shame on me." In other words, it should take only one hard-won lesson to make us forever wary. If we fail to be sufficiently on our guard after that, it is clearly our own fault.

Not surprisingly, that attitude does not lead to mutually satisfying business partnerships. It makes even less sense when it becomes the guiding principle of our personal lives. It turns once-loving, trusting relationships into bitter disappointments: "I cannot believe she said that about me. I will never trust her again!" "You swore you would never do that again. How can I ever believe another of your promises?" "He said he would not tell anybody—and he claimed to be my best friend!"

Relationships are built on trust. Once deception enters the picture—a violated confidence, a broken promise, an outright lie—trust is shattered, and the memory of the deceit taints everything that follows. Consider the way Laban treated Jacob concerning the issue of his planned marriage to Rachel. The excuse the uncle gave was offered flatly and without any sense of regret. The toxicity introduced during that early exchange tarnished the family dynamic for years to come.

Far too many Christians are involved in one or more relationships in which they are entangled in a web of deceit. The deceptions may be small or great, but they still do their relationships no good. The best course of action is set these dysfunctional relationships on the right path by dealing honestly and candidly with all forms of pretense and duplicity.

Esau and Jacob Reconciled

DEVOTIONAL READING

Psalm 133

DAILY BIBLE READINGS

Monday October 22
  Genesis 32:3-12 Jacob's Prayer

Tuesday October 23
  Genesis 32:13-21 Jacob's Presents to Esau

Wednesday October 24
  Genesis 33:1-4 The Brothers Wept Together

Thursday October 25
  Genesis 33:5-11 The Gift of Reconciliation

Friday October 26
  Genesis 33:12-15 Their Separate Ways

Saturday October 27
  Genesis 33:16-20 An Altar to God

Sunday October 28
  Psalm 133 The Blessedness of Unity

Scripture

Background Scripture: *Genesis 33*
Scripture Lesson: *Genesis 33:1-11*
Key Verse: *But Esau ran to meet Jacob and embraced him; he threw his arms around his neck and kissed him. And they wept.* Genesis 33:4.
Scripture Lesson for Children: *Genesis 33:1-11*
Key Verse for Children: *Esau ran to meet Jacob and . . . kissed him. And they wept.* Genesis 33:4.

Lesson Aim

To stress that experiencing God changes our relationships and our priorities.

Lesson Setting

Time: *1909 B.C.*
Place: *East and west sides of the Jordan River*

Lesson Outline

Esau and Jacob Reconciled

  I. The Meeting of Jacob and Esau: Genesis 33:1-4
      A. *Esau's Arrival with His Men: vs. 1a*
      B. *Jacob's Defensive Strategy: vss. 1b-3*
      C. *Esau's Display of Affection: vs. 4*
  II. The Reconciliation of Jacob and Esau: Genesis 33:5-11
      A. *Esau's Question about Jacob's Children: vss. 5-7*
      B. *Esau's Question about Jacob's Livestock: vs. 8*
      C. *Discussion Concerning Jacob's Gift: vss. 9-11*

Introduction for Adults

Topic: *Family Reunion!*

A friend related an experience that changed his life. As he awakened in his chair on an airliner to the words "We have a very serious emergency," James suddenly looked toward his eternity. Three engines on the plane had been rendered useless because of fuel contamination, and the remaining one would lose power any second.

James decided to bury his head in his lap and pull up his knees. Then he made what he thought would be his last earth-to-heaven communication: "Oh, Lord, thank You! Life has been wonderful. . . . Oh, Lord, please be with my wife and my children, whom I'll never see again!"

Miraculously, the plane landed and at least one dazed passenger—James—roamed the airport piecing things together. He concluded, "Here is the bottom line: relationship." Nothing else matters. At that moment the family relationships he thought he had cherished went to a much deeper level. God had underscored their importance.

Introduction for Youth

Topic: *Family Reunion*

As the Civil War drew to a close, President Lincoln stood with his little son, Tad, on the steps of the White House listening to a band. One of the soldiers approached with a noose and a knife. He stated that these items were both to be used on Jefferson Davis (the President of the Confederate States of America).

Lincoln told the soldier that reconciliation was hard to effect when one approached with a knife and a noose. His son Tad asked why Davis should not be hanged. Lincoln responded that Davis and all the others should not be hanged, and told the boy that he advocated a plan whereby all the rebels would be pardoned and not punished. Lincoln said that revenge was best left up to the Lord.

Lincoln saw an ideal way to resolve a conflict and restore a nation's citizens. Jacob and Esau, likewise, approached each other with open arms, not with a knife and a noose. Their family reunion became an occasion for rejoicing.

Concepts for Children

Topic: *Two Brothers Reunite*

1. Fear of Esau played a part in Jacob's reunion with his brother.
2. Esau showed a forgiving attitude when he saw Jacob.
3. Jacob offered a gift to Esau.
4. Jacob saw God's favor in Esau's response to his return.
5. The kindness and compassion between Esau and Jacob should reflect the way we treat each other.

Lesson Commentary

I. THE MEETING OF JACOB AND ESAU: GENESIS 33:1-4

A. Esau's Arrival with His Men: vs. 1a

Jacob looked up and there was Esau, coming with his four hundred men.

This week's Scripture passage concerns a later period of Jacob's life, when he had a large family, lots of servants, and many livestock. After leaving his father-in-law, Laban, in Haran, Jacob made his way back to Canaan, where he arranged to meet his brother, Esau. Two decades had passed since Jacob had seen Esau and taken his birthright and blessing; and Jacob certainly had not forgotten his brother's vow to kill him (Gen. 27:41). Did Esau still feel the same way?

Wisely, Jacob chose to settle the question once and for all before settling in Canaan. He hoped to reconcile with his brother. Thus, he headed for Esau's new homeland, Seir, by traveling southward on the eastern side of the Jordan River. From Mahanaim (32:1-2), Jacob sent servants bearing a message to his brother in Seir. The humbly worded statement informed Esau that Jacob and his people had separated from Laban. It also expressed Jacob's desire to set things right with his brother (vss. 3-5).

The servants faithfully performed their mission. When they returned, they did not have a reply for Jacob from his brother; but they did carry the news that Esau was coming to meet Jacob and was bringing with him a large force of 400 men (32:6; 33:1a). Jacob was so concerned that he prayed to God about the coming meeting. First, the patriarch recalled the Lord's initial command for him to return to Canaan and the divine promise to bless him (32:9). Jacob then threw himself on the mercy of God by admitting that he was not worthy of the Lord's commitment and unfailing love. God's faithfulness was evident in the material wealth He had given Jacob over the past 20 years (vs. 10). In an ardent plea, Jacob asked God to rescue him from Esau, whom he thought was coming to kill him and his entire family (vs. 11).

Jacob reasoned that since God had taken care of him in the past, God could take care of him in the present. Moreover, the patriarch recalled both the Lord's promises to him recorded in Scripture. God had appeared to Jacob in Bethel and promised to prosper him and give him many descendants (vs. 12; compare 28:13-15). Later, when the Lord directed Jacob to leave Paddan Aram, God also pledged to prosper Jacob in the promised land (32:9; compare 31:3). Jacob realized that neither of these covenantal blessings could be fulfilled if he and his family were wiped out by Esau.

B. Jacob's Defensive Strategy: vss. 1b-3

So he divided the children among Leah, Rachel and the two maidservants. He put the maidservants and their children in front, Leah and her children next, and Rachel and Joseph in the rear. He himself went on ahead and bowed down to the ground seven times as he approached his brother.

In Jacob's day, it was customary for an endangered caravan to divide into separate companies. If one company was attacked, the other could escape. Jacob took that normal precaution by dividing his children among Leah, Rachel, and the two female servants (Gen. 33:1b). The patriarch arranged the caravan into a column, with his two concubines and their children out in front. Next came Leah and her children. Last in line were Rachel and Joseph (vs. 2).

In that time period, ancient Near Eastern society was patriarchal; and someone such as Jacob, as the eldest male in the clan, would have been regarded as the leader of the family. With the privilege of leadership came the responsibility of providing for and protecting the more vulnerable family members. In the present circumstance, Jacob went in front of the entire caravan (vs. 3).

Earlier, Jacob had sent a message to Esau that the patriarch wanted to find favor in the sight of his brother (32:5). One way to signal this intent was for Jacob, as he approached Esau, to bow toward the ground seven times (33:3). According to ancient records recovered by archaeologists, it was customary to bow this many times when approaching a monarch. Thus, Jacob demonstrated his respect for Esau, who had become a ruler in a region of the south.

Jacob was also indicating that he regarded himself to be in a position of subservience to his brother. Such an attitude of humility had taken two decades to develop in the patriarch. Throughout most of his life, Jacob had been a struggler. For instance, he pitted himself against Esau and Laban; but those conflicts were just reflections of Jacob's continuing struggle with God over who would control his life.

A resolution of the issue occurred in the early morning hours before Jacob's reunion with Esau. The previous night, Jacob had dispatched the entire caravan across the Jabbok River, a main tributary on the Jordan River (32:22-23). Consequently, Jacob was left alone in the camp, which was east of the Jordan and north of the Jabbok rivers. We don't know why the patriarch stayed behind. Perhaps he intended to spend more time in prayer.

That night, Jacob had an unusual encounter. Verse 24 says that he wrestled with a mysterious man until daybreak, while verse 30 adds that Jacob had somehow seen God face to face. According to Hosea 12:4, this individual was an angel. Others conjecture this man was the Messiah before His birth at Bethlehem. One possibility is that Jacob wrestled with the angel of the Lord, a figure in the Old Testament who is identified as His messenger but speaks with the authority of God Himself.

In the unfolding episode, Jacob's opponent knocked his hip socket out of joint; nevertheless, the wrestling match continued, and the stranger's identity was about to be exposed by the early morning dawn. Before this could happen, however, the man told Jacob to release him. The patriarch refused to do so until his opponent blessed him (Gen. 32:25-26). In making this request, Jacob evidently suspected something was extraordinary about his adversary.

Next, the man blessed the patriarch by changing his name from Jacob to Israel (vss. 27-28). The name "Jacob" pointed to his struggle with people, while the name

"Israel" commemorated the wrestling match with the Lord's messenger. The new name signified a new beginning, a new opportunity, a new position, and a new person. Jacob's strength and tenacity would serve God anew, and the Lord would become the God of the patriarch's descendants. Also, it would be from Jacob's new name that the nation descended from him became known as Israel.

Despite Jacob's request, the stranger refused to disclose his name; instead, the man blessed Jacob, who suddenly realized that he had some sort of encounter with God (vs. 29). We don't know what form this blessing took. Perhaps it was a repetition of the blessings belonging to the Abrahamic covenant. To commemorate the event, Jacob named the place "Peniel" (vs. 30), which means "face of God." Though the patriarch had seen a manifestation of the Lord and expected to die (see Exod. 33:20; Judg. 13:22), God spared his life.

In terms of who won the wrestling match, the Lord's messenger acknowledged that he had been overcome by Jacob (Gen. 32:28). Nonetheless, Jacob wound up with a damaged hip and could only hold on to his adversary in a desperate embrace. If Jacob had let go in his injured state, God's emissary would have won. The conclusion of the match is a perfect image of Jacob's spiritual relationship with the Lord. The patriarch discovered that his need for the remainder of his life was to rely on the Lord.

As the sun rose, Jacob left Peniel limping because of his hip (Gen. 32:31). The account includes an interesting comment about the dietary custom that developed out of Jacob's struggle with the Lord's messenger. The people of Israel refused to eat the sinew that is attached to the socket of the hip (possibly the sciatic muscle) in memory of what happened to Jacob (vs. 32). This prohibition is not part of Old Testament law, but teachings of rabbis written hundreds of years later mention it.

A new day of trust in God dawned for Jacob. It formed the basis of his dependence on the Lord as the encounter with Esau drew closer. As the subsequent narrative of Genesis indicates, Jacob's character was transformed. From now on, he was truly God's servant, and Jacob's descendants, the Israelites, would be given the opportunity to serve the Lord and receive His covenantal blessings.

C. Esau's Display of Affection: vs. 4

But Esau ran to meet Jacob and embraced him; he threw his arms around his neck and kissed him. And they wept.

Years earlier, Esau held a grudge against Jacob for stealing the family blessing from him; and the elder brother made specific plans to bring about Jacob's demise (Gen. 27:41). Two decades later, as the reunion of the fraternal twins neared, we don't know what was Esau's intention. Most likely, he never planned to attack Jacob. Esau may have brought 400 men with him both to impress his younger brother with his power and to defend against Jacob in case Jacob attacked.

Whatever Esau's original aim, he was filled with emotion at the sight of his brother. Esau ran to meet Jacob and showered him with signs of genuine affection. This included a warm embrace, throwing his arms around Jacob's neck, and kissing him on each cheek. This was followed by both brothers weeping, perhaps in a mixture of relief and joy (33:4). The 20-year interval since the two had seen each other had brought about changes in the older twin as well as the younger. Esau's former bitterness had been replaced with a gracious and tender spirit toward Jacob.

II. THE RECONCILIATION OF JACOB AND ESAU: GENESIS 33:5-11

A. Esau's Question about Jacob's Children: vss. 5-7

Then Esau looked up and saw the women and children. "Who are these with you?" he asked. Jacob answered, "They are the children God has graciously given your servant." Then the maidservants and their children approached and bowed down. Next, Leah and her children came and bowed down. Last of all came Joseph and Rachel, and they too bowed down.

After the tears stopped flowing, the brothers naturally began to catch up on one another's lives. For the first time, Esau met Jacob's wives and children. When the elder twin asked about their identity, Jacob stated that the children were God's gracious gift. As a sign of submission, the patriarch was careful to refer to himself as Esau's "servant" (Gen. 33:5).

In last week's lesson, we learned Jacob had married two wives. The patriarch's first wife, Leah, initially bore him four sons—Reuben, Simeon, Levi, and Judah (29:32-35). In contrast, Rachel remained childless (vs. 31). For Rachel the situation felt unbearable. In fact, she became so jealous of her sister that she demanded that Jacob give her children of her own (30:1). This made the patriarch furious, especially since he realized that only God had the power to enable Rachel to conceive. In the unfolding drama, the patriarch slept with Bilhah, Rachel's maid, on two separate occasions. This led to the birth of two sons, whom Rachel named Dan and Naphtali (vss. 3-8).

When Leah realized that she was not getting pregnant anymore, she had Jacob sleep with Zilpah, her maid, on two different occasions. This led to the birth of Gad and Asher (vss. 9-13). Then, in response to Leah's prayers, God enabled her to conceive for the fifth time and give birth to Issachar (vss. 14-18). Leah's sixth pregnancy led to the birth of Zebulun (vss. 19-20). Later, Leah bore Jacob a daughter named Dinah (vs. 21). Finally, God took pity on Rachel by enabling her to conceive and give birth to her firstborn, whom she named Joseph (vss. 22-24). Tragically, Rachel would later die in giving birth to her second son, Benjamin (35:16-20).

In all these circumstances, the Lord was providentially at work. His enabling Jacob's wives to become pregnant led to the birth of the leaders of Israel's future 12 tribes. In turn, they would become God's chosen people, whom He would enable to enter and conquer the promised land. To them the Lord would reveal His glory, and with them He would establish the Mosaic covenant and law (Rom. 9:4). Indeed, they alone would be entrusted with the oracles of God (3:2).

Such a bright future was due in part to the Lord's gracious intervention at the reunion of Jacob and Esau. The first members of the patriarch's family to arrive were his two concubines with their children, who bowed low in submission before Esau (Gen. 33:6). Next, Leah came with her children and they bowed down. Finally, Rachel and Joseph appeared and they likewise bowed (vs. 7).

B. Esau's Question about Jacob's Livestock: vs. 8

Esau asked, "What do you mean by all these droves I met?" "To find favor in your eyes, my lord," he said.

The previous night, Jacob had selected a gift for his brother, Esau. In some contexts, the Hebrew noun rendered "gift" (Gen. 32:13) can refer to the tribute a vassal paid to a monarch. This may be the emphasis in this verse, for earlier Jacob had referred to Esau as his "lord" (vs. 4) and himself as Esau's "servant."

Jacob picked out 550 animals of different kinds as gifts for the elder twin. Furthermore, Jacob arranged things so that Esau would receive those valuable animals in herds, one after another. Each time Esau received one drove, one of Jacob's servants would deliver a courteous message from their master (vss. 14-21). Clearly, the patriarch's intent was to build goodwill toward himself before he and his brother met.

After the initial reunion and exchange of introductions were finished, Esau brought up the subject of the herds Jacob had sent him. Of course, the patriarch's servants had told Esau that the animals were gifts; but the elder twin politely inquired to be sure of Jacob's intentions for the flocks and herds. Jacob explained that the droves were meant as gifts to ensure the favor of Esau, whom Jacob deferentially referred to as his "lord" (33:8).

C. Discussion Concerning Jacob's Gift: vss. 9-11

But Esau said, "I already have plenty, my brother. Keep what you have for yourself." "No, please!" said Jacob. "If I have found favor in your eyes, accept this gift from me. For to see your face is like seeing the face of God, now that you have received me favorably. Please accept the present that was brought to you, for God has been gracious to me and I have all I need." And because Jacob insisted, Esau accepted it.

After Jacob offered his explanation, a battle of courtesy ensued (which was far better than a real battle). Esau declined the generous gift, stating he did not need the animals because he already had many of his own (Gen. 33:9); but Jacob insisted. The patriarch noted that by accepting the gift from his hand, Esau would also be demonstrating that his younger brother had found favor in his sight.

Jacob felt that seeing his brother's friendly face and warm acceptance was as if the patriarch had seen the face of God (vs. 10). Jacob was alluding to the incident at the campsite he had recently left. It was there he had seen God face to face (32:30); and with the favorable encounter with Esau, the patriarch realized that the Lord had answered his prayer for protection (vs. 11).

Understandably, then, while Jacob remained polite, he also was insistent that his brother accept the present the younger twin had offered. Jacob explained that God had enabled him to materially prosper, so much so that he had all he needed. In the original, "present" (33:11) is more literally rendered "blessing." Perhaps the patriarch's gesture toward his brother was his way of making restitution for what he had stolen two decades earlier. Custom also decreed that by receiving the gift, Esau would be confirming his kind intentions toward the giver. Thus, upon Jacob's continued insistence, Esau accepted the gift of animals.

Discussion Questions

1. Why did Jacob divide his family before meeting up with Esau?
2. What did Jacob initially think the encounter with his brother would be like?
3. What was the significance of Jacob bowing down to the ground seven times as he approached Esau?
4. How did Esau's greeting contrast with that of Jacob?
5. Why did Jacob insist on Esau accepting his gift?

Contemporary Application

In the early 1970s, the Watergate scandal toppled President Richard Nixon and his administration. Many of Nixon's aides were convicted of criminal charges and served time in prison. One of those who did was Charles Colson, a former Marine captain who served as the White House special counsel.

In the midst of being disgraced for his dealings in the Nixon White House and being sent to prison, Colson had a life-changing encounter with God, during which he became a devoted follower of Jesus Christ. Colson began to tell fellow inmates about the Savior and organize prison Bible studies.

Since departing from prison, Colson has been a leading voice for Christ not only among believers but also among unbelievers. He has written several best-selling books; and he has founded an effective prison ministry. Colson, who describes himself as a strong-willed and determined person, has determined to serve others in the name of Jesus instead of destroying or deceiving them.

Most of us do not have as interesting a testimony to share as Chuck Colson does, but the change God brings in us and in the way we relate to others is no less important. After Jacob encountered God at the Jabbok River, he faced his brother not with animosity and hatred, but with humility and courage. Jacob's encounter with God affected not only his character and identity, but also his relationship with others, particularly Esau.

Likewise, when we experience the Father through faith in the Son, we will change. It is impossible for God's touch not to have any affect on our lives and in how we relate to others, especially with those who are closest to us. As we continue to walk with the Lord, He blesses us by giving us the courage and humility to interact with others, even with those with whom we have a major contention.

Joseph's Dream

DEVOTIONAL READING

Psalm 70

DAILY BIBLE READINGS

Monday October 29
Genesis 37:1-4 The Favored Son

Tuesday October 30
Genesis 37:5-11 The Jealous Brothers

Wednesday October 31
Genesis 37:12-17 The Messenger

Thursday November 1
Genesis 37:18-24 The Dreamer

Friday November 2
Genesis 37:25-28 Sold into Slavery

Saturday November 3
Genesis 37:29-36 A Father's Distress

Sunday November 4
Psalm 70 A Prayer for Deliverance

Scripture

Background Scripture: *Genesis 37*
Scripture Lesson: *Genesis 37:5-11, 19-21, 23-24, 28*
Key Verse: *Joseph had a dream, and when he told it to his brothers, they hated him all the more.* Genesis 37:5.
Scripture Lesson for Children: *Genesis 37:3-8, 17, 18-21, 23-24, 28*
Key Verse for Children: *[Joseph's brothers] sold him for twenty shekels of silver to the Ishmaelites, who took him to Egypt.* Genesis 37:28.

Lesson Aim

To recognize that favoritism can have devastating effects.

Lesson Setting

Time: *1898 B.C.*
Place: *Canaan and Egypt*

Lesson Outline

Joseph's Dream

I. Joseph's Two Dreams: Genesis 37:5-11
   A. *The First Dream: vss. 5-8*
   B. *The Second Dream: vss. 9-11*

II. Joseph's Enslavement: Genesis 37:19-21, 23-24, 26
   A. *The Brothers' Plot to Kill Joseph: vss. 19-20*
   B. *The Intervention of Reuben: vs. 21*
   C. *The Selling of Joseph to Some Midianites: vs. 23-24, 28*

Introduction for Adults

Topic: *Interpreting a Call!*

"WANTED: Mother. Salary: $00. No retirement, no insurance, no guarantees. Bonuses for a job well done may include a few hugs and kisses. Skills required: Must love children, cats, dogs, hamsters, and fish. Must have nursing experience for kissing 'owies,' and lots of bandages. Must be able to love a kid, even when he's rotten." This tongue-in-cheek advertisement, from *What Kids Need Most in a Mom* by Patricia Rushford, is a good beginning of a never-ending job description. An equally overwhelming one would apply to a father.

Parents know that each child has a "love tank" that requires daily refueling. If this is neglected for any child, his or her "engine" can cut off. The same thing happens in other areas of life when we show undue partiality to particular coworkers, relatives, or even Sunday school students. Pray this week that God would disclose any people in your life whom you are paying more attention to at the expense of others; and consider it part of His call for you to make things right.

Introduction for Youth

Topic: *Dreamer in the Pit*

Favoritism is the practice of giving unfair preferential treatment to one person or group at the expense of another. This is exactly the case in the family of Jacob. He loved Joseph more than any of his other sons and gave him a special tunic to wear as a symbol of his preference. While this may have helped Joseph feel special, it infuriated his brothers. In fact, they threw Joseph into a pit because of their resentment for him.

Ultimately, no one in that family benefited from the presence of favoritism. Joseph was shunned and sold into slavery in Egypt. For years to come his siblings had to shoulder the guilt and moral taint of their misdeed against their younger brother; and their father had unimagined grief over the perceived loss of Joseph. From this we see that favoritism always produces destructive results.

Concepts for Children

Topic: *From Son to Slave*

1. Joseph's brothers hated him.
2. Jacob thought about the dream Joseph had experienced.
3. Joseph's life was spared because of Reuben's influence.
4. Because they were jealous, Joseph's brothers sold him into slavery.
5. Even in a seemingly hopeless situation God is still with us.

Lesson Commentary

I. JOSEPH'S TWO DREAMS: GENESIS 37:5-11

A. The First Dream: vss. 5-8

Joseph had a dream, and when he told it to his brothers, they hated him all the more. He said to them, "Listen to this dream I had: We were binding sheaves of grain out in the field when suddenly my sheaf rose and stood upright, while your sheaves gathered around mine and bowed down to it." His brothers said to him, "Do you intend to reign over us? Will you actually rule us?" And they hated him all the more because of his dream and what he had said.

Genesis 36 contains a list of Esau's descendants and the rulers of Edom, their nation. While the clan of Esau settled and expanded in Edom, Jacob and his family continued to move about Canaan without a permanent residence, hierarchal government, or growing line of distinguished monarchs (37:1). The account of Jacob, introduced in verse 2, spotlights the life of Joseph and the circumstances that led to the relocation of Jacob's entire family to Egypt. The narrative, coming as it does at the end of Genesis, serves as a bridge between the accounts of the patriarchs (Abraham, Isaac, and Jacob) and the material concerning the Israelites' exodus from Egypt and 40-year sojourn in the wilderness.

The narrative begins with Joseph as a young man of 17. He and some of his brothers were taking care of his father's flocks. The brothers had done something they shouldn't have (the text doesn't specify what) while away from home tending the sheep. Joseph saw the wrongdoing and let Jacob know about it. Commentators take different views of Joseph's action. Some censure him, calling him a tattletale, while others commend him, saying he was only acting as any conscientious son should. Although the text doesn't tell us so, the brothers undoubtedly had hard feelings toward their younger sibling because of his reporting of them.

Jacob increased the friction between the older brothers and Joseph by showing his preference for the firstborn of his favorite wife, Rachel. Verse 3 explains that the patriarch loved Joseph more because he was born to his father in his old age. As a matter of fact, Joseph was Jacob's youngest son, next to Benjamin. Jacob showed his favoritism by giving Joseph a special tunic. It's hard to know the exact nature of this outer garment because of the unclear meaning of the Hebrew word that describes it. Differing opinions conjecture that the robe had long sleeves or was richly embroidered. In any case, it distinguished Joseph as the favored son of Jacob and the future ruler over the family.

When Jacob was younger, his mother liked him more than Esau, while Jacob's father preferred Esau. This display of parental favoritism led to threats of murder and to a deep rupture between the fraternal twins. Having seen the damage such preferential treatment can do, Jacob should have known better than to repeat the same mistake among his children. Beyond question, as Joseph wore the ornate robe, it became a source of constant irritation to his siblings. They were reminded that their father loved Joseph best, a realization that fueled resentment and jealousy. The brothers' hatred of Joseph prevented them from being able to speak to him kindly (vs. 4).

Next, we read about two dreams. In the ancient world, people believed that dreams were a window into knowing the future. This sentiment proved to be true in the case of Joseph, for God sent the dreams to show the superior blessings He would give to Rachel's firstborn. After having the dream, Joseph told it to his brothers and in turn their hatred of him intensified (vs. 5). Some commentators allege that Joseph was gloating over his siblings, that his demeanor was arrogant, or that his manner was condescending. There is nothing in the text, however, to support these views.

In the first dream (vs. 6), Joseph saw himself and his brothers tying up sheaves of grain in the middle of a field. This was a normal harvest scene; but suddenly, Joseph's bundle stood up. Then, his siblings' bundles surrounded Joseph's sheaf and bowed down to it (vs. 7). The Hebrew verb used here denotes the kind of worship and obeisance servants would give to their master. The brothers correctly interpreted the dream to mean that one day they would bow down to Joseph as their ruler (vs. 8). This literally happened when Joseph became a ruler in Egypt.

As a result of the dream and Joseph's retelling of it, his siblings hatred of him rose a notch higher. Given the existing family dynamics, the response of the brothers is understandable. They may also have been unsettled by what Joseph related, especially if they genuinely wondered whether God was using the dream to disclose what He would do in the future.

B. The Second Dream: vss. 9-11

Then he had another dream, and he told it to his brothers. "Listen," he said, "I had another dream, and this time the sun and moon and eleven stars were bowing down to me." When he told his father as well as his brothers, his father rebuked him and said, "What is this dream you had? Will your mother and I and your brothers actually come and bow down to the ground before you?" His brothers were jealous of him, but his father kept the matter in mind.

In Joseph's second dream, he saw the sun and moon (the parents of the clan) as well as 11 stars (the siblings) bow down to him (Gen. 37:9). This time Joseph described the dream to his father as well as his brothers. Now even Joseph's indulgent father was upset with his favorite son. He expressed dismay at what he perceived was audacity and rebuked Joseph for it. Jacob accurately interpreted the dream to mean that he, his wife Leah (Joseph's mother, Rachel, had died by this time), and his sons would all bow down to Joseph (vs. 10). This dream, too, referred to the future when Joseph would be a ruler in Egypt. While Jacob kept in mind and pondered what Joseph said, his brothers grew all the more jealous of him (vs. 11).

In relating the dreams, Joseph was only telling the truth; but some commentators suggest that he was unwise to mention the dreams and that he was motivated by pride. There are few clues in the text, however, to support this view. Later in the Genesis narrative it is disclosed that Joseph had the ability to interpret dreams. Perhaps, then, he had an inkling of what his first and second dreams meant. Also, while he could have remained silent about the dreams, he chose to tell them. Of course, regardless of whether Joseph should have kept his mouth shut, his brothers were wrong to nurse feelings of jealousy and hatred against him.

II. JOSEPH'S ENSLAVEMENT: GENESIS 37:19-21, 23-24, 26

A. The Brothers' Plot to Kill Joseph: vss. 19-20

"Here comes that dreamer!" they said to each other. "Come now, let's kill him and throw him into one of these cisterns and say that a ferocious animal devoured him. Then we'll see what comes of his dreams."

Some time after Joseph's dreams, most of Jacob's sons took his flocks about 50 miles north to Shechem (Gen. 37:12). A desire to get away from Joseph may have been one reason why they traveled so far from their home in the Valley of Hebron; but if so, it did no good, for Jacob sent Joseph after them to find out how they were doing (vss. 13-14). Neither the father nor his favored son could have known that more than two decades would pass before they laid eyes on each other again.

When Joseph reached Shechem, a man noticed him wandering around the countryside. When the man asked Joseph what he was looking for, he explained that he was in search of his brothers. Joseph requested help from the stranger in finding where the group was grazing the flocks under their care. When the man mentioned overhearing them talk about going on about 15 miles north to Dothan, Joseph left for the place and found his brothers there (vss. 15-17).

Dothan was already over a thousand years old when Jacob's sons tended their sheep near it. The city lay on a major trade route between Damascus and Egypt, making it a common site for caravans to venture near the city as they made their way toward the south. The location of Dothan caused it to be destroyed and rebuilt a number of times. For instance, the city was nearly wiped out when the king of Aram (Syria) besieged Dothan to capture Elisha (2 Kings 6:13-19).

For some time feelings of ill will toward Joseph had been festering in the hearts of his brothers. Thus, when the siblings spotted Joseph from a distance wearing his ornate robe, they hatched a scheme to murder him (Gen. 37:18). The brothers literally referred to Joseph as "this master of dreams" (vs. 19). The sarcastic tone of their statement reflected the resentment they felt toward Joseph and the dreams God had given him. The plan involved throwing the younger sibling into a nearby dry cistern.

In the semiarid climate of ancient Palestine, the inhabitants regularly worried about the availability of water. Unlike wells, which were fed by underground water seepage, cisterns would catch and store runoff rainwater during the wetter months of the year for use during the long dry season that followed. In Jacob's day, the people of Canaan dug bottle- or pear-shaped reservoirs out of the soft limestone; but due to the porous nature of the rock, the underground tanks were prone to break and lose their contents.

Jacob's sons agreed to lie about the demise of Joseph. When asked about him, they would claim that a vicious, wild animal had attacked and devoured him. Their uncontrolled jealousy and hatred had brought them to such an intention. They thought they could get away with their scheme because Joseph was away from their father's protection, and there were no witnesses nearby to report their actions. They assumed that by getting rid of their dreaded younger brother, the siblings could prevent his dreams from coming true (vs. 20). They did not realize that God would use their actions to make the dreams a reality.

B. The Intervention of Reuben: vs. 21

When Reuben heard this, he tried to rescue him from their hands. "Let's not take his life," he said.

Based on Genesis 37:2, some think the sons of Bilhah and Zilpah (namely, Dan, Naphtali, Gad, and Asher; 30:4-13) were the instigators of the murderous plot. When Reuben (the firstborn son of Jacob through Leah) heard the plan, he came to Joseph's rescue by advising his brothers not to take the younger sibling's life (37:21). Rather than harm Joseph and thereby shed innocent blood, Reuben urged the rest to bind Joseph and place him in the cistern, presumably to die of thirst and hunger (vs. 22).

Reuben secretly planned to help Joseph escape and bring him back unharmed to Jacob. The tide of events, though, would wash away Reuben's good intentions. More effective would have been for him, as the elder son of the group, to put a complete end to the scheme. Despite whatever admirable qualities he had, Reuben previously compromised his integrity and standing in the family by becoming involved in incest with Bilhah, the concubine of his father (35:22). Perhaps the memory of that incident spurred Reuben to make a halfhearted attempt to rehabilitate himself in the situation involving Joseph.

C. The Selling of Joseph to Some Midianites: vs. 23-24, 28

So when Joseph came to his brothers, they stripped him of his robe—the richly ornamented robe he was wearing—and they took him and threw him into the cistern. Now the cistern was empty; there was no water in it. . . . So when the Midianite merchants came by, his brothers pulled Joseph up out of the cistern and sold him for twenty shekels of silver to the Ishmaelites, who took him to Egypt.

Joseph eventually reached his brothers; but rather than being greeted warmly, the older siblings stripped him of his ornate robe and consequently his status. This was the special tunic he wore out of respect for his father (Gen. 37:23). The brothers, by harming Joseph, dishonored Jacob. After removing Joseph's outer garment, the siblings threw him into a nearby empty cistern. Though there was no water in it (vs. 24), the underground tank would have been musty and moldy. For health reasons, it would not be a hospitable place to stay for very long.

The callous nature of the brothers is evident as they sat down to eat some food (vs. 25), seemingly indifferent to Joseph's pleas for mercy (42:21). Sometime during the meal, they spotted a caravan of traders. In ancient times, travel was extremely dangerous. The threat of robbers and wild animals discouraged most people from venturing out alone or even in small groups. For safety on the unmarked roads between Syria and Egypt, caravans such as the one mentioned in this verse were often formed.

A large caravan could number over 3,000 people and animals. As it journeyed from town to town, some persons and merchandise would leave the caravan, while other persons and merchandise would replace them. Often, slaves would be a part of the merchandise. The wealthier persons in a caravan would ride camels. These beasts of burden would also carry trading goods. The poorer travelers would walk or ride on donkeys.

The biblical text calls the traders spotted by the brothers both "Ishmaelites" (37:25, 27) and "Midianites" (vs. 28). Technically speaking, Ishmaelites were the descendants of Ishmael, the son of Abraham and Hagar (21:13; 25:12). The Midianites were the descendants of Midian, a son of Abraham and Keturah (25:2). The Midianites seem to have been centered in northwest Arabia, but in some periods they may have been found over a much larger area. Evidence suggests that all the desert tribes living east of the Jordan River were known as Ishmaelites.

Since Midian and Ishmael were both sons of Abraham, the terms referring to their respective descendants probably described an interrelated group of people who lived in the Sinai peninsula and the Arabian Desert east of the Red Sea. It was to this area called Midian that Moses fled after he killed the Egyptian who was beating a Hebrew slave (Exod. 2:15). There is evidence elsewhere in Scripture that the Midianites and Ishmaelites worked together. Specifically, the Midianites who later conquered the Israelites during the period of the judges (Judg. 6:1-6) were described as part of a coalition of "eastern peoples" (vs. 3) who included the Ishmaelites (8:24).

The traders spotted by Jacob's sons were carrying spices, balm, and myrrh down to Egypt (Gen. 37:25). These were goods used in medicine, cosmetics, and preparing the dead for burial. Judah, the fourth son of Jacob and Leah, questioned how he and his siblings would profit by murdering their brother and hiding his body. All they would gain from such an act was a guilty conscience (vs. 26). What the group failed to appreciate is that any harm they brought to Joseph would be a moral stain on their lives and an issue God would deal with as the Genesis narrative unfolded.

Judah's face-saving scheme involved not directly laying a hand on Joseph. Instead, they would sell their despised younger brother to the Ishmaelites. Archaeological records indicate that the Egyptians were always open to purchasing slaves, as well as other commodities, from traders such as the Ishmaelites. Judah's plan would not only get rid of Joseph, but also make some money for his brothers at the same time. The group liked Judah's idea and so went along with it (vs. 27).

When the siblings pulled Joseph out of the cistern, he initially may have thought that he would be freed; but perhaps to his dismay, his brothers sold him as slave to the Ishmaelites for 20 pieces of silver. The traders then took him to Egypt (vs. 28). Slavery was a common practice in the ancient world. Surviving records tell us that the amount paid for Joseph was the usual price for a boy between five and 20 years of age. An older slave would generally bring 30 pieces of silver.

Reuben was not present when his brothers sold Joseph. Perhaps Reuben was with a different part of the flocks; or maybe he was off making plans to rescue Joseph. At any rate, when he got back, Joseph was gone. Since it was too late to help him, Reuben went along with the plan to trick Jacob, the great trickster. The brothers dipped Joseph's cloak in goat's blood and, when they returned home, showed the garment to their father. They knew full well that Jacob would interpret the blood-ied tunic to mean that his favored son had been killed by a wild beast (vss. 29-33).

Discussion Questions

1. What was the response of Joseph's brothers to his first dream?
2. What was the response of Joseph's father to his son's second dream?
3. Why would Joseph's brothers want to bring harm to him?
4. How did Reuben try to intervene on behalf of his brother?
5. What alternative plan did Joseph's brothers adopt?

Contemporary Application

Whether we are doing it consciously or not, we may be showing favoritism toward one person at the expense of someone else. If one person receives most of the attention, others will go unnoticed. The favored one develops a "me first" attitude. An ignored child may cry "Notice me!" through rebellious behavior.

Overlooked people, like Joseph's brothers, can become withdrawn and resentful. The employee who knows that the boss's favorite will get all of the recognition eventually says "Why bother?" The student who is overlooked by his or her teacher stops learning or caring about an education.

The effects of favoritism may be hidden for years, especially if those not favored are afraid to voice their feelings. Accumulated hatred and bitterness almost caused Esau to kill Jacob (Gen. 27:41) and certainly motivated Joseph's brothers to sell him as a slave. Anger about preference may produce a "root of bitterness" (Heb. 12:15) that can contaminate families, groups, or even entire communities for a long time.

Perhaps you are the one who has been overlooked or ignored; or perhaps you know someone who has been rejected by a parent or superior. God's Spirit can heal even the most damaged person; and all Christians can help heal the victims of favoritism by loving them as God loves. Your friendship may help someone who has been rejected feel like a person of value.

Joseph's Dream Began to Come True

Scripture

Background Scripture: *Genesis 41:25-45*

Scripture Lesson: *Genesis 41:25-40*

Key Verse: *Then Pharaoh said to Joseph, "Since God has made all this known to you, there is no one so discerning and wise as you."* Genesis 41:39.

Scripture Lesson for Children: *Genesis 41:1-8, 15-16, 25, 29-31, 33, 41*

Key Verse for Children: *Joseph said to Pharaoh, . . . "God has revealed to Pharaoh what he is about to do."* Genesis 41:25.

Lesson Aim

To note that God's wisdom can enable us to help others.

Lesson Setting

Time: *1885 B.C.*

Place: *Egypt*

Lesson Outline

Joseph's Dream Began to Come True

  I. Joseph's Interpretation of Pharaoh's Dreams: Genesis 41:25-32

    A. *The Symbolism of the Cows and Heads of Grain: vss. 25-27*

    B. *The Significance of the Symbolism: vss. 28-32*

  II. Joseph's Advice to Pharaoh: Genesis 41:33-40

    A. *Appointing an Overseer: vss. 33-34*

    B. *Storing a Sufficient Amount of Grain: vss. 35-36*

    C. *Pharaoh's Agreement with Joseph: vss. 37-38*

    D. *Pharaoh's Selection of Joseph: vss. 39-40*

Introduction for Adults

Topic: *A Dream Unfolds!*

> Isambard Brunel had a dream of building a great ship to sail from England to Australia. In 1857, he launched the *Great Eastern*. She was 693 feet long, five times the size of any ship afloat! With five gilded and mirrored salons and 800 cabins, she was supposed to be a floating palace. While the predecessor of the modern ocean liner never made much money, she successfully laid the transatlantic cable that ushered in the age of modern instant communication.

> Joseph's dreams were greater than Brunel's. Joseph's dreams were of God's power and activity in the adult Hebrew's life and the lives of all those in the world around him. God is also able to unfold similar aspirations in our lives.

Introduction for Youth

Topic: *A Dream Come True*

> Fe Wale, a Presbyterian Filipino pediatrician, directs the Marina Clinic outside of Dumaguete in the southern Philippines. At one point she was captured by rebels, who insisted that she perform the surgery required to remove a bullet from their leader. They refused to accept the fact that as a pediatrician, the last surgery she had done was in medical school years earlier. So with a prayer, some boiling water, and a makeshift operating table, she successfully performed the operation.

> Today Fe Wale's community health workers, wearing identifying T-shirts, are free to work unhampered in the rural areas where many other services have ceased because of the threat of rebel activity. For this saved pediatrician, it is a dream come true. God is also able to make our dreams of service for Him come to pass in His time and in His way.

Concepts for Children

Topic: *From Slave to Ruler*

> 1. The two years Joseph waited in prison for his situation to change seemed like a long time.
> 2. Pharaoh realized the dreams that troubled him held some important meaning.
> 3. Joseph said that God gave him the ability to tell Pharaoh the meaning of his dreams.
> 4. Pharaoh made Joseph the second most powerful person in the land of Egypt.
> 5. God is pleased when we give Him the credit for all we do.

Lesson Commentary

I. JOSEPH'S INTERPRETATION OF PHARAOH'S DREAMS: GENESIS 41:25-32

A. The Symbolism of the Cows and Heads of Grain: vss. 25-27

Then Joseph said to Pharaoh, "The dreams of Pharaoh are one and the same. God has revealed to Pharaoh what he is about to do. The seven good cows are seven years, and the seven good heads of grain are seven years; it is one and the same dream. The seven lean, ugly cows that came up afterward are seven years, and so are the seven worthless heads of grain scorched by the east wind: They are seven years of famine."

Once Joseph became the slave of Potiphar, the quality of his character began to show itself. Joseph did not wallow in self-pity, but energetically carried out the tasks set before him (Gen. 39:1). Verse 2 stresses that the Lord was with Joseph. Although the young man was separated from everyone and everything familiar to him, God helped him to be successful in all he did. This enabled Joseph to respond positively to the turn of events in his life.

As an experienced leader of men, Potiphar was not long in noticing Joseph's abilities. The official promoted Joseph from common house servant to personal attendant and then to steward of the entire household. In each position, the young man's work was blessed by God. Joseph soon had Potiphar's complete confidence. Without supervision, Joseph ran everything in the house (vss. 3-6).

Joseph's smooth sailing eventually became turbulent when Potiphar's wife made bold sexual advances toward the handsome steward. Despite the repeated attempts of Potiphar's wife, Joseph refused to compromise morally. This so vexed Potiphar's wife that she falsely accused Joseph of trying to rape her. Potiphar's response was to commit Joseph to the prison reserved for political detainees—probably the most comfortable facility available (vss. 7-20).

Nonetheless, Joseph's experience was by no means easy. The injustice of his treatment must have wounded him as much as it would anyone; but he remained faithful to God because God remained faithful to him. In particular, the Lord blessed Joseph, which enabled him to gain the favor of the warden and rise to full responsibility over the prison (vss. 21-23).

While incarcerated, Joseph used his God-given abilities to interpret the dreams of two fellow prisoners, Pharaoh's cupbearer (or food taster) and baker. The baker's dream meant that he would die, while the cupbearer's dream meant that he would be reinstated to his post. Joseph asked the cupbearer to intercede on his behalf with Pharaoh; but when the cupbearer was released from confinement, he forgot about Joseph (40:1-23).

Two more years passed before Pharaoh experienced his own dreams. In the first one, he found himself standing on the banks of the Nile River, the source of Egypt's prosperity and power. He saw seven ugly, gaunt cows devour seven fat, healthy-looking cows (41:1-4). In Pharaoh's second dream, he saw seven heads of shriveled and withered grain swallow up seven heads of plump, well-formed grain (vss. 5-7). The next morning, the Egyptian ruler summoned all his priests who were experienced with magic, divination, and soothsaying, but none of them could interpret his dreams (vs. 8).

The incident triggered the memory of Pharaoh's cupbearer, who recalled his own prior experience with Joseph (vss. 9-13). This prompted the ruler to order Joseph's immediate release from prison. After he had shaved and changed clothes, Joseph found himself standing before the most powerful man in the known world. Pharaoh's request was straightforward. He needed Joseph to interpret his troubling dreams. The young man stated that while he didn't have any innate ability to do this, God would supply the interpretation the ruler desperately desired (vss. 14-16). Having this assurance, Pharaoh recounted his dreams (vss. 17-24).

We can only imagine how clearheaded the Egyptian ruler became as he focused his attention on the lowly, foreign prisoner appearing before him. Joseph explained that both dreams of Pharaoh had the same meaning. The God whom Joseph worshiped and served—despite his years of hardship and isolation—was using him to disclose to Pharaoh what the Lord would soon do (vs. 25). Joseph pointed out that the seven fat cows and the seven plumb heads of grain both represented seven years of prosperity (vs. 26). In contrast, the seven gaunt, ugly cows and the seven withered heads of grain represented seven years of famine (vs. 27).

Joseph's reference to the "east wind" merits further comment. In the Middle East, a hot wind off the desert often shrivels and destroys crops in agricultural areas such as Israel and Egypt. In Israel, this wind is called the *sirocco* and regularly blows from the east, off the Arabian deserts, in late spring and early fall, with devastating effects (Jer. 4:11-12; Ezek. 19:10-12; Hos. 13:15). Egypt has a similar scorching wind, called the *khamsin*, that blows in from the deserts and wilts crops in the Nile River valley.

B. The Significance of the Symbolism: vss. 28-32

"It is just as I said to Pharaoh: God has shown Pharaoh what he is about to do. Seven years of great abundance are coming throughout the land of Egypt, but seven years of famine will follow them. Then all the abundance in Egypt will be forgotten, and the famine will ravage the land. The abundance in the land will not be remembered, because the famine that follows it will be so severe. The reason the dream was given to Pharaoh in two forms is that the matter has been firmly decided by God, and God will do it soon."

By means of the explanation Joseph offered, he clarified the significance of the symbolism in Pharaoh's two dreams. God gave the Hebrew the correct interpretation so that he in turn could make known to the powerful ruler what the Lord was about to do (Gen. 41:28). In this regard, both dreams had identical messages. There would be seven years of abundance in the kingdom (vs. 29). Then, following the time of plenty, there would be seven years of terrible famine. In fact, it would be so widespread and horrific that all the prosperity would be forgotten and wiped out due to the devastating effects of the famine (vs. 30).

"Egypt" (Gen. 41:29) refers to the country in the northeast corner of Africa. In ancient times, its territory extended from the first waterfall of the Nile River in the south to the Mediterranean Sea in the north (about 650 miles). The only inhabitable areas were the narrow Nile Valley and the broad alluvial Nile Delta through which the long river reached the Mediterranean Sea. Egypt was the home of one of the earliest civilizations. Its culture was rich and complex, having developed over a period stretching from about 3000 B.C. to Roman times.

Joseph's announcement of a kingdom-wide famine posed a real threat to Egypt's dominance on the international scene. A brief episode of drought might be endured without much concern; but the disaster Joseph foretold would be so severe and prolonged that it could decimate the powerful nation situated along the Nile River (vs. 31). The Hebrew ex-prisoner noted that Pharaoh's experience of two versions of the same dream was God's way of signaling to the ruler that the matter was divinely decreed and would soon occur (vs. 32).

II. JOSEPH'S ADVICE TO PHARAOH: GENESIS 41:33-40

A. Appointing an Overseer: vss. 33-34

"And now let Pharaoh look for a discerning and wise man and put him in charge of the land of Egypt. Let Pharaoh appoint commissioners over the land to take a fifth of the harvest of Egypt during the seven years of abundance."

Because God was sure to act as He had declared through Joseph, the Hebrew urged Pharaoh to take immediate action. In particular, the Egyptian ruler was advised to find someone who was wise and discerning. Such an individual would be aware and informed as well as mature and experienced. This person would also exhibit keen insight and good judgment. Joseph recommended that this even-tempered and morally grounded overseer be placed in charge of a nationwide program (Gen. 41:33).

A consistent theme in Proverbs is the comparison between the way of wisdom and the way of foolishness. The way of wisdom leads to a clear conscience, meaningful relationships, and a full life. The path of foolishness leads to frustration, heartache, and eventual ruin. As the collection of wisdom sayings repeatedly remind us, being prudent is always the superior choice. The benefits of wisdom far outweigh the consequences of foolishness. People who follow the way of wisdom tend to succeed. Those who follow the way of foolishness eventually come to ruin.

Next, Joseph recommended that Pharaoh appoint officials throughout the land to collect one-fifth of the produce harvested during the seven plentiful years (Gen. 41:34). In ancient Egypt, farming followed a regular cycle. First, the Nile River would flood the land in September, October, and November, providing moisture and a layer of rich soil in which to plant crops. If the Nile did not flood because of low rainfall upstream, famine would follow. After the flood, farmers would plant their crops immediately, before the ground dried out. Then they would harvest the crops in March or April.

Some of the harvest would be given to the town temple for the priests. The rest would be stored in granaries for future use, but a portion was collected as annual taxes by government officials, who carefully counted the harvest. Much of the government's grain went to the pharaoh's storehouses. Consequently, the Egyptians would have been used to an official like Joseph collecting grain for Pharaoh; and Scripture says that Joseph used the circumstances of the famine to increase Pharaoh's influence in Egypt (47:23-26).

B. Storing a Sufficient Amount of Grain: vss. 35-36

"They should collect all the food of these good years that are coming and store up the grain under the authority of Pharaoh, to be kept in the cities for food. This food should be held in reserve for the country, to be used during the seven years of famine that will come upon Egypt, so that the country may not be ruined by the famine."

Joseph advised that commissioners be appointed to have responsibility for gathering all the excess food and grain during the seven years of abundance to come. In turn, the officials—operating under the authority of Pharaoh—were to stockpile these supplies in the royal storehouses located in various cities throughout the realm (Gen. 41:35). By adopting this strategy, Pharaoh would ensure that there would be enough food to eat when the seven years of famine came. To do otherwise would bring about widespread starvation, resulting in the eventual ruin of the nation. Joseph's proposed course of action was the only way for Egypt to survive the calamity (vs. 36).

There are no Egyptian records that can be linked to the specific drought and famine that Joseph described to Pharaoh, or to the storage and distribution plan he devised; however, an inscription has been found in the tomb of an Egyptian official who lived south of Thebes that describes a similar event. The writing in the tomb of Baba, governor of the city of El-Kab, says that the governor stored up corn during a time of plenty, "and when a famine arose, lasting many years, I distributed corn to the city, each year of the famine."

C. Pharaoh's Agreement with Joseph: vss. 37-38

The plan seemed good to Pharaoh and to all his officials. So Pharaoh asked them, "Can we find anyone like this man, one in whom is the spirit of God?"

The advice Joseph gave made sense to Pharaoh and all his officials (Gen. 41:37). As the royal court discussed who should be appointed to oversee the entire operation, Pharaoh openly wondered whether they could find a more suitable person than Joseph, someone in whom resided the Spirit of God (vs. 38). The ruler's rhetorical question expected a negative answer.

Throughout the ancient Near East, kingship was believed to have been established by the pagan gods of the people. The monarch was viewed as representing and often embodying the authority of the local deity. Therefore, the inhabitants of a region believed a king ruled by divine right. Monarchs were also believed to have direct access to divine wisdom. Pharaoh's remark in verse 38 implied that Joseph displayed unparalleled foresight and prudence, which even exceeded that of the king.

Moreover, throughout the ancient Near East, there were three distinct classes of wise men: enchanters, astrologers, and diviners. Enchanters were those who practiced conjuring and divination, the art of foretelling the future by signs. Astrologers were probably priests or magi who maintained the traditions of the native religion. Diviners, like enchanters, would interpret signs. In Joseph's day, these signs took many forms, including dreams or the casting of lots. Some diviners examined the patterns found in animal organs or the remains in a cup after the liquid was poured out. Joseph distinguished himself from all these pseudo wise men by receiving direct revelation from God about the future.

D. Pharaoh's Selection of Joseph: vss. 39-40

Then Pharaoh said to Joseph, "Since God has made all this known to you, there is no one so discerning and wise as you. You shall be in charge of my palace, and all my people are to submit to your orders. Only with respect to the throne will I be greater than you."

Joseph had spent a number of years in prison, which proved to be the watershed of his life. During that dark period, God humbled and matured him. The Lord also enabled him to acquire and refine his organizational and leadership skills. The former Hebrew prisoner came to see that God had a grander purpose for his hardships. The Lord permitted Joseph to be sold into slavery in Egypt to bring about the rescuing of many lives. This included those of his immediate family, through whom the blessings of the covenant would be transmitted to the world (Gen. 45:5). Thus, despite the harm his siblings intended to cause, God's nobler intent was to bring about widespread good (50:20).

Joseph's first meeting with Pharaoh was the starting point for all these things to happen. When the Hebrew was brought out of prison and taken to the Egyptian ruler, he stopped long enough to change clothes and shave (41:14). While he may have done this just to look nice for Pharaoh, it is likely that Joseph was following the social customs of the time. In ancient tomb paintings, Egyptians are almost always depicted as clean shaven, while Canaanites and other non-Egyptian peoples are shown with full beards. In fact, in most of the ancient Near East, men did not shave, unless it was a sign of mourning (Jer. 41:5); and an enemy could humiliate captured prisoners by shaving off their beards, as the Ammonites did when they captured some of David's men (2 Sam. 10:3-5).

Pharaoh took at face value Joseph's earlier statement that God had revealed to him the meaning of the king's dreams (41:16). Pharaoh was convinced that the Hebrew—though a foreigner—was the wisest and most discerning person throughout the entire realm (vs. 39). Thus, it made sense to appoint the 30-year-old to be the national overseer. In order for Joseph to direct the project, he would manage the household of Pharaoh and have charge over all his officials and inhabitants. They were to submit to the Hebrew's commands. Only the Egyptian ruler would rank higher than Joseph and retain supreme authority (vs. 40).

It was unusual for Pharaoh to appoint a foreigner for such a vital task as preparing for a famine and to give him so much power in the kingdom. It was especially unusual for the Egyptian ruler to place a relatively young, unknown, and unproven prisoner in an office of such great authority. Only God could have made such an act possible. Joseph had risen from slavery and prison to be the second most powerful person in Egypt, but God's plans for Joseph were just beginning.

Discussion Questions

1. To whom did Joseph give the credit for the ability to interpret Pharaoh's dreams?
2. What was God signaling by giving Pharaoh two dreams?
3. How did each of Pharaoh's dreams indicate that there would be seven years of plenty?
4. How did each of Pharaoh's dreams indicate that there would be seven years of famine?
5. How did Pharaoh respond to Joseph's advice?

Contemporary Application

The account of Joseph shows us how God gives us wisdom and how we can use that wisdom to help others. Even though he was only 30 when he went before Pharaoh, Joseph was already wise to God's ways, since he had learned to trust God in hard places. We are wise when we trust God through crises. We can then use that godly wisdom to help others—for instance, as we share with a struggling friend what God has done for us.

Opportunities to help others come when we least expect them. Joseph was brought quickly from the prison to the court of Pharaoh. That is why we must walk close to the Lord every day, so we will be ready when He calls us to serve. We must be prepared to alter direction if God suddenly changes our circumstances.

Moreover, we never know how far-reaching the effects of sharing our godly wisdom will be. Joseph interpreted Pharaoh's dream correctly and saved Egypt. Later, he saved his own family from starvation. Similarly, people will seek our help in times of need if they have seen God in us.

Pharaoh recognized that God spoke through Joseph. People should notice our humility, acts of kindness, and wise advice as God works through us—but He receives the glory for what we do for Him. Joseph gave God the credit for the correct interpretation of Pharaoh's dream. Likewise, when God gives us wisdom to help others, all the glory belongs to Him.

God Preserved a Remnant

DEVOTIONAL READING

Psalm 85

DAILY BIBLE READINGS

Monday November 12
Psalm 85 Restoration of God's Favor

Tuesday November 13
Genesis 42:1-20 Food in Egypt

Wednesday November 14
Genesis 43:1-15 Jacob's Difficult Decision

Thursday November 15
Genesis 43:16-34 Dining Together

Friday November 16
Genesis 44:1-13 Joseph Tests His Brothers

Saturday November 17
Genesis 44:14-34 Judah's Plea

Sunday November 18
Genesis 45:1-15 Brothers Reconciled

Scripture

Background Scripture: *Genesis 43:1—45:15*
Scripture Lesson: *Genesis 45:1-12*
Key Verse: *God sent me ahead of you to preserve for you a remnant on earth and to save your lives by a great deliverance.* Genesis 45:7.
Scripture Lesson for Children: *Genesis 45:1-12*
Key Verses for Children: *"I am your brother Joseph . . . it was to save lives that God sent me ahead of you."* Genesis 45:4-5.

Lesson Aim

To emphasize that God's purposes exceed our plans.

Lesson Setting

Time: *1876 B.C.*
Place: *Egypt*

Lesson Outline

God Preserved a Remnant

   I. Joseph's Disclosure: Genesis 45:1-7
     A. Joseph's Loud Weeping: vss. 1-2
     B. Joseph's Declaration: vs. 3
     C. Joseph's Realization: vss. 4-5
     D. Joseph's Explanation: vss. 6-7
  II. Joseph's Instructions: Genesis 45:8-12
     A. God's Sovereign Working: vs. 8
     B. Joseph's Exhortation: vs. 9
     C. Joseph's Promises: vss. 10-11
     D. Joseph's Assurance: vs. 12

Introduction for Adults

Topic: *Negative Actions, Positive Results!*

Jim Elliot, Nate Saint, Pete Flemming, Ed McCulley, and Roger Youderian were martyred in 1956, shortly after they arrived in the jungles of Ecuador to bring the Gospel to the Auca Indians. It was a witness that could not be ignored. They were a testimony that properly placed faith is more precious than life itself.

Five years after she watched those martyrdoms, a woman named Dawa became the first Auca Christian. Other conversions followed. Then, 36 years later, the Aucas (properly called the Huaoranis) received their first complete New Testament.

Some wonder if Elliot and his associates could have planned their missionary outreach better and thus worked longer for the Lord; yet God allows some candles to burn fast and brilliantly, while others burn long and steadily. Both are a part of His plan.

Introduction for Youth

Topic: *Gotcha!*

The sign on the high-school football team's locker room door read: "Everyone is welcome to play football! To play you must: 1. Give 110%! 2. Be at practice every-day! 3. Have a positive attitude! 4. Listen to your coach!" While the sign said *welcome,* there were conditions. Joseph welcomed his brothers unconditionally. Expressed differently, there were no "Gotchas!" to his offer of reconciliation.

Moreover, despite circumstances that looked less than favorable at first, God accomplished His purposes in Joseph's life; and God's plans for him went beyond his brother's intentions. Sometimes when our plans are frustrated, we feel that God is indifferent or has forgotten us; but we can trust that God loves us and that He has the ability to bring His best out of the worst circumstances.

Concepts for Children

Topic: *From Stranger to Family*

1. Joseph's brothers displayed both gratitude and guilt in their relationship with Joseph.
2. Joseph extended acceptance and forgiveness to his brothers and wanted them near him.
3. Joseph saw God's plan at work throughout his journey from slavery to a position of power.
4. Joseph saw himself as God's agent in preserving a remnant of the family of promise.
5. God also wants to work through us to do important things for Him.

Lesson Commentary

I. JOSEPH'S DISCLOSURE: GENESIS 45:1-7

A. Joseph's Loud Weeping: vss. 1-2

Then Joseph could no longer control himself before all his attendants, and he cried out, "Have every-one leave my presence!" So there was no one with Joseph when he made himself known to his brothers. And he wept so loudly that the Egyptians heard him, and Pharaoh's household heard about it.

Joseph used an elaborate test to see what kind of adults his brothers had become over the years. He began by accusing his siblings of being spies and imprisoning them for three days. Joseph then held Simeon as hostage and allowed the other brothers to return to Jacob with food for the family. Joseph also ordered that the money they had brought to buy food be hidden in their sacks of grain. He informed them that to buy more grain and save Simeon, they would have to return before him with Benjamin (Gen. 42:1-20).

Jacob thought he had already lost one of his sons born to Rachel—Joseph. Now the patriarch thought he was in danger of losing his other son born to Rachel—Benjamin—who was probably then in his twenties or early thirties; however, to save the family from starvation, a reluctant Jacob allowed Benjamin to return with his other sons to Egypt. The reformed brothers immediately attempted to return the money that had mysteriously appeared in their grain sacks on the last trip. They also purchased more grain for the family. Then, with Simeon returned to them, they all began their journey back to Canaan (42:21—44:3).

The siblings hadn't traveled far before they discovered another phase of Joseph's test. He had again hidden their money in the grain sacks and had hidden his silver cup in Benjamin's grain sack. Joseph's servant accused Benjamin of the crime and offered to let the other brothers go free while he took Benjamin to become Joseph's slave. Instead of saving themselves, the brothers risked their lives by returning to Egypt to plead for Benjamin's freedom. Judah functioned as the spokesperson for the group (44:4-32).

Judah pleaded with Joseph to be kept in Egypt as a slave in place of Benjamin. The young man, in turn, would be permitted to return with his other brothers to their home in Canaan (vs. 33). Judah explained that the alternative would involve him returning to his aged father without Benjamin, and Judah could not bear to witness the devastation Jacob would feel (vs. 34). Judah's speech proved that he was not the same man who earlier had come up with the idea of selling Joseph to Midianite traders. It had taken a long time, but the Lord had worked changes in his heart. Finally, the overseer could hide his feelings no more. Not for a minute longer could he stand in front of his brothers and pretend to have a merely official interest in them.

Joseph's brothers must have been stunned when they heard him command his Egyptian attendants to leave the room (45:1). All along, Joseph had probably been talking to his siblings through an interpreter to disguise the fact that he could understand their Hebrew speech. The tender reunion that was about to occur would be a family matter, and presumably Joseph didn't want any outsiders around to distract him and his brothers. Moses described Joseph's emotional release as so powerful that his weeping could even be heard by the servants who had departed from the area. Somehow the household of Pharaoh also learned about the incident, perhaps by means of an official report (vs. 2).

B. Joseph's Declaration: vs. 3

Joseph said to his brothers, "I am Joseph! Is my father still living?" But his brothers were not able to answer him, because they were terrified at his presence.

The sons of Jacob were shocked to hear the second-most powerful person in Egypt declare, "I am Joseph!" (Gen. 45:3). For more than 20 years, his siblings thought of Joseph as enslaved or dead. Since meeting Joseph, they never for a moment suspected that the ruler dressed in Egyptian finery and speaking the Egyptian language was their long-lost brother; but there he stood, saying in Hebrew that he was their sibling.

Joseph quickly followed up his self-revelation by asking about the father he had not seen for over two decades. Beyond question, this was the concern closest to the heart of the overseer. Thus, he was eager to have more news about his father. Until this point, Joseph would have aroused suspicion by showing too much interest in Jacob. Joseph's brothers made no reply to his question, for they were still in shock over finding themselves in the presence of their sibling. Evidently, they had not mentioned the name of the brother who—as the cover-up story went—had been killed by an animal (see 42:13; 44:28). Thus perhaps Joseph's using his own name convinced them of his true identity. Now they were confused and terrified and undoubtedly wondered if he would eliminate them for what they had done to him.

The biblical text portrays Joseph as an emotional, sensitive man. The moment when he revealed his identity to his brothers is not the first time in the narrative that he cried. He did so briefly but secretly when he had Simeon taken from his brothers and held prisoner (42:24). Then he showed even more emotion when he first saw his brother Benjamin. So his brothers would not see him cry, he left them and wept by himself for a while in his private room (43:30). Later, he would weep "for a long time" (46:29) when he saw and embraced his father Jacob after the passage of more than 20 years.

C. Joseph's Realization: vss. 4-5

Then Joseph said to his brothers, "Come close to me." When they had done so, he said, "I am your brother Joseph, the one you sold into Egypt! And now, do not be distressed and do not be angry with yourselves for selling me here, because it was to save lives that God sent me ahead of you."

Thinking that perhaps the brothers did not believe he was who he said he was, Joseph called them to him so that they could take a closer look at his face (Gen.

45:4). Then he repeated his claim to be Joseph, the sibling whom they long ago had sold into slavery. Only Joseph himself could have known the secret that they had mistreated him so shamefully.

Of course, Joseph's brothers were dumbfounded by his revelation. The person they had terribly wronged was now in a position of absolute power over them. He could imprison, enslave, or execute his siblings with just a word. The overseer's emotional outburst only added to their fear of his vengeance; however, like his brothers, he was a different person than the 17-year-old adolescent who was thrown into a cistern.

During their time of reunion, Joseph reassured his petrified brothers that he was not interested in revenge. He was able to forgive his siblings because he had learned to look at his trials from a godly perspective. Instead of Joseph concentrating on his brothers' evil intentions, he focused on God's supreme plan of blessing him with success and saving people from destruction. Thus Joseph urged his siblings not to be angry with themselves for their past misdeeds. Ultimately God had been working in the circumstances that had brought Joseph to Egypt. Though the brothers' actions in the past were despicable, God had used their decisions to place Joseph in a position of authority so that he could rescue Egypt and his own family (45:5).

The truth of God's oversight over all that occurred lay at the heart of the reconciliation between Joseph and his brothers. None of them could reverse the wickedness the siblings were guilty of committing against Joseph; but the realization that God can bring good out of evil paved the way for the severed relationship to be restored and rehabilitated. That which was humanly impossible to achieve the Lord sovereignly brought about in His own time and in His own way.

D. Joseph's Explanation: vss. 6-7

For two years now there has been famine in the land, and for the next five years there will not be plowing and reaping. But God sent me ahead of you to preserve for you a remnant on earth and to save your lives by a great deliverance.

Joseph explained that the two years of famine that had already past would extend to seven. (This means that he was now 39 years old.) During this time, the drought would be so severe that neither plowing nor harvesting would occur (Gen. 45:6). This would be just as true for the family of Jacob as for the entire nation of Egypt. Without assistance and long-term help, the Israelite clan would not likely survive.

Over the years, Joseph had plenty of time to reflect on the strange turn of events his life had taken. As a person of faith, he could discern God's purposes in what had happened to him. God would use Joseph to preserve a "remnant" (vs. 7) of His people. Joseph's words reminded his brothers of the great peril facing their family and implied that they would be rescued only because God had something special in store for the Israelite clan.

One of the most enduring concepts in Scripture is the remnant—a faithful minority who survive a catastrophe or judgment. This notion especially applied to the descendants of Jacob, whom Moses later said had been made "a people holy to the Lord your God" (Deut. 26:19). "Holy" renders the Hebrew word *qodesh*, which means "separation" or "set apart." In the Old Testament, *qodesh* is frequently applied to the Israelites as God's people. Thus, the descendants of Jacob, as the Lord's upright remnant, were to be separated from sin, impurity, and evil. They were also to be set apart for the sole use of their possessor, Yahweh.

In the ancient Near East, there was no greater goal than preserving the family line and no greater family sin than endangering the family line. Joseph's brothers endangered the family line by robbing the clan of Joseph, a male member. Jacob also endangered the family line by hesitating to let Benjamin go to Egypt to get grain (42:38). His selfish desire to protect Benjamin might have caused the starvation of the entire clan and the family line would have ended.

II. JOSEPH'S INSTRUCTIONS: GENESIS 45:8-12

A. God's Sovereign Working: vs. 8

"So then, it was not you who sent me here, but God. He made me father to Pharaoh, lord of his entire household and ruler of all Egypt."

The main point of Joseph's explanation is that ultimately God—not Jacob's sons—was responsible for sending the former Hebrew slave and prisoner to Egypt. Joseph said that the Lord had made him a "father to Pharaoh" (Gen. 45:8). Joseph was speaking figuratively of someone giving others advice, as parents would to their children. In the case of Pharaoh, he relied on Joseph's foresight and prudence. In the years since the Egyptian ruler had appointed him as second-in command, the Hebrew had proven his trustworthiness and dependability. Both the royal household and the entire land of Egypt were in good hands.

"Pharaoh" was the official title of the rulers of Egypt. The name itself derived from an Egyptian word meaning "great house." Before the name came to be applied to the person of the ruler himself, it was used to refer to the royal palace and the Egyptian court. By the time of Joseph, it was commonly used to refer to the ruler. The name *pharaoh* was a title, and as such, was not the personal name of the Egyptian rulers.

B. Joseph's Exhortation: vs. 9

"Now hurry back to my father and say to him, 'This is what your son Joseph says: God has made me lord of all Egypt. Come down to me; don't delay.'"

Since the first time Joseph's brothers had appeared before him, the overseer had worked out a plan for the family. He would settle them in Egypt. Joseph knew that the Israelite clan had to act quickly in order to survive the famine, which had several more years to go. Thus, he directed his brothers to exhort their father to not delay in relocating the entire family. As reassurance that this was the divinely ordained course of action, Joseph noted that God had made him "lord of all Egypt" (Gen. 45:9).

This statement was no exaggeration. After Pharaoh decreed that Joseph would be in charge of the entire realm (41:41), the king placed his own signet ring on the Hebrew's finger as a symbol of his authority. Also, Pharaoh dressed Joseph in fine linen robes and placed a royal gold chain around his neck (vs. 42). Moreover, the king had Joseph ride in the chariot used by the king's second-in-command (vs. 43).

All of this signified the Hebrew's high status and rank in the kingdom. We can only imagine the impression left on Joseph's brothers as they possibly heard attendants command everyone within earshot to kneel down in the presence of the nation's overseer. Pharaoh gave Joseph such extensive power that apart from his authorization no one was permitted to take any action, whether to move a hand or foot in the all the land of Egypt (vs. 44).

C. Joseph's Promises: vss. 10-11

"'You shall live in the region of Goshen and be near me—you, your children and grandchildren, your flocks and herds, and all you have. I will provide for you there, because five years of famine are still to come. Otherwise you and your household and all who belong to you will become destitute.'"

Joseph's plan was to settle the entire Israelite clan—family members, their livestock, and all their possessions—in the land of Goshen (Gen. 45:10). This region was located in the northeastern section of the Nile River delta. Although the area is not large (about 900 square miles), it was considered some of the best territory in Egypt. With irrigation, it was an excellent site for grazing and for growing certain crops. The Hebrew people were still living in the region at the time of the Exodus, four centuries later.

Joseph, as the second-in-command in Egypt, promised to provide the Israelite clan what they needed and would watch over them, especially in the five years of famine that remained. Left on their own in Canaan, Jacob's family would either die from starvation or scatter from the plight of their destitution. Joseph wanted to ensure that the entire group remain together and safe in Egypt (vs. 11).

When Jacob's family moved to Egypt, they had to cross barriers greater than the rocky Sinai peninsula to make this new land their home. Not only were Egypt and Canaan on different continents, but also they contrasted sharply in terms of agricultural practices and societal traditions. For instance, Egypt was rich in crops, livestock, and precious metals, but Canaan's primary enterprise was shepherding, which the Egyptians despised (46:34).

Egypt was an intellectual and cultural center of the ancient world, while Canaan was mostly an intellectual and cultural backwater. Most Egyptians were brown-skinned, with stiff brown hair. Most Canaanites had olive-colored complexions and dark brown or black hair. Without Joseph's power in the royal court, it is unimaginable that the Israelite clan of nomadic shepherds would have received such a gracious welcome from Pharaoh in the sophisticated, cosmopolitan nation over which he ruled (47:1-12).

D. Joseph's Assurance: vs. 12

"You can see for yourselves, and so can my brother Benjamin, that it is really I who am speaking to you."

Joseph wanted there to be no doubt among his siblings that he truly was their long-lost brother. Thus, he dispensed with an interpreter and spoke directly to his brothers (Gen. 45:12). With the important explanations over, Joseph embraced and wept with his brothers, beginning with the youngest. Benjamin was Joseph's only full brother and the only one innocent in regard to the overseer.

Earlier, when Joseph was pretending to be an Egyptian, he must have wanted more than anything to embrace Benjamin and the others. The high ranking official did not have to restrain himself anymore. This mutual display of emotion and the conversation that followed completed the family reunion (vss. 13-15). Whatever bitterness Joseph may have felt toward his brothers was all gone now. They had nothing to fear from him, for he had forgiven them.

Discussion Questions

1. Why did Joseph have all the Egyptian attendants leave his presence?
2. Why did Joseph weep so intensely?
3. Why were Joseph's brothers terrified in his presence?
4. What reason did Joseph give for being in Egypt?
5. What plan did Joseph have for the Israelite clan?

Contemporary Application

When leaders Mark and Jana set out with their youth group for Pennsylvania from Michigan, they knew the church's bus was not in the best shape. Still, they had not expected to stop dead in bumper-to-bumper traffic on an Ohio interstate exit ramp—on a Sunday morning. There was little the group could do but push the stalled bus onto the shoulder, raise the hood, and pray for help.

Soon a woman on her way to church stopped to find out how she could help. "Well," Mark said, "we need a mechanic." "There's a mechanic in our church," the woman said. "Let's see what I can do." Once at church, the woman interrupted the service to tell the congregation about the group's plight and ask for assistance. She returned to the broken-down bus with a few other churchgoers. "I can repair the bus," one man said. Another pulled Mark aside and said, "I would like to put your group up for the night at our church while you wait for the repair. I would also like to buy your dinner."

That breakdown taught the group important lessons about God's faithfulness. It could have been a time of grumbling and frustration. Instead, they were all reminded that God's purposes exceed our plans, especially as He works to accomplish His will in our lives. We must simply remember whose children we are—and enjoy the ride.

Jacob Blessed His Family

DEVOTIONAL READING

Psalm 145:1-13

DAILY BIBLE READINGS

Monday November 19
Genesis 45:16-20 Bring Your Father

Tuesday November 20
Genesis 46:1-4 God's Reassurance

Wednesday November 21
Genesis 46:28-34 The Reunion

Thursday November 22
Genesis 47:7-12 A Blessing

Friday November 23
Genesis 47:27-31 Joseph's Promise

Saturday November 24
Genesis 48:8-21 A Grandfather's Blessing

Sunday November 25
Psalm 145:1-13 The Greatness and Goodness of God

Scripture

Background Scripture: *Genesis 48:8-21*

Scripture Lesson: *Genesis 48:11-19*

Key Verse: *Israel said to Joseph, "I never expected to see your face again, and now God has allowed me to see your children too."* Genesis 48:11.

Scripture Lesson for Children: *Genesis 46:1-6, 28-30; 47:7, 11-12*

Key Verse for Children: *Joseph settled his father and his brothers . . . in the best part of the land.* Genesis 47:11.

Lesson Aim

To underscore that faith is a journey with God.

Lesson Setting

Time: *1859 B.C.*

Place: *Egypt*

Lesson Outline

Jacob Blessed His Family

   I. Israel's Meeting with Joseph's Sons: Genesis 48:11-14

      A. Manasseh and Ephraim's Appearance: vs. 11

      B. Joseph's Display of Respect: vs. 12

      C. Ephraim's Preeminence over Manasseh: vss. 13-14

  II. Israel's Blessing of Joseph's Sons: Genesis 48:15-19

      A. Israel's Pronouncement of Blessing: vss. 15-16

      B. Joseph's Disagreement: vss. 17-18

      C. Israel's Insistence: vs. 19

Introduction for Adults

Topic: *Leaving a Legacy*

What does God ask us to do? Plumbers, accountants, and athletes have been surprised when God called them to enter the ministry or become missionaries; but the Lord may ask us to do simpler things that are also challenging—for instance, sharing the Gospel with someone seated next to us on a bus or inviting a peer at work to go to church with us.

Living in faith means continually taking risks, stepping out of the familiar into the unfamiliar. We can learn from other believers how to respond when God calls. We need to heed His will at all times, no matter the consequences. Nothing less than the legacy we leave behind is at stake.

Introduction for Youth

Topic: *Blessed*

What keeps you from hearing someone call you? Distance, language, volume, or the level of anticipation may all be factors. Think of how quickly a mother can hear the soft cry of her child in another room. Obviously, she is tuned in to hear that call; nevertheless, how many times can that same mother call her older child to the dinner table before he or she hears the summons?

God is calling each one of us. He is calling some of us to take the first step on a lifelong journey of faith with Him. That step is admitting our sinfulness and accepting His Son, Jesus Christ, as our Savior. It's the most important first step we can take. For those who have already taken that first step, the journey has only begun. God continues to call and eternally bless us each step of the way.

Concepts for Children

Topic: *Together Again*

1. God reassured Jacob that the move to Egypt was the right thing to do.
2. God's promises to Abraham were renewed in God's promises to Jacob.
3. In obedience to God, Jacob took his family and his possessions to Egypt.
4. The ruler of Egypt allowed Jacob and his family to live in the best part of the land.
5. God fills our lives with eternal joy when we do His will.

Lesson Commentary

I. ISRAEL'S MEETING WITH JOSEPH'S SONS: GENESIS 48:11-14

A. Manasseh and Ephraim's Appearance: vs. 11

Israel said to Joseph, "I never expected to see your face again, and now God has allowed me to see your children too."

Although Joseph had sent the Egyptians out of the room before he disclosed his identity to his brothers, many outside heard his loud weeping (Gen. 45:2). This roused their interest. At some point they learned that Joseph's brothers had come to him, and the servants carried the news to the royal palace (vs. 16). Nine years after receiving his high post, Joseph still enjoyed Pharaoh's favor. As chapter 47 shows, Joseph was in the process of using the nation's grain reserves to make the king tremendously wealthy. Not surprisingly, Pharaoh was kindly disposed toward Joseph. Consequently, the news about the Hebrew overseer's brothers was greeted with pleasure in the royal court.

When Joseph next had an audience with Pharaoh, the matter of his brothers was discussed. Apparently, Joseph did not even get the opportunity to tell the king about the plan to bring the overseer's family to Egypt before Pharaoh instructed him to do just that. This would be a way for the king to reward his trusted second-in-command for his work (vss. 17-24). Jacob must have spent the weeks that his sons were away from home worrying about them, especially Benjamin; and the patriarch must have been overjoyed when all 11 returned safe and sound. Initially, though, Jacob was stunned by the news that Joseph was not only alive but also a high official in Egypt. Further persuasion, along with the sight of the carts, animals, and riches, finally convinced Jacob, and he vowed to go to his son in Egypt before the patriarch died (vss. 25-28).

Chapters 46 and 47 detail the journey of the Israelite clan from Canaan to Egypt. Joseph traveled to meet Jacob in the region of Goshen. After the reunion, Joseph escorted the Israelite caravan to Pharaoh and presented his brothers and father to Egypt's ruler. In keeping with Pharaoh's suggestion, Joseph then provided land and food for the Hebrew immigrants. Joseph himself, though, continued in his government position, saving lives while at the same time enriching Pharaoh.

Chapters 48 and 49 record a deathbed scene. With his last remaining strength, Jacob sat on the edge of his bed and spoke to his sons. They had been called to him because of his final illness (48:1-2). Even Joseph came from his palace with his two boys. Jacob knew death was closing in on him, so he performed the traditional duty of blessing his sons. This meant he divided the inheritance among them and invoked God's favor upon them. Since Jacob's family was in covenant with the Lord, the belief that their descendants would one day possess the promised land lies behind his words.

The patriarch began his speech by addressing Joseph, telling how Almighty God had blessed Jacob long ago at Luz or Bethel (48:3-4; compare 28:10-22). The Lord had promised that Jacob's descendants would become numerous. In light of that blessing, Jacob claimed Manasseh and Ephraim as his own sons. Any other sons Joseph might have would remain Joseph's own. They would not be equal with their uncles, as Manasseh and Ephraim were (vss. 5-6). In those days, the oldest son usually received twice as much of the inheritance as any other son. Jacob's oldest son was Reuben, but he had proven himself unworthy (35:22). Thus Jacob instead gave the double portion to Joseph by adopting Joseph's sons, Manasseh and Ephraim. Through them, Joseph's descendants would be two tribes, not one.

Next, Jacob mentioned the death and burial of his favorite wife, Rachel, the mother of Joseph and Benjamin. Perhaps Jacob mentioned Rachel to suggest that Manasseh and Ephraim would take the place of any other sons he would have had by Rachel if she had not died early. Finally, Jacob (whom the text begins referring to as Israel) saw two young men he did not recognize. Surely in the 17 years he had spent in Egypt, the patriarch had gotten to know the grandsons, Manasseh and Ephraim; but Israel's eyesight was failing, and he could not easily recognize them (48:7-9). Another possibility is that the patriarch's question was part of the ritual to formally identify the beneficiaries of the covenantal blessings.

Having been told who the two young men were, Israel had them come near. Then he kissed and embraced them (vs. 10). Next, the patriarch admitted that he had never anticipated seeing Joseph again. After all, years earlier the older brothers had convinced their father that Joseph was dead. Now the Lord graciously allowed Israel not only to see the face of Joseph but also his children (vs. 11).

B. Joseph's Display of Respect: vs. 12

Then Joseph removed them from Israel's knees and bowed down with his face to the ground.

Up until this point, Joseph's two sons probably had been standing by Israel's knees as he blessed them. Scholars think receiving children onto or beside one's knees was a symbol of adoption. At some point, Joseph moved Manasseh and Ephraim away from the knees of their grandfather. Then Joseph bowed down with his face to the ground before the elderly patriarch (Gen. 48:12). Although Joseph was a high official in one of the most powerful nations of the day in that region of the world, it did not get in the way of him humbly thanking his father for the honor he was showing Joseph in adopting and blessing his two sons.

C. Ephraim's Preeminence over Manasseh: vss. 13-14

And Joseph took both of them, Ephraim on his right toward Israel's left hand and Manasseh on his left toward Israel's right hand, and brought them close to him. But Israel reached out his right hand and put it on Ephraim's head, though he was the younger, and crossing his arms, he put his left hand on Manasseh's head, even though Manasseh was the firstborn.

Joseph's two sons were born to him before the seven years of famine came (Gen. 41:50). The name of the first son, "Manasseh" (vs. 51), possibly means "he who brings about forgetfulness" and served as a reminder that God had enabled Joseph to forget all his troubles and the family of his father. The name of the second son, "Ephraim" (vs. 52), means "to bear fruit" and served as a reminder of that God had made Joseph fruitful in the land of his suffering. The names the Hebrew overseer gave his children indicated that he held on to his heritage and faith even while in Egypt.

The Lord honored Joseph's devotion by allowing Jacob to adopt and bless Manasseh and Ephraim. Joseph positioned Ephraim on his right hand, which was across from Israel's left hand. Joseph also placed Manasseh by his left hand and across from Israel's right hand. As Joseph brought his sons closer to their grandfather, the overseer was quite intentional in wanting to maintain this arrangement (48:13). It would allow the firstborn, Manasseh, to receive the greater blessing, in accordance with ancient custom.

Israel, however, broke with tradition by stretching out his right hand and placing it on Ephraim's head. The patriarch deliberately did this, even though Ephraim was the younger son. Next, Israel crossed his hands so that he could place his left hand on Manasseh's head (vs. 14). Again, this defied conventional wisdom, for Manasseh was the older son. The patriarch's reversal of his hands did not mean that only Ephraim would be blessed. In fact, Israel invoked God's blessing on both young men (vss. 15, 16, 20); but in the providence and sovereignty of God, Ephraim would have the superior blessing.

II. ISRAEL'S BLESSING OF JOSEPH'S SONS: GENESIS 48:15-19

A. Israel's Pronouncement of Blessing: vss. 15-16

Then he blessed Joseph and said, "May the God before whom my fathers Abraham and Isaac walked, the God who has been my shepherd all my life to this day, the Angel who has delivered me from all harm—may he bless these boys. May they be called by my name and the names of my fathers Abraham and Isaac, and may they increase greatly upon the earth."

The Hebrew verb rendered "blessed" (Gen. 48:15) is *barak* and literally means "to kneel." When used of God toward people, the term generally refers to His bestowing a rich and abundant life on someone; and when used of people blessing people, the verb usually signifies a desire that God would shine His favor on a particular individual or group. Finally, when the verb describes people blessing God, it is an expression of praise to Him in recognition of His goodness and grace.

In the blessing that Israel conveyed to Joseph and his two sons, the patriarch made reference to the covenant-keeping God of Abraham and Isaac. Many years earlier, God came to Abraham in a vision and declared that He was the patriarch's shield of protection as well as the One who would reward him in great abundance (15:1). Later, the Lord referred to Himself as God Almighty and instructed Abraham to serve Him faithfully and live a blameless life (17:1). The testimony of Jacob's grandfather and father was that both of them lived faithfully in the Lord's presence (15:2; 48:15).

Like other people of faith, the patriarchs believed that God exists and that He rewards those who earnestly seek Him (Heb. 11:6). Their trust in the Lord enabled them to sojourn as foreigners in Canaan and embrace the covenant pledges connected with the promised land. They could live in this way because they looked forward to the heavenly city of the eternal God (vss. 7-16). Indeed, the lives of Abraham, Isaac, Jacob, and Joseph were all characterized by unwavering faith in the Lord (vss. 17-22). They and others like them died with the assurance that God would bring to pass everything He declared He would do (vss. 39-40).

It is this perspective of faith that lay at the heart of Israel's statements to Joseph. As the end of the patriarch's life drew closer, he could genuinely affirm that the Lord had been his shepherd (Gen. 48:15). When Jacob first ventured from Canaan to Paddan Aram, God pledged to watch over him and prosper him (28:10-22). Two decades later, as Jacob prepared to return to Canaan, the Lord promised to be with him (31:3). Before the patriarch's reunion with Esau, Jacob had a life-changing encounter with God's angel (vss. 24-30). Then, as Israel made the journey to Bethel, the Lord appeared to him and spoke reassuringly to him (35:1). Upon Israel's arrival, Almighty God again appeared to him and reiterated the covenant promises (vss. 11-13).

Even in the matter involving Joseph, Israel believed the Lord was sovereignly at work to bring about His will. Indeed, the patriarch was convinced that the angel sent by God had protected and delivered him from all harm. It may be that Israel thought the divine blessing he was conferring on Joseph's sons would be mediated through this angelic representative. It was Israel's expressed wish that they would be identified by the names of Abraham, Isaac, and Israel. An additional implication is that as the Lord enabled Joseph's sons to increase greatly on the earth and become a mighty nation, they would also preserve the honor associated with the names of the patriarchs (48:16).

B. Joseph's Disagreement: vss. 17-18

When Joseph saw his father placing his right hand on Ephraim's head he was displeased; so he took hold of his father's hand to move it from Ephraim's head to Manasseh's head. Joseph said to him, "No, my father, this one is the firstborn; put your right hand on his head."

Joseph was displeased to see that his father placed his right hand on the head of Ephraim, the younger of the two sons. The overseer saw his father's crossing of hands as a mistake and tried to correct it by moving Israel's hand to the head of Manasseh, the older son (Gen. 48:17). Joseph, perhaps assuming that his elderly and sight-impaired father was unaware of what he was doing, respectfully but straightforwardly explained that Manasseh was the firstborn and thus deserved to receive the greater blessing (vs. 18); but despite social custom, this was not God's will.

C. Israel's Insistence: vs. 19

But his father refused and said, "I know, my son, I know. He too will become a people, and he too will become great. Nevertheless, his younger brother will be greater than he, and his descendants will become a group of nations."

Israel calmly refused to give preferential treatment to Manasseh, Joseph's firstborn. With prophetic insight, the patriarch revealed that the descendants of both young men would become great, but Ephraim's offspring would be greater. In fact, the younger son's descendants would become a multitude of nations (Gen. 48:19). Centuries later, the tribe of Ephraim did end up being more powerful than the tribe of Manasseh. During the wilderness wandering, the tribe of Manasseh was led by the banner of the tribe of Ephraim. At the time of the divided kingdom, the northern 10 tribes were often collectively called Ephraim.

In blessing Joseph's sons, the patriarch said that the people of Israel would use the names of Ephraim and Manasseh to bless their fellow citizens in the nation (vs. 20). Perhaps as the grandfather of the two young men put Ephraim ahead of Manasseh, he thought back to the time he had stolen his brother's birthright. Like Ephraim, Jacob had been elevated above his older brother, Esau. Jacob knew from personal experience that sometimes God acts in ways that upset human conventions and ideas.

The pronouns translated "you" and "your" in verse 21 are plural in the Hebrew text. This suggests that Israel was directing his words not only to Joseph, but also to Manasseh, Ephraim, their descendants, and the rest of the offspring of Israel. The patriarch declared that God would be with the Hebrew people and one day bring them back to Canaan. In expectation of that return, Israel gave to Joseph and his sons an extra portion beyond what the patriarch had given his other sons.

The Hebrew for the phrase rendered "one more ridge of land" (vs. 22) is identical with the place name for Shechem. In light of this, some commentators have suggested that mountain slope Israel referred to was the plot of ground he purchased for a hundred pieces of silver from the sons of Hamor, the father of Shechem (33:18-20). The reference in 48:22 to the acquisition of the land by warfare (namely, by sword and bow) takes into account the events narrated in 34:25-29. Later, Joseph was buried in Shechem and the tract of land became the inheritance of Joseph's descendants (Josh. 24:32).

After Israel blessed his adopted sons, he proceeded to bless his natural sons (49:1-28). His words prophetically anticipated the characteristics of the tribes that would come from the men. According to Israel, the tribes of Judah and Joseph (that is, Manasseh and Ephraim) had the greatest future. These prophecies were borne out. The tribe of Manasseh would occupy the largest land area of any in the Hebrew nation. The tribe of Ephraim would become the leader of the northern kingdom of Israel. The tribe of Judah would possess the land that included Jerusalem, and would eventually become a separate kingdom. Greatest of all, the Messiah came from the tribe of Judah. After Israel finished the address to his sons, he repeated his request that he be buried in the cave of Machpelah along with his ancestors and his wife, Leah. Then the patriarch died at the age of 147 (vss. 29-33).

Joseph led the way in displaying grief over the death of his father. Then he gave orders for physicians under his management to embalm Israel's body (50:1-2). At the end of a 70-day mourning period, Joseph sought permission from Pharaoh to leave the country to bury his father. For some reason, the overseer did not make this request in person to the king (vss. 3-4). In Egypt, funeral processions were major spectacles. Jacob's funeral procession was no exception. His body was accompanied by Joseph, Joseph's brothers, and other members of their family. Out of respect for Joseph, many Egyptian officials also accompanied the body. To protect such an important crowd, mounted soldiers went along. Eventually, the body arrived at its final resting place: the cave of Machpelah, not far from Mamre. Then everyone in the party returned to Egypt (vss. 5-14).

Discussion Questions

1. How did Jacob feel about being able to see Joseph's two sons?
2. What is significant about Joseph bowing in the presence of his father?
3. What difference of opinion did Jacob and Joseph have about which of the sons should receive the blessing of the firstborn?
4. What sort of blessing did Jacob bestow on Joseph's sons?
5. What future awaited the descendants of Manasseh and Ephraim?

Contemporary Application

Bob remembers traveling as a child with his father, a regional salesman, to visit accounts throughout southern Illinois. "On those trips, my father relied as much on his date book as he did his map," Bob says. The book was filled with the names and addresses of his customers, directions to their businesses, their purchasing history, and of course, the date of their next appointment. "Without that book," Bob says, "my father would have been out of business in less than a week."

Today, millions in all walks of life hold tightly to their schedulers and planners, both paper and electronic. We use them to map out our future years in advance and plan our days down to the half hour. As a result, our journey through life is often driven by the calendar and the clock.

Sometimes, though, God has other plans for our lives than the ones we so carefully map out. Consider the future of the Israelite clan, especially the two sons of Joseph. He envisioned Manasseh, the firstborn, to receive the primary family blessing from his grandfather; but Jacob bestowed it on Ephraim, the second of Joseph's sons. In this case, God's will went against conventional wisdom and social customs.

In our lives, when things do not go according to our predetermined plans, it may be due to the fact that there is a lesson we need to learn, a person we need to meet, or a job only we can do. When God calls, the date books must be set aside. Ultimately, we are travelers with God on a lifelong journey of faith. Thus, His planner (so to speak) takes precedence.

Called to Believe!

DEVOTIONAL READING

Psalm 66:1-4, 16-20

DAILY BIBLE READINGS

Monday November 26
Psalm 66:1-4 Sing God's Praises

Tuesday November 27
Luke 1:5-7 Righteous before God

Wednesday November 28
Luke 1:8-13 Incense Offering Interrupted

Thursday November 29
Luke 1:14-17 A Ministry Foretold

Friday November 30
Luke 1:18-23 Zechariah Sees a Vision

Saturday December 1
Luke 1:24-25 Elizabeth Conceives

Sunday December 2
Psalm 66:16-20 God Listened to My Prayer

Scripture

Background Scripture: *Luke 1:5-25*
Scripture Lesson: *Luke 1:8-23*
Key Verse: *"And now you will be silent and not able to speak until the day this happens, because you did not believe my words, which will come true at their proper time."* Luke 1:20.
Scripture Lesson for Children: *Luke 1:8-23*
Key Verse for Children: *The angel said to him: "Do not be afraid, Zechariah; your prayer has been heard. Your wife Elizabeth will bear you a son, and you are to give him the name John."* Luke 1:13.

Lesson Aim

To become more expectant of God's blessings.

Lesson Setting

Time: *About 6–5 B.C.*
Place: *Jerusalem and the hill country of Judea*

Lesson Outline

Called to Believe!

   I. John's Birth Foretold: Luke 1:8-17
      A. *The Selection of Zechariah: vss. 8-10*
      B. *The Appearance of the Lord's Angel: vss. 11-12*
      C. *The Angel's Declaration Concerning John: vss. 13-17*
  II. Zechariah's Skepticism: Luke 1:18-23
      A. *The Doubt Voiced by Zechariah: vs. 18*
      B. *The Angel's Declaration of Censure: vss. 19-20*
      C. *The Inability of Zechariah to Speak: vss. 21-23*

Introduction for Adults

Topic: *Surprising Opportunities*

For a number of years, Zechariah and Elizabeth remained childless. But then a suprising opportunity came. The Lord's angel promised they would have a child in their old age. Regardless of whether anyone in your class is struggling with childlessness, most of them have gone through times of apparently fruitless praying. Unanswered prayer is an embarrassment to some Christian adults because they interpret it as a sign that their relationship with God has gone awry.

A few distressed adults will become so obsessed with their unfulfilled desire that they will pray about little else. Other adults go to the opposite extreme. They decide not to pray at all because they reason God did not respond the way they wanted.

Regardless of where we may be in our prayer life, we can learn much from Zechariah and Elizabeth. They were faithful to God, and He richly blessed them because of it. He will also shower us with His favor when we remain faithful to Him. In turn, this will prepare us for the surprising opportunities He wants to bring in our lives!

Introduction for Youth

Topic: *Called to Believe*

Teenagers, like adults, have unresolved problems in their lives. If you were to ask the adolescents in your class about the lingering issues they face, some might mention such problems as feeling ill, struggling with school work, or dealing with frustration over a broken relationship with someone of the opposite gender. Their outlook might include fear that a situation will get worse.

In this week's lesson, the students will learn about Zechariah and Elizabeth's childless condition. And the class members will also discover how God promised to bless this elderly couple through the birth of John the Baptist. This lesson will encourage the teens to respond favorably to God's call for them to believe that He can help them resolve the problems they face—in His time and strength.

Concepts for Children

Topic: *Believing in Miracles*

1. Zechariah was a priest who served before God.
2. The angel promised that Zechariah and Elizabeth would have a son in their old age.
3. Zechariah found it hard to believe what the angel had promised.
4. Because of his unbelief, Zechariah was unable to speak until that day when he would praise God for the fulfillment of the promise.
5. God is pleased when we believe His promises to us in His Word.

Lesson Commentary

I. JOHN'S BIRTH FORETOLD: LUKE 1:8-17

A. The Selection of Zechariah: vss. 8-10

Once when Zechariah's division was on duty and he was serving as priest before God, he was chosen by lot, according to the custom of the priesthood, to go into the temple of the Lord and burn incense. And when the time for the burning of incense came, all the assembled worshipers were praying outside.

The first accounts about Jesus circulated in oral form. Then, as more believers joined the church and as eyewitnesses began to pass from the scene, it became necessary to put His words and the accounts of His deeds into written form. Several narratives recounting the Messiah's teachings and accomplishments—probably including the Gospels of Matthew and Mark—had already been produced by the time Luke decided to write his own. In doing so, he endeavored to check all the facts for himself so that his account would remain objective, factual, and orderly.

Luke was a Gentile physician from elsewhere (Col. 4:14), but he certainly could have visited Palestine and talked with some of the people who had known Jesus. For instance, Luke may have learned many of the details surrounding the Messiah's birth from Mary, the mother of Jesus. A public official named Theophilus was the person for whom Luke penned his account. Some think Theophilus had not yet decided what to believe about Jesus and that Luke wrote his Gospel as an evangelism tool. Others think Theophilus may have been someone with influence in Rome and Luke hoped that by Theophilus reading this Gospel, he would be convinced to defend Christianity. Still others believe his name (literally, "lover of God") tells us he was already a believer in Christ. If so, perhaps he had recently been converted and needed more information in order to grow spiritually.

One common thread between people of the first century A.D. and people living today is their need for a Savior. Men and women are bruised and battered by life's disappointments and society's injustices, and so were the people of the first century. People today must face the awfulness of their own sin, just as people had to do in the first century. And people today can find strength and hope through trusting in Jesus, just as Luke's first reader, Theophilus, may have done when he read the third Synoptic Gospel.

Luke 1:1-4, which serves as the introduction to this Gospel, is followed by a recounting of the events connected with the birth of John the Baptizer. These occurred during the reign of Herod the Great, who was king of Judea from 37–4 B.C. Herod was confirmed by the Roman Senate as the ruler of the Jews despite his being only half Jewish. His crowning achievement was beginning the reconstruction of the temple in Jerusalem in 20 B.C. (The shrine complex was not completed until A.D. 64.)

Zechariah and Elizabeth, the parents of John the Baptizer, were both descended from Aaron (vs. 5). Levi was the original ancestor of Israel's priests, including those descended from Aaron. The Mosaic legislation, however, made a distinction between Aaronic priests and Levites. Only members of the first group were permitted to offer sacrifices in the tabernacle (Exod. 28; Lev. 8—10). The Levites assisted the Aaronic priests in their responsibilities (Num. 3:5-9; 16:8-9).

Zechariah also belonged to the priestly division of Abijah. This couple pleased the Lord by the way they lived (Luke 1:6). In fact, they consistently walked in the way of righteousness and obeyed all that God had commanded. Nonetheless, despite their blameless lifestyle, they were childless (vs. 7). In Bible times, children were regarded as God's reward for faithful service (Ps. 127:3-5). Some incorrectly believed the Lord was displeased with and punished those who lacked children. The experience of Zechariah and Elizabeth disproves that theory. From a human perspective, the barren condition of Elizabeth and the advanced age of her and her husband made it highly unlikely that she would ever get pregnant. The inability of this godly couple to have children must have been a deep disappointment for them.

During the reign of David, the Aaronic priests were divided into 24 groups, and Abijah was the leader of the eighth division (1 Chron. 24:10). The priestly groups served in the temple on a rotating basis, with each group ministering for a week twice a year and at the major festivals. Twice a day, before the morning sacrifice and after the evening sacrifice, priests burned incense on the altar in front of the holy of holies in the temple (Exod. 30:7-8). Because there were so many priests (estimated by some to be approximately 18,000 at that time), each priest would get to offer incense at the daily sacrifice only once in his lifetime (if at all) and the opportunity represented the pinnacle of one's ministerial career.

The priests performed a variety of important duties. For instance, they offered gifts and sacrifices for the sins of both themselves and others. The priests also read the law of Moses to God's people and reminded them of their obligation to keep the covenant (Deut. 31:9-13; Neh. 8:2-3). The priests revealed the will of God (Exod. 28:30) and blessed the people (Num. 6:22-26). Moreover, the priests were subject to special laws. For example, they could not drink wine when they went into the tabernacle (Lev. 10:9). They had to observe the difference between what was holy and what was common (vs. 10). A priest could only marry an Israelite, and she had to be either a virgin or a widow, not a divorced person (21:7)

The priests used lots to determine who from a certain group would be chosen to burn incense in the temple. Lots were small marked objects like pebbles, sticks, or pieces of pottery. Although the exact method of casting lots remains unclear, some think a priest placed the objects in a jar with a narrow neck. Then when he shook the container, only one piece came out. One day the division of Abijah was on duty, and Zechariah was fulfilling his priestly obligation (Luke 1:8). When the lot was cast, he was chosen to burn incense (vs. 9). He, along with the other priests, would enter the temple, but they would exit, leaving him alone to perform the offering. While Zechariah performed the ritual, pious Jews stood outside the building to worship and pray (vs. 10). The smoke drifting upward symbolized the prayers of the devout Jews ascending to the throne of God (Ps. 141:2; Rev. 5:8; 8:3-4).

B. The Appearance of the Lord's Angel: vss. 11-12

Then an angel of the Lord appeared to him, standing at the right side of the altar of incense. When Zechariah saw him, he was startled and was gripped with fear.

An angel from the Lord suddenly appeared to Zechariah on the south side of the incense altar, between it and the golden lampstand (Luke 1:11). The right side of the altar would have been regarded as the spot of divine favor (see Ps. 110:1; Mark 16:5). Upon seeing the heavenly being, Zechariah became shocked and terrified (Luke 1:12). A survey of Scripture indicates that being gripped with fear was a common response when messengers from God appeared to people (see Judg. 6:22-23; 13:6, 22; Luke 1:29-20; 2:9). The angel, whose name was Gabriel (Luke 1:19), would not leave Zechariah in a state of fear.

C. The Angel's Declaration Concerning John: vss. 13-17

But the angel said to him: "Do not be afraid, Zechariah; your prayer has been heard. Your wife Elizabeth will bear you a son, and you are to give him the name John. He will be a joy and delight to you, and many will rejoice because of his birth, for he will be great in the sight of the Lord. He is never to take wine or other fermented drink, and he will be filled with the Holy Spirit even from birth. Many of the people of Israel will he bring back to the Lord their God. And he will go on before the Lord, in the spirit and power of Elijah, to turn the hearts of the fathers to their children and the disobedient to the wisdom of the righteous—to make ready a people prepared for the Lord."

Before going any further, the angel from the Lord directed Zechariah not to be afraid. Then the supernatural emissary announced that the prayer of Zechariah had been heard (Luke 1:13). While the priest was offering the sacrifice in the temple, his immediate petition would have been for the nation. But the angel's statement indicates that the long hoped-for desire of Zechariah and Elizabeth would be fulfilled. Possibly this indicates the couple had been praying for the messianic redemption of Israel (see 2:25; 24:21). Another possibility is that they had asked God for a child. In turn, the Lord blessed their obedience by granting their deep desire.

The angel declared that Elizabeth's newborn son was to be named "John" (1:13). The Greek noun comes from the Hebrew name *Johanan*, which means "Yahweh has shown favor" or "Yahweh is gracious." This signifies the reason for John's birth, namely, to herald the advent of the Messiah, the gift of God's grace. God's naming John before his birth suggests that the Lord was singling him out for his important work. The angel also declared that Zechariah and Elizabeth would experience great joy over the birth and life of their son, and many others would rejoice with the godly couple at John's birth (vs. 14). The reason is stated in verse 15. John would "be great in the sight of the Lord." In fact, God would use John to persuade many Israelites to turn to the Lord in faith (vs. 16).

Instead of consuming and being controlled by wine and other fermented drink, John would be filled with the Holy Spirit, even before his birth. This fact has led some to surmise that John eventually took the vow of a Nazarite (Num. 6:1-4). Those making such a pledge even refrained from ingesting grapes, grape juice, and raisins. In the case of John, however, Luke did not specifically state that he took such a vow. Instead, the emphasis seems to be on John's ascetic lifestyle (see Luke 7:25, 33).

Regardless of one's view on the matter, it's clear that John had a uniquely God-given position. As a prophet in the stature of Elijah (Matt. 11:14; 17:10-13; Luke 7:24-28), John would go as a forerunner before the Lord. John's mission would be to turn the hearts of parents back to their children. He would also persuade disobedient minds to accept godly wisdom (Luke 1:17; see Mal. 3:1; 4:5-6). These two tasks cover all relationships, namely, those involving other people (the horizontal dimension of life) and those involving God (the vertical dimension of life). Furthermore, the Greek verb rendered "to turn" (Luke 1:17) highlights John's task of summoning people to repent, that is, to change the moral and spiritual direction of their lives in preparation for the advent of the Messiah (see 3:1-14; 24:47).

II. ZECHARIAH'S SKEPTICISM: LUKE 1:18-23

A. The Doubt Voiced by Zechariah: vs. 18

Zechariah asked the angel, "How can I be sure of this? I am an old man and my wife is well along in years."

Zechariah, being caught off guard by the angel's announcement, was filled with doubt and asked how he could be sure of what he had been told. When he considered the situation from his limited human perspective, he concluded that it was physically impossible for an elderly man such as himself to become a father or his wife, who was past the age of childbearing, to become a mother (Luke 1:18). The same sort of skepticism overtook Sarah when the Lord revealed that He would enable her to become pregnant through Abraham. The divine promise was made when both of them were advanced in years. In that episode, God declared that nothing He pledged was too difficult for Him to do (Gen. 18:10-14). Likewise, with the situation involving Elizabeth and Zechariah, the Lord was able to fulfill what He had promised.

B. The Angel's Declaration of Censure: vss. 19-20

The angel answered, "I am Gabriel. I stand in the presence of God, and I have been sent to speak to you and to tell you this good news. And now you will be silent and not able to speak until the day this happens, because you did not believe my words, which will come true at their proper time."

The angel who appeared to Zechariah announced that his name was "Gabriel" (Luke 1:19), which means "man of God," "God has shown Himself strong," or "God is my hero." The greatness of this messenger from heaven is seen in the fact that Gabriel stood in the presence of the Lord; and because God had sent the angel to announce to Zechariah the good news about John, Zechariah should have believed what he heard. Because the priest had used words to convey his doubt, the Lord would discipline him by preventing him from being able to speak (vs. 20). Evidently, Zechariah was also unable to hear, for as verses 61-63 indicate, others had to use gestures to communicate with him. He would remain deaf and mute until the time when God fulfilled what He had promised (vs. 20). This circumstance would also be a sign of assurance that what the angel had declared was true.

It is noteworthy that God broke 400 years of silence by sending Gabriel to a man whose name means "God remembers" (Zechariah). The Lord remembered Zechariah's prayer for a son (Luke 1:13), but more than that, He recalled the covenants He made with Abraham and David (Gen. 12:2-3; 2 Sam. 7:12-16; Gal. 3:16-17). Elizabeth's name is also significant in this regard, for it means "God's oath (or covenant)." To speak of her name was to remember that the Lord was a covenant-making, covenant-keeping God. Scripture teaches that the Lord remembers His people, answers their prayers, keeps His promises to them, and sent Jesus to redeem the lost, all because God is gracious.

C. The Inability of Zechariah to Speak: vss. 21-23

Meanwhile, the people were waiting for Zechariah and wondering why he stayed so long in the temple. When he came out, he could not speak to them. They realized he had seen a vision in the temple, for he kept making signs to them but remained unable to speak. When his time of service was completed, he returned home.

Under normal circumstances, the priest ministered in the temple for a short period of time and then came out to offer a blessing (see Num. 6:22-27). In the case of Zechariah, the pious Jews waiting outside began to wonder why he seemed to be delayed in the holy place (Luke 1:21). Eventually, the priest did leave the temple, and after he emerged, the people discovered that he was unable to speak to them. The signs he kept making with his hands made this clear and also indicated that he had seen a vision. Expressed differently, while Zechariah ministered in the holy place, he had a supernatural encounter, one involving an angel from the Lord (vs. 22). In due course, Zechariah's time of service in the temple ended. Then he returned to his home in the hill country of Judea, which was south of Jerusalem (vss. 23, 39-40).

Just as the angel had promised, Elizabeth became pregnant. For the next five months she did not leave her house, perhaps to reflect on what had happened and to quietly express her joy (vs. 24). Elizabeth concluded that the Lord had enabled her, a woman past the age of childbearing, to become pregnant. The favor God had shown her would remove the perceived disgrace of childlessness she bore. No longer would people look down on her because of her barrenness (vs. 23).

Discussion Questions

1. What was Zechariah's personal and professional background?
2. What were the people doing outside the temple as Zechariah ministered inside?
3. What announcement did the angel from the Lord make to Zechariah concerning Elizabeth?
4. What ministry awaited John the Baptizer?
5. Why did the angel declare that Zechariah would be unable to speak until John was born?

Contemporary Application

Zechariah and Elizabeth followed the Lord, and He blessed them. We can also expect Him to bless us as we follow Him faithfully. When we say we anticipate God's blessings, we do not mean we set the agenda or make arrogant demands of God. There is a difference between anticipating God's blessings and living as if we deserved to be blessed. Everything the Lord does for us is based on His undeserved favor.

Our attitude toward life can greatly influence how expectant we are of God's blessings. If we typically view circumstances through negative or pessimistic lenses, it might be harder for us to anticipate and recognize the blessings of the Lord in our lives. An overly critical or cynical attitude can blind us to the wonderful things God is doing and wants to do in our lives.

It takes time to become more expectant of God's blessings. Part of the process includes reflecting on what the Lord has done for us in the past and how He is presently working in our lives. At first, it might be hard for us to notice what God has done. Gradually, however, we should begin to recognize the wonderful ways the Lord has blessed us.

Our relationship with God can take on an added dimension of excitement as we anticipate new ways the Lord might bless us. We can cultivate an attitude of expectancy by keeping a log of prayer requests for ourselves, loved ones, and friends. As we record our petitions, we can look forward to God answering some of our prayers affirmatively. Another way we can become more expectant of God's blessings is by learning how the Lord has blessed other Christians. For example, by reading the biographies of other believers, we can see how God graciously worked in their lives. We might also consider asking godly Christians we know to share how the Lord has blessed them through the years. Such an investigation can help us to become more perceptive of ways God might bestow His favor on us.

Called to Be a Vessel!

Scripture

Background Scripture: *Luke 1:26-38*

Scripture Lesson: *Luke 1:26-38*

Key Verse: *"I am the Lord's servant," Mary answered. "May it be to me as you have said." Luke 1:38.*

Scripture Lesson for Children: *Luke 1:26-38*

Key Verse for Children: *"I am the Lord's servant," Mary answered. "May it be to me as you have said." Luke 1:38.*

Lesson Aim

To recognize and submit to the responsibilities God has given us.

Lesson Setting

Time: *About 6–5 B.C.*

Place: *Nazareth and the hill country of Judea*

Lesson Outline

Called to Be a Vessel!

I. The Heavenly Messenger: Luke 1:26-29
   A. *The Virgin Mary: vss. 26-27*
   B. *The Angel's Announcement and Mary's Response: vss. 28-29*

II. The Astonishing Message: Luke 1:30-38
   A. *Mary's Pregnancy Foretold: vss. 30-31*
   B. *Jesus' Greatness Foretold: vss. 32-33*
   C. *Mary's Miraculous Conception Explained: vss. 34-35*
   D. *Elizabeth's Pregnancy Declared: vss. 36-37*
   E. *Mary's Humble Response: vs. 38*

Introduction for Adults

Topic: *Significance and Purpose*

A man who lost his job found that he also had to face the protracted illness of his son and the death of his mother-in-law. The man thought about going back to a local university for an advanced degree, but in the meantime he took a temporary position. One day, the man answered the phone and the person on the other end offered him an attractive position. He had received an unexpected calling, one filled with significance and purpose. In this way, God was faithful and provided for him and his family.

God spoke to Mary out of the blue (so to speak), and she was unprepared for what He had to say. Nevertheless, because Mary knew God, she trusted Him to take care of her, despite the fact that she was going to become pregnant through the miraculous work of the Holy Spirit. Would we stagger and stumble at something like that? Probably. When God surprises us, we will want to say *yes*, especially if we are serious about obeying Him.

Introduction for Youth

Topic: *Called to Be a Servant*

The Bible's accounts regarding angelic-human encounters are designed not just to excite our interest, but also to inspire our faith and obedience. The Bible tells us about God's calls to many individuals under a variety of circumstances, yet somehow we find it hard to believe that He can and will summon any of us to serve Him.

When God calls, He always gives sufficient evidence for us to respond obediently and not turn away. Sometimes, we demand signs to confirm God's call, but Jesus rebuked those of His day who demanded signs.

The life of Jesus is sufficient to inspire our commitment, loyalty, and service. God has called us in His Son. Therefore, it is reasonable for Him to expect faithful obedience from us. God calls us first to trust in Jesus for salvation, and then to faithful service in our homes, churches, schools, and communities.

Concepts for Children

Topic: *Being God's Servant*

1. Gabriel, the Lord's angel, visited a young woman named Mary.
2. Gabriel said that God highly favored Mary.
3. Gabriel said that Mary would become pregnant with the Christ child.
4. Unlike Zechariah, Mary responded in faith, rather than doubt, to the divine promise announced by Gabriel.
5. Like Mary, God wants us to accept His plan for our lives.

Lesson Commentary

I. THE HEAVENLY MESSENGER: LUKE 1:26-29

A. The Virgin Mary: vss. 26-27

In the sixth month, God sent the angel Gabriel to Nazareth, a town in Galilee, to a virgin pledged to be married to a man named Joseph, a descendant of David. The virgin's name was Mary.

For several hundred years, God's voice through the prophets had been silent in Palestine. The Roman army had nearly crushed the Jews' hopes that the promised Messiah would come to deliver them. Had God forgotten His people? The Jews enjoyed limited political and religious freedom at that time. Roman administrators had appointed the civil and religious leaders of Judea. When small bands of zealots tried unsuccessfully to fight against foreign occupation, the Roman military quickly and brutally subdued their revolts. The average Jew found few reasons to be optimistic about the future.

But when the fullness of time came, God sent the angel Gabriel, whom we learned about in last week's lesson. The word "angel" means "messenger" and is used to identify supernatural beings whom God created to execute His will (Ps. 148:2-5; Col. 1:16). They neither marry nor are given in marriage (Matt. 22:30). In poetic passages, angels are literally called "sons of God" (Job 1:6; 38:7) and "holy ones" (Job 5:1; Ps. 89:5, 7). The two basic divisions of angels are good ones and evil ones. The latter refer to "demons," who rebelled against God.

Within these two divisions, the Bible mentions the following individuals and orders of angels: (1) *Angel of the Lord.* At crucial points in Jewish history, a figure called the Angel of the Lord protected and guided God's people. Many scholars believed this was the Second Person of the Trinity—Jesus Christ. (2) *Angel leaders.* The archangel, or leader of the angels, is Michael. His counterpart among the evil angels, the archdemon, is Satan. God's chief messenger is Gabriel. (3) *Cherubim.* Angels in this order appear to have some human and some animal features, along with multiple faces and wings. The cherubim function as guardians and as bearers of God's throne-chariot. (4) *Seraphim.* Members of this order of angels are possibly more human in appearance, but have six wings. They are servants of God's throne, praising Him and sometimes acting as His agents.

More incredible than Gabriel's announcement to Zechariah and Elizabeth was his message to a young woman in Nazareth (Luke 1:26). The timing of the visit, "the sixth month," refers back to Elizabeth's five-month seclusion (vss. 24-25). The small town of Nazareth was 16 miles west of the southern end of the Sea of Galilee. Located near a major trade route, the village was frequently visited by Roman soldiers and Gentile merchants. Mary was betrothed to a man who was descended from King David, the family from which the prophets had said the Messiah would come (vs. 27). For Jewish women at this time, betrothal could occur as early as 12 years old, and the betrothal period normally lasted for about a year.

We find little information about Joseph in the Gospels, though we do know that he was a descendant of David, the husband of Mary, and the legal guardian of Jesus (Luke 1:27). By trade, Joseph was a carpenter (Matt. 13:55). We can deduce from Scripture that Joseph possessed great integrity and firm moral conviction (1:19). Regardless of what God desired of him, Joseph was willing to obey (1:24; 2:14, 21). Because he was a devout Jew, Joseph no doubt made sure Jesus received good spiritual training during His adolescent years in Nazareth (Luke 2:39-40, 51-52). Joseph is last mentioned when Jesus was 12 years old (vss. 42-48). Many scholars think Joseph had died by the time Jesus entered His public ministry (4:14-15).

Long before Luke recorded the events of Jesus' birth, the Old Testament anticipated what the angel would tell Mary. The prophets pinpointed the place of the Messiah's birth (Mic. 5:2), and some commentators say even the time (Dan. 9:25) and the who—not Mary by name, but that the Redeemer would be born to a virgin (Isa. 7:14). Thus, Luke was careful in his Gospel to emphasize Mary's virginity even before he introduced her by name (Luke 1:27). "Mary" is the equivalent of the Hebrew name "Miriam" (Exod. 15:20) and means either "the exalted one" or "excellence."

B. The Angel's Announcement and Mary's Response: vss. 28-29

The angel went to her and said, "Greetings, you who are highly favored! The Lord is with you." Mary was greatly troubled at his words and wondered what kind of greeting this might be.

Gabriel appeared to Mary in an undisclosed indoor area, such as the entrance to a room or a house (Luke 1:28). The Greek participle translated as "highly favored" (literally, "one who is favored") draws attention to Mary as the recipient of God's grace. The Vulgate (an early fifth-century translation of the Bible into Latin made by Jerome) renders the same word as "full of grace," which gives the incorrect impression that Mary was a source of God's grace to others, rather than someone who received His unmerited blessings. Paul used the same term in Ephesians 1:6, where believers are told that God loved us in Christ "to the praise of his glorious grace, which he has freely given us." To be highly favored conveys more than just being shown grace. It is to have grace lavished upon us.

In terms of Mary, God promised to be with her and through her bestow His grace upon many. (The phrase rendered "Blessed art thou among women" [Luke 1:28, KJV] is not found in the earliest Greek manuscripts, so it is omitted from the NIV.) Mary's understanding of God's grace explains why she was taken aback at Gabriel's greeting. Mary's "why me?" kind of response reflected humility (vss. 29, 48), but also surprise. Mary seemed more startled by the angel's grace-greeting than his appearance. Mary didn't consider herself particularly special, but God did. Indeed, that's the surprise of grace. And the Lord is still surprising people with His grace. He has told us in His Word that even though we're sinners and undeserving of His grace, we are nonetheless highly favored in Christ.

It was vital for God to send Gabriel to speak with Mary before she became pregnant because she was a virgin and her pregnancy would cause her distress and shame. In addition, she would have no idea who this child was. Gabriel came to prevent any fears and anxieties that Mary might otherwise have felt. The angel also came so that the young woman could prepare for this great event.

II. THE ASTONISHING MESSAGE: LUKE 1:30-38

A. Mary's Pregnancy Foretold: vss. 30-31

But the angel said to her, "Do not be afraid, Mary, you have found favor with God. You will be with child and give birth to a son, and you are to give him the name Jesus."

Before Gabriel continued his message, he calmed Mary's fears. He had come to bring her good news, not to alarm her (Luke 1:30). The angel then told Mary how God was to bless her. She would give birth to a Son and was to call Him "Jesus" (vs. 31). In Jewish culture, a child's name was supposed to indicate the essence of his or her personality. *Jesus* is the Greek form of the Hebrew name *Joshua*, which means "Yahweh saves" and emphasizes the deliverance of the Lord. Mary's Son would save people from sin and death (Matt. 1:21). It was the hope of every Jewish woman that she might bear the Lord's Messiah. Since Jewish betrothal often took place soon after puberty, Mary was perhaps into her teens when Gabriel disclosed to her that she would be the mother of the Redeemer.

Some think Mary belonged to the tribe of Judah and was herself a descendant of David (Matt. 1:1-16; Luke 1:32). We see much of Jesus' early life through Mary's eyes, especially since she treasured many key events and pondered in her heart what they might mean (Luke 2:19, 51). This information, unique to Luke, has led some to conclude that Mary was one of the eyewitnesses Luke interviewed when he gathered material for his Gospel (1:2). Mary was also an eyewitness to Jesus' first miracle—the turning of water into wine at the wedding feast in Cana of Galilee (John 2:1-11). On another occasion, Mary and Jesus' brothers wished to see Him while He was teaching the multitudes (Luke 8:19). When Jesus was crucified, Mary stood near the cross. It was then that Jesus gave her over to the care of John (John 19:25-27). After Jesus' resurrection, Mary was in the upper room along with the rest of the disciples as they awaited the coming of the Holy Spirit (Acts 1:14).

B. Jesus' Greatness Foretold: vss. 32-33

"He will be great and will be called the Son of the Most High. The Lord God will give him the throne of his father David, and he will reign over the house of Jacob forever; his kingdom will never end."

The prophet Isaiah had promised that a virgin would conceive and bear a son (Isa. 7:14). Mary's Son would be that child, the absolutely great Messiah of Israel. This miracle was possible because He would also be the "Son of the Most High" (Luke 1:32). Furthermore, He would fulfill what Isaiah had prophesied about the one who would rule on David's throne (Isa. 9:6-7). God had promised David that his

kingdom would be established forever (2 Sam. 7:16). In fact, David's descendants reigned over Judah until the Exile (586 B.C.). The angel's reference to the "throne of his father David" (Luke 1:32) meant that God would now restore the broken line of David's succession. Indeed, Gabriel revealed to Mary that her Son would fulfill that promise, most of all as He ruled forever in majestic splendor (vs. 33).

C. Mary's Miraculous Conception Explained: vss. 34-35

"How will this be," Mary asked the angel, "since I am a virgin?" The angel answered, "The Holy Spirit will come upon you, and the power of the Most High will overshadow you. So the holy one to be born will be called the Son of God."

Mary asked the obvious question. How could she, who had not been physically intimate with any man, become pregnant (Luke 1:34)? While Mary's question provides Scripture's best verification for the virginal conception of Jesus, Mary's words also show a strong and thinking mind. She was confident enough in her relationship with God to ask appropriate questions. It's worth noting that both Mary and Zechariah asked Gabriel how God could do the seemingly impossible. The difference in their queries is that Mary asked how it was possible, while Zechariah (in doubt) asked, "How can I be sure of this?" (vs. 18). Also, Mary assumed an immediate fulfillment of what Gabriel told her, whereas Zechariah asked for a sign, which Gabriel granted in the form of Zechariah's muteness.

Gabriel anticipated Mary's initial confusion, for the angel was prepared to explain God's message to her. Gabriel said Jesus would need no man to father Him, for the Spirit of God would come upon Mary and act with creative power (vs. 35). In the Old Testament, the Hebrew counterpart to "overshadow" are the episodes in which the cloud covered the tabernacle when the glory of God descended upon it (for example, Exod. 40:34-35). When the Holy Spirit later came upon Mary, she became the instrument of Jesus' incarnation. Being the "Son of God" (Luke 1:35), Jesus is holy, not because He was dedicated to God, but because He is God.

The Savior's virginal conception and birth, which is essential to Jesus' deity, was likely even foreshadowed in the Garden of Eden. According to Genesis 3:15, God told the serpent that the woman's offspring would crush the serpent's head. This previews Christ's ultimate victory over sin, Satan, and death (see Rom. 16:20). Descendants were usually traced through fathers, but the unique designation of the woman's offspring implies that the Messiah would have no natural father. In fact, in Luke 3:23, the author was careful to qualify that Jesus was only "thought" to be Joseph's son.

D. Elizabeth's Pregnancy Declared: vss. 36-37

"Even Elizabeth your relative is going to have a child in her old age, and she who was said to be barren is in her sixth month. For nothing is impossible with God."

Although Mary had not asked Gabriel for a sign, he pointed toward evidence that God's power was already at work. He mentioned Mary's relative, Elizabeth (not necessarily a cousin), who had long been barren but was now pregnant (Luke 1:36). The angel assured Mary that what he said to her would come to pass, for with God nothing is impossible (vs. 37). Human promises sometimes fail, especially when people lack the resources or inclination to keep them. God, however, always fulfills His word. He always comes through. In this regard, Isaiah noted, "Surely the arm of the Lord is not too short to save" (Isa. 59:1).

E. Mary's Humble Response: vs. 38

"I am the Lord's servant," Mary answered. "May it be to me as you have said." Then the angel left her.

Mary's response to Gabriel perhaps helps explain why God had chosen her. Many disturbing questions may have been running through her mind: *Will Joseph believe the unimaginable? What will my friends and neighbors think when they learn I am pregnant? Will I be branded the worst of sinners, rather than God's chosen instrument?* Nevertheless, Mary did not argue with the angel. Instead, she humbly submitted to God when He gave her a responsibility (Luke 1:38). Scripture describes faith as "being sure of what we hope for and certain of what we do not see" (Heb. 11:1). Mary had such faith. Although she did not fully understand Gabriel's message, she accepted God's promise. Faith says, "I will believe the 'impossible' as fact because the Lord says so." We put our faith into action when we obey God in this way.

Mary's compliance with the will of God was supported by two assurances Gabriel gave the young woman. The first is, "The Lord is with you" (Luke 1:28). God often encourages His people by affirming His constant presence with them, particularly when they are facing something that is hard or challenging (see Hag. 1:13; 2:4; Matt. 28:20; Heb. 13:5). The second assurance was "nothing is impossible with God" (Luke 1:37). From this we see that the Lord will accomplish what He purposes to do in, through, and for us, no matter what the odds or the risks. He accomplished His plan with Mary, and He will with us.

A short time after Gabriel departed, Mary made preparations and quickly traveled from Nazareth to a town in the hill country of Judea where Elizabeth and Zechariah lived (vss. 39-40). Mary possibly journeyed 50 to 70 miles by herself, which would have been a considerable distance for a single, pregnant woman in her day. Mary might have planned to stay with Elizabeth to be secluded from intrusive friends and neighbors. The privacy at Elizabeth's home would give Mary an opportunity to reflect on all that was happening to her life. She would also have an opportunity to receive encouragement and support from Elizabeth.

In verse 41, we read that the Holy Spirit filled Elizabeth, which means He controlled and empowered her. He apparently gave her the insight to recognize that Mary's child was the Messiah. Elizabeth drew upon the Spirit's strength to praise God for His gift to Mary. Elizabeth joyfully exclaimed that God's favor rested on Mary uniquely among all women. Likewise, the Lord had uniquely blessed the child in her womb. Finally, Elizabeth commended Mary for believing that the Lord would keep His promise to her (vss. 42-45).

Discussion Questions

1. Why was it important for God to send Gabriel to speak with Mary before she became pregnant?
2. In what way is the name of Jesus significant?
3. What connection is there between David and Jesus?
4. How would it be possible for Mary, who was a virgin at the time, to conceive and give birth to the Christ child?
5. Why did the angel mention Elizabeth to Mary?

Contemporary Application

Through Gabriel, God revealed what He desired of Mary. Although few people have ever received such a celestial visit, God wants all His spiritual children to know the responsibilities He has given them. Any quest to discover our God-given responsibilities should include a study of Scripture. As a carpenter's plumb line measures the straightness of a wall, the Bible provides the standard against which all undertakings must be measured. Any course of action that contradicts scriptural teachings is not the will of God.

Knowledge of what God desires also comes through prayer. Praying puts our minds in tune with the Lord's so that we can receive direction from the Holy Spirit. At other times, circumstances or other people can help us recognize a responsibility that God has given us. A door of opportunity that suddenly opens after others have closed may indicate God's desire. Advice from a Christian friend whose spiritual insight maybe more clear than ours can provide understanding.

At first glance, Mary seems to have been a peculiar candidate to be used for one of God's greatest works. A nobody in her society, she had three strikes against her in that culture: she was young, poor, and female. In addition, she lived in Nazareth, a provincial village. Nevertheless, "one individual life may be of priceless value to God's purposes," said Oswald Chambers, "and that life may be yours." Therefore, we shouldn't ever feel too insignificant when God gives us a responsibility.

The best example of submission is how Jesus willingly did all His Father desired. While on the Mount of Olives, Jesus did not complain about the prospect of having to die on a cross. Instead, He yielded Himself to the Father's will (Luke 22:42). Regardless of the responsibility God gave Him, the Messiah humbly submitted. As those who believe in Jesus, we should also strive to do what the Lord desires.

Called to Proclaim!

DEVOTIONAL READING

Malachi 3:1-4

DAILY BIBLE READINGS

Monday December 10
*Malachi 3:1-4 A Messenger
Is Coming*

Tuesday December 11
*Luke 1:57-61 Elizabeth
Births a Son*

Wednesday December 12
*Luke 1:62-66 His Name Is
John*

Thursday December 13
*Luke 1:67-75 God Sends a
Powerful Savior*

Friday December 14
*Luke 1:76-80 Preparing the
Way*

Saturday December 15
*Luke 3:7-14 Warnings to the
Crowds*

Sunday December 16
*Luke 3:15-20 A Powerful
One Is Coming*

Scripture

Background Scripture: *Luke 1:57-80*
Scripture Lesson: *Luke 1:67-80*
Key Verse: *Immediately his mouth was opened and his
tongue was loosed, and he began to speak, praising God.*
Luke 1:64.
Scripture Lesson for Children: *Luke 1:57-67, 76-77, 80*
Key Verse for Children: *"And you, my child, will be called
a prophet of the Most High; for you will go on before the Lord
to prepare the way for him."* Luke 1:76.

Lesson Aim

To recognize the value of humble and faithful service
to the Lord.

Lesson Setting

Time: *6–5 B.C.*
Place: *Hill country of Judea*

Lesson Outline

Called to Proclaim!

    I.   Zechariah's Praise of God: Luke 1:67-75
       A. *Freedom for God's People: vss. 67-68*
       B. *The Standard of Salvation: vs. 69*
       C. *The Prophetic Picture: vs. 70*
       D. *Safety and Security: vs. 71*
       E. *Faithful and Merciful: vss. 72-73*
       F. *Delivered to Serve: vss. 74-75*
   II. Zechariah's Prophecy of John: Luke 1:76-80
       A. *Preparation for the Messiah: vs. 76*
       B. *Knowledge of Salvation: vs. 77*
       C. *God's Mercy to All: vss. 78-79*
       D. *John's Early Years: vs. 80*

Introduction for Adults

Topic: *Life-Changing Events*

John the Baptist's birth was a life-changing event. But before he prepared the way for Jesus, his godly parents—Zechariah and Elizabeth—prepared the way for him (in a manner of speaking). We don't find many details about John's home life recorded in Scripture. It was enough for Luke to tell us that John's parents were "upright in the sight of God, observing all the Lord's commandments and regulations blamelessly" (Luke 1:6). We also learn that John "grew and became strong in spirit" (vs. 80).

From this information it is evident that John's faithful, praying parents spiritually prepared the way for John's ministry. They had followed God for many years before John was born, and they undoubtedly continued to do so while he grew up. They did everything for John that they were supposed to do. Empowered by the Holy Spirit, he went on to urge many people to repent. God gives us many opportunities to prepare others spiritually—starting with our loved ones—to become the Lord's mighty servants in midst of numerous life-changing events.

Introduction for Youth

Topic: *Called to Spread the Word*

The high school band drum majorette stepped into her leading role at the head of the parade. Not too far along, however, she lost a step. As a result, her baton struck the trombone player's slide and knocked his instrument out of commission. Leading roles are great opportunities to show what we can do, but if we are not careful, we can make some devastating mistakes.

God gave John the Baptist the lead role in spreading the word about the advent of the Messiah. John did not fail, because he never boasted about himself, but always pointed people to Jesus. This is why John succeeded in his role. Pointing others to Jesus is the hallmark of true spiritual leadership. If we want to play a leading role in God's plan of spreading His Word, we must allow Jesus to have first place in our lives.

Concepts for Children

Topic: *Preparing for God's Messenger*

1. John's birth convinced people that he would do great things for God.
2. Elizabeth said that her newborn son's name was John.
3. Zechariah agreed that the infant's name was John.
4. Once Zechariah could speak again, he used his voice to praise God.
5. God also wants us to express our thankfulness to Him for what He wants to do in our lives.

Lesson Commentary

I. Zechariah's Praise of God: Luke 1:67-75

A. Freedom for God's People: vss. 67-68

His father Zechariah was filled with the Holy Spirit and prophesied: "Praise be to the Lord, the God of Israel, because he has come and has redeemed his people."

When the period of gestation ended, Elizabeth gave birth to a son (Luke 1:57). The mother's neighbors and relatives had heard how merciful the Lord had been to her, and they, too, were glad (vs. 58). Eight days after the child was born, Elizabeth and Zechariah had their infant son circumcised in accordance with the law of Moses (Gen. 17:9-14; Lev. 2:3). The ceremony signified that John belonged to the Lord and the community of His people.

This ceremony was a joyous occasion when family members and friends gathered together. Those present assumed the parents were going to name their newborn after Zechariah, his father (Luke 1:59). Elizabeth, however, objected, saying that the child's name was John (vs. 60). The guests were surprised by the mother's statement, for no one in her own or her husband's family was named John (vs. 61). Those present made gestures to Zechariah to discover what he wanted to name his son (vs. 62). From this verse it seems likely that Zechariah was deaf as well as mute.

The father asked for a writing tablet and indicated that the child's name was John. This decision amazed the guests, for it broke with the custom of the day (vs. 63). Gabriel had previously said Zechariah would be mute until his son was born (vs. 20). After the father indicated what his son's name would be, Zechariah immediately received back his ability to speak. Without hesitation he began to praise God for the birth of John and for the wonderful things the Lord would do through him (vs. 64).

All the neighbors became filled with awe, for they sensed that something unusual, perhaps even supernatural, had occurred. Moreover, throughout the entire hill country of Judea, the recent series of events became the topic of conversation (vs. 65). The locals pondered in their hearts what the Lord had in store for John, especially since it was clear that that the hand of the Lord was with him (vs. 66). The latter implies that God's favor, presence, and direction were evident in John's life from the time of his birth.

Verse 67 says that John's father, Zechariah, became "filled with the Holy Spirit" and began to prophesy. As the following verses make clear, the elderly father spoke God's will through a song of praise. Whereas Zechariah's previous words expressed unbelief, his subsequent words were filled with adoration and gratitude. His previous words had expressed doubt, but his song was full of assurance and faith. Zechariah's song closely followed the pattern of Old Testament prophecies about the coming Messiah. Also, Zechariah's poetry reveals that devout people of Israel prayed for and understood the significance of the messianic age.

Zechariah began with a common benediction: "Praise be to the Lord, the God of Israel" (vs. 68). The start of the psalm could also be rendered "blessed be," the Latin wording of which has given rise to Zechariah's hymn being called the *Benedictus*. Much of the language that the priest used echoes the poetic words found in the Psalms. For instance, Luke 1:68 sounds similar to Psalm 41:13 ("Praise be the LORD, the God of Israel") and 111:9 ("He provided redemption for his people"). Other parallels are Luke 1:69 and Psalm 132:17; Luke 1:70-72 and Psalm 106:10, 45; Luke 1:73-75 and Psalm 105:42; and Luke 1:79 with Psalm 107:10.

Zechariah not only enjoined praising God, but also gave reasons for doing so by amassing all the evidence he could remember about God (1:68). First, Zechariah praised God because He had turned His face towards His people and set them free. God had broken into the priest's life in such a special way that he could not miss its significance. He equated his experience with God's redemptive purposes for His people. God's saving intervention was the theme of the Old Testament prophecies. They painted glorious pictures of the Messiah's reign over Israel. Zechariah had imbibed deeply of these prophecies. Nothing in his mind superseded his hope of God's coming to redeem His people through the Messiah. In this regard, Gabriel had told Zechariah what John's role would be. He would be filled with the Holy Spirit to bring Israel back to God. John would also "make ready a people prepared for the Lord" (vs. 17). It's no wonder that Zechariah was excited about what God promised to do through John the Baptizer.

B. The Standard of Salvation: vs. 69

"He has raised up a horn of salvation for us in the house of his servant David."

Zechariah thanked God because He had raised up a standard of salvation through David's line. The godly Jews knew that the promised Messiah would be a descendant of King David. Prophecies about the Messiah's Davidic ancestry abound in the Old Testament (2 Sam. 7:12; Ps. 89:3; Jer. 23:5; 33:14). During Jesus' time, the people were astonished and asked, "Could this be the Son of David?" (Matt. 12:23). They knew that "the Christ will come from David's family" (John 7:42). Many cried "Hosanna to the Son of David" (Matt. 21:9) when He entered Jerusalem. Paul likewise declared that God's Son was "a descendant of David" (Rom. 1:3).

Undoubtedly, Zechariah had these sorts of messianic promises in mind when he made reference to God's "horn of salvation" (Luke 1:69). Zechariah and Hannah used similar terminology when they responded to God's blessing (1 Sam. 2:1; Luke 1:69); however, the image Zechariah had in mind was different from Hannah's. Her vision had to do with being freed from a burden and being able to lift her head up with pride. Zechariah's vision had to do with the power associated with a beast of burden such as an ox, an animal whose horns are indicative of strength.

Moses used this image to bless the descendants of Joseph. The lawgiver said, "he is like a firstborn bull; his horns are the horns of a wild ox. With them he will gore the nations, even those at the ends of the earth" (Deut. 33:17). Also, Micah used this image to picture how Israel will respond to those who attack her. The prophet declared, "Rise and thresh, O Daughter of Zion, for I will give you horns of iron . . . and you will break to pieces many nations" (Mic. 4:13). In the Old Testament, the "horn" also symbolized a destructive kind of power, for it pictured the horn of various wild animals (1 Kings 22:11; Ps. 22:21; 75:5; Dan. 8:5-7). From what has been said, it is clear that the image of a "horn of salvation" in Luke 1:69 referred to the powerful way in which the Father would redeem Israel through His Son.

C. The Prophetic Picture: vs. 70

"(As he said through his holy prophets of long ago)"

Zechariah praised God because He had promised "long ago" (Luke 1:70) through the "holy prophets" to provide redemption through the Savior. Zechariah now saw what had happened in the light of his understanding of the messianic prophecies recorded in the Old Testament. This might have included Micah 5:2, which foretold the advent of a Redeemer "whose origins are from of old, from ancient times." The promise was that God's people would eventually have a new Ruler, one who would bring success and not failure. God said this Ruler would be "for me," meaning that the Ruler would do God's will. The only king who was born in Bethlehem, sprang from Davidic stock, and has an eternal nature is, of course, Jesus Christ. He is the Ruler about whom Micah foretold and Zechariah offered praise.

D. Safety and Security: vs. 71

"Salvation from our enemies and from the hand of all who hate us."

Zechariah was thankful, for God had promised "salvation from our enemies" (Luke 1:71). Because Israel had suffered so much at the hands of foreign invaders, relief from their oppressing circumstances was uppermost in the minds of God's people. In John's time, the despised Romans ruled the Jews. God's chosen people vented their ill will by periodically rebelling against their captors. In fact, in A.D. 70, the Romans completely obliterated Jerusalem and its temple. The salvation God promised was not in terms of political deliverance, but spiritual liberation from Satan, sin, and death. Indeed, one day the Messiah will usher in a universal reign of peace and justice. It's true that at His first advent, He was rejected and crucified; yet, at His second advent, He will reign in great power and glory.

E. Faithful and Merciful: vss. 72-73

"To show mercy to our fathers and to remember his holy covenant, the oath he swore to our father Abraham."

Zechariah continued to emphasize that what had happened in the amazing birth of John was consistent with all God promised to do for His people. Zechariah was thankful for God's "mercy" (Luke 1:72), especially His steadfast love through which He fulfilled His promises. The priest also expressed gratitude that the Lord remembered "his holy covenant." This was in keeping with "the oath he swore" (vs. 73) with Abraham, the patriarch. God promised through Abraham that his descendants would possess and dwell in the land that eventually became Israel. In fact, the entire world would be blessed through one of the patriarch's descendants (Gen. 12:1-3; 22:16-18). Through what was about to happen in the lives of John and Jesus, God planned to fulfill His covenant promise to Abraham.

F.   Delivered to Serve: vss. 74-75

"To rescue us from the hand of our enemies, and to enable us to serve him without fear in holiness and righteousness before him all our days."

Zechariah was convinced God would "rescue" (Luke 1:74) His people "from the hand of [their] enemies" so that they could serve Him. Israel's service before God "without fear" was stamped with "holiness and righteousness" (vs. 75). Zechariah here emphasized the character of the Messiah's reign and the purpose of His coming. His ultimate mission was to restore Israel's people to their God-given duty to be holy. Holiness speaks of our relationship with God through faith in Jesus Christ, while righteousness has to do with how we respond to others. We are to serve God "all our days," striving to be consistent in our witness before the world.

Verses 74 and 75 indicate that the redemption of Israel and the fulfillment of the covenant would involve three things. The first was Israel's deliverance from their oppressors. Throughout its history, Israel was threatened and sometimes taken over by pagan nations. In particular, God's chosen people were in continual conflict with the Philistines, eventually overrun by the Assyrians, and taken into captivity by the Babylonians. In Zechariah's time, the enemy was the Roman Empire. Understandably, the Jews longed for the day when they would be free from any foreign rulers.

The second aspect for redemption was spiritual. At times, Israel had a good relationship with God and benefited from His blessings; but frequently the people turned their backs on the Lord and suffered the consequences. God wanted a personal relationship with His people, one where they would be totally devoted to Him. The Messiah would bring Israel back into this type of relationship with God. The third aspect of redemption was moral. Israel needed a change of heart. The Messiah would bring about a redemption of the heart, one that would allow Israel to serve God in a virtuous and upright manner.

II. ZECHARIAH'S PROPHECY OF JOHN: LUKE 1:76-80

A.   Preparation for the Messiah: vs. 76

"And you, my child, will be called a prophet of the Most High; for you will go on before the Lord to prepare the way for him."

At this point Zechariah focused his attention on John. He would be a "prophet" (Luke 1:76) to prepare the way for the Messiah. John was the forerunner who would tell Israel that the promised Redeemer had arrived in the person of Jesus. John clarified who the Messiah was, what role He would serve in the redemption of Israel, and what the people must do in response. When the crowds heard John preach, they recognized that he was indeed a "prophet of the Most High." The latter expression was a way to refer to the exalted, transcendent God without directly naming Him. First-century Jews adopted this convention out of reverence for the divine name. The task of the Lord's prophet was not pleasant, because he was called to expose people's sins. Preparing the way for the Messiah was rough business. It was like road building through mountains and valleys (Isa. 40:3-4).

B. Knowledge of Salvation: vs. 77

"To give his people the knowledge of salvation through the forgiveness of their sins."

Most of the Jews had erroneous ideas about the kind of salvation the Messiah would bring. They thought it would be political, not spiritual, in nature. God sent John to teach them the true and correct understanding of spiritual deliverance, which is based on the forgiveness of sins through faith in Christ. The people desperately needed this "knowledge of salvation" (Luke 1:77; see Jer. 31:34), for they were in spiritual darkness. As John went about the difficult task of preparing the people for the advent of the Messiah, the Baptizer would light their path and show them the proper direction to walk. Indeed, though John would cause people to face up to their sinful nature, his message would focus on God's offer of forgiveness, not on condemnation.

C. God's Mercy to All: vss. 78-79

"Because of the tender mercy of our God, by which the rising sun will come to us from heaven to shine on those living in darkness and in the shadow of death, to guide our feet into the path of peace."

Zechariah's song acknowledged that John's life and ministry would be blessed by the "tender mercy of our God" (Luke 1:78). Such steadfast love would be like the dawning of a new day. The priest knew that he himself had received God's grace, and he was overcome by the prospect of God's people being spiritually revived and restored under His merciful hand. John's amazing birth and his preaching of righteousness would be considerable evidence that God had not forgotten His people.

Like the "rising sun," the Father's mercy made available through His Son would bring light to people "living in darkness and in the shadow of death" (vs. 79). Like the rising sun, God's unfailing compassion in the Messiah would lead sinners "into the path of peace." These beautiful words reflect the majesty and glory of Zechariah's proclamation. He was filled with praise because he knew that God was about to do something special for His people through John.

D. John's Early Years: vs. 80

"And the child grew and became strong in spirit; and he lived in the desert until he appeared publicly to Israel."

At the conclusion of Zechariah's song, Luke the historian added a brief postscript about John (which mirrors similar growth summaries found in the Old Testament; see Gen. 21:8; Judg. 13:24; 1 Sam. 2:21, 26). We learn two main facts concerning the Baptizer. First, while growing up, he "became strong in spirit" (Luke 1:80). This indicates John imbibed his parents' vibrant faith, trust, and hope in the Lord. In fact, from birth John was filled with the Holy Spirit (vs. 15). Second, John chose a life of seclusion "in the desert" (vs. 80), that is, the barren Judean wilderness in the Jordan Valley west of the Dead Sea. This was part of his spiritual preparation for his mission. He was focused on God and on His calling. When John began to preach, his desert lifestyle gave power and authenticity to his words (Matt. 3:1-6).

Discussion Questions

1. How was Zechariah able to prophesy words of hope and promise to the people?
2. Why was it important for Zechariah to emphasize that the Savior would be of the lineage of David?
3. What was the "holy covenant" (Luke 1:72) that God had made with His people?
4. What was the message John would proclaim to the people?
5. How can we become more willing to let God speak through us to communicate the good news of salvation to those in our sphere of influence?

Contemporary Application

"What then is this child going to be?" (Luke 1:66), the neighbors of Zechariah and Elizabeth wondered. John's parents probably wondered the same thing too, and so do parents today concerning their children. The angel had told Zechariah that his son would be used in a significant way by God, but at first the priest didn't believe the angel. Then, after John's birth, Zechariah proclaimed that his son would prepare Israel for the coming of the Messiah.

Would parents today be as excited about this prospect as Zechariah and Elizabeth were? Wouldn't parents today be happier if God told them their child was going to be a rich financier, university president, professional athlete, musician, or leader of a country? Wouldn't it be a let down to learn that your child was going to be a preacher who would lead many people to find forgiveness through faith in the Lord Jesus?

Such mixed feelings spotlight our foremost priorities in life. What we seek for our loved ones, and all the things we give them, speak volumes about what we think is important. Isn't it ultimately better to be a humble and faithful servant of the Lord than to be rich, powerful, or famous in the eyes of the world? Zechariah and Elizabeth would say yes, and so should we.

Called to Rejoice!

DEVOTIONAL READING

Psalm 96:1-6

DAILY BIBLE READINGS

Monday December 17
Psalm 96:1-6 Sing a New Song

Tuesday December 18
Matthew 1:18b-21 Joseph and Mary

Wednesday December 19
Luke 2:1-5 Traveling to Bethlehem

Thursday December 20
Luke 2:6-7 Jesus, Firstborn Son

Friday December 21
Luke 2:8-14 Angels Proclaim the News

Saturday December 22
Luke 2:15-20 Shepherds Visit the King

Sunday December 23
Psalm 96:7-13 Judging with God's Truth

Scripture

Background Scripture: *Luke 2:1-20*
Scripture Lesson: *Luke 2:1-14*
Key Verse: *"Today in the town of David a Savior has been born to you; he is Christ the Lord."* Luke 2:11.
Scripture Lesson for Children: *Luke 2:1-14*
Key Verse for Children: *The shepherds returned, glorifying and praising God for all the things they had heard and seen, which were just as they had been told.* Luke 2:20.

Lesson Aim

To note that God's message is good news for everyone.

Lesson Setting

Time: *About 6–5 B.C.*
Place: *Nazareth and Bethlehem*

Lesson Outline

Called to Rejoice!

   I. The Birth of Jesus: Luke 2:1-7
     A. *The Decree of Caesar: vss. 1-3*
     B. *The Journey to Bethlehem: vss. 4-5*
     C. *The Savior's Humble Beginning: vss. 6-7*
  II. The Affirmation of Angels: Luke 2:8-14
     A. *The Angel of the Lord: vss. 8-12*
     B. *The Heavenly Host: vss. 13-14*

Introduction for Adults

Topic: *Reasons to Rejoice*

Charles Schultz's *Peanuts* characters frequently give insight into human nature. As a bewildered Charlie Brown thinks about Christmas, Lucy comments, "Who else but you, Charlie Brown, could turn a wonderful season like Christmas into a problem?"

For many, Christmas is a problem to be endured rather than a holiday over which to rejoice. Exhaustion from too much activity exaggerates family tensions. The parents are tired and the children are anxious. A demoralizing Christmas may also result from feelings of loss or incompleteness. Living with memories of happier holidays past, an elderly person may long for those who have died or are far away. The single person may feel miserably alone at Christmas, when everyone else seems to have someone. Even the weather can contribute to Christmas blues.

Although your students may not put their feelings into words, they will bring some of these thoughts to your class. Use this lesson to focus on the good news of Jesus' wondrous birth. Giving the Savior the central focus can turn a blue holiday into a joy-filled occasion.

Introduction for Youth

Topic: *Called to Greet the Messiah*

There are over millions of babies born each year in the United States. Most of these infants begin their lives in a hospital. The delivery room or birthing suite is the norm. Sixty years ago, however, a delivery outside the hospital would have been commonplace. And it's still the norm for much of the developing world.

There wasn't anything extraordinary about the place of Jesus' birth. It was humble and ordinary. Nevertheless, it was one of the most spectacular events in human history, and so is worthy of our remembrance and celebration. Encourage your students to use the Christmas holiday season to express thanks to the Father for the gift of His Son.

Concepts for Children

Topic: *Rejoicing about the Good News*

1. The Gospel of Luke is the only one that tells us about the visit of angels to shepherds on the night of Jesus' birth.
2. The account involving the shepherds is full of emotion.
3. God decided that humble, lowly shepherds would be the first to hear about Jesus' birth.
4. The shepherds were so filled with joy that they told others about the birth of Jesus.
5. God also wants us to tell others about the birth of the Savior.

Lesson Commentary

I. THE BIRTH OF JESUS: LUKE 2:1-7

A. The Decree of Caesar: vss. 1-3

In those days Caesar Augustus issued a decree that a census should be taken of the entire Roman world. (This was the first census that took place while Quirinius was governor of Syria.) And everyone went to his own town to register.

Luke 2:1 introduces Jesus' birth by setting it in its historical context. The author mentioned the emperor of Rome, Caesar Augustus. This refers to Octavian, who had established a reputation for being administratively skillful and adroit. As a result of an imperial edict issued by the Roman Senate, Caesar directed that the inhabitants of the empire be registered for the purpose of collecting taxes. The census was not so much to count people as to determine who owed taxes and who could serve in the Roman army (though Jews were not subject to military conscription).

This was the first registration taken when Publius Sulpicius Quirinius was governor of the Roman province of Syria (vs. 2). Caesar relied upon high-level administrators such as Quirinius to ensure that inhabitants throughout the empire journeyed to their hometowns to be registered (vs. 3). Luke's historical approach underscores the fact that at Jesus' birth the eternal God invaded temporal human affairs. Not only that, but also God used secular rulers and events to accomplish His purposes.

Most Bible scholars have concluded that Jesus was born sometime between 8 B.C. and 4 B.C. The following are some of the facts that must be considered: Caesar Augustus (Luke 2:1) was emperor of Rome from 27 B.C. to A.D. 14. (and succeeded by Tiberius, the Roman emperor at the time that Jesus ministered). One Roman inscription refers to an official who governed Syria sometime in the first decade B.C. and again for a while in the first decade A.D.; this may have been Quirinius (vs. 2). The earliest Roman census we know about, from sources other than the Bible, was conducted in A.D. 6. Since these censuses were probably conducted every 14 years, the "first census" would have been in 8 B.C. It may have been delayed, however, a year or more in Palestine. Finally, Jesus may have lived for as long as two years before Herod the Great died in the spring of 4 B.C. (Matt. 2:16, 19). Jesus was about 30 when He began His ministry in A.D. 26 or 27 (Luke 3:1, 23).

B. The Journey to Bethlehem: vss. 4-5

So Joseph also went up from the town of Nazareth in Galilee to Judea, to Bethlehem the town of David, because he belonged to the house and line of David. He went there to register with Mary, who was pledged to be married to him and was expecting a child.

Even such a seemingly obscure individual as Joseph was affected by the Roman census (Luke 2:4). At the time, Joseph was living in Nazareth, a town situated in lower

Galilee, roughly halfway between the Sea of Galilee and the Mediterranean Sea. Nazareth was sufficiently close to the main trade routes of Palestine to maintain contact with the outside world; but its rural setting in a high valley overlooking the Plain of Esdraelon enabled the town to remain somewhat independent and aloof from external influences. Indeed, people from Jerusalem regarded such a frontier town as Nazareth as being on the periphery of Israel's national and religious life (see John 1:46).

To comply with the census, Joseph had to travel about 90 miles—at least a three-day journey—from Nazareth to Bethlehem, the town of his ancestors (and possibly those of Mary). Bethlehem is located on the edge of the Judean desert about seven miles southwest of Jerusalem. The town of Jesus' birth is situated on a high ridge of mountains about 2,500 feet above sea level, near the main road linking Hebron and Egypt. The climate of Bethlehem is somewhat Mediterranean. However, the town's higher elevation moderates the summer temperatures it experiences. This milder climate, along with fertile surrounding hills, makes the area ideal for growing grapes and figs and for grazing sheep and goats.

Bethlehem was the burial place of Rachel, the wife of Jacob (Gen. 35:19). The city was also the setting for much of the Book of Ruth. Bethlehem later became the ancestral home of David, and it was there that Samuel the prophet anointed David as Saul's successor (1 Sam. 16:1, 13; 17:12). King Rehoboam later rebuilt and fortified the city (2 Chron. 11:5-6). Micah the prophet foretold that Bethlehem would be the birthplace of the Messiah (Mic. 5:2), and Luke 2:11 records the fulfillment of the prophecy. Micah 5:2 discloses that the origins of the Savior were in the distant past, which probably means that He would come from the royal lineage of David, who had been dead for more than two centuries in Micah's day; but the prophet's words may also hint at the eternal nature of the Ruler.

At the time Joseph made the journey, he was betrothed to Mary (Luke 2:5). Evidently, she was living with Joseph as his wife, though they had not yet consummated their relationship (Matt. 1:25). Because Mary was almost ready to give birth to Jesus, the trip from Nazareth to Bethlehem was not the best time for her; but there was no way Joseph could delay the journey. Thus, they decided Mary should go with him.

In Jewish culture, betrothal was as legally binding as marriage itself. Before the engagement could be finalized, negotiations took place between the groom and the family of the bride. In addition, the groom paid a dowry (usually money or property) to the father of the bride. For a virgin, the period of betrothal typically lasted a year and could be terminated only by divorce. If the groom died during this time, the bride would be regarded a widow. Sexual unfaithfulness during betrothal was considered adultery (Deut. 22:13-21). When the period of betrothal had ended, the groom claimed his bride. After the wedding rituals, the newly married couple could consummate their union.

C. The Savior's Humble Beginning: vss. 6-7

While they were there, the time came for the baby to be born, and she gave birth to her firstborn, a son. She wrapped him in cloths and placed him in a manger, because there was no room for them in the inn.

While Joseph and Mary were in Bethlehem, Mary's pregnancy ended and she delivered her child (Luke 2:6). At this time, Bethlehem was likely overflowing with travelers who sought to register in the census; thus, suitable accommodations were difficult to find. The "inn" (Luke 2:7) could have been a reception room in a private home or a space at a public outdoor shelter, but it was probably not a large building with several individual rooms. The traditional image of an apathetic innkeeper who turned away Joseph and Mary (as well as Jesus) at the door may or may not be accurate. According to tradition, Mary gave birth to her firstborn in a cave that had been made into a stable (vs. 6). Others, however, think Joseph and Mary stayed in the open courtyard of a crowded home, where there would have been a series of stalls along the walls. Travelers used the stalls as stables and lean-to shelters. Quite possibly, Mary gave birth surrounded by the activity of the courtyard.

Like many peasant children, Mary's son would have been washed in a mixture of water and olive oil, rubbed with salt, and then wrapped in strips of linen. These would be placed around the arms and legs of the infant to keep the limbs protected. (The custom of wrapping infants this way is still practiced in many Middle Eastern countries.) Mary then laid the child in a trough used for feeding animals. Being born in a stable was a humble beginning for one supposed to be the Savior of the world. He would not be the conquering Messiah the nation was anticipating. He would not mobilize the militant Zealots to throw off the Roman yoke. Instead, He came to serve (Mark 10:45), to seek and to save the lost (Luke 19:10).

Mary must have wondered how the angel's words about Jesus could come true (1:32-33). We can be thankful, however, that the Gospel of Luke gives us its distinctive version of Jesus' birth. The third Synoptic Gospel shows us how God stooped to lift fallen humanity. Jesus came as a poor, humble, and homeless baby. Between a humble birth and a debasing (but victorious) death, Jesus lived simply, spoke vividly, and was often in the company of people whom polite society either rejected or ignored (5:27-32; 7:36-50). Because He identified with the lowliest, He gives hope today to those who have no other source of hope.

II. THE AFFIRMATION OF ANGELS: LUKE 2:8-14

A. The Angel of the Lord: vss. 8-12

And there were shepherds living out in the fields nearby, keeping watch over their flocks at night. An angel of the Lord appeared to them, and the glory of the Lord shone around them, and they were terrified. But the angel said to them, "Do not be afraid. I bring you good news of great joy that will be for all the people. Today in the town of David a Savior has been born to you; he is Christ the Lord. This will be a sign to you: You will find a baby wrapped in cloths and lying in a manger."

An angel announced the Messiah's birth to ordinary shepherds, not the powerful rulers or religious leaders (Luke 2:8). In Bible times, shepherds had three basic responsibilities—to lead their sheep, to provide for the needs of the flock, and to protect it from danger. Shepherds could not ignore leading their sheep, for without the shepherd's gentle hand and familiar voice to give direction, the flock could become afraid, lost, and helpless (Isa. 40:11; John 10:3). In providing for the sheep, the shepherd guided them to green pastures, peaceful waters (Gen. 29:7; Ps. 23:1-2), and safe shelter (Num. 32:24; John 10:1-3).

Protecting the sheep was a difficult task. The shepherd had to deal with inclement weather (Gen. 31:40), unfriendly shepherds at common watering places (Exod. 2:16-19), and robbers (John 10:1, 8, 10). The shepherd also had to protect the flock from wild animals, such as wolves, lions, and bears (1 Sam. 17:34-35). Because of the inherent dangers, the job of shepherding was not for the cowardly. Those who were lazy or indifferent would not make good shepherds either, for the hours were long and personal comforts were few. Shepherds were continually on duty. It did not matter if they felt sick, struggled with loneliness, or disliked the weather. They had to tend the flock despite the meager pay, plain diet, and harsh living conditions.

Since shepherds in Bible times lived out in the open and were unable to maintain strict obedience to the law of Moses, they generally were considered to be ceremonially unclean. As a result, they were despised by religious legalists and were typically excluded from temple worship. Custom didn't even allow shepherds to serve as witnesses in legal cases. Interestingly, these shepherds may have been watching over flocks reserved for temple sacrifices in Jerusalem. Why then did God single out these Bethlehem shepherds? Perhaps He wanted to make a point. It's not normally the influential or the elite whom God chooses, but those who call for help and place their trust in the Lord.

According to verse 9, an angel of the Lord suddenly appeared near or in front of the shepherds and the radiance of God's glory surrounded them. The word "glory," when applied to God in Scripture, refers to the luminous manifestation of His being. In other words, it is the brilliant revelation of Himself to humanity. This definition is borne out by the many ways the word is used in Scripture. For example, brilliant light consistently went with manifestations of God (Matt. 17:2; 1 Tim. 6:16; Rev. 1:16). Furthermore, the word "glory" is often linked with verbs of seeing (Exod. 16:7; 33:18; Isa. 40:5) and of appearing (Exod. 16:10; Deut. 5:24), both of which emphasize the visible nature of God's glory.

The shepherds were terrified by the sight of the angel; but the heavenly emissary reassured them with good news of a joyous event (Luke 2:10), namely, the birth of Israel's "Savior," "Messiah," and "Lord" (vs. 11). (This combination of terms appears no where else in the New Testament.) The one who eternally existed in regal splendor had been born that night in Bethlehem. Indeed, He who is sovereign and all-powerful would make redemption available to humanity, including the weak and oppressed—even society's outcasts. Military and political leaders during those times were frequently called "saviors"; but Jesus was unique, being the Anointed One of God. The angel encouraged the shepherds to find the Christ child lying in a manger, wrapped snugly in strips of cloth (vs. 12). In fact, this would be a sign from the Father validating the birth of His Son.

It's worth mentioning that *Christ* is a word borrowed from Greek. It means "Anointed One," signifying divine commissioning for a specific task. In Old Testament times, kings and priests were anointed with oil as a sign of their divine appointment. The Hebrew word for the Anointed One is translated *Messiah*. It was used of the promised one who would deliver Israel from oppression. Most Jews thought He would be a political leader. They did not consider that His mission might be to free them from sin.

B. The Heavenly Host: vss. 13-14

Suddenly a great company of the heavenly host appeared with the angel, praising God and saying, "Glory to God in the highest, and on earth peace to men on whom his favor rests."

We can imagine the shepherds staring in amazement, trembling and trying to grasp the significance of the angel's announcement. Suddenly the night sky exploded with the sounds of a vast, heavenly army praising God (Luke 2:13). The angels gave glory (or honor) to the Creator and announced peace for all who receive His favor (vs. 14). In that day, Augustus was hailed as the source and sustainer of peace. Even today, people long for freedom from war as well as to enjoy a state of mental calm and serenity; but true and lasting peace cannot be achieved until individuals experience an ending of hostility with the Father, and this is only possible through faith in the Son (see John 14:27; Rom. 5:1-11).

The shepherds' initial response to the unusual sights and sounds was fear; but following the words about the birth of the baby, and after the praise of the angelic host, the shepherds moved from fear to curiosity (vs. 15). The angel had told the shepherds the location and specific situation of the holy birth. Now they decided to travel to Bethlehem and see for themselves what the Lord had told them. It's not easy to convey in English the urgency of the shepherds' words. We might paraphrase it by saying, "Come on, let's quickly go and see Him without delay!" Thus, the shepherds hurried off and successfully found Mary and Joseph (vs. 16). The shepherds also saw the baby lying on the bed of hay. These most common of all people had the privilege of being the first on record to see the holy child.

After the shepherds had seen Jesus, they became instant evangelists. Being in His presence must have convinced them that what the angel had said to them was true. Indeed, the shepherds felt compelled to tell every person they met that they had seen the Messiah (Luke 2:17). The shepherds could have responded differently to the wonderful things they had seen and heard. They could have been so paralyzed by fear that they told no one about the wonders. The shepherds could have remained quiet. Thankfully, they spread the good news about the Messiah's birth. Those who heard the news were astonished. The Greek word translated "amazed" (vs. 18) conveys the idea that when the people heard the testimony of the shepherds, chills ran down their spines. This was neither immediate belief nor disbelief; it was simply attention. The shepherds' message captured the interest of all who heard, but we are not told whether they actually believed the reports.

At first Mary, too, must have been amazed by what the shepherds said concerning her firstborn; but verse 19 suggests that she did more than just remember what took place. She also treasured the incident and sought to fathom its significance. This remained true even though she did not fully understand all the ramifications of the events that were happening around her.

Discussion Questions

1. What circumstances forced Joseph and Mary to travel to Bethlehem?
2. What sign did the angel give to the shepherds to confirm what he had declared?
3. How did the shepherds react to the angel's announcement concerning the baby Jesus?
4. How did Mary's response to the shepherds' story contrast with that of others?
5. What are some ways to glorify God for the gift of His Son?

Contemporary Application

The announcement of Jesus' birth was good news to the shepherds and anyone who believed that Jesus was the promised Savior. The birth of the Messiah should have the same impact on us. Our needs are just as great as the shepherds'. We may possess more than they; we may enjoy the pleasures of the world much more than they; but our need for the Savior is just as great. That is why we should value God's gift to humanity more than anything else in the world.

Although we need Christ and the salvation He offers, are we too preoccupied with the things of the world to care? The shepherds watched their flocks in the quietness of night. When the angel appeared, he had their undivided attention. In what ways can we quiet our spirits to give our attention to the greatest of divine gifts, the Savior?

The Lord not only wants us to receive His gift to humanity, but also to glorify Him for His gift. One way this can be done is by sharing the Good News about the Messiah with others. This can take place while walking with a friend in a park, while taking a midmorning break with a coworker, while talking casually across the fence with a neighbor, or while spending a quiet evening with a family member.

We can also use times of private prayer to glorify the Father for sending His Son. Moreover, we can give praise to God in group worship. One possibility is getting together with a handful of other Christians to sing hymns and offer praise to the Lord for the gift of His Son. This activity not only honors God but can also be mutually encouraging to all who participate.

Called to Witness!

DEVOTIONAL READING

Isaiah 49:5-6

DAILY BIBLE READINGS

Monday December 24
Isaiah 49:5-6 A Light to All Nations

Tuesday December 25
Luke 2:22-24 The Presentation to God

Wednesday December 26
Luke 2:25-26 The Consolation of Israel

Thursday December 27
Luke 2:27-28 A Sign from the Spirit

Friday December 28
Luke 2:29-33 A Light to the Gentiles

Saturday December 29
Luke 2:34-35 A Sign of Opposition

Sunday December 30
Luke 2:36-38 A Sign of Redemption

Scripture

Background Scripture: *Luke 2:22-38*
Scripture Lesson: *Luke 2:22-35*
Key Verse: *Then Simeon blessed them and said to Mary, his mother: "This child is destined to cause the falling and rising of many in Israel."* Luke 2:34.
Scripture Lesson for Children: *Luke 2:22-35*
Key Verse for Children: *Simeon took [the child] in his arms and praised God.* Luke 2:28.

Lesson Aim

To stress that God continues to use the elderly for His glory.

Lesson Setting

Time: *6 or 5 B.C.*
Place: *Jerusalem*

Lesson Outline

Called to Witness!
   I. The Presentation of Jesus: Luke 2:22-24
  II. The Prophecy of Simeon: Luke 2:25-35
     A. *The Messianic Hope of Simeon: vss. 25-26*
     B. *The Statement of Praise: vss. 27-33*
     C. *The Prophetic Declaration: vss. 34-35*

Introduction for Adults

Topic: *Hearing and Telling Good News*

The story is told of a village whose inhabitants incorrectly thought a vagrant passing through their town was the government inspector. They not only treated him as royalty, but also quickly set into motion a plan to cover up years of fraud. Their mistaking the man for someone else cost them dearly.

This fable is a reminder of how important it is to search for hope in the right place—namely, the Christ of the Bible—not some figment of our imagination. Jesus is no longer a newborn baby in a manger. He is also not just a wise and loving person. He is the Lord of life, the King of kings, and the Savior of the world.

Simeon and Anna are people who recognized these truths about Jesus. He was for them light, hope, and salvation. In fact, all who receive Christ by faith can partake of the forgiveness and grace He now offers. Certainly, this is wonderful news we can share with others!

Introduction for Youth

Topic: *Called to Be Faithful*

Young people hear many promises during their years of adolescence. For instance, if they do their schoolwork, they are told they will graduate from school. If they pass their driving test, they will be allowed to operate a car. And if they take care of themselves, they will enjoy a long life. How gratifying it is when all such statements come true!

As Christians, we trust the promises that God has made to us in Scripture. We need not doubt His ability or willingness to fulfill His pledges to us, for He is faithful to keep His Word. In turn, He calls us from the earliest days of our lives to be faithful to Him.

The advent of Christ is the fulfillment of one of God's greatest promises. Simeon and Anna recognized this. They could see that the Christ child was their Savior. Even today, Jesus saves all who come to Him in faith (including young people). Thus, when we are assailed by doubts and tempted to abandon our faith, we should turn our attention to the Lord and believe His promises. They are the only ones fully guaranteed by Him.

Concepts for Children

Topic: *Praising God for Promises Kept*

1. In ancient times, there was a Jewish hope that God would send the Messiah.
2. When Jesus was brought to the temple, both Simeon and Anna recognized Jesus as the Messiah.
3. Simeon had a sense of peace upon seeing Jesus.
4. Anna gave thanks to God at the sight of Jesus.
5. We can have joy and hope when we come to know Jesus as our Savior.

Lesson Commentary

I. THE PRESENTATION OF JESUS: LUKE 2:22-24

When the time of their purification according to the Law of Moses had been completed, Joseph and Mary took him to Jerusalem to present him to the Lord (as it is written in the Law of the Lord, "Every firstborn male is to be consecrated to the Lord"), and to offer a sacrifice in keeping with what is said in the Law of the Lord: "a pair of doves or two young pigeons."

After the birth of Jesus, Mary and Joseph stayed on for a while in Bethlehem. During that time, they traveled at least twice to the temple in nearby Jerusalem to fulfill religious duties. On one occasion they had Jesus circumcised. Another time they presented Him to the Lord. On the second visit, two elderly people—Simeon and Anna—recognized Jesus' special nature and made pronouncements concerning Him. In a sense, they served as two credible Jewish witnesses (one male and the other female) who affirmed the truthfulness of Jesus' status as the Messiah (see Deut. 19:15).

Mary and Joseph were careful to fulfill the requirements of the Mosaic law. In the case of Jesus, while He was God's Son, He was not born above the law. Thus it was fitting for Jesus' family to observe its customs. Accordingly, eight days after Jesus' birth, Mary and Joseph had Him circumcised (Lev. 12:3; Luke 2:21). Circumcision symbolized the Jews' unique relationship with God. It was also customary for Jewish boys to be named when they were circumcised. In the case of Mary's firstborn son, she and Joseph named Him "Jesus," in accordance with the directive of the Lord's angel before the Christ child was conceived in Mary's womb (see Luke 1:31).

A woman who had given birth to a male child was considered to be ceremonially unclean for seven days (Lev. 12:2). Then for 33 days more she was not to touch any sacred thing, nor was she to enter the sanctuary (vs. 4). After 40 days, she was required to go to the temple to be purified in the prescribed manner (Luke 2:22-24). The woman's purification included the offering of a sacrifice. According to Leviticus 12:6, this offering was to be a year-old lamb for a burnt offering and a young pigeon or a dove for a sin offering; but the law also said that if the woman could not afford a lamb, two pigeons or doves would suffice (vs. 8). Mary evidently chose the second option due to her modest financial situation (Luke 2:24).

According to the Mosaic law, the woman's firstborn son was considered holy and thus had to be dedicated to the Lord in service (Exod. 13:2, 11-16; Luke 2:23). This requirement went back to that night in Egypt when the firstborn sons were saved from death by blood applied to the doorposts (Exod. 12:12-13); but since the entire tribe of Levi was chosen for service, a firstborn son could be released from service by a payment of a ransom (Num. 3:11-13; 18:15-16). This act of buying back, or redeeming, the child from God was performed during a presentation ceremony at the temple, probably at the same time as the mother's purification ceremony (Luke 2:22).

A sacrificial offering was the means by which the ransom was paid. In this way the parents acknowledged that their firstborn belonged to God, who alone had the power to give life. In this special circumstance, however, Jesus was a gift from God to the whole world (John 3:16). Moreover, in the midst of the fulfillment of legal requirements, God put the stamp of approval on His Son with the unusual but blessed ministries of Simeon and Anna.

II. THE PROPHECY OF SIMEON: LUKE 2:25-35

A. The Messianic Hope of Simeon: vss. 25-26

Now there was a man in Jerusalem called Simeon, who was righteous and devout. He was waiting for the consolation of Israel, and the Holy Spirit was upon him. It had been revealed to him by the Holy Spirit that he would not die before he had seen the Lord's Christ.

While Mary and Joseph were at the temple with Jesus, they met a man named Simeon, whose name means "God has heard" (Luke 2:25). From verse 26 we get the impression that he was advanced in years. Throughout his adult life, Simeon had distinguished himself as being "righteous and devout" (vs. 25). This means he was morally upright in his behavior and zealous in his observance of the law. His faithfulness and sincerity in keeping God's ordinances is especially seen in his "waiting for the consolation of Israel." This phrase refers to Simeon's hope that the Messiah would come and deliver the nation (Isa. 40:1; 49:13; 51:3). Indeed, Simeon loved God so much that he looked with eager anticipation for the comfort the Redeemer would bring to all people.

Simeon was also filled with the Holy Spirit (Luke 2:25). This means Simeon had been given special insight by God's Spirit to recognize the Redeemer. Furthermore, the Spirit had disclosed to Simeon that he would not die until he had seen the Lord's Messiah (vs. 26). Thus, on the right day and at the right time, the Spirit led Simeon into the Jerusalem temple. This circumstance is just one of several examples in the first two chapters of the second Synoptic Gospel of a promise from God being fulfilled.

It's worth mentioning that *Christ* comes from a Greek word meaning "anointed one." It is equivalent to *Messiah*, a word derived from Hebrew. Both terms signify divine commissioning for a special task. For instance, in Old Testament times, kings and priests were anointed with olive oil as a sign of their divine appointment. The Hebrew word for the *Anointed One* is translated *Messiah*. It was used of the promised one who would deliver Israel from oppression. Many Jews believed that a man would appear as the Lord's anointed prophet, priest, and king to bring salvation to the people of God; and tragically, most had defined salvation in political terms (John 6:14-15). They did not consider that the Savior's mission would be to free them from sin. This explains why the majority of Jesus' contemporaries failed to recognize Him as the individual who fulfilled the most comprehensive definition of the Messiah (1:10-11).

B. The Statement of Praise: vss. 27-33

Moved by the Spirit, he went into the temple courts. When the parents brought in the child Jesus to do for him what the custom of the Law required, Simeon took him in his arms and praised God, saying: "Sovereign Lord, as you have promised, you now dismiss your servant in peace. For my eyes have seen your salvation, which you have prepared in the sight of all people, a light for revelation to the Gentiles and for glory to your people Israel." The child's father and mother marveled at what was said about him.

The Spirit led Simeon into the temple courts the day Mary and Joseph brought Jesus (Luke 2:27). What was the nature of the Spirit's work among the people of God in the Old Testament era (before the day of Pentecost)? While the Old Testament mentions the Spirit of God frequently, it tells little about people possessing the Spirit. The Hebrew sacred writings do, however, reveal that those who experienced the Spirit in that era included rulers, such as elders (Num. 11:25), judges (Judg. 3:10), and kings (1 Sam. 16:13). Prophets also experienced the Spirit (Ezek. 2:2). In at least one case, a craftsman experienced God's Spirit (Exod. 31:3). Nonetheless, the Holy Spirit was sometimes also withdrawn from people (1 Sam. 16:14).

When all the evidence is considered, the impression is conveyed that the Spirit mainly came upon selected individuals for specific jobs in the Old Testament era. This truth notwithstanding, the Hebrew prophets also entertained a lively hope that a time was coming when the Spirit of God would be given out more broadly (Isa. 32:15; 59:21; Joel 2:28-29). That hope, which was manifested in upright persons such as Simeon, was fulfilled on the day of Pentecost (Acts 2:14-21).

Because of the special insight Simeon had been given, he immediately recognized Jesus as the Messiah. The reference in Luke 2:27 is to the larger temple area, not to the Most Holy Place. Simeon was either in the court of the Gentiles or the court of women, since Mary was present. Amazingly, the parents allowed the elderly man to hold their son (vs. 28). Simeon's words of praise concerning the Christ child occurred at the epicenter of the Jewish religion. This implies that, far from being a foreigner and outcast, Jesus was accepted and worshiped by the most pious individuals in Israel.

Simeon's brief prophetic declaration in verses 29-32 is sometimes called the *Nunc Dimittis*, which comes from the opening phrase in Latin, "now dismiss" (in other words, "now permit to die"). In this short refrain, we see the heart of a humble and godly man. Simeon's hymn is a patchwork of passages and themes found in the Book of Isaiah (40:5; 42:6; 46:13; 49:6; 52:9-10). Isaiah's vision of the future included salvation for the Gentiles, along with God's chosen people, Israel. We also find similar strains in the Minor Prophets. Simeon's words were revolutionary and, in some respects, visionary. As a loyal and devout Jew to whom God had given special insight, Simeon recognized that because of the advent of the Messiah, God's redemption would now be available for all people—Jews and Gentiles alike.

Simeon said he was God's "servant" (Luke 2:29), a concept that did not imply a menial, servile existence, but rather privilege and honor in service to the Creator. Moreover, Simeon referred to God as the "Sovereign Lord" (Luke 2:29). The latter phrase renders the Greek word *despótes*, which means "master" or "absolute ruler," and from which we get our English term "despot." The divine promise to Simeon had been fulfilled, and now he could die in peace. He explained that he had seen God's salvation (vs. 30). The idea is that to see Jesus, the Messiah, is to see the deliverance of the Lord (see John 14:9). There is some debate as to whether the phrase "all people" (Luke 2:31) refers to Israel alone or to both Israel and the Gentiles. Verse 32 makes it clear that Simeon included non-Jews as well as Jews. This is a key thematic emphasis of Luke (see Luke 24:47; Acts 10:34-43).

There is also disagreement over the best way to structure Luke 2:32. The KJV sees "light" and "glory" being parallel, or corresponding, ideas; in other words, Jesus is a light to bring revelation to Gentiles and glory to the people of Israel. The NIV sees "light" as a summary statement that refers to the entire verse. In this case, "revelation" and "glory" would be parallel, or corresponding, ideas; in other words, Jesus is a light for all, but is a revelation for the Gentiles and glory for Israel (Luke 1:78-79; Acts 26:22-23). In either case, the central idea is clear that Jesus makes salvation available to all people. Interestingly, both Mary and Joseph were amazed at what Simeon had said about their infant son (Luke 2:33). Simeon's words tell us that in the birth of Jesus, the next stage of redemptive history has begun. Gentiles would experience the same deliverance promised to Jews. Indeed, for all who put their faith in Messiah, God promised to give them eternal life.

C. The Prophetic Declaration: vss. 34-35

Then Simeon blessed them and said to Mary, his mother: "This child is destined to cause the falling and rising of many in Israel, and to be a sign that will be spoken against, so that the thoughts of many hearts will be revealed. And a sword will pierce your own soul too."

After invoking God's blessing upon Joseph and Mary, Simeon prophesied concerning Mary and her son (Luke 2:34). Here we find the first hint in the third Synoptic Gospel that Jesus' advent would be accompanied with great difficulty. Perhaps God revealed to Simeon that Joseph would not be alive when the sorrows foretold would come to pass. Although the Scriptures do not give an account for the death of Joseph, no mention is made of him after Jesus began His public ministry. It is generally believed that Joseph died before that time.

The phrase "falling and rising" emphasizes that Jesus would bring division in the nation. Some would fall (or be judged) and others would rise (or be blessed) because of how they responded to the Messiah (Isa. 8:14-15; Mal. 4:2). Furthermore, others see in Simeon's words the fact that Jesus' preaching of repentance would cause many to fall from their self-righteous opinion of themselves to the point where they could recognize their sinfulness and be saved, or exalted, through faith in the Redeemer.

Simeon related that Jesus would be a sign against whom many would speak (Luke

2:34). This is based on the fact that God would appoint the Messiah as the provision for salvation from sin. While some (like Simeon) would receive Him with joy, others (like the religious leaders) would reject Him. As a result, the deepest thoughts of many people (namely, their reasonings and motives) would be exposed by the way they responded to Christ (vs. 35). Although Jesus came to be the Redeemer of His people, the majority would despise Him. Tragically, despite the glory of the salvation He would freely offer, many of His contemporaries would reject Him as the Messiah.

Simeon mentioned a sword piercing "your own soul." The remark seems directed specifically to Mary (as opposed to the entire nation of Israel). Simeon's reference to a sword (namely, a large, broad, two-edged weapon) is figurative and pictures great pain. The statement probably refers in part to the cross; but Simeon may also have been referring to the pain that all of Jesus' ministry would cause, especially in the opposition He would encounter throughout His ministry. The broader truth is that no would be able to remain neutral about Christ, and it's still the same today. We must have an opinion about Jesus. Either we are for Him or we are against Him. Either we surrender our lives to Him or we are at war with Him.

Mary, Joseph, and Jesus also met a woman named Anna. Verse 36 relates that Anna (whose name means "grace" or "favor") was a prophetess; in other words, she had the gift of prophecy and was recognized for having that gift. Anna was also the daughter of Phanuel, who was from the tribe of Asher. Thus Anna was a Galilean who lived in Jerusalem at the time of Jesus' birth. There is some dispute concerning Anna's age. Some think the Greek text indicates that she was 84 years old when she saw the Messiah. Others think she had been a widow for 84 years, having been married to her husband for seven years before he died. In either case, Anna was an exceptionally committed woman. She worshiped God so constantly with fasting and praying that she never left the temple (vs. 37). She may have lodged in one of the outer rooms of the temple complex, or at least she spent most of her waking hours at the temple.

During her lifetime, Anna had undoubtedly witnessed her share of war and national oppression. It is no wonder she had an intense longing for the "redemption" (vs. 38) promised through the Messiah. This hope of deliverance sustained Anna through many years of patient waiting. God honored Anna's faith in the birth of His Son; and as evidence of His miraculous timing, the Lord allowed Anna to cross paths with Mary and Joseph at the same moment they were talking with Simeon. Consequently, Anna became a grateful and continual witness to others who had been waiting for the promised King. The accounts of Simeon and Anna provide a valuable reminder that God rewards the faithful. He preserved the lives of that man and woman until they saw the Lord. Similarly, God's plan includes showing us kindnesses along the way in our lives.

Verse 39 indicates that by bringing Jesus to the Jerusalem temple to be presented before the Lord, His parents sought to perform everything required by the

Mosaic law (see vss. 22-24). This pious couple wanted to ensure that they reared Jesus according to the teachings and traditions of the Jewish faith. Now that their business in the capital was completed, Joseph and Mary returned to Galilee with Jesus, to their own town of Nazareth. Luke, however, neither mentioned the events recorded in Matthew 2 nor any specific event that may have happened until Jesus was 12 years old. We assume that Joseph and Mary had children of their own during this time, for the Scriptures mention four of Jesus' half-brothers, James, Joseph, Simon, Judas (Matt. 13:55), and Jesus' sisters (vs. 56).

Discussion Questions

1. Why was it necessary for Joseph and Mary to bring the infant Jesus to be presented to the Lord in the temple?
2. How did the spiritual qualities Simeon possessed equip him for a unique opportunity?
3. How was Simeon able to be in the right place at the right time?
4. Based on what Simeon said, what was God going to do through the Messiah?
5. How was there both glory and tragedy in Simeon's prophecy concerning the mission of the Savior?

Contemporary Application

All people are created by God and bear His image (Gen. 1:27). And as image-bearers of the divine, all people enjoy His earthly blessings (vs. 28). It stands to reason that the elderly are included in this group. Unlike our culture, which glorifies the young and strong and sets aside those who are older, God continues to use the elderly for His glory. In contrast to the young, senior citizens are filled with wisdom that comes from experience. The Lord knows they are capable of serving Him faithfully if given the opportunity. In His eyes they do not need to retire from being useful members of His kingdom.

Some mistakenly think that only the young have the energy and drive to honor God. Yet the Bible teaches that even in old age devoted believers can produce spiritual fruit for the Lord (Ps. 92:14). The Lord honors these faithful older people by giving them significant ministry opportunities. We cannot outlive God's purposes for us. He is not finished with any believer simply because he or she has reached an advanced age. His purposes for His children never end.

The fact that God values older Christians can dramatically improve their outlook on life. Also, despite society's sometimes disparaging view of them, godly seniors can rejoice in knowing that the Lord has confidence in their ability to serve Him. Furthermore, because God honors elderly members of the Christian faith, we should do the same. By doing so, we are stating that godly senior citizens should not be ignored and that their wisdom and experience are valuable to us. Indeed, God is pleased when we defer to older believers and pay attention to their needs for comfort and happiness.

Inspired to Inquire!

DEVOTIONAL READING
Psalm 148:7-14

DAILY BIBLE READINGS

Monday December 31
Psalm 148:7-14 A Horn for God's People

Tuesday January 1
Numbers 9:1-5 The Passover Feast Instituted

Wednesday January 2
Exodus 12:11-14 First Passover Observed

Thursday January 3
Luke 2:41-45 The Annual Pilgrimage

Friday January 4
Luke 2:46-50 About the Father's Business

Saturday January 5
Luke 2:51-52 Growing Up in Nazareth

Sunday January 6
Psalm 148:1-6 Praise the Lord!

Scripture

Background Scripture: *Luke 2:41-52*
Scripture Lesson: *Luke 2:41-52*
Key Verse: *"Why were you searching for me?" [Jesus] asked. "Didn't you know I had to be in my Father's house?"* Luke 2:49.
Scripture Lesson for Children: *Luke 2:41-52*
Key Verse for Children: *After three days they found [Jesus] in the temple courts, sitting among the teachers, listening to them and asking them questions.* Luke 2:46.

Lesson Aim
To help one another grow in favor with the Lord and others.

Lesson Setting
Time: A.D. *7–8*
Place: *Nazareth and Jerusalem*

Lesson Outline
Inspired to Inquire!
  I. Jesus at Twelve: Luke 2:41-50
    A. *The Passover: vss. 41-42*
    B. *The Lost Boy: vss. 43-45*
    C. *Among the Teachers: vss. 46-47*
    D. *The Parents' Concern: vs. 48*
    E. *Jesus' Answer: vss. 49-50*
  II. Jesus' Youth: Luke 2:51-52
    A. *Jesus' Obedience: vs. 51*
    B. *Jesus' Growth: vs. 52*

Introduction for Adults

Topic: *Questions and Answers*

Adults are prone to forget what it was like to grow up. But when they get older and suffer the consequences of broken bones and strokes (for example), they have to learn basic skills all over again. Amazingly, they can recover many of these, but it can be a long, painful process that requires hours of repetitive exercises.

Growing spiritually is also tough. We cannot grow in Christlikeness without following the disciplines of the Spirit. Sitting in a church pew one hour a week is no substitute for studying God's Word to find the answers to the questions we have about life, for praying, and for serving one another. Every day God gives us growth opportunities. If we fail to use them, we become stunted, unfruitful, and unhappy Christians.

Introduction for Youth

Topic: *Inspired to Inquire!*

The Marine Corps attracts recruits with images of youth who appear to be tall, bright, and tough. The implication is that by joining the Marines you will get tough mentally and physically. Many veterans testify that they also grew spiritually while serving in the armed forces.

God calls us to enlist in His kingdom service, and He desires to toughen us for spiritual warfare. In one sense, Jesus trained for 30 years before He began His earthly ministry. His training included hard work, study, and inquiry. Most of all, He remained faithful to God.

When we trust in Christ for salvation, He will do far more for us than any human organization can promise. He enables us to excel as believers when we follow the disciplines of the Spirit, which include exploring God's Word, sacrifice, prayer, and obedience (among other things).

Concepts for Children

Topic: *Inspired to Ask Questions*

1. Jesus grew up in a humble family where obeying God was stressed.
2. Jesus studied in the synagogue and learned the Scriptures.
3. Jesus talked with His Bible teachers about important truths and asked questions about what these truths meant.
4. Even when Jesus was 12, He had a strong desire to obey and follow God.
5. When we study and obey God's Word, He blesses us with His love and grace.

Lesson Commentary

I. JESUS AT TWELVE: LUKE 2:41-50

A. The Passover: vss. 41-42

Every year his parents went to Jerusalem for the Feast of the Passover. When he was twelve years old, they went up to the Feast, according to the custom.

During Jesus' childhood years, He physically matured and became strong (Luke 2:40). With reference to His human nature, Jesus experienced normal development in body, mind, spiritual awareness, and social acceptance. All these things occurred with the perfection that is suited to each phase of life through which He passed (vss. 40, 52). As Jesus gained knowledge through observation, asking questions, and seeking instruction, He progressively became filled with wisdom (vs. 40). Jesus' wisdom was more than mere intellectual knowledge. It included the ability to use the knowledge He acquired to the best advantage. Though He did not attend a rabbinical college, the Messiah received a common education, which was primarily religious and which prepared Him for the practical duties of life.

Luke also noted that "the grace of God" was upon Jesus. Because Jesus was human as well as divine, during His earthly life He depended on His heavenly Father for all things, just as we do. Nonetheless, Jesus was sinless, and God's favor upon Him was for reasons unique to His earthly life and ministry. Much of Jesus' growth and development from infancy to adulthood is difficult for us to fathom. Perhaps this is because, as a human being, Jesus was completely unhindered by those sinful influences that affect all of us who are descendants of Adam. Jesus' body and spirit responded to His heavenly Father much as a bud drinks in the sunshine and rain and grows into a beautiful and perfect blossom.

When Jesus was "twelve years old" (vs. 42), He went with His parents "to Jerusalem for the Feast of the Passover" (vs. 41). This detail calls attention to the piety of Joseph and Mary in obeying the law. About the age of 12, a Jewish boy such as Jesus became "a son of the (divine) law" (that is, a *bar mitzvah*), while a Jewish girl became a "daughter of the commandment" (that is, *bas mitzvah*). This meant the children pledged to learn and to obey the commandments of God. Similarly today, Jewish boys and girls spend their twelfth year studying the Torah (a Hebrew word normally translated "law") with rabbis and other Jewish scholars and teachers. After they turn 13, the adolescents are held accountable for knowing and heeding the law. They also may take part in leading religious services, form binding contracts, and testify in religious courts.

Jesus' visit to Jerusalem for Passover is the only account we have about Him between His birth and His baptism. The Passover was celebrated to remind the Jews what God did to free Israel from slavery in Egypt, when the angel of death "passed over" (Exod. 12:27) the Hebrew households and did not kill their firstborn children. The Jewish people in biblical times celebrated the Passover feast annually to

153

remember this event. Many of the elements reminded them of what God had done; but they were also required to dedicate their firstborn children and cattle directly to the Lord. This was a way of giving back to God what the angel of death could have easily taken away.

John the Baptizer, who came as a forerunner to prepare the way for the Messiah, declared Him to be "the Lamb of God, who takes away the sin of the world" (John 1:29). The sacrifice of the Passover lamb was a picture of what Jesus would ultimately do on the cross. Just as the lamb was sacrificed to allow the angel of death to "pass over," so Jesus' death would allow the judgment of sin to "pass over" those who believed in His sacrificial death. It was likely no accident that Jesus began His transition to adulthood during this particular feast time.

B. The Lost Boy: vss. 43-45

After the Feast was over, while his parents were returning home, the boy Jesus stayed behind in Jerusalem, but they were unaware of it. Thinking he was in their company, they traveled on for a day. Then they began looking for him among their relatives and friends. When they did not find him, they went back to Jerusalem to look for him.

Probably no job in the world is tougher than being a parent. Parent's don't always know what's right, and children don't always do what is expected. Under the best of circumstances, the relationship between a parent and a child can be filled with frustration. This week's Bible passage makes it clear that even the relationship between Jesus and His parents was not without difficulties. It was a learning experience for Jesus as well as for Joseph and Mary. In the episode under consideration, Joseph and Mary remained in Jerusalem the full seven days and then started for home, but Jesus stayed behind (Luke 2:43). It was not until the parents had walked a day's journey that they realized Jesus was not with them. So the parents started to look for Jesus, but without success (vs. 44). The parents then turned around and went back to Jerusalem to find Jesus (vs. 45).

The parents traveled to Jerusalem for Passover in a caravan that included their relatives and acquaintances as well as traders taking their goods to the crowds of pilgrims attending the religious festival. Caravans provided some safety for journeys in the Holy Land, since bands of robbers frequently attacked travelers (10:30). A caravan would be a noisy, busy group. If later custom was followed, the women and younger children were positioned at the front of the caravan, followed by the men and older boys. Thus, Joseph or Mary each could have thought Jesus was with the other parent, or that He was traveling with relatives and friends.

Luke did not blame either Jesus or His parents for what had happened. Perhaps from our standpoint we might assume that Jesus should have told His parents what He was doing. In God's plan, however, the unfolding events served to highlight Jesus' unusual spiritual giftedness. We can well imagine Jesus' thrill and exuberance on His visit to Jerusalem and the temple. This was no ordinary event. Perhaps it was the most dramatic thing that had occurred thus far in His life. Undoubtedly,

Jesus followed the inspiration of His heart and the unique genius that was His nature.

C. Among the Teachers: vss. 46-47

After three days they found him in the temple courts, sitting among the teachers, listening to them and asking them questions. Everyone who heard him was amazed at his understanding and his answers.

Joseph and Mary had traveled with the caravan one day north toward Galilee, and it required a day for them to return to Jerusalem. Then they spent a day searching throughout the city for Jesus. They finally found Him "in the temple courts" (Luke 2:46). Jesus was engaged in dialogue with the teachers of the law. Also, interested observers were "amazed at his understanding and his answers" (vs. 47).

It's quite possible that these sorts of discussions in the temple occurred on a daily basis. The opportunity to exchange questions and answers drew Jesus' interest. It was highly unusual for the scholars to invite a youth into their theological debates, but Jesus asked such intelligent questions that they included Him. Luke did not record the content of these discussions. Perhaps they concerned matters of rabbinical history and traditions. If so, this would have been more like a gathering of legal experts talking about matters of interest. Jesus, of course, listened and asked probing questions respectfully. He was able to follow the various arguments and, surprisingly, was also able to answer challenging queries put to Him.

D. The Parents' Concern: vs. 48

When his parents saw him, they were astonished. His mother said to him, "Son, why have you treated us like this? Your father and I have been anxiously searching for you."

The religious experts were taken aback by Jesus' understanding of the law and His ability to answer interpretative questions regarding it. Joseph and Mary were also "astonished" (Luke 2:48), but for quite a different reason. At this point, they weren't focusing on Jesus' ability to hold His own among the legal scholars of the day. Instead, Joseph and Mary were concerned for Jesus' well-being. Interestingly, when Jesus' parents found Him, it was Mary who addressed Him. There was surprise and frustration in Mary's words. This was the natural response of a mother who temporarily had lost her child.

Joseph and Mary were good parents, but they were not perfect. They were so focused on their search that they didn't understand why Jesus had to be at the temple. Though they could see that the gathered crowd was impressed with Jesus, His parents didn't make the connection between who Jesus was and the sacred place where He was. One fact we learn from this incident is that Joseph and Mary acted like normal parents and they loved their child deeply.

E. Jesus' Answer: vss. 49-50

"Why were you searching for me?" he asked. "Didn't you know I had to be in my Father's house?" But they did not understand what he was saying to them.

Jesus' answer, as recorded in Luke 2:49, must have cut deeply into the hearts of His parents. In essence, Jesus said, "You just don't understand me." These words, when voiced by a disobedient or rebellious child, are generally a reflection of the nature of that child; but when voiced by "the boy Jesus" (vs. 43), the world's only perfect child, they were true. In many ways, Joseph and Mary did not comprehend the unique nature of their son (vs. 50). Later, during Jesus' earthly ministry, His disciples would also fall short of understanding Him (see 9:45; 18:34).

Jesus' answer showed that He had a clear understanding of the relationship between Himself and His heavenly Father. Throughout Jesus' public ministry, He referred to this relationship again and again. Jesus knew that He was one with His Father. For instance, Jesus' statement to Mary, "Didn't you know that I had to be in my Father's house?" (2:49), reveals Jesus awareness of His status as the Son of God and the realization that His life was on a divine schedule. This is the first clue we find in the Gospels that Jesus was not just an ordinary child from Nazareth. His pilgrimage to Jerusalem was a divinely ordained mission. In fact, Jesus' response to God's call resulted in the Messiah engaging the highest level of learning in the Jewish nation.

Though Joseph and Mary had some awareness of the special relationship Jesus had with God, they did not fully grasp its implications. Jesus needed to talk to His Father. Jesus also needed to learn what His Father expected of Him. In fact, there was no better place to do this than at the temple, the sacred place where God uniquely manifested His presence. Perhaps Mary was for the first time learning what Simeon had told her about her heart being pierced (vs. 35). Some see this event as the first step in that painful separation. Ultimately, Jesus' divinely appointed mission would lead to His death on the cross.

II. Jesus' Youth: Luke 2:51-52

A. Jesus' Obedience: vs. 51

Then he went down to Nazareth with them and was obedient to them. But his mother treasured all these things in her heart.

After the brief visit to Jerusalem and its temple, Jesus returned to Nazareth to live with His parents. Luke 2:51 notes that over the next 18 years, Jesus obeyed His parents. This implies that in every way He submitted to their will. This is perhaps the strangest relationship that a person could ever imagine. How could a perfect individual, who is God incarnate, put Himself under the authority of imperfect human parents? Strange as it may seem, the Bible states that this is what Jesus did. The role of parents is so crucial in God's plans for relationships that Jesus was willing to model that role by being obedient to His earthly parents. Mary, for her part, "treasured all these things in her heart." She was a godly woman of great faith and humility. As she watched her son grow into manhood, she recalled the words of the angel and the prophecy of Simeon. No doubt Mary also reflected on the messianic prophecies.

During Jesus' time growing up, He learned the carpenter's trade (Mark 6:3). We can safely assume that Jesus continued His religious studies in the prescribed Jewish fashion. We know that He kept the law perfectly, for He was without sin (2 Cor. 5:21; Heb. 4:15; 7:26). He also observed the religious festivals and rituals of the Jews, for He said that He had come to fulfill the Mosaic law, not to break it (Matt. 5:17). From Jesus' later activities and associations, we know that He was familiar with the local customs of farmers and other sorts of trades people. From this we see that Jesus saturated Himself in the ways of ordinary people. He knew their stories and their traditions. He also moved among them comfortably.

Scholars tell us that accounts about Jesus' life initially circulated in oral form; but as eyewitnesses began to pass from the scene, it became necessary to put important reports about the activities and teachings of the Savior into written form (for example, His presentation at the temple). Several accounts of Jesus exist that are unreliable. For instance, in a document called the *Gospel according to the Hebrews*, Jesus is reported as referring to "my Mother, the Holy Spirit." Another document, the *Gospel according to the Egyptians*, teaches celibacy as ideal—even within marriage. The *Gospel of Thomas* tells of Jesus performing miracles as a child, which contradicts John 2:11. The questionable authenticity of such accounts underscores why someone such as Luke found it important to conduct a careful investigation and sort through the claims so that his version of the Gospel was objective, accurate, and reliable (Luke 1:1-4).

B. Jesus' Growth: vs. 52

And Jesus grew in wisdom and stature, and in favor with God and men.

In another concise statement, Luke noted that Jesus continued to develop spiritually, morally, and intellectually. Holiness and humility marked His life. In fact, "wisdom and stature" (Luke 2:52) indicate robust spiritual health. From this we see that Jesus wedded truth and conduct. He not only knew the truth, but also lived it. These things were so true in Jesus' life that He "grew . . . in favor with God and men." What more could be said of anyone than that they pleased God and others? Clearly, Jesus' life with His family bore the stamp of divine and human approval.

We can only imagine what an unusual situation existed in Joseph's home during Jesus' adolescent years. Was there sibling rivalry? How did Joseph and Mary deal with such problems in the home? These are issues that Scripture does not address. Despite this, the Bible sheds much light on the way in which Jesus related to His earthly parents during the early years of His life. Though endowed with wisdom, Jesus gained more under the tutelage of Joseph and Mary. Also, though knowledgeable, Jesus gained additional knowledge from His parents. God shows through this how crucial parents are in nurturing their children and helping them become what God intends them to be.

Many think Joseph died before Jesus began His public ministry. If so, Jesus probably cared for His mother and any members of the family who were still at home. He earned His living as a carpenter, a trade Joseph had taught Him. Jesus evidently did not do any miraculous works in the years preceding His public ministry. He lived a quiet, ordinary life, fulfilling His domestic, professional, and religious duties until the time when His Father summoned Him to complete His redemptive mission.

Discussion Questions

1. What is the difference between the way in which God's favor was manifested to Jesus and the way it is often shown to us?
2. How might Jesus have anticipated attending the Passover festival with His parents in Jerusalem?
3. In ancient times, what was the spiritual significance of a Jewish boy's twelfth birthday?
4. What caused the teachers of the law to be so impressed with the way Jesus responded to them?
5. What can parents learn from Jesus' childhood regarding the rearing of their own children?

Contemporary Application

Perhaps the best illustration of what life was like for Jesus as a boy is found in De La Tour's famous painting, "St. Joseph the Carpenter." It has caught the appreciation of many people. Here we see something of the warm relationship that must have existed between Joseph and Jesus. It's a refreshing scene, especially because most classical painters focused on the relationship between Mary and the infant Jesus.

Jesus did not live a pampered life on earth. For instance, carpentry in ancient times was a physically demanding occupation. Thus, as Jesus learned this trade from Joseph, the Savior developed a strong body in order to handle the demands of the trade.

It's important to note that the Messiah, at the age 12, was fully aware of His unique identity. He was also committed to obeying His heavenly Father. Jesus thus continued to honor His earthly parents by submitting to them. Moreover, after Jesus returned with them to their home in Nazareth, the Savior continued to grow physically toward adulthood.

The residents of Nazareth became increasingly aware of Jesus' dedication to God and desire to obey His commandments. It was also more and more evident that the grace of God was upon Jesus' life. Young people sometimes become impatient in their desire to break away from their home ties; but a loving Christian home atmosphere can help them develop the patience they need to wait for God's leading in their lives.

Inspired to Love!

Scripture

Background Scripture: *Luke 6:27-36*

Scripture Lesson: *Luke 6:27-36*

Key Verse: *"Love your enemies, do good to them, and lend to them without expecting to get anything back."* Luke 6:35.

Scripture Lesson for Children: *Luke 6:27-36*

Key Verses for Children: *[Jesus said,] "Love your enemies, do good to those who hate you, bless those who curse you, pray for those who mistreat you."* Luke 6:27-28.

Lesson Aim

To recognize that love is the hallmark of the Savior's followers.

Lesson Setting

Time: A.D. *28*

Place: *Galilee*

Lesson Outline

Inspired to Love!

   I. Love for Enemies Enjoined: Luke 6:27-31

      A. *Expressions of Love: vss. 27-28*

      B. *Examples of Love: vss. 29-30*

      C. *Essence of Love: vs. 31*

  II. Love for Enemies Explained: Luke 6:32-36

      A. *Minimal Efforts of Love: vss. 32-34*

      B. *Maximal Efforts of Love: vss. 35-36*

Introduction for Adults

Topic: *Questions and Answers*

Booker T. Washington, the noted African-American educator, was taking a walk with a Caucasian friend when a pedestrian roughly elbowed Washington into the gutter. His friend was furious and asked him, "How can you tolerate such an insult?" Washington replied, "I defy any man to make me hate him."

This is what true Christian love does—it defies all the bitterness and hatred in the world. It also sweeps aside all the barriers that separate people. Because Jesus makes a difference in our social relationships, Christians can extend the love of God to others.

Jesus' teaching on the importance of loving others forces us to look deep inside ourselves. How easy it is for us to say we love God, but then do nothing for our neighbors. Also, how hard it is for us to cast aside our own desires for the sake of helping those in great need.

Introduction for Youth

Topic: *Inspired to Love*

Every small group has certain individuals who can be identified as "extra-grace people." They invariably demand extra grace on our part to accommodate their personality. Even in a church setting, they require Christlike love. Maybe some people have come to mind as you read this. They are not enemies, just frustrating people who do not return the kindness you extend toward them.

Part of the reason we have difficulty responding in love to those who have irritated us is that we don't want to appear like a doormat to others. Thus we become defensive instead of exhibiting the fruit of the Spirit. Neil Anderson (a former aerospace engineer and current professor of practical theology at Talbot School of Theology) answers this issue of defending ourselves in his seminar "Resolving Personal and Spiritual Conflicts." He says, "If you are wrong, you don't have a defense. If you are right, you don't need one!" Isn't it liberating to know that we don't have to respond in kind to extra-grace people? God's love inspires us to be compassionate!

Concepts for Children

Topic: *Showing Love to Others*

1. Jesus teaches us about love for others.
2. Jesus shows us how to be kind to others no matter what they may do to us.
3. We must be willing to pray for our friends and our enemies.
4. When we love and expect nothing in return, we are living God's Word.
5. We show that we belong to God's family by being kind and showing forgiveness to others.

Lesson Commentary

I. LOVE FOR ENEMIES ENJOINED: LUKE 6:27-31

A. Expressions of Love: vss. 27-28

"But I tell you who hear me: Love your enemies, do good to those who hate you, bless those who curse you, pray for those who mistreat you."

According to Luke 6:12, Jesus spent the night on a mountainside praying to God. The Messiah's presence on a mountain (perhaps located at the northwest corner of the Sea of Galilee near Capernaum) might be intentionally reminiscent of Exodus 24:12. In this case, though, Jesus was not just a new Moses who was presenting a new law; insead, Jesus utterly transcended Moses as the Lord of the new covenant. While on the mountainside, Jesus selected 12 of His followers for special assignment as apostles. Some experts think the reason He chose 12—the same number as the Israelite tribes—was to indicate that He was creating a new people of God (Luke 6:13-16).

After that, Jesus came down from the mountainside with His disciples. In all probability, the level place or plateau on which Jesus stood was in the midst of a more mountainous region (vs. 17). This observation has prompted some to suggest that the message Jesus delivered in verses 20-49 (traditionally known as the Sermon on the Plain) is an abridgment of the Sermon on the Mount recorded in Matthew 5—7. Admittedly, experts remain undecided about the precise nature of the relationship between these two passages. Be that as it may, all agree there are literary and thematic parallels between Matthew's and Luke's accounts. For example, both Sermons begin with the Beatitudes and end with the lesson on the builders.

In Luke's version, Jesus opened His sermon with two lists—the first, a list of blessings, and the second, a list of woes (Luke 6:20-26). These lists match up item for item, and together they overturned widely accepted beliefs among Jews in Jesus' day. For example, wealth and social success were considered signs of God's favor, while poverty and hardship were considered signs of divine disfavor; however, too often wealth and social success were achieved by exploiting others. Obviously, God's favor had nothing to do with it. Probably the crowd listening to Jesus' sermon was made up largely of people from the lower classes. If so, perhaps Jesus wanted to assure His hearers that God saw their faith and would bless them, and that God would pull their oppressors down from their high places.

In verses 27-28, Jesus enjoined love for one's enemies. The experts of the day taught others to love their neighbors and hate their enemies (see Lev. 19:18; Pss. 139:19-22; 140:9-11; Matt. 5:43). The idea of hating one's enemies, however, was an extra-biblical injunction maintained by some. It was based on a narrow understanding that a neighbor included only one's fellow citizens. Jesus carried on His ministry in the midst of this intensely prejudiced, exclusivist, and intolerant environment. One of His goals was to tear down the walls that existed between sinners and

161

God. Doing this would enable God's love to flow freely and not be hindered by such potential barriers as nationality, race, party, age, and gender.

Thus, in Luke 6:27, Jesus commanded His followers to show kindness to their antagonists. Moreover, the disciples were to do good to those who hated them and return blessing for cursing (vs. 28). Cursing in the New Testament era was really an indirect form of prayer. The idea is that those who cursed called down divine judgment on others. This especially included excommunication from the temple and expulsion from the synagogue (see John 9:22, 34). In addition, Jesus' followers were to pray directly for those who mistreated them. Abuse included spiteful actions as well as malicious speech. When hurt in any of these ways, believers were to be kind and forgiving in return.

The principle of Christ's disciples returning good for evil is a teaching also found in Romans 12:17-21. The believers at Rome were to consider what was virtuous in the sight of all people and focus on doing those things (vs. 17). The behavior of Christians had a significant impact on the credibility of the Gospel, so they were to maintain a high moral standard at all costs. Jesus' followers were to do their best to live at peace with all people (vs. 18). They should use whatever means at their disposal to promote harmony. There are times, however, when even a believer's best efforts will fail to produce peace. Any hostility that prevails should be the fault of an unreasonable antagonist, not the Christian.

The Christian's desire for peace could be perceived as weakness, which might result in further exploitation. Even then, Paul urged his friends at Rome not to seek revenge when others abused them. Retaliation was not the answer. Instead, as Christians we are to wait patiently for God to right all injustices in His time (vs. 19). Paul's statement agreed with Deuteronomy 32:35, which says that it is God's responsibility to repay all wrongs and vindicate His people. In view of the fact that it is the Lord who takes vengeance and not His people, as Christians we should heed what is written in Proverbs 25:21-22, which Paul quoted in Romans 12:20. As believers we should give our hungry and thirsty enemies the nutrition they need, not deny them. By offering help instead of the expected retaliation, we might bring our enemies to repentance. Paul admonished his readers not to be defeated by evil. Instead, the believers at Rome were to defeat evil by doing good (vs. 21). By showing love and kindness rather than hatred and vengeance, we as believers might win the unsaved to Christ.

B.   Examples of Love: vss. 29-30

"If someone strikes you on one cheek, turn to him the other also. If someone takes your cloak, do not stop him from taking your tunic. Give to everyone who asks you, and if anyone takes what belongs to you, do not demand it back."

Luke 6:29-30 is paralleled by Matthew 5:38-42. The backdrop for these sets of verses was the ancient teaching that the punishment the authorities gave had to be equitable and match the crime, not exceed it. The original intent of Exodus 21:24

(see Lev. 24:20; Deut. 19:21) was to limit the occurrence of vengeance, to help the court mete out correction that was neither too strict nor too lenient, and to prevent having different penalties for different social classes. Scholars have labeled this ordinance the law of retaliation (*lex talionis* in Latin). The premise was to offer protection for the guilty party from disproportionate retaliation on behalf of the victim. The law also ensured that the victim had the right to equal recompense. In the absence of such an equitable enforcement of justice, lawlessness and turmoil would result.

God originally intended the law of retaliation to be carried out by the appointed judges, who were responsible for maintaining law and order. However, at the time of Christ some used the law to excuse their vendettas against others. They turned a negative injunction into a positive authorization for them to take justice into their own hands. Jesus, however, declared that God wanted His people to be characterized by humility and patience. This meant believers were not to resist someone who was violent against them. Christians were also not to exact revenge for any wrongs done against them.

A court of law probably would have been the context of Jesus' teaching. The implication is that He was not condemning the government's right to prosecute and punish those who were guilty of robbery and violence. Rather, Christ was denouncing a spirit of revenge. To illustrate His point, Jesus said that if a person slapped one of His disciples on the right cheek, the believer was to turn the other cheek so that the person might slap it, if he so desired (Luke 6:29). The slap on the right cheek would have been a backhanded one, and would have been both an insult as well as an injury. In the ancient Near East, people would have regarded the right side of the face as being more important than the left side. Thus, striking the right side would have been most humiliating and signified public rejection.

Within the context of verse 29, Jesus was indicating that His followers were not to seek restitution (see Isa. 50:6). Thus, for example, if a person chose to sue a follower of Christ with the intention of confiscating his coat, the believer was also to give him his cloak. Likewise, if a person asked one of Jesus' disciples for something, the believer was to give it to him. Moreover, if a person wanted to borrow something from a follower of the Savior, the believer was not to deny the request (Luke 6:30). It would be incorrect to take Jesus' comments as legal prescriptions. For instance, He was not commanding His disciples to give endless amounts of money to everyone who sought it (see Prov. 11:15; 17:18; 22:26). Rather, He was talking about being generous to the poor (see Deut. 15:7-11; Ps. 112:5, 9). The only limit to the believer's response is what love and the Scriptures imposed.

In brief, Jesus was stressing the importance of being more concerned about eternal matters than temporal matters. For example, the creaturely comfort and respect a believer had was less important than bringing glory to God. Likewise, ensuring that one never was insulted or taken advantage of was less important than heeding God's Word. Furthermore, preserving one's material wealth was not as crucial as helping other people in need. At issue here was being just and merciful. Instead of demanding their rights, Christ's disciples were to give them up freely.

C. Essence of Love: vs. 31

"Do to others as you would have them do to you."

Jesus urged His followers to do for others what they wanted others to do for them (Luke 6:31; see Matt. 7:12). Philosophers have called this truth the Golden Rule. This maxim is found in negative form in the ethical teachings of ancient Greeks, Romans, Jews, Hindus, Buddhists, and Confucianists. Among ancient non-Christian thinkers the Golden Rule went something like this: "Do not do to others what you do not want done to you." This formulation is restrictive in nature and premised on the fear of retaliation. Jesus, however, made the truth a positive obligation, one that was inclusive, not exclusive, in nature. Christ's statement is based on the generosity, forbearance, and forgiveness of God. Believers were to follow the example of their heavenly Father in the hope that others whom they treated kindly would respond with kindness.

Jesus' declaration implied that He did not want His followers to be preoccupied with protecting themselves from outside harm. Rather, He wanted them to concentrate on actively helping others in need. It may be a loving gesture to refrain from killing one's enemy. However, the ultimate act of love is to give one's life for one's enemy (see John 15:13). What Christ said, as articulated in the Golden Rule of Luke 6:31, encapsulated the teaching of the Law and the Prophets (that is, the entire Old Testament; see Exod. 23:4; Lev. 19:18; Deut. 15:7-8; Prov. 24:17; 25:21; Matt. 7:12). Expressed differently, this timeless truth did not do away with and replace the Mosaic law, but rather fulfilled it. The Golden Rule served as an integrating principle for understanding the Old Testament. Although the Golden Rule was not explicitly stated in the Hebrew Scriptures, it was implicitly contained in them and thus was a key to their proper interpretation.

II. LOVE FOR ENEMIES EXPLAINED: LUKE 6:32-36

A. Minimal Efforts of Love: vss. 32-34

"If you love those who love you, what credit is that to you? Even 'sinners' love those who love them. And if you do good to those who are good to you, what credit is that to you? Even 'sinners' do that. And if you lend to those from whom you expect repayment, what credit is that to you? Even 'sinners' lend to 'sinners,' expecting to be repaid in full."

Jesus reasoned that if God's people only loved those who loved them in return, there was nothing commendable or distinctive about that. Indeed, even "sinners" (Luke 6:32) operated in this way. The reference here might be to people who had little, if any, concern for heeding the Mosaic law. In the time of Jesus, such individuals were often regarded with contempt and treated as outcasts. Society might regard the display of mutual love to be normal, customary, and sufficient to fulfill moral expectations. Christ, however, stated that it was ethically inadequate. Merely responding in love to those who have first shown love is equivalent to an exchange of favors (vs. 33). Jesus called His followers to show the love of God without preconditions or self-imposed limitations.

Christ's disciples should not expect to receive any heavenly reward for displays of love that were narrowly focused and conditional in nature, for the most despised people of society—namely, those who made a sizeable profit by collecting taxes from their fellow citizens on behalf of the Roman government—showed love to the same extent (Matt. 5:46). Jesus also said there was nothing uniquely Christlike in greeting only one's brother, for even unsaved people did that. It was unusual to display kindness not only to one's brother but also to one's enemy (vss. 46-47). Moreover, if believers lent their money or goods only to people from whom they expected to receive an interest payment, there was nothing commendable about that, for sinners did the same thing (Luke 6:34). It was distinctively more godly not only to lend one's possessions to other people but also to expect to receive nothing in return for one's kindness.

B. Maximal Efforts of Love: vss. 35-36

"But love your enemies, do good to them, and lend to them without expecting to get anything back. Then your reward will be great, and you will be sons of the Most High, because he is kind to the ungrateful and wicked. Be merciful, just as your Father is merciful."

Rather than selfish love, Jesus promoted unselfish love. Toward that end, the Savior reiterated the importance of loving one's enemies, doing good to them, and lending to them, without any expectation of being repaid in kind. The irony in Luke 6:35 is that when Jesus' followers show love unselfishly, without the motive of getting something in return, they in fact do get something in return. The "Most High" (namely, God in heaven) regards them as the heirs of an eternal reward. Also, God considers them to be His spiritual children, for they reflect His grace and kindness to people who are ungrateful and evil.

Christ was stressing that goodwill must not allow itself to be limited by ill will. In fact, those who were genuine children of the Father demonstrated their parentage by their moral resemblance to Him who is love (1 John 4:8, 16). For example, those who regarded showing forgiveness as a sign of weakness were hypocritical in asking God to forgive them. Likewise, those who felt enmity toward others could hardly be effective peacemakers for the Lord.

God demonstrated His love for sinners by allowing His Son to die for them, even though they were His enemies (Rom. 5:8). The mercy, generosity, and fairness of God is also evident when one realizes that He provides sunshine for all people, regardless of whether they are evil or good. He likewise provides rain for the righteous and the unrighteousness (Matt. 5:45). These truths underscore the universal goodness of the Creator, which is to be the model for the believer's conduct. In short, believers are to be merciful toward others, just as their Father in heaven is merciful (Luke 6:36). Theologians have used the phrase "common grace" to refer to the merciful favor that God bestows without discrimination on all people.

Despite what has been said, it would be incorrect to conclude from Jesus' teaching that God's love is amoral. It would also be mistaken to deduce that He shows love without any distinction toward people and that, therefore, all people must be saved. Jesus taught otherwise (see 25:31-46), and the rest of the New Testament reveals that some aspects of God's love are linked to His moral character and the prerequisite of obedience (see John 15:9-11; Jude 21).

Discussion Questions

1. How is it possible for believers to love their enemies?
2. What sorts of things can believers pray for on behalf of those who mistreat them?
3. To what extent are believers to give to others who ask for things from them?
4. Why does God consider it wrong for us to love with preconditions?
5. How has God been merciful to us? How should this influence the way in which we treat our enemies?

Contemporary Application

Jesus' band of followers were a close-knit group who daily witnessed the greatest demonstration of love in their Lord's words and actions. Nonetheless, there must have been numerous times when they got on each other's nerves. Rivalry, jealousy, and bickering surfaced on several occasions. For instance, Peter and the other disciples were seething when James and John sought the heavenly seats next to the Lord (Mark 10:35-45).

The group probably had to deal with their personal prejudices as well. Who knows how many arguments occurred between Simon the Zealot, who was probably against the government, and Matthew, who had been a government tax collector? Meanwhile, Jesus' enemies certainly hurled verbal abuse at His followers throughout His public ministry.

As believers, we still have lapses in showing the love with which Jesus has blessed us. Can we love the people who live around us and work with us, especially those who have been unkind to us, or even other believers who have offended or hurt us in some way? We know we will always encounter situations in which it takes more than our own strength to demonstrate love to others; yet that is just what our Lord requires His disciples to do.

Jesus wants us to heed His command to love others unconditionally and He empowers us to do so. When we submit to Him, God will uplift our hearts. We will also be a witness to the world of Christ's love, and sometimes we will heal torn relationships. We can—and we must—love others because Jesus first loved us.

Inspired to Pray!

Scripture

Background Scripture: *Luke 11:5-13*

Scripture Lesson: *Luke 11:5-13*

Key Verse: *"So I say to you: Ask and it will be given to you; seek and you will find; knock and the door will be opened to you."* Luke 11:9.

Scripture Lesson for Children: *Luke 11:5-13*

Key Verse for Children: *[Jesus said,] "Ask and it will be given to you; seek and you will find; knock and the door will be opened to you.* Luke 11:9.

Lesson Aim

To emphasize the importance of prayer in the life of believers.

Lesson Setting

Time: A.D. *29*

Place: *Judea*

Lesson Outline

Inspired to Pray!

  I. The Parable about Boldness in Prayer:
      Luke 11:5-8
      A. *The Demand: vss. 5-6*
      B. *The Rebuff: vs. 7*
      C. *The Grudging Acquiescence: vs. 8*
  II. The Motivation to Pray: Luke 11:9-13
      A. *The Exhortation to Ask: vss. 9-10*
      B. *The Compassion of God: vss. 11-13*

Introduction for Adults

Topic: *Finding a Listening Ear*

People learn new skills all the time. People like to talk about how they learned to use a computer. We laugh about the mistakes we made and how we inadvertently wiped out some important material. We keep taking refresher courses to upgrade our computer skills.

Learning to pray is like that, because praying is a new skill. It's not something you fall into. Prayer is a developed discipline that expresses our desire to listen to God. Prayer takes the same kind of training and discipline that is required in learning how to use a computer. While we pray, we learn more about it and find new pleasure in it, but it requires time and concentration.

Prayer is not like technology, however, because anyone can pray. That's because prayer is having a talk with God. But for the conversation to be satisfying, we have to think about what we say and how we say it. We have to use our best thoughts and skills, conditioned by a proper attitude, as we listen for God's response.

Introduction for Youth

Topic: *Inspired to Pray!*

The concept of prayer as conversation with God has tremendous appeal. We have to take prayer out of the realm of stuffy, pious jargon. We have to show teenagers that prayer is not limited to the people who do the praying in public services. Rather, prayer pleases God because it shows that we love Him and His fellowship.

Many times Christian teens pray for the first time on retreats, or in small campus and church groups. They touch levels of intimacy in prayer because they are vulnerable to each other, more so than many adults. Therefore, our concern is not with the right words and tone of voice, but in practicing our faith with honesty and integrity. That's what Jesus talked about.

Our goals for youth are to develop strong daily prayer habits, as well as quality prayer in fellowship groups. Then, as they pray, they can develop the strength and stamina they need for standing up in spiritual battles.

Concepts for Children

Topic: *God Hears and Answers Prayer*

1. Jesus teaches that praying is talking to God.
2. Jesus encourages us to pray to God every day.
3. Jesus teaches that God listens to our prayers.
4. Jesus teaches that God loves us and cares for us.
5. Jesus teaches that sometimes we have to wait for answers to our prayers.

Lesson Commentary

I. The Parable about Boldness in Prayer: Luke 11:5-8

A. The Demand: vss. 5-6

Then he said to them, "Suppose one of you has a friend, and he goes to him at midnight and says, 'Friend, lend me three loaves of bread, because a friend of mine on a journey has come to me, and I have nothing to set before him.'"

Numerous scholars have noted that the theme of prayer is strong in the Gospel of Luke, as exemplified by this week's Scripture passage. In 11:1, we learn that one day Jesus was praying in an unnamed spot. When He finished, one of His disciples asked Him to teach the Twelve how to pray, just as John the Baptizer had done for his followers. In that day, Jewish groups typically would express their corporate identity by means of a distinctive prayer. Evidently, the disciples of John the Baptizer had adopted a prayer as their own, and now Jesus' followers requested from Jesus the opportunity to do something similar.

In response, Jesus outlined a model prayer (vss. 2-4). Although this is traditionally known as the Lord's Prayer (see also the longer version in Matt. 6:9-13), it more accurately represents how Jesus' followers should approach God. A fuller understanding of what Jesus taught can be obtained by considering both Luke's and Matthew's versions of the Lord's Prayer. We discover that God wants us to address Him in a way that reflects our close, personal relationship with Him. Like a father, God has authority over us and yet at the same time loves us and wants to give us the things we legitimately ask for. Because He lives in heaven, He is transcendent (namely, going beyond our earthly existence) and has the ability to grant our requests.

The Greek phrase rendered "hallowed be your name" (Luke 11:2) emphasizes how important it is for us to honor and revere the Lord, as represented by His name. Thus, the initial focus of prayer is not on one's personal needs, but on God's glory. The one who prays also desires that God's rule over His creatures will extend to its fullest bounds and that people on earth will come to obey the Lord as perfectly as do the angels in heaven. Some think that the reference to "kingdom" denotes a time when Christ will physically rule over the earth. They maintain that the official rejection of Jesus did not negate the promises to Israel regarding the kingdom. Others, however, think that this kingdom refers to Jesus' spiritual rule and that the disciples would someday share close fellowship with Jesus at a future time in this realm.

Luke 11:3-4 indicates that we are to look to God for our needs—no matter how basic—on a day-to-day basis. Accordingly, while our foremost priority should be giving God the honor that is due Him, there's nothing wrong with asking Him to give us the things we think we need, whether they are material or spiritual in nature. Three personal requests are delineated in the Lord's Prayer. The first petition is for bread, which was a staple of the Jewish diet in Jesus' day. Bread stands for all the basic needs people have. The second personal request is for forgiveness. God is the one who can cancel our spiritual debts because Christ paid them in full on the cross; but as Jesus stated, before we ask God to forgive our sins, we should first forgive the wrongs others have done to us. The third request is for protection from temptation and Satan. This reminds us that we should ask for God's help in preserving our spiritual health.

Perhaps the model prayer Jesus offered prompted some of His disciples to wonder how confident they should be in bringing seeming small, personal matters to God. Also, if it is permissible for God's spiritual children to make specific requests to Him, then why doesn't He seem to answer all their petitions? These are some of the concerns Jesus addressed in His parable on being persistent in prayer. From this story, they learned that if they prayed, God would answer.

Jesus used parables as a favorite teaching technique. The parables were effective because they appealed to the entire person by touching the emotions, challenging the mind, and igniting the imagination. The Synoptic Gospels record 40 parables told by Jesus. They are short stories and sayings drawn from everyday life; but Jesus used these parables to communicate spiritual truths that may have been unfamiliar to His audience. He would start by commenting on something in the physical world and then compare it to something in the spiritual realm. Jesus' parables usually emphasized one primary concept that could be applied in a variety of ways. In fact, not all the details of a parable necessarily had significance. This observation serves as a caution against reading too much into a parable.

Jesus' parable recorded in verses 5-13 differs from other stories He told in that He made His point by means of contrasts, rather than similarities. In particular, God is not like the friend or the father in these stories, but rather different from them. The parable about the unexpected guest spotlights a typical, though embarrassing, situation in the time of Jesus. It's late at night when a hungry traveler arrives at the home of a friend and requests some food to eat. The friend, however, does not have anything to feed his friend; and since showing hospitality was important in that culture, the friend would feel ashamed if he could not satisfy his guest's request for a meal. This prompts the host to go to a neighbor around midnight to pester him for a loan of three loaves of bread (vss. 5-6). In a simple Galilean village such as this, in which women baked bread in common courtyards, all the residents would know who had a fresh supply of bread.

B. The Rebuff: vs. 7

"Then the one inside answers, 'Don't bother me. The door is already locked, and my children are with me in bed. I can't get up and give you anything.'"

In the parable Jesus told, the head of the household told his neighbor not to bother him. The former explained that the wooden door was already bolted shut, and he and his children were in bed. Moreover, the homeowner declared that he was unable to get up and give his neighbor anything to eat (Luke 11:7). This scene can be better understood with some background information about the typical sleeping arrangements of a home in Jesus' day. The dwelling was probably a peasant's cottage made up of one large room that served the entire family's needs. The bedding was kept in a recessed part of a wall and taken out at night and spread on reed mats on the floor. The parents would sleep in the center of the room, with the male children positioned on the father's right-hand side and the female children on the mother's left-hand side. Even with a modest-sized family, the father's getting up would have disturbed the whole household, especially any children sleeping closest to him.

C. The Grudging Acquiescence: vs. 8

"I tell you, though he will not get up and give him the bread because he is his friend, yet because of the man's boldness he will get up and give him as much as he needs."

As noted earlier, it was a matter of cultural honor for a neighbor to be a good host to visitors. Thus, the host in Jesus' parable continued to nag his friend for food to give to the hungry traveler. The Savior noted that the inconvenienced fellow would not comply with the request out of friendship; instead, he caved in to the demand because of the neighbor's "boldness" (Luke 11:8). Indeed, the worn-down head of the household gave his neighbor not just three loaves of bread, but whatever he requested.

The Greek term *anaideia*, which is rendered "boldness," is used only here in the Greek New Testament. It denotes a lack of sensitivity to what others would consider proper. Such ideas as "shamelessness," "impertinence," and "impudence" are wrapped up in the NIV translation. Other possible renderings include "sheer persistence" and "shameless audacity." The idea is that the neighbor gave his friend as much bread as he needed because the man kept harassing him. In addition, the head of the household possibly wanted to avoid the shame that would come from a breach of hospitality (see Prov. 3:27-28).

It would be incorrect to infer from Jesus' story that God will eventually answer our prayers if we keep pestering Him. He is not like a sleepy man who does not want to be troubled and has to be shamed into responding. In reality, our heavenly Father is completely opposite the friend in the house. Jesus' point is that if this man was willing to respond to the pleas of his friend, how much more willing is God to give us the things we really need. He is not reluctant to give us what we ask, but instead is eager to do so.

James 4:2-4 adds further insight regarding the issue of prayer. In the last part of verse 2, James explained that his readers did not receive what they desired because they left God out of their pursuits. Perhaps these believers recognized the selfish or immoral nature of what they desired, so they felt that asking God's assistance would be futile. Of course, if this was true, they would have been correct. Some of those who did make their requests known to God were attempting to use prayer as a means of self-gratification. Their motives were impure because they sought pleasure for its own sake—not the pleasure one derives from implementing the will of God (vs. 3).

James's anger over this matter is revealed by his referring to his readers as adulterous or unfaithful people (vs. 4). He used this harsh tone in order to shock his readers into an awareness of what they were really doing. Again James drove his point home with a question: "Don't you know that friendship with the world is hatred toward God?" To be friends with the world—that is, to court its godless beliefs and value systems—is to make oneself an enemy of God. As we see in John 17:15, Jesus asked His Father not take believers out of the (physical) world, but to protect them from the evil one who cultivated worldly thinking.

II. THE MOTIVATION TO PRAY: LUKE 11:9-13

A. The Exhortation to Ask: vss. 9-10

"So I say to you: Ask and it will be given to you; seek and you will find; knock and the door will be opened to you. For everyone who asks receives; he who seeks finds; and to him who knocks, the door will be opened."

In moments of discouragement or distress believers can receive consolation and encouragement from their heavenly Father. Although He is the all-powerful and sovereign Lord, they should not be timid or fearful about praying to Him, for Jesus will intercede on their behalf (Heb. 4:14-16; 1 John 2:1). Likewise, believers should not worry about petitioning God in a religiously acceptable manner or framing their words in exactly the proper way, for the Spirit will help them to communicate with God (Rom. 8:26-27).

It thus was fitting for Jesus to encourage His disciples to pray. He stated that when they asked the Father for something, it would be given to them. This meant He delighted to hear and answer their requests. It also meant the disciples were totally dependent on the Lord. The more they looked to God to meet their needs, the less inclined they would be to covet what others had. Whatever Christians sought from God would be found, and whatever door of ministry opportunity they accessed in His will would be opened to them (Luke 11:9). The idea of knocking suggests that a certain urgency should accompany the disciples' praying. The Greek verb tenses used in this verse (present imperatives) indicate continuous action—*keep on asking, keep on seeking,* and *keep on knocking.*

The Savior explained that His followers need not fear being rejected or ignored, for God would answer their petitions (vs. 10). Moreover, Jesus' comments implied that His followers were to persist until the answer came. Perseverance in prayer would produce tangible results, for no prayer went unheard or unanswered by God (see 18:1). The Lord would neither disregard the petitions of His people nor treat them as insignificant. In fact, the prayers of His children were important and would get His personal attention. It would be mistaken to assume from what the Son said that the Father would fulfill unbiblical requests. In that regard, Luke 11:9-10 (see also Matt. 7:7-8) are not a blank check that God issues to people for them to fill in as they please. Before the Lord will answer a believer's request, she or he should be seeking to live and pray in His will (see 1 John 5:14-15).

B. The Compassion of God: vss. 11-13

"Which of you fathers, if your son asks for a fish, will give him a snake instead? Or if he asks for an egg, will give him a scorpion? If you then, though you are evil, know how to give good gifts to your children, how much more will your Father in heaven give the Holy Spirit to those who ask him!"

Jesus ultimately intended His comments to encourage, not discourage, His followers to pray. The Savior illustrated His Father's eagerness to fulfill the requests of His children by referring to the sensible practices of all parents. Normally when a child asked for a fish, a reasonable parent would not hand him a water snake, for that would be cruel and insensitive (Luke 11:11). Moreover, if a child asked for an egg, he would not get something as inappropriate and harmful as a scorpion (vs. 12; see Matt. 7:9-10). Similarly, God was not cruel and insensitive toward His children; rather, He was sensible and reasonable in handling their requests.

Human beings, who are fallen and inclined to do evil, understand how to give beneficial and appropriate things to their children. This being true, believers were to consider how much more their heavenly Father would do for them when they brought their requests to Him. He would always give them what was sensible and appropriate to meet their needs for that moment. This would include such virtues as righteousness, purity, and wisdom (Matt. 7:11; Jas. 1:5). Luke 11:13 specifies that the Holy Spirit is the ultimate good gift one can receive from God. From the Spirit believers receive wisdom and guidance to live in a godly manner in a fallen world (see 1 Cor. 2:10-16).

Jesus' teaching unveiled the heart of God. The Savior revealed that the Father was not stingy, selfish, or begrudging. Likewise, His children did not have to grovel and beg as they brought Him their requests. They knew He was a compassionate Father, who understood their needs and cared for them deeply. If human parents could be kind to their children, God, the heavenly Father of believers, was infinitely more considerate in hearing their petitions and meeting their needs.

Jesus' teaching serves as a reminder about the true nature of God. He is not a reluctant stranger who has to be coaxed and harassed into bestowing His gifts. He is also not a malicious tyrant who takes vicious glee in playing tricks on others. God is not even like an indulgent grandparent who provides whatever one asks of him. Rather, God is the believer's heavenly Father and the Lord of an eternal kingdom. He is also the one who graciously and willingly bestows the good gifts of His kingdom in answer to prayer (Jas. 1:17).

Discussion Questions

1. In Jesus' parable, what prompted one friend to go to another friend and request some food?
2. Why was the neighbor initially unwilling to satisfy his neighbor's demand for bread?
3. What eventually persuaded the neighbor to give in to his friend's request?
4. In what way is the Father in heaven *unlike* the reluctant neighbor?
5. What is the point of Jesus' comparison between earthly fathers and the heavenly Father of believers?

Contemporary Application

Praying is *talking to God*. The act of praying does not change what God has purposed to do. Rather, it is the means by which He accomplishes His will. Talking to God is not a method of creating a positive mental attitude in ourselves so that we are able to do what we have asked to be done. Instead, prayer creates within us a right attitude with respect to the will of God. Prayer is not so much getting God to do our will as it is demonstrating that we are as concerned as He is that His will be done (Matt. 6:10).

Perhaps the most unpopular concept regarding the practice of prayer is persistence. Whatever our misgivings about coming before the all-knowing, all-powerful God with the same specific petitions over and over, persistence is scriptural (Luke 18:1-8). God does not become more willing to answer because of perseverance. Rather, the petitioner may become more capable of receiving God's answer to his or her request. Also, perseverance can clarify in our minds deep-seated desire from fleeting whim. Additionally, talking to God about the deepest desires of our heart can prepare our soul to more fully appreciate the answer He gives to our request.

Thanksgiving is to be a regular part of our prayer life (1 Thess. 5:18). Thanksgiving is an aspect of praise in which we express gratitude to God. It should spring from an appreciative heart, though it is required of all believers, regardless of their initial attitude. We can thank God for His work of salvation and sanctification, for answering our prayers, and for leading us in the path of righteousness (Phil. 1:3-5; Col. 1:3-5). We can also express gratitude to God for His goodness and unending mercy, and for leading us to spiritual victory in Christ (Ps. 107:1; 1 Cor. 15:57).

Inspired to Trust!

Scripture

Background Scripture: *Luke 12:22-34*

Scripture Lesson: *Luke 12:22-34*

Key Verse: *"Therefore I tell you, do not worry about your life, what you will eat; or about your body, what you will wear."* Luke 12:22.

Scripture Lesson for Children: *Luke 12:22-34*

Key Verse for Children: *[Jesus said,] "For where your treasure is, there your heart will be also."* Luke 12:34.

Lesson Aim

To encourage focusing on God, not the worries of this world.

Lesson Setting

Time: A.D. *29*

Place: *Judea*

Lesson Outline

Inspired to Trust!

I. Prohibition Against Worrying: Luke 12:22-26
   A. *Anxiety about Life: vs. 22*
   B. *Our Value to God: vss. 23-24*
   C. *The Futility of Worry: vss. 25-26*

II. Remaining Focused on God's Kingdom: Luke 12:27-34
   A. *Wild Flowers versus Human Life: vss. 27-28*
   B. *God's Awareness of Our Needs: vss. 29-30*
   C. *Kingdom Priorities and Promises: vss. 31-32*
   D. *Heavenly Treasure: vss. 33-34*

Introduction for Adults

Topic: *Combating Anxiety and Worry*

It's common knowledge that excessive and prolonged worrying is not good for our health. We also know that worrying can rob us of peace and contentment. It should come as no surprise, then, that Jesus told us not to worry. He saw it as an exercise in futility. How then can we stop worrying?

Many books and sermons on tape give us good practical advice. The simplest answer, of course, is to focus our attention on the Lord. When we start the day with praise and thanks to God as well as meditation on His Word, we are in good shape to deal with the problem of worrying.

It also helps to have some good friends. These would not be people who dream up more stuff for us to worry about, but rather those who are good listeners and who can draw us back to our resources in Christ. Occasionally, we all need encouragement to let go of our worries and give them to the Lord.

Introduction for Youth

Topic: *Inspired to Trust*

Jesus gives at least seven reasons why saved teens should not worry: (1) the same God who created life in us can be trusted with the details of our life; (2) worrying about the future impedes our efforts for today; (3) worrying is more harmful than helpful; (4) God does not ignore those who depend on Him; (5) worrying shows a lack of faith in and understanding of God; (6) worrying keeps us from real challenges God wants us to tackle; and (7) living one day at a time keeps us from being consumed with worry.

The adolescents you teach need to know that fretting and trusting are both chosen patterns of behavior. To build a stronger spiritual "savings account," they must reject fear and choose faith. True security and freedom from worry come from daily, conscious decisions to live in the light of God's care and provision.

Concepts for Children

Topic: *Trusting God*

1. Jesus teaches us not to worry but to put our trust in Him.
2. Jesus teaches us to be thankful for all we have.
3. Jesus teaches us that God will provide for our needs.
4. Jesus teaches us that God knows what we need.
5. God is pleased when we encourage others to trust Him to meet their needs.

Lesson Commentary

I. Prohibition Against Worrying: Luke 12:22-26

A. Anxiety about Life: vs. 22

Then Jesus said to his disciples: "Therefore I tell you, do not worry about your life, what you will eat; or about your body, what you will wear."

The parable of the rich fool (Luke 12:13-21) forms the context of Jesus' remarks about worrying (vss. 22-34). Near the midpoint of His journey to Jerusalem, a crowd of many thousands had gathered to listen to Him denounce the hypocrisy of the Pharisees (vs. 1). At an opportune moment, someone asked Jesus to settle a family dispute over an inheritance (vs. 13). Making such a request of a rabbi was not unusual, for rabbis often served as impartial advisers; but Jesus refused to become involved in the dispute (vs. 14). Perhaps this surprised those who saw Him as being more insightful and fair than any rabbi they had ever known. While He wouldn't become a judge in the case, He saw that the dispute was rooted in greed. So just as He had warned against hypocrisy (vs. 1), He now warned against greed (vs. 15).

Jesus used a parable to illustrate His point (vss. 16-20). An ambitious man invested all his energy and talents in accumulating wealth. He looked forward to retirement, when he could take life easy and enjoy what he had accumulated; but the man forgot to consider God in his plans. Even though he had barns full of grain and thought he could provide for his every need, his life would end that night. When it came right down to it, he could not control what happened to him. Jesus said everyone who lived like this foolish, rich man would end up the same way (vs. 21). In contrast, when people invested their energy, talents, and possessions in the divine kingdom, they became "rich toward God." Indeed, the return on their spiritual investments stretched into eternity.

Jesus was urging His followers to decide who was going to be their real master, for He knew that divided loyalties between God and money would plunge them into spiritual turmoil. Christ also realized that selfishness and greed would leave them spiritually blinded. It would be mistaken to conclude from Jesus' teaching that riches are inherently evil. The Savior was not condemning wealth, but greed and the hoarding of money. Moreover, He viewed the desire to accumulate wealth as a substitute for faith.

The Savior wanted His disciples to live contentedly with whatever they possessed, for they had chosen what was eternal and lasting. Those who ignored Jesus' teaching on this matter would remain snared in their worship of a pseudo-deity. Although they might think they could worship the true God while being the slave of money, they were incorrect. Serving materialistic goals forever remains incompatible with serving the living God. Furthermore, once money is given power, it crowds out everything else and leaves the worship of God as an empty gesture (see Matt. 6:24).

Regretfully, the vast majority of people in the world are preoccupied with getting more money and possessions. The poor want to become rich and escape their poverty, while the rich want to become wealthier so they can preserve their affluence. Both groups fear being out of control or overwhelmed by life-threatening circumstances. Jesus taught that the believer's outlook on life was to be radically different from that of the unsaved.

Christians were not to be anxious, for it was counterproductive and prevented them from fully trusting God. Jesus was not condemning proper stewardship and forethought; rather, He was censuring nervousness over the future (vs. 25). In view of that concern, the Savior urged believers not to be panicky about their lives. For instance, the provision of food, drink, and clothes—matters that the unsaved constantly fretted over—were not to preoccupy the thoughts of Jesus' followers (Luke 12:22). This is because there is more to life than these things.

B. Our Value to God: vss. 23-24

"Life is more than food, and the body more than clothes. Consider the ravens: They do not sow or reap, they have no storeroom or barn; yet God feeds them. And how much more valuable you are than birds!"

Jesus explained that the lives of believers were of more significance and value than what they wore and ate (Luke 12:23; see Matt. 6:25). We can imagine Him pointing to some wild ravens or crows flying in the sky at that moment. These creatures, which the Jews considered to be unclean (Lev. 11:15; Deut. 14:14), were not involved in planting and harvesting crops. They also did not have a storeroom or barns; yet the Father in heaven amply supplied their material needs (Luke 12:24; see Matt. 6:26). The point of Jesus' illustration was not to encourage idleness, but rather freedom from anxiety. The birds could find everywhere around them the insects they needed to eat—all provided by God. It stood to reason that the person of faith was of more value to God than a bird. This being the case, God would not fail to provide graciously for His people's needs, just as He never failed to provide for the needs of creatures such as birds.

C. The Futility of Worry: vss. 25-26

"Who of you by worrying can add a single hour to his life? Since you cannot do this very little thing, why do you worry about the rest?"

Sadly, the tendency of believers was to be consumed with worry over the most insignificant details of life. Christ declared that being anxious was powerless and useless, and thus a waste of time (Matt. 6:27). Some Bible scholars think Luke 12:25 should be translated as it appears in the NIV: "Who of you by worrying can add a single hour to his life?" Others think the verse should be rendered as it appears in the NIV margin: "Who of you by worrying can add a single cubit to his height?" In ancient times a cubit varied in length from 18 to 21 inches. It was the measure taken from the length of a person's arm from the elbow to the tip of one's middle finger. Jesus' point comes through clearly in either translation—worry does not change things. It not only was futile to be anxious about small matters one could not control, but also the larger matters of life that lie even further beyond one's control (vs. 26).

II. REMAINING FOCUSED ON GOD'S KINGDOM: LUKE 12:27-34

A. Wild Flowers versus Human Life: vss. 27-28

"Consider how the lilies grow. They do not labor or spin. Yet I tell you, not even Solomon in all his splendor was dressed like one of these. If that is how God clothes the grass of the field, which is here today, and tomorrow is thrown into the fire, how much more will he clothe you, O you of little faith!"

Those who were paranoid about where their clothing, food, and shelter would come from, never had any inner peace and rest. This condition is far different from the one Jesus offered to believers. He was their source of eternal, spiritual rest (see Heb. 4:9-11). To illustrate this truth, Christ pointed to the lilies of the field (which possibly represent of all types of wild flowers) and asked His audience to consider how such delicate plants grew. These flowers did not labor to provide protective covering for themselves; yet the great King Solomon in all his splendor had not been clothed as magnificently as the lilies (Luke 12:27; see Matt. 6:28-29). To Christ's Jewish audience, Solomon would have been the foremost example of human glory. It stood to reason that the person of faith was more valuable to God than wild flowers. This being the case, God would not fail to provide for His people's needs, just as He never failed to clothe the grass of the field.

Next, Jesus stated that the life span of wild grass was very short. One day it was alive and the next day people removed it to burn as fuel (along with wood) in the rounded clay ovens of Palestine. If God was willing to do so much to ensure the growth and development of something as seemingly insignificant as the grass found in a field, would He not do unbelievably more for His people? Jesus assured His listeners that the Lord would provide for the basic needs of His children, individuals who were typically characterized by little faith (Luke 12:28; see Matt. 6:30). Since God abundantly cared for His lesser creatures, it stood to reason that He would care even more for His highest creatures—human beings. That is why it was irrational to worry even in the face of transitoriness and death. The Savior's comments were intended to enhance the confidence of His followers' trust in God.

B. God's Awareness of Our Needs: vss. 29-30

"And do not set your heart on what you will eat or drink; do not worry about it. For the pagan world runs after all such things, and your Father knows that you need them."

Since the Lord would always meet His children's needs, they were not to be overly concerned about obtaining such essential items as food, drink, and clothing (Luke 12:29; see Matt. 6:31). The more they remained uneasy about these things, the less able they would be to serve the Lord effectively. Likewise, as long as they lived in anxiety, they would miss what true life in Christ was all about. Indeed, worry could become so destructive that it actually became sinful, for a life consumed by anxiety indicated a lack of trust in God and His promises. Jesus stated that the basic necessities of life were constantly preoccupying the thoughts of the nations of the world. Believers, however, were not to be like the unsaved, for the Son promised that the Father would supply His children's needs (Luke 12:30; see Matt. 6:32).

C. Kingdom Priorities and Promises: vss. 31-32

"But seek his kingdom, and these things will be given to you as well. Do not be afraid, little flock, for your Father has been pleased to give you the kingdom."

While the unsaved spent their lives seeking after the things of the world, which were destined to pass away, Jesus urged His followers to make seeking God's kingdom and righteousness their foremost and unending priority (Luke 12:31). Some think the emphasis here is mainly prophetic and thus understand Jesus to be referring to the future expansion of God's active reign on earth, the vindication of the upright, and the punishment of the wicked. More likely, the connotation is ethical in nature. This means the principal goal of believers is the establishment of God's rule in their lives and in the lives of the unconverted. Put another way, the highest aim of any disciple is the imputation of Jesus' righteousness to repentant, believing sinners, along with its manifestation in the lives of His people.

In Jesus' day, the concept of the kingdom was rooted in the Old Testament. For instance, God's rule was eternal (Ps. 145:13) and universal (103:19), but it was only partially recognized on earth. In fact, all nations would not serve the Lord until the last days (Zech. 14:9). Jewish people prayed daily for the coming of God's reign. Also, when they prayed for His kingdom, they did not doubt that God presently reigned over His creation; yet they longed for the day when God would rule unchallenged and all people would acknowledge Him.

Other portions of the New Testament describe God's kingdom as being heavenly (2 Tim. 4:18) and unshakable (Heb. 12:28). It is also inseparably linked to righteousness, peace, and joy (Rom. 14:17). Moreover, the divine kingdom is associated with suffering and patient endurance (Rev. 1:9), supernatural power (1 Cor. 4:20), promise (Jas. 2:5), glory (1 Thess. 2:12), and "the renewal of all things" (Matt. 19:28). God's kingdom is not the product of human striving or invention (John 18:36). It is given as a gift (Luke 12:32) and humbly received (Mark 10:15). The Lord brings His people into His kingdom (Col. 1:13), makes them worthy of it (2 Thess. 1:5), and preserves them for it (2 Tim. 4:18).

Christians need not fear making heavenly concerns their greatest priority, for the Lord would not neglect their needs (Luke 12:31; see Matt. 6:33). When they truly honored God by their faith, He would honor their dependence on Him by supplying their needs. His children might not become wealthy in earthly treasures, but He would ensure they did not lack anything to serve Him effectively. When God had the foremost place in the life of His children, they would turn to Him first for help, fill their thoughts with His desires, make His character the pattern for their behavior, and obey His commandments.

In Luke 6:32, Jesus compared His followers to a flock of weak and vulnerable sheep whom the Father in heaven cared for, guided, and protected. In fact, He was well pleased to give them the kingdom. The Savior's teachings about the kingdom show it was both present with Him on earth (Matt. 4:17) and also something that would be completely fulfilled at the end of the ages (13:24-30; 16:28). Jesus revealed that entrance into His kingdom is something that God gives to those who believe (25:34), but (paradoxically) it can cost a person everything he or she has (19:16-24).

D. Heavenly Treasure: vss. 33-34

"Sell your possessions and give to the poor. Provide purses for yourselves that will not wear out, a treasure in heaven that will not be exhausted, where no thief comes near and no moth destroys. For where your treasure is, there your heart will be also."

Jesus urged His followers to sell their possessions and give alms to the poor. Expressed differently, the less attached they were to material riches, the more generous they would be to others in need. The provision of "purses" (Luke 12:33) is a figurative reference to bags used by business owners for storing money. Earthly treasuries were susceptible to wearing out and being depleted. There was also no guarantee that such temporal wealth would escape being confiscated by thieves or destroyed by cloth-eating moths. In first-century Palestine, the poorer inhabitants made their homes out of mud bricks. Thus, it was easy for robbers to break into these dwellings and steal things. Jesus alluded to this fact to point out how easy it was for people to lose what they owned (Matt. 6:19).

Sadly, this truth did not prevent multitudes of people in Jesus' day from continually hoarding greater and greater amounts of earthly treasures. Despite their efforts, this did not bring them real satisfaction. If anything, it filled the greedy rich with increased anxiety, for they were engrossed with preserving their temporal fortunes from being depreciated, lost, or stolen. No one, of course, can escape the fact that everything in this world is subject to ruin. Nevertheless, some people imagine they can prevent this from happening to their material goods. The Savior made it clear, however, that everything one owns will one day be destroyed. Thus, from an eternal perspective, it is foolish to amass earthly possessions.

Jesus declared that it was far better to accumulate heavenly treasures, for these were immune to decay, destruction, and confiscation (Luke 12:33). The reference here is to whatever one does in this life that has eternal value. Likewise, the spiritual riches of God's kingdom could never be devalued, lost, or stolen (Matt. 6:20). Other portions of Scripture teach similar truths. For instance, God preserves the believer's inheritance in Christ forever in heaven, allowing nothing to jeopardize

God's bestowal of His eternal blessings (see 1 Pet. 1:3-5).

The Savior announced that wherever one's treasure was, that was also where his or her aspirations and desires were located (Luke 12:34). Expressed differently, where people invested their time, talents, and resources was a barometer of what concerned them the most (Matt. 6:21). People who spent their time amassing material wealth had their interests and aims anchored in temporal concerns, whereas people who spent their time gaining spiritual treasures had their interests and aims anchored in eternal concerns.

Discussion Questions

1. Why is it so tempting to worry about our lives?
2. In what sense is life more than the food we eat and the clothes we wear?
3. Why is it pointless to worry about the length of our lives?
4. Why is our heart an accurate indicator of what we treasure most?
5. What is the difference between worry and proper concern for the future?

Contemporary Application

In his book *Come Before Winter*, Chuck Swindoll writes, "I don't have many temptations to worship evil things. It's the good things that plague me. It isn't as difficult for me to reject something that is innately bad or wrong as it is to keep those good and wholesome things off the throne."

Although many adults try to meet the demands of living, they seem to pile up like unfolded laundry. Since each day has only 24 hours, believers need to be selective. Meanwhile, their use of the time and energy that God gives them indicates where their priorities lie. Jesus' teaching in this week's lesson Scripture will help them to understand how they can spend their time and energy in ways that have eternal value.

Consider this. In the financial world, investors use money to make more money. In a sense, the Spirit is like a broker who is continually reinvesting God's resources in His children's lives. The Father first invested in us when He sent His Son to buy us back from Satan's kingdom. Now the resulting "dividends" include the fruit of the Spirit (Gal. 5:22-23).

Since everything we have belongs to God, we are stewards, obligated to use our possessions, time, and energy as investments for our Master. Every act of faithful stewardship adds to our spiritual treasure. Where, then, is our heart focused? Do our spiritual lenses need cleaning? Are we using our resources to invest in God's kingdom? Where have we stockpiled our treasures? The answers to these questions indicate that the contents of our character matter more to God than the size of our stock portfolio.

Summoned to Labor!

Scripture

Background Scripture: *Luke 10:1-12, 17-20*
Scripture Lesson: *Luke 10:1-12, 17-20*
Key Verse: *[Jesus] told them, "The harvest is plentiful, but the workers are few. Ask the Lord of the harvest, therefore, to send out workers into his harvest field."* Luke 10:2.
Scripture Lesson for Children: *Luke 10:1-12*
Key Verse for Children: *[Jesus said,] "The harvest is plentiful, but the workers are few. Ask the Lord of the harvest, therefore, to send out workers into his harvest field."*
Luke 10:2.

Lesson Aim

To stress that people respond to Jesus' message with either acceptance or rejection.

Lesson Setting

Time: A.D. *29*
Place: *Judea*

Lesson Outline

Summoned to Labor!

   I. The Mission of the Disciples: Luke 10:1-12
      A. *The Appointment of the Disciples: vs. 1*
      B. *The Need for Prayer: vs. 2*
      C. *The Potential for Danger: vss. 3-4*
      D. *The Disciples' Conduct and Provisions: vss. 5-7*
      E. *The Disciples' Response to Acceptance: vss. 8-9*
      F. *The Disciples' Response to Rejection: vss. 10-12*
  II. The Report of the Disciples: Luke 10:17-20
      A. *The Disciples' Joy: vs. 17*
      B. *The Savior's Response: vss. 18-20*

Introduction for Adults

Topic: *Response Requires Work*

"Hang in there!" is a relative newcomer to our English lexicon. You won't find it in the Bible, but the idea is there. And Jesus is our model for how to do it. He did not quit when others refused to believe in Him. And He is ever present to help us prepare for and carry out the job God has given us to do.

Joni Eareckson Tada tells how she refused to abandon her faith even when she was paralyzed after an accident. Her life was transformed by God's love and the love of her friends and family. She has since encouraged countless numbers of believers to prepare themselves for their God-given tasks in life.

When Jesus is firmly embedded in our hearts, He gives us strength to overcome ridicule and rejection. Opposition reinforces our determination to do God's will and fulfill His plans for our lives. We can do so, for we know that Jesus will never leave or forsake us (Heb. 13:5).

Introduction for Youth

Topic: *Summoned to Labor*

Ever since the days of Jesus, Christians have given their lives in response to the divine summons to share the Gospel; yet, despite the hope of the good news, the Savior's disciples have a tough time convincing unbelieving peers to welcome the truth.

In some parts of the world, the church's labor of love is exercised in the face of serious political and religious opposition. Even when Christians do deeds of mercy for victims of disasters, their religious foes do all they can to keep the people from hearing about Jesus. For many Christians, rejection takes the form of subtle discrimination in their offices, factories, and schools.

Jesus accomplished His mission despite opposition and unbelieving peers. And so can we. He lives in us. He empowers our mission. When we do His will, regardless of the opposition, He will honor and bless our faithfulness. As 1 Corinthians 15:58 reminds us, our "labor in the Lord is not in vain."

Concepts for Children

Topic: *Trusting God*

1. Jesus sent out 72 of His followers in groups of two and gave them important tasks.
2. Jesus told His followers to take with them only what they needed.
3. Jesus told His followers to stay only where they were welcomed.
4. Jesus' followers did everything He commanded.
5. Jesus also wants us to be busy serving Him each day.

Lesson Commentary

I. THE MISSION OF THE DISCIPLES: LUKE 10:1-12

A. The Appointment of the Disciples: vs. 1

After this the Lord appointed seventy-two others and sent them two by two ahead of him to every town and place where he was about to go.

The broader context of this week's Scripture passage is Jesus' steady progress to Jerusalem to die on the cross as an atoning sacrifice for the lost (Luke 9:51). The journey leading up to His divinely appointed end involved Him traveling from one town or village to the next and teaching the residents about the kingdom of God (13:22; 17:11; 18:31; 19:28, 41). The Greek of 9:51 literally says that Jesus "set His face" to go to the capital, which is an idiomatic way of indicating the Messiah's steadfast resolve to complete the mission of redemption His Father had given Him (see Isa. 50:7). In short, Jesus came to earth to give His life as a ransom for many, and nothing would deter Him from that end (Matt. 20:28; Mark 10:45).

Along the way, He devoted time and energy to prepare His disciples for His eventual return to heaven. He wanted to ensure they would be able to proclaim the good news of salvation even without Him being physically present. Doing this would require firm, unwavering devotion to Him. In fact, that is why in Luke 9:57-62, Jesus challenged several would-be disciples with the high cost of following Him. Those who wanted to be His followers might have to endure deprivation. They had to be willing to set aside all earthly loyalties for the sake of the kingdom and not look back once such a momentous decision was made. The forward look of the divine call to Christian service would settle for nothing less than this.

Previously, Jesus had summoned and commissioned the Twelve to proclaim the kingdom of God and heal the sick (Luke 9:1-2). This mirrored Jesus' own ministry, in which He taught others and restored people to health (for example, 4:16-44). Only the Gospel of Luke records a second episode in which Jesus appointed and dispatched a larger number of followers to be His official delegates.

There is a textual problem, however, in 10:1 and 17. Some Greek manuscripts read "seventy" as the number of disciples Jesus chose and commissioned, while other manuscripts put the figure at "seventy-two." These different textual traditions are reflected in the renderings of the KJV and NIV, respectively. Specialists think "seventy-two" is the more difficult reading and has slightly better manuscript support. It is conjectured that some scribes tried to harmonize these verses with several Old Testament passages that refer to groups of 70 people (for example, Num. 11:13-17; Deut. 10:22; Judg. 8:30; 2 Kings 10:1).

In any case, it's clear that Jesus made use of others, in addition to the Twelve, to spread the good news of the kingdom, a decision that foreshadowed the future mission of the church to the nations (Luke 24:47; Acts 1:8). By this time, the Messiah had a large group who followed Him as He journeyed along the way.

Understandably, the residents of a modest-sized village would have felt over-whelmed by the sudden appearance of so many people. Thus, Jesus gave advanced notice by sending pairs of disciples ahead of Him into every town and place where He intended to journey (Luke 10:1).

Previously, Jesus had dispatched the Twelve in pairs (Mark 6:7). One reason for doing this in both situations might have been the law that a minimum of two wit-nesses was needed to establish the credibility of a testimony (Deut. 17:6; 19:15). In addition, ministering as partners provided companionship and support (Eccl. 4:9-12). This pattern can be seen in the missionary activity of the early church, which included the joint ministries of Peter and John (Acts 3:1; 4:1; 8:14), Paul and Barnabas (11:30; 13:2), Barnabas and Mark (15:39), and Paul and Silas (15:40).

B. The Need for Prayer: vs. 2

He told them, "The harvest is plentiful, but the workers are few. Ask the Lord of the harvest, therefore, to send out workers into his harvest field."

From Jesus' own ministry experience, He recognized that the multitudes were like fragile, vulnerable sheep without a shepherd (Matt. 9:35-36). Put another way, if the sheep were left to themselves, they could easily get confused and lost. Jesus also real-ized that people were not being adequately guided by their religious leaders. As in Matthew 9:37-38, Christ's words to the 72 disciples recorded in Luke 10:2 indicated that the harvest of potential converts was abundant, though the workers were few. He instructed His followers to pray to the Father, who was the owner and master of the harvest, for workers to do the spiritual reaping. It is good for us to pray the same thing, for the harvest is still plentiful; but it's unreasonable for us to pray for more workers unless we ourselves are already busy working in the field or are willing to begin working (see John 4:35-38).

C. The Potential for Danger: vss. 3-4

"Go! I am sending you out like lambs among wolves. Do not take a purse or bag or sandals; and do not greet anyone on the road."

As Jesus' sent out His delegation of followers, they would experience opposition and threats from unbelievers. The Messiah used the metaphor of helpless and defense-less lambs being exposed to ravenous wolves (Luke 10:3). The implication is that the Lord Jesus was asking His disciples to risk their lives because the work was impor-tant. There would be danger and hardship for those invading Satan's territory. Despite this reality, the Savior's followers were commanded to go, trusting God for safety.

As with the Twelve (Luke 9:3; see Matt. 10:9-10; Mark 6:8-9), Jesus' instructions to the larger group of His followers indicated that their mission was important and that they were not to be distracted by lesser concerns (Luke 10:4). In fact, there's a sense of urgency conveyed by Jesus' directives that required His disciples to be frugal and remain focused on the task at hand. This demeanor contrasted with the flamboyant and pretentious manner in which itinerant philosophical teachers of the day conducted themselves. Because the Savior wanted His followers to travel light, He told them not to take a moneybag, traveler's knapsack, or extra footgear (such as sandals). These unnecessary items would have slowed them down. Also, He wanted them to trust God to provide for their needs day by day.

Moreover, Jesus forbid His disciples from greeting anyone they met as they traveled along the dusty roads of Palestine (Luke 10:4; see 2 Kings 4:29). By saying this, the Savior was not authorizing them to be rude, unfriendly, or antisocial. Instead, Jesus wanted them to hurry along and not squander their time on lengthy traditional greetings. Formal Eastern greetings between strangers were always time-consuming. It wasn't enough to say "Hello. How are you?" Instead, people who met on the road were expected to ask and answer detailed questions, such as the following: "What is your name?" "Where are you from?" "Where are you going?" "How many children do you have?" This long-winded custom could easily delay someone on urgent business.

D. The Disciples' Conduct and Provisions: vss. 5-7

"When you enter a house, first say, 'Peace to this house.' If a man of peace is there, your peace will rest on him; if not, it will return to you. Stay in that house, eating and drinking whatever they give you, for the worker deserves his wages. Do not move around from house to house."

While the disciples were not to greet others on the road, Jesus wanted them to lodge in the homes of those receptive to their ministry. Upon entering a dwelling, it was customary for a guest to say, "May peace be on this house" (see 1 Sam. 25:5-6). This greeting of peace (equivalent to the Hebrew concept of *shalom* or well-being) was similar to a benediction in which God's blessing was requested (Luke 10:5). The head of the house would show himself to be a peace-loving person by his positive response to the disciples' message. In turn, this determined how the blessing of God was bestowed. Those who refused to welcome the disciples would not have God's peace remain on their household (vs. 6; see Matt. 10:11-13). As a matter of fact, the forfeiture of such was equivalent to a curse.

Jesus also told the disciples to stay in one house and accept the provisions offered by their hosts. This was appropriate, for workers deserved the wages they earned (vs. 7), a principle reiterated elsewhere in Scripture (Deut. 25:4; 1 Cor. 9:14; Gal. 6:6; 1 Tim. 5:18; 3 John 5-8). In this case, Jesus' disciples were undertaking an important task, one that required considerable sacrifice on their part. Furthermore, the Savior barred His disciples to move around from house to house within a town (Luke 10:7; see Mark 6:10; Luke 9:4). Possibly Jesus gave this instruction so that the disciples would not insult a host by leaving if they were offered better accommodations elsewhere. Besides, the disciples were to be mainly concerned about their ministry, not their own comfort.

E. The Disciples' Response to Acceptance: vss. 8-9

"When you enter a town and are welcomed, eat what is set before you. Heal the sick who are there and tell them, 'The kingdom of God is near you.'"

What Jesus said with respect to households visited by His followers also applied equally to entire towns. For example, if the residents of a village welcomed His disciples, this meant they welcomed the message and ministry of the Savior, whom the disciples represented. Jesus told His followers to eat whatever they were served (Luke 10:8). Even if they were offered food not prepared according to the Jewish dietary laws, they were to overlook this (see Acts 10:9-16; 1 Cor. 10:27). After all, the principle focus of the disciples was to heal the sick and proclaim good news of the divine kingdom (see Matt. 10:7-8; Mark 6:12-13; Luke 9:6). Ultimately, the Messiah empowered His disciples to perform miracles of healing.

Depending on how one renders the Greek of Luke 10:9, the message is either that the kingdom of God has come upon the recipients or that it is near. The latter emphasis seems more likely. To be specific, the reign of God was at hand (though not yet fully manifested) in the person of the Messiah at His first advent. The full consummation of the kingdom awaits Jesus' second advent, when He returns as the sovereign King and Lord (2 Thess. 1:7-10; Rev. 19:16). Even so, through the victory Jesus achieved at Calvary, the power of Satan has already been overcome and the cause of the righteous has already been vindicated (Luke 10:18; 11:14-23).

F. The Disciples' Response to Rejection: vss. 10-12

"But when you enter a town and are not welcomed, go into its streets and say, 'Even the dust of your town that sticks to our feet we wipe off against you. Yet be sure of this: The kingdom of God is near.' I tell you, it will be more bearable on that day for Sodom than for that town."

Not all towns would welcome the missionary pairs. In those places where the residents rejected Jesus' disciples, they were to go to the main road, street corner, or public square of the town and declare God's condemnation on the townspeople for their refusal of His kingdom (Luke 10:10). In that day, pious Jews reentering Palestine would cleanse their feet and clothes so as not to pollute the Holy Land with the dust of Gentile territory. Jesus instructed His disciples to use this custom to symbolize the judgment of God on a town's Messiah-rejecting inhabitants. The only remaining responsibility for Jesus' followers was to declare to these towns that the divine kingdom was near. In this case, though, it was not coming to bring salvation, but judgment (vs. 11; see Matt. 10:14; Mark 6:11; Luke 9:5; Acts 13:51).

Jesus declared that on the day of judgment, these towns would be worse off than Sodom. The solemnity of Christ's words is evident by the fact that in the Greek text of Luke 10:12, the noun "Sodom" is in an emphatic position. Jesus was referring to Genesis 19:1-29, which relates God's destruction of two of the most wicked cities mentioned in the Old Testament—Sodom and Gomorrah (see Matt. 10:15). The allusion to Sodom reflects the fact that people who hear and reject the message of

God's kingdom, as presented in the Gospel, bear more responsibility than do people who don't hear the good news of salvation. Indeed, to spurn the truth about Jesus is a more serious transgression than any of the worst sins committed in the Old Testament era and will result in more severe condemnation on judgment day.

II. THE REPORT OF THE DISCIPLES: LUKE 10:17-20

A. The Disciples' Joy: vs. 17

The seventy-two returned with joy and said, "Lord, even the demons submit to us in your name."

The thought that Jesus' followers would sometimes be rejected reminded the Savior of times He had been spurned. Like an Old Testament prophet, He warned of judgment for the people of Korazin, Bethsaida, and Capernaum (Luke 10:13-15). These towns were evidently places where Jesus had concentrated much of His ministry and yet had met considerable resistance. With such episodes in mind, Jesus reassured the 72 that they represented Him fully. Indeed, the responses people gave His disciples were really responses to the Messiah (vs. 16).

When the larger group of Jesus' followers returned from their mission, they were full of joy and enthusiastically made their report to the "Lord" (vs. 17), a title that affirmed Jesus' status and authority as God's agent. As Christ's disciples proclaimed the message of the kingdom, even the demons submitted to them (vs. 17). These evil, supernatural beings were the henchmen of Satan; but when the disciples commanded them to depart from their human hosts, the fallen angels obeyed, for Jesus' followers were operating in His name and under His sovereign authority. This success in ministry reflected the experience of the Savior (11:20) and the Twelve (Mark 6:13).

Some people have said that the disciples' mission trips provide the model for Christians who are trying to obey the Great Commission (Matt. 28:19-20); but that is probably a mistaken notion, for Jesus sent His disciples on limited, temporary excursions. They traveled for a few days among the towns of Galilee to introduce the Jewish people to the Messiah. In contrast, the Great Commission applies to all peoples and is relevant until the Savior returns.

B. The Savior's Response: vss. 18-20

He replied, "I saw Satan fall like lightning from heaven. I have given you authority to trample on snakes and scorpions and to overcome all the power of the enemy; nothing will harm you. However, do not rejoice that the spirits submit to you, but rejoice that your names are written in heaven."

Jesus' statement of having seen "Satan fall like lightening from heaven" (Luke 10:18) might be an allusion to Isaiah 14:12. Some think Jesus was warning His disciples about spiritual pride, which was the cause for Satan's fall from heaven. The more likely view is that Jesus believed that Satan and his demonic cohorts had suffered defeat as a result of the ministry of the 72. Expressed differently, because of their faithful service in Jesus' name, they had won a victory against the devil. Moreover, the disciples' expulsion of the demons anticipated the greater defeat of

Satan at the hands of Jesus through His redemptive work on the cross.

In Luke 10:19, Jesus told the 72 that He had given them authority to tread or trample on "snakes and scorpions" and to prevail over the full force of "the enemy." Furthermore, nothing at all would harm them. (Jesus' statement in the Greek text is an emphatic double negative.) Bible students disagree over how literally to interpret this. Some say Christ was referring to literal protection from poison and satanic power (see Mark 16:8; Acts 28:3-6). Others say the "snakes and scorpions" (Luke 10:19) represent Satan.

As Genesis 3:15 promises, the offspring of the first woman—specifically, the Second Adam, Jesus Christ— secures the victory of the redeemed over the devil. Also, Paul noted that the "God of peace" (Rom. 16:20) will "soon crush Satan" under the feet of the saints. From a human standpoint, the delay seems long; but from the divine standpoint it is imminent, being one of the next series of events on the prophetic calendar (2 Pet. 3:8). While victory over the forces of evil was something to rejoice about, Jesus said it was more significant that the disciples' names were written in heaven (vs. 20). The biggest triumph we can have over the enemy is to escape his clutches through salvation in Christ.

Discussion Questions

1. Why did Jesus send out the 72 in pairs?
2. What did Jesus say His disciples were to pray for from the Lord of the harvest?
3. What did the disciples' greeting of peace signify?
4. What did it mean for the disciples to shake off the dust from their feet?
5. In what sense did Jesus see Satan fall from heaven?

Contemporary Application

The 72 weren't drafted or forced into service. Rather, Jesus chose each disciple to serve Him in a special way. Likewise, Jesus wants every member of your class to follow Him and be committed to doing His will. He doesn't twist their arms to get them to submit. Instead, He wants them to respond willingly to His summons. This is one way in which the Christian faith is different from all other world religions.

Moreover, these faith traditions demand that their followers improve themselves through rituals, sacrifice, and good deeds. This human "righteousness" counts at the end on whether a person becomes a god or achieves some higher level of existence; in contrast, Jesus offers people not some kind of glorified status based on keeping all the rules, but a personal relationship with Him based on faith.

This Gospel message is empowering to some people and offensive to others. Christians must be prepared for both responses. Sometimes the peer at work whom they thought would laugh them off for talking about Jesus, instead listens intently to them. In contrast, the neighbor whom the adult thought would trust in Christ, orders him or her to never again mention God.

Summoned to Repent!

DEVOTIONAL READING

Psalm 63:1-6

DAILY BIBLE READINGS

Monday February 4
Psalm 63:1-6 My Soul Is Satisfied

Tuesday February 5
Luke 3:7-14 Turn from Your Ways

Wednesday February 6
Mark 1:14-15 Jesus Calls for Repentance

Thursday February 7
Luke 13:1-5 Repent or Perish

Friday February 8
Luke 13:6-9 Bear Fruit of Repentance

Saturday February 9
Acts 26:19-23 Paul Calls for Repentance

Sunday February 10
Psalm 1:1-6 Choose God's Way

Scripture

Background Scripture: *Luke 13:1-9*

Scripture Lesson: *Luke 13:1-9*

Key Verse: *[Jesus said,] "I tell you . . . unless you repent, you too will all perish."* Luke 13:3.

Scripture Lesson for Children: *Luke 13:6-9*

Key Verse for Children: *[Jesus] told this parable: "A man had a fig tree, planted in his vineyard, and he went to look for fruit on it, but did not find any."* Luke 13:6.

Lesson Aim

To make repentance from sin a high priority.

Lesson Setting

Time: A.D. *29*

Place: *Judea*

Lesson Outline

Summoned to Repent!

  I. The Summons to Repent: Luke 13:1-5
    A. Pilate's Massacre of Galileans: vss. 1-3
    B. Deaths Caused by the Siloam Tower's Collapse: vss. 4-5

  II. The Parable of the Spared Fig Tree: Luke 13:6-9
    A. The Vineyard Owner's Command: vss. 6-7
    B. The Worker's Request: vss. 8-9

Introduction for Adults

Topic: *Turning Our Lives Around*

Do you think about sins you have committed in the past? Rather than dwelling on those sins and feeling guilty about them, it is better to approach God in repentance. Doing wrong slows us down, makes us look more closely at the direction we're traveling, and prompts us to ask ourselves some hard questions: *How can I avoid this in the future? Is there anything I can do now to rectify the matter?*

We can let a negative experience teach us to avoid making that error again. But if we choose to wallow in guilt, instead of returning to the Lord and experiencing His forgiveness, it is like making the same mistake twice. If any of your students are afraid that God might not be willing to forgive them, encourage them to recall the words of 1 John 1:9. This verse tells us that if we confess our sins, God will forgive us and purify us.

Introduction for Youth

Topic: *Summoned to Turn Around*

A Christian teen once declared to me that he had no fear of God because Scripture teaches "there is no fear in love," "perfect love drives out fear," and "fear has to do with punishment" (1 John 4:18). Sadly, because the adolescent had misunderstood this verse, his sins rarely disturbed him. Since he felt God loved him so much, he also believed God would naturally and promptly forgive him whenever he sinned.

Most saved young people do not share this teen's attitude, but can they safely say they are as contrite as they should be when they ask for God's forgiveness? If not, then they need to learn from this week's lesson to be more sincere and humble when they repent before the Lord.

Concepts for Children

Topic: *Given Another Chance*

1. Jesus told a story in which a man had a fig tree growing in his vineyard.
2. The owner was sad because he did not find any fruit growing on the tree.
3. The worker who took care of the tree asked that the plant be given another year to grow fruit.
4. The owner was willing to give the fig tree one more chance to grow rather than be cut down.
5. Jesus gives us many opportunities to become more like Him in what we think, say, and do.

Lesson Commentary

I. THE SUMMONS TO REPENT: LUKE 13:1-5

A. Pilate's Massacre of Galileans: vss. 1-3

Now there were some present at that time who told Jesus about the Galileans whose blood Pilate had mixed with their sacrifices. Jesus answered, "Do you think that these Galileans were worse sinners than all the other Galileans because they suffered this way? I tell you, no! But unless you repent, you too will all perish."

During one episode in which Jesus taught a crowd of thousands about the signs of the times (Luke 12:1, 13, 54), some listeners mentioned an atrocity committed by Pontius Pilate. It was reported that he had massacred a group of Galileans, with the result that some of their blood mixed with the sacrifices they had been offering near the temple in Jerusalem, perhaps during the season of Passover (13:1). There is no other historical record of this event, though it mirrors similar incidents chronicled in the writings of the ancient Jewish historian, Josephus. Pilate was the fifth Roman prefect or governor of Judea (A.D. 26–36) and was notorious for his role in sentencing Jesus to die on the cross. It is generally thought that Pilate was an Italian-born, middle-class Roman citizen from the region of Samnium in central Italy.

By all accounts, Pilate was harsh in the way he dealt with his Jewish contemporaries. This was due in part to his contempt for their religious convictions. For instance, in one episode the prefect brought into Jerusalem military insignia that bore the image of the emperor. This created a firestorm of protest from the Jewish people, who regarded the effigies as an idolatrous presence that violated their law. Unwavering Jewish resolve in the face of being slaughtered eventually caused Pilate to remove the offensive insignia.

The prefect again incited ill will when he raided the temple treasury to fund the construction of an aqueduct to bring water to Jerusalem. Pilate used brute force to squash the protests that ensued, which in turn resulted in appalling bloodshed. Later, at the prefect's residence in Jerusalem, he mounted a pair of golden votive shields that were inscribed with the names of Tiberius and himself. The Jewish elite lodged a formal complaint with Tiberius, which prompted him to order the immediate relocation of the shields to Caesarea.

In A.D. 36, Vitellius, the legate of Syria, deposed Pilate, ordered him to appear before the emperor in Rome, and explain his actions. Pilate's dismissal from office stemmed from his violent response to a group of Samaritans who had assembled at Mount Gerizim. They did so in anticipation of finding sacred items they believed had been lost from the Samaritan temple (which the Hasmoneans destroyed about a century and a half earlier). The people superstitiously thought Moses had buried these treasures at the foot of the mountain. A Samaritan delegation to Vitellius accused Pilate of cruelly slaughtering innocent lives. Episodes such as these left the prefect with a reputation for being arrogant, vindictive, and easily provoked to anger.

If those listening to Jesus thought they would get a sympathetic response, they were mistaken. The Savior declared that the Galileans whom Pilate massacred had not experienced this tragedy because they were worse sinners than their peers (vs. 2). When considering the atrocities committed by the depraved, intellectually curious believers are prompted to ask why God allows evil in the world (see Hab. 1:13). Whether one is considering evil attitudes, actions, or aims, this wickedness results from the absence of the moral perfection that God originally intended to exist between good things.

Ultimately, only God knows why He has allowed wickedness to exist in the world. Nevertheless, it remains true that the Lord may use ungodliness to bring home to us the distressing fact of our mortality, to warn us of greater evils, to bring about a greater good, or to help defeat wickedness. The last two reasons are especially evident in the cross of Christ. Despite the tragedy of the Messiah's suffering at Calvary, His atoning sacrifice resulted in a greater good (the salvation of the lost) and the defeat of evil (for instance, sin and death).

Jesus declared to the crowd that unless each of them repented and received eternal life (by trusting in Him), they faced the prospect of death, namely, eternal separation from God. The word "repent" in Luke 13:3 translates the Greek word *meta-noeite*. The term conveys the idea of changing one's mind. In a religious sense, it signifies a turnabout in attitude toward God and life's priorities. Repentance is part of the conversion process. Through the working of the Holy Spirit, sinners come to the point at which they are ready to turn away from sin and place their trust in Christ for salvation.

B. Deaths Caused by the Siloam Tower's Collapse: vss. 4-5

"Or those eighteen who died when the tower in Siloam fell on them—do you think they were more guilty than all the others living in Jerusalem? I tell you, no! But unless you repent, you too will all perish."

Jesus brought up another incident in which 18 individuals perished when the tower of Siloam collapsed on them (Luke 13:4). This structure was near the reservoir of Siloam and built into the southeast corner of the wall of Jerusalem; however, the precise location of the tower remains unknown. In contrast to the event Jesus previously mentioned, this disaster was an accident beyond anyone's control. It raised the question of whether God was judging the victims for being worse offenders than all the other residents of Jerusalem. As before, in this case Jesus said the answer was no. Moreover, He told the crowd that unless they repented of their sin, eternal condemnation was their end (vs. 5).

A number of Old Testament writers address the issue of why some people prosper while others experience tragedy for no apparent reason (see Job 21:7-26; 24:1-17; Ps. 73:1-14; Eccl. 8:14; Jer. 12:1-2; Hab. 1). While none of the writers offered a comprehensive solution to the problem, they all affirmed that in the end God will punish the wicked and reward the righteous (see Job 24:22-24; 27:13-23; Ps. 73:16-20; Eccl.

8:12-13; Jer. 12:7-17; Hab. 2:3; 3:2-19). Indeed, this is how Solomon ended the Book of Ecclesiastes: "Here is the conclusion of the matter: Fear God and keep his commandments, for this is the whole duty of man. For God will bring every deed into judgment, including every hidden thing, whether it is good or evil" (12:13-14).

The longing of the righteous is centered in one day experiencing the salvation of the Lord. From a temporal standpoint, this meant being freed from the oppression of the wicked. From an eternal standpoint, God's salvation would result in the righteous remnant experiencing unbroken fellowship with Him in heaven (see Rev. 21:7, 22; 22:3-5). In the face of all adversity, whether due to natural or human causes, an understanding of the Redeemer's just will and unfailing love should elicit hope and confidence in His plan for us. No matter how dark things may appear at the moment, we can have confidence that someday God will make His glorious presence known to us once again. This is the basis for us quietly and patiently waiting for the salvation of the Lord (Lam. 3:26).

II. THE PARABLE OF THE SPARED FIG TREE: LUKE 13:6-9

A. The Vineyard Owner's Command: vss. 6-7

Then he told this parable: "A man had a fig tree, planted in his vineyard, and he went to look for fruit on it, but did not find any. So he said to the man who took care of the vineyard, 'For three years now I've been coming to look for fruit on this fig tree and haven't found any. Cut it down! Why should it use up the soil?'"

To emphasize the importance of repenting and receiving eternal life, Jesus told the parable of the spared fig tree. A parable is essentially a comparison. It uses a brief story or illustration to help people understand a concept. Parables are effective because they appeal to the entire person, touching the emotions, challenging the mind, and igniting the imagination. Jesus used vivid illustrations to keep the people's interest, help them remember His teaching, and enable them to think seriously about their relationship to God.

In the parable under consideration, Jesus said that a Jewish landowner regularly inspected one of the fig trees in his vineyard for fruit (Luke 13:6). He complained to the worker who tended the vineyard that after three years, the tree had enough time to become viable and fruitful; yet it remained barren. Some have suggested that the total elapsed time could have been six years, given the fact that it was common practice in Jesus' day for three years to transpire before a farmer even began to look for fruit on a fig tree. In any case, because the tree in Jesus' parable remained unproductive, the landowner did not want the plant to continue depleting the soil of nutrients to prolong its growth. Instead, he ordered the worker to cut down the tree (vs. 7).

Some think Micah 7:1 forms the backdrop of Jesus' parable. This verse records the Lord's lament over Judah's sin, as symbolized by a grove of unfruitful fig trees. Others have noted that the fig tree in Jesus' parable is a variant of the more familiar picture of a vine representing the nation. In fact, there are several places in the Old Testament where Israel is referred to as a vineyard. For example, in Isaiah 5:4 we read that God desired His vineyard (Israel) to bring forth grapes (righteousness); instead, the people brought forth wild grapes (unrighteousness). As a nation ready for exile, Israel's behavior was not pleasing to God. The Father, whom Jesus called "the gardener" in John 15:1, planted the true vine by sending His Son to dwell among us. Unlike the nation of Israel, the Lord Jesus lived a life of fruitfulness that was pleasing to the Father. For instance, Christ voluntarily offered up His life as the acceptable sacrifice for the sins of the world.

Ancient farming practices are part of the cultural context of Jesus' parable. In Bible times, both city dwellers and villagers were involved in agriculture, and it influenced many facets of the nation's social behavior, law, and religion. Practically every family owned a piece of land in Israel, and many families farmed a small area of their own. Outside the cities, most Israelites lived in villages rather than on farms. The land they cultivated was perhaps miles away from the village and situated near the water supply or on western or northern hillsides, where rainfall was greatest.

The variety of plants cultivated included cereal grains (such as barley and wheat), legumes (such as lentils and peas), and fruit trees (such as grapes, olives, dates, pomegranates, and figs). The conditions in Palestine were not always favorable for the cultivation of crops. The rainy season tended to be short (from mid-October to April) and unpredictable. Also, farm work was made more difficult by the presence of hilly ground and stony soil. To overcome these obstacles, the people terraced the uneven soil to catch rain run-off on the hillsides. Moreover, there were times when certain plants or trees failed to yield any fruit due to diseases, locust attacks, and other pests such as mice, worms, fruit bats, and weeds. These plants or trees were not allowed to remain in the soil. Farmers eventually uprooted or chopped down and burned the ones that yielded worthless fruit.

The sowing of plants took place in the fall. Early autumn rains softened the soil and enabled farmers to till the ground. On larger plots, they used wooden-frame plows pulled by a team of animals (for example, oxen, cows, or donkeys), while on smaller plots, they used hand-held hoes. They would set aside two months to sow cereal grains and two more months to plant legumes and vegetables, and start cultivating grapes in the vineyards.

Vines required constant care to keep them productive. For instance, farmers had to gently place vines that had fallen to the ground back into position. They also had to constantly repair trellises and poles supporting the vines and regularly pull the weeds. If farmers did not regularly prune healthy branches and remove dead ones, the plant would not produce a good crop of fruit. The grapes that grew on the plants needed to sufficiently ripen before the farmers could pick them. Otherwise, if they prematurely harvested the fruit, it would taste quite sour.

Produce harvesting occurred in the spring. The farmers would first gather the barley, then the wheat, grapes, and other fruit. Next, the farmers processed the grapes and other fruits. Some of it would be dried in the sun and used to make cakes, but most of it would be used to make wine. People would tread the grapes on a flat, hard surface and allow the juice to run of into a reservoir cut out of rock or made out of stones and clay. The juice was then transferred to large jars, which the farmers put in a cool storage place to allow the contents to ferment. To find workers for tilling, sowing, harvesting, and processing, a Jewish landowner would go to the center of town early in the morning and hire those who were waiting there and willing to work. Usually, those were the poor people, who depended on someone hiring them each day in order to make enough money to live.

B. The Worker's Request: vss. 8-9

"'Sir,' the man replied, 'leave it alone for one more year, and I'll dig around it and fertilize it. If it bears fruit next year, fine! If not, then cut it down.'"

Jesus said that the worker who tended the vineyard petitioned the landowner to give the barren fig tree one more opportunity to bear fruit. Specifically, the worker wanted another year to dig around the tree. His efforts to loosen the soil near the roots would increase the likelihood of the tree obtaining the nutrients it needed to become fruitful. This process would be aided by the addition of manure, which he wanted to toss around the tree as fertilizer (Luke 13:8). The worker hoped that by giving the tree extra time and attention, it would bear fruit during the next growing season; but if it failed to do so, he would be fine with the landowner's decision to cut down the tree (vs. 9).

The Savior's point is that God, in His grace, does not immediately punish transgressors. Nonetheless, it would be incorrect to assume that His patience and forbearance are a license to sin. Instead, the truth is that the Lord is dealing mercifully with the lost by giving them additional time to repent and receive eternal life (2 Pet. 3:9). While Jesus' parable had immediate application to the people of Israel, the story remains timeless in its relevance to all people throughout history.

For Christians today, Jesus' parable encourages them to be fruitful members of God's kingdom. Admittedly, there is debate over the exact nature of the fruit being referred to by Christ. Some think Jesus was talking about leading many people to Him in faith, while others think He was referring to the moral virtues and characteristics of a godly life. Probably, Jesus had both ideas in mind when He talked about being spiritually fruitful.

The concept of fruitful and unfruitful trees can be illustrated by two of Jesus' disciples. The Messiah chose Judas as a follower. Possibly because of the latter's ability as a businessperson, he was given the job as treasurer for the group (John 12:6; 13:29); but Judas's abilities helped lead to his downfall because of his greed. Though Judas was associated with Jesus, heard His teaching, and witnessed His works, Judas did not have an abiding spiritual union with Jesus; rather than bearing fruit, Judas's life ended in destruction. Christ also chose Peter to be one of His disciples. Jesus taught him the same truths and gave him the same opportunities to witness that He had given Judas. Peter did not begin his life as a disciple with great success, but after some pruning (such as his denial of Christ and reinstatement later), Peter bore much fruit. He found the key to a productive life in a living relationship with the Savior.

Discussion Questions

1. Why do you think some who were listening to Jesus told Him about the tragedy involving some Galileans?
2. What assumption had some in the crowd possibly made about the spiritual status of the Galileans who perished at the hands of Pilate?
3. What was the point of Jesus bringing up the incident involving the collapse of the tower in Siloam?
4. What does it mean to repent?
5. What point was Jesus making by telling the parable of the spared fig tree?

Contemporary Application

In modern life, there is a strong tendency for people to blame others for anything bad that happens, but to take credit for anything good. In God's law court, however, everyone stands or falls on the basis of their own conduct and decisions. God is not swayed by excuses, buck passing, or blame shifting. While it is certainly true that every believer has an obligation to share the Gospel with the lost, in the end, all stand solely responsible for themselves before the Lord.

Jesus warned the people of His day to guard against twisted and perverted ways of living. He also urged them not to forsake God's upright path. Moreover, other biblical writers encouraged their readers to seek wisdom as one would seek hidden treasure. They were careful to point out that, though wisdom can be sought through human effort, finding it is a gift from God. Tragically, while no one wants to be a fool, people keep on doing foolish, destructive things. The problem is that by ignoring God, they fail to realize that wisdom and folly have moral dimensions. Amazingly, an uneducated person may easily surpass an educated person in wisdom, according to God's standards.

What can believers do in a climate of perversion and folly? The only sensible option is for them to turn away from sin in their life and demonstrate the positive values of wisdom represented in the teachings of Jesus and the rest of Scripture. People need to see what wisdom looks like in godly individuals, not just in theory. Christians do not offer simply a better philosophy but a superior code of wise conduct. The Lord calls His people to repent and do what is right, just, and fair. They seek to avoid the crooked ways of those who mock God. His wisdom is the hallmark of their lives. When our churches are filled with people hungry for learning and doing God's commands, the unbelieving world will take notice.

Summoned to Be Humble!

Scripture

Background Scripture: *Luke 14:1, 7-14*

Scripture Lesson: *Luke 14:1, 7-14*

Key Verse: *[Jesus said,] "For everyone who exalts himself will be humbled, and he who humbles himself will be exalted."* Luke 14:11.

Scripture Lesson for Children: *Luke 14:1, 7-14*

Key Verse for Children: *[Jesus said,] "Everyone who exalts himself will be humbled, and he who humbles himself will be exalted."* Luke 14:11.

Lesson Aim

To respond with humility and generosity to the needs of others.

Lesson Setting

Time: *A.D. 29*

Place: *Perea*

Lesson Outline

Summoned to Be Humble!

I. Silence Over a Sabbath Healing: Luke 14:1

II. Humility and Generosity Enjoined: Luke 14:7-14

   A. *The Importance of Humility: vss. 7-11*

   B. *The Importance of Generosity: vss. 12-14*

Introduction for Adults

Topic: *The Necessity of Humility*

Arrogance and greed cause people to do strange things. For instance, most of us have seen a community of family members split over the handling of estates. We have seen landlords cheat tenants. We have seen quarreling over insignificant accounts.

On the other hand, most of us have been greatly blessed by humble and generous people within our respective faith communities. Prosperous farmers have given away property and wealth. Wealthy businesspeople have given huge amounts to Christian causes.

What makes the difference? The difference is that greedy people are too arrogant to release themselves to God's care, while generous people humbly trust God to take care of them. How liberating it is to give everything to God. When we do that, we don't have to worry about stockpiling wealth, and we don't have to worry when we stand before God's judgment.

Introduction for Youth

Topic: *Summoned to Be Humble*

The values of young people are strongly shaped by role models in sports and entertainment. They see the stars revel in unparalleled wealth. They watch as athletes refuse to show up for practice because they are being paid only three million dollars a year.

Against this popular culture comes the teaching of Jesus, who said we are fools if all we work for is money and possessions. Young people are driven, not for millions, but for cars, stereos, clothes, and sports equipment. Jesus said it's all a lot of stuff that in the end does not mean a thing.

Real life is found not in things but in knowing God and living for Jesus. Money and possessions cannot buy happiness, and they deceive us into thinking all is well with our souls, when we really are in grave danger. That's why Jesus urges us to be humble and hospitable in our dealings with others.

Concepts for Children

Topic: *Putting Others First*

1. One Sabbath, Jesus was having dinner in the home of an important religious leader.
2. Jesus saw how the guests tried to take the best seats.
3. Jesus taught that we should do good things for others, especially those in need.
4. Jesus wants us to accept others as they are.
5. God is pleased when we put others before ourselves.

Lesson Commentary

I. SILENCE OVER A SABBATH HEALING: LUKE 14:1

One Sabbath, when Jesus went to eat in the house of a prominent Pharisee, he was being carefully watched.

The focus of Luke 14:1 is Jesus accepting an invitation one Sabbath (perhaps around midday after a synagogue service) to dine at the house of a leader of the Pharisees. The Jewish Sabbath began at sunset on Friday and ended at sunset on Saturday. Sabbath restrictions kept people from carrying any loads or traveling great distances until sunset. The Sabbath regulations began in the time between the Old and New Testaments as a way to protect and preserve the spirit of the day.

The scribes who first wrote the rules wanted to guarantee a proper observance of the Sabbath and ensure that people did not break the fourth commandment; but the Sabbath regulations became a burden rather than a blessing. They deprived people of many opportunities to enjoy the day and serve the Lord. Several times during His earthly ministry, Jesus confronted the legalistic views of the Pharisees concerning the Sabbath.

The Pharisees arose in the second century B.C. and shaped much of the religious thinking of Jesus' day. They consisted mostly of middle-class men drawn from the merchants and tradesmen of the day. Before being fully accepted as a Pharisee, each candidate's behavior was closely watched for obedience to the law. The Pharisees' greatest desire was to bring all people into total obedience to the law, especially as they interpreted it. This explains why some Pharisees scrutinized and ultimately condemned the person and work of Jesus.

Luke 14:1 is a case in point. We learn that religious leaders dining at the home of a prominent Pharisee (possibly a synagogue official) were watching the Lord Jesus closely to detect any Sabbath-breaking conduct. The Gospels reveal that over the course of Jesus' earthly ministry, the Pharisees and scribes grew increasingly opposed to Him. They envied His popularity, resented His challenges to their traditions, and hated His exposure of their hypocrisy. Undoubtedly, the Jewish leaders wondered whether Jesus had political aspirations and worried about how His increasing influence would affect their control over the people. The Pharisees and scribes allowed their petty concerns to blind them to the truth that Jesus was their Messiah.

The Sabbath regulations the religious leaders wanted Jesus to observe were part of the so-called "tradition of the elders." During the captivity of the Jews in Babylon (605–445 B.C.), there was a renewed interest in the Mosaic law. At that time, an unwritten but highly developed body of teachings and commentary about the law began to develop among the rabbis. The original intention of this tradition was good. The rabbis wanted to prevent violations of the law. They tried to enforce God's Word by setting up humanly devised regulations for all of life, like a hedge around the law of Moses.

For example, to clarify the commandment to honor the Sabbath and keep it holy (Exod. 20:8; Deut. 5:12), specific rules were developed to tell people which actions were Sabbath-honoring and which were Sabbath-breaking. With each new generation, more and more of these stipulations were devised until they were gathered in a written collection called the Mishnah two centuries after Jesus' death. Even during Jesus' life, the tradition had become so overvalued that it obscured what the law was meant to safeguard.

This fact is evident in the episode under consideration. Luke 14:2 says that a man (either another guest or a bystander) suffering from dropsy was right in front of Jesus. This ailment (also known as edema) involved the abnormal swelling of limbs, which resulted from excessive amounts of fluid accumulating in the cavities and tissues of the body, especially the legs.

By today's standards, the best-educated people in ancient times had a diminished understanding of human anatomy and physiology. Physicians had little comprehension of the nature of disease and its effects on the body. For instance, the existence and function of bacteria and viruses were unknown. Therefore, it's not surprising that people would attribute illness to sin or to a curse by an enemy. The main diagnostic tools were observation and superficial physical examination. Physicians had few aids to use in their work. In fact, the majority of people probably were born and died without ever being treated by a medical professional.

In Jesus' day, the religious leaders believed restoring someone to health on the Sabbath was work and thus violated their longstanding traditions (see 13:14). Jesus, being aware of this, asked the Pharisees and experts in the interpretation of religious law whether they thought it was legal to heal someone on the Sabbath (14:3). Would they end up defending tradition or advocate doing good? Their silence indicated they chose the first option, while Jesus approved the second one.

Accordingly, the Redeemer took hold of the man, healed him, and sent him away (vs. 4). Then Jesus turned to the religious leaders and asked which of them did not work on the Sabbath (vs. 5). After all, if they had a child (some manuscripts read "donkey") or an ox that had fallen into a well on a Sabbath day, they would immediately pull out the person or animal. In short, deeds of mercy were permissible on the Sabbath. Again, Jesus' critics chose to remain silent (vs. 6), rather than be humiliated by His words of censure (see 13:17).

II. HUMILITY AND GENEROSITY ENJOINED: LUKE 14:7-14

A. The Importance of Humility: vss. 7-11

When he noticed how the guests picked the places of honor at the table, he told them this parable: "When someone invites you to a wedding feast, do not take the place of honor, for a person more distinguished than you may have been invited. If so, the host who invited both of you will come and say to you, 'Give this man your seat.' Then, humiliated, you will have to take the least important place. But when you are invited, take the lowest place, so that when your host comes, he will say to you, 'Friend, move up to a better place.' Then you will be honored in the presence of all your fellow guests. For everyone who exalts himself will be humbled, and he who humbles himself will be exalted."

A variety of attitudes and noms formed the context of what is recorded in Luke 14:7-11. For instance, social distinctions in first-century Palestine were much different from those existing in our culture today. It was thoroughly a man's world. Jewish men ranked higher than women in all forms of public life. Even within the home, the man was master, and boys ranked higher than girls. By way of example, only boys received formal schooling. Except for those of nobility, Jewish women took no part in public life. They were to stay indoors and live in seclusion. However, where economic necessity dictated, wives helped their husbands with their work. Rules of propriety forbade a man to look at a married woman or to greet her. Also, it was disgraceful for a scholar to speak to a woman in the street. While rural women had a little more freedom, they did not speak to men they did not know.

Moreover, the Jewish social spectrum was broad and layered. The upper class consisted of the priestly and lay aristocracies and the scribes. The priestly nobility included the high priest, any retired high priests, and the chief priests who administered temple affairs. The middle class consisted of Jews of pure descent, among whom were found the ordinary priests (who served in the temple), the Levites (who served as temple musicians and servants), merchants, artisans, and farmers. The lower classes embraced all Jews who were not of pure descent as well as Jewish slaves, Jews with slight blemish (proselytes), Jews with a grave racial blemish (eunuchs), and Jews who worked in despised trades. Gentile slaves and Samaritans held the lowest rank in this social order.

The Jews in Jesus' day felt that a person's lot in life was a measure of God's approval. If a person was wealthy, it was regarded as a sign that God was on his or her side. Oppositely, if a person lived in poverty, it was assumed that person had sinned and was suffering God's judgment. Jews also measured people by their role in society. The people most respected were the religious leaders (such as the Pharisees and the priests) and the ruling classes. Affluent lay persons and the working middle class were respected, but they were a little lower in the social order and tended to look up to the Pharisees and other religious leaders.

Jesus, who was familiar with these attitudes and norms, observed how the guests intentionally chose places of honor at the table of the prominent Pharisee hosting the meal (vs. 7). In New Testament times, the seating arrangement at gatherings indicated much about the honor and respect extended to those present. At dinner feasts, the closer one sat to the host, the higher the honor. In fact, many Jewish homes had two levels, with honored guests seated on the higher floor. The seat to the right of the host was a place of special honor, with the seat to the left next in rank (see Matt. 20:20-21). Other seats were ranked in descending honor, with the seat on the lower floor and next to the door being the lowest. To be left standing, or seated on the floor, was the humblest position of all (see Jas. 2:3-4).

To emphasize the importance of humility, Jesus told a parable involving those present receiving an invitation to a wedding feast. He urged them to resist the temptation to recline in the place of honor (Luke 14:8). In that day, meals were not eaten while sitting in upright chairs at a table. Instead, people would recline on their left elbows on the cushioned floor, with their head being closest to the low table and their feet being farthest away. Jesus raised the possibility that the host might ask a guest who had presumptuously taken one of the best spots to vacate it for someone else who was more distinguished or highly respected. Social convention would then require that the person who had been publicly disgraced to move to a place of least importance (for example, whatever spot was left at the foot of the table; vs. 9).

In that culture, avoiding public embarrassment and shame was important. For that reason, Jesus emphasized the wisdom of taking the place of least importance at a banquet. Then, when the host approached, the humble individual would be asked in the presence of all the other guests to move to a more important spot—at the head of the table. As a result, the deferential guest would be honored in front of all those sharing the meal with him or her (vs. 10). The moral of Jesus parable appears in verse 11. God will humble the proud, who strive to exalt themselves before others. In contrast, God will exalt or honor the humble. This principle, which is repeated elsewhere in Scripture (Prov. 3:34; 25:6-7; Matt. 18:4; 23:12; Luke 11:43; 18:14; 20:46; Jas. 4:10; 1 Pet. 5:6), was not worldly advice on how to manipulate a situation to make oneself look good. Rather, Jesus was advocating the cultivation of genuine humility among His followers.

B. The Importance of Generosity: vss. 12-14

Then Jesus said to his host, "When you give a luncheon or dinner, do not invite your friends, your brothers or relatives, or your rich neighbors; if you do, they may invite you back and so you will be repaid. But when you give a banquet, invite the poor, the crippled, the lame, the blind, and you will be blessed. Although they cannot repay you, you will be repaid at the resurrection of the righteous."

Perhaps Jesus was one of those seated in a place of honor near the head of the table. If so, we can imagine Him turning to His host to emphasize the importance of showing unconditional generosity. For instance, when the leader of the Pharisees hosted a dinner or a banquet, Jesus urged him to break with social convention. The goal should not be to invite friends, close family members, other relatives, or rich neighbors (in other words, the powerful and well-to-do), who would feel obliged to extend an invitation in return as a repayment for the display of hospitality (Luke 14:12).

Instead, when planning an elaborate meal, the host was urged to invite people who did not have the means or the ability to reciprocate—"the poor, the crippled, the lame, the blind" (vs. 13). God would take note of and approve this display of unselfish graciousness. He would also eternally bless His followers for acting in this way. In verse 14, the Greek term rendered "blessed" conveys the idea of endowing someone with productivity or fruitfulness in service to the Lord. Although the kind and caring host would receive no recompense from his or her guests, God would reward him or her at the resurrection of the righteous (Dan. 12:2; John 5:28-29; Acts 24:15). The latter event will occur at the return of Christ, who will sit on His glorious throne and honor those who served others in His name (see Matt. 25:31-46).

God's kingdom is defined by His righteousness. The latter means that God acts justly and fairly in all His decisions and actions (Dan. 9:14). God declares as righteous those who acknowledge their sin and put their faith in Him for forgiveness and eternal life (Mark 2:17; Luke 18:14). In contrast, the unsaved have a false sense of righteousness, for they trust in their moral accomplishments to make others think they are living in accordance with God's holy standards (Matt. 23:38; Luke 18:9). Thus, it is clear that people cannot attain a right relationship with God based on their merits. Instead, God must impute, or transfer, to them an upright standing. This takes place through faith in the Son; in other words, the Father sees us as righteous because of our identification with His Son (Rom. 3:21-26; Gal. 3:6; Phil. 3:9). Those who lack God's righteousness, but hunger and thirst for it, will receive it in full (Matt. 5:6). Also, those who are burdened with the load of self-righteousness are invited to find their rest in the Savior (11:28-30).

The righteousness Jesus commanded included showing hospitality to others. Jews in the Old Testament and Christians in the New Testament were encouraged to be kind to strangers and to take care of the needs of passersby. Hospitality was shown in many ways. The most common was to wash the feet of visitors. This offered much-needed relief to those who traveled long distances over the dusty roads in Israel. It was also common to prepare meals for visitors. This often consumed a great deal of time as hostesses baked bread, cooked meat, and did whatever else was necessary to provide substantial meals for guests. Animals accompanying visitors were also looked after and were given food, water, and shelter. When guests left, they were often given supplies to help them in their travels. This could include food, water, and articles of clothing. The host might even accompany departing visitors for a short distance as they continued their journey. Showing hospitality in a practical way met the physical needs of visitors. It was also crucial for maintaining social relationships.

As far back as the law of Moses, God told His people to give alms (or gifts) to the poor and needy (Exod. 23:11; Deut. 15:7, 11). The prophets of the Old Testament saw alms as a right of the poor. Several prophets warned that when the poor were not taken care of, there was no justice in the land (Isa. 10:1-4; Jer. 5:26-29; Amos 5:12-15). This type of thought led to the idea that righteousness could be obtained through giving alms, and it could also help in obtaining forgiveness of sins. The Pharisees of Jesus' day also believed that almsgiving entitled them to divine favor in moments of trouble. By the time of Jesus' earthly ministry, righteousness and almsgiving were seen as the same thing by many Jews. Jesus encouraged giving to the poor, for He said in Matthew 6:2, "*when* you give," not "*if* you give"; but Jesus also stressed the need for the right motive. The giver should not take a pious act, such as giving to the poor, and make it a sign of spirituality for others to see.

Discussion Questions

1. What restrictions did the religious leaders in Jesus' day place on activities performed on the Sabbath?
2. Why was Jesus being closely watched by the religious leaders?
3. Why would people in Jesus' day want to be seated in places of honor at a feast?
4. Why would being asked to vacate a seat of honor at a banquet be a social embarrassment during the time of Christ?
5. Why would inviting the poor and the crippled to a banquet represent a break with what was normally done in Jesus' day?

Contemporary Application

I have several acquaintances who have shared that they would like to write a book. I try to encourage them by saying, "Work up an outline and then write one or two sample chapters. Next, start sending the entire manuscript to book publishers." Usually they are amazed to learn that they do not need to write an entire nonfiction book before they sell it to a publishing house. The typical response is, "That does not sound too hard." Later, however, when I inquire about their book project, the answer is always the same: "I have not gotten around to it yet."

What went wrong? These would-be authors were not willing to sit down and actually manuscript anything; yet, if they had made the effort to write their thoughts down, their words could have touched countless lives. This serves as an illustration of what Jesus is saying to us in terms of demonstrating through our lives the reality of our commitment to Him. It's almost as if He were saying, "You call yourselves Christians? Unless there is evidence of your faith in the way you act, I question the truth of your claim. You may believe there is a God who saves, but has He touched your behavior as well as your mind?"

Consider this. Apple trees produce apples, orange trees produce oranges, bankers invest money, and Christians are known by their good works. The good news is that, as long as we have breath, even the unfruitful can choose to change, opening themselves up to bearing the fruit of God's good works. Our hands, feet, backs, and pocketbooks are some of the means by which we can help our fellow Christians. These sorts of resources enable us to comfort those in sorrow, accompany those who are lonely, and contribute to those in dire financial straits. People can see by our actions that our faith is real and vibrant.

In order for us to respond with humility and generosity to the needs of others, we must first be aware of those needs. Sadly, too many believers are so caught up in their own feelings about their faith that they have lost the art of observation. By opening our eyes—and hearts—to the needs of others, we show that the God we serve also cares about them.

Summoned to Be a Disciple!

DEVOTIONAL READING

Psalm 139:1-6

DAILY BIBLE READINGS

Monday February 18
Psalm 139:1-6 You Know Me

Tuesday February 19
Luke 14:25-27 Conditions of Discipleship

Wednesday February 20
Luke 14:28-33 First, Count the Cost

Thursday February 21
Luke 18:18-25 The Rich Ruler's Response

Friday February 22
Luke 18:28-30 Rewards of Discipleship

Saturday February 23
Luke 5:1-11 First Disciples Called

Sunday February 24
Acts 9:1-6, 11-16 Saul Called to Be a Disciple

Scripture

Background Scripture: *Luke 14:25-33*
Scripture Lesson: *Luke 14:25-33*
Key Verse: *[Jesus said,] "And anyone who does not carry his cross and follow me cannot be my disciple."* Luke 14:27.
Scripture Lesson for Children: *Luke 14:25-33*
Key Verse for Children: *[Jesus said,] "Any of you who does not give up everything he has cannot be my disciple.* Luke 14:33.

Lesson Aim

To consider what it means to be a full-time disciple of Jesus.

Lesson Setting

Time: *A.D. 29*
Place: *Perea*

Lesson Outline

Summoned to Be a Disciple!

  I. Discipleship Mandated: Luke 14:25-27
      A. *Discipleship and Family: vss. 25-26*
      B. *Discipleship and Sacrifice: vs. 27*
 II. Discipleship Illustrated: Luke 14:28-33
      A. *Building a Tower: vss. 28-30*
      B. *A King and His Army: vss. 31-33*

Introduction for Adults

Topic: *Becoming Passionate Supporters*

Insurance agents tell us it's wise to make an inventory of everything in our home in case we suffer loss from a fire or theft. It's also a good idea to make an inventory of our lives. In so doing, we might ask ourselves what we are willing to give up and what we can't do without.

Items we'd be willing to give up may include an old radio, used exercise equipment, or outdated clothing. But when it comes to our family and friends, we know we couldn't bear the thought of parting from them. In fact, we wouldn't even listen to an offer to exchange them for something or someone else.

But as Christians, we know that even our loved ones must take second place to Jesus. Yes, it's counter-intuitive to think this way. Nevertheless, Jesus must have first place in our lives. This means we willingly give everyone and everything to Him. Doing this frees us from the sin of idolatry, for our worship is ardently centered in God, not the people and possessions of the world.

Introduction for Youth

Topic: *Summoned to Be a Disciple*

The young man faced a critical juncture in his life. He had been active in his church as a teenager and college student. Then, after he graduated from school, he was offered an attractive position at a large company. But he wondered whether he should first consider Christian ministry. He was hesitant, for he feared the risks involved and the negative opinion of others.

Then the young man heard a sermon on the meaning of discipleship that changed his thinking. He decided to follow Jesus into full-time ministry, not because the business world was wrong or evil, but because he believed the Lord's will for him lay in a different area. (Many other believers, of course, have honored God by serving Him in the business world.)

Later, after more than 50 years of devoted service to Christ, the minister thought about God's faithfulness to him. He recognized that discipleship means trusting Jesus to take care of us, no matter what.

Concepts for Children

Topic: *Becoming a Follower*

1. Large crowds were walking along with Jesus.
2. Jesus said that if we want to be His followers, we have to love Him completely.
3. Jesus wants us to give up everything that keeps us from being close to Him.
4. Jesus is looking for a commitment from us to follow Him.
5. Jesus also wants us to encourage others to become His followers.

Lesson Commentary

I. DISCIPLESHIP MANDATED: LUKE 14:25-27

A. Discipleship and Family: vss. 25-26

Large crowds were traveling with Jesus, and turning to them he said: "If anyone comes to me and does not hate his father and mother, his wife and children, his brothers and sisters—yes, even his own life—he cannot be my disciple."

No one knows for certain when Luke wrote his Gospel and Acts; however, since Acts ends with Paul still under house arrest in the capital of the empire, it seems likely that Luke penned both of his works from Rome during the apostle's confinement there (A.D. 60–62). Luke recorded Jesus' prophecy of Jerusalem's destruction in A.D. 70 (19:42-44; 21:20-24), yet there is no mention of the fulfillment of the prophecy. Also, Luke's writings make no mention of the persecution that began under Nero in A.D. 64. In any case, it's clear from the Gospel's prologue that Luke sought to give an ordered, detailed, and accurate account of the key events in Jesus' life, especially His earthly ministry, death, burial, and resurrection.

Luke portrayed Jesus as the Son of Man, the answer to the needs and hopes of the human race, and the One who came to seek and save the lost. Luke's Gospel also has a universal outlook. For example, Luke traces Christ's genealogy back to Adam, the father of the human race. Moreover, Luke is very socially minded. For instance, Jesus' citation of Isaiah 61:1-2 (Luke 4:18-19) talks about His ministry to those who are poor, blind, and oppressed. Luke's Gospel is concerned with the theological importance of Jesus' first advent. In fact, this event is portrayed as being characterized by joy.

Luke's Gospel places a significant emphasis on the ministry of the Spirit, especially His activity in the ministry of the Lord Jesus. Also, Luke's Gospel emphasizes the importance of prayer, especially in the life of the Messiah. Luke's own Gentile roots and his Gentile audience explain why his Gospel has a universal perspective. It speaks to the condition of the entire human race, not just to Jews. Luke either omitted Jewish phrases and practices found in the other Gospels or explained them carefully, making his Gospel helpful and readable for those less familiar with Jewish ways.

This broad, multicultural perspective is evident in Luke 14:25. An increase in Jesus' popularity resulted in large crowds enthusiastically following Him as He made His way toward to Jerusalem, where He faced death on a cross (see 13:22). The implication is that what He said concerning the cost of discipleship was not just directed to the Twelve, but also to the throngs gathered around Him. Many of His disciples had given up everything to follow Him; but Jesus knew that not all those present were true believers. He was headed for Jerusalem and a cross; however, many were tagging along because they thought He was headed for a throne.

Jesus, after turning around to face the large crowds, called them (and us) to a radical consideration of what it means to follow Him. He declared that coming to Him meant hating one's own parents, spouse and children, and siblings. It even meant hating one's own "life" (literally, "soul"; 14:26). It is unlikely that the Savior was advocating literal hatred of one's family, for this would violate the Ten Commandments (compare also a similar saying of Jesus in Matt. 10:37-38). One possibility is that Jesus was speaking rhetorically by using a customary teaching method called hyperbole. This refers to intentional exaggeration to make a point. Jesus frequently spoke in this manner, perhaps to hold His listeners' attention, to touch their imagination, or to show a bit of humor.

Another possibility is that Jesus was speaking comparatively, in the sense of relative value. He was saying that the kingdom of God should take precedence over everything, including one's family. In the New Testament, the contrast between love and hate can also refer to value placed on things by comparison. For example, if we love our lives too much, we will not think of things other than our lives. In essence, that is hating the kingdom of God, because if our minds are on ourselves, they cannot be on God. Conversely, if we have our minds set on Jesus and the divine kingdom, we will not have as much time for selfish pursuits. Thus, in a sense, we will be "hating" our lives here on earth in anticipation of life with the Savior for eternity in heaven.

B. Discipleship and Sacrifice: vs. 27

"And anyone who does not carry his cross and follow me cannot be my disciple."

The Lord Jesus declared that those who were not willing to carry their own cross and follow Him could not be His disciples (Luke 14:27). In 9:23, Jesus stated that this had to be done on a daily basis. In both passages, Jesus was speaking metaphorically against the backdrop of being rejected. Put differently, even in the face of denunciation, our allegiance remains with Christ. In a sense, discipleship involves a figurative form of death that is similar to crucifixion.

Jesus did not need to describe the details of crucifixion to His audience. No doubt most of them had seen several, since the Romans had made this mode of death common in Jesus' day. Crucifixion as a means of torture and execution was invented in the East and adopted by the Romans, who used it for slaves and lower-class persons. A victim of Roman crucifixion typically had to carry the crossbeam of his cross to the place of execution. He or someone else would also often carry a tablet citing the charge against him, which was then sometimes nailed to the top of the cross.

At the execution site, the crossbeam would be attached perpendicularly to a longer beam (the stake), at or near the top of it, while it was lying on the ground. The condemned was then nailed to the cross with spikes driven through the wrists and feet. The torso would face forward, but the feet would sometimes be nailed sideways, thus twisting the waist in an unnatural position. A rope was often tied around the victim's chest, knotted between the shoulders, and then tied to the beam behind the body. This was done to prevent the body from falling forward, especially as the muscles weakened. Finally, the cross would be lifted and dropped into a hole.

Death was excruciatingly slow and bloody, with the naked victim exposed to the withering heat of the sun by day and temperatures at night dropping between 40 and 50 degrees Fahrenheit for a spring crucifixion in Palestine. Victims sometimes lasted for two or three days, finally succumbing to death due to poor blood circulation and heart failure. If the crucifiers wanted to make the victim last longer, they would have first outfitted the cross with a block of wood as a seat or a footrest, which would give the victim support and improve circulation. If the crucifiers wanted to shorten the victim's life, they would break his legs with a club to remove his ability to support himself with his legs.

Jesus frequently called on His disciples or others in the crowds to follow Him wholeheartedly (Mark 10:21); but what Jesus meant by this and what others thought He meant are two different things. For instance, after Jesus finished talking with the rich ruler, Peter said he had already done the very things that Jesus required. Peter said he had given up everything and was already following Jesus (vs. 28). Later, when Jesus asked James and John whether they could drink the bitter cup of sorrow the Messiah was about to drink, or undergo the baptism of suffering He was about to experience (vs. 38), they said they were able (vs. 39), not understanding what they were asserting.

Being a true follower of the Savior is demanding. Jesus' disciples agree not only to obey Him in all He has said, but also to order their priorities for His sake. They seek to serve Him as a slave would serve a master. The followers of Christ want to be like Him in their thoughts and actions. Furthermore, their desire is to abide in His words and heed His commands. The disciples of Jesus do not merely perpetuate His teachings, transmit His sayings, or imitate His life. They bear witness in their own words and actions that their Lord dwells within them. Thus Jesus is much more than a mere teacher or guru to His followers; for them He is the indwelling presence of God.

Bible students have long considered what it means to deny oneself in the manner referred to by Jesus. It might mean giving up control of our lives to the Lord. It might mean rooting out aspects of our sinful nature that are slowing down our spiritual growth. It might mean being willing to give up our own comfort to serve others. In all likelihood, it means all these things. Every day, Christians must be willing to follow the Lord's will, even if it leads to pain and death. We must acknowledge our helpless state, much like a condemned person, in order to receive the fullness of Christ.

In Luke 9:24-25, we have one of the many paradoxes that arise in Jesus' teaching. Here He said that those who save their life will lose it, while those who lose their life will save it. The cross is not an attractive object, so the natural reaction would be to recoil from it and avoid it; but Jesus said that to seek life by avoiding the cross would in the long run result in spiritual death. Eternal life is of much more value than success, prosperity, or even a long earthly existence. The one who wins without Jesus still loses. The shame of the cross might cause some people to avoid the Redeemer and not want to be identified with Him (vs. 26); but those who are ashamed of Jesus now will have to face His rejection when He comes in glory.

II. DISCIPLESHIP ILLUSTRATED: LUKE 14:28-33

A. Building a Tower: vss. 28-30

"Suppose one of you wants to build a tower. Will he not first sit down and estimate the cost to see if he has enough money to complete it? For if he lays the foundation and is not able to finish it, everyone who sees it will ridicule him, saying, 'This fellow began to build and was not able to finish.'"

Jesus used two illustrations (or parables) to explain what He had previously said. In the first one, Jesus mentioned the issue of undertaking a building project, in this case the construction of a watchtower (perhaps to guard a vineyard) or a building on a farm. Wise landowners first computed the cost to ensure there were sufficient funds to complete the job (Luke 14:28). Otherwise, once the foundation was laid, there would not be enough money to finish the structure (vs. 29). Then, all who saw this embarrassing spectacle would make the shortsighted owners the object of joking and ridicule (vs. 30).

It's true that salvation is free; but Jesus told people first to count the cost of serving Him before becoming His disciple. Just as a person planning a building project should first make sure he or she can complete the job, Jesus told His followers that they must have a full appreciation of what is demanded of them to be His disciples. One who began to follow Jesus and turned back would not be fit for the kingdom of heaven and would also be ridiculed by the world. Moreover, one must remain distinct from the world, and the world's wrong ways of thinking, in order to be recognized as a member of God's kingdom.

B. A King and His Army: vss. 31-33

"Or suppose a king is about to go to war against another king. Will he not first sit down and consider whether he is able with ten thousand men to oppose the one coming against him with twenty thousand? If he is not able, he will send a delegation while the other is still a long way off and will ask for terms of peace. In the same way, any of you who does not give up everything he has cannot be my disciple."

Jesus' second illustration involved one monarch confronting another monarch, whether in a single battle or a drawn-out engagement. Before going to war, though, the ambitious king was wise to determine beforehand whether his small army of 10,000 soldiers would be able to prevail against a larger fighting force of 20,000 combatants (Luke 14:31). If the monarch with the smaller army concluded that he could not succeed in such a military engagement, he was prudent to dispatch a representative, while his antagonist was still a long way off, and ask for terms of peace (vs. 32).

With respect to following Jesus, He wanted potential disciples to consider what they were doing. On the one hand, there is sacrifice involved in committing oneself to Him. On the other hand, to refuse God (by way of example, the most powerful King) placed one's life in eternal jeopardy. In a sense, Jesus was warning the crowds to opt for peace with the Father through faith in the Son. Doing so included a willingness to give up everything for cause of Christ (vs. 33). The Greek verb translated "give up" literally means "to say farewell to" or "to take leave of" of one's possessions. The idea is that we must not rely on our earthly belongings or who we are, but instead rely on Christ alone both for salvation and for our direction as His disciples.

Jesus was willing to give up everything in order provide eternal life for us. According to Mark 10:45, by means of His sacrifice on the cross, Jesus paid the price (the "ransom") to free humanity (the "many," as opposed to the single life that is being sacrificed) from the bondage of sin and death. The "ransom" He offered is not said to be paid to anyone, but the Greek verb it translates (*lytron*) pictures the price given to release slaves. The irony of prominence in Jesus' kingdom is that the greatest are the servants of others, and Jesus Himself is the ultimate example of that principle in His substitutionary death.

The key to this week's lesson is radical commitment to the kingdom of God. Jesus called the first disciples to complete and absolute surrender of their lives to His lordship. Still today, if we hold on to things in our lives, and even our own lives, we cannot totally abandon ourselves to Jesus as His disciples. In Jesus' day, many people followed Him because He was a dynamic teacher and because He performed amazing miracles. Today, people may belong to church because of a dynamic pastor, or because there are other things they can get out of that congregation. Just as church membership today does not make one a Christian, just being part of the crowd that followed Jesus did not make anyone a disciple. Jesus wants us to understand that to fully experience Him, we must recognize all things are under His control (even good things like family) in order to be totally filled with Him.

Giving up everything to follow Jesus may or may not mean giving up our literal physical possessions. In our modern culture, often we become enslaved to our possessions because we think we must have them. Consequently, they occupy more and more of our time and energy; but Jesus told the people of His day that they must give up all of those things in order to be His disciples. The real question, then, is one of priority and focus. There is nothing inherently wrong with having possessions; but the problem comes when the possessions are the main focus of our lives. Jesus declared that wherever our treasure is, there our heart and thoughts will also be (Matt. 6:21). Thus, if our treasure—what we value in life—is the kingdom of God, then naturally our affections and focus will be there. The problem comes when we see our worldly possessions as our treasure and not the kingdom of God.

Discussion Questions

1. Why was it necessary for Jesus' followers to "hate" (Luke 14:26) others in order to be His disciples?
2. What did Jesus mean by carrying one's cross as part of the process of being His disciple?
3. What was the point of Jesus' illustration about building a tower?
4. What was the point of Jesus' illustration about one king going to war against another?
5. In what sense must Jesus' disciples give up everything they have to be His followers?

Contemporary Application

Some people think that discipleship is for super zealous Christians, not ordinary ones. This incorrect way of thinking has led to a wishy-washy form of Christianity in the lives of countless believers. Rather than serve Him wholeheartedly, they are superficial in their devotion. They fail to realize that following Jesus is an all or nothing proposition.

Jesus never distinguished between disciples and ordinary Christians. To Him, true believers are also His disciples. They cast everything on Jesus and trust in Him for their salvation. They willingly forsake their old life of sin to experience new life in Him. They have counted the cost and determined that serving Jesus is eternally more valuable than striving for fame, wealth, and power.

These disciples are not disappointed with their decision, for they have found new life, hope, and purpose in the Son. They are freed from sin and its consequences. They have the hope of eternal salvation, and their purpose in life is to worship and glorify God. Those who choose to follow Jesus aren't sidetracked by earthly comforts, confused priorities, or divided loyalties. Instead, they are totally submitted, steadfast in their commitment, and absolute in their devotion to the Savior.

The Ark Comes to Jerusalem

Scripture

Background Scripture: *1 Chronicles 15:1-28*
Scripture Lesson: *1 Chronicles 15:1-3, 14-16, 25-28*
Key Verse: *David assembled all Israel in Jerusalem to bring up the ark of the LORD to the place he had prepared for it.* 1 Chronicles 15:3.
Scripture Lesson for Children: *1 Chronicles 15:1-3, 14-16, 25-28*
Key Verse for Children: *All Israel brought up the ark of the covenant of the LORD with shouts.* 1 Chronicles 15:28.

Lesson Aim

To emphasize that God is present to help us be successful in our service for Him.

Lesson Setting

Time: *997 B.C.*
Place: *Jerusalem*

Lesson Outline

The Ark Comes to Jerusalem
I. Preparing to Move the Ark:
 1 Chronicles 15:1-3, 14-16
 A. *Constructing Buildings in Jerusalem: vs. 1*
 B. *Selecting Levites for Their Special Task: vs. 2*
 C. *Assembling All Israel in Jerusalem: vs. 3*
 D. *Consecrating the Priests and Levites: vss. 14-15*
 E. *Appointing the Levites as Musicians: vs. 16*
II. Successfully Moving the Ark:
 1 Chronicles 15:25-28
 A. *Going to the House of Obed-Edom: vs. 25*
 B. *Offering Sacrifices: vs. 26*
 C. *Being Properly Attired: vs. 27*
 D. *Transporting the Ark with Great Fanfare: vs. 28*

Introduction for Adults

Topic: *A Symbol of God's Presence*

Little Ammar, a 9-year-old with terminal leukemia, couldn't smile. His facial nerves were damaged to the point where the muscles just wouldn't work. He was a Muslim child who had been receiving treatment in a Baghdad hospital for four months. One special day, Ammar got the opportunity to hear about Jesus and His love when he received his very own copy of the *Arabic Picture Bible*.

On this same visit to the Children's Teaching Hospital, the team met the administrator who welcomed them, received his own copy of the *Picture Bible*, and allowed them to distribute *Picture Bibles* to the children in the different wards. When they started giving the books out, everyone wanted a copy. They only had 80 copies that day. The next day they took 120 more. Suddenly, all the physicians, nurses, and staff said they wanted their own copy of the *Picture Bible* for their children. The literature became a tangible symbol of God's loving presence.

Introduction for Youth

Topic: *God Is with Us!*

A little boy was afraid to sleep alone. He did not like the darkness, and he could not stand the idea that he was in his bed, his room, all by himself. His mother tried to console him by reminding him that he was not alone and that God would be with him to protect him at all times. The little boy thought about this truth for a while. Then he said, "But I need somebody in here who has skin on him!"

God knew that we would be that way and that we could never conceive the fact He is Spirit (John 4:24). The Lord also knew that we could never feel secure with the reality of His presence until His Son appeared in time "with skin on him" (in a manner of speaking).

Concepts for Children

Topic: *King David Leads Worship*

1. King David led the nation of Israel in worshiping God.
2. King David prepared a special place for the sacred chest in Jerusalem.
3. King David followed God's instructions in completing the task of returning the sacred chest.
4. The people worshiped God as the sacred chest was brought back into the city.
5. God is pleased when we join other believers to worship Him.

Lesson Commentary

I. PREPARING TO MOVE THE ARK: 1 CHRONICLES 15:1-3, 14-16

A. Constructing Buildings in Jerusalem: vs. 1

After David had constructed buildings for himself in the City of David, he prepared a place for the ark of God and pitched a tent for it.

The events of 1 Chronicles 15 concern King David transporting the ark of the covenant to Jerusalem. The time was about 997 B.C., which was 13 years after he began his reign as king at Hebron in 1010 B.C. (It wasn't until 1003 B.C. that his reign was acknowledged throughout all Israel.) During that initial period, David conquered Jerusalem from the Jebusites, made the fortress complex his home, and renamed it the City of David. He also fortified the city from the supporting terraces (or the Millo) to the surrounding walls and had a palace built for himself. Meanwhile, Joab, the military commander of David's army, supervised the rebuilding of the rest of Jerusalem (11:4-8; 15:1).

At some point, David sensed it was time to relocate the ark of the covenant from Kiriath Jearim, which was a fortified city nine miles north of Jerusalem. After the Philistines returned the ark, it remained in the house of Abinadab at Kiriath Jearim for about two decades (see 1 Sam. 6:19—7:2). Throughout the reign of Saul, David's predecessor, the sacred chest was ignored (1 Chron. 13:1-3). This was regrettable, for the ark was originally intended to be the place where the sovereign Lord met with Israel and provided the people with guidance (see Exod. 25:22). David's proposal to bring the sacred chest to Jerusalem met with the approval of all the Israelites (1 Chron. 13:4).

The plan to move the ark involved bringing it outside Abinadab's house and placing it on a new ox cart. While Abinadab's sons, Uzzah and Ahio, guided the cart, David and a crowd of people danced and sang praises to the Lord; but when the procession came to the threshing floor of Kidon, the oxen stumbled. To prevent the chest from falling, Uzzah reached out and took hold of it; however, the Lord was very angry at Uzzah for doing this and struck him dead right there beside the ark (1 Chron. 13:5-10; see 1 Sam. 6:1-7).

Despite David's anger over what God had done (1 Chron. 13:11), the king bore responsibility for the mishap. After all, he violated the instructions recorded in the Mosaic law. To be specific, Levites were supposed to carry the ark on poles inserted through rings permanently attached to the side of the chest (Exod 25:12-14). Also, none of the sacred objects was to be touched, with death being the penalty for violating the injunction (Num. 4:5-6, 15). In this regard, Uzzah showed irreverence for God's holy presence by indiscriminately grabbing the ark. Because of this incident, David decided to temporarily store the ark in the house of a Levite named Obed-Edom, where it remained for three months (1 Chron. 13:13-14; see 15:18, 21, 24). The king also set up a special tent to shelter the ark (15:1).

217

Concerning the sacred chest, it was rectangular in shape and made out of acacia (a dark, hard, and durable desert wood). It was entirely covered with pure gold (in other words, with all of its alloys and impurities carefully removed; Exod. 25:10-15). The various items deposited within the ark were the two stone tablets on which were inscribed the Ten Commandments (vss. 16, 21), Aaron's rod which budded (Num. 17:10), and a golden jar holding the wilderness manna (Exod. 16:32; Heb. 9:4). The various items placed on top of the ark included a pure gold lid (namely, the mercy seat, atonement cover, or place where divine satisfaction was made; Exod. 25:17; Lev. 16:15-17) and a pair of winged lions with human heads called cherubim (that is, guardians and protectors of God's kingly presence; Exod. 25:18-20; see Gen. 3:24; 1 Sam. 4:4; 2 Sam. 6:2; 2 Kings 19:15; Ps. 99:1).

B. Selecting Levites for Their Special Task: vs. 2

Then David said, "No one but the Levites may carry the ark of God, because the LORD chose them to carry the ark of the LORD and to minister before him forever."

As a result of the previously unsuccessful attempt to move the ark, David decided to do exactly what the Mosaic law commanded. In particular, only Levites were allowed to carry the sacred chest, for the Lord had chosen them to do this and to minister in His presence perpetually (1 Chron. 15:2). The Levites received their priestly status centuries earlier when they distinguished themselves as loyal followers of Moses during the episode involving the golden calf. This incident occurred not long after the Israelites had left Egypt (Exod. 32:28-29; Deut. 33:8-11).

The Lord set apart the Levites to maintain and transport the tent of meeting, the altar, and other sacred vessels (Num. 3—4). They also served as special assistants to the Aaronic priests, who officiated in worship rituals and offered sacrifices on the altar (Num. 1:50; 3:6, 8; 16:9; 1 Chron. 23:28; Ezra 3:8-9). Both groups ministered in a cooperative fashion to represent the entire covenant community before the Lord. When the Israelites conquered and settled Canaan, the Levites did not receive any permanent land of their own. Instead, 48 towns were set aside for the Levites (Num. 35:1-8; Josh. 21:4, 13-19).

Although Moses had taken a census of all the male Levites who were a month old or more (Num. 3:15, 39), the actual number of those who were to do the work at the tabernacle was smaller. Only those between the ages of 25 and 50 were eligible for service. Once the Israelites had become established in the promised land and had set up the tabernacle in Jerusalem, King David expanded the Levites' work force by changing the age requirements for service. All males more than 20 years old became eligible to serve in the tabernacle (1 Chron. 23:24-27). David explained that the reason for enlarging the Levites' work force was because the Levites no longer had to carry the tabernacle and its articles. Seemingly, their labor was less strenuous in Jerusalem than was the labor of their ancestors in the wilderness.

C. Assembling All Israel in Jerusalem: vs. 3

David assembled all Israel in Jerusalem to bring up the ark of the LORD to the place he had prepared for it.

The relocation of the ark of the covenant to Jerusalem was a special occasion. Undoubtedly, time and attention were invested in choosing the site where the chest would be placed. The spot also needed to be prepared for the ark, the vessels and furniture connected with it, and the tent sheltering it. To commemorate this historic event, David summoned all the Israelites to assemble at Jerusalem (1 Chron. 15:3). The king also sent for Aaron's descendants and for the Levites (vss. 4-10).

D. Consecrating the Priests and Levites: vss. 14-15

So the priests and Levites consecrated themselves in order to bring up the ark of the LORD, the God of Israel. And the Levites carried the ark of God with the poles on their shoulders, as Moses had commanded in accordance with the word of the LORD.

A total of 862 priests from the tribe of Levi assembled at Jerusalem. The three main divisions were present (descendants of Kohath, Merari, and Gershon), along with three distinct subgroups among the Kohathites (descendants of Elizaphan, Hebron, and Uzziel; 1 Chron. 15:4-10). David summoned six of their leaders (Uriel, Asaiah, Joel, Shemaiah, Eliel, and Amminadab) and the two Aaronic high priests who served during his reign (Zadok and Abiathar). Then, he directed these leaders of the clans of the Levites to consecrate themselves in preparation for transporting the ark. By this David meant they had to go through a set procedure to make them ceremonially clean and acceptable to the Lord (vss. 11-12). Most likely, this included washing their body and garments and abstaining from sexual relations (Exod. 19:14-15).

In Bible times, certain activities, practices, and physical conditions were believed to place the worshiper in an undesirable status before God (Lev. 5; 11; 12:2-5; 13; 14:25; 15; 18:24-30; 21:17-21). This condition was primarily ceremonial or ritualistic in character. The desire was to be fully restored in one's status before God and to live in harmony with the customs and traditions established in His law (see Ps. 51:7; Ezek. 36:25; Heb. 1:3; 9:13-14, 23; 1 John 1:7). Any type of departure from the norms instituted by the Lord could create an undesirable condition. In everything they did, whether individually and as a covenant community, God's people were to reflect His moral purity and separation from sin (Lev. 10:10; 11:44-45).

David said that after purifying themselves, the Levitical priests would be allowed to carry the sacred chest to the spot the king had designated in Jerusalem (1 Chron. 15:12). The king had learned from his previous attempt to move the ark how important it was to do exactly what the Mosaic law commanded. David noted that he and the other civil and religious leaders failed to ask God about the proper way to relocate the chest. As a result, the anger of the Lord broke out against the procession (vs. 13). The Aaronic priests and Levites fully complied with David's injunction to make themselves ceremonially clean (vs. 14). The descendants of Levi also did exactly what the law said by carrying the ark on poles that rested on their shoulders (vs. 15).

E. Appointing the Levites as Musicians: vs. 16

David told the leaders of the Levites to appoint their brothers as singers to sing joyful songs, accompanied by musical instruments: lyres, harps and cymbals.

In ancient times, people used music to commemorate major events in the life of their community and to express their joy on such special occasions. For the Israelites, music was also used to worship the Lord in formal, prescribed ways. This typically involved a choir of singers, choral music, and a full array of instruments, such as lyres, harps, and cymbals. (Like trumpets, the cymbals were not used for musical accompaniment, but to announce the beginning of a song.) Undoubtedly, as the occasion permitted, there was also plenty of spontaneity, in which participants sang and danced with reverence and exuberance to the Lord. This lively medley of elements was evident in David's appointment of Levites to serve as musicians during the transport of the ark to Jerusalem (1 Chron. 15:16). Verses 17-24 list the names of those who ministered on that occasion.

II. SUCCESSFULLY MOVING THE ARK: 1 CHRONICLES 15:25-28

A. Going to the House of Obed-Edom: vs. 25

So David and the elders of Israel and the commanders of units of a thousand went to bring up the ark of the covenant of the LORD from the house of Obed-Edom, with rejoicing.

Eventually, all the preparations were finalized for the momentous event. A procession from Jerusalem traveled to the house of Obed-Edom to move the ark of the covenant. Those in the entourage included David, the leaders (or elders) of Israel, and the army officers who commanded units of a thousand troops (1 Chron. 15:25). Unlike the previous occasion, the king was far more cautious the second time around. Out of reverence for the Lord, David wanted to make sure that nothing went wrong.

B. Offering Sacrifices: vs. 26

Because God had helped the Levites who were carrying the ark of the covenant of the LORD, seven bulls and seven rams were sacrificed.

The Lord gave the Levitical priests the strength they needed to carry the ark of the covenant (1 Chron. 15:26). After taking the first six steps, they stopped and waited until David sacrificed a bull and a fattened calf (2 Sam. 6:13). In this way, the king expressed thanks to God that the procession had started. He was also depending on God to bless the journey to Jerusalem with success. By the end of the journey, seven bulls and seven rams were sacrificed (1 Chron. 15:26). In ancient Israel, the presentation of burnt, grain, and peace offerings provided the people with a formal means of approaching the Lord in the place where He manifested His presence (namely, the tabernacle). Also, the sacrifices (both animal and vegetable) helped the covenant community to preserve their ritual holiness and purity before the Lord.

C. Being Properly Attired: vs. 27

Now David was clothed in a robe of fine linen, as were all the Levites who were carrying the ark, and as were the singers, and Kenaniah, who was in charge of the singing of the choirs. David also wore a linen ephod.

David, the Levites who carried the ark, the singers, and Kenaniah (the music director) were all wearing robes made out of fine linen. The king also wore a linen ephod (1 Chron. 15:27). Some think David's garment extended from the waist to the knee (like a skirt). More likely, it resembled a closely fitting sleeveless vest usually worn by the high priest as part of his ceremonial robes.

Concerning the latter, it was made of gold, blue, purple, and scarlet, and finely twisted linen (Exod. 28:6). The fabric of the ephod was the same as the curtains and veil of the tabernacle. This stressed the intimate connection between the high priest and the sanctuary. Its front and back were fastened to the priest's body by two shoulder pieces and a woven waistband (vss. 7-8, 32). Two clear, bright, multicolored stones were placed on the shoulder pieces of this vest. These onyx stones had the names of the 12 tribes of Israel engraved on them (vss. 9-13). This stressed the fact that the high priest represented all Israel when he ministered in the tabernacle. Pure gold chains attached a breastpiece to the ephod. The breastpiece had 12 precious stones in four rows. A blue robe reaching to the feet of the priest was worn underneath it. The ephod was part of the attire used to seek the Lord's will, especially in times of crisis (Exod. 28:30; 1 Sam. 23:9; 30:7).

D. Transporting the Ark with Great Fanfare: vs. 28

So all Israel brought up the ark of the covenant of the LORD with shouts, with the sounding of rams' horns and trumpets, and of cymbals, and the playing of lyres and harps.

David, while wearing the linen ephod, was dancing with all his strength before the Lord (2 Sam. 6:14). Meanwhile, the procession accompanying the transport of the ark celebrated the historic event by shouting, blowing rams' horns and trumpets, sounding cymbals, and playing stringed instruments such as lyres and harps (1 Chron. 15:28). When the entourage reached Jerusalem, the ark was put in its place in the middle of the special tent that David had pitched for it.

Next, the king worshiped the Lord by sacrificing burnt offerings and fellowship (or peace offerings) in His presence. Once David was finished, he pronounced a blessing over the people in the name of the sovereign Lord. The king then handed to all the men and women in the crowd a portion of bread, a cake of dates (or a portion of meat), and a cake of raisins. After that, all the people returned to their homes (1 Chron. 16:1-3; see 2 Sam. 6:17-19).

Discussion Questions

1. Why did David feel the need to prepare a place in Jerusalem for the ark of the Lord?
2. Why did David stress that only the Levites could carry the ark of the covenant?
3. Why did the priests and Levites consecrate themselves?
4. What purpose did it serve for the musicians to make a joyful sound while the ark was being transported?
5. What was the significance of the linen ephod that David wore?

Contemporary Application

The consistent teaching of Scripture is that all people have sinned and fallen short of God's glory (Rom. 3:23). The Bible also reveals that if we confess our sins, the Lord is faithful and just to forgive our sins and cleanse us from all unrighteousness (1 John 2:9). The people of God in the Old Testament (including David) were aware of these truths. For instance, during the king's first attempt to move the ark of the covenant to Jerusalem, he did not follow the strictures recorded in the law of Moses; and this sin led to the death of at least one Israelite. It also prevented David from fulfilling his plans for three months.

Though the king was troubled by this turn of events, he came to realize he had transgressed against the Lord. Undoubtedly, it was God's forgiveness and grace that gave David the courage to try again to relocate the sacred chest to Jerusalem. This time, however, he relied on the Lord to make the undertaking a success. The king also made sure that he and all who were with him did everything in accordance with God's Word. Even the priests and Levites sought to minister before the Lord in holiness and purity. God honored their devotion by helping them carry the ark without any mishaps.

We who have trusted in Christ for salvation have the assurance of Scripture that God is always with us and will never forsake us (Heb. 13:5). The Bible teaches us that the Lord is our helper, even in the most difficult of circumstances (vs. 6). Indeed, He has given us His Spirit as a deposit guaranteeing our eternal inheritance in the Savior (Eph. 1:14). Moreover, the indwelling Spirit helps us in our weakness and intercedes for us through wordless groans (Rom. 8:26). With the Lord ever present in our lives and eternally on our side, there is nothing that can prevent us from succeeding in all that He calls us to do (vs. 31). Thus, we can give ourselves fully to the work of the Lord, for we know that our Christian service is not in vain (1 Cor. 15:58).

God's Covenant with David

Scripture

Background Scripture: *1 Chronicles 17:1-27*

Scripture Lesson: *1 Chronicles 17:1, 3-4, 6-15*

Key Verses: *"I took you from the pasture and from following the flock, to be ruler over my people Israel. I have been with you wherever you have gone, and I have cut off all your enemies from before you. Now I will make your name like the names of the greatest men of the earth."* 1 Chronicles 17:7-8.

Scripture Lesson for Children: *1 Chronicles 17:1, 3-4, 6-15*

Key Verse for Children: *"O LORD, you are God! You have promised these good things to your servant."* 1 Chronicles 17:26.

Lesson Aim

To trust and obey the Lord, no matter how He answers our prayers.

Lesson Setting

Time: *995 B.C.*

Place: *Jerusalem*

Lesson Outline

God's Covenant with David

   I. David's Desire: 1 Chronicles 17:1, 3-4, 6
       A. *David's Concern: vs. 1*
       B. *Nathan's Encouragement: vs. 2*
       C. *God's Restriction: vss. 3-4, 6*
  II. God's Promise: 1 Chronicles 17:7-15
       A. *David's Rise to Power: vss. 7-8*
       B. *Israel's Homeland in Canaan: vss. 9-10a*
       C. *David's Perpetual Dynasty: vss. 10b-12*
       D. *God's Abiding Presence: vss. 13-14*
       E. *Nathan's Faithful Reporting: vs. 15*

Introduction for Adults

Topic: *Covenanting*

Promises are the great stuff of life. We make promises when we get married. Our children exact promises from us. And we obtain promises from our employers. God's covenantal promises to David were so astonishing that we find it hard to relate to them. God pledged to give him a great name, a homeland for the Israelites, and an enduring dynasty. Perhaps these promises sound too much like the pledges that politicians make during their election campaigns.

Promises are only as good as the one who makes them. (Nothing is worse than a broken pledge!) In David's case, he believed what God promised to him. David, in turn, has left an enduring legacy to encourage us in our faith. We, too, can be refreshed and encouraged by God's covenantal promises to us. We live in hope because we believe in the total reliability and trustworthiness of God. And like David, the Lord can enable us to leave a legacy of faith to those who follow after us.

Introduction for Youth

Topic: *God's Special Promise*

We love to ask children, "What do you want to be when you grow up?" Later on, when they finish high school, we may ask, "What are your career goals?" That's when youth begin to wrestle with their dreams. Sometimes it takes years for them to figure out what they want to do with their life.

Since we build our lives on God's will and His special promises to us in Scripture, it's good to remind ourselves what He told David: "I took you from the pasture and from following the flock to be ruler over my people Israel" (2 Sam. 7:8). No high school or college guidance counselor could ever have predicted that career for David.

While it's wise to get all the counseling we can, in the end we must trust God to help us make something out of our lives. After all, we are His people forever and have the assurance of His covenantal promises to us. Thus, we can be sure that God's desire for our success as Christians far outweighs our own. Obedience to Him right now will lead to greater opportunities to serve Him in the future.

Concepts for Children

Topic: *David Accepts God's Covenant*

1. God used used Nathan, His messenger, to tell something special to King David.
2. David wanted to build a temple, or house of worship, to store the sacred chest.
3. God said that David's son, Solomon, would build the temple.
4. God promised to give David a long-lasting kingdom.
5. David is an example of someone who accepted God's will and worshiped Him.

Lesson Commentary

I. DAVID'S DESIRE: 1 CHRONICLES 17:1, 3-4, 6

A. David's Concern: vs. 1

After David was settled in his palace, he said to Nathan the prophet, "Here I am, living in a palace of cedar, while the ark of the covenant of the Lord is under a tent."

After David became king over Israel, he built a palace for himself and moved into it (1 Chron. 17:1). This was possible because the Lord had brought peace to the land (2 Sam. 7:1). Inasmuch as Israel's king had relief from all his enemies, he had the opportunity to step back and think about what had happened to him up to this point in his life and career. He openly shared his concerns with a trusted advisor in the royal court, Nathan the prophet. David lamented the fact that while he lived in a palace made from cedar, the ark of the Lord's covenant sat in the middle of a tent (1 Chron. 17:1; see 2 Sam. 7:2). The king felt as if this large disparity was unacceptable and had to be remedied. The logical solution was for him to oversee the building of a temple in Jerusalem.

B. Nathan's Encouragement: vs. 2

Nathan replied to David, "Whatever you have in mind, do it, for God is with you."

Prophets were people who communicated messages from God, often in times of crisis that involved divine judgment or deliverance (or both). The Lord commissioned these individuals (both men and women) to be His spokespersons. In turn, they conveyed His declarations in written, dramatic, or oral form. The messages of the prophets could contain elements of proclamation (namely, forthtelling) or prediction (namely, foretelling). The importance of those who served in this capacity is evidenced by the fact that the word "prophet" occurs over 300 times in the Old Testament and almost 125 times in the New Testament.

An examination of Deuteronomy 13:1-5 and 18:15-22 surfaces at least five indicators by which true prophets of God could be confirmed. They had to be Israelites, speak in the name of the Lord, foretell both the near as well as the distant future, announce signs and wonders, and make declarations that agreed with previous revelations from God. It would be incorrect to assume that they were zombie-like automatons who mechanically mouthed God's words. Instead, when the Lord spoke through His prophets in various portions and in a number of ways (for example, through visions, dreams, and riddles; Heb. 1:1-2), He did so without excluding their human intelligence, individuality, literary style, personal feelings, or any other human factor.

We can infer from 1 Chronicles 17:1 that Nathan was a true prophet of the Lord whose ministry encompassed the reigns of David and Solomon. Scripture highlights three particular episodes involving Nathan: his declaration of the Lord's

promise to David of a perpetual dynasty (2 Sam. 7; 1 Chron. 17); his announcement that God would punish David for his sin involving Bathesheba and Uriah the
Hittite (2 Sam. 12); and David's intervention on behalf of Solomon in his efforts to
succeed his father as king (1 Kings 1). Nathan also penned historical accounts
about the reigns of David and Solomon (1 Chron. 29:29; 2 Chron. 9:29). Moreover,
Nathan was pivotal in establishing the playing of music in the worship liturgy used
at the temple (2 Chron. 29:25).

As a prophet in David's royal court, Nathan had relatively free access to the king.
Even so, Nathan was not a proverbial "rubber stamp" for David. Indeed, Nathan
did not hesitate to speak with God-given authority and courage, especially at critical junctures in the life of the monarchy. Though a true spokesperson for the Lord,
Nathan was far from perfect and could make mistakes. For instance, when David
voiced his desire to build a temple to house the ark of the covenant (1 Chron.
17:1), Nathan misspoke when he encouraged the king to do whatever he had in
mind. While it's true that the Lord was with David, it was not God's will for him to
build a shrine for the ark (vs. 2; see 2 Sam. 7:3).

C. God's Restriction: vss. 3-4, 6

*That night the word of God came to Nathan, saying: "Go and tell my servant David, 'This is what the
LORD says: You are not the one to build me a house to dwell in.'" . . . "Wherever I have moved with all
the Israelites, did I ever say to any of their leaders whom I commanded to shepherd my people, 'Why
have you not built me a house of cedar?'"*

That night Nathan received a revelation from the Lord (1 Chron. 17:3). Perhaps
God's word came in a vision while the prophet was awake; or it might have been in
a dream while Nathan slept. Whatever the case, God referred to David as His servant, which in itself was a great honor. The Lord stated that the king would not be
the person to build a temple in Jerusalem (vs. 4; see 2 Sam. 7:4-5).

One reason is that David was too busy waging wars in an effort to expand and
consolidate his kingdom (1 Kings 5:3). A second reason is that while fighting many
battles, he had become defiled due to all the bloodshed that resulted (1 Chron.
22:8; 28:3). Expressed differently, his being a person of violence, rather than peace,
disqualified (but not necessarily condemned) him. While David would not have
the privilege of honoring the Lord by building a shrine in the nation's capital, the
plans and provisions he made for its construction helped his son, Solomon, successfully complete the endeavor (22:2-5; 28:2).

There is one Hebrew term, which is usually rendered "house," that lies at the
heart of chapter 17. The same word refers to the "palace" (vs. 1) of David, the
"house" (vss. 4-6; or temple) of the Lord, and the "house" (vs. 10; or dynasty) of
David. In brief, the king saw his own palace and desired to build a temple for God;
but the Lord declared that He would build a dynasty for David and enable his son,
Solomon, to build a shrine in Jerusalem.

Notice this play on words in verse 5. The Lord declared that He had not lived in a "house" from the time He liberated the Israelites from Egypt to the day of David's reign. Instead of confining Himself to one location, God traveled with the Israelites as they moved the tabernacle from one place to the next during their 40 years of wandering in the wilderness of Sinai. Then, after the chosen people settled in Canaan, the Lord never censured any of their leaders, whom He appointed to shepherd the Israelites, for not building a "house" (vs. 6) made from cedar. Instead, the higher priority was for Israel's judges to care for those whom God had entrusted to their care.

II. GOD'S PROMISE: 1 CHRONICLES 17:7-15

A. David's Rise to Power: vss. 7-8

"Now then, tell my servant David, 'This is what the LORD Almighty says: I took you from the pasture and from following the flock, to be ruler over my people Israel. I have been with you wherever you have gone, and I have cut off all your enemies from before you. Now I will make your name like the names of the greatest men of the earth.'"

Nathan referred to God as the one who commanded heaven's armies. The all-powerful Lord had taken an obscure shepherd named David and made him the leader of the Israelites, the divinely chosen people (1 Chron. 17:7). David did not lobby for this position or do anything noteworthy to receive the honor of being the Lord's servant-king; rather, it was the grace of God that led Him to direct Samuel to anoint David as Israel's next monarch (1 Sam. 16:12-13) and for the entire nation to confirm him as their shepherd-leader (1 Chron. 11:1-2). The path to kingship was neither straightforward nor easy. Regardless, even in the darkest moments, the Lord was with David wherever he went and defeated his enemies right in front of his eyes. And now God pledged to make the name of Israel's king one of the most famous in the world (17:8; see 2 Sam. 7:8-9).

B. Israel's Homeland in Canaan: vss. 9-10a

"And I will provide a place for my people Israel and will plant them so that they can have a home of their own and no longer be disturbed. Wicked people will not oppress them anymore, as they did at the beginning and have done ever since the time I appointed leaders over my people Israel. I will also subdue all your enemies."

God originally promised to Abraham that his offspring would inherit the land of Canaan (see Gen. 13:14-17). In 15:18-20, God defined the extent of the land He would give. It lay between the river of Egypt (probably one of the seasonal rivers in the Negev) in the south to the Euphrates River in the north. At that time, this region was occupied by at least 10 different people groups. Centuries later, the Lord chose David to be the person to bring stability and peace to the Israelites in the promised land (2 Sam. 7:1). As 1 Chronicles 18—20 reveals, this undertaking lasted for much of David's reign.

God's long-term goal was to establish a place for His chosen people, Israel, and to settle them in Canaan. He wanted them to live there permanently and not be disturbed anymore (17:9). From the time God chose His people right up until the days of the judges, violent groups oppressed the Israelites; but with the establishment of David as king, the Lord would subdue all His people's enemies (vs. 10) and give His people rest (2 Sam. 7:11). Psalms 44:2 and 80:8 record the fulfillment of these promises to God's people.

Tragically, the Israelites violated the stipulations of the Mosaic covenant and eventually went into exile because of their sin (see 2 Kings 17:1-23; 2 Chron. 36:15-20). This attitude of unbelief and disobedience could be seen from the very beginning of Israel's existence as a people. For example, at the end of Hebrews 3, the author concluded that the wilderness generation of Israelites failed to enter God's rest. Then the writer began chapter 4 by saying that Christians can possess the promise to enter God's rest.

The "rest" the author of Hebrews was referring to is both spiritual and eternal. This rest that had been offered to the Israelites hundreds of years earlier was symbolic of the spiritual rest that culminated in the salvation offered by the Messiah. The author warned the readers against failing to accept the rest provided by the Lord Jesus, telling them not to be like the generation of Israelites who had failed to accept God's rest in the promised land. Thus, the writer said to take care not to fall short of God's promise (vs. 1).

C. David's Perpetual Dynasty: vss. 10b-12

"I declare to you that the LORD will build a house for you: When your days are over and you go to be with your fathers, I will raise up your offspring to succeed you, one of your own sons, and I will establish his kingdom. He is the one who will build a house for me, and I will establish his throne forever."

First Chronicles 17:10-12 (see 2 Sam. 7:11-13) records the establishment of God's covenant with David, which amplifies and confirms the promises of His covenant with Abraham (Gen. 12:1-3; 17:4-8, 16). Although the word *covenant* is not specifically stated in 1 Chronicles 17, it is used elsewhere to describe this occasion (2 Sam. 23:5; Pss. 89:3, 28, 34; 132:11-12), and the promises associated with it have enduring significance. Clearly, the issues of 1 Chronicles 17 are of immense theological importance. They concern not only the first coming of the Messiah, but also the Savior's eternal rule on the throne of David (see Isa. 9:6-7; 11:1-5; Jer. 23:5-6; Luke 1:32-33).

In particular, the Lord declared that He would build a dynastic house for David (1 Chron. 17:10). When the time came for the king to die, God would raise up one of his sons to succeed him. Solomon, of course, is the person who became Israel's next ruler and for whom the Lord established the Davidic dynasty (vs. 11). God would let Solomon build a temple for God's "Name" (2 Sam. 7:13). In the Old

Testament, God's "Name" stood for His presence in the tabernacle or temple, often represented by a visible "cloud" around the Holy Place. According to the Lord's express declaration to David and Solomon, the temple was to serve as the dwelling place for His name (see 1 Kings 9:3). That is how God abided with the Israelites.

David did not have to worry whether his kingdom would endure after his death, for the Lord pledged to establish the throne of Solomon's dynasty permanently (1 Chron. 17:12). The New Testament reveals that God's promises to David are fulfilled in the Messiah. He keeps the conditions of the covenant perfectly (Heb. 4:15), serves as the Mediator of the covenant (9:15), and promises to return as the conquering King (Matt. 24:29-31).

D. God's Abiding Presence: vss. 13-14

"I will be his father, and he will be my son. I will never take my love away from him, as I took it away from your predecessor. I will set him over my house and my kingdom forever; his throne will be established forever."

God pledged to establish an intimate Father-son relationship with David's descendants, beginning with Solomon (1 Chron. 17:13). When a Davidic king did wrong, the Lord would punish him just as parents discipline their rebellious children (2 Sam. 7:14). God's punishment of David's successors would culminate in the loss of land and temple (see 1 Kings 9:6-9); yet the Lord would never withdraw His loyal love from David's dynastic successors. In contrast, God rejected David's predecessor, Saul, and his dynasty (1 Chron. 17:13) because Saul was unfaithful to the Lord. To be specific, Israel's first king failed to heed God's commands and even consulted a medium, rather than direct his inquiries to God (10:13-14; see 1 Sam. 28:7).

Through Nathan, the Lord declared that He would make sure David's son, Solomon, and his descendants ruled God's chosen people and kingdom permanently. Indeed, the Davidic dynasty would endure forever (1 Chron. 17:14). God's promise to establish forever the throne of David would not fail (2 Sam. 7:16), being one day fully realized in the Messiah (see Jer. 33:14-26; Mic. 5:2-5). God, who promised to do great things for David, has also done great things for us through Christ. Because we trust in Him, our sins are totally forgiven and we look forward to a glorious future with God in heaven.

E. Nathan's Faithful Reporting: vs. 15

Nathan reported to David all the words of this entire revelation.

Nathan told David all that the Lord had revealed to him in his vision (1 Chron. 17:15; see 2 Sam. 7:17). Nathan, whose name means "[God] has given," proved to be a necessary and helpful gift from God to David. Indeed, throughout Nathan's career, he displayed wisdom in his counsel and bravery in his confrontation of injustice. In light of what God promised to David, we can more fully appreciate the king's profound sense of awe and gratitude. He entered the tent that housed the ark of the covenant, sat before the Lord, and prayed (1 Chron. 7:16). Throughout David's prayer, he referred to himself as the servant of the all-powerful Lord. David realized that he was just an earthly vessel whom the God of the universe had chosen to reign over His people. Here we clearly see the humble heart of David.

Discussion Questions

1. What prompted David to desire to build a temple for the Lord?
2. Why did Nathan counter his original statement to David regarding the building of a temple?
3. Why did God not want David to build a temple for Him?
4. How would God use David to bring peace and stability to Israel?
5. What sort of future awaited the dynasty of David?

Contemporary Application

At first, it was probably hard for David to accept what God had said through Nathan. Though David had desired to do a good thing, it wasn't the Lord's will for him. This undoubtedly tested the faith and patience of David. His humble response indicated that he truly was a person after God's own heart (1 Sam. 13:14).

There are times when God says *no* to our plans. It would be incorrect, however, to assume that God doesn't want us to serve Him. Rather, He wants us to do something else for Him. Like David, we should accept the part God has for us in His eternal plan and not try to go beyond it. We do this by taking full advantage of the present opportunities that God gives us to serve Him.

At other times, God says *yes* to plans for us we did not anticipate. Consider the case of Steve. He was asked to serve on the board of directors of an interdenominational organization. At first, he was reluctant because of the work, but his boss wanted him involved in the community, so he agreed to give him that one afternoon a month off.

Still, after the first meeting, Steve felt reluctant. Reading reports seemed boring! But as time passed, he became more involved in the cause of the organization and saw how much he believed in it. He met people who gave of themselves sacrificially, and they became role models for him—spurring him on to greater faith and service. After his first term, Steve said, "This is exactly what I needed in my life to pull me out of my shell and get busy for God."

Jesus assures us that His love will always be with us. This remains true, even when some of our noble dreams crumble. Such circumstances remind us to live by faith, not by sight. In fact, the entire Christian life is based on eternal truths, which we cannot see. That is the essence of our faith (Heb. 11:1). Like David, we did nothing to deserve God's blessings, whether past, present, or future. Thus, our foremost response is to praise and thank the Father for giving us eternal life with Him through faith in His Son, Jesus Christ.

God Calls Solomon to Build the Temple

Scripture

Background Scripture: *1 Chronicles 28:1-28*
Scripture Lesson: *1 Chronicles 28:5-10, 20-21*
Key Verse: *"Consider now, for the LORD has chosen you to build a temple as a sanctuary. Be strong and do the work."*
1 Chronicles 28:10.
Scripture Lesson for Children: *1 Chronicles 28:1-3, 5-10*
Key Verse for Children: *"Consider now, for the LORD has chosen you to build a temple as a sanctuary. Be strong and do the work."* 1 Chronicles 28:10.

Lesson Aim

To be courageous in carrying out our God-given tasks.

Lesson Setting

Time: *About 970 B.C.*
Place: *Jerusalem*

Lesson Outline

God Calls Solomon to Build the Temple

I. Solomon as David's Successor: 1 Chronicles 28:5-7
   A. *God's Choice of Solomon: vs. 5*
   B. *God's Pledge to Solomon: vss. 6-7*

II. David's Exhortations to Solomon:
   1 Chronicles 28:8-10, 20-21
   A. *The Importance of Heeding God's Commands: vs. 8*
   B. *The Necessity of Remaining Wholehearted in Devotion: vss. 9-10*
   C. *The Assurance of God's Abiding Presence: vs. 20*
   D. *The Willingness of the People to Obey: vs. 21*

Introduction for Adults

Topic: *Chosen for a Specific Task*

During a broadcast of *MotorWeek*, correspondent Henry Kopacz described how some law enforcement officers learn to drive safely and professionally. The training occurs at the Maryland Police and Correctional Commission's Driver Training Facility in Sykesville. The campus provides "more than just an opportunity to learn how to drive fast for pursuits." Students are given the opportunity to "hone their skills at car control on a closed course."

The staff who teach the curriculum realize they have been chosen to perform an important task. The administrator of the facility, Al Liebno, believes what the instructors teach students is vital. It's this mind-set that helps explain why the program is so comprehensive. According to Kopacz, when law enforcement officials are "out on the road, they can expect to perform anything from traffic stops to high-speed chases." And with the instruction provided at the facility at Sykesville, they learn "exactly what to do."

God has also chosen believers to perform important tasks. Indeed, the eternal future of countless unsaved people is at stake, which is why Christians need to take their God-given responsibilities all the more seriously.

Introduction for Youth

Topic: *Called for a Purpose*

Dwight Moody was an evangelist in the second half of the nineteenth century. As a teenager, he was a hard worker and ambitious. It was his dream to become a millionaire. At seventeen, he moved to Boston and worked in his uncle's shoe store, putting in long hours while still determined to go from rags to riches.

It was then that a Sunday school teacher challenged Moody to commit his life to living in a way that would honor God. This challenge profoundly affected Moody, forcing him to think about a purpose for his life. Thus, on April 21, 1855, through the influence of this teacher, Moody trusted in Christ for his salvation. It was the beginning of a spiritual journey that would end in 1899, but not before Moody himself had stirred up the faith in Christ in the hearts of untold numbers of people. God has also called each of us for a purpose and to bring glory to Him.

Concepts for Children

Topic: *Solomon Is Given a Task*

1. God selected David's son, Solomon, to build the temple (or house of worship).
2. David told Solomon to remain focused on God's call upon his life.
3. David passed on his plans for the construction of the temple to Solomon and encouraged Solomon to follow those plans.
4. David reminded Solomon that if he were obedient, God would be with him as he built the temple.
5. Regardless of the tasks we are given, God can also help us to finish them.

Lesson Commentary

I. SOLOMON AS DAVID'S SUCCESSOR: 1 CHRONICLES 28:5-7

A. God's Choice of Solomon: vs. 5

"Of all my sons—and the LORD has given me many—he has chosen my son Solomon to sit on the throne of the kingdom of the LORD over Israel."

The building of the temple is a major theme of 1 and 2 Chronicles, especially in light of the amount of space the writer devoted to this topic. Although David did not build the Jerusalem shrine, he made extensive preparations for its construction before he died. For instance, he appointed some of Israel's foreign residents to cut blocks of limestone for the sanctuary. He also supplied a large amount of the iron for the nails that would be needed for the doors in the gates and for the clamps. He provided more bronze than could be weighed and more cedar logs than could be counted (1 Chron. 22:2-4). There was also a seemingly endless supply of gold and silver (vs. 14). Moreover, at Solomon's disposal would be many stonecutters, masons, carpenters, and an innumerable array of other artisans skilled in using a wide variety of metals (vss. 15-16).

David wanted to ensure that the temple was so magnificent that it would become famous and be regarded as splendid by the surrounding nations (vs. 6). And yet, while David invested a great deal of time, effort, and resources to ensure the successful building of the shrine, this was not his foremost concern; rather, it was the building of an enduring dynasty founded on wholehearted devotion to the Lord and uncompromising adherence to the stipulations of the Mosaic law. Accordingly, the king prayed that the Lord would give Solomon, who was relatively young and inexperienced (vs. 5), insight and understanding so that he might obey God's decrees. In fact, the success of the new monarch hinged on his careful observance of all the Lord had commanded (vss. 12-13).

In Hebrew, the name *Solomon* is similar to *shalom*, the word for peace (vs. 9). Because Solomon's reign would be a time of peace, the Lord had chosen him to build His temple. David quoted to Solomon part of the Lord's promise about the Davidic dynasty found in 17:11-14 (22:10). The latter part of 22:10 implies that David's immediate son, Solomon, foreshadowed the king's later descendant, Jesus Christ, also known as the Son of David (see Matt. 1:1).

King David next extended his challenge to include other leaders of Israel whose help his son would need to accomplish the construction of the temple (1 Chron. 22:17-18). The old monarch wanted a pledge from all the leaders that they would devote themselves to the Lord and His sanctuary (vs. 19). David urged them, as he had urged Solomon, simply to begin building (compare vs. 16). David seemed convinced that if the leaders and people started the project, the Lord would see that it was completed.

Whereas the meeting with selected officials in verses 17-19 seems to have been a private hearing aimed at encouraging Solomon, the assembly in chapter 28 was a public announcement of Solomon's succession to the throne. The leaders whom David assembled in Jerusalem for a final address appear to have been the military, tribal, and cabinet officials described in chapter 27, along with the heroes of David's army (28:1). Even in such a setting, the theme of temple construction dominated David's thinking.

David reiterated his longstanding desire to build a temple for the Lord and God's veto of the idea because of the bloodshed in David's extensive military career (vss. 2-3). The monarch added that the temple would be a place of rest for the ark of the covenant in comparison to the restlessness of the portable tabernacle. He also referred to the ark as "the footstool of our God." The presence of the Lord in some way localized itself over the mercy seat atop the ark (see Exod. 25:22; Num. 7:89; 1 Sam. 4:4; 2 Sam. 6:2; 2 Kings 19:15; Ezek. 10:4).

David next stated how Solomon fit into God's plans. The Lord, through Jacob, designated Judah as the tribe of from which future kings arise (see Gen. 49:10). God pointed out the family of Jesse to Samuel as the source of the successor to Saul (see 1 Sam. 16:1). The Lord directed Samuel to anoint David as the future king of Israel (vss. 7, 11-13). First Chronicles 3:1-9 lists 19 sons born to David by seven wives. Solomon was at least the tenthborn, but the Lord chose him to rule on David's throne (28:4-5). This was a crucial requirement for a legitimate monarch of Israel (Deut. 17:15). David acknowledged that the kingdom really was not his. The throne Solomon inherited was "the throne of the kingdom of the Lord over Israel" (1 Chron. 28:5). When Israel originally insisted on having a king, the people were rejecting the rule of God over them (see 1 Sam. 8:7). David, however, understood that he ruled as God's representative.

B. God's Pledge to Solomon: vss. 6-7

"He said to me: 'Solomon your son is the one who will build my house and my courts, for I have chosen him to be my son, and I will be his father. I will establish his kingdom forever if he is unswerving in carrying out my commands and laws, as is being done at this time.'"

The Lord declared that Solomon would build God's "house" (1 Chron. 28:6) and "courts." The future temple is called a "house" because it would be permanent in comparison to the movable tent-tabernacle. The house was for God's name (see 22:7-8). God's name represented His attributes, especially His visible glory, which settled on the temple after its dedication (see 2 Chron. 6:20; 7:1). Solomon would build the temple of God and be known as God's son in anticipation of the Son of God who would be born in Bethlehem, the City of David, nearly 1,000 years later (1 Chron. 28:6).

The Lord pledged to permanently establish the kingdom of Solomon, if he remained as unswervingly committed as David was to obeying the divine commands and regulations (vs. 7). The elderly monarch cherished the messianic language of the promises of the Lord that could begin to come true in Solomon if he would govern by the law of God. Solomon needed to remain true to God's Word, even as he had been doing as a young man. At this time, he was probably in his twenties.

II. DAVID'S EXHORTATIONS TO SOLOMON: 1 CHRONICLES 28:8-10, 20-21

A. The Importance of Heeding God's Commands: vs. 8

"So now I charge you in the sight of all Israel and of the assembly of the LORD, and in the hearing of our God: Be careful to follow all the commands of the LORD your God, that you may possess this good land and pass it on as an inheritance to your descendants forever."

The writer of 1 and 2 Chronicles was deeply influenced by the theology of the Book of Deuteronomy. As a matter of fact, the historical narratives of 1 and 2 Chronicles reflect the belief that God blessed Israel's leaders and people when they obeyed the covenant that He had made with Moses. Conversely, God disciplined them severely when they transgressed the law. Indeed, the dominant theological idea seems to be that sin brought punishment, while repentance brought restoration.

This mind-set is reflected in 1 Chronicles 28:8, which records David's final instructions to Israel's leaders. The witnesses to the proceedings included God and "all Israel," the latter referring to the assembly of the Lord's chosen people. David gave the leaders the same mission he had given Solomon. They were to carefully observe everything the sovereign Lord had commanded through Moses. If they did so, they would possess Canaan, which was a "good land."

According to Exodus 3:8, Canaan was good in terms of quality as well as large in terms of size. The land was also "flowing with milk and honey," which is a picturesque way of saying the land abounded with the most delectable products of animals and of the earth, of herders and farmers. Israel's civil and religious leaders had the opportunity to pass on Canaan as a permanent inheritance for their descendants. The key was to revere the Lord by obeying His statutes and commandments (Deut. 6:2-3).

Constant and unwavering vigilance was necessary, otherwise God's people might succumb to the temptation to forget the Lord and fail to heed His ordinances. Then, as feelings of self-importance emerged, the Israelites would deceive themselves into thinking their own ability and skill were the reasons for their material abundance. This arrogant attitude would lead to disdain for God and His covenant. The people would abandon Him and venerate false gods. This apostasy, in turn, would lead to their annihilation (8:11-20).

B. The Necessity of Remaining Wholehearted in Devotion: vss. 9-10

"And you, my son Solomon, acknowledge the God of your father, and serve him with wholehearted devotion and with a willing mind, for the LORD searches every heart and understands every motive behind

the thoughts. If you seek him, he will be found by you; but if you forsake him, he will reject you forever. Consider now, for the LORD has chosen you to build a temple as a sanctuary. Be strong and do the work."

To Solomon, David stressed the conditional nature of the immediate blessings of God on his reign. The young monarch was urged to know God, acknowledge Him, and worship Him alone. When the Lord was the center of Solomon's life, he would be able to serve God with a submissive attitude and a willing spirit. This was the only sensible way to operate, for the Lord knew all the thoughts of every person and the motives for their actions. Solomon had the assurance that if he sought God, He would be found. Put another way, if the king inquired of the Lord in humility and sincerity, He would hear Solomon's petitions. However, if the king abandoned God, He would permanently reject Israel's ruler (1 Chron. 28:9).

The Lord directly emphasized these truths to Solomon when He appeared to the king at Gibeon early in his reign (1 Kings 3:4-15) and later after the temple was built (9:1-9). Tragically, while God remained faithful to His promise to bless Solomon, the king eventually wavered in his commitment. When he grew old, he refused to follow the Lord completely, but instead did what was evil in God's sight. The king's growing apostasy angered the Lord, especially since He had warned Solomon about worshiping false gods. The monarch's refusal to heed the stipulations of the Mosaic covenant would result in the breakup of the kingdom after his death (11:1-13).

This historical background information indicates how important David's final statements were to Solomon. The aging father wanted his son to take his words of admonition seriously. Solomon had a bright and promising future ahead of him. After all, the Lord had chosen him to build the temple and make it the official sanctuary where the people would worship Him. David wanted Solomon to be confident and energetic as he did the work assigned to him (1 Chron. 28:10).

C. The Assurance of God's Abiding Presence: vs. 20

David also said to Solomon his son, "Be strong and courageous, and do the work. Do not be afraid or discouraged, for the LORD God, my God, is with you. He will not fail you or forsake you until all the work for the service of the temple of the LORD is finished."

As God had given plans for the tabernacle to Moses (see Exod. 25:9), so He gave plans for the temple to David (1 Chron. 28:11-12). The plans included an entry porch whose roof was apparently supported by columns, extensive storage areas in and around the temple proper, and the Holy Place and Most Holy Place where annual atonement was made for the sins of the people.

The Spirit of God had guided the thoughts of David in designing the elaborate complex that comprised the temple area (vs. 12). The Spirit had also inspired the division of priests, Levites, singers, doorkeepers, and other worship leaders recorded in chapters 23—26. Further, the Spirit of God had designated how much precious metal to put into each of the items of furniture and vessels of worship and sacrifice for the temple service (28:13-17).

The last item of temple furnishing that the Holy Spirit instructed David about was the mercy seat for the ark of the covenant, here called "the chariot" (vs. 18). In several places in the Old Testament, the cherubim whose images adorned the mercy seat on the ark are said to transport the glory of the Lord (see 2 Sam. 22:11; Ezek. 1; 10:18-19). The temple furnishings that might seem static to us were filled with dynamic imagery to the people of the day.

Interpreters understand 1 Chronicles 28:19 differently. Some take this verse to mean that God's Spirit guided David in drafting detailed plans for the temple. Others see in this verse evidence that God presented David with plans He Himself had drawn and written in the same way He had presented the tabernacle layout to Moses. Whichever view is correct, the Lord also gave David insight into the temple pattern that enabled him to give especially valuable advice to Solomon and the other leaders of Israel.

David issued one last word of encouragement to his son. The elderly monarch directed the young king to be strong and brave, rather than afraid and discouraged. The reason is that the Lord, Israel's covenant-keeping God, would abide with Solomon, not forsake him. Yahweh would ensure that all the work to related to the building the temple was finished correctly so it could be used for worshiping Him (vs. 20). Implicit in David's challenge was his realization that any spiritual weakness, fear, or lack of courage on Solomon's part would prevent the temple construction. Equally implicit was the assumption on David's part that the presence and faithfulness of the Lord would give Solomon strength, peace, and courage to succeed in the work.

David's exhortation to Solomon mirrors what Moses said to Joshua, which indicates that the Lord's presence and power to help had not decreased with time. In particular, the lawgiver urged his successor to be strong and courageous in leading a new generation of God's people into the promised land. Joshua would prosper by remaining faithful to the Lord and heeding His commands. The protégé of Moses had the assurance that God would be with him wherever he went (Deut. 1:37-38; 31:1-8; Josh. 1:1-9). For both Joshua and Solomon, a common goal was to remain morally equitable and upright as they led the heirs of God's covenant promises into a new phase of their existence in Canaan.

D. The Willingness of the People to Obey: vs. 21

"The divisions of the priests and Levites are ready for all the work on the temple of God, and every willing man skilled in any craft will help you in all the work. The officials and all the people will obey your every command."

In Joshua's day, a new generation of Israelites wholeheartedly supported the nation's leader as he shouldered the task of conquering and settling Canaan. They pledged to obey him just as they had fully obeyed Moses (Deut. 34:9; Josh. 1:16-18). In a similar way, "all Israel" (1 Chron. 29:23) was ready to obey Solomon's "every command" (28:21). All the royal officials, the army commanders, and David's other sons pledged their loyalty to Solomon as king (29:24). In addition, the various divisions of priests and Levites were ready to carry out their assigned duties in the temple. Moreover, all the skilled workers were prepared to do their work (28:21). If Solomon would commit himself to the Lord and the temple work, no one in Israel would lay a stumbling block in his path.

Discussion Questions

1. Why do you think the Lord chose Solomon to succeed David as king?
2. Why did God want Solomon to be unswerving in carrying out His commands?
3. What did the leaders of Israel need to do to ensure their ongoing prosperity in Canaan?
4. Why did David want Solomon to acknowledge the Lord as his God?
5. What support would Solomon enjoy from those under his command?

Contemporary Application

Within two months, two of Al and Dellene Stucky's adult children experienced personal tragedy. Michelle was paralyzed from the waist down as a result of a plane crash. Marlyn, hospitalized with acute motor azonal neuropathy, couldn't move at all. Six months later, both were in wheelchairs. Despite their hardships, Michelle and Marlyn, along with their parents, were eager to get back to work. Together, they had been translating the New Testament into the Melpa language of Papua, New Guinea.

Dellene recalls, "Many people thought we were crazy, taking two people in wheelchairs to Papua, New Guinea. It's not wheelchair accessible, let alone an easy place to live. But it's where God wanted us. The Lord performed no end of miracles as we traveled to Los Angeles, Honolulu, Cairns, Australia, and on to Papua, New Guinea. The prayers of God's saints carried us through." It took faith and courage for Michelle and Marlyn to return to their work. Together, they typeset the Melpa New Testament, which was then dedicated and distributed to many people.

As we journey with God on the road of life, He asks us to accept new challenges, such as reaching out to others in need, loving a difficult child or spouse, going the extra mile for a friend, or making decisions full of integrity but lacking in other advantages. Sometimes God directs our steps in gentle nudges, while at other times it is through the stern words of a friend. In every situation, the Lord wants us to be courageous in carrying out our God-given tasks. We can do so knowing that He is with us every step of the way and will enable us to be successful in what He wants us to do.

Fulfillment of God's Promise

DEVOTIONAL READING

Psalm 135:1-5

DAILY BIBLE READINGS

Monday March 17
Psalm 135:1-5 Praise for God's Goodness

Tuesday March 18
2 Chronicles 6:1-11 Dedication of the Temple

Wednesday March 19
2 Chronicles 6:12-17 Solomon's Prayer

Thursday March 20
2 Chronicles 6:18-31 Pray toward This Place

Friday March 21
2 Chronicles 6:36-39 Repent and Pray

Saturday March 22
2 Chronicles 6:40-42 God's Promise Remembered

Sunday March 23
Luke 24:44-49 God's Promise Fulfilled

Scripture

Background Scripture: *2 Chronicles 6; Luke 24*
Scripture Lesson: *2 Chronicles 6:12-17; Luke 24:44-49*
Key Verse: *"The LORD has kept the promise he made. I have succeeded David my father and now I sit on the throne of Israel, just as the LORD promised, and I have built the temple for the Name of the LORD, the God of Israel."*
2 Chronicles 6:10.
Scripture Lesson for Children: *Luke 24:1-12*
Key Verse for Children: *"[Jesus] is not here; he has risen!"*
Luke 24:5.

Lesson Aim

To affirm that we are witnesses to the reality of the risen Messiah.

Lesson Setting

Date: *958 B.C. (Solomon's prayer of dedication);* A.D. *30 (Jesus' resurrection)*
Place: *Jerusalem*

Lesson Outline

Fulfillment of God's Promise

  I. Solomon's Prayer of Dedication:
      2 Chronicles 6:12-17
      A. *Solomon's Presence Before the People: vss. 12-13*
      B. *God's Faithfulness to His People: vss. 14-15*
      C. *Solomon's Petition for God's Blessing: vss. 16-17*
  II. Jesus' Final Words to His Disciples: Luke 24:44-49
      A. *Jesus' Fulfillment of the Old Testament Messianic Prophecies: vs. 44*
      B. *Jesus' Explanation to His Disciples: vss. 45-47*
      C. *Jesus' Commissioning of His Disciples: vss. 48-49*

Introduction for Adults

Topic: *Whose Promises Can You Trust?*

Our world is filled with pundits and politicians who routinely make and break promises. Thankfully, it is far different with the Father. He promised to raise His Son from the dead, and He fulfilled that promise to the letter.

The wonderful news is that we celebrate the resurrection of a rejected King. His resurrection brought victorious life out of dark death and despair. This is perhaps the greatest reversal in history! Christians do not worship a dead hero. They do not idolize a man who fought for a just cause but lost. Many others have suffered terrible ends for their ideals, but none of them ever came back from the grave.

God's love, wisdom, and power provide forgiveness, hope, and eternal life out of apparent defeat. And Jesus' incomparable triumph from tragedy stands as the greatest event of all time. But it is more than a historical incident. Jesus lives in the hearts of all those who trust in Him.

Introduction for Youth

Topic: *God Keeps Promises*

On school trips to Washington, D.C., I used to stand in awe before the memorials to the United States' greatest heroes—Washington, Jefferson, and Lincoln. I admired their courage and wisdom. They spoke to me in their speeches and proclamations. I owe them a great debt.

Nevertheless, these greats from the past are dead and gone. We cannot know them personally. We cannot invite them into our hearts. In contrast, we can know Jesus in an intimate and personal way.

That's because, thanks to the Father keeping His promises to us, the Son is alive in heaven. There is a real person in heaven, the same person who came to earth two thousand years ago. Jesus invites our trust, worship, hope, and obedience. We can talk to Him in prayer. He is our supreme confidant and helper.

Concepts for Children

Topic: *Jesus Is Alive*

1. The Father fulfilled His promise to raise His Son from the dead.
2. Several women visited the tomb and found it empty.
3. The Father sent messengers from heaven to tell the women that He had fulfilled His promise.
4. God's methods of doing what He promised sometimes involve the miraculous and unexpected.
5. God wants us to tell others the wonderful news of Jesus' resurrection.

Lesson Commentary

I. SOLOMON'S PRAYER OF DEDICATION: 2 CHRONICLES 6:12-17

A. Solomon's Presence Before the People: vss. 12-13

Then Solomon stood before the altar of the LORD in front of the whole assembly of Israel and spread out his hands. Now he had made a bronze platform, five cubits long, five cubits wide and three cubits high, and had placed it in the center of the outer court. He stood on the platform and then knelt down before the whole assembly of Israel and spread out his hands toward heaven.

Before David's death in 970 B.C., the kingship had been successfully transferred to his son, Solomon. He in turn firmly secured his control over the throne so that all the tribes of Israel were obedient to him (1 Chron. 29:22-24). Moreover, the Lord greatly magnified the newly appointed monarch over the nation and bestowed on him greater royal splendor than any king of Israel before him (vs. 25). Thus, it was God who permitted His chosen people to stand in awe of Solomon and for him to have more wealth and honor than even his father (2 Chron. 1:1).

Early in his reign, Solomon and the representative leaders of Israel went to the high place at Gibeon, for the tabernacle and bronze altar for burnt sacrifices were located there (1 Chron. 21:29; 2 Chron. 1:2-5). Gibeon was about six miles northwest of Jerusalem and functioned as a major center of worship before Solomon built the temple. While at the high place, Israel's king offered sacrifices and prayed to the Lord. Then, that night, God appeared to Solomon and invited him to ask for anything he wanted. The young monarch asked for wisdom and discernment so he could be effective in leading the chosen people. The Lord not only granted this request, but also made him richer and more famous than any ruler before or after him (vss. 7-12).

Verses 14-17 catalog the riches and possessions of Solomon. In 966 B.C., he used his wealth and power to begin construction on a temple to honor the Lord (2:1). Chapters 2 through 4 detail this massive building project, which was completed seven years later in 959 B.C. (1 Kings 6:37-38). While the design of the Jerusalem shrine bore some resemblance to that of other temples of the day, it was most closely patterned after the tabernacle. In particular, three main areas comprised Solomon's temple: the outer courtyard, the Holy Place, and the Most Holy Place (the latter being cubical in shape).

The king put in the treasuries of the Jerusalem shrine the holy items that belonged to his father David (the silver, gold, and all the objects used in worship; 2 Chron. 5:1). Solomon also relocated the ark of the covenant, the tabernacle, and all the sacred furnishings to the temple (vss. 4-6). This happened in the twelfth year of his reign (958 B.C.; 1 Kings 8:2). As the priests carried the ark to the temple, Solomon and the elders of Israel sacrificed countless sheep and cattle along the way in thanksgiving (2 Chron. 5:4-6).

The king waited nearly a year to transfer the ark so he could do it at the time of the day of Atonement and the Feast of Tabernacles. On the day of Atonement, the blood of the sin offering was sprinkled on the atonement cover of the ark. The Feast of Tabernacles celebrated God's blessing on Israel by taking them from a wandering existence to a permanent place to inhabit. The priests placed the ark in the Holy Place under the wings of the cherubim (vs. 7). When the priests left the Holy Place, the cloud of God's glory filled the temple (vss. 13-14).

Those who assembled with Solomon included all the leaders of the Israel (vs. 2). As they stood before him, he pronounced a blessing over them (6:3). Then he recalled the promise God made with David that his son would build a temple to honor Yahweh. Solomon affirmed that the Lord had fulfilled His pledge to establish the young monarch as Israel's ruler and to enable him to complete the task of building a shrine in Jerusalem to house the ark of the covenant (vss. 4-11).

Earlier, Solomon had a bronze platform made that was about seven and one-half feet long and wide and four and one-half feet high. He had it placed in the center of the temple's outer courtyard near the altar so that he could be easily seen and heard. Most likely, the platform was erected temporarily for use during the ceremony in which the shrine was dedicated. Here we see that as Solomon officiated over this special occasion, he sought to focus attention on the place of sacrifice. After his initial comments, the king stood with his hands spread out before the altar in front of the entire assembly. Then, he knelt down on his knees and lifted up his hands toward the sky in a gesture signifying prayer (vss. 12-13; see Exod. 9:29, 33; Ezra 9:5; Isa. 1:15; 1 Tim. 2:8).

B. God's Faithfulness to His People: vss. 14-15

He said: "O Lord, God of Israel, there is no God like you in heaven or on earth—you who keep your covenant of love with your servants who continue wholeheartedly in your way. You have kept your promise to your servant David my father; with your mouth you have promised and with your hand you have fulfilled it—as it is today."

As the representative and shepherd of God's people, Solomon publicly interceded on their behalf. In his prayer, he affirmed that there was no deity in heaven or on earth like Yahweh, the all-powerful God of Israel. The Hebrew of 2 Chronicles 6:14 literally says, God is the "one who keeps the covenant and the loyal love." The idea is that He never forgot the covenantal promises He made with His chosen people. He also showed unfailing compassion and favor toward His servants who obeyed His teachings in a wholehearted, sincere manner. These truths were evident in the circumstance involving Solomon and his completion of the temple. The young monarch acknowledged that the Lord had kept every promise He made to His servant, David (vs. 15).

C. Solomon's Petition for God's Blessing: vss. 16-17

"Now Lord, God of Israel, keep for your servant David my father the promises you made to him when you said, 'You shall never fail to have a man to sit before me on the throne of Israel, if only your sons

are careful in all they do to walk before me according to my law, as you have done.' And now, O LORD, God of Israel, let your word that you promised your servant David come true."

The past faithfulness of Yahweh toward His chosen people was the basis for Solomon's petition for God's blessing. The king appealed to the Lord to keep the promise He previously made to David, His servant. Specifically, God pledged that David would never fail to have a successor ruling before the Lord on the throne of Israel. The key provision was that David's descendants guarded their behavior and obeyed the Mosaic law, just as he had done throughout his reign (2 Chron. 6:16-17; see 2 Sam. 7; 1 Chron. 17).

It would be incorrect to assume that the rule of David's descendants would never be interrupted. In fact, an interruption occurred when Judah was exiled to Babylon (2 Kings 25:1-21; Hos. 3:4-5); nevertheless, the right to rule would always belong to the Davidic dynasty (see Ps. 89:20-37). Luke 1:31-33 says that Jesus would receive the dynasty, throne, and kingdom promised to David and his posterity. This promise will be fully realized when Jesus returns to reign with His people in the kingdom age (Rev. 20:1-6).

II. JESUS' FINAL WORDS TO HIS DISCIPLES: LUKE 24:44-49

A. Jesus' Fulfillment of the Old Testament Messianic Prophecies: vs. 44

He said to them, "This is what I told you while I was still with you: Everything must be fulfilled that is written about me in the Law of Moses, the Prophets and the Psalms."

In Solomon's prayer, he declared that there was no one who had acted in history as had the God of Israel. He sovereignly directed the long-term course of events so that His covenant promises to His people would be fulfilled. Also, His fidelity was not temporary, and His power was not limited to a particular country or region. These truths are seen in the Lord Jesus, especially His resurrection from the dead.

While Luke's account of the Resurrection includes much of the same factual information as the other Gospels, it contains some different elements as well. For instance, while all the Gospel writers mention the women's visit to the tomb, only Luke relates details of Jesus' encounter with the disciples on the road to Emmaus, which was a village about seven miles from Jerusalem (24:13). These two devout followers of the Savior were talking about what had happened to Jesus. No doubt they were disappointed and depressed. Their conversation was interrupted by a wonderful opportunity: Jesus came up and joined in their discussion; but at first they didn't recognize Him (vss. 14-16).

The pair opened their hearts to this stranger, telling Jesus about their confusion, their fears, and their broken dreams. Amazed that He seemed so uninformed, they recounted what had happened to Jesus. They also explained that the Crucifixion had dashed all their hopes that He would be the person who would redeem Israel (vss. 17-21). Their desires for the nation's redemption came from a misconception about the Messiah taken from selected Hebrew prophecies. Most first-century A.D. Jews looked for the Messiah to come as a political hero who would deliver their nation from Roman rule and reestablish the throne of David. They knew about the glory, but they didn't see the suffering of the Savior.

Eventually, the three travelers reached Emmaus; but since it was late in the afternoon, the two disciples insisted that Jesus stay the night with them. When they sat together to eat the evening meal, Jesus broke the bread and gave thanks for it. At once, they knew who He was, but then He disappeared (vss. 28-31). Though it was late, they couldn't wait to tell the disciples back in Jerusalem what had happened. They hurried out into the night, prepared to hike seven miles through darkness. When the Emmaus disciples arrived in Jerusalem, the others were talking about another appearance of the risen Messiah. Peter had seen Jesus! We don't know any details of Jesus' visit to Peter, but it is fascinating to realize that the one who denied the Lord was one of the first Jesus wanted to see (vss. 32-35).

As the disciples talked excitedly about the latest developments, Jesus stood in the room with them. They were shocked by His sudden appearance and thought they were seeing a ghost (vss. 36-27), probably because the doors to the room were locked (John 20:19). Jesus wanted to calm His disciples' fears by convincing them He was not a ghost. He showed them the marks left by the nails in His hands and feet. The disciples saw Him with their eyes, but they couldn't believe what they were seeing. So Jesus asked for something to eat, and by eating a piece of broiled fish gave them proof that He was indeed not a ghost (Luke 24:38-43).

Jesus reminded His followers that while He was previously with them, He told them how the messianic promises recorded in the Old Testament were ordained by God to be fulfilled. The Law, the Prophets, and the Psalms—the three sections of the Hebrew Scriptures—reveal truths about the Redeemer that had to occur. Verse 44 affirms that there is a strong interrelationship between the Old and New Testaments. Succinctly put, the triune God brought the universe into existence; humankind sinned, bringing moral and spiritual corruption to themselves and their world; and now the Godhead has made redemption possible through the atoning work of the Son. The divine plan of redemption began at Calvary, continues even now, and will one day be complete when God creates a new heaven and new earth.

B. Jesus' Explanation to His Disciples: vss. 45-47

Then he opened their minds so they could understand the Scriptures. He told them, "This is what is written: The Christ will suffer and rise from the dead on the third day, and repentance and forgiveness of sins will be preached in his name to all nations, beginning at Jerusalem."

At this point, Jesus opened the minds of the disciples to comprehend the Scriptures (Luke 24:45). While the specific texts are not listed in this verse, it's possible they included the many Old Testament passages appearing elsewhere in the

Gospel of Luke and the Book of Acts. The threefold thrust of those prophecies was that the Messiah had to die on the cross (see Pss. 22; 31; 69; 118; Isa. 53), rise from the dead on the third day (see Ps. 16:10; 110:1), and have the good news of salvation heralded to the lost (Luke 24:46; see Matt. 28:19; Mark 13:10).

Part of the Gospel proclamation included an emphasis on repentance for the forgiveness of sins (Luke 24:47). This Hebrew concept included the idea of turning from wrongdoing as a prelude to experiencing the Father's offer of pardon through faith in the Son. Beginning at Jerusalem (the initial center and focus of the Gospel), the followers of the Savior were to announce the Good News to the nations of the world (see Isa. 49:6; Luke 2:32; Acts 13:47). Acts 2 records how all this got started on the day of Pentecost.

The disciples must have been surprised at Jesus' words. Generally, Jews believed that Gentiles were outside the favor of God, or that if Gentiles were to receive God's favor, they first had to become Jews; but here was Jesus telling His disciples to disperse into the world and make disciples of people from all over (see Matt. 28:19). The Father had thrown His arms wide to graciously receive all people who love and believe in His Son.

C. Jesus' Commissioning of His Disciples: vss. 48-49

"You are witnesses of these things. I am going to send you what my Father has promised; but stay in the city until you have been clothed with power from on high."

Jesus declared to His followers that they were witnesses of all that had occurred (Luke 24:28). The idea of proclaiming all that happened in connection with the Savior is a key concept in the Book of Acts (see 1:22; 2:32; 3:15; 5:32; 10:39, 41; 13:31; 22:15, 20; 26:16). In 1:8, for instance, the risen Lord told His disciples they and future believers would testify about Him in Jerusalem, in all Judea and Samaria, and to the farthest regions of the earth. They would not do this alone and in their own strength; rather, the Holy Spirit would empower them for effective Christian service.

The Greek word translated "witnesses" (Luke 24:48; Acts 1:8) is the origin of the English word *martyr* and means to testify to something on the basis of what one has seen or heard. After Jesus' ascension, the Eleven plus other disciples gathered to choose someone to replace Judas as an apostle. Peter said that this person should be a "witness" (Acts 1:22) to the Resurrection and someone who had been with Jesus since His baptism. In one sense, then, a witness was someone who actually saw the risen Lord and could testify, as in a courtroom, to the reality of the Resurrection. Nonetheless, the writer of Hebrews also called anyone who perseveres for the faith a "witness," and says all believers are surrounded by a "great cloud of witnesses" (Heb. 12:1). These witnesses include those who have testified to the reality of the Gospel, and their witness encourages us to testify today.

In Luke 24:29, Jesus referred to the Spirit as the one whom the Son was sending and whom the Father had previously promised to His people. This divine pledge is rooted in such Old Testament passages as Jeremiah 31:31 and Ezekiel 36:26-27.

Also, when John prepared the way for the advent of the Messiah, the messenger declared that Jesus would baptize people with the Holy Spirit (3:16). As the disciples heralded the Good News, they helped to fulfill what God had promised to do. Moreover, Jesus pledged to clothe His followers with "power from on high" (24:49), which is a reference to the Holy Spirit. He would enable them to bear much fruit by leading many lost people to put their trust in the Redeemer for salvation.

Discussion Questions

1. Who was present in the assembly at the dedication of the Jerusalem temple?
2. Why do you think Solomon proclaimed the uniqueness of Israel's God?
3. What covenant promises had God made to David?
4. What prophecies about the Messiah can be found in the Old Testament?
5. What does it mean to be a witness to the reality of the risen Messiah?

Contemporary Application

At the dedication of the newly built Jerusalem temple, Solomon testified to the uniqueness and power of the living God. Similarly, the earliest followers of the Messiah faithfully declared that the Father had raised the Son from the dead. We are not witnesses to the Resurrection in the same sense as Mary Magdalene, Peter, and the Emmaus disciples. Put differently, we are not *eyewitnesses* of the risen Lord; but we have firsthand reports in the New Testament of those who saw Jesus alive from the dead. By comparing these accounts, we can see why it's much more reasonable to conclude that Jesus did indeed rise than that He did not.

Over the centuries, many skeptics have tried to disprove the truth of the Resurrection. Some, such as Josh McDowell and Lee Strobel, concluded that the evidence for the Resurrection is far stronger than the evidence against it. And perhaps most conclusive of all is the reality of Jesus manifesting His resurrection life through us. There is no better news than the Resurrection. It means victory over death. It signifies new life that begins now and goes on for eternity.

And so the question for us is the following: *What are we doing with this great news?* We wouldn't keep the news of the birth of a new child or grandchild to ourselves. We also wouldn't fail to mention that we'd been promoted at work. Are we telling others of the even greater news that Jesus lives?

This might be a good time to read Acts 2 to see how the apostles witnessed to the Resurrection once they were clothed with power from on high. Let's recognize their boldness, sense their excitement, and be in awe of their results. We also have the same Spirit empowering us for faithful and effective Christian service. He will enable us to witness to the reality of the Resurrection with the same fervor.

Josiah Renews the Covenant

DEVOTIONAL READING

Psalm 119:25-40

DAILY BIBLE READINGS

Monday March 24
  Psalm 119:25-32 Revive Me

Tuesday March 25
  2 Chronicles 34:1-7 Josiah Seeks God's Way

Wednesday March 26
  2 Chronicles 34:8-18 A Big Discovery

Thursday March 27
  2 Chronicles 34:19-21 Josiah Repents

Friday March 28
  2 Chronicles 34:22-28 God Hears Josiah

Saturday March 29
  2 Chronicles 34:29-33 The Covenant Renewed

Sunday March 30
  Psalm 119:33-40 Teach Me

Scripture

Background Scripture: *2 Chronicles 34*

Scripture Lesson: *2 Chronicles 34:15, 18-19, 25-27, 29, 31-33*

Key Verse: *The king stood by his pillar and renewed the covenant in the presence of the LORD—to follow the LORD and keep his commands, regulations and decrees with all his heart and all his soul, and to obey the words of the covenant written in this book.* 2 Chronicles 34:31.

Scripture Lesson for Children: *2 Chronicles 34:14, 19, 21-23, 27, 29-31*

Key Verse for Children: *The king stood by his pillar and renewed the covenant in the presence of the LORD—to follow the LORD.* 2 Chronicles 34:31.

Lesson Aim

To recognize that godly leaders honor the Lord.

Lesson Setting

Time: *622 B.C.*

Place: *Jerusalem*

Lesson Outline

Josiah Renews the Covenant

I. A Stern Warning: 2 Chronicles 34:15, 18-19, 25-27
    A. *Finding the Book of the Law: vs. 15*
    B. *Reporting the Discovery to the King: vss. 18-19*
    C. *Foretelling Impending Judgment: vs. 25*
    D. *Sparing the King of Judgment: vss. 26-27*
II. A Sincere Response: 2 Chronicles 34:29, 31-33
    A. *Convening the Nation's Leaders: vs. 29*
    B. *Renewing the Covenant: vss. 31-32*
    C. *Enacting Widespread Reforms: vs. 33*

Introduction for Adults

Topic: *Mending a Broken Relationship*

Correspondent Reed Abelson of *The New York Times* reported that in early April 2006, Massachusetts "enacted legislation to provide health insurance for virtually every citizen within the next three years." The landmark bill is the first in the United States requiring "people to buy health insurance if they don't get it at work." The legislation enjoys support from representatives across the political spectrum. Indeed, it was approved by "a Republican governor and a Democrat-dominated House." House Speaker Sal DiMasi compared "the new health law to the Mayflower Compact," which the pilgrims created after landing "on Plymouth Rock in 1620." He noted that the intent of the colonists was to forge a "community of people where laws were made for the common wealth." He says "the new law reflects that original idea."

The notion of a community of people existing in a covenantal relationship mirrors what we find in this week's lesson. Josiah led the officials and populace of Judah to renew their commitment to the Lord and each other, as expressed in the Mosaic Covenant. Then, as now, they realized that a community is benefited most when the basic human needs of everyone are met.

Introduction for Youth

Topic: *Mending a Broken Relationship*

"When I was a boy, my father, a baker, introduced me to the wonders of song," tenor Luciano Pavarotti relates. "He urged me to work very hard to develop my voice. Arrigo Pola, a professional tenor in my hometown of Modena, Italy, took me as a pupil. I also enrolled in a teacher's college. On graduating, I asked my father, 'Shall I be a teacher or a singer?'

"'Luciano,' my father replied, 'if you try to sit on two chairs, you will fall between them. For life, you must choose one chair.' I chose one. It took seven years of study and frustration before I made my first professional appearance. It took another seven to reach the Metropolitan Opera. And now I think whether it's laying bricks, writing a book—whatever we choose—we should give ourselves to it. Commitment: that's the key. Choose one chair." This bit of advice applies even to successfully mending broken relationships. It requires undivided commitment.

Concepts for Children

Topic: *Josiah Obeys the Law*

1. In Josiah's time, the Book of the Law, which had been lost, was found.
2. Josiah was sad when he heard the Law, for he realized the people were not obeying it.
3. Josiah sought to restore the nation's relationship with God.
4. God's messenger, Huldah, explained the Lord's expectations to Josiah.
5. God wants us to be serious about obeying Him.

Lesson Commentary

I. A Stern Warning: 2 Chronicles 34:15, 18-19, 25-27

A. Finding the Book of the Law: vs. 15

Hilkiah said to Shaphan the secretary, "I have found the Book of the Law in the temple of the Lord." He gave it to Shaphan.

Josiah, one of Judah's most godly kings, was only eight years old when he began to reign in 640 B.C. About 82 years had passed since the northern kingdom of Israel had been conquered by Assyria in 722 B.C. Sixty-one years had elapsed since the Lord had answered King Hezekiah's prayers by destroying the Assyrian army threatening Jerusalem in 701 B.C. Josiah enjoyed a long reign of 31 years, but simple arithmetic shows he died at the age of 39 (2 Chron. 34:1). A great deal happened in the life of this king, whose tragic end prefigured the fate of the nation.

Josiah's rule followed the short, two-year reign of his father Amon (33:21). King Amon followed the earlier example of Manasseh by worshiping and sacrificing to idols (vs. 22). Perhaps his evil example caused some of his own officials to assassinate him after only a couple of years (vss. 23-24). The Chronicler recorded that Josiah began to seek the Lord in the eighth year of his rule, when he was only 16, and that he was destroying idols and shrines in the Jerusalem area by his twelfth year on the throne (34:3-4). Soon his zeal for destroying idols reached even into the northern territory that had been Israel (vss. 6-7).

In the eighteenth year of Josiah's reign (622 B.C.), when he was 26, he began to repair the Jerusalem temple (vs. 8). He delegated the task to three prominent officials in his royal court: Shaphan, who served as a scribe and treasurer to the king, and would have been among one of the highest ranking civil servants; Maaseiah, the governor of Jerusalem; and Joah, the historian who kept the government records. These three men went to Hilkiah the high priest and gave him the money (literally, silver) that had been collected by the Levites who served as gatekeepers at the Jerusalem shrine (vs. 9).

In turn, the money was entrusted to the men assigned to supervise the restoration efforts. With some of the money, they paid the workers who did the repairs and renovation (vs. 10). The remainder of the money was given to the carpenters and masons to purchase chiseled stone for the walls and timber for the rafters and beams, all of which had fallen into disrepair (vs. 11). Some Levites were put in charge of the laborers of the various trades, while other Levites assisted as secretaries, scribes, and gatekeepers. Together, they ensured that the laborers remained honest and diligent in their work (vss. 12-13).

Verse 9 states that people from both Judah and Israel contributed money for the restoration effort. When workers removed the money that had been brought to the temple, Hilkiah the high priest discovered what was called the "Book of the Law of the Lord that had been given through Moses" (vs. 14). Later, it is called the "Book

249

of the Covenant" (vs. 30). That would indicate the scroll contained the laws that the Lord had given to Moses, particularly those recorded in Exodus 19—24; however, the curses Josiah was about to hear seem to have come from Leviticus and Deuteronomy. Thus, what was likely found was either all three books or Deuteronomy, which contains a retelling of the events of the Exodus and a reiteration of God's instructions through Moses. Hilkiah informed Shaphan about the discovery of the law scroll and gave it to the court secretary (2 Chron. 34:15).

B. Reporting the Discovery to the King: vss. 18-19

Then Shaphan the secretary informed the king, "Hilkiah the priest has given me a book." And Shaphan read from it in the presence of the king. When the king heard the words of the Law, he tore his robes.

Much earlier, Moses told the Levites who carried the ark of the covenant to take the scroll containing the law and place it beside the ark of the covenant (Deut. 31:26). Also, every seven years the priests were to read the decrees and teachings of the law in the hearing of all Israel during the Feast of Tabernacles (vss. 10-11).

Tragically, in the days of King Ahaz (732–715 B.C.), the temple in Jerusalem had been closed and the ark of the covenant, along with other temple objects, may have been stored or hidden (see 2 Chron. 28:24). It had been replaced when Hezekiah restored and rededicated the temple (see 29:18-19). Then, during the evil reigns of Manasseh and Amon, it's likely that the ark had been removed from the temple again for protection, because Josiah ordered its restoration to the Most Holy Place during his great Passover celebration (see 35:1-3). During this turmoil, it is not surprising that the Book of the Law, which was to be stored beside the ark, had been misplaced long enough to be forgotten.

In the course of Josiah's reign, Shaphan reported to the king that his officials were doing everything that had been assigned to them (34:16). The scribe specifically mentioned the money that was collected at the temple and entrusted to the the supervisors of the construction foremen undertaking the repairs (vs. 17). Shaphan told Josiah that Hilkiah the high priest had given him a scroll containing the Mosaic law. Then the scribe read it out loud before the king (vs. 18).

When Josiah heard what was written in God's Word, he tore his clothes as a sign of mourning and repentance (vs. 19). The king's great concern suggests he probably heard a passage from the Mosaic law dealing with how God would judge the Israelites if they did not obey His Word. Deuteronomy 28:15-68 is one such passage. In it Moses warned Israel about all the dire consequences that would come upon the people if they rejected the Lord and turned to idolatry.

C. Foretelling Impending Judgment: vs. 25

"Because they have forsaken me and burned incense to other gods and provoked me to anger by all that their hands have made, my anger will be poured out on this place and will not be quenched."

Josiah next summoned several of his trusted officials and related his concerns. The king ordered the priest and his company to seek an oracle from the Lord about the future of the kingdom, including the remnant in Israel and Judah. Josiah figured out that his ancestors had disobeyed the Lord and violated His commands. They thus deserved God's righteous judgment (2 Chron. 34:20-21). Based on what Josiah had heard, he could discern how far the Lord's people had fallen from His holy standards. Judah's king did not offer any excuses. He could see that God's wrath had resulted in the destruction of the northern kingdom and the dispersion of its people. Josiah sensed that the same end would befall Judah. Therefore, he confessed and sought God's will.

Hilkiah and some other court officials left right away and went to talk with Huldah, a previously unnamed prophetess. She was the wife of a court official, Shallum, the keeper of the wardrobe (vs. 22). Huldah may also have been the prophet Jeremiah's aunt, since Jeremiah had an uncle named Shallum (see Jer. 32:7). Huldah lived in the Second District of Jerusalem, probably a new working-class suburb west of the temple area and inside new walls added by Hezekiah and Manasseh (see 2 Chron. 32:5; 33:14).

Josiah wanted to know the implications of the scroll containing the law for himself, for the people, and for the existence of Judah (34:23). Huldah responded first about the people and the place. The prophetess revealed that the Lord would punish Judah, its capital, and its people in accordance with all the curses recorded on the scroll that had been read aloud to Judah's king (vs. 24). These calamities would happen because the people abandoned the Lord to burn incense and offer sacrifices to pagan deities. God was angered by all the idols they had made. Indeed, His wrath was so intense that it would blaze against Jerusalem and its temple and not be extinguished (vs. 25).

D. Sparing the King of Judgment: vss. 26-27

"Tell the king of Judah, who sent you to inquire of the LORD, 'This is what the LORD, the God of Israel, says concerning the words you heard: Because your heart was responsive and you humbled yourself before God when you heard what he spoke against this place and its people, and because you humbled yourself before me and tore your robes and wept in my presence, I have heard you, declares the LORD.'"

Huldah replied in more detail about the future of Judah's king. The prophetess explained that her words were not her own; rather, they came from "the LORD, the God of Israel" (2 Chron. 34:26). Yahweh had taken note of Josiah's tender spirit and responsive heart. In particular, when the king heard that Judah and its people would be completely wiped out, he humbled himself, expressed his despair by tearing his clothes, and wept in repentance before the Lord (vs. 27).

Huldah declared that because Josiah was genuinely distressed by what he had heard, the Lord would not bring His promised judgment until after the king had died and was buried in peace. The officials who received Huldah's message reported what she had said to Josiah (vs. 28). Since he would meet his death in a losing battle against Egypt, it's appropriate to ask in what sense he was "buried in peace."

When he died, he was at peace with God and in harmony with his subjects, who loved him and honored him in death (see 2 Kings 23:30; 2 Chron. 35:24-25). Also, his kingdom was still secure and intact.

II. A Sincere Response: 2 Chronicles 34:29, 31-33

A. Convening the Nation's Leaders: vs. 29

Then the king called together all the elders of Judah and Jerusalem.

The king summoned the leaders of the nation and the capital city to lead the populace of Judah in renewing their long-neglected and forgotten covenant with the Lord (2 Chron. 34:29). Josiah then led a royal procession the short distance from the palace to the temple. This group included representatives from all the inhabitants of Judah, the residents of Jerusalem, the priests, and the Levites. In fact, the solemn gathering included the least important to the most important people of the day, for the king knew that spiritual reform had to change everyone (vs. 30). Josiah's intent was to review the stipulations of the law and urge the leaders and people of Judah to heed them.

The temple was the place where God had pledged to show His presence among His people. Thus, it was a fitting spot for the king and his subjects to meet and rededicate themselves in service to God. Interestingly, Josiah himself—not Hilkiah the priest, Shaphan the scribe, or Jeremiah the prophet (who served as a spokesperson for God at this time)—read the Book of the Covenant to the assembly. Whether the Book of the Covenant was the same as the Book of the Law (see vss. 14-15) or just the part of it detailing the covenant and its attendant blessings and curses is unclear. If the Book of the Law was Deuteronomy, the Book of the Covenant may have been all or parts of chapters 5 through 28. Exodus 24:7 attaches the title "Book of the Covenant" to Exodus 20—23, a concise statement of Israel's covenant with the Lord.

B. Renewing the Covenant: vss. 31-32

The king stood by his pillar and renewed the covenant in the presence of the LORD—to follow the LORD and keep his commands, regulations and decrees with all his heart and all his soul, and to obey the words of the covenant written in this book. Then he had everyone in Jerusalem and Benjamin pledge themselves to it; the people of Jerusalem did this in accordance with the covenant of God, the God of their fathers.

Josaih's hope was that the people would be stirred to confession and repentance. The audience had to be instructed and awakened by the power of God's Word. They also had to be alerted to the coming dangers. Josiah knew they had to change course if they were to avert disaster. The king, realizing that he alone could not change the heart of the nation, hoped the people would follow his example.

Josiah positioned himself by one of two massive bronze pillars, Jakin and Boaz, in the portico at the temple entrance (see 2 Chron. 3:17). This was the usual place for royal activities that pertained to the Lord. For instance, kings were customarily crowned by the pillar (see 2 Kings 11:14). It was there that Josiah openly entered into a covenant before the Lord. This means the king made a binding agreement with God.

Josiah and those with him specifically pledged to follow the Lord with all their heart and soul, that is, to observe every aspect of the Mosaic law. This included the "commands, regulations and decrees" (2 Chron. 34:31). The king, along with all the people living in Jerusalem and in the territory of Benjamin, promised to do so (vs. 32). In this way, Josiah followed in the steps of Moses (see Exod. 24:3-8), Joshua (see Josh. 24), Samuel (see 1 Sam. 11:14—12:25), and Jehoiada the priest (see 2 Kings 11:17). Josiah also set the stage for later reformers, such as Ezra and Nehemiah (see Neh. 9—10).

C. Enacting Widespread Reforms: vs. 33

Josiah removed all the detestable idols from all the territory belonging to the Israelites, and he had all who were present in Israel serve the LORD their God. As long as he lived, they did not fail to follow the LORD, the God of their fathers.

In such a huge gathering, there would be tremendous pressure to conform. No one could see into the hearts of others. No one could tell who was sincere and who was hypocritical. Promises would be easy to make in the heat of the moment, but hard to keep when the lure of idolatry beckoned. Nevertheless, Josiah did all he could to bring God's laws into the conscious awareness of the people. The portion of Scripture discovered in the temple was the spark that brought the king and his people to repentance, confession, and commitment to follow the Lord. For the rest of Josiah's rule as king, the people did not turn away from the God of their ancestors (2 Chron. 34:33).

Part of the king's reform efforts included embarking on a systematic campaign to root out idolatry in Jerusalem, Judah, and the part of Israel to which he had access (see 2 Kings 23:4-14, 24). Josiah's demolition included tearing down the altars of the Baals (see 2 Chron. 34:4). Josiah's demolition also involved smashing of the Asherah poles (vss. 3-7).

Josiah took such harsh and drastic measures because he knew that pagan practices were deeply ingrained in the lives of Judah's citizens. He understood that if his renewal efforts were to have any lasting impact, he would have to weed out all ungodly practices. His sincere desire was that everyone under his rule would worship and serve the Lord rather than the things of the world. The three decades of Josiah's reign were characterized by peace and prosperity as well as spiritual reform. Given the years preceding and following it, Josiah's tenure as Judah's monarch were among the most pleasant experienced by the nation.

Discussion Questions

1. What was the Book of the Law that was found in the temple?
2. Why did Josiah's officials think it was important to tell him about the discovery of the scroll?
3. Why did the Lord plan to judge His people?
4. How had Josiah humbled himself before the Lord?
5. Why did the king think it was important to renew the covenant?

Contemporary Application

Mark R. Watkinson was a minister of the First Baptist Church in Ridleyville, Pennsylvania, and as a shepherd of a dynamic Christian congregation, he was well respected by his flock. Nevertheless, Watkinson did not restrict his influence to his church. Because the struggle between the North and the South was becoming increasingly hostile and religious sentiment was high, Watkinson deeply felt that someone or something had to turn the people's attention back to their Creator.

During this tense political climate in 1861, Watkinson believed the nation needed to be reminded of its spiritual roots. Thus, he wrote a letter to the secretary of the treasury, Salmon P. Chase, noting that the United States coinage omitted any reference to God. Watkinson suggested that a religious motto be inscribed on American coins that would indicate the nation's faith in God.

President Abraham Lincoln's administration enthusiastically welcomed Watkinson's advice, and subsequently, a number of mottoes were considered, including *God Our Trust, Our God and Our Country*, as well as Watkinson's own *God, Liberty, Law*. Finally, Secretary Chase selected *In God We Trust*, which has been printed on United States coinage and currency ever since.

Because of the godly action of one Christian leader, verbal homage is constantly visible to the people of the United States. Indeed, most Americans hold in their hands this sacred statement on a daily basis. Regardless of whether a person subscribes to this creed, these words still boldly indicate how every true Christian should live his or her life.

Leading God's people is not an easy task. Josiah kept the people on God's path, but later they wandered off it. If we are to stay on the Lord's path, we must first have God-honoring leaders like Josiah, and then we must do our part by following that leader and being a good example ourselves.

Daniel Keeps Covenant

DEVOTIONAL READING

Psalm 141:1-4

DAILY BIBLE READINGS

Monday March 31
  Psalm 141:1-4 A Prayer for God's Support

Tuesday April 1
  Daniel 1:1-2 God's House Besieged

Wednesday April 2
  Daniel 1:3-7 The King's Plan

Thursday April 3
  Daniel 1:8-10 Daniel's Resolution

Friday April 4
  Daniel 1:11-14 The Ten-Day Test

Saturday April 4
  Daniel 1:15-17 Four Fine Young Men

Sunday April 5
  Daniel 1:18-21 Tested and True

Scripture

Background Scripture: *Daniel 1*
Scripture Lesson: *Daniel 1:8-20*
Key Verse: *But Daniel resolved not to defile himself with the royal food and wine, and he asked the chief official for permission not to defile himself this way.* Danel 1:8.
Scripture Lesson for Children: *Daniel 1:3-4, 6-17*
Key Verses for Children: *Daniel resolved not to defile himself with the royal food and wine . . . God had caused the official to show favor and sympathy to Daniel.* Daniel 1:8-9.

Lesson Aim

To affirm that we can obey God even in complex situations.

Lesson Setting

Time: *605–602 B.C.*
Place: *Babylon*

Lesson Outline

Daniel Keeps Covenant

  I. Devotion to God: Daniel 1:8-14
      A. *The Request Made by Daniel: vs. 8*
      B. *The Official's Alarm: vss. 9-10*
      C. *The Suggestion Offered by Daniel: vss. 11-14*
  II. Appointment to Royal Service: Daniel 1:15-20
      A. *The Healthy Appearance of the Four: vss. 15-16*
      B. *The Remarkable Wisdom and Intelligence of the Four: vs. 17*
      C. *The Exceptional Talent of the Four: vss. 18-20*

Introduction for Adults

Topic: *Holding to Your Convictions!*

Every temptation promises us relief from some form of "hunger" inside us. What allures us in our weakest moments can include enticements such as eating, spending, and lusting (to name a few things). One way to get through temptation is this: look steadily at what is being offered and ask yourself, *Is this what I really want?* If we let that question sink in, we can discover a deeper need beneath our pressing desire of the moment: our hunger for unconditional love and fulfillment. It's a need only God can meet.

Perhaps it will also help to view sin in a different light—not as something we must constantly steel ourselves against, but as something we can finally gain the freedom to abandon, especially as we recognize its self-destructive effects. We find a glorious New Testament promise to encourage us: 1 Corinthians 10:13. Consider that Scripture as a promise that gives us the encouragement we need to hold to our convictions. As God did with Daniel, the Lord will always show us a way out—if we are open to taking it.

Introduction for Youth

Topic: *Go Along to Get Along?*

These days, adolescence is like entering a foreign land where new rules for survival must be learned. Saved teens discover that their faith and their culture often offer competing rules for that survival. Also, they come to see that schools and teachers have an influence on their lives that may at times encourage priorities that are at odds with their Christian faith. In fact, many youth feel great pressure to go along to get along with their friends and peers.

Consider Cheryl. She wants to be a Christian at school, but she's afraid of how her peers might respond to her openly living out her faith. She remembers another student named Jan who shared her faith with someone else in her science class. That student in turn complained to their teacher, who then scolded Jan for trying to "convert others to Jesus."

Being a saved teen in a non-Christian society can create situations in which it is difficult to serve God. This week we will study how Daniel obeyed the Lord despite the possible consequences of his actions. God calls us to display the same kind of obedience in difficult circumstances.

Concepts for Children

Topic: *Daniel Makes a Choice*

1. Daniel and his friends faced making a choice about who to obey.
2. Daniel resolved to follow God despite the consequences.
3. God gave Daniel favor with the palace official.
4. Even nonbelievers recognized the wisdom of Daniel's choice.
5. God blesses those who faithfully follow His Word.

Lesson Commentary

I. DEVOTION TO GOD: DANIEL 1:8-14

A. The Request Made by Daniel: vs. 8

But Daniel resolved not to defile himself with the royal food and wine, and he asked the chief official for permission not to defile himself this way.

In 605 B.C., Nebuchadnezzar conquered Judah and Jerusalem (Dan. 1:1-2). In keeping with a common practice of the time, the king had the best educated, most attractive, most capable and talented among Judah's citizens sent back to Babylon. In essence, only the poorer, uneducated people were left behind to populate conquered lands (see 2 Kings 24:14). Included among those deported from Judah to Babylon, were Daniel, Hananiah, Mishael, and Azariah (Dan. 1:3, 6). Most likely, they would have been about 14 or 15 years of age at this time.

Nebuchadnezzar commanded Ashpenaz, who was in charge of the king's court officials, to bring in some of the Israelites. The king specifically wanted to see members of the "royal family" (vs. 3) referring to princes descended from David, and others who came from the ranks of nobility. Nebuchadnezzar was obviously looking for the "cream of the crop" (so to speak) among the captives. He wanted young men of such physical and mental superiority that they would be "qualified" (vs. 4) for service to him.

Ashpenaz was charged with teaching the young men the Babylonian language (Akkadian) and literature. The latter was written in cuneiform (a complex syllabic writing system made up of wedge-shaped characters) and mainly engraved on clay tablets. The intent was to assimilate the captives into their new culture. In addition to this, they were to undergo an intensive three-year study program to prepare them for royal service. The course of study most likely included mathematics, history, astronomy, astrology, agriculture, architecture, law, and magic. During the course of their education, the young men would receive "food and wine" (vs. 5) rations directly from the table of the king.

The number of captives enrolled in the king's educational program is not stated. Only the names of the four young men from Judah are given. All four of the names referred to and honored the God of Israel in some way. In Hebrew, the ending "-el" means "God" and "-iah" is an abbreviation for "Yahweh." The God-honoring names of the four men could indicate that they all had God-fearing parents. But since their captors wanted their patron gods to be honored (for instance, Marduk, Nebo, and Ishtar) rather than the God of Israel, the names of the four youths were changed (vss. 6-7).

Daniel, meaning "My judge is God," was changed to Belteshazzar, possibly translated "Bel, protect his life" or "Lady, protect the king." Hananiah, meaning "Yahweh is gracious," became Shadrach, possibly translated, "The command of Aku" (the Sumerian moon-god) or "I am very fearful [of God]." Mishael, meaning

"Who is what God is?," was changed to Meshach, possibly translated, "Who is what Aku is?" or "I am of little account." Azariah, meaning "Yahweh has helped," became Abednego, possibly translated, "Servant of Nego" (a corruption of the name of the god Nebo, elsewhere called Nabu, the god of writing and vegetation) or "Servant of the shining one." If changing the names was a ploy to shift the young men's allegiance from the God of Israel to the gods of Babylon, it failed.

Those who were being groomed for service in the king's court received the best of everything, including food and drink from the king's own table. But because Daniel was certain the king's provisions would bring ritual uncleanness, he made up his mind not to partake of them. Daniel's concern centered on the realization that the king's food was not prepared in compliance with the law of Moses. Even the simple fact that it was prepared by Gentiles rendered it unclean. The king's diet included pork and horseflesh, which were forbidden by the Mosaic law (see Lev. 11; Deut. 14). Furthermore, the Gentile monarch's food and wine would have been offered to Babylonian gods before they reached his table. Consuming anything offered to pagan deities was strictly forbidden in Exodus 34:15.

Accordingly, Daniel resolved not to defile himself by breaking the Mosaic law. The word translated "resolve" (Dan. 1:8) denotes a determined, committed stand. When Daniel took this position, it was simply the natural result of a life-long pledge to be obedient to God's will in every situation. With boldness and courage, Daniel asked Ashpenaz for permission not to eat the king's delicacies or drink his wine. Evidently, Daniel's three companions shared his resoluteness and made the same commitment as well.

B. The Official's Alarm: vss. 9-10

Now God had caused the official to show favor and sympathy to Daniel, but the official told Daniel, "I am afraid of my lord the king, who has assigned your food and drink. Why should he see you looking worse than the other young men your age? The king would then have my head because of you."

Both Daniel 1:8 and 9 contain a phrase that can be rendered "the commander of the officials" or "the chief of the eunuchs." The earliest-known eunuchs lived in Mesopotamia, where they worked as servants in the women's quarters of the royal household. They could also serve as palace or government officials, even generals. They were castrated in the belief that this would make them more compliant to their superiors. While the Hebrew term for "eunuch" appears 47 times in the Old Testament, it is used in the technical sense of a castrated man on only 28 of those occasions. The rest of the time it appears to be used more broadly to refer to an official representative of the king. Its use in Daniel is probably meant to emphasize the official capacity of those who cared for Daniel, rather than their physical state.

As 1:3 states, Ashpenaz was in charge of the court officials. According to verse 9, God caused the overseer to be sympathetic to Daniel. Despite the respect, kindness, and compassion of Ashpenaz, he was afraid of violating the edict of his master, the king. Nebuchadnezzar had assigned the trainees a daily ration from his royal delicacies and from the wine he himself drank (vs. 5). Ashpenaz realized the monarch would hold him responsible if Daniel and his three Israelite associates looked malnourished in comparison to the other young men their age. The chief official also knew he would be decapitated for neglecting his duties (vs. 10).

C. The Suggestion Offered by Daniel: vss. 11-14

Daniel then said to the guard whom the chief official had appointed over Daniel, Hananiah, Mishael and Azariah, "Please test your servants for ten days: Give us nothing but vegetables to eat and water to drink. Then compare our appearance with that of the young men who eat the royal food, and treat your servants in accordance with what you see." So he agreed to this and tested them for ten days.

Since Daniel got nowhere with Ashpenaz, the young Israelite captive turned his attention to the guardian or warden placed over him by the chief official (Dan. 1:11). The petition was for the guardian to put Daniel and his friends on a 10-day trial diet. In the Old Testament, the number 10 was sometimes used as an ideal figure to denote completeness. Daniel proposed that the four be given nothing but vegetables to eat and water to drink (vs. 12). The Hebrew word for "vegetables" meant "that which grows from sown seed." Thus, grains, bread made from grain, and even fruit would also have been included. Since no plants were designated unclean by the law of Moses, there was no danger of ceremonial defilement with this diet.

At the end of 10 days, the warden could compare the appearance of the test subjects with that of the young men who were eating the royal delicacies. Based on what the guardian saw, he would decide what to do with Daniel and his friends (vs. 13). The warden agreed to Daniel's proposal (vs. 14). Perhaps the guardian was reassured by Daniel's confidence that the Jews would fare better on the vegetarian diet than those who ate the king's food. In any case, the warden probably reasoned that 10 days was not enough time for the health of the four youths to suffer any permanent damage.

II. Appointment to Royal Service: Daniel 1:15-20

A. The Healthy Appearance of the Four: vss. 15-16

At the end of the ten days they looked healthier and better nourished than any of the young men who ate the royal food. So the guard took away their choice food and the wine they were to drink and gave them vegetables instead.

At first, Ashpenaz worried that Daniel and his friends would become pale and thin compared to the other youths their age (Dan. 1:10); but at the end of the 10 days, the four looked healthier in appearance and their bodies looked better nourished than the rest of the young men who had been eating the royal delicacies (vs. 15). So after that, the warden removed the rich foods and wines from their diet and instead gave them only vegetables to eat (vs. 16).

Without compromising his principles or lowering his standards, Daniel managed to negotiate his way to an acceptable solution to a difficult problem. He undoubtedly petitioned the Lord for divine guidance in this matter. That he received God's assistance is obvious. Daniel's very life depended on his faith. Since he requested a specific amount of time, a specific method, and a specific result, he knew that only God could bring the necessary results. In one sense, Daniel was pitting God against the Babylonian king himself. Daniel would have seen in the Babylonian literature he was being taught many stories in which the gods and goddesses affirmed the king as a deity. So God was the ultimate reason for the success of Daniel's plan.

This incident illustrates the truth that God blesses those who obey and trust Him. Perhaps the lesson was not lost on the Israelite people as a whole. They had disobeyed God's laws and were severely judged because of it. Their nation was destroyed and they were now captives. Daniel and his friends, on the other hand, obeyed God by refusing to eat Nebuchadnezzar's food. They did this even though they knew their stand might cost them their lives. But because of their faithfulness and obedience, the four youths experienced God's blessing, and continued to thrive even in a hostile, ungodly environment.

B. The Remarkable Wisdom and Intelligence of the Four: vs. 17

To these four young men God gave knowledge and understanding of all kinds of literature and learning. And Daniel could understand visions and dreams of all kinds.

While Daniel and his three friends were being groomed for service in the royal court, God was preparing them for service to Him and to His people. The Lord gave the four Israelites "knowledge and understanding" (Dan. 1:17). They had a special ability to reason clearly and logically, and to approach any subject with insight and discernment. Under royal tutelage and with divine assistance, the four youths excelled in a wide range of subjects in the arts and sciences. Daniel, however, surpassed all the other students in a special field. God gave him insight into all kinds of dreams and visions.

It was commonly believed in ancient times that the gods spoke to human beings in dreams. Divine guidance was anticipated and sometimes actively sought through the medium of heaven-sent visions. In addition to the Babylonians, this was part of the culture of the Egyptians, Assyrians, Greeks, and Israelites. Through the ages, people's fascination with dreams and visions has focused especially on omens and oracles that supposedly reveal the future. Tragically, such activity has most often been associated with occultic practices.

Thus, when God's people entered the land of Canaan, where the occult permeated all areas of pagan society, they were strictly forbidden to adopt those practices (see Deut. 18:9-13). In Babylon, however, Daniel found himself immersed in a culture where that kind of occultic activity was woven into the fabric of everyday life. By God's Spirit and special commission, Daniel was able to interpret dreams without being tainted by any occultic associations.

C. The Exceptional Talent of the Four: vss. 18-20

At the end of the time set by the king to bring them in, the chief official presented them to Nebuchadnezzar. The king talked with them, and he found none equal to Daniel, Hananiah, Mishael and Azariah; so they entered the king's service. In every matter of wisdom and understanding about which the king questioned them, he found them ten times better than all the magicians and enchanters in his whole kingdom.

At the conclusion of the three-year educational program implemented by Nebuchadnezzar, Ashpenaz brought all the court trainees, including Daniel, Hananiah, Mishael, and Azariah, before the king for a final interview (Dan. 1:18). When the Babylonian monarch spoke with the graduates, he discovered that none of the others were as outstanding as the four Israelite captives. Because they impressed him so much, Nebuchadnezzar appointed them to serve among his staff of advisers in his royal court (vs. 19).

The Babylonian king found these four godly young men not only to be the best and brightest among the trainees, but also "ten times better" (vs. 20) than any of the magicians and enchanters throughout his empire. The phrase "ten times" was an expression in the Old Testament meaning "many times" (see Gen. 31:7; Num. 14:22; Job 19:3). "Magicians" (Dan. 1:20) was perhaps a general designation for all practitioners of the occult. "Enchanters" may refer to men who performed exorcisms by reciting special spells. In addition to "magicians" and "enchanters," in the next chapter and elsewhere, reference is made to "sorcerers," "astrologers," and "diviners." All of these seem to be covered by the ironic designation "wise men" (2:12-14).

Most cultures in the ancient world had an elite group of men who were trained in languages, court protocol, and international relations. The counsel and advice offered by these courtiers was highly regarded and widely sought after, especially by kings. The "wisdom" of such men was usually derived from many sources, most of which were connected with the occult or other pagan rites and rituals. Such men were among the king's closest advisors. They were glib, master communicators who knew how to impress the king with lofty messages from phony gods. Next to the true wisdom and knowledge imparted by the God of Israel, the best the occult specialists could offer looked anemic and uninspired.

Daniel, Hananiah, Mishael, and Azariah achieved prominence even though forced to live in a foreign land and culture. They honored God by applying themselves to their studies and striving for excellence in everything they did. They honored Him most, however, by their dedicated prayer, unwavering trust, and steadfast loyalty to godly convictions.

Daniel's service in the royal court continued until Cyrus overthrew the Babylonian empire in 539 B.C. (1:21). Other kings would come and go between Nebuchadnezzar and Cyrus; but it mattered little to Daniel which earthly monarch he was compelled to serve at any given time. His allegiance was to the King of all the earth. To God alone would Daniel kneel in prayer, bow in worship, and look for wisdom and guidance.

Discussion Questions

1. Why did Daniel resolve not to defile himself by eating food and wine provided by Nebuchadnezzar?
2. Why would Daniel take the risk of approaching the guardian with the proposal of a vegetarian diet?
3. What was the reason for the superior intellectual abilities of Daniel and his three friends?
4. How was it possible for Daniel and his friends to be without equal among their peers?
5. How was Daniel's faith in God evident throughout the entire episode?

Contemporary Application

The first chapter of Daniel teaches several important practical lessons. The first lesson is the value of discernment. The four Israelite youths knew exactly what was wrong with eating the king's food. Most likely, they learned this from pious parents (Deut. 6:4-9). Because of their early training in godly living, the young men knew precisely what they had to do the moment the crisis presented itself. Resisting temptation is easier and more effective if our principles are established ahead of time. The very moment at which temptation presents itself is a poor time to take a crash course in convictions.

The second lesson we learn from Daniel and his friends is the true character of courage. They were not afraid to speak up when their principles were challenged. But it was more than just talk. The guardian was right. Their refusal to eat the king's food could have cost them their lives. The same courage of conviction was revealed later in a fiery furnace and den of lions.

The third lesson is the power of perseverance laced with humility and common sense. Daniel and his companions were determined to overcome any obstacle in order to follow God. With respect and humility, Daniel presented his request to Ashpenaz that he not be made to defile himself with the king's food. But when Ashpenaz refused, Daniel in quiet persistence went to the guard and proposed a test that was both reasonable and feasible.

Many Christians seem to believe that God has called them to be either meek and mild milquetoasts, or loud, obnoxious, "in your face" witnesses for Christ. Neither approach seems to be very effective. God wants us to hold to our convictions with courage, and to witness for Him with love, humility, and a healthy dose of common sense. The lives of Daniel and his friends proved that divine wisdom is the best possible guide. Daniel demonstrated what wisdom coupled with quiet confidence and gentle persuasion can accomplish.

Three Refuse to Break Covenant

Scripture

Background Scripture: *Daniel 3*

Scripture Lesson: *Daniel 3:10-13, 16-18, 21, 24*

Key Verses: *"If we are thrown into the blazing furnace, the
God we serve is able to save us from it, and he will rescue us
from your hand, O king. But even if he does not, we want you
to know, O king, that we will not serve your gods or worship
the image of gold you have set up."* Daniel 3:17-18.

Scripture Lesson for Children: *Daniel 3:8-9, 12-13,
12-13, 16-18, 21, 24-26*

Key Verse for Children: *"Praise be the God of Shadrach,
Meshach and Abednego, who has . . . rescued his servants!
They trusted in him.* Daniel 3:28.

Lesson Aim

To stand for what is right, regardless of the consequences.

Lesson Setting

Time: *About 603 B.C.*

Place: *Babylon*

Lesson Outline

Three Refuse to Break Covenant

   I. Taking a Stand for What Is Right:
       Daniel 3:10-13, 16-18

      A. *The Decree of the King: vss. 10-11*

      B. *The Insubordination of the Three: vs. 12*

      C. *The Ultimatum of the King: vs. 13*

      D. *The Resolve of the Three: vss. 16-18*

  II. A Willingness to Face Death: Daniel 3:21, 24

      A. *Tossed into the Blazing Furnace: vs. 21*

      B. *Delivered from the Blazing Furnace: vs. 24*

Introduction for Adults

Topic: *Holding on to Your Faith*

When new offices or shopping centers are built today, they can be "instantly" landscaped with bushes, rolls of sod, and even large trees. That kind of portable landscaping is not what the prophet Jeremiah described when he told his audience to "plant" themselves in God (Jer. 17:7-8). Like firmly rooted trees, those who trusted God could remain faithful to Him regardless of the circumstances.

Always standing for what is right challenges our faith. It is tempting to follow the crowd instead. Yet just as a tree burrows its roots deep into the soil to brace itself against the storm and rain, so we believers can anchor ourselves in the Lord Jesus to withstand attacks against us. In this week's lesson, we see how three Jewish men stood against the wrath of King Nebuchadnezzar. Just as the Lord was with them, so He will be with us, especially as we honor Him in all that we say and do.

Introduction for Youth

Topic: *Standing Up to False Gods*

Correspondent Barry Petersen of the television program *Sunday Morning*, filed a report from Defan Art Village in China. He noted that the country now has "factories for a popular new export: art." It isn't original, one-of-a-kind art, either. These are copies of such famous works as Van Gogh's "Starry Night." He may have "sold one painting in his lifetime," but today they "come off the line by the dozens."

"Mass reproduction" is the operational mandate of the factory where these pieces are churned out. One finds "gallery after gallery, painter after painter, art for the masses by masses of artists." For example, there's Cheng Pei, who took four days to copy the "Mona Lisa," a piece that consumed four years of Leonardo Da Vinci's life. The replica Cheng will sell costs $36. Factory workers such as this can "even take a small photo from a computer e-mail and turn it into fine art."

Thankfully, Daniel's three friends—Shadrach, Meshach, and Abednego—were not fooled by cheap imitations of the living God. They didn't settle for counterfeit, manufactured deities when they could know by faith the Creator of the universe. In turn, He enabled them to stand up to the false gods of their day.

Concepts for Children

Topic: *Three Friends Take a Stand*

1. Three friends of Daniel—Shadrach, Meshach, and Abednego—refused to worship King Nebuchadnezzar's gold statue.
2. The king was so angry that he threw the three into a very hot furnace.
3. God honored the faith of the three by keeping them alive.
4. In this way, God showed the unbelieving king that He is all-powerful.
5. God is pleased when we do what is right, even when the outcome might be unpleasant.

Lesson Commentary

I. TAKING A STAND FOR WHAT IS RIGHT: DANIEL 3:10-13, 16-18

A. The Decree of the King: vss. 10-11

"You have issued a decree, O king, that everyone who hears the sound of the horn, flute, zither, lyre, harp, pipes and all kinds of music must fall down and worship the image of gold, and that whoever does not fall down and worship will be thrown into a blazing furnace."

Early in the reign of Nebuchadnezzar, the king became obsessed with his own power and grandeur. He decided to have a golden statue made. The image was 90 feet tall (about the size of a nine-story building) and nine feet wide (Dan. 3:1). Most likely, the object was not solid gold, but made from a less valuable metal or wood and overlaid with gold (see Isa. 40:19; 41:7; Jer. 10:3-4). When placed on a pedestal, the statue's imposing height would have been a striking statement to the greatness of Nebuchadnezzar and his lofty achievements.

Given the extremely narrow and high dimensions of the image, some have suggested it was an obelisk, that is, a pole-shaped tower of stone. Others think the statue represented either the king himself or a Babylonian deity. If the latter option was the case, it remains unclear which pagan god was honored by this object. Three possibilities include Marduk, Bel, or Nabu, with the third forming the first element of Nebuchadnezzar's name and being his patron deity.

In any case, Daniel 3:1 says that Nebuchadnezzar's dazzling image sat on the plain of Dura in the province of Babylon. It's unclear where this plain was located, but several sites have been suggested. One was the spot where the Harbor and Euphrates Rivers met. A second option is that Dura was located near Apollonia, north of Babylon and east of the Tigris River. A third possibility is that the location is to be associated with *Tulûl Dûra* (meaning "tells of Dura"), which is about 16 miles south of Babylon. Some think the name "Dura" could also have referred to a circular enclosure or fortress.

Despite these ambiguities, there is no doubt about the king's intent. He ordered a variety of international delegates to assemble, seven categories of whom are mentioned in verse 2 (see vss. 3, 27). While the specific duties each of these groups performed is debated, their loyalty to Nebuchadnezzar is not questioned. They complied with his order to gather for the dedication, stand before the image, and pledge their complete allegiance to the Babylonian monarch (vs. 3).

When all these important dignitaries had arrived, a herald made a loud proclamation. Those present represented the people of all races, nations, and languages whom Nebuchadnezzar had vanquished in order to establish his empire (vs. 4). The attendees learned that a variety of musical instruments would begin playing, including horns, flutes, zithers, lyres, harps, and pipes. (This indicates how important music was in the worship at ancient temples and palaces.) The sound of the music would be their signal to bow down to the ground and pay homage to the gold-plated colossus the king had erected (vs. 5). Falling prostrate in worship of the statue was not optional, either. Those who refused to obey would immediately be thrown into a furnace of blazing fire (vs. 6). Not surprisingly, as soon as the officials heard the music, they did exactly as they were told (vs. 7).

Imagine in the background a kiln with smoke roaring from its top. At once, a vast number of standing people bow in unison to the ground. It would not be difficult to spot any individuals who failed to comply. This proved to be the case with Daniel's three friends. Perhaps their Babylonian counterparts suspected they would refuse to fall prostrate before the statue. Also, some of the astrologers might have been jealous of the fact that Nebuchadnezzar followed Daniel's request to appoint Shadrach, Meshach, and Abednego as administrators over the province of Babylon (2:49).

In any case, certain Babylonians used this as an opportunity to come forward and bring malicious accusations against their Jewish peers. In 3:8, some think the word rendered "astrologers" denotes an order of priests who looked to the stars to foretell the future; but others note that the word can also be translated "Chaldeans" and used to refer to a particular ethnic group. This would imply the informants stigmatized the Jews simply because of their race (see Esth. 3:5-6). The word rendered "Jews" is a shortened form of "Judahite" and refers to the remnant of God's chosen people who once inhabited the southern kingdom of Judah.

Before the astrologers pressed forward with their agenda, they addressed the Babylonian monarch with the typical court greeting, "O king, live forever!" (vs. 9). Following this prescribed protocol did not necessarily reflect the real sentiments of the informants. They reminded Nebuchadnezzar of the edict he issued in which he commanded everyone to bow down and worship the gold-plated statue when the music was played (vs. 10). He also decreed that anyone who was insubordinate would be burned alive in a fiery furnace (vs. 11).

B.   The Insubordination of the Three: vs. 12

"But there are some Jews whom you have set over the affairs of the province of Babylon—Shadrach, Meshach and Abednego—who pay no attention to you, O king. They neither serve your gods nor worship the image of gold you have set up."

The Chaldeans brought to the king's attention three Jewish men he had appointed to high positions in the province of Babylon. Shadrach, Meshach, and Abednego were charged with failing to show proper respect to Nebuchadnezzar. Furthermore, the young men refused to serve his gods and pay homage to the golden statue he had erected (Dan. 3:12). As loyal citizens of Babylon, the Jewish exiles were expected to promote any cause connected with Nebuchadnezzar's deities and worship the image of gold. Of course, the king had no idea that their first duty was to the God of Israel, not to the patron gods of the state. Good polytheist that he was, the king couldn't understand why the Jewish nobles refused to worship his deities along with theirs, for that was the way everybody did it.

C. The Ultimatum of the King: vs. 13

Furious with rage, Nebuchadnezzar summoned Shadrach, Meshach and Abednego. So these men were brought before the king.

The whereabouts of Daniel in this episode remain unclear. Some suggest that because of his high position within Babylon, he was exempted from demonstrating his loyalty. Previously, Nebuchadnezzar had promoted Daniel to be the governor over the entire province of Babylon and put him in charge of the rest of the wise men (Dan. 2:48). Others speculate that either sickness or official business elsewhere prevented him from being able to attend the dedication ceremony. Regardless of which explanation is preferred, Daniel's position of power and influence did not exempt his friends from experiencing the wrath of the king.

Upon hearing the informants' report, Nebuchadnezzar became enraged at Shadrach, Meshach, and Abednego and ordered that they be brought before him (3:13). Perhaps as the three Jewish officials stood in front of the monarch's throne, he questioned them sharply to be sure that his informers had told him the truth (vs. 14). It was incomprehensible to him that anyone would disobey him, especially his trusted administrators. They were supposed to set the example for others, not break the laws.

Nebuchadnezzar stated that if the three refused to comply, they would be tossed at once into a flaming furnace. The king then threw down his final challenge. He dared them to even think that their God could save them from the wrath of his judgment; in other words, if they did not worship his god, they were doomed. Was Nebuchadnezzar really jealous for the worship of his gods, or was he outraged because the three had defied his order? Probably his authority was at stake. He could not tolerate the idea that even his choicest appointees would violate his decrees and get away with it.

D. The Resolve of the Three: vss. 16-18

Shadrach, Meshach and Abednego replied to the king, "O Nebuchadnezzar, we do not need to defend ourselves before you in this matter. If we are thrown into the blazing furnace, the God we serve is able to save us from it, and he will rescue us from your hand, O king. But even if he does not, we want you to know, O king, that we will not serve your gods or worship the image of gold you have set up."

Here is the beginning of a remarkable confession. Shadrach, Meshach, and Abednego were not daunted by the king's threats (Dan. 3:16). Note that initially they did not make any excuses for their refusal to worship the golden idol. In fact, their answer was a courageous acknowledgment that what their enemies had said about them was indeed true. Logic and survival would dictate that the Jewish officials had to defend themselves before the king. But they punctured the king's pride and power by telling him that they did not need to answer to him for their conduct in this matter. Of course, if they had placed top priority on their lives, they would have come up with some weak explanation and begged for mercy.

Instead of defending themselves and trying to save their lives, Shadrach, Meshach, and Abednego chose the path of unwavering faith. They testified that God was able to save them, and that if He so chose, He could rescue them (vs. 17). How did the three come by their strong faith? They had walked in obedience to God. They saw the Lord as personal, as someone whom they were bound to serve. They did not waffle, trying to worship Nebuchadnezzar and God. When the situation looked bleak, they went with God. To do otherwise would amount to idolatry.

Of course, Shadrach, Meshach, and Abednego were strengthened by standing together. They supported each other in their momentous decision. When the law was first passed, they had decided not to worship the idol. They probably had time to think, discuss, and pray together before being hauled before the king. They assured each other that they would remain faithful to Israel's God, no matter how terrible the punishment. Mutual support and encouragement are vital to unwavering faith. These men were prepared to die for their convictions. The bottom line for them was refusal to engage in false worship of any kind. Even though they owed their positions to the king, they would not compromise and worship his gods.

Part of the Jewish officials' strong faith must have sprung from their firsthand experience of being captured and deported. They probably knew how the prophets Isaiah and Jeremiah had warned Israel that idolatry would bring certain judgment from the Lord. Although Israel and Judah failed to repent, the lessons taught by the prophets had begun to take hold. After the captivity in Babylon, Israel was never again as prone to idolatry. Although these Jewish officials might die, it was not worth it to compromise. Israel and Judah had tried to mix idolatry with worship of God. That effort had brought catastrophe. Therefore, it did not make sense to try the same thing again.

Regardless of what Nebuchadnezzar might do, Shadrach, Meshach, and Abednego stood firm in their faith in the Lord and their obedience to His laws about worshiping other gods. Also, while the three were confident in their reply to the king, they were not presumptuous. They were personally convinced that God could rescue them, but recognized the possibility that they may have misunderstood His plans. Either way, their response would be the same. Whether it meant deliverance or death, they would never compromise in their faith (vs. 18).

II. A WILLINGNESS TO FACE DEATH: DANIEL 3:21, 24

A. Tossed into the Blazing Furnace: vs. 21

So these men, wearing their robes, trousers, turbans and other clothes, were bound and thrown into the blazing furnace.

Perhaps Nebuchadnezzar had never before encountered such stiff resistance. Didn't these young Jewish officials understand what the powerful Babyonian king could do with them? He was in no mood to back down and, because of his pride and position, he could not back down. He became so furious that his face became distorted with rage. To vent to his fury, he ordered his servants to heat up the furnace seven times hotter than usual (Dan. 3:19).

To make sure that nothing could upset his plans, the king ordered his toughest soldiers to bind Shadrach, Meshach, and Abednego and hurl them into the fiery furnace (vs. 20). Perhaps even then Nebuchadnezzar wasn't totally sure about his scheme. He certainly wasted no time on reflection or logic. He had put himself in a corner, and there was no way out. We don't know how long it was between the initial interrogation and the king's decision. While the monarch's face twisted with anger, no doubt the three young Jewish officials were deep in prayer, asking for God's intervention and for courage to remain true to their convictions. Faced with the prospect of certain death, they did not cave in, recant their faith, or beg for mercy from the authorities.

Consequently, the three were tied up while still wearing their full court attire and tossed into the superheated oven (vs. 21). The king's command was so urgent and the furnace so hot that the flames leaped out and incinerated the soldiers as they threw in the three men (vs. 22). That Nebuchadnezzar was willing to sacrifice his strongest troops to carry out the execution shows the intensity of the king's fury. It was probably the monarch's anger more than a sense of duty that compelled the soldiers to endanger their lives in this way. Humanly speaking, nothing now seemed to prevent Shadrach, Meshach, and Abednego from experiencing a similar gruesome end. There is no indication in the narrative that the three Jewish officials had any kind of spiritual vision or revelation that they would be saved from the furnace. They simply trusted in God even as they fell down into the roaring flames (vs. 23).

B. Delivered from the Blazing Furnace: vs. 24

Then King Nebuchadnezzar leaped to his feet in amazement and asked his advisers, "Weren't there three men that we tied up and threw into the fire?" They replied, "Certainly, O king."

"Seven times hotter" (Dan. 3:19) was enough to consume the soldiers, but not enough to destroy Shadrach, Meshach, and Abednego. Nebuchadnezzar realized that something astounding had taken place. He had to check his arithmetic. He was sure that he had sentenced three men to die in the furnace, and his advisers said this was true. Even though the king's soldiers had cast three men into the fire (vs. 24), Nebuchadnezzar saw four unharmed, unbound men in the blazing furnace.

The fourth figure the king described as "a son of the gods" (vs. 25). This answer fit his theology, which included the possibility of many gods. The monarch did not have a name for this person in the furnace, but he was sure the one he saw was not a mere mortal, but a supernatural being. According to verse 28, it was an angel. Some think the Lord Jesus Christ made a special appearance before His incarnation to save these faithful men. In any case, God had vindicated the unwavering faith of these Jewish officials with a mighty miracle. By definition this was an act

269

performed in the external world by the supernatural power of God, contrary to the ordinary course of nature, and designed to be a sign. In this incident, the deliverance of the three men from the fiery furnace was intended to show God's sovereignty over the Babylonians who had captured Israel.

After the three walked out of the fire (vs. 26; the fourth did not for he had evidently disappeared), the king and the members of his royal court gathered around them and marveled that the ropes binding them were the only things scorched. Not a hair on the Jewish officials' heads was singed. There was not even the smell of fire on them (vs. 27). Instead of losing their ability to influence the king, Daniel's three friends—who were willing to die rather than serve another god—were given a promotion, and God was honored throughout Babylon (vss. 29-30).

Discussion Questions

1. What was the consequence for disobeying the decree issued by Nebuchadnezzar?
2. Who brought the charge of insubordination against Shadrach, Meshach, and Abednego and why did they do so?
3. Why would the three refuse to defend themselves before the king?
4. What was the basis for the three deciding to defy the king?
5. How did God rescue the three from their fiery ordeal?

Contemporary Application

Shadrach, Meshach, and Abednego clearly understood that King Nebuchadnezzar would punish them if they refused to submit to his demand to commit idolatry. Yet despite the severe consequences, they were unwavering in their devotion to God.

Christians around the world today are suffering and even dying for their faith. Most of us, however, will never face a deadly threat as a result of standing for our Christian convictions. But we are often in situations where we must pay some kind of price for our faith when we stand up for what the Bible teaches to be true and right. At times, the price may be as costly as losing a job or alienating a loved one, but more often we may suffer a smirk or a derisive laugh.

When we put our religious beliefs on the line, we must always stand on our Christian principles regardless of the consequences. After all, Jesus was resolute in saving us from God's wrath despite encountering every kind of hostility and indignation. Therefore, we must have the same kind of attitude as His apostles, who rejoiced "because they had been counted worthy of suffering disgrace" (Acts 5:41) for Christ.

Keeping an unwavering faith in Christ when we are alone can be difficult. We need to remember that one straw can easily be broken, but many straws joined together are unbreakable. That is why God provides us with Christian brothers and sisters to strengthen us when we stand up for what is right in the Lord.

Daniel's Life-and-Death Test

DEVOTIONAL READING

Psalm 119:57-64

DAILY BIBLE READINGS

Monday April 14
Psalm 119:57-64 Prayer and Commitment

Tuesday April 15
Daniel 6:1-4 An Honest Leader

Wednesday April 16
Daniel 6:5-9 A Dishonest Plot

Thursday April 17
Daniel 6:10-14 The King's Distress

Friday April 18
Daniel 6:15-18 The Charge Stands

Saturday April 19
Daniel 6:19-23 Daniel Trusted in God

Sunday April 20
Daniel 6:24-28 The Living God

Scripture

Background Scripture: *Daniel 6*
Scripture Lesson: *Daniel 6:4-7, 10, 16, 19, 21, 25-26*
Key Verse: *Now when Daniel learned that the decree had been published, he went home to his upstairs room where the windows opened toward Jerusalem. Three times a day he got down on his knees and prayed, giving thanks to his God, just as he had done before.* Danel 6:10.
Scripture Lesson for Children: *Daniel 6:4-7, 10, 16, 19, 21, 25-26*
Key Verse for Children: *"My God sent his angel and shut the mouths of the lions . . . because I was found innocent."* Daniel 6:22.

Lesson Aim

To decide, when faced with a decision to choose between God and people, to choose God.

Lesson Setting

Time: *Between 539–537 B.C.*
Place: *Babylon*

Lesson Outline

Daniel's Life-and-Death Test

  I. The Dastardly Plan: Daniel 6:4-7
      A. *The Innocence of Daniel: vs. 4*
      B. *The Treacherous Plot of the Officials: vss. 5-7*
 II. The Divine Deliverance:
     Daniel 6:10, 16, 19, 21, 25-26
      A. *Daniel's Decision to Pray: vs. 10*
      B. *Daniel's Night in the Lions' Den: vs. 16*
      C. *Daniel's Deliverance from the Lions: vss. 19, 21*
      D. *Darius' Decree: vss. 25-26*

Introduction for Adults

Topic: *Faith without Compromise!*

Adults in your class probably consider themselves law-abiding citizens. It would be extremely difficult for them not to conform to the laws and regulations of society. They may fudge here and there, such as driving five miles over the speed limit, but they wouldn't flagrantly disregard the laws of the land, such as driving through red lights.

At times, however, your students are faced with situations in which they must obey God or submit to an authority that challenges their commitment to the Lord. When that occurs, they need to understand that they should set aside their desire to be "good" citizens, "good" employees, "good" adult children, or even "good" spouses if they are to be obedient children of God. This is neither easy nor pleasant, but with God's help it can be done. Daniel's life is proof of that.

Introduction for Youth

Topic: *Defiance!*

Fourteen years ago this month, Juvenal Habyarimana, the Hutu president of the central African nation of Rwanda, was returning by plane to Kigali, the country's capital. But as the aircraft was about to land, it was shot down. In response, the political opponents of the deceased president were murdered. Then, over the next 100 days, members of the rival Tutsi clan were also slaughtered.

During this horrendous bloodbath, one extraordinary person stood out—Paul Rusesabagina. He recounts in his book, *An Ordinary Man*, how he stood up to the insane actions unfolding around him by giving refuge to over 1,200 Tutsis and Hutus within the confines of the luxury hotel he managed. This was his way of defying the bands of murderers who hacked their victims to death with machetes. It is the same sort of ethical fortitude that saved teens should applaud, especially as they take a stand for justice and equity in our sometimes morally topsy-turvy world.

Concepts for Children

Topic: *Daniel Faces the Lions*

1. In defiance of civil authority, Daniel continued his practice of prayer.
2. Daniel's faith in God helped him stand firm even in the face of death.
3. God stood with Daniel in the lions' den and saved his life.
4. Daniel, who lived out his faith, influenced the king to proclaim the power of God.
5. God can help us choose the best way to respond to changing situations in our lives.

Lesson Commentary

I. THE DASTARDLY PLAN: DANIEL 6:4-7

A. The Innocence of Daniel: vs. 4

At this, the administrators and the satraps tried to find grounds for charges against Daniel in his conduct of government affairs, but they were unable to do so. They could find no corruption in him, because he was trustworthy and neither corrupt nor negligent.

In 539 B.C., Babylon fell and Darius the Mede took over the kingdom (Dan. 5:31). The exact identity of Babylon's new ruler remains debated (see 6:1, 6, 9). According to 9:1, he was the "son of Xerxes" ("Ahasuerus" in Hebrew), who was a "Mede by descent" (not to be confused with the person by the same name mentioned in Esth. 1:1). Apart from Scripture, Darius is not referred to in the surviving historical sources. Some think "Darius the Mede" (Dan. 5:31) was the throne name for Cyrus, the founder of the Persian empire (see 6:28). Others suggest the reference in 5:31 was a designation for Gubaru (or Gobryas), who was appointed governor over the territories the Persians had seized from the Babylonians.

When Darius came to power, he decided to divide the kingdom into 120 provinces, and he appointed "satraps" (6:1) to rule over each region of the empire. Each of these officials answered to a supervisor, who similarly was accountable to Darius. Initially, the monarch appointed three administrators, one of whom was Daniel, to watch out for the ruler's interests and ensure that the government ran properly (vs. 2). This included minimizing any loss of territory due to insurrections and erosion of tax revenue due to corruption. From the earliest days of Daniel's career, he had shown considerable promise (see 1:17-21; 4:8; 5:12). Not surprisingly, then, this exceptionally gifted and morally upright elder statesman distinguished himself above the rest of his peers, regardless of whether it was the other administrators or the satraps.

In turn, Darius took note of Daniel's exceptional qualities; and because he did his work so much better than the other officials, Darius intended to appoint Daniel over the entire kingdom (6:3). The king's plan, however, did not sit well with the other administrators and satraps, who became envious of the positive turn of events for Daniel. They thought they could undermine his standing with Darius by trying to find damaging evidence of negligence or corruption against Daniel in his "conduct of government affairs" (vs. 4). Yet, despite their efforts (which we can assume were extensive and exhaustive), the courtiers were unable to find any pretext for charging Daniel with a crime. In every area of his professional and personal life, he proved to be faithful and honest in fulfilling his responsibilities.

B. The Treacherous Plot of the Officials: vss. 5-7

Finally these men said, "We will never find any basis for charges against this man Daniel unless it has something to do with the law of his God." So the administrators and the satraps went as a group to the

273

king and said: "O King Darius, live forever! The royal administrators, prefects, satraps, advisers and governors have all agreed that the king should issue an edict and enforce the decree that anyone who prays to any god or man during the next thirty days, except to you, O king, shall be thrown into the lions' den."

Many years earlier, when Daniel was a younger Jewish captive being trained for a life of service in the government of Babylon, he resolved to follow the Lord whole-heartedly, regardless of the consequences; and God honored his devotion (see Dan. 1). Now almost six decades later, the elder statesmen faced a new challenge from the ministers who served alongside him in the court of the Persian government. The administrators and satraps concluded that the only grounds for charges they could trump up against Daniel had to be in connection with the requirements of his religion, as expressed in the Mosaic law (6:5).

The idea of how to entrap Daniel met with the approval of all the courtiers, and they conspired together to petition the king (vs. 6). Perhaps a representative body of the ministers sought audience with Darius. After entering his presence, they followed the custom of the day by declaring their hope that the monarch would live forever. Then, the government officials concisely stated their proposal that a royal edict be issued, which would also be strictly enforced. They exaggerated, though, when they claimed that all the ministers were in unanimous agreement. Obviously, Daniel was not in collusion with the rest of his peers.

Five different classes of important state officials are listed in verse 7. "Royal administrators" denotes commissioners who served in the uppermost echelons of government. "Prefects" would be high-ranking appointees, who were directly responsible to the "satraps." The latter oversaw larger divisions of the empire. "Advisers" were counselors who ministered in the royal court, while "governors" were lower-ranking administrators of outlying regions of the kingdom. In all probability, the majority of these officials were unaware of the plot against Daniel that had been devised by a smaller number of conspirators.

The plan was straightforward. The king's loyal subjects were forbidden to pray to any god or human being, other than the monarch. Also, the duration was reasonable, lasting just 30 days, after which it would expire. Those who violated the decree would be thrown into a den filled with lions. Verse 17 suggests the latter would have been a pit below ground level with a modest-sized opening at the top that was covered by a stone. This would make it impossible for a detainee such as Daniel to escape from the den.

The collaborators petitioned Darius to issue and sign the decree, which would ensure that it could not be altered or revoked. This conformed to the practice of the day (as attested in extra-biblical ancient writings), in which no one could repeal or revoke a law of the Medes and Persians (vs. 8; see Esth. 1:19; 8:8). Such a proposal would have met with the king's approval because he thought it would strengthen his political, military, and religious authority over the newly conquered territories once controlled by Babylon. Thus, he approved the request and signed the decree into law (Dan. 6:9). By doing so, he actually undermined his own power as king, for he allowed himself to be duped by subordinates who were manipulating him to achieve their own end.

II. THE DIVINE DELIVERANCE: DANIEL 6:10, 16, 19, 21, 25-26

A. Daniel's Decision to Pray: vs. 10

Now when Daniel learned that the decree had been published, he went home to his upstairs room where the windows opened toward Jerusalem. Three times a day he got down on his knees and prayed, giving thanks to his God, just as he had done before.

Given Daniel's high-ranking status in the government, it probably did not take long for him to learn about the issuance of the decree (Dan. 6:10). He was now in a quandary. Would he remain loyal in his devotion to the God of Israel and risk certain death in the lions' den, or would he succumb to the pressure by praying only to King Darius? The biblical text leaves no doubt about the decision of the elder statesman. He returned to his home, went upstairs, and kneeled in prayer in front of the latticed window that faced Jerusalem. He repeated this practice three times a day, which involved offering petitions and thanks to the God of his ancestors. This customary practice finds its basis in other Old Testament passages (see 1 Kings 8:44, 48; 2 Chron. 6:37-39; Pss. 5:7; 55:17-18; 138:2).

Incidentally, by this time, Zerubbabel had led a group of Jews back to the demolished former capital of Judah to rebuild it (see Ezra 1—2). Daniel would have been aware of this and regarded it as a sign of God's faithfulness to His chosen people (see Dan. 9). After more than eight decades of life under the Lord's care, there was no way that Daniel would suddenly now abandon his devotion. Not even the threat of torture and execution would prevent him from going before the Lord in prayer. Undoubtedly, his conspirators were familiar with the religious practices that characterized Daniel's piety and virtue; and sure enough, they found him on his knees in prayer, asking God for help (6:11).

B. Daniel's Night in the Lions' Den: vs. 16

So the king gave the order, and they brought Daniel and threw him into the lions' den. The king said to Daniel, "May your God, whom you serve continually, rescue you!"

The courtiers now had the evidence they needed to frame Daniel. The government officials approached the king and queried him about the seemingly innocuous decree he had enacted. He not only affirmed doing so, but also declared that it could not be revoked (Dan. 6:12). Imagine how chagrined Darius must have felt when the entourage of subordinates mentioned Daniel, whom the king highly admired. The courtiers noted that Daniel was one of the captives from Judah (vs. 13). This might have reflected their own prejudice against his ethnic identity. Despite the presence of such animosity, Daniel refused to compromise his Jewish heritage to achieve temporal gains.

The conspirators accused the elder statesman of refusing to obey the king or heed the royal edict he issued, as evidenced by Daniel's insistence on praying three times each day (most likely, early in the morning, then at midday, and finally at night). Rather than be enraged at his trusted subordinate, Darius became very upset and began thinking about how he might rescue Daniel. Evidently, the law mandated that the prescribed punishment be inflicted on a criminal the same day a transgression was committed. This meant the king had until sundown for his attendants to find any legal means of delivering Daniel from the predicament he faced (vs. 14). We can only imagine how much more agitated Darius felt when a bloodthirsty delegation reminded him of the irrevocable nature of the decree he had signed into law (vs. 15).

If this was a game of chess, the king would have been checkmated by the conspirators. In a sense, he acknowledged this when he ordered Daniel to be arrested and thrown into a pit containing hungry lions. Darius tried to console the aged Jewish exile with the possibility that the God whom he continually worshiped and served might rescue him (vs. 16). Then, a stone was rolled over the opening of the pit. Also, the king sealed it with his signet ring and with those of his nobles. This involved rolling the object against soft clay, which left the unique mark of the dignitary's seal. Unauthorized tampering would be a violation of the law and discourage any one from trying to rescue Daniel from his ordeal (vs. 17).

We can only imagine how Daniel must have felt. While most of us would have become distraught, it seems reasonable to assume that the Spirit of God overshadowed Daniel with an incomprehensible sense of peace (see Phil. 4:6-7; 1 Pet. 3:14). Perhaps like Paul and Silas during their imprisonment (see Acts 16:25), Daniel could be heard praying and singing hymns to God. The Spirit might have also interceded on his behalf with inexpressible groanings (Rom. 8:26). In contrast, Darius enjoyed no such peace of mind as he departed to his palace. Though he was surrounded by the safety and comfort of his plush dwellings, neither these nor his countless royal attendants could ease the anxiety he felt as his most trusted minister spent the night in a pit filled with ravenous beasts. Daniel 6:18 states that the monarch would not eat, and he refused his usual entertainment. In fact, all night he could not sleep.

C. Daniel's Deliverance from the Lions: vss. 19, 21

At the first light of dawn, the king got up and hurried to the lions' den. . . . Daniel answered, "O king, live forever!"

Very early the next morning, at daybreak, the monarch got up and rushed out of the palace to go to the lions' pit (Dan. 6:19). At some point, he ordered the removal of the heavy stone from the mouth of the den. He cautiously made his way to the pit, his voice filled with anxiety and distress as he called out to Daniel. Darius referred to the Jewish exile in the lions' pit as the "servant of the living God" (vs. 20). The king, hoping that Daniel was still alive, asked whether his God had rescued him from his predicament. Imagine the monarch's relief when he heard his most trusted minister respond with the customary wish that the king might live forever (vs. 21).

Then, Daniel explained that his God knew he was innocent of the charges his peers had maliciously brought against him. That is why the Lord sent His angel to keep the starved animals from devouring His faithful servant. Daniel ended with the assurance that he never did anything to defraud or harm Darius (or anyone else, for that matter; vs. 22). The king, perhaps feeling relieved at the sound of Daniel's voice, was delighted when he learned that his minister was safe.

Now that the stipulations of the royal edict had been fulfilled, it was permissible for Daniel to be hauled out of the pit by the king's attendants. Once they did this, they discovered he had no injury of any kind, for he had placed his trust in God (vs. 23). Like other saints of old, Daniel believed that God exists. The Lord, in turn, was pleased with and rewarded such faith (see Heb. 11:6).

This happy ending contrasted sharply with the fate awaiting those who had used the king to achieve their diabolical goal. The custom of the day was to inflict punishment on both the criminals and the families' members they represented. That is why the conspirators and their loved ones were tossed into the pit, where the half-starved beasts devoured them, bones and all (vs. 24). There is an ironic sense of justice here. Daniel's detractors had "falsely accused" him, which literally means they had "eaten the pieces of" him. In turn, they and their loved ones were overpowered and torn to pieces by the lions at the bottom of the pit.

D. Darius' Decree: vss. 25-26

Then King Darius wrote to all the peoples, nations and men of every language throughout the land: "May you prosper greatly! I issue a decree that in every part of my kingdom people must fear and reverence the God of Daniel. "For he is the living God and he endures forever; his kingdom will not be destroyed, his dominion will never end. "

Perhaps Daniel formally petitioned the king to issue a royal edict in which the God of the Jews was affirmed. We can only imagine how much of an encouragement this would be to the exiles returning to Judah from many years of captivity in Babylon. The decree, which Daniel beyond question helped to draft, was directed toward all the peoples, nations, and language groups living in the Persian empire. After a customary opening in which the monarch wished peace and prosperity to his loyal subjects (Dan. 6:25), he directed all inhabitants to tremble with fear before the "God of Daniel" (vs. 26).

Such reverential worship and honor was appropriate, for Yahweh had proven Himself to be the living God, who endured forever. Moreover, no one could destroy His kingdom or bring His authority to an end. The all-powerful God of the

Jewish captives had distinguished Himself above all other entities by rescuing Daniel, His faithful servant, from the lions' pit. This was just one example of God delivering people and performing miraculous signs and wonders, both in heaven and on earth (vs. 27). He is the same God who enabled Daniel to be promoted to prime minister and prosper in that position during the reigns of Darius the Mede and Cyrus the Persian (vs. 28). The latter continued as king until 530 B.C. He was followed by Cambyses, Darius I the Great, and Xerxes (Ahasuerus).

Discussion Questions

1. Why did Daniel's peers want to find a reason to bring charges against him?
2. Why did the conspirators try to frame Daniel in his religious practices?
3. Why did the king finally decide to have Daniel arrested and thrown into the lions' pit?
4. How did God rescue Daniel from the ravenous lions?
5. What was the nature of the decree the king issued?

Contemporary Application

The issue of choosing to obey God goes far beyond mere legal matters. Many "laws" are unwritten—cultural expectations, prevailing attitudes in society, pressure from peers, the influence of traditions, and so on. All these weigh heavily upon believers, who must choose between the ways of people and the ways of God. When the ways of people are morally neutral, there's no problem. But when they violate God's principles, a choice is required.

To choose for God in the face of popular opinion requires great courage and conviction. That is why we, like Daniel, need the indwelling power of the Spirit. And that is why we, like him, need to bath our circumstances in prayer. We may never be placed in a pit full of hungry lions, but every day we face other kinds of challenges to our faith. Also, every day we need the same devotion to God that motivated Daniel.

Overcoming challenges to our faith is a two-stage process. It begins with a clear understanding of God's will as revealed in Scripture and exemplified in the Lord Jesus. This understanding clarifies our purpose in this world so that we can recognize our God-given task in any situation. And we experience victory by drawing upon the Holy Spirit's enabling power to fulfill God's purpose for us regardless of the opposition we encounter.

Daniel's Prayer for the People

DEVOTIONAL READING

Psalm 130

DAILY BIBLE READINGS

Monday April 21
Psalm 130 The Assurance of Redemption

Tuesday April 22
Daniel 9:1-3 Preparing to Pray

Wednesday April 23
Daniel 9:4-10 A Righteous God

Thursday April 24
Daniel 9:11-14 God's Response to Sin

Friday April 25
Daniel 9:15-19 Hear, O God

Saturday April 26
Daniel 9:20-23 A Word Gone Out

Sunday April 27
Daniel 9:24-27 God's Strong Covenant

Scripture

Background Scripture: *Daniel 9*
Scripture Lesson: *Daniel 9:1-7, 17-19*
Key Verse: *"Now, our God, hear the prayers and petitions of your servant. For your sake, O Lord, look with favor on your desolate sanctuary."* Daniel 9:17.
Scripture Lesson for Children: *Daniel 9:1-7, 17-19*
Key Verse for Children: *"O Lord, listen! O Lord, forgive! O Lord, hear and act! For your sake, O my God, do not delay."* Daniel 9:19.

Lesson Aim

To affirm that God holds people responsible for their own behavior.

Lesson Setting

Time: *539–538 B.C.*
Place: *Babylon*

Lesson Outline

Daniel's Prayer for the People

I. Affirming the Righteousness of God: Daniel 9:1-7
   A. *The Concern of Daniel: vss. 1-3*
   B. *The Confession of Daniel: vss. 4-7*

II. Appealing to the Mercy of God: Daniel 9:17-19
   A. *The Petition for Divine Favor: vs. 17*
   B. *The Plea for a Divine Response: vss. 18-19*

Introduction for Adults

Topic: *Intercession in Crisis*

Even when we go through the painful process of repentance, we must never forget that God shows mercy and graciously bestows blessings upon us because it pleases Him to do so, not because we deserve it. Many people, believers and unbelievers alike, act as if God is somehow obligated to grant any and all requests made of Him. But since sin placed all humanity under a death sentence, it would be unwise indeed to demand that a just and holy God give us what we deserve.

The wonderful truth arising from this week's lesson is that God still answers the prayers of His children today, whether for themselves or for others in crisis. But there is a condition. He expects us to be walking in obedience to His will when we come to Him with our requests (see John 15:7). If there is unconfessed sin in our lives, the first prayer the Lord wants to hear from us is one of confession and repentance. Then the way is clear for prayers of petition and intercession. Clearly, that was Daniel's practice when he approached the throne of grace and God responded favorably to him. The same can also be our experience, if we so desire.

Introduction for Youth

Topic: *Confess!*

Daniel knew how to pray. Unreserved confession of sin opened his heart to the Lord. Complete submission to God's will also prepared the prophet for divine direction. Like Daniel, we should first go to the Lord in confession, then listen with an attitude of submission and openness to hear what He wants to say to us.

Quite often, God uses circumstances and other people to get our attention and draw us back to Him. In difficult times, we should be especially sensitive to how God may want to speak to us through them. Tragically, though, when trouble comes, it is all too easy for us to point the finger of blame and guilt toward others while excusing ourselves. It is difficult to imagine anyone among the Israelites more righteous and blameless than Daniel. Yet he was the one on his knees begging God's forgiveness for his sin and that of his people. If we want renewal and revival in our churches, the first step is for us to look into a mirror and ask the Lord to begin with the one we see.

Concepts for Children

Topic: *Daniel Asks God for Help*

1. We learn from Daniel's prayer that God's love for believers is firm.
2. We also discover that despite God's love, the people of Israel continued to rebel against Him.
3. Daniel sensed his duty to pray on behalf of God's people.
4. Daniel understood that God cares about how His people live.
5. God will listen to our prayers, regardless of what is going on in our lives.

Lesson Commentary

I. AFFIRMING THE RIGHTEOUSNESS OF GOD: DANIEL 9:1-7

A. The Concern of Daniel: vss. 1-3

In the first year of Darius son of Xerxes (a Mede by descent), who was made ruler over the Babylonian kingdom—in the first year of his reign, I, Daniel, understood from the Scriptures, according to the word of the LORD given to Jeremiah the prophet, that the desolation of Jerusalem would last seventy years. So I turned to the Lord God and pleaded with him in prayer and petition, in fasting, and in sackcloth and ashes.

The events of Daniel 9 took place during the first year of the reign of Darius the Mede (Dan. 9:1). That began in 539 B.C., the year Babylon was conquered by the Medo-Persians. Daniel had been in captivity for 66 years, since 605 B.C. At this time, he would have been about 82 years old. The last date recorded in the Book of Daniel is 536 B.C., "the third year of Cyrus king of Persia" (see 10:1). Media was a region northeast of Babylon. Almost nothing is known about the origins of the ancient people known as the Medes, and only a few words of their language have survived. Persia, modern Iran, was located south of Media.

While the kings of Persia and Media had made joint military campaigns into southwest Asia in 559 B.C., 20 years later Darius overthrew Belshazzar to gain control of the Babylonian empire. Belshazzar knew about his own fall in advance because of a handwritten message inscribed on his palace wall (see Dan. 5). The rise of the Medo-Persians was a providential act of God. Daniel apparently knew that the rise of Darius paved the way for the return of the Israelites to their homeland. Daniel understood from Jeremiah's prophecies (which the elder statesman regarded as being verbally inspired) that the 70-year exile begun by the "desolation of Jerusalem" (9:2), was nearing its end (see Jer. 25:11-12; 29:10).

The writer of Chronicles saw those 70 years as the sabbath rest for the land, time accumulated during 490 years when the people had neglected to allow the land to rest every seventh year, according to the law (see 2 Chron. 36:20-23; compare Lev. 25:1-7). With no specific way to measure the 70 years, some interpret this as a round number, perhaps denoting either a complete generation or an entire human lifetime (see Ps. 90:10). Others see it as the time period extending from 605 B.C. (the first attack on Jerusalem) to 536 B.C. (when Jerusalem was resettled). Still others calculate the 70 years from 586 B.C. (when the temple was destroyed) to 516 B.C. (when Zerubbabel dedicated the new temple; Ezra 6:13-18; Zech. 1:12).

In any case, Daniel's expectation for his people drove him to his knees in prayer. Two distinct terms appear in Daniel 9:3. The first, simply rendered "prayer," was a general word often used in intercessory entreaties. The second word, translated "petition," denoted a supplication for mercy and compassion. On behalf of his people, Daniel pleaded with God for mercy. Daniel also cried out to the Lord first in confession, and then in petition.

In describing how he prayed, Daniel said that he turned his face to the Lord. This could mean Daniel set aside his normal routine and devoted himself entirely to prayer. It may also allude to the practice of praying in the direction of Jerusalem. Earlier in this book, we read how Daniel prayed in his upstairs room, where the latticed windows opened toward Jerusalem (6:10). Daniel approached the throne of grace with fasting, adorned in sackcloth (a rough material similar to burlap), and ashes. All three of these were signs of deep repentance or personal grief and loss (Dan. 9:3; see Ezek. 27:29-31).

B. The Confession of Daniel: vss. 4-7

I prayed to the LORD my God and confessed: "O Lord, the great and awesome God, who keeps his covenant of love with all who love him and obey his commands, we have sinned and done wrong. We have been wicked and have rebelled; we have turned away from your commands and laws. We have not listened to your servants the prophets, who spoke in your name to our kings, our princes and our fathers, and to all the people of the land. Lord, you are righteous, but this day we are covered with shame—the men of Judah and people of Jerusalem and all Israel, both near and far, in all the countries where you have scattered us because of our unfaithfulness to you."

Daniel recognized that the exile in Babylon was God's judgment for Israel's sin. The prophet also understood what God's covenant with His people required if they were to receive forgiveness, restoration, and divine blessing. The nation had to confess its sin and obey the commands of God (Dan. 9:4-5). In this knowledge, Daniel confessed the sins of the people, not once but four times (vss. 5, 8, 11, 15). He included himself as if he were personally involved in Israel's wickedness, rebellion, and disobedience. Even though God had graciously sent the prophets to turn His people back, the nation as a whole had ignored their message. According to Daniel, all Israel was guilty before God (vss. 6, 8-11).

The elder statesman began his prayer by making reference to the "Lord" (vs. 4), a term that renders the four Hebrew letters making up the divine name, YHWH (or *Yahweh*). Incidentally, it appears eight times in this chapter, but nowhere else in the rest of the book. This special name for the covenant-keeping God of Israel emphasizes His eternal existence, supreme power, and active involvement in human history. In short, He is the ever-present, ever-living God (see Exod. 3:13-14). The second Hebrew term rendered "Lord" in Daniel 9:4 is *adonai*. It emphasizes the authority, rule, and majesty of Yahweh over all creation.

"God" is the rendering for *elohim* in the Hebrew. In addition to being used for rulers, judges, and pagan deities, the word is the most common way the writers of the Old Testament referred to God. Despite the plural form of the noun, it is consistently used in the Hebrew sacred writings as a singular term. As a matter of fact, when used as a proper name for the divine, *elohim* portrays the Lord as the one, true, and unique God. The totality of Scripture leaves the impression that He is unique in His being or essence, the fountain and source of all things, and the one who unifies all the forces of time and eternity.

These truths form the theological foundation of Daniel's confession. He affirmed that God is both great and awesome as well as faithful to fulfill His covenant promises with those who loved and obeyed Him. In contrast, God's chosen people had sinned against Him by doing what is wrong and wicked. They also rebelled by turning away from His commands and scorning His teachings (vs. 5). The covenant community refused to listen to the Lord's prophets, who humbly served Him. They spoke as His representatives in the authority of His name to a wide audience of people, including monarchs and princes who ruled the inhabitants of the promised land (vs. 6).

Daniel affirmed the righteousness of the Lord in His person and actions. His chosen people, though, suffered public disgrace as a result of their disloyalty to God. Because they transgressed His ways, He was in the right to scatter them far and wide (vs. 7). All the chosen people experienced the humiliation of being dragged away to foreign lands because of their sin (vs. 8). Yet despite their rebellion, the sovereign Lord remained merciful and forgiving (vs. 9). His compassion was evident when He gave the Mosaic law; but the recipients of His favor refused to heed His stipulations and listen to His teachings, as set before them through His prophets (vs. 10).

Before the destruction of Jerusalem by the Babylonians, many people of Judah did not believe that God would destroy His own temple and His holy city until it actually happened. They continued in their worship of other gods. The prophets repeatedly pointed out that the people's unfaithfulness would bring judgment, and it did, namely, their 70-year exile in Babylon. The rejection of the prophets proved the people's unfaithfulness. Although the Lord's representatives occasionally foretold future events, their primary responsibility was calling the nation to obey God in the present. They spoke to Israel's leaders and, through them, to all the people.

Tragically, the entire nation was guilty of stubbornly refusing to follow the Lord's will (vs. 11); and because God is just in everything He does (vs. 14), He had no other choice but to pour out on His wayward people the judgment solemnly threatened in the Mosaic law (see Deut. 28:15-68). God had given His people a very simple choice—obey Him and be blessed or disobey Him and suffer terrible curses. Because Israel had chosen the latter course, the people were dispersed and Jerusalem fell (Dan. 9:12). These horrible calamities were meant to bring God's people back to Him, but they refused to respond. Yet in spite of the unparalleled "disaster" (vs. 13) brought upon the nation, the people were still not turning away from their sin and submitting themselves to God's "truth."

II. Appealing to the Mercy of God: Daniel 9:17-19

A. The Petition for Divine Favor: vs. 17

"Now, our God, hear the prayers and petitions of your servant. For your sake, O Lord, look with favor on your desolate sanctuary."

Daniel's petition for divine favor was grounded in an awareness of how God had faithfully acted throughout the course of Israel's history. The premier example of this was the Lord's deliverance of His people out of the land of Egypt with great power. Because of that mighty act, God brought lasting honor to His name; but this did not prevent His chosen people from sinning and behaving wickedly (Dan. 9:15). As a consequence of this sobering truth, the only thing Daniel could do was appeal to the Lord on the basis of His justice.

In view of all of God's faithfulness and mercy in connection with His covenant promises, the elder statesman humbly asked the Lord to turn His raging anger away from Jerusalem. It was the chosen city built on His holy mountain (vs. 16) and thus the place where God decided to dwell and reign (Pss. 43:3; 68:16; Isa. 24:23). As such, it was intended to be the sacred site where the people could enjoy a transcendent encounter with God, in addition to finding refuge, peace, and joy in His presence (Isa. 2:1-5; Mic. 4:1-5).

In short, Daniel was entreating the Lord to end Jerusalem's condition as an object of scorn among the surrounding nations. Suggested here is the idea that the fortunes of a country, whether good or bad, were an indicator of its deity's power and might. A positive outcome for Judah would require God to forgive the sins of the current generation of Jews and the iniquities committed by their ancestors (Dan. 9:16). With humility and courage, Daniel petitioned God to "hear" (vs. 17) the prayer of His servant. Expressed differently, the prophet asked the Lord to graciously accept his request to show favor on His devastated sanctuary. Daniel was convinced that God would bring honor to His name by smiling once again on His temple. Though it lay in ruins, the Lord could enable His people to rebuild it.

B. The Plea for a Divine Response: vss. 18-19

"Give ear, O God, and hear; open your eyes and see the desolation of the city that bears your Name. We do not make requests of you because we are righteous, but because of your great mercy. O Lord, listen! O Lord, forgive! O Lord, hear and act! For your sake, O my God, do not delay, because your city and your people bear your Name."

Daniel concluded with an entreaty to God to "give ear" (Dan. 9:18) to his prayer, as if the Lord would turn His ear to listen attentively to the prophet's request. Daniel also asked God to open His eyes and see the ruined condition of Jerusalem. The Hebrew word translated "desolation" usually describes devastation that results from divine judgment. Daniel was not implying that God was not listening or had closed His eyes to the exiles' problems. The Lord was fully aware of these issues. This prayer, however, came from the human perspective on the circumstances. It appeared to the Jews still in exile in Babylon as if God had stopped listening and had closed His eyes.

Although Daniel hoped God would show compassion, the prophet recognized that Israel deserved its current suffering. Therefore, his prayer request appealed to divine mercy; but the petition also showed a concern for God. Daniel reminded

Him that both the city of Jerusalem and His people carried His "Name" as a mark of ownership. The Hebrew word can signify reputation or renown, as in God's name being praised and known for what He has done (2 Sam. 7:25-26). The Lord's deliverance of His people from Babylon would show who He was to the people who were called by His name. Also, since God's reputation rested with His people and His holy city, the neighboring peoples would recognize who the Lord is by His deliverance of the Jews and restoration of Jerusalem and its temple.

Daniel acknowledged that he was not basing his requests on the righteous deeds of himself or his fellow Jews, whether they were living in the past or present; rather, it was due to the Lord's abundant compassion (Dan. 9:18). This truth mirrors what is recorded in Deuteronomy 7:7-8, which is part of Moses' address to the Israelites on the plains of Moab. The lawgiver declared that the Lord did not favor or choose them because they were more numerous and mighty than all other peoples. In fact, they were the least numerous and weakest among the surrounding nations. To the contrary, God lavished His affection on His people because of His unconditional love for them and His faithfulness to the promise He solemnly vowed to their ancestors. In keeping with that pledge, the Lord used His great power to redeem the Israelites from slavery in Egypt and the control of Pharaoh.

Daniel was not trying to manipulate God; rather, the prophet showed a concern for the glory of the Lord. Daniel realized that God's reputation was inevitably tied to the fortunes of His exiled people. Thus, the prophet was convinced that even though they had disowned God, He would not disown them. This truth emboldened Daniel to plead with the Lord to hear his request and forgive the sins of His people. The prophet entreated God to act quickly in restoring the exiles to the promised land and enable them to bring honor to His name by rebuilding their sanctuary and capital (Dan. 9:19).

Daniel reviewed the content of his prayer once again. He had started by confessing his own sins and the sins of Israel. While nothing negative is recorded about the prophet in Scripture, he still identified himself with the sins of Israel. In his petition, he asked God to consider the state of "his holy hill" (vs. 20), meaning Jerusalem. Daniel requested that the Lord not delay in acting upon his prayer. And the divine response could hardly have come more quickly.

While Daniel was still making his entreaty, he was interrupted by the angel, Gabriel, who had appeared to him earlier with an interpretation of the ram and goat vision (vs. 21; see 8:15-16). Throughout the Bible, we see how God used angels as one way to communicate with people. When they appeared, it was in human form. For instance, Daniel referred to Gabriel as a "man" (Dan. 9:21). Gabriel is one of only two angels who are named in the Bible (the other being Michael). Gabriel is the celestial messenger who appeared in the New Testament to announce the births of John the Baptizer and the Lord Jesus.

Gabriel said he had come to give Daniel insight and understanding about God's plans for Israel (vs. 22). Because of the high esteem the Lord had for Daniel,

Gabriel was dispatched with an answer to the prophet's prayer at the very moment he had begun his supplication. Indeed, God had a very important message for Daniel about the future of the chosen people (vs. 23). Gabriel revealed that God's program for the Jews would be completed in "seventy 'sevens'" (vs. 24). Daniel would naturally have understood the "sevens" to signify actual years. Thus, "seventy 'sevens'" would equal 490 years.

Daniel was told that during the course of the 490 years, God would do several things for Israel (Dan. 9:24). He would end the people's rebellion and sin, make atonement for their "wickedness" (through the atoning sacrifice of the Messiah), and establish a permanent state of righteousness (at the return of the Lord Jesus to establish His kingdom). Furthermore, God would "seal up vision and prophecy" (by fulfilling His covenant promises to Israel), and "anoint the most holy" (by enthroning the Messiah as Israel's King). Gabriel unfolded God's 490-year program for Israel by using key events as chronological beginning and ending points. The angel said the program would begin with a "decree to restore and rebuild Jerusalem" (vs. 25) and end when "the Anointed One" returns.

Discussion Questions

1. What understanding did Daniel have concerning Jeremiah's prophecy?
2. Why did Daniel begin his prayer by referring to the Lord as the "great and awesome God" (Dan. 9:4)?
3. How had God's chosen people responded to His covenantal love?
4. In what sense were the Jewish exiles covered with shame?
5. What specifically did Daniel ask God to do for His people?

Contemporary Application

If you were to interview the students in your class, you would discover that they shoulder a wide variety of personal responsibilities. Many are married, have children, and hold at least one job. The class members have to deal with financial obligations, work-related deadlines, and health matters.

Your students have a multitude of complex and controversial decisions to make as they shoulder their responsibilities. For instance, administrators in large organizations often have to make decisions about who to hire or fire, what projects to begin or end, and how to expand or contract certain business ventures.

What happens when a decision that is made backfires? When things go wrong, it is all too common for people to shift the blame to others. It is much rarer to find individuals who hold themselves accountable for their actions. One reason for this is that people do not want to endure the negative consequences associated with a mistake or error in judgment they have made.

In this week's lesson, we discover that it is wrong to blame others for mistakes we have made. God wants us to take personal responsibility for our own lives. When we do, He is glorified and immensely pleased.

The Temple Rebuilt

DEVOTIONAL READING

Psalm 84:1-4

DAILY BIBLE READINGS

Monday April 28
Psalm 84:1-4 In God's House

Tuesday April 29
Haggai 1:1-11 Time to Rebuild the Temple

Wednesday April 30
Haggai 1:12-15 The Work Begins

Thursday May 1
Ezra 3:8-13 Rebuilding the Foundation

Friday May 2
Ezra 4:1-4 Help Rejected

Saturday May 3
Ezra 5:1-5 The Rebuilding Questioned

Sunday May 4
Ezra 5:6-17 The Decree of King Cyrus

Scripture

Background Scripture: *Haggai 1; Ezra 5*
Scripture Lesson: *Haggai 1:1-4, 7-10, 12-15*
Key Verse: *"Go up into the mountains and bring down timber and build the house, so that I may take pleasure in it and be honored," says the LORD.* Haggai 1:8.
Scripture Lesson for Children: *Haggai 1:1-4, 7-10, 12-13*
Key Verse for Children: *[The people] came and began to work on the house of the LORD Almighty.* Haggai 1:14.

Lesson Aim

To understand that God blesses us when we give first priority to His purposes and plans.

Lesson Setting

Time: *520 B.C.*
Place: *Jerusalem*

Lesson Outline

The Temple Rebuilt

I. The People's Neglect: Haggai 1:1-4, 7-10
   A. *The Lord's Commission of Haggai: vs. 1*
   B. *The Lord's Question to His People: vss. 2-4*
   C. *The Lord's Exhortation to Begin Rebuilding: vss. 7-8*
   D. *The Consequence of the People's Disobedience: vss. 9-10*

II. The People's Response: Haggai 1:12-15
   A. *The People's Reverential Obedience: vs. 12*
   B. *The Lord's Encouraging Word: vss. 13-15*

Introduction for Adults

Topic: *First Things First!*

Merriam Webster's Collegiate Dictionary says that procrastination is "to put off intentionally the doing of something that should be done." God has called us to do His work in the church and in the world. At first, we might be eager and energetic; but when obstacles and hardships arise, our enthusiasm fades and we begin to put off doing what the Lord wants.

How can God bless us as long as we procrastinate in serving Him? We need to remember that the Lord blesses us when we give first priority to His purposes and plans. When we set our minds on doing His will before all other things, He gives us the strength and resources we need to get the job done. God will watch over us in times of difficulty and encourage us when we feel dejected. With the Lord on our side, we can do all that He asks of us.

Introduction for Youth

Topic: *Rebuild!*

A teacher once wrote the word *apathy* in large letters across the entire chalkboard of his classroom. One of his students broke his conversation with another student long enough to glance at the word on the board, slowly sounding the word out. Then the student turned to the guy slouched next to him and asked what the word meant. The classic response came: "Who cares?"

The story may be funny, but the truth it conveys is tragic. Apathy can be like a crippling disease among teens, especially believers. In fact, when it comes to doing the work of God in the church and surrounding community, too many Christians are apathetic. They would rather form "holy huddles" than do all that the Lord desires of them.

Apathy might feel comfortable and safe, but it accomplishes little of value. The people of Haggai's day had grown apathetic about rebuilding the temple, and God used the prophet to spur them to action. Once they overcame their complacency, they did a great work for God and experienced His blessing.

Concepts for Children

Topic: *The People Go to Work*

1. God sent Haggai to tell the people that they were wrong for not rebuilding the house of worship in Jerusalem.
2. Haggai showed the people that they were to blame for not finishing the work they had started.
3. The people obeyed the words of the Lord that Haggai had spoken to them.
4. Haggai promised the people that God would remain with them as they rebuilt the house of worship.
5. God is also with us as we seek to obey Him.

Lesson Commentary

I. THE PEOPLE'S NEGLECT: HAGGAI 1:1-4, 7-10

A. The Lord's Commission of Haggai: vs. 1

In the second year of King Darius, on the first day of the sixth month, the word of the LORD came through the prophet Haggai to Zerubbabel son of Shealtiel, governor of Judah, and to Joshua son of Jehozadak, the high priest.

In 538 B.C., King Cyrus of Persia allowed a group of Jews under the leadership of Zerubbabel to return to Jerusalem (Ezra 1—3). Then, in 536 B.C., with the permission of the king, the Jews began to rebuild the temple. The books of Ezra and Nehemiah, together with the prophecies of Haggai and Zechariah (both dated about 520 B.C.) and Malachi (about 432 B.C.), comprise the main Hebrew records of those years.

Ezra 1:7 reveals that King Cyrus brought out the bowls and pans that had once been in the temple of the Lord. Nebuchadnezzar had taken these articles from Jerusalem and placed them in the shrine of his own god. Verse 8 notes that Cyrus had Mithredath, his chief treasurer, return the stolen items to Sheshbazzar, the "prince of Judah." This particular title "prince" does not necessarily imply descent from royalty. Sheshbazzar probably was a Jewish deputy of the governor of the Persian province of Samaria, from which a new province, Judah, was being carved to accommodate the returning exiles (see 5:14).

Eventually Sheshbazzar loses importance in the biblical narratives to Zerubbabel. He is identified as "governor" in the description of the return recorded in Haggai 1:1. The Persian government authorized this person of Davidic lineage to spearhead the return of the Jewish exiles and the restoration of Judah. Some have suggested that Sheshbazzar and Zerubbabel are the same person, but it is more likely that Sheshbazzar was an elderly governor while Zerubbabel was the younger, more popular leader (Ezra 3:8-11). In fact, some have suggested that Sheshbazzar is to be identified with Shenazzar (1 Chron. 3:18), the fourth son of King Jehoiachin. Sheshbazzar would then have been Zerubbabel's uncle.

Under the leadership of Zerubbabel and Joshua, the high priest, the foundation of the Jerusalem temple was laid. Before the exile, a monarch ruled God's people; but in the period after the exile and return to Judah, the leadership was jointly shared by two office holders, one civil and the other religious. The latter was the son of Jehozadak or Jozadak (who had been taken captive by Nebuchadnezzar) and thus a descendant of Zadok, the high priest (Hag. 1:1; see 1 Chron. 6:8, 15). At the end of David's reign over Israel, Zadok distinguished himself by remaining faithful to the king and helping to anoint Solomon as the next monarch (1 Kings 1:7-8, 32-45). This led to the removal of Abiathar as high priest and the appointment of Zadok as the sole holder of the sacred office (2:26-27). In short, Jehozadak was the member of a priestly family with an honorable history. Undoubtedly, this placed him in high regard among the Jews returning from exile in Babylon.

Tragically, the rebuilding of the shrine was interrupted for a number of years due to opposition from the Samaritans and the indifference of many of the returned exiles who had never worshiped in the temple of Solomon. In 521 B.C., King Darius Hystaspes ascended the Persian throne (ruling from 521–486 B.C.). After crushing a number of revolts, he consolidated his control over the empire and restored political stability. He also discovered the decree of Cyrus for rebuilding the Jerusalem temple and reactivated the mandate. Shortly thereafter, on August 29, 520 B.C., God raised up the prophet Haggai to exhort Zerubbabel, Joshua, and the people of Judah to resume rebuilding of the shrine (Hag. 1:1). Through the ministry of Haggai and Zechariah, his contemporary, the endeavor was completed in four years (516 B.C.).

B.   The Lord's Question to His People: vss. 2-4

This is what the LORD Almighty says: "These people say, 'The time has not yet come for the LORD's house to be built.'" Then the word of the LORD came through the prophet Haggai: "Is it a time for you yourselves to be living in your paneled houses, while this house remains a ruin?"

The prophet began his message by stating, "This is what the LORD Almighty says" (Hag. 1:2). He did not want anyone to mistake his words; they came with the full authority of God Himself. The phrase "LORD Almighty" (traditionally rendered "LORD of hosts") occurs 91 times in the books of Haggai (14), Zechariah (53), and Malachi (24). The term "Almighty" can refer to the Lord as the leader of heaven's armies (1 Sam. 17:45). It stresses His sovereign majesty as the divine warrior who is forever victorious. The all-powerful God of Israel declared that the time had come for His people to resume work on rebuilding the temple. The Lord revealed His displeasure with the inhabitants of Judah, referring to them as "these people" (Hag. 1:2) rather than "my people."

The Jewish inhabitants of Jerusalem excused their apathy by declaring that the time had not yet come for them to rebuild the Lord's house of worship in the holy city. Some believed that the 70 years of captivity were not yet up (see Jer. 25:11-12; 29:10). Though they claimed to be waiting for a better time to proceed, the real problem was the people's lack of concern. In effect, they were saying, "We'll work on the shrine when we get around to it." The people were aware of their ambivalence, but it did not seem to bother them. It is true that times were not the best for rebuilding the temple. After all, political turmoil, local opposition, civil war, poor communication with the central government, famine, and a sinking economy all combined to put a damper on such an ambitious construction project. God's people lumped all these factors together and concluded the time wasn't right. In fact, they were willing to put things off indefinitely.

Haggai exposed the reason why the work of rebuilding the temple wasn't finished by comparing the people's homes to God's house of worship (Hag. 1:3-4). If conditions weren't satisfactory for building the temple, then why were they able to remodel and beautify their own homes with cedar paneling (or possibly a protective plastering)? With God's sanctuary in ruins, the people should have given less priority to the rebuilding of their homes. Haggai's penetrating question shows that the inhabitants put their own interests before God's. Their own well-being took precedence over the public testimony to the Lord as represented by the temple.

C. The Lord's Exhortation to Begin Rebuilding: vss. 7-8

This is what the LORD Almighty says: "Give careful thought to your ways. Go up into the mountains and bring down timber and build the house, so that I may take pleasure in it and be honored," says the LORD.

Apparently, Haggai did not wait for excuses or confessions. He forged ahead beyond the obvious answer and told the people to look at themselves and their circumstances (Hag. 1:5). The prophet exhorted them to consider the results of the investment of their time and strength in their own needs. The inhabitants had sown much seed, but harvested meager crops (such as grapes, figs, and pomegranates, which were picked at that time of year). They were eating and drinking without satisfaction. They had clothes, but were cold. They had money, but could not hold on to it (vs. 6).

It was proper for the Lord to withhold His blessings. After all, His people had lopsided priorities in which they crowded out God. In response, the Lord of hosts reversed the normal process of things, so that the harder the people worked for themselves, the less they got in return. Their crops, food, clothes, and wages seemed to disappear. In light of these facts, Haggai again told the people to consider their ways (vs. 7). Then he urged them to swing into action. Once they admitted their unwise decisions, they would be ready to rebuild the temple. They would recognize that further delays would be self-defeating and dishonoring to God.

The people had gone to the hills to get timber for their houses. Now it was time for them to gather lumber for the temple (vs. 8). Since the exterior of the shrine was primarily made out of large stones, the wood was probably used for the structure's interior paneling (see Ezra 5:8; 6:4). Often, getting started is the most difficult part of a project. Gathering timber from the forests would show obedience and initiate the rebuilding process. Previously, Solomon's temple had been built with cedars from Lebanon; but now, because of the limited resources available to the people, trees in the nearby rugged hills around Jerusalem (which were well wooded at this time) would provide lumber.

The issue was not simply the building, but pleasing God by giving Him priority instead of always attending to one's own needs. Haggai reminded the resettled inhabitants that their majestic and sovereign Lord would be pleased by their work on His house of worship. His pleasure related to the fact that the temple represented His glory to the people. It was an outward sign of God's presence among them.

D. The Consequence of the People's Disobedience: vss. 9-10

*"You expected much, but see, it turned out to be little. What you brought home, I blew away. Why?"
declares the LORD Almighty. "Because of my house, which remains a ruin, while each of you is busy
with his own house. Therefore, because of you the heavens have withheld their dew and the earth its
crops."*

For emphasis, Haggai returned to his previous theme: because of the people's
delay in rebuilding the temple, the all-powerful Lord had withheld His blessings.
The people "expected much" (Hag. 1:9); however, the greater their greediness, the
more bitter was their disappointment, because they were poorer than ever. As long
as they remained unrepentant, the Lord would thwart their efforts to become more
prosperous. They failed to recognize that God was judging them for their disobedience, in accordance with the stipulations of the Mosaic covenant (see Lev. 26:20;
Deut. 11:8-15; 28:29, 38-40).

The prophet's explanation of the people's hard times focused on their agricultural economy. When they brought their harvest home, God blew it all away (Hag.
1:9). This may be a reference to windstorms or possibly to the small size of the
grain, which caused it to disappear with the chaff. This circumstance served as a
reminder of the transitory nature of all human accomplishments (see Isa. 40:7). As
long as the returnees to Judah continued to delay rebuilding of the temple, it
would prove to be costly.

During the dry summers, farmers in Judah relied on dew to water their crops
(see 2 Sam. 1:21; 1 Kings 17:1). The air, full of moisture from the Mediterranean
Sea, condensed during the cool nights, and usually provided enough water for the
crops; and being good farmers, the people planted with high hopes of reaping an
abundant harvest. God, however, kept back the dew, which in turn brought withered crops and widespread famine (Hag. 1:10). Moreover, the Lord sent a severe
drought that affected everything—the fields and terraced hillsides; the grain (most
likely, barley and wheat), the grapes (used to make new wine), the olives (used for
food, ointment, and medicine), and all the other crops; and the people, livestock,
and all that they labored to produce (vs. 11).

This calamity occurred because the people put their homes ahead of God's
house of worship. Their zeal to beautify their own places of residence was contrasted with their apathy toward the Jerusalem temple. The people had only to look at
the ruins of the temple to find the reason for their devastated crops. Again, the
contrast was plain. This should have been a signal to them to repent; but because
they did not discern the will of God through the drought, He sent the prophet
Haggai to make the connection clear (vss. 1, 12).

II. THE PEOPLE'S RESPONSE: HAGGAI 1:12-15

A. The People's Reverential Obedience: vs. 12

Then Zerubbabel son of Shealtiel, Joshua son of Jehozadak, the high priest, and the whole remnant of the people obeyed the voice of the LORD their God and the message of the prophet Haggai, because the LORD their God had sent him. And the people feared the LORD.

Haggai's message produced the desired result. Within a modest period of time, Zerubbabel, Joshua, and all the people recognized that God's hand was upon His messenger, the prophet. The Hebrew word translated "remnant" (Hag. 1:12) denoted all the people who returned from exile in Babylon. More generally, it referred to those among God's chosen people who remained loyal to Him despite widespread apostasy and disobedience. The survival of some of the people of Judah was God's gracious provision to avert the nation's complete disappearance (Isa. 1:9). If it were not for this group of survivors, Judah would have been utterly destroyed for its sin—just as the cities of Sodom and Gomorrah had been destroyed long before (Gen. 18:16—19:29; see Ezra 9:14; Isa 10:20-22; 11:11, 16; Jer. 23:3; 31:17).

A closer examination of Haggai 1:12 suggests that Zerubbabel and Joshua had been remiss in not strongly urging the people to get on with their rebuilding efforts. The returnees obeyed the voice of the Lord through Haggai, for they recognized that the Lord had sent him. Indeed, "the voice of the LORD" and "the message of the prophet Haggai" are one and the same, a sign of true prophecy. The people responded in reverence and obedience. Their proper view of God brought a change of heart and mind. This led to worship, renunciation of their old, selfish priorities, and a willingness to resume the hard work of rebuilding the temple.

B. The Lord's Encouraging Word: vss. 13-15

Then Haggai, the LORD's messenger, gave this message of the LORD to the people: "I am with you," declares the LORD. So the LORD stirred up the spirit of Zerubbabel son of Shealtiel, governor of Judah, and the spirit of Joshua son of Jehozadak, the high priest, and the spirit of the whole remnant of the people. They came and began to work on the house of the LORD Almighty, their God, on the twenty-fourth day of the sixth month in the second year of King Darius.

All the old problems and obstacles persisted, but the people's attitude had changed. They gave priority to rebuilding God's temple over concerns about their houses, crops, food, drink, clothes, and financial holdings. In response to this remarkable change of heart, mind, and will, God promised them His presence in the work that loomed ahead: "I am with you" (Hag. 1:13), He said. That was the most valuable component of all.

Before the Exile, Ezekiel had seen a vision of the glory of the Lord leaving Jerusalem prior to the destruction of the city and its temple (Ezek. 10:1—11:23). Haggai's messages reassured the remnant that the Lord was indeed with them, and most importantly, His glory had returned to His temple (Hag. 1:13). Their obedience in rebuilding and His desire to honor the covenant He made at Mount Sinai had brought His blessings to them (2:4-5).

What a sense of relief the people must have felt as God's tone changed from reproof to tenderness. He hastened, as it were, to forget the remnant's previous unfaithfulness and to assure them that He was and would be with them. God's presence was the best blessing, because it included all the others. Contrast "they came and began to work" (1:14) with "the time has not yet come" (vs. 2). The civil and religious leaders, along with the entire remnant of God's people, moved from selfish excuses to sacrificial labor. The reason for the change in attitude was the stirring of God's Spirit in the hearts of His people. They were now energized and encouraged to undertake their divinely appointed task.

Haggai specified the day the work began was September 21, 520 B.C., namely, 23 days after he delivered his initial message (vss. 1, 15). Some suggest that the intervening days were spent in planning, obtaining building materials (such as wood), and getting a sufficient number of skilled artisans. The "sixth month" was also the time when summer crops were harvested in the orchards and fields, so the people may have needed to complete that task first. Still, three weeks was remarkably fast, especially considering that the work had been halted for years.

Discussion Questions

1. What excuse did the people give for not rebuilding the temple?
2. In what way were the priorities of the people misplaced?
3. What was the result of the people's misplaced priorities?
4. How did the people respond to the exhortation of Haggai?
5. Why is it important for us to keep our priorities straight when it comes to the things of God?

Contemporary Application

How do we know what people believe? A fair test is to look at what they value as most important in their lives. We are not called to judge one another's lifestyles. Only God has the authority to do that. Nevertheless, we are called to serious self-evaluation about the signals we send to others concerning the way we use our time, talents, and treasures. The Bible speaks clearly about the necessity of making Jesus Lord of all.

Thus, as Christians, we should be careful to ensure that our faith is not double-minded. After all, it's so easy to try to serve both God and material wealth. But we know deep down inside that it is impossible. We cannot serve two masters. That's why God must come first in our lives.

If we run after material wealth, invariably we will neglect the Lord. In pursuit of careers, possessions, and comfortable lifestyles, we risk losing out on what is most important—our obedient walk by faith in Christ. That's why Haggai's warning is still important today. We cannot expect to avoid God's displeasure if we keep on postponing our obedience to His good and perfect will.

Rebuilding the Wall

Scripture

Background Scripture: *Nehemiah 1:1—2:20*
Scripture Lesson: *Nehemiah 2:1-8, 11, 17-18*
Key Verse: *I also told them about the gracious hand of my God upon me and what the king had said to me. They replied, "Let us start rebuilding." So they began this good work.* Nehemiah 2:18.
Scripture Lesson for Children: *Nehemiah 2:1-8, 11, 17-18*
Key Verse for Children: *Because the gracious hand of my God was upon me, the king granted my requests.* Nehemiah 2:8.

Lesson Aim

To note that if God's work is to get done, sometimes we must be bold and take the lead.

Lesson Setting

Time: *445–444 B.C.*
Place: *Susa and Jerusalem*

Lesson Outline

Rebuilding the Wall
  I. Nehemiah Prepares for Jerusalem: Nehemiah 2:1-8
    A. *The First Question and Response: vss. 1-3*
    B. *The Second Question and Response: vss. 4-5*
    C. *The Third Question and Response: vss. 6-8*
  II. Nehemiah Motivates Jerusalem: Nehemiah 2:11, 17-18
    A. *The Secret Inspection: vs. 11*
    B. *The Summons to Rebuild the Wall: vss. 17-18*

Introduction for Adults

Topic: *Following a Visionary Leader!*

Challenging tasks come in many forms. We meet them early in our school years, then in college, then in our jobs, and finally in our families and churches. Often, it seems easier to accept new challenges when we are younger than when we are older. But we're never too old to take on hard tasks.

A veteran of many years in the U.S. Navy chaplains' corps retired. Instead of looking for a comfortable place where he could relax and take it easy, this visionary leader chose a run-down church in a tough, urban neighborhood. When his friends asked him why, he said, "It was the toughest thing I could find to do."

That's the attitude with which we must always be open to God's leading. We need the Holy Spirit's guidance, as well as courage and faith, to follow the Lord, regardless of our age or circumstance. The thrill of living for God is always there when we offer ourselves for His service.

Introduction for Youth

Topic: *Rebuild!*

"Racers, start your engines!" With that announcement, the crowd roared and the race car drivers zoomed down the speedway. But before the event started, highly skilled engineers, mechanics, and drivers had spent many hours and lots of money in preparation.

How foolish it is to start a road race without adequate equipment and trained drivers. Yet sometimes that's how we try to get ahead in our spiritual lives. We think we know how to run the race of faith. We think we can jump in at any time and succeed with little preparation and effort. But we are incorrect. We cannot start and finish unless we trust in God and obey His Word.

Nehemiah did not start his rebuilding project without first going to God in prayer. Nehemiah knew God's promises, and he knew about the presence of sin in his life. Nehemiah also knew the importance of God's name and honor. Only then was the governor ready to start doing great work for the Lord.

Concepts for Children

Topic: *Nehemiah Sees a Need*

1. An official named Nehemiah asked some men from Judah about Jerusalem and the people living there.
2. When Nehemiah learned how difficult things were, he cried for days.
3. Nehemiah got permission from King Artaxerxes to return to Judah and rebuild Jerusalem's broken-down wall.
4. Nehemiah encouraged the people of Jerusalem to join him in the task.
5. With God's help, we can work together to do great things for Him.

Lesson Commentary

I. NEHEMIAH PREPARES FOR JERUSALEM: NEHEMIAH 2:1-8

A. The First Question and Response: vss. 1-3

In the month of Nisan in the twentieth year of King Artaxerxes, when wine was brought for him, I took the wine and gave it to the king. I had not been sad in his presence before; so the king asked me, "Why does your face look so sad when you are not ill? This can be nothing but sadness of heart." I was very much afraid, but I said to the king, "May the king live forever! Why should my face not look sad when the city where my fathers are buried lies in ruins, and its gates have been destroyed by fire?"

When the first Jewish exiles returned from Babylon to Jerusalem with Sheshbazzar in 537 B.C., they may have expected to establish the blessed messianic community anticipated by Isaiah and other prophets after the Lord purified His people (see Isa. 40; 54; Zeph. 3). Instead, they faced disappointment, failure, and disillusionment. Malachi preached against a cynical spirit among the remnant who felt that it didn't much matter whether they served the Lord (see Mal. 2:17; 3:13-14).

After 20 years, in response to the urging of the prophets Haggai and Zechariah, the Jewish remnant managed to complete a small version of the former temple (see Ezra 6:14). During this time, Ezra strengthened the commitment of the exilic community in Judah to the Law of the Lord (see 7:14, 25-26). However, nearly a full century after the first exiles arrived in Judah, Jerusalem still lay unfortified, the spiritual reforms of Ezra were only skin-deep, and powerful enemies surrounding Judah were committed to keeping the remnant weak and disgraced.

At the time Nehemiah lived, the wall surrounding Jerusalem was completely destroyed. This was tragic, for it represented the protection of the Lord and also illustrated His fidelity in reestablishing His people. During the time of Ezra, attempts to rebuild the wall may have been started and then were stopped by orders from the king (Ezra 4:21-23; 9:9). Perhaps any progress that had been made in restoring the city wall had been reversed.

The Book of Nehemiah begins by relating what happened in the city of Susa (the winter capital of Persia) and the resort center of its kings. It was November-December, 445 B.C. Nehemiah's blood-brother Hanani (7:2) and representatives from the territory of Judah came to Susa to see him. The Jewish patriot asked about the situation for the resettled Jews in their homeland (1:1-2). It was then that the Lord laid a burden for the welfare of Jerusalem on the heart of Nehemiah. Like Daniel before him in Babylon, Nehemiah had risen to prominence in the imperial court of Persia. The Hebrew name *Nehemiah* meant "the Comfort of the Lord." Nehemiah is related to the biblical names *Nahum* ("Comfort") and *Menahem* ("Comforter").

Nehemiah was so overwhelmed with grief by what he had heard that he sat down and wept (vs. 4). He also expressed his concern for days, through fasting and praying before the Lord, whose dwelling is heaven. In the address recorded in verses 5-

297

11, Nehemiah affirmed both God's surpassing greatness and His involvement in the lives of His people. Nehemiah acknowledged that the Lord kept His covenant with those who loved and obeyed Him.

Nehemiah 2 brings us to the following spring, namely, April–May, of 444 B.C. (2:1; see 1:1). Artaxerxes I was the king of Persia (465–424 B.C.) and possibly hosting an opulent banquet. He had winter palaces in Susa and Babylon, and he may have been in Babylon during the four months of Nehemiah's fast. The latter was serving as the king's cupbearer (2:1; see 1:11). In this capacity, Nehemiah tasted all the wine before it was served to the monarch. Nehemiah certified that none of it was poisoned or contaminated. The position of cupbearer often included advisory responsibilities. As a trusted and loyal servant, Nehemiah had a considerable amount of influence in the imperial court.

On previous occasions, Nehemiah's appearance was pleasant, not depressed. Regardless of their personal problems, servants of the king were expected to keep their feelings concealed and to appear cheerful in his presence. To do otherwise might leave the impression that a courtier was discontented with the monarch and planning a seditious act. In this situation, however, Artaxerxes I noticed a change in Nehemiah's countenance and asked why he seemed sad. The king surmised that Nehemiah was distressed about something. Nehemiah became even more concerned, for it was uncertain what the emotionally volatile ruler might do (vs. 2).

Court protocol required one to give the emperor a wish for a very long and prosperous reign (see 1 Kings 1:31; Dan. 2:4; 3:9; 6:21). Nehemiah gave this wish and then quickly but carefully connected his sadness, inappropriate as it was in the throne room, to the tragedy of knowing that his ancestral city was desolate and defenseless. Without the protection of walls, it would be too difficult to rebuild Jerusalem, for such efforts were subject to attack and vandalism (Neh. 2:3).

B. The Second Question and Response: vss. 4-5

The king said to me, "What is it you want?" Then I prayed to the God of heaven, and I answered the king, "If it pleases the king and if your servant has found favor in his sight, let him send me to the city in Judah where my fathers are buried so that I can rebuild it."

Artaxerxes' blunt "What is it you want?" (Neh. 2:4) may have been more than the cupbearer hoped for so early in the conversation. In the space of a deep breath, Nehemiah's heart reached for God's hand even as his mouth started forming the words of his petition to the emperor. Perhaps he asked for wisdom about what to say and that God would grant him favor in his earthly master's sight (vss. 3-4). Nehemiah knew he needed the "LORD, God of heaven, the great and awesome God" (1:5) to shape Artaxerxes' attitude toward the project and toward himself as a petitioner.

In the exchange between Artaxerxes I and Nehemiah, the emperor was brusque and demanding, while the courtier was formal and deferential. In a masterstroke of diplomacy, Nehemiah did not mention Jerusalem by name but always tied the city to himself and his family. He did not waste the emperor's time with wishful gen-eralities. God had helped him formulate a specific plan during those months of fasting and prayer. Indeed, Nehemiah used few words when he asked for permis-sion to go back to Judah and to the city of his ancestors. He also asked for permis-sion to rebuild the city, including its walls (vs. 5). It had been 71 years since the temple was rebuilt in 516 B.C. Now, to succeed in rebuilding Judah's capital signi-fied an important aspect of restoring the Jewish remnant in their homeland.

C. The Third Question and Response: vss. 6-8

Then the king, with the queen sitting beside him, asked me, "How long will your journey take, and when will you get back?" It pleased the king to send me; so I set a time. I also said to him, "If it pleas-es the king, may I have letters to the governors of Trans-Euphrates, so that they will provide me safe-conduct until I arrive in Judah? And may I have a letter to Asaph, keeper of the king's forest, so he will give me timber to make beams for the gates of the citadel by the temple and for the city wall and for the residence I will occupy?" And because the gracious hand of my God was upon me, the king grant-ed my requests.

At this point in his narrative, Nehemiah mentioned the presence of one of Artaxerxes' consorts. Perhaps the queen played a role in the emperor's decision in Nehemiah's favor. Artaxerxes I gave permission by asking how long it would take Nehemiah to get to Judah and when he would be back (Neh. 2:6). Although Nehemiah may have anticipated a brief leave of absence from service in the impe-rial court, his actual stay in Jerusalem lasted 12 years (5:14; 13:6).

Artaxerxes I was moved by Nehemiah's sincerity and perhaps by reasoning that the prosperity of Judah (at that time a province of Persia) would benefit the king; but the monarch's favorable response was a remarkable example of the power of prayer. Earlier, when the trouble had arisen over the first efforts to rebuild Jerusalem, Artaxerxes I himself had issued the decree that ended the exiles' efforts to completely restore their city (Ezra 4:17-23). Nehemiah's faith in God and bold-ness to approach the king had effectively reversed that decree, an outcome that was highly out of the ordinary in a culture in which governmental policies were rarely repealed (see Esth. 1:19; 8:8; Dan. 6:8, 12, 15).

Because the king was amenable to dispatching Nehemiah, the cupbearer asked for official documents to present to the governors assigned in the Trans-Euphrates region of the empire (Neh. 2:7). The papers Nehemiah requested would authorize whatever his rebuilding efforts required. In this situation, he would need permis-sion to travel freely through various territories without any complications. Nehemiah also needed an escort to safeguard his journey. He requested a letter to Asaph (the keeper of the monarch's royal park or nature preserve) giving him access to the required building supplies he needed to restore Jerusalem. These included timber to make beams for the gates of the citadel on the north side of the temple (later to become the site of the Fortress of Antonia built by Herod), to con-struct the city wall, and to build a palace for the governor to live. While Nehemiah's words and actions suggest his careful thought and planning, he nevertheless acknowledged that the gracious hand of God upon him led to the king granting these requests (vs. 8).

There is some debate about the location of "the king's forest." The best-known source of fine timber in the Persian Empire was in Lebanon, where Zerubbabel secured materials for the temple (Ezra 3:7). However, it is improbable that these costly, imported cedar logs were used to rebuild the gates of Jerusalem. A likely location of the king's forest is Solomon's garden (2 Kings 25:4; Eccl. 2:5), which the early historian, Josephus, located at Etham, roughly six miles south of Jerusalem. Native oak, poplar, or terebinth in this area would have made good construction timbers for gates.

Nehemiah didn't bother to describe his journey to Jerusalem, although it should have been quicker than Zerubbabel's and Ezra's, for the governor was unencumbered by children, livestock, and household possessions. Nehemiah presented documents authorizing his mission to the authorities in Trans-Euphrates (vs. 9). His status was enhanced by the presence of an armed imperial escort.

Ominously, Nehemiah introduced into his narrative two characters who were upset that he had arrived to promote the welfare of the Jews (vs. 10). Sanballat's name was Babylonian; he was likely named after Sin, the moon god. He was probably from Upper or Lower Beth Horon, two villages about 12 miles northwest of Jerusalem on the main road to the Mediterranean coast. He was the governor of Samaria and a leader of the Samarian opposition. Tobiah was a Jewish name meaning "The Lord Is Good." He was probably a worldly Jew living in and controlling the territory associated with Ammon east of the Jordan River (vs. 10). These two men would be Nehemiah's bitter enemies for years to come.

II. NEHEMIAH MOTIVATES JERUSALEM: NEHEMIAH 2:11, 17-18

A. The Secret Inspection: vs. 11

I went to Jerusalem, and after staying there three days.

After contacting the officials of the satrapy of Trans-Euphrates, Nehemiah went on to Jerusalem (Neh. 2:11). As Ezra had done before him, Nehemiah rested three days before initiating any activity (see Ezra 8:32). Before telling anyone in Jerusalem what he had come to do, Nehemiah surveyed the most damaged portion on the city walls. As an outsider, he wanted to be able to give the leaders of Jerusalem an informed account of what needed to be done when he revealed his mission.

B. The Summons to Rebuild the Wall: vss. 17-18

Then I said to them, "You see the trouble we are in: Jerusalem lies in ruins, and its gates have been burned with fire. Come, let us rebuild the wall of Jerusalem, and we will no longer be in disgrace." I also told them about the gracious hand of my God upon me and what the king had said to me. They replied, "Let us start rebuilding." So they began this good work."

Perhaps the greatest challenge Nehemiah faced was transmitting his conviction that rebuilding Jerusalem's walls at this time was God's idea—not the fantasy of a government official who would go home in a while and leave the locals to live with the trouble he had stirred up. Nehemiah took a few trusted associates—probably men who had accompanied him from Susa—and set out to inspect the walls at night, perhaps by moonlight (Neh. 2:12-13). The governor knew there were enemies all around, and he needed to keep his plans a secret until they were fixed in his mind. Only when his plan was formulated would he disclose it to the residents of Jerusalem.

Nehemiah rode a horse or mule, while the others with him walked. The inspection party went out through the ruins of the Valley Gate on the west side of the southern point of Jerusalem and turned to the left toward the Jackal Well near the city's southern extremity. They passed the Dung Gate before reaching the well. After rounding the southern side of Jerusalem, Nehemiah turned north up the Kidron Valley along the eastern wall (vs. 14). Here the Fountain Gate exited to the King's Pool (the Pool of Siloam; see 3:15). The hillside from Jerusalem into the Kidron Valley is steep. The old wall of Jerusalem had been far down the hill and a system of terraces that supported buildings had been anchored against that wall. When the old wall was destroyed, the terraces had also crumbled. Nehemiah had to dismount and continue on foot because the slope along the east side of Jerusalem was choked with rubble that even a donkey could not negotiate in the moonlight.

Nehemiah's inspectors picked their way an unspecified distance farther along the ruins of the eastern wall (2:15). This side would be the most daunting section to rebuild. Much of the rest of the wall stood on relatively level ground. Finally, they turned back, retraced their steps over the rocks, rounded the southern point of Jerusalem, and reentered the Valley Gate to the southwest. Neither Persian officials nor Jewish leaders were informed about Nehemiah's investigation before it occurred (vs. 16).

When the time was right, Nehemiah gathered everyone and surprised them. First, he outlined the problem and then suggested the solution. The problem was plain to see. For about 150 years, much of the city lay in ruins, with only a broken-down wall and charred timbers for gates. The solution was to rebuild Jerusalem's wall and remove the residents' feeling of disgrace and defeat (vs. 17). In Old Testament times, the condition of a city's wall indicated its power and prosperity. Since the wall was the primary means of defense against an enemy, the quality of its construction and maintenance reflected the financial condition and vulnerability of the city's inhabitants.

Nehemiah challenged the people to rebuild the wall and thus restore the standing of the Jewish community in the holy city. As his clincher, the governor shared the amazing account of God's intervention with Artaxerxes I to secure official sanction for this task (vs. 18). The vision and decisiveness of Nehemiah were what the remnant had needed to get started. The response of the priests, nobles, officials, and ordinary people was profoundly united: "Let us start rebuilding." In the books of Ezra and Nehemiah, the concept of "the hand of the LORD my God" (see Ezra 7:6, 28; 8:31) or "the gracious hand of my God" (see 7:9; 8:18, 22; Neh. 2:8, 18) explains the influencing force behind everything that happens. Emperors, nations, and the people of God are all tools in that gracious hand.

Discussion Questions

1. Why was Nehemiah sad in the presence of Artaxerxes I?
2. Why was Nehemiah afraid when the king asked him about his dejected demeanor?
3. What difference do you think prayer made in Nehemiah's interaction with the king?
4. What did Nehemiah do after arriving in Jerusalem?
5. How did Nehemiah see the Jewish community removing the disgrace of their ruined city?

Contemporary Application

Nehemiah was a man who had a burden—a God-sent desire—to restore the walls of Jerusalem. The circumstances, however, did not seem to warrant any hope of success. But Nehemiah overcame the obstacles with God's help—just as your students can if they will depend on Him.

Consider, for example, Henry Stenhouse, an ophthalmologist from Goldsboro, North Carolina. When he was 100 years old, he decided to run for the United States Congress. He was prompted to take such a bold step by his concern for the young children who attended his party. Stenhouse said he was distressed about the quality of life in the country, and he wanted to do something to make life better for the children.

Some of the adults in your class may think their options are closed when they reach a certain age; or they may feel confined by circumstances. Yet here is the story of a man who proved that constructive action begins with a person who has a strong desire and concern. If your students are willing to act on their ministry desires, God will give them the courage and ability they need to start new ventures, despite what may appear to be overwhelming obstacles.

Of course, we cannot do the Lord's work unless we trust in Him and obey His Word. Consider Nehemiah. He did not start his building project without first going to God in prayer. Nehemiah knew God's promises, and he knew about the presence of sin in his life. Nehemiah also knew the importance of God's name and honor. Only then was he ready to start doing a great work for the Lord. The same holds true for us.

Up Against the Wall

Scripture

Background Scripture: *Nehemiah 4—6*

Scripture Lesson: *Nehemiah 4:1-3, 7-9, 13-15; 6:15*

Key Verse: *So we rebuilt the wall till all of it reached half its height, for the people worked with all their heart.* Nehemiah 4:6.

Scripture Lesson for Children: *Nehemiah 4:1-3, 7-9, 13-15; 6:15*

Key Verse for Children: *We rebuilt the wall . . . for the people worked with all their heart.* Nehemiah 4:6.

Lesson Aim

To learn that as we are doing God's work, we need to prepare for opposition.

Lesson Setting

Time: *444 B.C.*

Place: *Jerusalem*

Lesson Outline

Up Against the Wall

  I. A Vigilant Strategy: Nehemiah 4:1-3, 7-9, 13-14

     A. *Dealing with Sarcasm: vss. 1-3*

     B. *Responding to a Threatened Attack: vss. 7-9*

     C. *Emboldening the Workers: vss. 13-14*

  II. A Victorious Achievement: Nehemiah 4:15; 6:15

     A. *Divine Intervention: 4:15*

     B. *God-Ordained Success: 6:15*

Introduction for Adults

Topic: *Finishing the Task!*

As we endeavor to finish our God-given tasks, we should expect opposition, just as Nehemiah and his colleagues faced opposition from their neighbors. If opposition doesn't come, we can thank the Lord for His mercy. But most often, opposition will arise in one form or another.

The devil and those who follow him don't like to see effective work carried out for the cause of Jesus. Yet we need not lose hope. If we take steps to prepare for the opposition, Jesus can help us thwart it. Consider the situation in Nehemiah's day. When the Jerusalem wall was halfway up, many must have wondered if it would ever be finished. But as a result of the governor's careful planning and God's grace, it was finished. Remember, then, to never give up in doing the Lord's work.

Introduction for Youth

Topic: *Keep on Building*

The third verse of "Amazing Grace" says: "Through many dangers, toils, and snares I have already come." That verse is particularly appropriate for the hostility that Nehemiah and his colleagues encountered. And it is likewise true when we are doing God's work.

If we're content to let things go on in a routine sort of way, nobody bothers us. But when we dare to throw down the challenge of a great opportunity for God's glory, opposition suddenly appears. Nehemiah knew what John Newton wrote about in "Amazing Grace." In this week's Scripture passage, we discover that the nature and intensity of the opposition were quite different than before. Nehemiah was not looking for trouble. He wanted to do God's will—build the wall. But Nehemiah's enemies would not let his project go uncontested. Thankfully, he refused to give up. And neither should we!

Concepts for Children

Topic: *The People Complete the Work*

1. Nehemiah had enemies who tried to stop the rebuilding of the wall.
2. When others plotted against them, Nehemiah and the workers prayed and set up a guard.
3. Nehemiah believed that God could be trusted to give hope, power, and strength to those who are faithful.
4 Our vision for action should be motivated by our desire to follow through with God's plan.
5. When we do so, God will provide everything we need to be successful in our efforts.

Lesson Commentary

I. A Vigilant Strategy: Nehemiah 4:1-3, 7-9, 13-14

A. Dealing with Sarcasm: vss. 1-3

When Sanballat heard that we were rebuilding the wall, he became angry and was greatly incensed. He ridiculed the Jews, and in the presence of his associates and the army of Samaria, he said, "What are those feeble Jews doing? Will they restore their wall? Will they offer sacrifices? Will they finish in a day? Can they bring the stones back to life from those heaps of rubble—burned as they are?" Tobiah the Ammonite, who was at his side, said, "What they are building—if even a fox climbed up on it, he would break down their wall of stones!"

Last week, we learned how Nehemiah convinced the leaders and inhabitants of Jerusalem to join him in rebuilding the walls of the city (Neh. 2:17-18). Their support was crucial for the success of the undertaking. Three potent human enemies opposed to the gracious hand of God (vs. 19). The company of Sanballat and Tobiah (who were first mentioned in verse 10) was joined by Geshem the Arab. Ancient sources reveal that Geshem led an assortment of Arab tribes that controlled the deserts south of Judah from Egypt to the Arabian peninsula. He was more powerful than Sanballat and Tobiah combined, but his hostility to the Jews appears to have been less intense.

Sanballat to the north, Tobiah to the east, and Geshem to the south forged a hostile boundary around Judah. Together they launched a campaign of ridicule and mockery against the small Jewish community. Their initial charge was the old standby: rebellion against the emperor (see Ezra 4:11-16). Nehemiah shrugged off his adversaries as though they were minor annoyances (Neh. 2:20). He was used to dealing with the real political heavyweights of Persia; comparatively speaking, Sanballat, Tobiah, and Geshem were lightweights. On the other hand, Nehemiah looked at the situation in Jerusalem through a theological lens. The God of heaven wanted the walls built. By terms of a covenant, Nehemiah and the Jews were the servants of the God of heaven. Their enemies had no covenant status. Jerusalem belonged to God and His people. The blustering nations around them had no part in God's plan for Jerusalem.

Nehemiah 4:1 picks up where 2:20 left off. Sanballat, the Samarian leader, assembled his army in his capital city to agitate Nehemiah and his workers. Along with all the petty bureaucrats, Tobiah joined Sanballat on the speakers' platform as a visiting dignitary. The intensity of Sanballat's anger at the Jews exposed the lie behind his ridicule. Under the veneer of his propaganda, Sanballat was worried about what Nehemiah was doing. This tenacious exile threatened his power over Judah.

"Samaria" (4:2) was a region of central Israel first occupied by the tribe of Ephraim and part of the tribe of Manasseh. One of the region's most prominent centers, the ancient town of Shechem (near Mount Gerizim, Samaria's highest peak), became the capital of the northern kingdom of Israel under Jeroboam I

(931-910 B.C.; 1 Kings 12:25). Later, a city named Samaria (begun by Omri around 880 B.C.) became the capital of the northern kingdom, and remained so through several monarchies until it fell to the Assyrians in 722 B.C.

When the northern kingdom collapsed, most of its prominent citizens were deported to Assyria, Aram (Syria), and Babylon. The deported Israelite population was then replaced with foreigners from Babylon and elsewhere (2 Kings 17:24). Through intermarriage between the newcomers and those left in the land, the group later known as the Samaritans was created. Because of their mixed Jewish-Gentile blood, early pagan worship (vs. 29), and later religious ceremonies that centered on Mount Gerizim rather than the temple in Jerusalem (John 4:20-22), the Samaritans were generally despised by the Jews throughout their history. Interestingly, the Jewish historian, Josephus, claimed that Sanballat was the founder of the Samaritan temple on Mount Gerizim, and that his brother-in-law, Manasseh, was the high priest.

In a rapid series of five questions, Sanballat made Nehemiah and the Jews seem ridiculous in the eyes of the army of Samaria (Neh. 4:2). Sanballat implied that the Jews were powerless to do anything. He scoffed at the idea that such a bunch could fortify a city. He suggested they were religious fanatics trusting God to raise the walls in response to sacrifices. Sanballat claimed they had barely strength for one day, so they had better work fast. He mocked the wall as a fortress made of charcoal bri-quettes. The native limestone, when subjected to fire, turned brittle and crumbly.

The Samarian army must have responded favorably to Sanballat's taunts, because Tobiah followed them up with the kind of joke that assumed his audience was ready to hear it (vs. 3). Allegedly, if a nimble fox jumped up on that ridiculous wall, the whole thing would totter and collapse from the shock. Imagine the clash of swords on wooden shields and battle yells from the assembled army as they responded to the jibes and jeers of their leaders.

B. Responding to a Threatened Attack: vss. 7-9

But when Sanballat, Tobiah, the Arabs, the Ammonites and the men of Ashdod heard that the repairs to Jerusalem's walls had gone ahead and that the gaps were being closed, they were very angry. They all plotted together to come and fight against Jerusalem and stir up trouble against it. But we prayed to our God and posted a guard day and night to meet this threat.

At this point in his memoir, Nehemiah inserted a prayer. He had no time to both-er with the empty words of posturing opponents. He committed these hecklers to God, who alone has the right to take vengeance on those who oppose His purpos-es (see Deut. 32:35; Rom. 12:19). Nehemiah asked God to take note of the abuse hurled at His servants and to deflect that spite back on those who initiated it. The governor prayed that the enemies of God's people might know the horrors of the kind of captivity the Jews had survived (Neh. 4:4). Nehemiah also requested that their offense might never be forgiven, because they had opposed the purposes of God, the divine warrior, to protect His people (vs. 5). Nehemiah prayed as

Jeremiah and certain of the psalmists had when they asked God to bring calamity on their enemies (see Pss. 79:12; 94:1-3; 137:7-9; Jer. 18:23).

While Sanballat and Tobiah waged a war of words, the Jewish laborers from Jerusalem and the surrounding towns were mounting stone on stone all around the two-mile perimeter of Jerusalem. Before the opponents knew what was happening, the wall had reached half its planned height all the way around. The wall went up quickly because the exilic community toiled hard. Indeed, the last phrase of Nehemiah 4:6 could be rendered as "they had a heart to work."

Perhaps to their dismay, Sanballat and Tobiah had to change their strategy, for their saber-rattling mockery clearly had discouraged no one. First, they recruited more allies. Sanballat and his Samarians to the north, Tobiah and his Ammonites to the east, and Geshem and his Arabs to the south were joined in angry opposition to Jerusalem's walls by the Ashdodites, people of the strongest Phoenician city on the Mediterranean coast to the west of Judah (Neh. 4:7).

Second, the alliance that ringed Judah and Jerusalem started planning attacks on Jerusalem. Nehemiah heard rumors about the impending raids; perhaps this was something Sanballat and Tobiah wanted him to hear. Their biggest problem was that Nehemiah had Artaxerxes' permission to rebuild the walls of Jerusalem. An actual attack would risk bringing Persian wrath on their heads, while a threatened attack might do what taunts had not—demoralize the Jews (vs. 8).

C. Emboldening the Workers: vss. 13-14

Therefore I stationed some of the people behind the lowest points of the wall at the exposed places, posting them by families, with their swords, spears and bows. After I looked things over, I stood up and said to the nobles, the officials and the rest of the people, "Don't be afraid of them. Remember the Lord, who is great and awesome, and fight for your brothers, your sons and your daughters, your wives and your homes."

In response to the threat of an attack, the Jews started praying (Neh. 4:11). Clearly, Nehemiah organized the prayer vigil, because it was accompanied by around-the-clock sentries to detect any raiders. Even as they prayed and watched, the builders were feeling the cumulative effect of the pressure of the task and the opposition. They were exhausted from the toil and discouraged by the rubble they had to work in. In response, the opponents engaged in psychological warfare by claiming they could use the cover of the rubble to send terrorists in among the builders to kill them before they knew the attackers were at hand (vss. 10-11).

When Sanballat and Tobiah sensed that rumors of war were affecting the morale of the builders, the antagonists planted more rumors in Jewish villages that bordered enemy lands (vs. 12). Soon Nehemiah had repeated intelligence reports that together indicated attacks from every point of the compass. In response, the governor stopped the construction and posted heavy guards inside Jerusalem wherever the wall was still low or where there were open spaces. Nehemiah's "army" was his corps of builders, grouped by family units. Their armaments consisted of the weapons that were their personal property, namely, swords, spears (lances with long shafts), and bows (vs. 13).

At this point, the governor took time to look over the situation. Then, after completing his inspection, he mustered the nobles, officials, and the rest of the workers and gave them a three-part battle instruction. First, they were not to fear the enemy (see Exod. 14:13; Num. 14:9; Deut. 20:3; Josh. 10:25). Second, the Jews were to keep their minds fixed on the great and awesome Lord. Third, they were to fight for their families and homes (Neh. 4:14). Nehemiah never prayed without working nor worked without praying. Like him, we should approach opposition with confidence in God. But we should not stop there. We also should use every ounce of our courage and ability to overcome that opposition in God's name.

II. A VICTORIOUS ACHIEVEMENT: NEHEMIAH 4:15; 6:15

A. Divine Intervention: 4:15

When our enemies heard that we were aware of their plot and that God had frustrated it, we all returned to the wall, each to his own work.

Nehemiah showed great organizational skill when he devised the initial plan for portioning out the work on the walls and gates among the labor crews. He displayed flexibility in the face of daunting opposition, especially as he anticipated and headed off the various schemes of the encircling foes. There came a time, however, when he needed to put in place a more robust approach that could handle a variety of threats. Otherwise, the rebuilding of the walls and gates wasn't going to be completed.

After waiting an unspecified number of days for a surprise attack, Nehemiah somehow heard the news that Sanballat, Tobiah, Geshem, and the Ashdodites had given up on ambushing the workers. Nehemiah took no credit for the failure of the numerically overwhelming enemies. He knew only God could have frustrated their plans to attack (Neh. 4:15).

After receiving the good news, Nehemiah encouraged everybody to get back to work. From this point on, until the walls and gates were finished, half the people worked while the other half served as armed sentries (vs. 16). Officers ready to take charge in the event of a military emergency waited at intervals behind the workers and guards. The carriers who transported materials to the various work stations around the walls kept one hand free to carry their weapons. The builders wore swords on their belts (vss. 17-18a). A trumpeter stayed with Nehemiah at all times so that he could signal everyone to gather at any point on the walls where trouble developed.

This "trumpet" was most likely the ram's horn, or *shofar*, and was the standard signal for assemblies or attacks (see Exod. 19:16-17; Josh. 6:20; Judg. 6:34). The instrument measured about 18 inches in length and was made from the left horn of one of the most common breeds of sheep in Judah, the fat-tailed sheep. In appearance, the horn was somewhat flattened and curved backward in a sort of semicircle so that its point faced forward under the sheep's left ear. To bend the horn into the desired shape, it was first softened in hot water to make it pliable.

The Mosaic law prescribed the blowing of the ram's horn as part of feast days and other special dates on the Jewish calendar. In a more ordinary way, the trumpet summoned the people of Israel to assemble (Jer. 4:5). Perhaps the most famous use of the ram's horn involved Joshua and the conquest of Jericho. Ironically, whereas Nehemiah employed the trumpet as part of his strategy to ensure that the wall of Jerusalem would continue to go up, Joshua used the ram's horn to help bring down the walls of Jericho (Josh. 6). After the Israelites marched around the fortified city for seven days, seven priests blew seven trumpets on the seventh circuit. Then, with a loud shout from the people, the walls of Jericho collapsed.

Nehemiah's plans included round-the-clock protection. In the daytime (as we have noted), the wall was protected by soldiers and by armed soldiers. At night, the workers were supposed to be available to serve as sentries (Neh. 4:21). The governor felt compelled by the gravity of the security issue to have workers from neighboring towns remain in Jerusalem at night rather than return to their homes (vs. 22). Jerusalem and its temple were the twin focal points of the faith and history of the Jews, but most of the exiles lived in other towns. The sparseness of Jerusalem's population would continue to be a problem for Nehemiah throughout his governorship (see 7:4; 11:1-2). Nehemiah and his closest associates also endured great hardships as they set the pace for all the workers on the wall project (4:23). When they could catch some sleep, they slept in their clothes. They kept their weapons with them at all times so they could be in the front lines if an attack materialized at any point.

B. God-Ordained Success: 6:15

So the wall was completed on the twenty-fifth of Elul, in fifty-two days.

The opponents of Jerusalem's refortification abandoned their strategy of direct confrontation. They turned to attempts of subtle deception and betrayal. They tried several times to lure Nehemiah out of Jerusalem into their hands at a "peace conference." They insinuated he was orchestrating a plot to rebel against the Persian Empire and eventually proclaim himself king. They hired false prophets to convince Nehemiah to do something damaging to his reputation. But the governor was too focused on what God wanted him to accomplish to fall for any of their ploys (Neh. 6:1-14).

Nehemiah told surprisingly little about building the wall of Jerusalem. He included an honor roll of the dedicated builders, but he told mostly about the obstacles overcome from without and within in the process of building. That's what he remembered. That's what God wanted every generation of His spiritual children to keep in mind as they do His work. Success comes after facing foes in the strength of His name.

All of the commotion reported in Nehemiah 4 through 6 occurred in the 52 days from the second of the month of Ab to the twenty-fifth of the month of Elul—approximately August 11 to October 2, 444 B.C. (vs. 15). Everyone in the coalition opposed to the construction of the walls was informed instantly by their intelligence network. They were awed because such an outcome was humanly impossible. In their hearts, they knew the God of Israel had been at work. Tinges of terror colored their thoughts of the future, and they doubted whether good things lay ahead for them (vs. 16).

Discussion Questions

1. Why was Sanballat enraged when he heard that the Jews were rebuilding the walls of Jerusalem?
2. What sort of sarcastic remarks did Nehemiah's adversaries use to demoralize the Jews?
3. Why did Nehemiah and his associates resort to prayer in the face of intense opposition?
4. What plan did Nehemiah put into place to deal with the threat from antagonists?
5. How was it possible for God's people to rebuild the Jerusalem wall in such a short period of time?

Contemporary Application

The Lord's work in any era advances against opposition. Jesus made this clear when He said hell itself would attack, but not prevail against His church (Matt. 16:18). Each generation needs wisdom to discern the enemy's strategy and to develop plans to resist.

Christian adults are often surprised by the opposition they encounter in striving to serve the Lord. They wrongly assume the path will be easy. But even though the sources of opposition may not be obvious when they begin their work, opposition will appear. It may be as subtle as discouragement or as blatant as outward attempts to interfere with a believer's service for the Savior.

Sometimes, the attacks are obviously physical, such as what Nehemiah and his people faced. Other times, the attacks are psychological and emotional. We have to be prepared for both. If the enemy cannot sidetrack us with suffering or persecution, for example, we may find ourselves being subverted by sinful attachments. The usual avenues of such attacks are immorality, money, and power.

Therefore, to be strong for God we need wisdom, courage, and faith. We need the kind of wise instructions Nehemiah gave. We need leaders who will call us to battle and show us how to protect ourselves. They will call us to prayer, obedience, and disciplined study of God's Word. Our greatest need in the face of hostility is to know how to put on and use the complete armor of God (Eph. 6:10-18).

Call to Renew the Covenant

DEVOTIONAL READING
  Psalm 27:11-14; 19:7-14

DAILY BIBLE READINGS
  Monday May 19
    Psalm 27:11-14 Take
    Courage
  Tuesday May 20
    Leviticus 23:33-43 The
    Festival of Booths
  Wednesday May 21
    Deuteronomy 16:13-17 Do
    Not Appear Empty-handed
  Thursday May 22
    Nehemiah 8:1-6 Hear the
    Word
  Friday May 23
    Nehemiah 8:7-12 Teach the
    Word
  Saturday May 24
    Nehemiah 8:13-18 Study the
    Word
  Sunday May 25
    Psalm 19:7-14 Delight in
    God's Law

Scripture

Background Scripture: *Nehemiah 8*
Scripture Lesson: *Nehemiah 8:1-3, 5-6, 13-14, 17-18*
Key Verse: *[Ezra] read it aloud from daybreak till noon as he faced the square before the Water Gate in the presence of the men, women and others who could understand. And all the people listened attentively to the Book of the Law.* Nehemiah 8:3.
Scripture Lesson for Children: *Nehemiah 8:1-3, 5-6, 13-14, 17-18*
Key Verse for Children: *"Do not grieve, for the joy of the LORD is your strength."* Nehemiah 8:10.

Lesson Aim

To discover that recommitment to God's Word produces celebration and confession.

Lesson Setting

Time: *444 B.C.*
Place: *Jerusalem*

Lesson Outline

Call to Renew the Covenant
  I.   The Reading of the Law: Nehemiah 8:1-3, 5-6
        A. *The People Assembled: vss. 1-2*
        B. *The Reading Done by Ezra: vs. 3*
        C. *The People's Worship: vss. 5-6*
  II. The Feast of Booths: Nehemiah 8:13-14, 17-18
        A. *The Feast of Booths Commanded: vss. 13-14*
        B. *The Feast of Booths Observed: vss. 17-18*

Introduction for Adults

Topic: *Restored and Renewed*

We all accept the axiom that ignorance is no excuse when we break the law. Yet we tend to tolerate ignorance of God's laws and wonder why our lives and our churches seem to lack spiritual authority and power.

A researcher in church growth has noted that preaching is pretty much useless unless people first confess their sins. But why should they confess when they have no standard by which to measure their behavior?

God's laws are that standard. Unless we know those laws and respect them, there's not much likelihood for confession to occur. Our task is to make God's Word clear and applicable to all of life. Only then will we see spiritual restoration and renewal and strong discipleship in our lives and in our churches.

Introduction for Youth

Topic: *Rebuilding the Relationship*

All of us use favorite send-off words to encourage our friends, like "Keep your chin in the wind." There must be a collection of these sayings somewhere. Right words do make a difference. The best words to remember are found in the Bible.

"The joy of the Lord is your strength" (Neh. 8:10) is one of those classic biblical promises. It means a lot more when we recall its original setting. When God's people wept for their sins, Nehemiah told them that it was now time for them to experience God's joy and let that be the foundation for rebuilding their relationship with Him and others within the faith community.

Scripture brings us to confession and joy. Divine words of truth are always the right and best ones for us. When we neglect them, it's like neglecting food and drink for our bodies. The Bible helps us to overcome our sins, to find joy, and to give joy to others.

Concepts for Children

Topic: *Ezra Reads the Law*

1. Ezra led God's people in worship.
2. God's purpose became clear through prayer and the reading of the Bible.
3. The people offered sacrifices to God in a sincere manner.
4. The people felt moved to observe the Festival of Booths.
5. Like God's people in the past, we should take the opportunity to remember and give thanks to God.

Lesson Commentary

I. THE READING OF THE LAW: NEHEMIAH 8:1-3, 5-6

A. The People Assembled: vss. 1-2

All the people assembled as one man in the square before the Water Gate. They told Ezra the scribe to bring out the Book of the Law of Moses, which the LORD had commanded for Israel. So on the first day of the seventh month Ezra the priest brought the Law before the assembly, which was made up of men and women and all who were able to understand.

It had taken over 80 years after the Exile for the Jerusalem wall to be completed (Neh. 6:15). Some of this delay was due to opposition from enemies, but the returnees were as much to blame for the delay as anyone else. They became discouraged when they faced hardship and they also easily fell into sin. Accordingly, while the first half of the Book of Nehemiah concentrated on the physical preservation of God's people, the second half focused on the spiritual preservation. Ezra plays a prominent role in this endeavor. He was a Jewish scribe and priest who traced his ancestry to Aaron (Ezra 7:1-5). In 458 B.C., he received permission from Artaxerxes I to travel to Jerusalem with 1,800 exiles and carry out religious reform.

While in the capital of Judah, Ezra wept bitterly over the sins of the people. In response, many Jews gathered to confess their sins and to weep alongside their spiritual leader. The people then made a covenant to obey God and to put away the foreign wives who had caused them to abandon the Lord (10:1-4). The efforts of Ezra to initiate a spiritual renewal lasted for a short period; but by the time Nehemiah returned, the spiritual fire had fizzled. As a matter of fact, in the 13 years between the end of the Book of Ezra and the beginning of the Book of Nehemiah, the Jewish people once again fell into their sinful ways. They intermarried into foreign religions and neglected to support the temple.

Thankfully, God was at work in the hearts of His people. They had seen the Lord's hand on Nehemiah, and they knew that to survive, they needed God's help. They also understood that to receive God's help, they needed to dedicate themselves to obeying His commands. Rather than waiting for Ezra or Nehemiah to start another spiritual revival, the people started it themselves. The Jews assembled in Jerusalem on October 8, 444 B.C. The event was timed to coincide with the Feast of Trumpets, the New Year's Day of the Jewish civil calendar (later known as Rosh Ha-Shanah; Neh. 7:73—8:1). This was one of the most noteworthy seasons on Israel's religious calendar (Lev. 23:23-43), and it was celebrated by the blowing of horns or trumpets from morning until evening. After the Exile, the festival was observed by the public reading of the Law and by general rejoicing.

The people gathered in an open plaza in front of the Water Gate, an entryway leading to the Gihon spring (Jerusalem's primary source of water). The gate was located on the eastern side of the city, slightly south of the wall's midsection, and directly opposite the temple. This area was not considered sacred, which meant

313

laypeople could participate with priests in the gathering. Women and children, who did not always attend temple ceremonies, were present in accordance with Moses' instructions in Deuteronomy 31:10-13 (Neh. 8:2; see 2 Chron. 20:13). The occasion for the assembly was Ezra's reading of the "Book of the Law of Moses" (Neh. 8:1), which the Lord had given Israel to obey. Several suggestions have been made concerning the identity of this document, but most likely it was a scroll (or scrolls) containing the first five books of the Old Testament—Genesis, Exodus, Leviticus, Numbers, and Deuteronomy. Scrolls were made from long strips of leather or papyrus. Scribes would use a pen to write in columns on one or both sides of these materials.

In the Hebrew canon, these documents are known as the Torah (or Law) and comprise the first of three major divisions of the Jewish sacred writings. The other two are the Prophets and the Writings. Both Jewish and Christian traditions assert that Moses was the human author of the Torah (which are also called the "Pentateuch" or five books). The Law is not only a compilation of the decrees of God entrusted to Moses, but also the history of humanity and the Israelites. Moses probably wrote these books in the fifteenth century B.C. A thousand years later, the Book of Nehemiah was being created as the wall of Jerusalem underwent rebuilding.

The purpose of having Ezra read from the Law was not only to preserve the Torah, but also to encourage every generation to revere and obey God's decrees and teachings. This public reading led the Jews to renew their commitment to God's covenant and to instruct their children to do the same. The Jews did not own personal copies of the law. The main way they were able to become familiar with it was by hearing it read and explained. This is what Ezra had returned to Jerusalem to do; but during the 52 days when the wall of Jerusalem was being rebuilt, there was little time for an assembly. After the wall's completion, however, the people expressed a desire to hear more instruction from the Torah.

B. The Reading Done by Ezra: vs. 3

He read it aloud from daybreak till noon as he faced the square before the Water Gate in the presence of the men, women and others who could understand. And all the people listened attentively to the Book of the Law.

Ezra faced the open square just inside the Water Gate from early morning until noon and read aloud from the Torah scroll to everyone who could understand. In ancient times, this was the customary practice. All the people, in turn, paid close attention to what they heard (Neh. 8:3). Imagine standing for five or six hours in reverential silence while attentively listening to the Bible being read! From this incident comes the modern Jewish tradition of standing as the Torah scroll is read in the synagogue (a ritual some Christian churches also observe). Everything that was done and the way it was reported points to the deep commitment and devotion of God's people. Ezra the scribe was standing on a high wooden platform that had been built for this occasion. He wasn't alone, either. Standing next to him was Nehemiah, and they were flanked on their right and left by priests, Levites, and other Jewish leaders (vs. 4; see vs. 9). They evidently stood alongside Ezra to assist in the long time that it took to read, translate, and interpret God's Word.

C. The People's Worship: vss. 5-6

Ezra opened the book. All the people could see him because he was standing above them; and as he opened it, the people all stood up. Ezra praised the LORD, the great God; and all the people lifted their hands and responded, "Amen! Amen!" Then they bowed down and worshiped the LORD with their faces to the ground.

Ezra stood on the elevated platform in full view of the people. When they saw the scribe unroll the Torah scroll, they rose to their feet in unison out of respect for the reading and exposition of God's Word (Neh. 8:5). This spontaneous reaction from the crowd must have warmed the scribe's heart. These Jews were far different from the ones he had addressed years earlier. They were now eager to hear God's Word and willing to do whatever He asked of them.

When Ezra gave praise to the Lord, "the great God" (vs. 6), the people chanted "Amen! Amen!" (to indicate emphatic agreement with and acceptance of the law) and lifted their palms heavenward (perhaps in unison, to denote expectation and dependency). Then the attendees bowed down and worshiped the Lord "with their faces to the ground." In this way, the people indicated their humble and willing submission to their God and Creator. As a matter of fact, the Hebrew word translated "worshiped" originally meant "to prostrate oneself on the ground."

A number of Levites instructed the people who were standing as Ezra read the Mosaic law (vs. 7). Jewish tradition says the Levites were translating the words from ancient Hebrew to Aramaic, the international diplomatic and trade language of the day. Most likely, at intervals between the readings, the assistants circulated freely among the crowd and gave the sense of the text (perhaps paragraph by paragraph and sentence by sentence) so that the people could grasp what was being read (vs. 8). The goal of the expositors was to make the interpretation God's Word clear and its application understandable.

The reading and teaching of the law took place under the watchful eyes of Nehemiah, Ezra, and the Levites, which indicated there was unity among the Jewish leaders. Unexpectedly, something quite remarkable happened. The people began to weep and mourn. The Holy Spirit used the words of the law to bring strong conviction of sin to their hearts and minds (vs. 9). Perhaps for the first time, the returnees comprehended how far short they fell of God's righteous moral standard (see Rom. 3:23). Incidentally, the Hebrew word rendered "mourn" (Neh. 8:9) often describes the reaction of those who are suddenly aware that they deserve judgment (Exod. 33:4; Ezra 10:6).

Although the people's weeping and confessing of their sin (and possibly the transgressions of their ancestors) was an understandable response, this occasion called for a different reaction. The Jewish leaders encouraged the people not to be sorrowful at this time. Because it was a sacred day before the Lord, the appropriate response was for the community of the redeemed to sing praises to the God of Israel. That's why Nehemiah, in concert with the other officials (vs. 11), urged the people to celebrate the occasion with "choice food and sweet drinks" (vs. 10). The former reference is to festive, tasty morsels prepared with the fat of sacrificial animals. Nehemiah also encouraged the attendees to share gifts of food with those who had nothing prepared. This reflects the Jewish tradition of remembering the disadvantaged on joyous occasions (2 Sam. 6:19; Esth. 9:22).

While the returned exiles experienced a renewed devotion to the law of God and sincerely repented of their sins, this devotion eventually led to close study of the law and then to a legalistic interpretation of it. This phenomenon became the seedbed for the development of the Pharisees and their strict adherence to the Torah. Jesus later rebuked the Pharisees for obeying the letter of the law while neglecting to obey the spirit of the law.

II. The Feast of Booths: Nehemiah 8:13-14, 17-18

A. The Feast of Booths Commanded: vss. 13-14

On the second day of the month, the heads of all the families, along with the priests and the Levites, gathered around Ezra the scribe to give attention to the words of the Law. They found written in the Law, which the LORD had commanded through Moses, that the Israelites were to live in booths during the feast of the seventh month

The audience departed to do all that the leaders had said. They ate and drank at a festive meal, shared gifts of food with the disadvantaged, and celebrated the occasion with "great joy" (Neh. 8:12) because they had both heard and understood the Word of God that had been read and expounded to them. The next day, the leaders of each family along with the priests and Levites assembled to meet with Ezra. He helped them understand the law better (vs. 13). They discovered that the Feast of Booths was celebrated during the fall season five days after the Day of Atonement (vs. 14).

The leaders announced in Jerusalem and Judah that the people were to observe the sacred day. This involved going out to the hill country and obtaining a variety of branches—from cultivated and wild olive trees, myrtle trees (evergreen shrubs that gave off a pleasant fragrance), date palms, and other leafy trees—to construct temporary shelters for living outside. This was done in accordance with the Law (vs. 15). The Feast of Booths (also called Tabernacles or Ingathering) was characterized by a week of celebration for the harvest in which God's people lived in booths and offered sacrifices. This observance memorialized the Israelites' journey from Egypt to Canaan (when they lived in tents) and gave them an opportunity to thank the Lord for the productivity of the land (see Exod. 23:16; Lev. 23:33-43; John 7:37).

B. The Feast of Booths Observed: vss. 17-18

The whole company that had returned from exile built booths and lived in them. From the days of Joshua son of Nun until that day, the Israelites had not celebrated it like this. And their joy was very great. Day after day, from the first day to the last, Ezra read from the Book of the Law of God. They celebrated the feast for seven days, and on the eighth day, in accordance with the regulation, there was an assembly.

The people complied with the directive. They went out, cut branches, and used them to build shelters in every possible location of the city—on the flat roofs of their houses, in the courtyards of their homes, in the outer and inner courtyards of God's temple, and in the plazas around the Water Gate and the Ephraim Gate (the latter being on the north side of the city and facing toward the territory of Ephraim; Neh. 8:16). The people living in the surrounding villages also built temporary shelters. This holiday had not been observed in quite this way and with this much joy since the time of Joshua. The people were once again giving thanks to God for His blessings with the same enthusiasm and zeal as the Israelites of Joshua's day had done (vs. 17).

Understanding of biblical truth is dry without the joy that God produces. Likewise, feasting and joy are meaningless without the firm foundation of God's Word. That is why Ezra read from the law each day throughout the entire seven-day period of celebration. On the eighth day, a solemn assembly took place in accordance with the law (vs. 18). The purpose of the reading was not only to preserve the law but also to encourage every generation to revere and obey God's Word. This public reading led the Jews to renew their commitment to God's covenant and to instruct their children to do the same.

The ninth chapters of Ezra, Nehemiah, and Daniel all contain prayers of confession dealing with the national sins that led to the Babylonian captivity and the loss of Israel's sovereignty over its own affairs. These confessions of the transgressions of people long dead were not requests that the original sinners be forgiven. They were statements of identification with the past. Through the prayer in Nehemiah 9, Ezra helped his contemporaries rehearse the sins of the past, recognize the present results of those sins, and prepare to move into a future marked by faithfulness and blessing. As Christians today, we, too, can find it helpful to face the past in order to understand the present and move into the future with God's fullest blessing.

Two days after the last joyous day of the Feast of Booths, the people of Judah and Jerusalem gathered once again in Jerusalem (vs. 1). Earlier, Ezra and Nehemiah had discouraged mourning over sin during the festival days when the people were to draw spiritual strength from the joy of knowing the Lord (see 8:9-10). Now they came again to explore another aspect of being the people of God through fasting, separation from idolatry, and confession of sin. The remnant was prepared to connect their personal sins with the obvious rebelliousness of their ancestors before the Exile.

The people stood for three hours of reading from the law and three hours of confession and worship, just as they had stood all morning on the first of the month to hear Ezra read the law (Neh. 9:2-3; see 8:3, 5). The Levites called on the people to stand for worship (vs. 5a). This worship consisted of praise that focused on the covenant relationship between God and His people Israel. "The LORD"— *Yahweh*—was God's covenant name, and indeed the following recitation of Israel's history is an account of God's covenant faithfulness and Israel's covenant faithlessness. Jewish tradition and many Christian commentators attribute the beautiful prayer of Nehemiah 9:5b-37 to Ezra. The prayer was structured carefully to guide the worshipers of Judah and Jerusalem in contrasting themselves with the Lord.

Discussion Questions

1. What do you think it would have been like to be a participant at the reading of the law?
2. How would you describe the reaction of the people?
3. What connection do you see between the law of God and celebration?
4. Have you ever been through a phase of your life when you neglected to read the Bible? What effect did it have on you?
5. What can you do to renew a commitment to know and do God's will?

Contemporary Application

Nehemiah and his fellow Jews understood the importance of launching their resolve to obey God with the strongest possible beginning. Do your students have the same attitude about obeying God? This week's lesson stresses that when a strong commitment is absent, believers are more prone to violate His Word.

Missionaries tell stories that resemble Nehemiah's account about the public reading and teaching of God's Word. People who have never heard it before are amazed and overcome. They seek God's forgiveness for their sins and welcome Jesus Christ as their Lord and Savior. On the other hand, people who have heard the Bible read and taught again and again sometimes find it hard to be moved. The Word of God becomes so familiar to them that it loses its initial forcefulness on their consciences.

We also face the problem of Bible ignorance and neglect. Public opinion polls show that among Christians, regular Scripture reading is largely neglected. Yet we can be thankful that local Bible study groups flourish in many churches and communities. Those who hunger and thirst for righteousness will be spiritually satisfied (Matt. 5:6). When we seek God and put Him first in our lives, we will listen to, study, obey, and teach God's Word. Compared to the upright remnant in Nehemiah's day, we are surfeited with Bibles and Scripture study materials. Therefore, our judgment will be severe if we neglect these gifts and opportunities from the Lord.

Jesus as God's Son

DEVOTIONAL READING

Proverbs 8:22-31

DAILY BIBLE READINGS

Monday May 26
  Proverbs 8:22-31 From the Beginning

Tuesday May 27
  Hebrews 1:1-5 Appointed Heir

Wednesday May 28
  John 1:1-5 In the Beginning

Thursday May 29
  Hebrews 1:6-9 The Firstborn

Friday May 30
  Hebrews 1:10-12 The Work of God's Hands

Saturday May 31
  John 1:14-18 Full of Grace and Truth

Sunday June 1
  Hebrews 1:13-14 Heir of All Things

Scripture

Background Scripture: *Hebrews 1*
Scripture Lesson: *Hebrews 1:1-4, 8-12*
Key Verse: *The Son is the radiance of God's glory and the exact representation of his being, sustaining all things by his powerful word.* Hebrews 1:3.
Scripture Lesson for Children: *Matthew 3:13-17*
Key Verse for Children: *"This is my Son, whom I love; with him I am well pleased."* Matthew 3:17.

Lesson Aim

To sort out the implications of worshiping Jesus as God.

Lesson Setting

Time: *Before* A.D. *70*
Place: *Possibly Rome*

Lesson Outline

Jesus as God's Son

  I. The Father's Revelation in the Son: Hebrews 1:1-4
      A. *Divine Disclosure through the Prophets: vs. 1*
      B. *Divine Disclosure through the Son: vs. 2a*
      C. *Divine Superiority of the Son: vss. 2b-4*
  II. The Son's Superiority to Angels: Hebrews 1:8-12
      A. *The Sovereign Rule of the Son: vss. 8-9*
      B. *The Eternal Existence of the Son: vss. 10-12*

319

Introduction for Adults

Topic: *Finding Deeper Meaning in Life*

An irate woman approached the receptionist's desk at the ophthalmologist's office. "Yesterday, while I was having surgery, someone stole my wig," she said accusingly. The physician came out and tried to calm down the woman. "I assure you that no one on my staff would have done such a thing. Why do you think it was taken from here?" "Well," the woman huffed, "after the operation, I noticed that the wig I had on was ugly and cheap-looking." The surgeon gently remarked, "Ma'am, I think that means that your cataract operation was a success."

When we come to know Jesus by faith, it should serve as a lens through which to view our entire lives. In the light of our new birth, the truth of the Gospel functions like a new pair of eyeglasses through which we see ourselves and our world in a different light and with a fresh perspective. It's a light in which we find deeper meaning, especially as we recognize the love of God in every moment, in every place, and in every relationship.

Introduction for Youth

Topic: *Here Comes the Son!*

The little girl's voice echoed across the hallway to the master bedroom. "Daddy, I'm scared!" The father tried his best to focus his thoughts. "Honey, don't be afraid. Daddy's right across the hall." After a brief pause, the girl said, "I'm still scared." The father, being theologically astute, replied, "You don't need to be afraid. God is with you. God loves you." Then, after a longer pause, the girl said in a quivering voice, "Daddy, I want someone with skin on."

When Jesus, the Son, became a human being, He "put skin" on the glory and character of God the Father so that He might reveal Him to us.

Concepts for Children

Topic: *God's Son, Jesus*

1. John prepared people for Jesus to come.
2. John called for the people to change their sinful ways.
3. Jesus said that John should baptize Him in order to carry out all that God requires.
4. At the moment of Jesus' baptism, the Holy Spirit descended on Him like a dove.
5. God is pleased with us when we obey His Son.

Lesson Commentary

I. THE FATHER'S REVELATION IN THE SON: HEBREWS 1:1-4

A. Divine Disclosure through the Prophets: vs. 1

In the past God spoke to our forefathers through the prophets at many times and in various ways.

The writer of Hebrews began his letter by commenting on God's disclosure of Himself to humankind. Since the creation of the world (see Gen. 1:1), people have been aware of God's invisible attributes. In particular, they could infer His eternal power and divine nature through what He has made (Rom. 1:20; see Ps. 19:1-6). While this general revelation of God enables people to know that He exists, it does not impart divine truths leading to salvation. The latter is only made possible by God revealing Himself and His will in a special way.

Hebrews 1:1 declares that during the era of the Old Testament, God spoke redemptively to His people through His prophets on a number of occasions. The Lord did so in various portions and in a variety of ways (for example, through visions, dreams, and riddles). The idea is that His revelation was fragmentary, partial, and incomplete, though fully inspired and authoritative. Prophets used a variety of means to convey God's message to people, including oral, dramatic, and written forms. Prophets did not spend all of their time predicting the future. Much of their efforts went into observing what was taking place around them and declaring God's message concerning those situations. The prophets were not speaking on their own behalf or for their personal benefit. Rather, they were God's messengers, whom He authorized to convey vital truths to others.

B. Divine Disclosure through the Son: vs. 2a

But in these last days he has spoken to us by his Son.

The basis for God choosing to reveal Himself in progressive stages rests on the fact that He works with us according to the level of our understanding. At first, He revealed Himself only in shadows and symbols; but as people came to know more about Him and the way He works, He became more explicit in His dealings and revelations. It's important to acknowledge these ancient revelations for what they taught people about God, while simultaneously noting that they pointed to a time when God would reveal Himself more fully and finally in "his Son" (Heb. 1:2).

The candid statements appearing in verse 1 were not meant to diminish the value of God's revelation through the Hebrew prophets. The fact that He considered them the transmitters of divine revelation is evidence of just how much respect He held for these faithful servants of the Lord; but the same God who had partially revealed Himself in times past, now had disclosed Himself totally and ultimately in His Son. With the advent of the Messiah, everything is centered in Him. He in turn gives full and final expression to all that was previously revealed (see

Luke 24:44), and He does so in a way that is focused, clear, and eternally relevant.

"In these last days" (Heb. 1:2) would carry a special significance for the readers, who probably interpreted the phrase to mean that Jesus, as the Savior, had ushered in the messianic age. He is not merely the end of a long line of Old Testament prophets, but also the one for whom the Hebrews had waited for centuries. He is the complete and distinct revelation of God. Even with the coming of the Savior, the inspired nature of God's communication has not changed. The messages He conveyed through the prophets to the community of faith were graced by His power and love; and this remains true now that the Son has revealed the Father to us. In fact, what the Messiah has unveiled is in harmony with all that appears in the Old Testament, for what the prophets foretold finds its fulfillment in the Messiah (see Rom. 1:2; 3:21).

C. Divine Superiority of the Son: vss. 2b-4

Whom he appointed heir of all things, and through whom he made the universe. The Son is the radiance of God's glory and the exact representation of his being, sustaining all things by his powerful word. After he had provided purification for sins, he sat down at the right hand of the Majesty in heaven. So he became as much superior to the angels as the name he has inherited is superior to theirs.

Having pointed out Jesus' distinction as the Son of God, the author of Hebrews proceeded to explain ways in which God's revelation through the Savior is superior to all other revelations of the Lord. To show this superiority, the writer made a number of statements describing the Son. First, the Father appointed His Son as "heir of all things" (1:2). In Hebrew culture, the firstborn son was the highest ranked of all children. Therefore, he was also the family heir. Jesus is the heir, owner, and Lord of God's creation. Second, it is through the Son that the Father "made the universe." The Greek term rendered "universe" refers to the temporal ages and includes the spatial realm, which exists in those time periods. Before time and matter were created, the Messiah eternally preexisted.

Third, the Son is the "radiance" (vs. 3) of the triune God's glory. This does not mean Jesus is merely a reflection of the Lord's majesty. The Messiah is God Himself, for the glory of God is His radiance. In Jesus' incarnation, He unveiled to humankind the majesty of the divine. Fourth, the Son is the "exact representation" of the triune God's being. The Greek word behind this translation originally referred to the die used in minting coins. The term later came to refer to the impression on coins. The writer of Hebrews was saying that who Jesus is corresponds exactly to that of the Godhead. Thus, He alone is the precise image of God's essence. While the Son is one with the Father and the Spirit in terms of their being, there remains a distinction of the divine persons of the Trinity. Fifth, not only did the Son create the universe, but He also holds it together by His powerful word. Through His sustaining royal decree, He prevents the cosmos from destruction. Clearly, the Son has a continued interest in the world and loves it. Thus, He is carrying it toward the fulfillment of His divine plan.

Sixth, at the heart of the divine plan and revelation to humankind is making redemption available for the lost. This is why the Son died to wash us from the stain of our sins. The Greek verb for "purged" is *katharismon*, from which we derive the term *catharsis*, meaning a purging that brings about spiritual renewal. The idea is that through His atoning sacrifice at Calvary, Jesus accomplished cleansing for humanity's transgressions. The writer expressed his thoughts in the past tense to underscore that the Messiah's redemptive work on our behalf has already been accomplished.

Seventh, because Jesus completed the task for which He was sent, He was granted the place of highest honor—to sit at God's right hand in a posture of rest (as opposed to endlessly ministering in a standing position; see 10:11). The Lord Jesus did once and for all what the Hebrew priests were required to do on a regular basis. Now, as our great High Priest, the Messiah continually applies to us the purification for sins He obtained at the cross. This enables us to worship in God's presence.

For the various reasons given by the writer of Hebrews, the Son is to be considered superior to all things, including "the angels" (1:4). The Hebrew people had long held angels in high esteem because these heavenly beings were instrumental in the giving of the law at Mount Sinai. The author told his readers that God's Son is absolutely above all angels. To emphasize Jesus' superiority, the writer of Hebrews said Christ's name (most likely, "Son") is superior to that of the celestial beings in heaven. The idea is that Jesus' character and work—which were summed up in His name—were far superior even to those of God's cosmic messengers.

II. THE SON'S SUPERIORITY TO ANGELS: HEBREWS 1:8-12

A. The Sovereign Rule of the Son: vss. 8-9

But about the Son he says, "Your throne, O God, will last for ever and ever, and righteousness will be the scepter of your kingdom. You have loved righteousness and hated wickedness; therefore God, your God, has set you above your companions by anointing you with the oil of joy."

The author of Hebrews quoted a number of Old Testament passages to show how and why the Lord Jesus is superior to the angels. Apparently, the writer of the epistle intended to imply that the Messiah is to be seen throughout the Old Testament. This was a strategically important decision, for the Jewish readership of the letter highly regarded the Hebrew Scriptures. There was no better way to substantiate the superiority of Christ than by citing pertinent verses from the Old Testament. Those reading Hebrews would have to admit that even their sacred writings affirmed that Jesus was better than anyone else.

The author began his series of citations with a question: "For to which of the angels did God ever say" (1:5). By quoting first a messianic psalm (Ps. 2:7) and then 2 Samuel 7:14 (which is parallel to 1 Chronicles 17:13), the author indicated that God had never singled out an angel and applied to that being the status He had accorded His Son (Heb. 1:5). Most likely, the Israelites applied Psalm 2:7 to the descendants of David, whom they crowned king. However, the verse ultimately refers to the Savior. This is made clear in Acts 13:33. When God raised Jesus from the dead, He conferred great dignity on Him by declaring Him to be His Son (something that Jesus had been for all eternity). No angel could claim this honor. In short, the writer of Hebrews was making a clear distinction: the angels are created heavenly beings, but Jesus is the only Son of God, the long-awaited Messiah who gives salvation to those who trust in Him. The quote from 2 Samuel 7:14 records the Lord telling David that He would relate to the descendants on his throne (for example, Solomon) as a father would to a son. This familial bond finds its ultimate expression in the relationship between God and Christ. The Father chose His Son to rule on His throne and serve as His official representative. From Hebrews 1:5 we discover that the Messiah enjoys a unique, one-of-a-kind, Father-Son relationship with God (see John 1:14, 18), something the angels cannot claim.

Commentators debate whether "and again" (Heb. 1:6) refers to Jesus' first advent, His ascension and exaltation to heaven, or His second advent. Another possibility is that the phrase is used as a simple connective without any specific reference to time. Regardless of which option is preferred, the writer's reference to the Savior as God's "firstborn" is unmistakable. Here the idea is not of the Messiah being first in order of birth, but highest in rank. The Son's unique relationship as an heir to God the Father is the point of emphasis. As God's firstborn heir, Jesus is the source of both righteousness and eternal life for all those who will come after Him—in essence, for all those who place their faith in His atoning work.

The source of the quotation in verse 6 is disputed by Bible scholars. Some say it was taken from Deuteronomy 32:43 of the Septuagint (a pre-Christian Greek version of the Hebrew Scriptures) and was not included in other ancient texts of the Bible. Others say it was taken from Psalm 97:7, and still others say the author of Hebrews combined the Deuteronomy and Psalm passages. Whatever the case, the author's purpose in using the quotation was to show that the Son is worthy of the angels' worship in the same way that God the Father is worthy of the angels' worship. The quotation also affirms Christ's deity. This worship of the Son was no small matter. Indeed, all of God's angels would participate in it.

While still addressing the Son's superiority to angels, the author then cited a quotation—the Septuagint version of Psalm 104:4—describing the character of the angels (Heb. 1:7). In the original Hebrew version, that Psalm's verse appears to describe the wind and lightning of a storm as God's servants. The Septuagint version, however, identifies angels as God's servants, and that's the point the author of Hebrews wanted to make. They are much lower in existence than the royal Son of David, who is enthroned in the heavens as the eternal Creator and King (see vss. 10-12). While the angels are God's servants, Jesus is God's Son and the divine King. This truth is stressed in Hebrews 1:8-9, which contain a quotation from Psalm 45:6-7. Here we find one of the Bible's strongest affirmations of the deity of Christ. In

Hebrews 1:8-9, the Son is addressed as God; and His royal status is alluded to in the words "throne," "scepter," and "kingdom." As the Father's representative and co-regent, the Son rules over all creation forever. His scepter symbolizes His regal authority, which is characterized by justice and equity. Because these virtues are the basis of His unending rule, He enjoys an infinitely exalted status as King.

The latter emphasis can be found in the phrase "oil of joy" (vs. 9). The allusion is to an ancient Israelite practice of anointing the head of a king with olive oil at his coronation. The event was a time of great celebration and renewed hope. The ultimate focus, of course, is Jesus Christ, who reigns as King over the cosmos. Like the Father, the Son loves righteousness and hates wickedness. Because of these characteristics, the Father set His Son above all other people and beings, and anointed Him to carry out the most sacred function of all time—to bring people to salvation.

B. The Eternal Existence of the Son: vss. 10-12

He also says, "In the beginning, O Lord, you laid the foundations of the earth, and the heavens are the work of your hands. They will perish, but you remain; they will all wear out like a garment. You will roll them up like a robe; like a garment they will be changed. But you remain the same, and your years will never end."

Hebrews 1:10-12 quotes Psalm 102:25-27. These verses declare that at the dawn of time, Yahweh (the covenant-keeping God of Israel) laid the foundations of the earth. Likewise, He made the heavens with His hands. We learn from Hebrews 1:10 that the Messiah acted as God's agent in Creation (see John 1:1-3; Col. 1:15-17). One day, the heavens and the earth will perish and disappear. The Son will roll up the Creation like a worn-out robe that is to be discarded, and replace this tattered garment with a new heaven and earth (see 2 Pet. 3:10-13; Rev. 21:1). In contrast, the Son (like the Father and the Spirit) will remain the same throughout all eternity (Heb. 1:11-12).

When Paul talked about "visions and revelations" (2 Cor. 12:1) he had "from the Lord," he disclosed he had been caught up to "the third heaven" (vs. 2) or "paradise" (vs. 4). Contemporary Jewish writings subdivided the heavens into three or more layers. It is unclear how much of this thinking the apostle accepted, though his wording here suggests he embraced the Jewish belief in the plurality of the heavens. If we assume that the first heaven is the sky and the second heaven the more distant stars and planets, the third heaven refers to the place where God dwells. Paradise is the abode of blessedness for the righteous dead. For believers, it also signifies dwelling in fellowship with the exalted Redeemer in unending glory.

In Hebrews 1:13, the writer quoted Psalm 110:1. In ancient Israel, the verse was applied to each successive monarch in the dynasty of David. Various New Testament references understand the Messiah to be the ideal Davidic king to which the verse ultimately points (see Matt 22:43-45; Mark 12:36-37; Luke 20:42-44; Acts

2:34-35). The Lord Jesus is God's vice-regent who sits in the place of honor at His right hand. The Father has pledged to humble the enemies of the Son and force them into subservience, as if they were a footstool under His feet (Heb. 1:13). No angel has such a privilege given to them. In fact, angels have a lesser role as "ministering spirits," serving those who are saved through faith in the Son (vs. 14).

Discussion Questions

1. What was the nature of God's revelation in the past through the Old Testament prophets?
2. In what sense is the Son the heir of all things?
3. In what sense does Jesus sustain all things by His powerful command?
4. What virtues characterize the reign of the Son?
5. How does the existence of the Son contrast with that of Creation?

Contemporary Application

When we read the opening verses of the Book of Hebrews, we learn that Christ is supremely great. Our natural response should be to worship the risen Lord; but there are times when we do not feel inclined to do so. In those instances, our will should direct the actions of our hearts.

One reason we should worship Jesus is that Scripture commands us to do so. At first we might react negatively to this; but we can see the wisdom of the biblical directive when we realize how inclined we are to worship ourselves and others, rather than the Lord (Rom. 1:25).

Another reason for worshiping Jesus is that it remains such an integral part of our relationship with Him. He created and saved us to adore Him. When we give praise to Christ, we will come to know and enjoy Him more. Moreover, we should worship Jesus out of love and gratitude. He loved us enough to die on the cross for our sins. We in turn demonstrate our love by adoring Him as our divine Creator and King.

It is part of our redeemed nature to want to worship Christ. Imagine buying an expensive piano and using it only as a coffee table or a place to shelve knickknacks and pictures of loved ones. What an inappropriate use of the piano that would be! A believer who does not worship Christ and a piano that is never used to play music are abnormal. If we commit ourselves to worshiping Jesus, we will discover more of what it means to be a person created in the image of God.

Finally, we should worship Christ in order to be united in love with other believers. Too often, we want to base our unity in the faith on how much we like one another, rather than on our common relationship with our Savior. Worship brings us back to the true basis for our unity.

Christ as Intercessor

Scripture

Background Scripture: *Hebrews 7*
Scripture Lesson: *Hebrews 7:20-28*
Key Verse: *[Christ] is able to save completely those who come
to God through him, because he always lives to intercede for
them.* Hebrews 7:25.
Scripture Lesson for Children: *John 17:6-11, 20-21*
Key Verse for Children: *[Jesus said,] "Holy Father, protect
them by the power of your name . . . so that they may be one as
we are one."* John 17:11.

Lesson Aim

To emphasize the importance of relying on Jesus as our
great High Priest.

Lesson Setting

Time: *Before A.D. 70*
Place: *Possibly Rome*

Lesson Outline

Christ as Intercessor

   I. The Son's Appointment: Hebrews 7:20-25
     A. *The Father's Solemn Oath: vss. 20-22*
     B. *The Son's Permanent Priesthood: vss. 23-25*
  II. The Son's Perfection: Hebrews 7:26-28
     A. *The Son's Perfect Moral Status: vs. 26*
     B. *The Son's Perfect Sacrifice: vs. 27*
     C. *The Son's Perfect Priesthood: vs. 28*

Introduction for Adults

Topic: *Who Can Speak for Us?*

We can have confidence in our Christian life because we have a Savior who understands us and takes an active interest in our well-being. He knows the problems we face. He experienced the same sorts of things we experience. Most important, He's here for us right now.

There's nothing wrong with turning to the pastor or our friends when we have problems. But we need to understand that our greatest source of strength is Jesus Christ. True, we cannot see Him. But like the anchor on the ocean floor, Jesus is still doing His high priestly work, providing the stability we need to face the issues of life.

Introduction for Youth

Topic: *We Have a Friend in High Places*

There are many crisis hot lines across the country that teens can call. When adolescents have a problem, they can call a hot-line telephone number and talk to someone who is sympathetic and understands their problem. Why is the counselor able to relate so well? Usually it's because the person answering the phone has been through the same problem as the caller or is familiar with others who have had similar problems.

Jesus is the teens' ultimate friend in the highest place of all—heaven. He's there right now to intercede on their behalf. But at the same time, He's right here with the adolescents in your class, providing them with advice, encouragement, and support. This should give them the confidence they need to face their problems.

Concepts for Children

Topic: *Jesus Prays for Us*

1. The Son prayed for God's chosen people.
2. The Son said He had fulfilled His mission.
3. The Son asked for protection for His followers when He returned to the Father.
4. The Son included all of His followers in His prayer.
5. The Son cares so much for us that watches over us every day of our lives.

Lesson Commentary

I. THE SON'S APPOINTMENT: HEBREWS 7:20-25

A. The Father's Solemn Oath: vss. 20-22

And it was not without an oath! Others became priests without any oath, but he became a priest with an oath when God said to him: "The Lord has sworn and will not change his mind: 'You are a priest forever.'" Because of this oath, Jesus has become the guarantee of a better covenant.

Humanity's need for a priesthood is rooted in people's consciousness of sin. Those whose hearts and lives had been stained by sin could not enter the presence of a holy God. They needed a mediator, a go-between, a representative—someone who could approach God with sacrifices and prayers on their behalf. In ancient Israel, the priest was authorized to come before God and intercede on behalf of His people.

The priests were to be from among Aaron's descendants and were to be free of physical defects. Priests were required to dress in designated attire and to live in strict obedience to the law. Besides upholding the civil and religious codes that applied to the Israelites, they had to execute those laws applying to their vocation as priests. The high priest was at the top of this religious hierarchy. While priests in general represented the people before God, the high priest was their supreme representative. He was uniquely set apart to God through the anointing of his head with sacred oil (Lev. 8:12; 21:10; Ps. 133:2). Other priests had oil sprinkled only on their garments, but the high priest became the "anointed priest."

Perhaps the Hebrew Christians were having a hard time believing that there could be any priesthood other than the one associated with Aaron. The writer of Hebrews revealed that the Lord Jesus is a priest forever in the order of Melchizedek (5:6, 10; see Ps. 110:4). Melchizedek is mentioned only three times in the Bible—in Genesis 14, in Psalm 110, and in Hebrews. The only biblical background for the life of Melchizedek is found in Genesis 14:18-20. The writer of Hebrews summarized the biblical data by noting that Melchizedek was not only the king of Salem, but also a priest of God Most High (7:1). The key factor is that he was both a king and priest. Here was a person outside the boundaries of God's revelation to Israel and yet he worshiped the Lord.

The author recounted how Melchizedek met with Abraham (probably before 2000 B.C.) when the patriarch was returning from his defeat of the kings of Elam, Goiim, Shinar, and Ellasar. During their meeting, Mechizedek blessed Abraham. The patriarch responded by presenting Melchizedek with a tenth of the spoils he had taken in his victory over the four kings (vs. 2). In ancient times, the person who collected the tithe was greater than the one who presented it. Also, the person who blessed was greater than the one who received the blessings (vss. 4-7). The implication is that Melchizedek was higher in rank than Abraham, along with all his descendants, including Levi and the priesthood originating from him (vss. 8-10).

The recipient of Abraham's gift was both a king of righteousness and peace (vs.

2). Interestingly, there is no record in Scripture of Melchizedek's parents and ancestors. It's almost as if his life and priesthood had no beginning or ending. In these ways, he resembled the Son of God (vs. 3). The implication is that Christ, the King-Priest in the order of Melchizedek (vs. 17), is superior to all Levitical priests. The latter, along with the Mosaic law, were unable to make anyone perfect in God's eyes (vs. 11). The entire system was weak and useless (vs. 18). Also, all the sacrificial rituals performed by the priests had really done little toward securing the peace of the souls of humanity (vs. 19). Consequently, God annulled the old system and replaced it with the high priesthood of Christ (vss. 11-15). Jesus did not attain His priestly status on the basis of the Mosaic law, but by the power of a life that cannot be destroyed (vs. 16). As a human being, He died on the cross, but He rose again to new life and now lives forever. He is the "better hope" (vs. 19) whom God introduced to give people complete and lasting access to Him. In essence, the Gospel of salvation through Christ is better than the ritualistic law.

The author said that God did not make an oath when Levites became priests (vs. 20). On the other hand, God did make an oath in appointing Christ to His priesthood. Quoting once again from Psalm 110:4, the author showed his readers how this oath was worded: "The Lord has sworn and will not change his mind: 'You are a priest forever'" (Heb. 7:21; see 5:6, 10; 7:17). In Psalm 110:1, God the Father tells David's Lord (the Messiah) to occupy a kingly position at God's right hand. Therefore, God the Father is recorded as addressing God the Son in this passage. In verse 1, the Messiah is affirmed to be a king, and in verse 4, He is declared to be a priest. Expressed differently, Christ is the perfect combination of a king-priest in one person. Whereas the Levitical priesthood had as its inception God's command, the high priesthood of Christ had as its inception the promise God made to His Son. Unlike the Levitical priesthood, Christ's priesthood will not fall short of its goal, and thus will never come to an end.

In the ancient world, people took an oath to back up a statement's truthfulness. Oaths were used as a guarantee that a promise would be kept. Sometimes they were even used as evidence in court. Oath takers often called for some punishment to be inflicted upon them if they broke the oath. Israelites would swear by someone greater than themselves, usually the king or the Lord. Adapting Himself to a human custom, God sometimes made an oath as a guarantee of performance (see Heb. 6:17). When His oath was accompanied by a promise of blessing, it was given for assurance. With a promise of judgment, it amounted to a curse.

Because of God's oath concerning Jesus' eternal priesthood, Christ is the guarantee of a new and better covenant (7:22). He takes full responsibility for ensuring that the divine promises associated with it will be fulfilled. What God specifically pledged can be found in the new covenant recorded in Jeremiah 31:31-34 (see Heb. 8:8-12; 10:16-17). In contrast with the old covenant inaugurated at Mount Sinai, the new covenant ratified through Jesus' atoning sacrifice bestows greater blessings on the righteous and executes more severe judgments on the wicked. In short, the final covenant is more complete in nature and comprehensive in scope.

There are two ways in which Christ is the guarantee of a better covenant. First, He assures humanity that God will fulfill His promise to forgive. Second, Jesus assures God that those who believe in Him are acceptable and may enter God's presence. The Greek word translated "guarantee" came from the word for *hand*. What a person could see in another's hand was guaranteed. (In that way, the word is comparable to our phrase, "A bird in the hand is worth two in the bush.") In Greek sources outside of the Bible, the same word was used for someone who acted as an undersigner, namely, someone who agreed to pay a banking debt or post bail if the debtor or prisoner defaulted. Through Jesus' sacrifice on the cross, He paid off our debt of sin, and by doing so, has provided us eternal salvation.

B. The Son's Permanent Priesthood: vss. 23-25

Now there have been many of those priests, since death prevented them from continuing in office; but because Jesus lives forever, he has a permanent priesthood. Therefore he is able to save completely those who come to God through him, because he always lives to intercede for them.

The author explained that under the old system, there had been many high priests to serve the Israelites; but death prevented them from continuing in that office (Heb. 7:23). By contrast, death cannot stop Jesus' service as our great High Priest. Because He lives forever, "he has a permanent priesthood" (vs. 24). The salvation that Christ offers is ongoing in extent and eternal in intent. Through His sacrifice, He is "able to save completely those who come to God" (vs. 25). No matter what the need of the sinner, the Messiah is capable of saving that person and making him or her worthy of entering into God's presence. And because He lives forever, His intercession for (or pleading on behalf of) humanity before God never ends.

Rather than turning haughtily away from sinners, the sinless one invites such people to His throne of grace. In fact, the author encouraged his readers to approach the Messiah with confidence, not in what they had achieved, but in what Jesus had achieved (Heb. 4:16). After all, He is a "merciful and faithful high priest" (vs. 17). The author said those who confidently and faithfully approach Christ for mercy and grace find that for which they approached Him. Therefore, instead of turning away from the Lord (see 3:12), the Hebrews were told to draw nearer to Him (4:16).

II. THE SON'S PERFECTION: HEBREWS 7:26-28

A. The Son's Perfect Moral Status: vs. 26

Such a high priest meets our need—one who is holy, blameless, pure, set apart from sinners, exalted above the heavens.

Our great High Priest is perfectly suited to meet our temporal and eternal needs. His ability to do so is based on four characteristics. First, Jesus is "holy" (Heb. 7:26). Second, Christ is blameless, meaning that He is innocent and without evil. Third,

He is pure, in the sense that He is undefiled. Fourth, He is set apart from sinners in that He is "exalted above the heavens." His sacrificial work on earth has been accomplished, and He now sits at the right hand of the throne of God. When taken together, these four characteristics imply that Jesus possesses the morally spotless character of God. Whether in motives, thoughts, words, or acts, the Messiah is upright and pure. He is free from all forms of evil, and also loves all goodness and truth. Accordingly, He abhors every aspect of wickedness, ethical impurity, and duplicity.

Our great High Priest is not austere, aloof, or fear-inducing, but is one who can empathize with our weaknesses because He became one of us and experienced life—with its joys and sorrows, highs and lows—just as we do. In fact, He even faced temptations as we do (4:15). But unlike us, our High Priest remained sinless despite being "tempted in every way" (see John 8:46; 2 Cor. 5:21; 1 Pet. 2:22; 1 John 3:5). Some have objected that, if Jesus did not sin, He was not truly human, for all humans sin. But those making that objection fail to realize that human beings are in an abnormal state. God did not create Adam and Eve as sinful, but as holy and righteous (Gen. 1:26-27). It was their willful disobedience that introduced sin into the human race (Gen. 3:1-24; Rom. 5:12).

The question is sometimes raised, "Was it possible for Christ to have sinned?" Some people argue for the impeccability of Christ, in which the word *impeccable* means "not able to sin." Others object that, if Jesus were not able to sin, His temptations could not have been real, for how can a temptation be real if the person being tempted is not able to sin at all? In thinking our way through the divine mystery associated with the sinlessness of Christ, it is prudent to affirm what Scripture teaches: (1) that Christ never actually sinned; and (2) that Jesus was tempted with real enticements to sin.

B. The Son's Perfect Sacrifice: vs. 27

Unlike the other high priests, he does not need to offer sacrifices day after day, first for his own sins, and then for the sins of the people. He sacrificed for their sins once for all when he offered himself.

In the Old Testament era, the Mosaic law required God's people to offer a number of specific kinds of sacrifices. On some occasions, the leaders and citizens of Judah could bring the objects to be offered, but only the priests were authorized to perform the actual sacrifice. In all circumstances, these were to be made only to the Lord. The Book of Leviticus describes five types of sacrifices. Burnt offerings consisted of a bull, an unblemished male sheep or goat, or a dove or pigeon. The entire object was to be burned as an expression of worship to God, to show devotion to Him, and to ask for His forgiveness (see 1:1-17; 6:8-13; 8:18-21; 16:23-24).

Fellowship (or peace) offerings could be the fat and specific inner organs from an unblemished bull, cow, sheep, or goat. The object could also be various kinds of bread made without yeast. Such was given in worship to God and to ask for His blessing (see 3:1-17; 7:11-26). Grain offerings consisted of a mixture of wheat flour, olive oil, and incense. It was sometimes presented in conjunction with burnt or peace offerings. The intent was to worship God by expressing thanks. Another aim was to recognize the Lord as the source of blessings and provider of all that is good (see 2:1-16; 6:14-23).

Sin offerings could be a young goat (for the high priest and the entire nation), a male goat (for a tribal elder), a female goat or lamb (for the common people), two doves or pigeons (for the poor), or two pounds of fine flour (for the very poor). These were presented to God to seek His forgiveness or to become cleansed from ritual impurity (see 4:1—5:13; 6:24-30; 8:14-17; 16:3-22). Guilt offerings consisted of an unblemished ram. It could also be the price of the animal, along with making restitution for whatever was stolen or destroyed, plus 20 percent. The intent was to make things right with the Lord after He had been defrauded, whether deliberately or unintentionally. Another goal was to make amends to those who had been robbed or cheated (see 5:14—6:7; 7:1-6).

Hebrews 7:27 presents a bit of a problem for some interpreters because the Jewish high priests, strictly speaking, did not provide sin offerings on a daily basis. However, in 9:7 the author revealed that he was aware of the sacrificial regulations (see also 9:25; 10:1). Therefore, for the sake of argument, he must have been combining the annual Day of Atonement sacrifices with the daily burnt offerings (see Num. 28:1-8). Of course, any time a high priest himself sinned, he might offer a sacrifice for his sin, but rarely on a daily basis. Christ stands in stark contrast to the earthly priests. Unlike the high priests of Israel, He does not have to offer sacrifices for His own sins, because He is sinless. And He does not have to offer ritualistic sacrifices for our sins, because He offered a sacrifice once for all when He offered Himself for our transgressions (Heb. 7:27). Jesus' sacrifice on the cross, for the sins of the world, was final. No other sacrifices need follow it.

C. The Son's Perfect Priesthood: vs. 28

For the law appoints as high priests men who are weak; but the oath, which came after the law, appointed the Son, who has been made perfect forever.

Two types (or orders) of priests are mentioned in Hebrews 7:28. Those appointed by the Mosaic law the author called "weak." The one High Priest sworn in by the oath of God the author called "perfect forever." The priests appointed by the law were limited, just as all ordinary people are limited. They were mortal and sinful and could only offer animals for sacrifices, which could never provide a real substitute for the sins of humanity. The High Priest appointed by divine oath, on the other hand, is unlimited. He is immortal and sinless. And He offered Himself as the perfect sacrifice for the sins of all human beings.

Hebrews 2:10 and 5:9 reveal that it was through Jesus' suffering on the cross that He was made perfect in connection with His divinely appointed mission of redemption. The author of Hebrews did not intend to imply that the Savior was ever morally or spiritually imperfect. Rather, the writer meant that through suffering, Jesus was perfectly able to carry out the task God had given Him. Because Jesus so thoroughly identified with us—even with our pain—He became qualified to be sacrificed on behalf of sinful humanity.

Discussion Questions

1. What point was the writer of Hebrews making when he noted that the high priesthood of Christ was established with an oath?
2. In what sense is Jesus the guarantor of a better covenant?
3. How is it possible for Jesus to have a permanent priesthood?
4. Why is it important for our great High Priest to be sinlessly perfect?
5. Why did Jesus offer Himself on the cross?

Contemporary Application

We used to derive much strength and support from family and friends. But for many families today, divorce and frequent relocation have severed the supportive ties upon which former generations relied. There are adults who feel more lonely now than they ever did before. Some are unable to socialize as much as they would like because of their demanding work schedules. Others are unwilling to take the risk of getting to know people because they fear being rejected or misunderstood.

In the midst of these difficulties, it's easy to wonder whether there really is anyone who cares. In his book on trends facing society, John Naisbitt discussed the emotional coldness that a technological society produces. In an increasingly impersonal world, there's a heightened need for personal contact and emotional support.

One of the great needs today is for people to know that God is there, and that He wants to hear about their needs. For the believer, Jesus Christ meets this need. As our perfect and faithful High Priest, He is sympathetic to our concerns and burdens. Rather than letting us shrink back from God in times of distress because we think our problems are insignificant or we're unworthy, the writer of Hebrews encouraged us to come boldly to the throne of grace and receive timely help from the Savior (see 4:14-16).

Christ as Redeemer

DEVOTIONAL READING

John 4:21-26

DAILY BIBLE READINGS

Monday June 9
  John 4:21-26 "I Am He"

Tuesday June 10
  *Hebrews 9:11-15 Mediator of
  a New Covenant*

Wednesday June 11
  *Hebrews 9:16-24 On Our
  Behalf*

Thursday June 12
  *Hebrews 9:25-28 Once for
  All Time*

Friday June 13
  *Hebrews 10:1-10 A One-
  Time Sacrifice*

Saturday June 14
  *Hebrews 10:11-14 For Our
  Sanctification*

Sunday June 15
  *Hebrews 10:15-18
  Forgiveness Forever*

Scripture

Background Scripture: *Hebrews 9:11—10:18*
Scripture Lesson: *Hebrews 9:11-18; 10:12-14, 17-18*
Key Verse: *[Christ] did not enter by means of the blood of
goats and calves; but he entered the Most Holy Place once for
all by his own blood, having obtained eternal redemption.*
Hebrews 9:12.
Scripture Lesson for Children: *Mark 2:1-12*
Key Verse for Children: *[Jesus said,] "Son, your sins are
forgiven."* Mark 2:5.

Lesson Aim

To explain the lasting benefits of Jesus' once-for-all sacrifice.

Lesson Setting

Time: *Before* A.D. *70*
Place: *Possibly Rome*

Lesson Outline

Christ as Redeemer

  I. The Blood of the New Covenant: Hebrews 9:11-18
      A. *Entering the Heavenly Tabernacle: vss. 11-12*
      B. *Cleansing the Consciences of Believers: vss. 13-14*
      C. *Mediating the New Covenant: vs. 15*
      D. *Inaugurating the New Covenant: vss. 16-18*
  II. The End of Old Testament Sacrifices:
      Hebrews 10:12-14, 17-18
      A. *The All-Sufficiency of Jesus' Single Sacrifice:
         vss. 12-14*
      B. *The Promises of the New Covenant: vss. 17-18*

Introduction for Adults

Topic: *Guilt Removed*

When we think about King David's notorious sins of adultery and murder, we may be surprised to learn that he wrote songs about these terrible crimes he committed. Even more astounding is that, through the marvels of God's grace and mercy, David found his guilt removed, and this prompted him to rejoice in the Lord.

David's experience stands as a strong corrective to those who think that God could not possibly forgive them for all the awful things they have done. Tragically, many people are caught in the deadly snare of believing they are beyond redemption. Jesus' provision of pardon and restoration can give them sorely needed hope.

Christians have the immense responsibility to point the way to God's forgiveness. And as pardoned sinners, we never outgrow the need to give our testimony to others who want to know the way to salvation and forgiveness.

Introduction for Youth

Topic: *Jesus to the Rescue*

One afternoon after school, Joe decided to do some target shooting with his father's shotgun. The lad had been allowed to use the gun for hunting game, but not for anything else. His father and mother were not at home, and so Joe felt it would not matter if he blasted away at some old metal cans along a tree line at the back of their lot. No sooner had he fired the weapon than his parents pulled into the driveway.

Joe became rigid. What should he do? Should he say he was hunting rabbits, for example? The lad decided to tell the truth. He admitted that he had been shooting at some metal cans. With this admission, Joe anticipated that he would lose his hunting privileges. But instead, his parents forgave him and asked him not to be irresponsible again.

To be forgiven is a wonderful feeling. It's one of the reasons for experiencing joy in the Christian life. When we sin, we should confess our wrongdoing to our loving and wise heavenly Father. God promises to forgive us and restore us to fellowship with Him. He can do this because of what Jesus did for us on the cross.

Concepts for Children

Topic: *Jesus Forgives*

1. A crippled man's friends brought him to Jesus.
2. Jesus forgave the crippled man's sins and gave him the ability to walk.
3. The teachers of the law questioned Jesus' motives.
4. Jesus responded to the teachers' unvoiced questions.
5. Jesus' loves us so much that He forgives our sins.

Lesson Commentary

I. THE BLOOD OF THE NEW COVENANT: HEBREWS 9:11-18

A. Entering the Heavenly Tabernacle: vss. 11-12

When Christ came as high priest of the good things that are already here, he went through the greater and more perfect tabernacle that is not man-made, that is to say, not a part of this creation. He did not enter by means of the blood of goats and calves; but he entered the Most Holy Place once for all by his own blood, having obtained eternal redemption.

By describing Christ as the High Priest in the order of Melchizedek, the author of Hebrews had established a basis by which he could emphasize that Jesus' priestly ministry is far better than that of the Levitical priests. For instance, unlike all other priests, our High Priest is so great that He has now taken His rightful place in heaven, God's dwelling place, at the right hand of the Father (Heb. 8:1). That Jesus sat down implies that He has completed His work of salvation. And to sit down at the right hand of the Father implies that the Son has earned and deserves to be in the place of highest honor.

At Mount Sinai, God told Moses to construct a tabernacle, a tent that was to be set up in the center of the Israelites' encampments as they traveled toward the promised land. It was also to be the focal point of the Israelites' worship. The writer said that the sanctuary of that earthly tent was modeled after the sanctuary in heaven, at which Christ serves as our High Priest. In fact, the author called the earthly tabernacle a copy and shadow of the real one in heaven (vs. 5; see Exod. 25:40). Because humans constructed the earthly tabernacle, it was imperfect and temporary. In contrast, because God established the heavenly sanctuary, it is perfect, permanent, and the true place of worship (Heb. 8:2).

To better understand and appreciate the superiority of the new covenant, the author explained the details of the sacrificial system under the old covenant. He described the layout of the outer room of the tabernacle and depicted the contents of the inner room (9:1-5). The lower ranking priests moved in and out of the holy place, carrying out such responsibilities as burning incense, setting the bread loaves out on the table of showbread, and trimming the lamps (vs. 6). Only the high priest could enter the inner sanctuary on just one day of the year: the day of Atonement (*Yom Kippur*). He was required to take with him an offering of blood to atone for both his sins and the sins of the people (vs. 7).

The Holy Spirit used the regulations about access to the most holy place to teach important truths to the Israelites. Most notably, they had no direct access to the presence of God; and they could never gain that access as long as the first tabernacle was still in operation (vs. 8). Thus, the tabernacle and its sacrificial system were an illustration of how the old covenant failed to effectively deal with the sins of humanity and clear the worshiper's conscience (vs. 9). The sacrifices that were part of the old covenant were external actions, and so had only an external effect. In fact, the author called these rituals "external regulations" (vs. 10). The writer implied that these rituals had served their purpose in times past. But now "a new order" is in place. This better system is the new covenant, and it revolves around internal essentials rather than externals, for no external ritual or action can ever substitute for our having a direct, personal relationship with Christ.

Under the old covenant, the main purpose of a priest was to sacrifice for sin. Therefore, as our High Priest, Christ must also offer a priestly sacrifice. Other priests offered animals as a sacrifice for sins, but those sacrifices were not able to cleanse the consciences of the people who brought them (vs. 9). Christ sacrificed Himself by dying on the cross and so secured God's forgiveness and blessing for believing sinners. Jesus has now become the High Priest over all the good things that are already here (for example, such eternal blessings as direct access to God and the perfecting of the conscience). Indeed, He has entered the greater, more perfect tabernacle in heaven. Humans didn't make this celestial sanctuary and it is not part of this created world (vs. 11). We should not think of Christ as engaged in some elaborate ritual in heaven. Rather, those external, earthly elements in the tabernacle below find their spiritual and eternal counterpart in the reality of Christ and His work.

The Messiah was not counted worthy of entering God's presence—and making a way for all humanity to enter God's presence—by sacrificing animals such as goats and calves and sprinkling their blood on the mercy seat in the most holy place of the earthly tabernacle. This was, of course, how the Levitical priests were counted worthy, and they were required to offer such sacrifices year after year. Christ made His passage into the heavenly sanctuary by shedding His own blood on the cross. He does not have to offer sacrifices year after year because He gave His own life, once for all, to secure our redemption from sin forever (vs. 12). This means His sacrifice was decisive and final. It does not have to be repeated. After paying the ransom for people's sins, Christ ascended into the true heavenly sanctuary. From there His salvation is continually offered to all human beings.

B. Cleansing the Consciences of Believers: vss. 13-14

The blood of goats and bulls and the ashes of a heifer sprinkled on those who are ceremonially unclean sanctify them so that they are outwardly clean. How much more, then, will the blood of Christ, who through the eternal Spirit offered himself unblemished to God, cleanse our consciences from acts that lead to death, so that we may serve the living God!

The writer briefly recounted how the high priests under the old covenant made atonement for the sins of the people, especially by means of two types of sacrifices (Heb. 9:13). On the day of Atonement, goats and calves were slaughtered and their blood shed (see Lev. 16). But that annual ceremony was different from the ashes of a sacrificed calf (a young adult animal) being sprinkled on those who were ceremonially defiled (Heb. 9:13). This purification rite could take place any time during the year. In it the priest slaughtered a red heifer, burned its carcass, and stored its ashes. Whenever a person became ritually impure by touching a corpse or being in contact with a foreigner, he or she could be cleansed by being sprinkled with these ashes mixed into water (see Num. 19).

The effectiveness of these ceremonies was limited in duration and superficial in benefit. Jesus' atoning sacrifice, in contrast, was eternal in its saving benefit and provided inward spiritual cleansing. When compared to the many offerings sacrificed by the priests under the old covenant, the shed blood of Christ was infinitely more valuable. He offered Himself as a perfect sacrifice to the Father through the power of the "eternal Spirit" (Heb. 9:14). Another possibility is that the author was referring to Christ's own spirit (that is, His divine nature). This means Jesus gave Himself on the cross as an eternal and spiritual sacrifice to God. In either case, the greatness of Christ and of His offering is incomparable. Because His shed blood was unblemished and undefiled, He could purify our consciences from "acts that lead to death" (including useless rituals). Jesus' crucifixion at Calvary also enables us to serve God. No longer hampered by our sins, we are able to engage in service to our Lord with all our heart and soul.

C. Mediating the New Covenant: vs. 15

For this reason Christ is the mediator of a new covenant, that those who are called may receive the promised eternal inheritance—now that he has died as a ransom to set them free from the sins committed under the first covenant.

Christ mediates the new covenant between God and humanity (Heb. 9:15). Like the arbitrator between two alienated factions, Jesus represents both sides. God, who is righteous, cannot accept unrighteous human beings into His presence. Therefore Christ, who is both God and man, lived a perfectly righteous life and then died as a ransom so that believers can be set free from the penalty of the sins they committed under the first covenant (see Rom. 3:23-26). So great is Christ's sacrifice that it enables all who are called to receive the eternal inheritance God has promised them (Heb. 9:15). These individuals are Jesus' spiritual brothers and sisters, who will inherit salvation (see 1:14; 6:17).

D. Inaugurating the New Covenant: vss. 16-18

In the case of a will, it is necessary to prove the death of the one who made it, because a will is in force only when somebody has died; it never takes effect while the one who made it is living. This is why even the first covenant was not put into effect without blood.

The Greek word translated "will" in Hebrews 9:16 is *diatheke*. Where it appears in other New Testament passages, however, this same Greek word is usually translated "covenant." The Greeks used *diatheke* when referring to a last will and testament. When the testator had died, his or her will was read to people who had no choice but to accept it. In that way, the testator's words carried a sense of finality. Among Jews who spoke Greek, the word was also used to refer to divine covenants. In a compact, God issued the terms and the people accepted them. So just as in a last will and testament, in a covenant God's words carry a sense of finality. The author may have used the term *diatheke* in Hebrews 9 as a rhetorical device to enhance the eloquence of his argument. He smoothly moved from using the word to mean "covenant" (vs. 15) to using it to mean "will" (vs. 16).

It is a universally accepted idea that a will goes into force only when it can be confirmed that the testator has died. A will never goes into effect while the one who made it is still living (vs. 17). Accordingly, even the old covenant was put into effect with the blood of an animal (vs. 18). In essence, the writer meant that something living must die—which is what is really being emphasized by the author's use of the term "blood"—for a covenant to be inaugurated. Exodus 24:3-8 records the ceremony described in Hebrews 9:18-21. The presence of additional details not in the original account suggests the author relied on other dependable sources of information. Also, at times he changed the wording of the biblical text from what appears in the Septuagint (the Greek translation of the Hebrew Scriptures). The author wanted to stress that when Moses performed a sacrificial ritual to confirm the covenant, blood was shed for the sake of human purification. In fact, the Mosaic law required almost everything to be cleansed by the shedding of blood, for apart from this happening, there is no forgiveness (vs. 22).

II. The End of Old Testament Sacrifices: Hebrews 10:12-14, 17-18

A. The All-Sufficiency of Jesus' Single Sacrifice: vss. 12-14

But when this priest had offered for all time one sacrifice for sins, he sat down at the right hand of God. Since that time he waits for his enemies to be made his footstool, because by one sacrifice he has made perfect forever those who are being made holy.

In Hebrews 9:23-28, the writer explained why Jesus' sacrifice for sin is superior to that of the old covenant. His death on the cross was once for all and ushered in the final state of affairs, namely, the messianic era, the age to which all preceding ages led. Against the backdrop of the author's comments was the religious regimen that was probably being carried out in the temple at Jerusalem even while he penned his masterpiece. He said that priests perform their rituals day by day. By writing that the priests stand while offering their sacrifices, the author implied that their work is never finished. The cumulative effect of all the sacrifices of all the priests could still not remove sins (10:11).

Jesus, as our High Priest, offered Himself as the one-time-for-all-time sacrifice for our sins. With His great and perfect work accomplished, He "sat down at the right hand of God" (vs. 12). Jesus occupies the position of utmost power and the place of highest honor. As a result of His completed work, Christ is now waiting until an appointed time, when He will overthrow all His enemies (vs. 13). While drawing upon Psalm 110:1, the author did not explain who Christ's enemies are. Some conjecture that the writer was referring to Jesus' bringing an end to all evil. Others say the author's intent was to issue a warning to his readers. In essence, he told them to take care that they were not numbered among the enemies of the Lord.

Whatever the case, this waiting has been called Christ's "unfinished work." This is based upon the finished work of His supreme sacrifice. By the all-sufficiency of Jesus' single offering, He forever made perfect those who are being made holy (Heb. 10:14). Most likely, this refers to all people who, at various intervals throughout the ages, are being added to the body of Christ, His church. They are the ones who trust in Christ for salvation. They are also the ones being set apart forever for God's service.

B. The Promises of the New Covenant: vss. 17-18

Then he adds: "Their sins and lawless acts I will remember no more." And where these have been forgiven, there is no longer any sacrifice for sin.

Christ, as the mediator between God and humanity, has established a new and better covenant than the old one based on the Mosaic law. The new covenant is better precisely because it is "founded on better promises" (Heb. 8:6). If the first covenant had sufficiently met the needs of people and had adequately provided for their salvation, then there would have been no need for a new covenant to replace it (vs. 7). But the old covenant was insufficient and inadequate. It wasn't adequate in bringing people to God, and therefore a new covenant had to be established.

God had found fault with the people under the old covenant (vs. 8), primarily because they did not continue in that holy compact (vs. 9). In turn, human failure rendered the old covenant inoperative. Although Ezekiel had written about God's establishing an "everlasting covenant" (Ezek. 16:60), only Jeremiah had spoken of a "new covenant" (Jer. 31:31). Jeremiah did not say that the covenant God made with the Israelites would be renewed. Rather, the prophet said that a completely new compact would be established (Heb. 8:8).

As 8:10-12 and 10:15-17 reveal (see Jer. 31:33-34), the new covenant would be inward and dynamic. God's Word would actually have a place inside the minds and hearts of His people. The old covenant had been inscribed on tablets of stone and was external. But in regard to the new covenant, God vowed that His teachings would be internalized by His people. The new covenant would also provide a way for believers to have an intimate relationship with God. Jeremiah echoed several Old Testament promises (see Gen. 17:7; Exod. 6:7; Lev. 26:12). But the life, death, and resurrection of Christ opened a new avenue for human beings to relate to their heavenly Father. Because of the salvation Jesus provided, all believers can enter into God's presence.

The new covenant would enable believers to have a deeper knowledge of God. An inclusiveness concerning knowing and learning about God will exist under the new covenant that was foreign to people under the old. No longer will this knowledge be limited to some people; all believers will have a personal knowledge of the Lord. Finally, through the new covenant, the forgiveness of sins is an eternal reality. Amazingly, an omniscient God has amnesia when it comes to our transgressions! He will never again remember our sins and lawless deeds. Through Christ's sacrifice, our iniquities have been dealt with once for all. Because our sins have been finally and effectively atoned through the sacrifice of Christ, there is no need for any other sacrifice (Heb. 10:18).

Discussion Questions

1. In what way is the heavenly tabernacle greater and more perfect than the one that formerly existed on earth?
2. How were the people of God in Old Testament times made outwardly clean?
3. When will Jesus finally vanquish His enemies?
4. What is the basis of believers being made perfect forever?
5. Why are the Old Testament sacrifices no longer necessary?

Contemporary Application

No one spent more time around the church than Ed. He was the congregation's Mr. Fix-it. He was also the best volunteer. Others would sign up for an evening, maybe two, to help paint Sunday school rooms. Ed would be there every evening.

Ed accepted the tedious job of keeping the financial records, tallying the Sunday school offerings, recording pledges, sending out the statements, making monthly reports, arranging the annual audit, and writing the checks. He volunteered at the local hospital on Saturdays. Most holidays, he delivered Meals on Wheels when others wanted time off.

One summer evening, Ed returned home complaining of chest pains. Tests revealed coronary problems, and physicians insisted on a heart bypass operation. The pastor came to call. The minister said, "You looked worried." Ed said, "Yeah, I guess I am." The pastor replied, "Well, of all people in the church, you've showed you're a man of faith."

After a long silence, Ed spoke. "Pastor, I really am not. In fact, I haven't ever been able to feel that Lord wanted me, because I'm not a good enough person. So I've been trying to get right with Him. I've sacrificed so much, even my family. But I still don't feel as though I've done enough to be accepted by the Lord."

In the next half hour, the pastor quietly explained to Ed that no human could hope to make an adequate sacrifice in order to be right with the Lord. The sacrifice has already been made at the Cross. No system of human offerings could accomplish what needs to be done. Ed's face gradually brightened with hope, and the two prayed. Ed went into surgery the next morning a changed man.

This story illustrates the way of number of adults—maybe even some in your class—think about their relationship to God. So pray for your students as you prepare the lesson. Also, be sure to encourage them to receive the benefits of Jesus' once-for-all sacrifice by trusting in Him for salvation.

Christ as Leader

Scripture

Background Scripture: *Hebrews 12:1-13*
Scripture Lesson: *Hebrews 12:1-13*
Key Verses: *Let us run with perseverance the race marked out for us. Let us fix our eyes on Jesus, the author and perfecter of our faith.* Hebrews 12:1-2.
Scripture Lesson for Children: *Luke 5:1-11*
Key Verse for Children: *[The disciples] left everything and followed [Jesus].* Luke 5:11.

Lesson Aim

To become more holy as we experience God's discipline.

Lesson Setting

Time: *Before A.D. 70*
Place: *Possibly Rome*

Lesson Outline

Christ as Leader

   I. Running the Race: Hebrews 12:1-3
       A. *Persevering in the Faith: vs. 1*
       B. *Keeping Our Mind on Jesus: vss. 2-3*
   II. Accepting God's Discipline: Hebrews 12:4-13
       A. *The Chastening of the Lord: vss. 4-6*
       B. *The Analogy of Human Parents: vss. 7-9*
       C. *The Benefit of God's Discipline: vss. 10-11*
       D. *The Exhortation to Stay the Course: vss. 12-13*

Introduction for Adults

Topic: *Trustworthy Leadership*

A minister shared his experience as a small boy when he went to his first symphony orchestra concert. He marveled at the different musicians as they came onto the stage and sat down. They all seemed so different. Some were young, while others were old. Some were thin and others were fat. Some had lots of hair, but others were bald. There were women and men.

One by one, the musicians picked up their instruments and began to play a few notes. It sounded like a dozen cats fighting on a hot night in the middle of the city. None of them were playing the same notes, let alone the same music. Then the boy saw a man in a long black coat walk to the center of the stage. When he raised a long, thin, black stick, the noise immediately stopped. With a sweep of this man's hand, the musicians began to play again and the sound this time was incredibly beautiful.

Jesus represents the Conductor who gives order and meaning to our lives. He is our Leader and Guide, who watches over and provides for us throughout our life journey. He alone is sufficiently qualified, capable, and trustworthy to do this for us; and that is why He is to be the sole focus of our faith.

Introduction for Youth

Topic: *Supreme Commander*

For decades, athletes and scientists agreed that no human being would ever run a mile in less than four minutes. And their predictions proved accurate. No one did. But one young man believed that he could go beyond that limit. On May 6, 1954, Roger Bannister broke the four-minute barrier. Now, among world-class male runners, several athletes beat Bannister's one-time record in nearly every mile race. But it took someone of Bannister's determination to be the first. He set the pattern. He became a great leader whose example others follow.

This week's Scripture text reminds us that Jesus is the best example of what it means to be a great leader. As the supreme commander of our salvation, He endured the shame of the cross. And though the authorities executed Jesus as a criminal, the Father raised Him from the dead so that all who trust in Him can have eternal life. As the pioneer and perfecter of our faith, Christ alone demonstrates that He is a leader who can be trusted.

Concepts for Children

Topic: *Follow the Leader*

1. Jesus used every opportunity to teach.
2. Jesus told Peter how to make a big catch of fish.
3. Jesus invited Peter and his friends to follow the Savior.
4. Jesus told His followers to encourage others to trust in Him.
5. Jesus wants us to tell others about the salvation He offers.

Lesson Commentary

I. RUNNING THE RACE: HEBREWS 12:1-3

A. Persevering in the Faith: vs. 1

Therefore, since we are surrounded by such a great cloud of witnesses, let us throw off everything that hinders and the sin that so easily entangles, and let us run with perseverance the race marked out for us.

Chapter divisions, which were placed in the Bible centuries after it was written and compiled, can prove misleading. For instance, Hebrews 12:1-3 piggybacks perfectly onto chapter 11. In fact, the first word in 12:1 ("Therefore") alerts us to the fact that what we are reading proceeds directly from what comes before it. The writer said, "Therefore, since we are surrounded by such a great cloud of witnesses." Presumably, the witnesses were people of faith mentioned in chapter 11.

The term rendered "witness" in the Bible is filled with significance. The Greek word is *martus* and comes from the verb *martureo*, which means "to testify" or "to bear witness." The idea is one of affirming what he or she has seen or experienced. The New Testament writers sometimes applied *martus* to those believers in Christ who were attesting to their faith while enduring persecution. Thus, in time such believers came to be known as martyrs, that is, those who voluntarily suffered death as the penalty for their allegiance to Christ.

The writers of the New Testament often used *martureo* to refer to believers who personally testified to Jesus' work on earth, regardless of whether suffering was present. John, in particular, noted the various witnesses who testified about Jesus. These included God the Father (John 5:31-32, 37; 8:18), the Holy Spirit (15:26), Jesus Himself (8:14, 18), Scripture (5:39), Jesus' own works (5:36), John the Baptist (1:34), and Jesus' disciples (15:27). The concept of witness is prominent not only in the New Testament but also the Old Testament. For example, Jacob used a pile of rocks to serve as a reminder that God was a witness to the patriarch's agreement with Laban (Gen. 31:45-50). In addition, the Mosaic law required that at least two witnesses had to support a charge of wrongdoing (Num. 35:30; Deut. 17:6).

This background information helps to clarify the reference in Hebrews 12:1 to the huge crowd of witnesses testifying to the life of faith. From the perspective of runners in a stadium, the spectators all around them in the stands might look something like a cloud of people. In a sense, Christians also have a cloud of people watching us: the saints in heaven. As "witnesses," they watch us and cheer us on in our race. They are also motivating examples of faithfulness.

In the ancient world, runners in a long-distance race competed in the nude. They would strip themselves of anything that might weigh them down or entangle their arms and legs. Similarly, the Hebrew Christians were to rid themselves of every encumbrance that might prevent them from living for the Redeemer. While some of these hindrances were not inherently sinful (for example, longstanding religious traditions), others were. The latter included the fear of being persecuted, resentment toward others, and sexual immorality (10:38-39; 12:15-16).

In mentioning "the sin that so easily entangles" (12:1), the writer may have had in mind the danger of defection resulting from discouragement—in other words, apostasy. The presence of opposition from others tempted some first-century Christians to revert to their former way of life. In light of this possibility, the writer urged his readers to remain steadfast in their faith even when they encountered hostile forces. We are also to "run with perseverance" our race of faith. This goes to show that our spiritual race is more like a marathon than a sprint. We must have the determination and the fortitude to keep running a long time and not quit.

B. Keeping Our Mind on Jesus: vss. 2-3

Let us fix our eyes on Jesus, the author and perfecter of our faith, who for the joy set before him endured the cross, scorning its shame, and sat down at the right hand of the throne of God. Consider him who endured such opposition from sinful men, so that you will not grow weary and lose heart.

The Letter to the Hebrews is directed to Christians who faced adverse circumstances and challenges to their faith. The author encouraged them to live wholeheartedly for the Messiah. Some of the original recipients, who were professing Jewish Christians, may have been on the brink of relinquishing their commitment to the Lord. They had begun to consider leaving the church and reintegrating fully into the Jewish synagogue worship of the day. In response to their circumstances, the writer of Hebrews encouraged them to remain firm in their faith in Christ.

From the text of this letter, we can surmise that readers were confronting a choice. Should they persist in Christianity, or should they renounce their Christian beliefs and settle into a more conventional lifestyle? The writer stressed the importance of persevering by keeping their faith in God's Son. Though these believers were no doubt steeped in the Jewish traditions, the writer reminded them that Christ is God's full and final revelation (1:1-2). The Messiah is the supreme and sufficient revealer and mediator of God's grace (vss. 3-4). Furthermore, Jesus is the "great high priest" (4:14).

With respect to the athletic metaphor appearing in 12:1, every race has a definite goal, a tape to break. The wise runner is one who keeps his or her eyes on the finish line and doesn't look back. As Christians, we too have a goal; we are heading for Jesus. And so the writer of Hebrews urged, "Let us fix our eyes on Jesus" (vs. 2). After all, Christ is "the author and perfecter of our faith." While we must persevere in our running, it is Jesus who enables us to both begin and complete the race.

One way Jesus helps us to start, continue, and finish our race is by being an example. He is the champion runner of the ages. As we struggle in our race, we can know that He has already been there and has shown that the race can be won. Just as we are to focus our attention on Jesus, so He kept His eyes fixed on the joy of completing the mission the Father had given to Him. And just as we are to persevere in the race marked out for us, so Jesus "endured the cross, scorning its shame."

The cross brought great suffering and disgrace, but Christ kept in mind that the glory of enduring the cross would be much greater. Despite facing the highest hurdle anybody has ever had—the Cross—Jesus successfully completed His race. And instead of receiving the wreath of leaves awarded to a victorious runner in the ancient world, Christ was rewarded with supreme authority. He took His seat in the place of highest honor beside His Father's throne in heaven.

The writer of Hebrews, knowing that his readers would sometimes feel weary and lose heart because of opposition, urged them to reflect earnestly on what Jesus experienced (vs. 3). Throughout the course of His earthly ministry, the Lord had to endure terrible opposition from sinners, and yet He persevered until He won the victory. Taking inspiration from Christ, we can persevere in our race no matter what obstacles wicked people may place in our way. Jesus, the pioneer and perfecter of our faith, is our supreme example.

II. ACCEPTING GOD'S DISCIPLINE: HEBREWS 12:4-13

A. The Chastening of the Lord: vss. 4-6

In your struggle against sin, you have not yet resisted to the point of shedding your blood. And you have forgotten that word of encouragement that addresses you as sons: "My son, do not make light of the Lord's discipline, and do not lose heart when he rebukes you, because the Lord disciplines those he loves, and he punishes everyone he accepts as a son."

The Hebrew Christians had endured persecution for their faith (Heb. 10:32-34). Yet they had not suffered to the extent that Jesus had. They also had not gone through the horrors cataloged in 11:35-38. Though his readers were tempted to return to their former way of life, the writer of the epistle urged them not to give up. He reminded them that no matter how difficult their situation had become, it had not yet led to bloodshed; in other words, none of them had died for their faith (12:4). A schoolmaster was once asked what would be the ideal curriculum for children. He answered, "Any program of worthwhile studies, so long as all of it is hard and some of it is unpleasant." The original readers of Hebrews had been experiencing what was hard and unpleasant in their "struggle against sin" (12:4). Thankfully, however, none of them had so far been martyred.

Despite the fact that their struggle was not as bad as it could be, the Hebrews were being tempted to look on their suffering in the wrong way. Once more, the author referred to some Old Testament Scripture to validate his point. This time he focused on Proverbs 3:11-12. This passage teaches those being disciplined by the Lord to respond properly. We are not to err by making light of it. Neither are we to err by losing heart, taking it too seriously. We should recognize that discipline from the Lord is a sign that He loves us and considers us His spiritual children (Heb. 12:5-6). And therefore, we should accept His discipline and pay attention to what He's trying to teach us through it.

At first, it might be hard for us to accept the truth that God's discipline of us is a sign of His love. We might mistakenly assume that His chastisement is solely to punish us, not educate us. Nevertheless, His foremost purpose is to bring about our character formation. The Lord cares for us so much that He corrects us for our eternal good. The suffering He allows us to experience can cause us to stop and take another look at our lives. It can force us to reevaluate our priorities and put first things first. Through God's hand of discipline, we learn to renounce sin in our lives and to become more holy in our conduct and grow in Christlikeness.

B. The Analogy of Human Parents: vss. 7-9

Endure hardship as discipline; God is treating you as sons. For what son is not disciplined by his father? If you are not disciplined (and everyone undergoes discipline), then you are illegitimate children and not true sons. Moreover, we have all had human fathers who disciplined us and we respected them for it. How much more should we submit to the Father of our spirits and live!

The author's aim was to make his audience aware of suffering as a teaching tool used by God; in other words, discipline is pedagogical. This insight makes the writer's statement in the first part of Hebrews 12:7 all the more forceful—"Endure hardship as discipline; God is treating you as sons." Since the dawn of time, good parents have been actively involved in disciplining their children. Likewise, God disciplines all His spiritual children.

In the first century of the Christian era, many Roman nobles had illegitimate children to whom they gave financial support but made little effort to educate. Rigorous training was reserved for the children of the aristocrat's legal wife, for her offspring would bear the family name and inherit the nobleman's estate. When God subjects us to His hand of discipline, He shows that He cares even more for us, who are co-heirs with Christ (see Rom. 8:17). Also, when the Lord corrects us, it demonstrates that we are legitimate members of His heavenly family (Heb. 12:8).

Notice the way in which the writer argued from the lesser reality to the greater reality ("how much more")—from human parents upward to the heavenly Father (vs. 9). If we respect our earthly parents when they discipline us, we should much more "submit to the Father of our spirits and live." Discipline by God should not cause us to think worse of Him, but rather to respect Him all the more. When He corrects us, His wise and loving purposes undergird His actions.

C. The Benefit of God's Discipline: vss. 10-11

Our fathers disciplined us for a little while as they thought best; but God disciplines us for our good, that we may share in his holiness. No discipline seems pleasant at the time, but painful. Later on, however, it produces a harvest of righteousness and peace for those who have been trained by it.

In human discipline, there is always the element of imperfection, even though our parents disciplined us as well as they knew how (Heb. 12:10). By an upgraded contrast, divine discipline is always "for our good, that we may share in his holiness." God's discipline is always prudent, and we can be sure it is needed and contributes to our spiritual growth. When we submit to the Lord's hand of correction, we experience greater moral fitness. We also become increasingly conformed in every aspect of our lives to the image of Christ.

The author admitted that no discipline is pleasant while it's occurring; in fact, it's downright painful. The benefit only appears later, when it produces the fruit of righteousness and peace by allowing ourselves to be spiritually trained in this way (vs. 11). The Greek verb rendered "trained" is based on the word from which we get *gymnasium*. We could say discipline gives us a tough workout, but helps us get into shape. As the saying goes, "No pain, no gain."

On the surface, it might seem counterintuitive to imagine that the griefs springing from tragedies, persecutions, and conflicts can have any temporal or eternal benefit. Yet Scripture teaches that God uses these hardships to prepare us to be at peace in all situations and to respond rightly to Him and other people in the face of difficulties. For instance, sufferings can teach us humility and patience. Also, through hardships we learn to trust God more and draw upon His strength to endure the trials we're experiencing.

Because God is our loving heavenly Father, He never disciplines us for sadistic reasons. And He does not enjoy seeing us experience pain. When God disciplines us, His intent is to help us grow and succeed in our walk with Christ. When we try to avoid God's discipline, we sacrifice long-term spiritual maturity for short-term ease. The real joys and victories of the Christian life will elude us, unless we yield to God's loving hand of discipline in our lives.

D. The Exhortation to Stay the Course: vss. 12-13

Therefore, strengthen your feeble arms and weak knees. "Make level paths for your feet," so that the lame may not be disabled, but rather healed.

The writer of Hebrews, perhaps returning to the running imagery, exhorted his readers to strengthen their limp hands and enfeebled knees (12:12). Verse 13 extends the imagery by quoting from Proverbs 4:26. The Hebrews were to smooth out the racetrack so that even the lame could get around it without falling and hurting themselves. The idea is that, as we are running our own race, we should look out for our fellow believers and try to help them succeed in their races as well. By God's grace, the Christian life is one in which we all can eventually wear the wreath of victory—no matter what disabilities we start with.

Here we see that a holy response to God's discipline is realistic, not naive, about life. We should not minimize the pain and loss we or others are experiencing. Instead, we should remain confident that God will bring good out of evil and that He will not forsake us. We become more holy when we remain calm after being terminated from work. And we grow in holiness when we respond with kind words to those who hurl abusive comments at us. Furthermore, when we show love, not hatred, after being harassed by others, we become more holy.

Hebrews 12:14 pulls together two threads from preceding verses. Verse 10 mentions "holiness," while verse 11 refers to "peace." Both words reflected strategic Hebrew ideas that, when taken together, carry the connotations of a life of wholeness. Both peace and holiness are to be goals for Christians. We are to strive to be at peace with everyone (vs. 14). That includes our fellow believers, our non-Christian neighbors, and even our enemies. We are also to seek personal purity. The author provided an incentive for seeking holiness when he said that those who are not holy will not see the Lord. God is all-holy, and He cannot tolerate moral impurity in His presence.

The twin virtues in verse 14 are the opposites of two vices in the following verses. Peace's opposite is the troublemaking of sinners (vs. 15). And holiness's opposite is sinfulness, such as immorality and godlessness (vss. 16-17). The author explained some of the things involved in seeking peace and holiness. Verses 15 and 16 begin similarly: "See to it that no one . . ." and "See that no one . . ." These verses show us the responsibility Christians have for helping one another become the men and women God wants us to be.

Discussion Questions

1. In your opinion, what is the relationship between Hebrews 11 and 12?
2. What kind of weight do you think prevents believers from running their race ?
3. Why is it appropriate for God to discipline us as His spiritual children?
4. In what ways has God disciplined you? How have you responded?
5. What can you do to help other believers run their race of faith better?

Contemporary Application

You have probably heard sermons in which the speaker defined holiness as being set apart to God for His use. The basic idea is that we belong to God and exist to do His will. Because we are His children, He disciplines us so that we might become more holy in our thinking, in our acting, and in our witness for Him.

The way we respond to God's discipline can shape our view of life. For instance, we become more worldly in our thinking if we respond to God's discipline with bitterness and anger. In contrast, we become more holy in our thinking when we respond to His discipline with humility and trust.

Our growth in holiness can enhance our witness to others; for instance, imagine a friend at church who gets angry with you over something you said. If you lash out in anger, you could worsen the situation. By remaining calm and respectful, you give God the opportunity to enhance your witness and move you along to spiritual maturity.

As we run the race of Christian living with perseverance, we leave an example for others to follow. We encourage them to break with sinful habits and become more Christlike in their behavior. We also spur them on to spiritual maturity. As an outcome of our marathon of faith, we not only possess the fruit of an upright life, but also assist those who are coming after us to grow in godliness.

The Eternal Christ

DEVOTIONAL READING

Psalm 118:5-9

DAILY BIBLE READINGS

Monday June 23
Psalm 118:5-9 Take Refuge in God

Tuesday June 24
Colossians 1:15-20 Christ as Supreme and Eternal

Wednesday June 25
Hebrews 13:1-6 Show Hospitality and Courage

Thursday June 26
Hebrews 13:7-9 True Leaders to Imitate

Friday June 27
Hebrews 13:10-16 Confess Christ's Name

Saturday June 28
Philippians 3:12-16 A Leader Who Professes Christ

Sunday June 29
Philippians 3:17-21 A Leader Looking to Christ Eternal

Scripture

Background Scripture: *Hebrews 13:1-16*
Scripture Lesson: *Hebrews 13:1-16*
Key Verse: *Jesus Christ is the same yesterday and today and forever.* Hebrews 13:8.
Scripture Lesson for Children: *Luke 24:36-49*
Key Verse for Children: *Jesus Christ is the same yesterday and today and forever.* Hebrews 13:8.

Lesson Aim

To learn that God wants us to honor Him by doing good to others.

Lesson Setting

Time: *Before* A.D. *70*
Place: *Possibly Rome*

Lesson Outline

The Eternal Christ

   I. Extraordinary Love: Hebrews 13:1-3
      A. *Love Commanded: vs. 1*
      B. *Love Demonstrated: vss. 2-3*
  II. Extraordinary Integrity: Hebrews 13:4-7
      A. *Honoring Marriage: vs. 4*
      B. *Finding Contentment in the Lord: vss. 5-6*
      C. *Appreciating Our Church Leaders: vs. 7*
 III. An Extraordinary Lord: Hebrews 13:8-16
      A. *Remaining Devoted to Christ: vss. 8-10*
      B. *Honoring the Sacrifice of Christ: vss. 11-14*
      C. *Living for God and Others: vss. 15-16*

Introduction for Adults

Topic: *Finding Stability and Permanence Today*

Joel Best, the author of *Flavor of the Month: Why Smart People Fall for Fads*, noted that every major discipline has its fads. In medicine, "there are fad diagnoses and fad treatments." In elementary and secondary education, "faddish teaching methods abound." And in business, the shelves of bookstores groan under the weight of new "titles explaining this month's revolutionary management scheme."

Best says that at their inception, "fads follow a parallel trajectory." Consider the hula hoop craze of the 1960s. At first, not many people had them. But then, "the number of people using hula hoops rises rapidly to a peak." After this, the "decline begins." This pattern indicates that each fad is characterized by "short-lived enthusiasm." Best observes that "while any novelty is spreading, it is always possible for its advocates to insist that this innovation will endure." In most instances, however, they prove to be incorrect.

The presence of fads reminds us that we live in a world filled with rapid change. So where can we go to find stability and permanence? The answer is Jesus Christ. The Father gave us His Son so that through faith in Him, we could have a firm foundation for living in relationship with Him and others.

Introduction for Youth

Topic: *Someone You Can Count On*

Her shoulders slumped as she waited to talk with me after church. Deep worry lines tugged her face into a furled, forlorn expression of grief. A three-year-old swung from her coat sleeve like a pint-sized Tarzan, whining so loudly that I could hardly hear the "secret" spoken from her despondent lips: "My husband is an alcoholic." Crushing despair overwhelmed Barb. She was trapped in a meaningless vortex. Life had become dismal, depressing, and seemingly hopeless.

As I listened to Barb's story, I realized that the eternal Christ, who is the same yesterday, today, and forever (Heb. 13:8), alone could give Barb the hope to dispel her heavy clouds of gloom. Regardless of the saved teens' circumstances, Jesus is someone they can always count on to help them through their ordeal.

Concepts for Children

Topic: *Jesus Is Forever*

1. After Jesus' resurrection, He appeared to His disciples.
2. Jesus allowed His followers to touch Him.
3. Jesus said He had done what was foretold in the Old Testament.
4. Jesus assured His followers that they would receive power from God.
5. Jesus promises to give us the ability to share the Gospel with others.

Lesson Commentary

I. EXTRAORDINARY LOVE: HEBREWS 13:1-3

A. Love Commanded: vs. 1

Keep on loving each other as brothers.

Hebrews 13:1 tells the readers to keep on loving each other as brothers and sisters. Often in the New Testament we read that Christians are, in effect, members of the same spiritual family, and should treat each other that way. The Hebrews were already exercising kindness and compassion toward one another, but the writer felt an encouragement to continue would be appropriate.

B. Love Demonstrated: vss. 2-3

Do not forget to entertain strangers, for by so doing some people have entertained angels without knowing it. Remember those in prison as if you were their fellow prisoners, and those who are mistreated as if you yourselves were suffering.

Hebrews 13:2 urges readers to show hospitality to strangers, which most likely refers to itinerant Christian preachers. In the first century A.D., there weren't many inns, and those that did exist often had an unsavory reputation. So travelers had to rely on householders if they were to get good accommodations during a journey. As an encouragement toward hospitality, the writer reminded his readers that some have unwittingly hosted angels.

The Bible relates many incidents in which angels visited both men and women. Sometimes these people did not realize they were talking to angels until they had time to ponder their encounters. During the Old Testament period, two angels accompanied the Lord when He called upon Abraham. The Lord told the patriarch that his wife, Sarah, would bear him a son, and God fulfilled the promise a year later (Gen. 18:1-2, 10; 21:1-2). After the Israelites had settled in Canaan, they turned away from the Lord, and their enemies oppressed them. An angel of the Lord visited Gideon and commissioned him to lead the Israelites in victory over the Midianites (Judg. 6:1, 11-16). On another occasion, an angel of the Lord twice visited the wife of a man named Manoah. Although this woman was barren, the angel promised she would bear a son. When the child was born, she named him Samson (13:2-21, 24).

During the New Testament period, the angel Gabriel told a priest named Zechariah that his barren wife, Elizabeth, would give birth to a son, whom the couple was to name John. Because Zechariah doubted this good news, he was not able to speak until his son was born (Luke 1:11-20, 64). God also sent Gabriel to Mary to tell her that though she was a virgin, she would give birth to the Son of God (vss. 26-38). When Mary's pregnancy became obvious, Joseph, who was pledged to marry her, decided to privately divorce her. An angel of the Lord appeared to

353

Joseph in a dream, revealed that Mary's pregnancy was due to the work of the Holy Spirit, and encouraged Joseph not to be afraid of marrying her (Matt. 1:18-20).

We understand from our study of Scripture that Christian love goes the second mile by displaying kindness to others. Everybody of course loves friends, but Jesus urged us to love our enemies as well (5:41-44). The unconditional love advocated by Jesus is reflected in Hebrews 13:1, where we learn that we should treat other believers as members of God's spiritual family. In verse 2, we discover that travelers will visit our homes if we show them hospitality.

In order to fulfill the command of verse 3, we will need to travel a bit. This directive is to remember two groups: prisoners and the mistreated. Probably with both groups the writer had in mind Christians who were being persecuted for their faith. Thus, visiting and identifying oneself with such people, as the writer urged, could have entailed considerable risk. But it was important for the Christian community to present a united front—believers supporting one another and maintaining the links within the body of Christ, regardless of the danger. The recipients of the letter had already suffered persecution and had stood with others who were being persecuted (see 10:33-34), so they knew just what the writer was talking about.

II. EXTRAORDINARY INTEGRITY: HEBREWS 13:4-7

A. Honoring Marriage: vs. 4

Marriage should be honored by all, and the marriage bed kept pure, for God will judge the adulterer and all the sexually immoral.

From relationships with individuals mostly outside the home (Heb. 13:1-3), the author turned to the primary relationship within the home—marriage (vs. 4). Evidently, some people were hawking the virtues of sexual fulfillment outside of the spousal relationship. The author taught that marriage was to be honored by everyone in the Christian community, and adultery was to have no place among them. In warning, the writer said that God will one day judge fornicators (a general reference to those committing a wide range of sexually immoral acts) and adulterers (a specific reference to those violating their marital vows). Elsewhere, the New Testament warns against Christians becoming promiscuous and debased in their behavior (see Acts 15:28-29; 1 Cor. 5:9-11; Eph. 5:3, 5; 1 Thess. 4:3-7; 1 Tim. 1:10; Rev. 21:8; 22:15).

B. Finding Contentment in the Lord: vss. 5-6

Keep your lives free from the love of money and be content with what you have, because God has said, "Never will I leave you; never will I forsake you." So we say with confidence, "The Lord is my helper; I will not be afraid. What can man do to me?"

Just as there is a danger in wanting more than our mate, there is also a danger in always wanting more and more money. The Bible is never anti-money, but it does warn against "the love of money" (Heb. 13:5; compare 1 Tim. 6:10). Too many today love money and use people, but for us, it should be the reverse: we should use money and love people. And so we should look out for any sign of greed entering our hearts.

Contentment with our material condition should characterize Christians. And the writer provided Old Testament quotes to show why Christians have every reason to be content. First, he quoted Deuteronomy 31:6 (see also Gen. 28:15; Deut. 31:8; Josh. 1:5; 1 Chron. 28:20), which contains a promise that God will never leave nor forsake His people. Why should we go crazy over dollars when the God who owns the whole universe is our constant companion? Next, the author cited Psalm 118:6-7 (Heb. 13:6). This quote contains the psalmist's declaration that since he had God, he would not be afraid, because no person had the power to hurt him (unless it was God's will). Why should we look to money for our security when we have Almighty God for our helper?

C. Appreciating Our Church Leaders: vs. 7

Remember your leaders, who spoke the word of God to you. Consider the outcome of their way of life and imitate their faith.

Hebrews 13:7-17 opens and closes with references to spiritual leaders. The reference in verse 7 appears to be to the Hebrews' past leaders, who had probably died. Verse 17 evidently refers to their present leaders. In the first case, the author urged the Hebrews to recall the leaders who had preached the Gospel to them, considering the results of how these people had lived (vs. 7). The Greek verb translated "remember" referred to calling to mind what one knew about a person, while the verb translated "consider" referred to carefully observing something.

The readers had evidently been blessed in the past with excellent Christian leaders. But just because these people were gone did not mean that one could no longer benefit from them. Alone or together, the Hebrews could recall these people, especially the Christlike character they had achieved and the good they had done for the Savior's cause. In this way, the departed leaders could still be heroes and models for the believers. Indeed, the author urged his readers to follow the example of their former leaders' faith.

III. An Extraordinary Lord: Hebrews 13:8-16

A. Remaining Devoted to Christ: vss. 8-10

Jesus Christ is the same yesterday and today and forever. Do not be carried away by all kinds of strange teachings. It is good for our hearts to be strengthened by grace, not by ceremonial foods, which are of no value to those who eat them. We have an altar from which those who minister at the tabernacle have no right to eat.

Human leaders come and go, but our great leader, the Lord Jesus, never changes. The Messiah is the contemporary of all the centuries, for He is the same yesterday, today, and forever (Heb. 13:8). The Hebrews' leaders undoubtedly made Christ the subject of their teaching, and the Hebrews were to cling to Him just as their leaders had. They could do so for they knew that He remains faithful to His followers. They could rely on Him even when circumstances seemed overwhelming. Because Jesus is reliable, believers can remain faithful to Him and cultivate integrity in their lives.

With Christ as their spiritual anchor and eternal guide, the recipients of Hebrews were not to be fooled by any kind of strange teachings (vs. 9). The Greek word rendered "strange" refers to notions that were foreign to the truth of the Gospel. We don't know precisely what the "strange teachings" were, but the Greek word for "strange" might be woodenly rendered "many-colored." It suggests the rainbow assortment of false teachings that confront believers. Those enticements that come dressed in canary yellow or flaming flamingo aren't too difficult to detect, but what about those that insinuate themselves in familiar shades of pastel?

Evidently, some of the heretical teachings current in the Hebrews' day involved eating "ceremonial foods" (for instance, what to eat, who could eat, and the manner in which to eat). Other portions of the New Testament provide instruction for believers confused about participating in the ritualistic meals of pagan religions (see Rom. 14; 1 Cor. 8; 10-11). Mostly likely, though, Hebrews 13:9 has Jewish practices in mind. Legalistic Jews maintained that because the Hebrew Christians did not participate in the ritual life of the temple, including the sacrificial feasts, they had no access to God. The writer responded that God's grace, not ritualistically prepared meals, strengthened the hearts of believers. And it was by grace that they participated in worship at the heavenly sanctuary where Jesus ministered.

In Old Testament times, priests had the right to a portion of the animals sacrificed as fellowship (or peace) offerings (Lev. 3; 7:11-34). As long as those priests and others depended on the old system of animal sacrifices for atonement and peace with God, they couldn't benefit from what the Lord Jesus did at Calvary. The cross was the "altar" (Heb. 13:10) on which the Messiah, the believers' great High Priest, sacrificed Himself to atone for their sins. Through faith in Christ, they could partake of the benefits of His redemptive offering. The priests who ministered under the old covenant never enjoyed such a privilege. To put all this another way, Christians are not to be bound by the food laws of non-Christian religions (since many religions have dietary regulations). Instead, we are to eat the "food" of grace, which is ours because of the Cross. And this "food" is a privilege to eat, being even greater than the sacrificial food that the priests of the tabernacle ate.

B. Honoring the Sacrifice of Christ: vss. 11-14

The high priest carries the blood of animals into the Most Holy Place as a sin offering, but the bodies are burned outside the camp. And so Jesus also suffered outside the city gate to make the people holy through his own blood. Let us, then, go to him outside the camp, bearing the disgrace he bore. For here we do not have an enduring city, but we are looking for the city that is to come.

When the Israelites were wandering in the wilderness, they carried a tabernacle with them. When they stopped, they would set up camp, and within the camp they would put up the tabernacle. Once a year, on the day of Atonement, the high priest carried the blood of a bull and a ram into the holiest part of the tabernacle to sprinkle it on and in front of the ark of the covenant (see Lev. 16:11-16). This served as a reminder that only through the death of a blameless substitute could anyone approach the holy God. The bodies of the animals that were sacrificed for this ritual were to be burned outside the camp (4:12; 16:27). They had been associated with sin, and therefore were considered unclean. In a sense, the substitute became the bearer of the people's sins. Likewise, taking away the body of the dead animal symbolized the removal of sin from the midst of the people.

The writer of Hebrews saw a parallel between these practices and the way the Lord Jesus was sacrificed for people's sins outside the walls of Jerusalem (Heb. 13:12; see also Matt. 27:32; Mark 15:20; John 19:17, 20). His suffering outside the holy city served as a reminder that He bore the curse of sin. His death outside Jerusalem also meant that most of the Jewish religious establishment had rejected Him as the Messiah. The repudiation that Christ endured was mirrored in the lives of His followers. The leaders of the Jews had evidently expelled them from the synagogues and the temple. The writer of Hebrews summoned his readers to accept this situation with courage.

In order to offer us grace, the Redeemer underwent great disgrace. Therefore, Christians should be willing to share Jesus' disgrace, in a sense following Him outside the camp (13:13). Are we willing to share His unpopularity when necessary? Are we willing to endure rejection for the Gospel as He did? Indeed, we should not expect to be entirely comfortable and satisfied with earthly life. There is no complete security, no permanence on this earth for us.

While the Jews venerated their holy city of Jerusalem, that city wouldn't last forever. In fact, in A.D. 70, four Roman legions under the command of Titus sacked Jerusalem, destroyed the temple, and either killed or dispersed much of the population. In contrast, believers long for "the city that is to come" (vs. 14). This is probably what the writer earlier referred to as "the city . . . whose architect and builder is God" and the "heavenly Jerusalem" (see 11:10; 12:22; see also Isa. 65:17-25; Rev. 21). The fact that the "city" theme crops up several times in Hebrews implies that some readers felt rejected from their community because they had identified with Jesus as the Messiah.

C. Living for God and Others: vss. 15-16

Through Jesus, therefore, let us continually offer to God a sacrifice of praise—the fruit of lips that confess his name. And do not forget to do good and to share with others, for with such sacrifices God is pleased.

Because of our relationship with Christ, we should give God glory. But instead of offering animal sacrifices, we are to offer to God a sacrifice of praise. And we aren't supposed to do this on our own. Rather, we offer such sacrifices through the Lord Jesus. The content of our offering is "praise—the fruit of lips that confess his name" (Heb. 13:15). The latter refers to an open acknowledgment of our belief in Him as the Messiah (to be voiced even when we face public abuse and scorn). What we do with our lips is not the sum total of our commitment. Our sacrifice also includes what we do with our lives (vs. 16). First, we are to "do good." The word *good*, when the letters are reordered, becomes *go do*. To do good we must go do; in other words, activism is required. Second, we must "share with others" as part of our Christian sacrificial system. This is also the way of life in God's eternal city.

Discussion Questions

1. Why did the writer of Hebrews stress the importance of showing brotherly love?
2. How would the truth that Jesus never changes have encouraged the Hebrew Christians?
3. How far should the Hebrew Christians have gone in following their leaders?
4. Why does Hebrews draw a sharp contrast between Christ's sacrifice and that of animals?
5. Why does Hebrews say that praising God and doing good works are sacrifices?

Contemporary Application

Hebrews 13:16 reminds us of the importance of doing good to others. Sometimes we can become so preoccupied in meeting our own needs—whether physical or spiritual—that we forget to meet the needs of others. And sometimes we can become so absorbed in our worship of God that we can forget to show His love to others. For us as Christians, doing good to others cannot be torn from the context of spiritual reality. Our faith in Christ should never be a matter of "pie in the sky by and by." The teaching and example of the Savior demand a practical out-working of faith in our relationships with others.

Just as travelers can bounce from city to city without really getting involved in the lives of others, so we can rush through life without taking the time to do good to others. We can bounce from relationship to relationship and from experience to experience without making the effort to see how God can use us in meeting the needs of others. A number of years ago, a popular song urged us to "stop and smell the roses." Jesus would want us to stop, take an interest in others, and do good things for them.

How can we do good to others? We can show love to those whom others have rejected and open our homes to people who have nowhere else to go. We can visit those in halfway houses, prisons, or nursing homes and share God's love with them. We can affirm the value of our loved ones and be supportive of our church leaders.

Christ as Teacher

Scripture

Background Scripture: *Luke 4:31-37; 20:1-8*
Scripture Lesson: *Luke 4:31-37; 20:1-8*
Key Verse: *They were amazed at [Jesus'] teaching, because his message had authority.* Luke 4:32.
Scripture Lesson for Children: *Luke 4:31-37; 6:17-22*
Key Verse for Children: *They were amazed at [Jesus'] teaching, because his message had authority.* Luke 4:32.

Lesson Aim

To discover that Jesus' message can be freeing or threatening.

Lesson Setting

Time: A.D. *26 and 30*
Place: *Capernaum and Jerusalem*

Lesson Outline

Christ as Teacher

  I. Jesus' Authority Demonstrated: Luke 4:31-37
      A. *Teaching in the Synagogue: vss. 31-32*
      B. *Encountering a Demon: vss. 33-34*
      C. *Expelling the Demon: vs. 35*
      D. *Acknowledging Jesus' Authority: vss. 36-37*
 II. Jesus' Authority Challenged: Luke 20:1-8
      A. *The Religious Leaders' Question: vss. 1-2*
      B. *The Savior's Counter-Question: vss. 3-4*
      C. *The Mutual Non-Response: vss. 5-8*

Introduction for Adults

Topic: *Teaching That Transforms*

Jean Rhys was the author of a series of popular novels during the 1920s and 1930s, but then fell into obscurity. She was re-discovered and showered with fame after the publication of her fifth and last novel, *Wise Sagasso Sea*, in 1966. She died in 1979. Her unfinished autobiography, which appeared in 1980, revealed an intensely self-centered woman. Critics and readers had suspected that Rhys was herself the subject of her fiction, but the depth of her egotism was disclosed in her candid remarks about herself. "People have always been shadows to me," she wrote. "I have never known other people. I have only ever written about myself."

Contrast this person to Jesus. He always regarded others, not as mere "shadows," but as beloved fellow members of the human race. Unlike people such as Rhys, Jesus would never arrogantly disregard others and focus on His own comfort and security. Though He is the Lord of heaven and earth, Jesus cared about the blind, the mute, and the distressed. He did not hesitate to help others in need so that they might come to a life-transforming knowledge of the truth.

Introduction for Youth

Topic: *Christ Tells It Like It Is!*

The Kansas-Nebraska Act of 1854 was designed to open the new western territories to slavery. It was championed by Stephen A. Douglas. Standing in opposition was a new politician, Abraham Lincoln. He wanted to check the extension of slavery and to preserve the Union, which was rapidly dividing over the issue of slavery.

In 1858, Lincoln accepted the Republican nomination for the Senate. His acceptance reiterated his desire to preserve and defend the Union, amidst rumblings of seccession from various southern states. His speech began, "A house divided against itself cannot stand. I believe the government cannot endure permanently half slave and half free."

Lincoln was right. The United States could not withstand division. His quote, which was based on the teachings of Jesus, proved to be tragically correct. Both men were not afraid to declare the truth as it is, regardless of how unpopular doing so might be.

Concepts for Children

Topic: *Jesus Taught with Power*

1. Jesus taught with great authority and power.
2. Jesus showed extraordinary love as He taught and healed people.
3. Jesus ordered the evil spirit to depart from a man.
4. Jesus used His voice as well as His hands to heal people.
5. Jesus wants to bless us with His healing touch.

Lesson Commentary

I. JESUS' AUTHORITY DEMONSTRATED: LUKE 4:31-37

A. Teaching in the Synagogue: vss. 31-32

Then he went down to Capernaum, a town in Galilee, and on the Sabbath began to teach the people. They were amazed at his teaching, because his message had authority.

Sometime after Jesus' baptism and victory over temptation (Luke 4:1-13), He returned to Galilee. Luke didn't provide details about what Jesus did in Galilee, but we know that He ministered in the power of the Spirit and taught in the synagogues (vss. 14-15). Wherever 10 Jewish families lived, they formed a synagogue (literally "congregation" or "assembly"). Sacrifices could be made only at the temple, but from the time of the Exile, teaching of the law and worship took place in synagogues situated wherever Jews had been scattered throughout the world.

People who saw and heard Jesus spread the news about what He was doing. Eventually, Jesus returned to His hometown of Nazareth, and following His custom, He went to the synagogue on the Sabbath. His reputation had mushroomed, and the locals turned out to hear the homegrown boy who had made good. But no doubt many were skeptical. They came doubting He could be as good as the stories painted Him to be. As a visiting rabbi and hometown celebrity, Jesus was invited to be the guest speaker at the local synagogue. At the appropriate time in the service, He was handed the scroll of Isaiah, which He unrolled and from which He read in Hebrew (vss. 16-17). Presumably, He then translated the passages into Aramaic, which was the common language of the people. Jesus read Isaiah 61:1-2, which was a messianic prophecy. The passage predicted that the era of the Messiah would be a time of liberation and change. Then Jesus gave the scroll back to the attendant and sat down to teach (Luke 6:18-20).

Most Jews hoped for a powerful leader to arise and deliver them from the Romans, who dominated them. So when Jesus announced that this messianic prophecy was now being fulfilled (vs. 21), He had the worshipers' full attention. Some were impressed. But others were not so sure. Amazed by Jesus' message, they began to talk among themselves (vs. 22). Jesus knew He had a skeptical audience on His hands, but He met their doubts head-on. He acknowledged that they would want Him to prove Himself, to see dramatic evidence of His power. But because they couldn't imagine God's raising up one of their own to be a prophet, He would not show them God's power (vss. 23-24; see Matt. 13:58).

Jesus drove His point home, reminding the skeptical worshipers that because God's chosen people doubted, they had missed blessings the Gentiles then received. Jesus cited an instance in the time of Elijah and another in the time of Elisha (Luke 4:25-27; see 1 Kings 17:8-16; 2 Kings 5:1-14). Hearing about the widow of Zarephath and the leper from Syria infuriated Jesus' hearers. It was bad enough for Jesus to say He was the fulfillment of messianic prophecy. Now He was saying that His audience was unworthy of God's blessings! The people surged toward Jesus. They pushed and shoved, moving Him toward a bluff at the edge of town, intending to toss Him over the side. But He slipped away from the mob and escaped (Luke 4:28-30). Luke doesn't say this escape was a miracle, but it probably was. By rejecting Jesus, the Nazarenes allowed the blessings of God to slip away from them. And by refusing to listen, they showed they were unworthy. In obstinate pride, they thought they knew better than Jesus.

Next, Jesus descended from the elevated region where Nazareth was located to the town of Capernaum, a fishing village located near the northwest shore of the Sea of Galilee, 680 feet below sea level (vs. 31). Capernaum hosted a Roman garrison that maintained peace in the region. Major highways crisscrossed at Capernaum, making it militarily strategic. Because of its fishing and trading industries, the city was something of a melting pot of Greek, Roman, and Jewish cultures. After leaving Nazareth, Jesus made Capernaum the headquarters of His Galilean ministry. Since the city was also the home of His first disciples, it makes sense that Jesus often returned to His home base. He may have stayed in Peter's house there (Mark 1:29; 2:1). Matthew collected taxes in Capernaum (Matt. 9:1, 9), and it was probably the home of a high-ranking official of Herod (John 4:46). A centurion in the Roman army was also located in the city (Matt. 8:5).

As was Jesus' custom, He taught on the Sabbath in the synagogue at Capernaum (Luke 4:31). As in Nazareth, the people of Capernaum were amazed at His teaching, for He spoke with authority (vs. 32). The Greek word rendered "authority" denotes the ability and right to perform an action. Permission could be obtained from a government official, a court of law, or one's master (to name a few possibilities). As Jesus proclaimed the imminence of God's kingdom, He exercised the divinely given right and power to forgive sins, expel demons, and teach. In His day, it was typical for rabbis to appeal to tradition and a list of experts to support one's point. What impressed Jesus' audience is that He spoke directly to the issues at hand, basing His remarks solely on His own understanding (see Matt. 7:28-29). He could do so, for His authority came directly from God.

B. Encountering a Demon: vss. 33-34

In the synagogue there was a man possessed by a demon, an evil spirit. He cried out at the top of his voice, "Ha! What do you want with us, Jesus of Nazareth? Have you come to destroy us? I know who you are—the Holy One of God!"

Once, when Jesus was in the synagogue at Capernaum, a man possessed by a demon began shouting at Him (Luke 4:33). This is one of numerous encounters Jesus had with persons who were possessed by unclean or evil spirits. Some commentators have dismissed the existence of demon-possession. They say that in Jesus' time, illnesses were described in this way. But there seems to be a difference between demonism itself and the spirits' effects. Diseases and demons were mentioned separately in descriptions of Jesus' healings (Matt. 4:24; Mark 1:34). And Jesus' triumphs over demons emphasized the authority He has over evil as well as disease.

Some claim that demons are helpful beings from other planes of existence who have come to aid people on their evolutionary journey to enlightenment. Others have said that demons are the personification of an innate intelligence within humankind. Still others call demons hallucinations of our unconscious minds that are maintained in thought and action. In contrast to these incorrect notions is the clear teaching of Scripture. From it we learn that demons are any of the angels of God's creation who chose to side with Satan in his rebellion against the Lord. These spirits are real, supernatural beings who strive to deceive people, thwart the will of God, and undermine the work of the Church (1 Cor. 10:20-21; 1 Tim. 4:1; Jas. 2:19; Rev. 9:20; 16:14). Because of Christ's atoning sacrifice, Satan and his demonic cohorts are defeated foes (Luke 10:17-18; John 12:31; 16:11; Col. 2:15; Heb. 2:14) awaiting certain doom (Matt. 25:41; 2 Pet. 2:4; Jude 6; Rev. 20:10). At the end of the age, demons will be forced to bow to the lordship of Christ (Matt. 22:44; Phil. 2:10).

In a display of defiance, the demon Jesus encountered in the synagogue at Capernaum, forced its victim to demand that the Savior go away. Only one entity spoke, though it spoke for "us" (Luke 4:34), perhaps as one spirit speaking for all the demons whom Jesus ultimately defeats on the cross. The unclean spirit reasoned that "Jesus of Nazareth" (Luke 4:34) was interfering in matters that supposedly were none of His concern. The idea is that Christ and the demon really had nothing to do with one another. Thus, Jesus should leave the evil entity alone. The demon feared the Son of God had come to "destroy" it. Expressed differently, the unclean spirit realized that the Messiah sent from God would cause it to perish by bringing it to eternal ruin. As the Holy One (see John 6:69), Jesus was filled with God's Spirit and lived in holiness. Likewise, Jesus was uniquely qualified and empowered to deal with all forms of moral and spiritual impurity.

C. Expelling the Demon: vs. 35

"Be quiet!" Jesus said sternly. "Come out of him!" Then the demon threw the man down before them all and came out without injuring him.

Episodes such as this make it clear that demons possess a great deal of power. Manifestations of demonic possession in Scripture included supernatural strength, multiple personalities, and physical and mental afflictions. The latter involved muteness, deafness, blindness, seizures, crippling, and symptoms of mental illness. It was not always possible to distinguish between the personality of the victim and the influence of the demons within them.

The demon who called Jesus the "Holy One of God" (Luke 4:34) was trying to gain control of the Messiah, in keeping with the ancient belief that to know a person's name gave one power over him. The attempt, however, failed, for Jesus was not intimidated by the evil entity. The Son of God ordered the unclean spirit to be quiet and leave its victim. This command was appropriate, for Jesus did not need the forces of darkness to bear witness to His status as the Messiah. He also did not want such testimony from demons to give people an incorrect impression of His identity as the promised Redeemer of Israel (for example, that He was a revolutionary seeking to free the Jews from the control of Rome). The demon responded by throwing the man to the ground in front of everyone. Then, the unclean spirit departed without further hurting its victim (vs. 35).

D. Acknowledging Jesus' Authority: vss. 36-37

All the people were amazed and said to each other, "What is this teaching? With authority and power he gives orders to evil spirits and they come out!" And the news about him spread throughout the surrounding area.

This incident is an example of Jesus' ability to completely deliver and protect an individual oppressed by the evil one. In contrast with the exorcists of the day, the Messiah did not resort to rituals or incantations. Neither did He conjure up someone else's name to bring about the cure. He simply gave the command and expelled the demon from its host. All the people in the synagogue were amazed at the authority and power Jesus' words possessed. In fact, it was so great that He could rebuke an unclean spirit and expel it from its tormented victim (Luke 4:36). Understandably, the news about Jesus spread throughout every village in that part of Galilee (vs. 37).

II. Jesus' Authority Challenged: Luke 20:1-8

A. The Religious Leaders' Question: vss. 1-2

One day as he was teaching the people in the temple courts and preaching the gospel, the chief priests and the teachers of the law, together with the elders, came up to him. "Tell us by what authority you are doing these things," they said. "Who gave you this authority?"

The episode involving the religious leaders' challenge to Jesus' authority occurred in the Savior's final week before His crucifixion. One Sunday, He entered Jerusalem triumphantly and surveyed the temple (Matt. 21:1-11; Mark 11:1-11; Luke 19:28-44). Then, on Monday, the Savior cursed a fig tree and cleared the temple (Matt. 21:12-22; Mark 11:12-19; Luke 19:45-48). The challenge to Jesus' authority took place on Tuesday of Passion Week, while He was teaching the people and proclaiming the Good News in the temple courts (Luke 20:1). The Jewish religious leaders resented the way Jesus had entered Jerusalem, purged the temple, and began teaching within its precincts. They thought He had overstepped His bounds. Weren't they in charge? Yet this "country preacher" acted like He owned the place!

The "chief priests" were members of the religious aristocracy who traced their authority to the law of Moses, which states that only descendants of Aaron could serve as priests. They resented Jesus' intrusion into temple activities, which they claimed as their area of responsibility. The "teachers of the law" (also known as scribes) were the law's interpreters. They resented Jesus because He explained the law differently than they did. The "elders" were heads of the most influential lay families of the nation. They resented Jesus because His popularity tended to undermine their influence. In short, the three leading social groups of the Sanhedrin approached Jesus. (When Judea was made a Roman province in A.D. 6, the Romans granted this council almost exclusive control of Jewish affairs.) Since Jesus had challenged the religious leaders' authority, they now challenged His. They demanded that He tell them who had given Him permission to act as He did in the temple (vs. 2). Apparently, they hoped His response would expose Him as a fraud with no legitimate authority.

B. The Savior's Counter-Question: vss. 3-4

He replied, "I will also ask you a question. Tell me, John's baptism—was it from heaven, or from men?"

The Savior knew His interrogators had sinister motives. He thus responded to their question with one of His own (Luke 20:3). In doing so, He was using a common debating technique of the rabbis. His query also put the religious leaders on the defensive. Their attitude toward John the Baptizer had revealed that these men would not recognize anyone's authority unless it served their own purposes. So Jesus forced the religious leaders into an impossible position by asking them about the authority behind John's baptism. If they answered Jesus' question, He said He would reveal who had given Him permission to act as He had. In particular, He wanted to know whether they thought John's authority to baptize came from heaven or was merely human in origin (vs. 4).

C. The Mutual Non-Response: vss. 5-8

They discussed it among themselves and said, "If we say, 'From heaven,' he will ask, 'Why didn't you believe him?' But if we say, 'From men,' all the people will stone us, because they are persuaded that John was a prophet." So they answered, "We don't know where it was from." Jesus said, "Neither will I tell you by what authority I am doing these things."

The delegation from the Sanhedrin found themselves in the same type of bind they had tried to place on Jesus. They discerned they could not answer His question without either alienating the crowd or supporting His position. Despite their contempt for the common people, the religious leaders feared them. The multitudes had held John in high esteem as a prophet during his lifetime, and still did. So the leaders were afraid to say anything against John. But if they acknowledged that John's authority came from heaven, then they would also have to acknowledge Jesus' authority, for John had told the nation to accept Jesus as the Messiah. And Jesus would ask the leaders why they had refused to believe the message John had declared (Luke 20:5-6).

In the end, the religious leaders were too duplicitous and cowardly to answer Jesus' question. By professing ignorance and conveying an attitude of indifference (vs. 7), they revealed that they were not interested in the truth, only in eliminating Jesus. Ironically, their response discredited them in the eyes of the people. Since the Jewish authorities had refused to answer the Savior's question, He refused to reveal the source of His authority (vs. 8). If He had revealed it, He undoubtedly would have been accused of blasphemy. We should never read of the hostile leaders without being concerned about making the same mistake they did. When God's will does not match up with our ideas or wishes, we should not question His right to do as He pleases. We should look for the fault in ourselves rather than question His sovereignty. We must trust the Lord, for He is God.

Discussion Questions

1. What was the significance of Capernaum to Jesus' earthly ministry?
2. Why did the demon want Jesus to go away?
3. How was it possible for Jesus to expel the unclean spirit from its victim?
4. Why were the religious leaders upset with Jesus for His activities in the Jerusalem temple?
5. Why did Jesus respond to the query of the religious leaders with a question about John the Baptizer?

Contemporary Application

After years of ministry, I have seen that people perceive the message of Jesus in different ways. Some people see it as freeing, liberating, comforting, and life-giving. Others somehow see it as inhibiting, limiting, restrictive, and life-diminishing.

On one occasion, I spoke for quite some time with a man who was in the midst of a bitter divorce, due chiefly to his alcoholism, his physical abusiveness, and his infidelity. As I told him about the salvation that Jesus offers him and how our church would accept him and nurture him with open arms, tears began to flow down his cheeks. A light seemed to go on in his eyes. I'm convinced that this man saw for the first time how freeing it would be to accept the salvation and peace that Christ offers. At that moment, the man seized the opportunity to accept Jesus' message.

On another occasion, I spoke for quite some time with a different man whose life was apparently spinning out of control after some unethical business dealings, an ensuing court case, and some embarrassing personal revelations. As I told him, too, about the salvation that Jesus offers and how our church would accept him with open arms, tears began to flow down his cheeks as well. But there was no light in his eyes. He desperately wanted a way out of his misery, but he was convinced that Jesus was not that way out, and he felt "unworthy" to accept any love or encouragement. At that moment, this person rejected Jesus' message.

Christ no more forces Himself on us today than He forced Himself on the people in His own day. His salvation is offered as a gift. If we see His offer for the deliverance and liberation that it is, we will gladly accept it. But so many view His offer as the people of His day did—with skepticism, doubt, and unbelief, and as a threat to their desire to run their own lives.

Christ as Healer

DEVOTIONAL READING

Isaiah 61:1-4

DAILY BIBLE READINGS

Monday July 7
  Isaiah 61:1-4 Anointed by God

Tuesday July 8
  Mark 1:29-34 He Cured Many

Wednesday July 9
  Mark 1:35-39 To Neighboring Towns

Thursday July 10
  Mark 1:40-45 The Word Spread

Friday July 11
  Mark 2:1-2 The Needs for Healing Grow

Saturday July 12
  Mark 2:3-5 Healed by Faith

Sunday July 13
  Mark 7:31-37 Astonished beyond Measure

Scripture

Background Scripture: *Mark 1:29-45*
Scripture Lesson: *Mark 1:29-45*
Key Verse: *Jesus healed many who had various diseases. He also drove out many demons.* Mark 1:34.
Scripture Lesson for Children: *Mark 1:29-34, 40-45*
Key Verse for Children: *Jesus healed many who had various diseases.* Mark 1:34.

Lesson Aim

To understand that Jesus is uniquely able to help the afflicted.

Lesson Setting

Time: *About A.D. 26*
Place: *Capernaum and the whole region of Galilee*

Lesson Outline

Christ as Healer
  I. Jesus Heals Many People: Mark 1:29-34
      A. *Healing Peter's Mother-in-Law: vss. 29-31*
      B. *Healing the Afflicted: vss. 32-34*
  II. Jesus Travels throughout Galilee: Mark 1:35-39
      A. *Praying in an Isolated Place: vss. 35-37*
      B. *Ministering in Galilee: vss. 38-39*
  III. Jesus Heals a Man with Leprosy: Mark 1:40-45
      A. *The Leper's Request: vs. 40*
      B. *The Savior's Response: vss. 41-42*
      C. *The Proclamation of the Healing: vss. 43-45*

Introduction for Adults

Topic: *Finding Healing and Wholeness*

We should be thankful that Jesus heals us, as sinners, to spiritual wholeness, for otherwise none of us would be saved. Yet once we become Christians and settle down among the nice people in church, we often forget that Jesus wants to touch the lives of all people with His reconciling power. Sometimes those whom He calls embarrass us, and we feel uncomfortable in their presence. We don't approve of the way they look and the things they do. Would we ever sit down to dinner with people like them?

The church's hardest task is to expand its vision to unlikely candidates for salvation and fellowship. Once our lives get cleaned up, we don't want to get dirty again. But if we refuse to reach sinners like Jesus did, then the church becomes a holier-than-thou club. It fails to fulfill its divine mission. Perhaps once in a while we need to put a banner behind the pulpit that says JESUS HEALS SINNERS TO SPIRITU-AL WHOLENESS.

Introduction for Youth

Topic: *The Doctor Is In!*

All children reach the stage when they realize they cannot fix everything on their own. They need their parents to bandage the scrape, clean up the spill, or ease them through painful trials. As children grow up, suddenly it's humiliating for them to think they cannot help themselves. They may pretend that there is nothing wrong or that they don't need anyone's help. Regrettably, they refuse to reach out.

As we move through the twenty-first century, there still remain physical and spiritual ailments that even the marvels of modern science cannot remedy. Thankfully, Jesus, the divine healer, is able to do what medicine cannot. He alone is uniquely able to help the afflicted.

Concepts for Children

Topic: *Jesus Healed*

1. Jesus' touch healed Peter's mother-in-law.
2. Jesus healed many with various diseases.
3. Jesus touched a leper before healing him.
4. Jesus gave the healed leper instructions, but the man disobeyed them.
5. Jesus can meet all our physical and spiritual needs.

Lesson Commentary

I. JESUS HEALS MANY PEOPLE: MARK 1:29-34

A. Healing Peter's Mother-in-Law: vss. 29-31

As soon as they left the synagogue, they went with James and John to the home of Simon and Andrew. Simon's mother-in-law was in bed with a fever, and they told Jesus about her. So he went to her, took her hand and helped her up. The fever left her and she began to wait on them.

It would be difficult to imagine a better introduction to the essence of Christianity than the Book of Mark. It is a concise, vivid, and moving presentation of the good news that Jesus Christ brought and proclaimed, and that is about Him as the Son of God (1:1). Verse 14 notes that after the authorities had arrested and imprisoned John the Baptizer, Jesus went into Galilee, where He proclaimed the Good News that comes from God and is about God. In particular, the Messiah declared that the time promised by the Lord had finally arrived. Indeed, His kingdom was already at hand. Jesus was referring to God's sovereign rule over His creation. This involved bringing His plan of redemption to completion through the Savior.

Here we see that a new era had begun. And when that era reaches its completion, the kingdom of God will have come in all its fullness. History is not in the unbroken grip of evil. Satan is powerful and active now, but his doom is certain. Neither is history moving in pointless circles, with all things being as they always have been and always will be. God is moving history toward a just conclusion. In light of these truths, Jesus urged everyone to turn back to God in repentance and believe the Good News (vs. 15).

After announcing the start of a new era, Jesus set out to summon His disciples. First, He called Simon (Peter) and Andrew (vs. 16). These brothers certainly were not perfect. But Jesus did not summon them because of who they were. He called them because of who they could become. Such people are the raw material with which Christ builds His kingdom. Jesus spoke to the brothers in language they could understand. They knew how it feels to catch fish—the thrill of hauling in a full net. Now they were being summoned to a task that offered deeper fulfillment: fishing for people (vs. 17). Jesus' words went straight to the hearts of Peter and Andrew. Here was what the brothers had been longing for! So they immediately followed Jesus, laying aside the nets they had used in their daily work as fishermen (vs. 18). Jesus continued walking until He found James and John at work with their father, Zebedee (vs. 19). Jesus called this pair of brothers too and they followed Him (vs. 20). Zebedee had the help of hired servants, and therefore presumably was able to maintain his fishing business without his sons.

From reading only Mark's Gospel, we might conclude that Jesus' first contact with Peter, Andrew, James, and John was when He said "Follow me" (vs. 17). However, the Gospel of John suggests that at least some of these fishermen already were part-time followers of Jesus (1:35-42). Therefore, when Jesus directed them to follow Him, He wanted them to be unreservedly committed to Him on a full-time basis. This was a call to make a difference in this world. That's a call every person finds challenging. Nets are not evil, and neither are possessions or careers. But we must cast aside anything that would keep us from following the Lord Jesus.

Mark 1:21-28 spotlights the episode we studied last week, in which Jesus expelled a demon from a man in attendance at a synagogue service in Capernaum. Then, after leaving the synagogue, Jesus walked with James and John to the home of Peter and Andrew to eat a Sabbath meal, which was customarily served at that time (vs. 29). Part of the reason for this visit was the illness of Peter's mother-in-law. She was lying down in bed, being sick with a high-grade fever (vs. 30; see Luke 4:38). In that day, a fever was considered to be an illness itself, rather than a symptom of many kinds of illness. We don't know precisely what was wrong with Peter's mother-in-law, but Jesus knew what to do. He went over to her bedside and ordered the fever to go away (vs. 39). Here the woman's malady is personified as an entity that held her captive and that Jesus rebuked and cast out by the power of His command. Next, He took Peter's mother-in-law by the hand and gently helped her up. In the process, Jesus healed her. With her fever now gone, the grateful host prepared an evening meal for her guests (Mark 1:31).

B. Healing the Afflicted: vss. 32-34

That evening after sunset the people brought to Jesus all the sick and demon-possessed. The whole town gathered at the door, and Jesus healed many who had various diseases. He also drove out many demons, but he would not let the demons speak because they knew who he was.

Later that Saturday evening, many local people came to Jesus, bringing the sick and the demon-possessed (Mark 1:32). The widespread occurrence of the latter might have been due to the presence of pagan occult practices in Galilee. According to Jewish law, now that the Sabbath was over (having ended at sunset), the people could travel and carry a burden. The crowd was so large that it looked as though the entire town had turned out (vs. 33). Jesus healed the sick and drove out demons. Here we see a distinction made between healing and exorcism, which implies that Jesus was dealing with two separate issues—one physical and the other spiritual in nature.

The Savior would not allow the demons to identify Him, for they knew He was the Messiah (vs. 34; see Luke 4:41). After all, He didn't need the testimony of the demonic world to establish His credibility. He also did not want unclean spirits to give people the false impression that He had any political aspirations to liberate Israel from their Gentile taskmasters. It would be incorrect to assume from Jesus' growing popularity that He was widely received as the promised Messiah of the Jews. Most of those who came to Him at this stage were not seeking Him because they appreciated who He is. Some just wanted to be healed, while most of the rest were curiosity seekers. Jesus was calling them to His eternal kingdom, but they were chiefly interested in a comfortable existence within the kingdoms of this world.

We face the same temptation. Often our goal for ourselves is an easy life. But Jesus' goal is to transform us, making us fit for His kingdom. And usually that transformation involves hardship and suffering, enabling us to grow spiritually. As we continue to study the words and works of the Messiah, we must look beyond the events themselves and ask what those events mean in light of Jesus' stated mission: "The Son of Man [came] to serve, and to give his life as a ransom for many" (10:45). Jesus' mission was not simply to provide earthly happiness. He came to offer eternal life.

II. JESUS TRAVELS THROUGHOUT GALILEE: MARK 1:35-39

A. Praying in an Isolated Place: vss. 35-37

Very early in the morning, while it was still dark, Jesus got up, left the house and went off to a solitary place, where he prayed. Simon and his companions went to look for him, and when they found him, they exclaimed: "Everyone is looking for you!"

Jesus knew the value of renewing His spiritual vitality. That's why, before daybreak the next morning, He got up, went out to an isolated place, and spent time in prayer (Mark 1:35). The demands of His ministry were already pressing upon Him, so it made sense for Him to commune alone with the heavenly Father. Perhaps the Son focused on the holiness of the Father, the advent of His kingdom, and the fulfillment of His will throughout creation. Jesus possibly also entreated the Lord to provide the disciples with sufficient food to eat, strength to endure temptation, and protection from all forms of evil (see Matt. 6:9-13; Luke 11:2-4).

Eventually, Peter and the other disciples got up. When they noticed that Jesus had left the house, they decided to track Him down (Mark 1:36). When the disciples found Jesus, they interrupted His prayer, exclaiming, "Everyone is looking for you!" (vs. 37). They could not understand why He would ignore the call of the crowd, even for prayer. Undoubtedly, they assumed the success of His mission required approval from the masses. But Jesus knew better. The success of His mission required approval from the Father. The Gospel of John reveals that many people believed in Jesus because they saw the miraculous signs He performed. However, the Messiah would not entrust Himself to them, for He understood the fickleness of human nature. No one had to tell Him what people were like, for He already knew (2:23-25). Later in His earthly ministry, many of His would-be disciples would turn away and desert the Savior (6:66).

B. Ministering in Galilee: vss. 38-39

Jesus replied, "Let us go somewhere else—to the nearby villages—so I can preach there also. That is why I have come." So he traveled throughout Galilee, preaching in their synagogues and driving out demons.

In response to His disciples, Jesus stated that it was imperative for them to go on to the "nearby villages" (Mark 1:38). His mission was to confront the people living in those places with the Good News. For this reason, He did not want to see the Gospel confined to one place. Consequently, Jesus traveled throughout the region of Galilee. As He made His way from town to town, He preached in the synagogues and expelled demons from their victims (vs. 39). These are just some of the signs Jesus performed in the presence of His disciples. And while the four Gospels do not record every miracle, what they do report is intended to convince everyone to believe that Jesus is the Messiah, the Son of God, and thereby have life in His name (John 20:30-31).

As Jesus taught and preached in the towns of Galilee, John the Baptizer heard in prison what the Savior was doing. John decided to send some of his disciples to ask whether Jesus was the promised Messiah of Israel. Jesus directed these emissaries from John to report what they had seen and heard. This included Jesus proclaiming the Good News to the poor and performing many miracles of healing and exorcism (Matt. 11:1-5; Luke 7:18-22). Jesus' point seems to be that since He was fulfilling prophecies about the Messiah (see Isa. 61:1-2), He must be the Messiah.

III. JESUS HEALS A MAN WITH LEPROSY: MARK 1:40-45

A. The Leper's Request: vs. 40

A man with leprosy came to him and begged him on his knees, "If you are willing, you can make me clean."

In Mark's continuing presentation of Jesus the Messiah (see Mark 1:1), we next find Him encountering a leper. This man had heard of Jesus' power, but evidently knew little about His compassion. The leper came to the Savior, knelt in front of Him, and begged Him for help. The leper reasoned that if Jesus was willing to do so, He could cleanse the leper of his affliction (vs. 40). The wording of the Greek text indicates that the leper was not presuming that Jesus would heal him, only that the Messiah had the power to do so.

The Greek word translated "leprosy" (Mark 1:40) refers to several types of inflammatory skin diseases. Judging by the excitement that followed the healing (vs. 45), the leper who approached Jesus was probably suffering from true leprosy (Hansen's disease), not just a mild skin ailment. Old Testament laws covered how to treat people with many skin diseases like leprosy (Lev. 13:1-46; 14:1-32). But what we label leprosy was distinct from other skin diseases because some rabbis taught that it was a punishment for sin. To them, leprosy was the visible sign of inward corruption. The Jews feared leprosy, not only because it was disfiguring, but also because lepers were treated as outcasts. Lepers lived in communities outside the city gates and were not allowed contact with others.

B. The Savior's Response: vss. 41-42

Filled with compassion, Jesus reached out his hand and touched the man. "I am willing," he said. "Be clean!" Immediately the leprosy left him and he was cured.

"Filled with compassion" (Mark 1:41) translates the reading found in many manuscripts of the Greek New Testament. A smaller number of other manuscripts, however, contain a reading that could be translated "moved with anger." It's not hard to imagine that Jesus simultaneously felt a mixture of pity and indignation. For instance, He might have been upset by the leper's apparent doubt over the Savior's desire to heal him (vs. 40). As well, Jesus could have felt sorry for the man's intolerable condition. In either case, there's no doubt concerning the Messiah's response. He was willing and able to heal the leper. Thus, Jesus stretched out His hand, touched the leper, and made him clean.

The man probably had not been touched by a nonleper in months or even years. Religious law declared that a person became "unclean" by touching a leper. Jesus could have healed the leper without touching him, but He did touch him, instantly healing him (vss. 41-42). Here we see that Jesus' compassion ignored ritual defilement. As He was with the crowds in Capernaum, Jesus was moved by kindness at the sight of suffering and willingly removed its cause.

C. The Proclamation of the Healing: vss. 43-45

Jesus sent him away at once with a strong warning: "See that you don't tell this to anyone. But go, show yourself to the priest and offer the sacrifices that Moses commanded for your cleansing, as a testimony to them." Instead he went out and began to talk freely, spreading the news. As a result, Jesus could no longer enter a town openly but stayed outside in lonely places. Yet the people still came to him from everywhere.

Jesus did not waste any time sending the former leper on his way with the stern warning to tell no one about the healing (Mark 1:43). In the time of Jesus, the Jews wanted freedom from Rome. Expectations ran high that God would raise up a warrior-prince who would throw off the yoke of pagan rule and usher in a Jewish kingdom of worldwide proportions. John 6:15 and Acts 1:6 show traces of this hope among the people. This explains why Jesus was careful not to give false impressions about the exact nature of His messiahship (John 18:33-37). He saw His destiny in terms of service to God and sacrificial suffering (Mark 8:31; 9:31; 10:33-34; Luke 24:45-46).

Jesus told the former leper to go to a priest, let him examine the once afflicted bodily area, and verify that a genuine healing had occurred. Jesus also directed the man to take along the offering required in the Mosaic law for those who had been cleansed from leprosy (Mark 1:44; see Lev. 13:6, 13, 17, 23; 14:2-32; Luke 5:14). Not only would such verification fulfill a requirement of the Mosaic law, but also it would testify to the religious establishment of Jesus' authority and His respect for the law. Indeed, the sight of a fully healed leper would attest to the religious leaders that Jesus is the Messiah, for the Jews believed only God could cure such a disease (2 Kings 5:1-7).

The former leper may have obeyed the priestly verification part of Jesus' orders, but he did not obey the Lord's command to remain silent. He proclaimed to everyone what had happened, which led to large crowds swarming around Jesus wherever He went. The presence of so many miracle seekers (along with the intensifying opposition of the religious leaders) hindered Jesus' ability to publicly enter a town or synagogue anywhere in Galilee. Instead, He had to confine Himself to "lonely places" (vs. 45), that is, secluded, remote areas. Even then, the people were so desperate that they kept coming to Him from everywhere to be healed.

Discussion Questions

1. What did Jesus do to heal Peter's mother-in-law?
2. Why did crowds of people seek out Jesus?
3. Why do you think prayer was important to Jesus?
4. How did Jesus respond to the leper's request to be healed?
5. Why did Jesus sternly warn the former leper not to tell anyone else about the healing?

Contemporary Application

In all the episodes highlighted in this week's lesson, physical needs mirrored deeper spiritual needs. For instance, in the case of those who were possessed by unclean spirits, their behavioral problems were a direct result of their spiritual bondage. And even in the case of the man with leprosy, his ailment was a result of the fallen condition of all creation. In fact, his physical condition reflected his spiritual helplessness.

Every person needs the deliverance and forgiveness only the Lord Jesus can provide. Those who have never placed their trust in the Messiah for salvation are as helpless as the large number of sick and demon-possessed who came to Jesus for assistance. Unsaved men and women need to be rescued from the terrible effects of Satan, just as those afflicted by evil spirits needed deliverance and healing.

Christian men and women stand in need of situational deliverance and forgiveness. Even though the eternal issue of salvation has been dealt with, physical disease and personal sins are still realities of life. Believers need to look to the Lord for help in time of sickness, and for forgiveness of the transgressions that damage fellowship with the heavenly Father.

People can only provide what amounts to a flimsy bandage for our physical and psychological afflictions. As physicians, they can try to treat our bodily ailments—sometimes successfully for a while and sometimes not. As counselors, they can try to treat our psychological problems—again, sometimes successfully for a while and sometimes not. But none of them can deal with any of our problems completely and permanently. They simply do not have that kind of healing power. Only Jesus does, because He is the God who heals. How can we not go to such a loving Savior for help and hope?

Christ as Servant

DEVOTIONAL READING

Isaiah 53:4-6

DAILY BIBLE READINGS

Monday July 14
Isaiah 53:4-6 The Suffering Servant

Tuesday July 15
John 13:1-2a To the End

Wednesday July 16
John 13:2b-11 Unless I Wash You

Thursday July 17
John 13:12-17 An Example

Friday July 18
John 13:18-20 Whoever Receives Me

Saturday July 19
Matthew 20:20-23 What Do You Want?

Sunday July 20
Matthew 20:24-28 Not to Be Served

Scripture

Background Scripture: *John 13:1-20*
Scripture Lesson: *John 13:1-8, 12-20*
Key Verse: *[Jesus said,] "I have set you an example that you should do as I have done for you."* John 13:15.
Scripture Lesson for Children: *John 13:1-16*
Key Verse for Children: *[Jesus said,] "I have set you an example that you should do as I have done for you."* John 13:15.

Lesson Aim

To emphasize that love does what pride does not.

Lesson Setting

Time: *A.D. 30*
Place: *Jerusalem*

Lesson Outline

Christ as Servant

I. The Setting: John 13:1-3
  A. *Jesus' Love for His Disciples: vs. 1*
  B. *Jesus' Awareness of Unfolding Events: vss. 2-3*

II. The Foot Washing and Its Significance: John 13:4-8, 12-20
  A. *The Act of Foot Washing: vss. 4-5*
  B. *The Necessity of the Foot Washing: vss. 6-8*
  C. *The Significance of the Foot Washing: vss. 12-17*
  D. *The Prediction of Jesus' Betrayal: vss. 18-20*

Introduction for Adults

Topic: *To Be a Servant*

"We try hard. We fail. We are sure we can succeed if we try harder tomorrow. We fail again. And if we succeed, it is only half success, half of what it would have been with God. We are all guilty. . . . The world has yet to see what God can do with one person wholly committed to Him."

Those words, spoken in the 1860s by Henry Varley in a prayer meeting, burned into the heart of ex-shoe salesman, Dwight L. Moody. He was already involved in ministry in Chicago, but Varley's words helped to change the self-sufficient Moody into a humble, God-directed evangelist and servant who went on to preach the Gospel to more people than anyone else in his time. And even though his crusade hymnbook royalties amounted to a million dollars, Moody lived on $120 a year, donating the rest to Christian charity and education. Moody followed his Redeemer's example of being a Christian servant to others.

Introduction for Youth

Topic: *Stooping Down to Lift Up*

"If you scratch my back, I'll scratch yours." This is an idiom that means if you do something for me, I'll return the favor. It's the kind of self-focused arrangement Jesus alluded to in Matthew 5:43-47. He declared that there is nothing praiseworthy about only loving those who can reciprocate our kindness and compassion. God's love is perfected in our lives when we minister to others in a humble and sacrificial manner.

Consider the foot-washing episode where Jesus modeled what He taught. He loved His disciples so much that He even knelt before them and cleaned their feet. It was His way of showing them how to love each other. We should not allow our pride to dictate when, how, and who we should love. Those around us are just waiting for us to show we can be the loving servants God has called us to be.

Concepts for Children

Topic: *Jesus, a Serving Example*

1. Jesus gave His followers an example of servanthood.
2. Peter did not understand what Jesus was doing.
3. When Jesus offered an explanation, Peter welcomed Jesus' act of servanthood.
4. Jesus encouraged those with Him to follow His example of humble service to others.
5. A willingness to serve others is one way we can glorify God.

Lesson Commentary

I. THE SETTING: JOHN 13:1-3

A. Jesus' Love for His Disciples: vs. 1

It was just before the Passover Feast. Jesus knew that the time had come for him to leave this world and go to the Father. Having loved his own who were in the world, he now showed them the full extent of his love.

The events in this week's lesson took place on the night before the official start of the Passover. Jesus knew the time had come for His departure from the world. The cross had always been on the horizon for Him, but now He was fully aware of its imminence. This was the time appointed by the Father for His Son's saving work to be completed. Throughout Jesus' earthly ministry, He loved those entrusted to His care. His compassion for the disciples was not superficial; instead, it was unselfish, unconditional, and unbounded. Jesus demonstrated His love completely and to the very end of His life. He knew that after His crucifixion and burial, He would be resurrected from the dead and exalted to the right hand of the Father (John 13:1).

B. Jesus' Awareness of Unfolding Events: vss. 2-3

The evening meal was being served, and the devil had already prompted Judas Iscariot, son of Simon, to betray Jesus. Jesus knew that the Father had put all things under his power, and that he had come from God and was returning to God.

Experts debate whether the "evening meal" (John 13:2) refers to the feast that was eaten at Passover (known to Jews as Pesach or Pesah; see Matt. 26:18; Mark 14:14; Luke 22:11). Passover normally began on the 15th day of Nisan (or Abib in the Torah), namely, the first month of the Hebrew calendar. The observance included the killing and eating of a lamb, along with consuming foods such as bitter herbs and bread made without leaven. The Jews ate this meal to remind them that the Lord had rescued them from slavery in Egypt. The first Passover, celebrated in Egypt (Exod. 12:1-20), had marked the turning point in God's plan of redemption for His people. The Crucifixion would fulfill the Passover's symbolism (John 1:35; Acts 8:32; 1 Cor. 5:7; 1 Pet. 1:19).

The farewell meal that Jesus ate with His disciples probably followed a well-established Jewish pattern for celebrating the Passover feast. During an opening prayer, the first of four cups was blessed and passed around. Each person at the table then took herbs and dipped them in salt water. Next, the host took one of three flat cakes of unleavened bread, broke it, and laid some of it aside. Typically, the youngest member of the group then asked the question "What makes this night different from all others?" The host responded by recounting the events of the Passover. This was usually followed by the singing of Psalms 113 and 114 and by the filling and passing around of the second cup.

Before the actual meal was eaten, all the participants washed their hands. Thanksgiving to God was prayed, and more of the bread was broken apart. The host dipped bread in a sauce usually made of stewed fruit, and then distributed a portion to each person gathered at the table. Finally, the time for the meal arrived. Eating a roasted lamb was the high point of the evening. It was after Jesus and His disciples had eaten the Passover meal that He instituted the Lord's Supper. Jesus took the third cup, which was known as the "cup of blessing," and uttered a prayer of thanks. He then instructed each of His disciples to take the cup and share its contents among themselves. Then He took a flat cake of unleavened bread, broke it, and passed it around so that each of His disciples could eat a portion of it.

Prior to the start of Jesus' farewell meal, Satan had put it into the mind of Judas Iscariot to betray his loyalty to the Savior (John 13:2). Judas is identified as the son of Simon (see 6:71; 13:36). Most likely, the term "Iscariot" refers to the town of Kerioth, which was located near Hebron in southern Judah (Josh. 15:25). Among Jesus' 12 disciples, Judas was their treasurer. He carried the moneybag and sometimes would steal from it (12:6). The three Synoptic Gospels detail how Judas plotted with the Jewish leaders to bring about Jesus' arrest. Judas received a payment of 30 silver coins (Matt. 26:14-16; Mark 14:10-11; Luke 22:3-6) for leading the authorities to Jesus (John 18:1-2). It's unlikely that Jesus felt any personal sense of defeat about this, for He was aware that the Father had given Him authority over everything. Jesus also knew that nothing could happen to Him apart from the will of God, from whom He had come and to whom He was returning (13:3).

II. THE FOOT WASHING AND ITS SIGNIFICANCE: JOHN 13:4-8, 12-20

A. The Act of Foot Washing: vss. 4-5

So he got up from the meal, took off his outer clothing, and wrapped a towel around his waist. After that, he poured water into a basin and began to wash his disciples' feet, drying them with the towel that was wrapped around him.

Without warning, Jesus rose from the table during the meal. Perhaps His disciples were preoccupied with eating and talking when they saw the Lord stand a short distance from them and remove His outer robe. Undoubtedly, they were shocked by this action. But even more unexpected was Jesus' decision to tie a towel (a long piece of linen cloth) around His waist (John 13:4). As the disciples watched in silence, they saw the Lord pick up a basin and a jar of water, which He then set down on the ground near the table. Next, He filled the large bowl with water, washed the feet of every disciple, and dried their feet with the towel around His waist (vs. 5).

The unpaved roads of Palestine required that particular care be given to the feet of travelers. If people were walking barefoot or wearing sandals, their dusty or mud-coated feet would have needed bathing several times a day. Upon the entrance to any house, the host customarily provided a servant to wash the visitor's feet.

Because people of that day considered dirt and dust on the feet to be defiling, the task of foot washing was viewed as the most menial duty a servant could perform. Since the Last Supper was conducted in secret, apparently there were no servants available to do the lowly task and none of those present volunteered to perform it.

Perhaps initially, none of the disciples dared to ask Jesus why He had chosen to wash their feet. Despite all His teaching on servanthood, He may have felt the need to do this task because the Twelve still did not understand the concept of being a servant. Luke records that even at the Last Supper, the disciples were arguing about who was the greatest (Luke 22:24-27), as they had several times before (Matt. 18:1-5; 20:20-28; Mark 9:33-37; 10:35-45; Luke 9:46-48). Although Jesus knew He was in His last hours before His death on the cross, He remained calm, reflective, and serious. He took the time to show His followers how much He loved them and how much they were to love others.

B. The Necessity of the Foot Washing: vss. 6-8

He came to Simon Peter, who said to him, "Lord, are you going to wash my feet?" Jesus replied, "You do not realize now what I am doing, but later you will understand." "No," said Peter, "you shall never wash my feet." Jesus answered, "Unless I wash you, you have no part with me."

Peter could not imagine that the person he served should humiliate Himself by washing the feet of His disciples. In a previous episode, Peter voiced his belief that Jesus is the "Holy One of God" (John 6:69). But what Peter did not realize is that God the Son voluntarily chose to set aside His divine privileges, take the humble position of a slave, and be born as a human being. Indeed, Jesus was willing to die a criminal's death on the cross (Phil. 2:6-8).

When Jesus knelt down in front of Peter, he asked the Lord whether He intended to wash the feet of His disciple (John 13:6). The Savior explained that even though Peter failed to grasp the significance of the foot-washing episode, he would later (after Jesus' resurrection) understand the meaning of what had been done (vs. 7). Because Peter was unable to fathom Jesus' intent, he strongly protested what his Lord was doing. The Greek literally says, "You will never wash my feet forever." Jesus, while maintaining His composure, replied matter-of-factly that if Peter did not permit Him to wash his feet, Peter would no longer really belong to Him. Expressed differently, Peter would not be Jesus' disciple (vs. 8). Christ's reply probably referred to His gift of cleansing in His blood, of which the foot washing was a symbol.

Perhaps at this point there was considerable tension and anxiety among the rest of the disciples over the exchange that had occurred between Jesus and Peter. The mood may have lightened up considerably as the group heard Peter beg the Lord to wash not just his feet, but also his hands and head (vs. 9). This reaction showed not only Peter's respect for Jesus, but his devotion as well. Most likely, Peter wanted to demonstrate to Jesus that he was one of His loyal followers.

Jesus responded to Peter by describing a situation in which a person went to a feast after having taken a bath. This person did not need to wash again, except for his feet, which had gotten dirty on the way to the feasting place (vs. 10). In a spiritual sense, Peter had already been cleansed of sin through faith in Christ. Thus, the disciple did not need to be cleansed again. At this point, none of those present understood the meaning of Jesus' words about who was "clean" and who was not. He meant that, except for Judas (vs. 11), all the disciples had experienced spiritual cleansing through faith in Him (15:3). Jesus' explanation to His disciples implies that the foot-washing incident was more than just an example of humble service. It also pointed to His atoning sacrifice at Calvary. Those who accepted Jesus' act of humiliation also embraced by faith His redemptive work on the cross.

C. The Significance of the Foot Washing: vss. 12-17

When he had finished washing their feet, he put on his clothes and returned to his place. "Do you understand what I have done for you?" he asked them. "You call me 'Teacher' and 'Lord,' and rightly so, for that is what I am. Now that I, your Lord and Teacher, have washed your feet, you also should wash one another's feet. I have set you an example that you should do as I have done for you. I tell you the truth, no servant is greater than his master, nor is a messenger greater than the one who sent him. Now that you know these things, you will be blessed if you do them.

After Jesus had washed the feet of His disciples, He stood up, put on His outer garment, and returned to His place at the table. Once Jesus was seated, He took the opportunity to explain the significance of His actions. He asked His followers whether they grasped the importance of the foot-washing incident (John 13:12). Jesus referred to the typical terms with which His disciples respectfully addressed Him. Jesus fully approved of being recognized as their "Teacher" (vs. 13; which is equivalent to "Rabbi") and "Lord." Yet, even though they rightfully submitted to His authority and instruction, He was willing to humbly and unselfishly serve them.

If Jesus ministered to His subjects in this most unassuming and sacrificial way, what should be their response? The Redeemer said they were obligated to follow His example (vs. 14). He had given them a demonstration of humility by washing their feet. Likewise, a generous and sacrificial attitude should characterize His followers in their relationships with each other (vs. 15). Because the foot washing also symbolized the spiritual cleansing that comes through Jesus' blood (which He was about to shed on the cross), He was urging His disciples to be willing to lay down their lives for one another, if necessary, as an act of sacrificial love (see 15:13).

In the Old Testament, servanthood is a common concept. In many places, Scripture mentions hired laborers and slaves. But more important are references to servants of God. People who were in covenant with the Lord considered Him their master. For example, Elijah declared to God, "I am your servant" (1 Kings 18:36). And when God spoke, He sometimes called one of His followers "my servant" (for instance, see 2 Kings 21:8). This servant-master relationship between a person and God is also in the New Testament. Believers are servants of Christ, who is Himself the servant of His Father. But in the New Testament, a related idea occurs. Believers are not only servants of God but also servants of one another (see Mark 10:43; 2 Cor. 4:5).

If any of Jesus' followers thought they were too good to stoop to any menial task of serving others, they did so only by placing themselves above their Lord. He was the suffering Servant, who had come to minister to others and give His life as a ransom for the sins of the world (Mark 10:45). Jesus solemnly assured the Twelve (and all who trust in Him for eternal life) that slaves are not greater than their master. Likewise, messengers are not greater than the person who sends them (John 13:16). Jesus' use of the word "sent" reminded His disciples that He had been sent to them by the Father. In turn, Jesus was sending His followers out to serve others, beginning with the proclamation of the Gospel (see 20:21-23).

The Lord Jesus, by example as well as by precept, introduced to His followers this principle of servanthood toward one another. Therefore, He is the believers' model of unselfish service. Those who willingly, consistently, and wholeheartedly follow His example are promised blessings (John 13:17). Thus, the only way for believers to be truly fulfilled and satisfied in their relationship with Christ is for them to be willing to accept and perform the role of a servant.

D. The Prediction of Jesus' Betrayal: vss. 18-20

"I am not referring to all of you; I know those I have chosen. But this is to fulfill the scripture: 'He who shares my bread has lifted up his heel against me.' I am telling you now before it happens, so that when it does happen you will believe that I am He. I tell you the truth, whoever accepts anyone I send accepts me; and whoever accepts me accepts the one who sent me."

It is unclear how Judas felt as Jesus talked openly about the importance of humble and sacrificial service. Perhaps Judas reacted with calloused indifference, especially as Satan took control of him (see John 13:27). In any case, Jesus explained that His statements were not directed to all of those present at the Last Supper (vs. 18). He was well aware of the fact that Judas would hand Him over to the authorities. Jesus also knew the ones He had chosen to receive eternal life.

Jesus stated that the decision made by Judas to betray Him was foretold in Scripture. In John 13:18, Jesus quoted Psalm 41:9. In this prayer for mercy, David noted that a trusted associate who served in his royal court and ate at his table, had lifted up his heel against the king. There are differing views concerning the meaning of this idiom. Most likely, the idea is that one of David's closest friends had acted treacherously by taking cruel advantage of him. What Israel's monarch lamented found its ultimate fulfillment in Jesus, the Son of David, when Judas Iscariot became His enemy by turning against him.

The Savior was predicting this act of betrayal before it ever happened so that when it occurred, His disciples would believe that He is the Messiah (vs. 19). The Greek is literally rendered "that I am." Some think Jesus was making reference to Exodus 3:14, and in so doing, declaring Himself to be the all-powerful, ever-living God. Other "I am" statements appear throughout the Gospel of John. Jesus said He is the following: the bread of life (6:35); the light of the world (8:12; 9:5); the gate of the sheep (10:7, 9); the good shepherd (vss. 11, 14); the resurrection and the life (11:25); the way, the truth, and the life (14:4); and the true vine (15:1, 5).

The Messiah solemnly announced that anyone who welcomed His messengers also welcomed Him. In turn, those who welcomed Him were welcoming the Father, who had sent the Son (13:20). Earlier, in the episode involving the nighttime visit that Nicodemus made to Jesus, we learn that God sent His only Son to die for our sins (3:16). God calls us to believe in Jesus—not just assent to what Jesus said as true, but to entrust our lives to Him. Those who believe in the Messiah will not suffer eternal separation from God, but enjoy a reconciled, deeply satisfying relationship with Jesus and His heavenly Father that will last forever.

Discussion Questions

1. In what way did Jesus show that He loved His followers to the very end?
2. Why did Judas Iscariot decide to betray Jesus?
3. How do you think the disciples felt as they saw Jesus washing their feet?
4. What explanation did Jesus give for wanting to wash the feet of His disciples?
5. What did Jesus say was the significance of the foot-washing episode?

Contemporary Application

Both "love" and "pride" have biblical meanings that are sometimes lost in our society. Jesus' kind of love goes beyond the sentimental kind of love found in valentines and romance novels. And the pride the Bible often describes is not like taking pride in one's work or being proud of one's accomplishments, but being so full of oneself that the individual cannot see the needs of others (1 Sam. 2:3; Isa. 13:11). Therefore, when God's Word encourages us to love and to not be full of pride, we need to look for our definitions in what Jesus taught His followers about these two ideas through His words and deeds.

One of the most vivid illustrations in Scripture is found in this week's passage from John, which describes Jesus' dropping to His knees and washing the filthy feet of His beloved disciples. Jesus showed them—and us—the power of love. What a memorable example of servanthood the Master demonstrated to His friends! This illustration of humility and love is pertinent for all Christians. We realize, of course, that it is not easy for us to set aside our pride and express love by being a servant to others. But since the Lord of the universe could do it, we can do so as well.

Indeed, Jesus' love for us empowers us so that we can break free from the kind of pride that demands that we never appear lowly or vulnerable. We are then able to display the kind of love that inspires us to care for the needs of others, especially those who are least able to help themselves. The power of love is being kind to others in the way that Jesus was kind. When we have such compassion, we can do all that pride urges us not to do. Those around us are just waiting for us to show we can be the loving servants God has called us to be.

Christ as Messiah

Scripture

Background Scripture: *Matthew 16:13-23*
Scripture Lesson: *Matthew 16:13-23*
Key Verse: *[Jesus] said to [the disciples,] "Who do you say I am?"* Matthew 16:15.
Scripture Lesson for Children: *Matthew 16:13-20*
Key Verse for Children: *Peter answered, "You are the Christ, the Son of the living God."* Matthew 16:16.

Lesson Aim

To discover that acknowledging Jesus as the Messiah calls for in-depth change.

Lesson Setting

Time: A.D. *30*
Place: *Caesarea Philippi*

Lesson Outline

Christ as Messiah

   I. The Confession of Peter: Matthew 16:13-20
      A. *Jesus' Question: vss. 13*
      B. *Various Responses: vss. 14-16*
      C. *Jesus' Pronouncement of Blessing on Peter: vss. 17-20*
  II. The Prediction of Jesus: Matthew 16:21-23
      A. *Jesus' Foretelling of His Death and Resurrection: vs. 21*
      B. *Jesus' Response to Peter's Rebuke: vss. 22-23*

Introduction for Adults

Topic: *Getting to Know a Person*

Helen Keller grew up without being able to see or hear. Despite her visual and auditory handicaps, she became one of America's most famous women. She graduated from college and had an illustrious career as a writer and speaker. As a young girl, she was told the good news about Jesus for the first time. It was reported that upon hearing the Gospel, Helen Keller exclaimed, "I already knew that such a God existed. I simply did not know His name!"

In the life, death, and resurrection of the Lord Jesus, we learn the name and personality of the eternal, living God.

Introduction for Youth

Topic: *What's My Line?*

Have you ever noticed how Jesus is portrayed in literature, on stage, or on screen? In *Jesus Christ Superstar*, He is an idealistic, but deluded, would-be Messiah. In *Godspell*, Jesus is a lovable innocent who becomes a crucified clown. Jesus is a well-intentioned charlatan in *The Passover Plot*, while He is a fierce champion in the film titled *The Gospel According to Saint Matthew*. And in *The Last Temptation of Christ*, Nikos Kazantzakis portrays Jesus as a man who did not want to be the Messiah.

So, who is Jesus to the teens in your class: a superstar, a sap, or a Savior? Peter had no difficulty whatsoever in affirming Jesus as the Messiah. Hopefully, your students can say the same.

Concepts for Children

Topic: *Jesus Is the Messiah*

1. Jesus asked His followers who people said He is.
2. Jesus' followers indicated that people were unsure.
3. Peter, through the Holy Spirit, said that Jesus is the Messiah.
4. Jesus did not yet want His identity made known.
5. Jesus said He would build the Church on the kind of faith Peter expressed.

Lesson Commentary

I. THE CONFESSION OF PETER: MATTHEW 16:13-20

A. Jesus' Question: vss. 13

When Jesus came to the region of Caesarea Philippi, he asked his disciples, "Who do people say the Son of Man is?"

Jesus left Galilee and went north to the region around the city of Caesarea Philippi (Matt. 16:13). Caesarea Philippi was a city located in the upper Jordan Valley and along the southwestern slope of Mount Hermon. Behind the town, which was about 1,150 feet above sea level, rose bluffs and rugged mountain peaks. The area was one of the most lush in Palestine, with an abundance of grassy fields and groves of trees. The city was also strategically located, standing as a sentinel over the plains in the area. For many years, a cave and spring there had been associated with the worship of Canaanite gods. Later, a shrine was built on the site and dedicated to the Greek nature gods. Herod the Great built a temple to Rome and Augustus in the town, and later Herod's son, Philip the tetrarch, refurbished the city and named it Caesarea Philippi. Jesus may have chosen this spot to ask His disciples who He was so He could draw a stark contrast between Himself and the pagan worship for which this area was famous.

In questioning the disciples about His identity, Jesus referred to Himself as the "Son of Man." This phrase was His most common self-description. He wanted to teach that, as the Messiah, He combined two Old Testament roles: Son of Man (Dan. 7:13-14) and Servant of the Lord (Isa. 52:13—53:12). Daniel described a Son of Man to whom God gives an everlasting kingdom, while Isaiah described a Servant of the Lord who suffers on behalf of others. Jesus knew that He must perform the role of the suffering Servant. But He also knew that eventually He would receive glory as the Son of Man.

At the heart of Jesus' reference to Himself as the Son of Man is the presence of divine authority. God the Father had chosen and commissioned His Son to bring about His plan of redemption, which included having the authority to forgive sins (Mark 2:10) and exercise lordship over the Sabbath (vs. 28). The Father also gave the Son of Man the authority to judge and the power to grant eternal life (John 5:27; 6:27). Jesus' redemptive mission as the Son of Man involved serving others and giving His life as a ransom for many (Mark 10:45). One day, the Son of Man will be seen sitting at the right hand of Almighty God (14:62). Indeed, the Savior will return in the clouds with great power and glory, accompanied by the holy angels (8:38; 13:26). Those who put their faith in the Son of Man (John 9:35) must be willing to endure the deprivation and derision He experienced during His earthly ministry (Matt. 8:20; 11:19).

B. Various Responses: vss. 14-16

They replied, "Some say John the Baptist; others say Elijah; and still others, Jeremiah or one of the prophets." "But what about you?" he asked. "Who do you say I am?" Simon Peter answered, "You are the Christ, the Son of the living God."

Jesus undoubtedly knew what the people were saying about Him, but He asked the question as a prelude to help the Twelve obtain a clearer understanding of His identity. The disciples reported a variety of opinions concerning who Jesus was. It seems that popular opinion stated that Jesus was one of the great figures of the past reincarnated, though there was no agreement on which great figure. Some thought He was John the Baptist, while others thought He was an earlier prophet, such as Elijah or Jeremiah (Matt. 16:14).

While mistaken about Jesus being a reincarnation, the people recognized correctly that Jesus was a prophet and that He stood in line with God's faithful servants of the past. If they had understood Him more fully, though, they would have known that He was someone totally new. People today, of course, are still uncertain about Jesus' true identity. Those who think of Him as a great reformer (like John the Baptist), a great miracle worker (like Elijah), or a great teacher (like some other Old Testament prophets) usually imagine they are holding Jesus in high esteem, when in reality they have misunderstood Him altogether. In short, Jesus did not receive a pleasing report. But He expected better from the Twelve. Thus, He put the question directly to them: "Who do you say I am?" (vs. 15). Peter responded (perhaps for the Twelve) with an affirmation of Jesus' identity that revealed greater insight than that of the people at large. Peter answered correctly, "You are the Christ" (vs. 16).

The title *Christ* comes from the Greek term *christos*, which means "anointed (with ointment or oil)." It is equivalent to *Messiah*, a word derived from the Hebrew term *mashiach*. The latter initially referred to persons installed in a special office, such as a king or priest. The anointing with oil implied that the Lord approved the person to undertake his or her divinely appointed role. Eventually, *mashiach* (and *christos*) came to designate God's royal agent, whom He would send to free Israel and restore the nation in righteousness. The Jewish hope for a messiah to deliver and purify the nation was defined mainly in political terms. Consequently, most of Jesus' contemporaries failed to recognize His true identity as the promised Messiah of Israel. In accordance with Old Testament prophecy, the Savior's mission included dying on the cross and rising from the dead (Luke 24:7, 44-47).

Matthew 16:16 relates that Peter also called Jesus the "Son of the living God." This phrase draws attention to the divine, exalted status of Jesus as the Messiah (Matt. 1:20-23; Luke 1:31-33; Acts 13:33; Rom. 1:3-4). When the Gospels refer to Him as the Son of God, the emphasis is on His unparalleled knowledge and saving work. The divine Son enjoyed intimate fellowship with the Father, obeyed the will of the Father, and experienced the Father's love, mercy, and blessings. In Peter's role as the spokesperson for the Twelve, he recognized Jesus as the true Messiah of Israel, even though He wasn't fulfilling popular expectations of the Savior as a political figure. Peter also understood that Jesus is more than just human; He is divine.

C. Jesus' Pronouncement of Blessing on Peter: vss. 17-20

Jesus replied, "Blessed are you, Simon son of Jonah, for this was not revealed to you by man, but by my Father in heaven. And I tell you that you are Peter, and on this rock I will build my church, and the gates of Hades will not overcome it. I will give you the keys of the kingdom of heaven; whatever you bind on earth will be bound in heaven, and whatever you loose on earth will be loosed in heaven." Then he warned his disciples not to tell anyone that he was the Christ.

"Simon" (Matt. 16:17) refers to Peter, a fisherman from Galilee. He was the son of Jonah (see John 1:42; 21:15-17) and one of the Twelve whom Jesus called to be His disciples (Matt. 4:18-20; Mark 1:16-17; Luke 5:1-11; John 1:40-42). Jesus said that Peter was "blessed" (Matt. 16:17); in other words, he was highly favored by God because his spiritual awareness did not come to him through any human agency or power, but from the heavenly Father. In light of Peter's blessing, Jesus commented on his name. The Savior made a play on words when He declared, "You are Peter, and on this rock I will build my church" (vs. 18). "Peter" translates the Greek word *petros*, which means "stone." "Rock" translates *petra*, which refers to a massive formation of bedrock. "Church" renders the Greek word *ekklesia*, which literally refers to those who are "called out." In verse 18, the term denotes the global community of Christians, while in 18:17 it refers to a local congregation of believers.

There are differing views concerning what Jesus meant by His statement in 16:18. One option is that Peter's confession is the "rock" upon which the church is built. A second option is that Jesus Himself is the "rock" (see Acts 4:11-12; 1 Cor. 3:11; Eph. 5:23; 1 Pet. 2:5-8). A third option is that Peter, as a representative and leader of the Twelve, is foundational to the church (see Eph. 2:20-21). Regardless of which view is preferred, there is no ambiguity to Jesus' declaration that the "gates of Hades" (Matt. 16:18) will not "overcome" His church. "Hades" (like "sheol," its Hebrew counterpart) is used to denote the place of the dead. The Greek verb translated "overcome" refers to one entity winning the victory over another entity. Through this figure of speech, Jesus was promising that not even the forces of evil and death will vanquish the community of the redeemed. More broadly speaking, while the apostles played a foundational role in the spiritual construction of the church, Jesus is the most important stone of the edifice. Also, those who affirm Jesus as the Messiah and trust in Him for salvation (as Peter did in his confession) represent the type of spiritually regenerate people on which the church is built. In turn, the Savior enables them to prevail against the forces of darkness.

In verse 19, the Lord promised to give the "keys of the kingdom of heaven" to Peter. In Jesus' day, keys were a symbol for authority and power. In this verse, "keys" probably refers to the exercise of spiritual authority in God's kingdom. The nature of this spiritual authority is elaborated upon in terms of binding and loosing. There would be a correspondence between binding and loosing on earth and binding and loosing in heaven. But what, exactly, is the binding and loosing? One possibility is that as Peter heralded the Gospel, he would play a part in determining who would not believe in Jesus (binding) and who would believe (loosing). Another possibility is that Peter would have authority in church discipline cases to determine whether a sinner had not repented (binding) or had repented (loosing). A third possibility is that Peter would have the authority to tell Christians what they could not do (binding) and what they could do (loosing).

The question of the meaning in verse 19 is complicated by uncertainty over the proper way to translate the verse. Some render it as the NIV does ("will be bound . . . will be loosed"), which might imply that God will ratify decisions made on earth. Others translate the verse as the NASB does: "Whatever you shall bind on earth shall have been bound in heaven, and whatever you shall loose on earth shall have been loosed in heaven." This rendering implies that decisions made on earth would be in keeping with decisions already made by God. The ideas of binding and loosing are referred to again in 18:15-18. That connection implies that Peter and the other disciples had the authority to confront sin among the members of the church. Put another way, God sanctioned the leaders of a congregation to discern (based on the teaching of Scripture) and declare who had repented of a sin that had been committed (and was therefore loosed) and who had not repented (and was still bound; see John 20:23). This observation suggests that the "keys" (Matt. 16:19) Jesus gave to Peter were also given to all other believers.

Jesus strictly warned Peter and the rest of the Twelve not to tell anyone that He was the Messiah (vs. 20). Why? Possibly because Jesus knew His followers needed additional time to learn more about Him before they could accurately declare the truth of His messiahship. Also, Jesus may have wanted to avoid drawing excessive attention to Himself at this time, the kind of attention that might make people think He would free them from the control of Rome. Furthermore, Jesus probably wanted to avoid intensifying the opposition of the religious leaders against Him, for doing so might lead to His arrest before the divinely appointed time. Should that happen, Jesus' enemies probably would have openly denounced Him as a heretic and tried to kill Him before He had intended.

II. THE PREDICTION OF JESUS: MATTHEW 16:21-23

A. Jesus' Foretelling of His Death and Resurrection: vs. 21

From that time on Jesus began to explain to his disciples that he must go to Jerusalem and suffer many things at the hands of the elders, chief priests and teachers of the law, and that he must be killed and on the third day be raised to life.

It's true that Jesus was the fulfillment of Old Testament prophecies concerning Israel's Savior. In addition, He was the suffering Servant—something His disciples did not yet understand. Jesus thus moved swiftly to tell them why He had come to this world. He came to die. This was Jesus' first specific teaching about His death. It was not a brief speech; rather, it gave particular details surrounding His crucifixion. In this regard, Jesus made five points about His future: (1) He would go to Jerusalem, (2) He would suffer, (3) He would be rejected by the religious leaders, (4) He would be executed by the authorites, and (5) He would rise from the dead (Matt. 16:21).

It's worth noting that three religious groups would be involved in Jesus' rejection and crucifixion: the elders, the chief priests, and the teachers of the law. The three groups comprised the Sanhedrin, namely, the Jewish supreme court. Although answerable to the Roman governor, the Sanhedrin of Jesus' day did possess power in dealing with Jewish affairs as well as complete control in dealing with religious matters. As Jesus foretold, the Council eventually rejected Him and sentenced Him to death. But the members apparently could not carry out that sentence without Roman authority. The implication is that the official religious and political establishment within Palestine would choose to have the Messiah executed.

B. Jesus' Response to Peter's Rebuke: vss. 22-23

Peter took him aside and began to rebuke him. "Never, Lord!" he said. "This shall never happen to you!" Jesus turned and said to Peter, "Get behind me, Satan! You are a stumbling block to me; you do not have in mind the things of God, but the things of men."

Peter was so shocked by Jesus' prediction of His suffering, rejection, and death, that the statement concerning His resurrection apparently meant nothing to the disciple. In Peter's mind, Jesus had violated all he understood about the mission of the Savior. Along with the majority of the Jews, Peter evidently was looking for a Messiah who would defeat Rome and establish Israel as the dominant power in the region (if not the entire world). As a result, Peter took upon himself the role of counselor. As Jesus talked openly about the future with His disciples, Peter took Him aside and "began to rebuke him" (Matt. 16:22). The Greek verb rendered "rebuke" means "to express strong disapproval of someone." In Peter's case, he was sternly censuring Jesus not to talk in the way He had.

The Greek phrase rendered "Never, Lord!" is more literally translated "[God be] merciful to you." It's as if Peter was wishing that the Father, in His mercy, would spare His Son from having to endure the Crucifixion. In contemporary English, we might say, "Heaven forbid, Lord!" Peter also declared that God would never let anything as horrible as this happen to the Messiah, especially since the disciple imagined that a glorious, earthly reign awaited his Master. It's amazing that, despite Peter's recent confession, he now utterly failed to understand that it was necessary for Jesus to suffer and die.

As Peter was in the process of chastising Jesus, the Savior did an amazing thing. He turned and declared that Peter's words were satanic. In fact, Peter was behaving as Jesus' adversary. Thus, Jesus referred to him harshly as "Satan" (vs. 23).

Expressed differently, Satan was using Peter to tempt Jesus to abandon the Father's will. Peter's ideas about the career of the Messiah were worldly, not godly. Indeed, Peter's words echoed the same kind of temptation Satan used in the wilderness to try to get Jesus to stumble (4:1-11). Peter had not become Satan; but by Peter's words, he had become an unknowing agent of Satan. Later, Peter warned his readers of the devil's tactics in attempting to devour his prey (1 Pet. 5:4).

Discussion Questions

1. What popular views existed concerning Jesus' identity?
2. What view of Jesus' identity did His disciples voice?
3. Why was it necessary for Jesus to die?
4. Why did Peter rebuke Jesus for predicting His death?
5. What did Jesus imply by referring to Peter as Satan?

Contemporary Application

Many people see Jesus as a wise philosopher, a social revolutionary, or a kind healer, but their knowledge makes no difference in the way they live. They neither love the Lord nor serve Him. In fact, they don't really see Jesus clearly. We will have difficulty understanding Jesus' teachings—especially about His suffering messiahship and heavenly glory—if we are not committed to obeying Him.

Have we strengthened our commitment to Jesus so we can see Him more clearly and love Him more dearly? We may have known about Jesus since we were young children, but do we recognize Him as the Son of God so we can follow Him more nearly? Being committed to Jesus does not mean being devoted to Him occasionally. It does not come and go like the wind. No, full commitment affects every phase of our lives. Such commitment to Jesus illumines His teachings more and more, day by day.

As we become more committed to Jesus, we desire to spend more time studying God's Word, are more attentive when God's Word is taught, and discuss God's Word with family and friends. The more interaction we have with God's Word, the more we understand Jesus' teachings. In addition, our commitment to Jesus deepens, and our experiences make Jesus' teachings more clear. We gain new God-given insights into the same teachings.

Oswald Chambers said, "Our Lord's making of a disciple is supernatural. He does not build on any natural capacity at all. God does not ask us to do the things that are naturally easy to us. He only asks us to do the things we are perfectly fitted to do by His grace." In short, we can commit to knowing and following the Lord Jesus, but not by trusting in ourselves to keep that commitment. We need His grace. The apostle Paul had this truth in mind when he noted in Philippians 2:13 that God is working in us, giving us both the desire to obey Him and the power to do what pleases Him.

Doers of the Word

DEVOTIONAL READING

Psalm 92:1-8

DAILY BIBLE READINGS

Monday July 28
James 1:1-4 The Full Effect of Endurance

Tuesday July 29
James 1:5-8 Ask in Faith

Wednesday July 30
James 1:9-11 How to Boast

Thursday July 31
James 1:12-15 Endure Temptation

Friday August 1
James 1:16-21 Everything Is from God

Saturday August 2
James 1:22-27 Blessed in Doing

Sunday August 3
Psalm 92:1-8 How Great Are Your Works

Scripture

Background Scripture: *James 1*
Scripture Lesson: *James 1:17-27*
Key Verse: *Do not merely listen to the word, and so deceive yourselves. Do what it says.* James 1:22.
Scripture Lesson for Children: *James 1:19-25*
Key Verse for Children: *Do not merely listen to the word, and so deceive yourselves. Do what it says.* James 1:22.

Lesson Aim

To explore the implications of heeding God's Word.

Lesson Setting

Time: *The early 60s of the first century* A.D.
Place: *Jerusalem*

Lesson Outline

Doers of the Word

   I. Recognizing God as Creator and Redeemer: James 1:17-18
     A. *God as Creator: vs. 17*
     B. *God as Redeemer: vs. 18*
  II. Heeding God's Word: James 1:19-27
     A. *Managing Our Anger: vss. 19-21*
     B. *Putting Scripture into Practice: vss. 22-25*
     C. *Striving for Purity and Compassion: vss. 26-27*

Introduction for Adults

Topic: *Committed Living*

When we walk into our health clubs, we check our file folders. After finishing our workouts, we mark what we have done. We want to see how we measure up to our trainer's expectations.

The Letter of James is like that workout checklist. The epistle is our spiritual trainer, pushing us to new levels of strength and competence. If we want to see how we are doing as Christians, we go to the Letter of James. The author tells us exactly what to do and what not to do to be committed in living for Christ.

The health club's workout checklist is meant for living people. It won't do the dead any good. It's too late for them. In a similar way, the author of James wanted to be sure his readers were alive spiritually. His list is a life-and-death list. Read it to find out how you stand.

Introduction for Youth

Topic: *Right on Living*

One of life's cruelest lessons is that words can be meaningless. Parents say they love their kids, but fail to spend time with them. Coaches promise to give you an opportunity to play football, but forget you are warming the bench. Conductors promise you a solo part, but you never get it. "I'll help you," your teacher declares, but disappears. "I love you," your girlfriend or boyfriend gushes, and then goes out with someone else

In many cases, that's what our words mean to God. We say we believe in Him. We say that Jesus is our Savior. But we find it hard to do what Jesus wants us to do. It's painfully hard to keep our word. The Letter of James tells us to stop being phonies. If we really are alive in Christ, we will do what He says, no matter how risky or embarrassing.

Concepts for Children

Topic: *Obey God's Word*

1. It is better to listen and learn before we talk.
2. When we become angry as we talk with one another, we displease God.
3. When God's truth is firmly planted in us, we are better able to obey God.
4. God blesses those who obey His Word.
5. We can encourage others to obey God's Word.

Lesson Commentary

I. RECOGNIZING GOD AS CREATOR AND REDEEMER: JAMES 1:17-18

A. God as Creator: vs. 17

Every good and perfect gift is from above, coming down from the Father of the heavenly lights, who does not change like shifting shadows.

After giving his name, James identified himself only by the title of "servant" (Jas. 1:1). He did not refer to his apostolic authority or to his sibling relationship with Jesus. As God's bond servant, James was acknowledging that he had voluntarily submitted himself to the Lord's service. This written correspondence was intended for Jewish believers scattered throughout the nations of the Mediterranean world. James readily identified with the plight of these people when he greeted them as "my brothers" (vs. 2).

Verse 3 says that believers should it "consider it pure joy" when they face hardships. James was not telling his readers that trials bring joy in a person's life. Instead, he meant that we are to cultivate a joyful attitude in the midst of life's difficult times. Trials serve as tests of our faith by which we develop patience. Spiritual maturity is the result of responding properly to this testing. This spiritual maturation makes us fit to do God's work in the world. In verse 12, James said that God blesses those who patiently endure afflictions. In turn, He is glorified when we persevere under trials. James did not say "if" but "when" we face temptations. Nevertheless, God promises to reward with an eternal "crown of life" those who love and serve Him despite life's obstacles.

Evidently, many of these early Christians blamed God for their troubles. James sternly rebuked this idea as false. God's divine and absolute goodness as the sovereign Lord renders evil powerless before Him. Thus, He is never tempted to do wrong; and because He acts in accordance with His holy nature, He never tempts anyone else (vs. 13). The blame for temptation that produces sin rests squarely upon the evildoer's own shoulders (vs. 14). Notice that James did not blame the devil here. If Satan and his cohorts didn't exist or were rendered powerless, evil could still exist in the world. First and foremost, temptation comes from within. James used a fishing metaphor when he referred to a person being "dragged away and enticed." Like a glimmering lure that attracts a fish from the deep, dark waters, the inner desire to sin entices the person to do what he or she knows is wrong. Sin results when a person is snared by a trap built and baited by his or her own hand.

James shifted from a fishing metaphor to that of the reproductive cycle. The process leading to sin begins with an enticement to transgress. If the temptation is entertained, then those evil desires conceive and the embryo of sin develops. After the sin is born, it matures and then produces its own terrible offspring—physical and spiritual death (vs. 15). In light of this, James admonished his readers not be deluded by the false notion that God is the source of temptation (vs. 16). Instead,

He is the origin of "every good and perfect gift" (vs. 17). Without question, the needs sin promises to fulfill can be met, without guilt, by the provisions God sends. This same generous God is the Father, or sovereign Creator, of the celestial lights (namely, the sun, moon, and stars). Since He was able to create these magnificent sources of illumination and life, surely He can provide every other good gift. But unlike the variations of light and darkness produced by those heavenly bodies, God's virtue and goodness never fluctuate. The same power the unchanging Lord demonstrated at Creation is available to believers today to enable them to resist enticements and bear fruit for His glory.

B. God as Redeemer: vs. 18

He chose to give us birth through the word of truth, that we might be a kind of firstfruits of all he created.

Our Creator has provided redemption through the Lord Jesus. Indeed, by God's sovereign plan, He chooses to give us spiritual birth through the message of truth (Jas. 1:18). First Peter 1:23 reveals that we are spiritually reborn, not from perishable but from imperishable seed, namely, by means of the "living and enduring word of God." Through the proclamation of the Good News about Christ, the power of God works to save everyone who believes (Rom. 1:16). The Spirit inwardly recreates our fallen human nature (John 3:5-8) so that we become a kind of "firstfruits" (Jas. 1:18) of God's redemptive plan for all of creation (see 1 Cor. 15:20).

In Old Testament times, the firstfruits were both the initial and best portion of the entire harvest (Exod. 23:19; 34:26; Lev. 23:9-14; Ezek. 44:30). Metaphorically speaking, the redeemed are God's most prized possessions in all creation. They also are the guarantee of God's plan to liberate the entire creation at the second advent of Christ (Rom. 8:19-21; Col. 1:20). The regeneration of believing hearts gives a snapshot picture of what the new heavens and the new earth will be like when touched by the redeeming hand of God.

II. HEEDING GOD'S WORD: JAMES 1:19-27

A. Managing Our Anger: vss. 19-21

My dear brothers, take note of this: Everyone should be quick to listen, slow to speak and slow to become angry, for man's anger does not bring about the righteous life that God desires. Therefore, get rid of all moral filth and the evil that is so prevalent and humbly accept the word planted in you, which can save you.

James instructed his fellow believers that even in the midst of trials, they should be quick to listen and slow to speak (Jas. 1:19). In the middle of a heated exchange, it is natural for us to begin forming our response to the other person even while he or she is still talking. Consequently, we tune out what this person is really saying. Patience and deference in speech takes concentrated effort, but in the long run pays great dividends in relationships. We usually walk away from such conversations feeling as if we've been understood and appreciated.

James also exhorted his readers to be slow to get angry. Human anger is a volatile emotion that can easily get out of control, especially in tense situations. When inappropriate forms of anger erupt, whether toward evildoers or unwanted circumstances, it does not accomplish God's "righteousness" (vs. 20). This means the aftermath of human anger falls short of God's righteous moral standard, does not reflect the upright standing He gives believers in Christ, does not result in any of the good things God wants done, and is contrary to the equity and justice He will establish in His future eternal kingdom. In short, human anger does not produce the righteousness God desires, regardless of its form.

For many Christians, the concept of righteousness might seem too abstract to understand. This difficulty is decreased as they grow in their appreciation of what it means to live in a holy, or morally pure, manner. People are considered righteous when their personal behaviors are in harmony with God's will as it is revealed in Scripture. The righteous person voluntarily serves the Lord (Mal. 3:18), takes delight in Him (Ps. 33:1), and gives thanks to Him for His mercy and love (140:13). The righteous are blessed by God (5:12) and upheld by Him (37:17). The righteous may experience hardships and trials in life, but God promises to help them through the difficulty (Ps. 34:19).

No matter how severe the believers' afflictions might be, the Lord will never forsake them (37:25) or allow them to fall (55:22). The prospect for the righteous is joy (Prov. 10:28) and the way of the Lord is their strength, or refuge (vs. 29). The Lord promises to be with them in their darkest moments (11:8) and to be a refuge for them in death (14:32). In summary, James was urging his readers to leave whatever sinful path they might have been on, and to follow the path of uprightness. Otherwise, they would be sinning by refusing to do what they knew to be "good" (Jas. 4:17). Here we see that sins of omission (neglecting to do what is right) are just as inappropriate as sins of commission (opting to do what is wrong).

Inappropriate anger is just one example of immoral behavior and evil excess that arise when believers follow the desires of their sinful nature (see Gal. 5:19-21). James told his readers to set aside such vices. The phrase "to get rid of" (Jas. 1:21) was often used of casting off burdensome clothing. Only a humble heart that acknowledges its own sinfulness and God's holiness is ready to accept and fully appropriate the message of His saving truth. It is like a seed that the Lord has planted deep in the soil of our hearts. If we allow the Good News to take root and grow, we will thrive spiritually and experience the fullness of our redemption in the Lord Jesus.

B. Putting Scripture into Practice: vss. 22-25

Do not merely listen to the word, and so deceive yourselves. Do what it says. Anyone who listens to the word but does not do what it says is like a man who looks at his face in a mirror and, after looking at himself, goes away and immediately forgets what he looks like. But the man who looks intently into the perfect law that gives freedom, and continues to do this, not forgetting what he has heard, but doing it—he will be blessed in what he does.

James told his readers that passively listening to God's Word was not enough to promote spiritual growth. It was just as important for them to obediently act upon what it says (Jas. 1:22). To hear the Good News without implementing its teachings is nothing but self-deception. Indeed, the devil's primary weapon against Christians is deceit. He often comes disguised as an angel of light (2 Cor. 11:14) and tries to lure us away from God with whatever feels good. James 4:4 reminds us that friendship with the world (namely, secular human society and culture under the guidance and control of Satan) is actually enmity, or antagonism, toward God.

At the close of the Sermon on the Mount, Jesus compared those who heeded His Word with wise builders who built their houses on firm foundations (Matt. 7:24-27). He later rebuked the Pharisees and called them hypocrites because even though they honored Him with their lips, their hearts were far from Him (15:8). Finally, Paul warned against making a show of being religious, but rejecting the power of the Lord that alone could enable people to become more godly (2 Tim. 3:5). From these verses we see that action always makes our faith authentic and believable.

Those who hear but do not heed the Gospel are like people who observe what they look like in a mirror, walk away, and quickly forget the image they saw (Jas. 1:23-24). In Bible times, a typical mirror was made of polished metal (such as copper, bronze, silver, or gold). Due to imperfections on the surfaces of these mirrors, they gave a distorted image of what they were reflecting. James exhorted his readers to look carefully into and fix their attention on the "perfect law that gives freedom" (vs. 25). They were to live out, not forget, what the law of liberty taught. The sustained and thoughtful study of God's Word would bring them true liberty, spiritual vitality, and abundant blessing in whatever they undertook.

"Law" translates the Greek noun *nomos*. In some contexts, it refers to a formalized set of rules that prescribe what people must do. These can range from ordinances and commands to customs and traditions sanctioned by society. In the New Testament, *nomos* usually refers to the Pentateuch (the first five books of Moses), but it can also denote the Old Testament as a whole. While *nomos* primarily refers to that which regulates behavior, it can also denote the promise of God (see Luke 24:44). Additionally, *nomos* refers to a word of instruction that is divine, not human, in origin and that indicates the path of righteousness and blessing.

James 1:25 specifically uses *nomos* to denote the moral and ethical teachings of the Old Testament, especially as expressed in the Ten Commandments (2:10-11; see Ps. 19:7). This is the same law that Jesus said He came to fulfill, not abolish (Matt. 5:17), and which finds its culmination in Him (Rom. 10:4). He perfectly obeyed the law and brought to pass its types and prophecies. Also, in Him, the law finds its significance and continuity. Through the Savior's ministry of teaching and His redemptive work on the cross, those who are united to Him by faith are able to understand and apply the precepts of Scripture, as expressed in the law.

Before trusting in Christ, believers were slaves to sin (John 8:34). God used the law to make them aware of their transgressions and their need for a Savior (Gal. 3:19-24). Thus, rather than being an agent of sin, the law gives perfect expression to God's holiness, righteousness, and goodness (Rom. 7:7-12). It is true that believers are no longer under the condemnation of the law (Rom. 6:14; 7:4, 6; 1 Cor. 9:20; Gal. 2:15-19; 3:25). Nevertheless, the law continues to disclose whether believers are living for God as much as they should. They can do so when they allow the Spirit, rather than the sinful nature, to control them (Rom. 8:4). Indeed, believers who are genuinely led by the Spirit and manifest the love of Christ fulfill the intent of the law (13:9-10). For them, heeding the precepts embodied in the law results in spiritual freedom, not bondage (Jas. 1:25; 2:12).

C. Striving for Purity and Compassion: vss. 26-27

If anyone considers himself religious and yet does not keep a tight rein on his tongue, he deceives himself and his religion is worthless. Religion that God our Father accepts as pure and faultless is this: to look after orphans and widows in their distress and to keep oneself from being polluted by the world.

James continued the theme of active Christianity with a look at the meaning of true religion. The Greek word translated "religious" (Jas. 1:26) denotes the practice of external rituals and observances of a spiritual tradition, such as attendance at worship, prayer, fasting, and giving to the poor. Merely doing these things does not in itself constitute true religion. Those who are genuinely pious demonstrate their faith by controlling what they say. On the other hand, failure to bridle the tongue betrays the self-deception in those who regard themselves as religious and exposes a form of spirituality that has no eternal value.

Verse 27 shifts the focus from outward observances to service for others, particularly "orphans and widows." In Scripture, widows, orphans, and aliens are usually depicted as the most helpless among people. Often, they had none but God as their patron and protector (see Exod. 22:22-23; Deut. 10:18; Isa. 1:17). Moreover, in Bible times, there was no social safety net to catch the dispossessed and homeless when their source of support was suddenly gone. Widows, orphans, and foreigners were frequently reduced to begging, especially if there was no friend, relative, or benefactor to care for them (see Gen. 38:11; Ruth 1:8).

Often, the disadvantaged were ignored by their neighbors, but Job strongly rebuked those who "sent widows away empty-handed and broke the strength of the fatherless" (Job 22:9). The psalmist, however, reminded widows and orphans that God cared for them (see Ps. 146:9). And the law made provision for widows to glean grapes, grain, and olives from the bounty of others (see Deut. 14:28-29; 24:19-21). In the end, according to Malachi 3:5, God's judgment will include those "who oppress the widows and the fatherless, and deprive aliens of justice."

James 1:27 reflects this biblical perspective by focusing attention on orphans and widows who live in a state of distress. The writer maintained that clean and undefiled religion is demonstrated, not just in rituals and observances, but in upright conduct and righteous character. Examples of this type of behavior include caring for those in anguish and keeping oneself clean in a morally polluted world. The writer's intention in this passage was not to give a formal definition of religion. Rather, his aim was to draw a contrast between religion as mere ritualistic observance and faith in action that pleases God. Religion that demonstrates genuine spirituality and Christian maturity is an active faith motivated by love.

Discussion Questions

1. In what sense does God never change?
2. In what sense are believers a kind of firstfruits of all God has created?
3. In what way is the Word that is planted within us able to save us?
4. In what sense is God's law perfect and a source of freedom?
5. What sort of religion does God accept as pure and faultless?

Contemporary Application

By heeding God's Word, Christians are to grow in grace. Spiritually mature persons are not born that way; neither do these individuals reach a maturity level overnight. Growth necessitates that we endure over a period of time and overcome whatever obstacles stand in our way. Growth (both physical and spiritual) also requires that we be faithful to our task. Children must regularly eat balanced and healthy meals, exercise, and get proper amounts of sleep, if they are to grow into healthy adults. Likewise, we must daily engage in prayer, Bible study, and Christian fellowship to grow in Christ.

Heeding God's Word requires that we are to be mindful of how we talk to one another. The manner in which we speak to someone can draw or repel him or her from wanting to serve the Lord Jesus. Is our manner of conversation kind? Do we exemplify the spirit of Christian love? It is surprising what a smile or a simple "hello" can do to the disposition of a person. Paul tells us to be careful how we talk, to guard against talk that tears others down, and to use our words to build up other people (Eph. 4:29).

Furthermore, we are to actively concern ourselves with helping those who are less fortunate than we. True worship (what James calls pure religion) goes beyond the four walls of the church building. Who is hungry, homeless, and sick in our community? Jesus says what when we have ministered to these sorts of individuals, regardless of how unimportant they might seem, we have also done so for Him (Matt. 25:40). Our Lord was concerned with ministering to the total person. When we neglect the physical needs of those around us, our witness is not complete. God calls us to prayerfully and faithfully seek out these persons and minister to their hurts.

Impartial Disciples

Scripture

Background Scripture: *James 2*

Scripture Lesson: *James 2:1-13*

Key Verse: *Has not God chosen those who are poor in the eyes of the world to be rich in faith.* James 2:5.

Scripture Lesson for Children: *James 2:1-9*

Key Verse for Children: *"Love your neighbor as yourself."* James 2:8.

Lesson Aim

To agree to treat all people respectfully and justly, especially the poor.

Lesson Setting

Time: *The early 60s of the first century* A.D.

Place: *Jerusalem*

Lesson Outline

Impartial Disciples

  I. The Believer and Favoritism: James 2:1-7
     A. *Favoritism Prohibited: vs. 1*
     B. *Discrimination Illustrated: vss. 2-4*
     C. *God's Blessing on the Poor: vs. 5*
     D. *Excesses of the Rich: vss. 6-7*
  II. The Believer and the Law: James 2:8-13
     A. *Keeping the Law: vs. 8*
     B. *Breaking the Law: vss. 9-11*
     C. *Respecting the Law: vss. 12-13*

Introduction for Adults

Topic: *Honoring All People*

How many poor people do you know personally? Unfortunately, as adults grow older, our circle of friends often becomes more homogeneous. It becomes more difficult to bridge our socioeconomic strata. When asked about the poor, many adults respond with "Hey, it's not my fault. . . . They aren't really trying hard enough. . . . I could get a job if I were them. . . . Let them pull themselves up by their own bootstraps. . . . We're just weakening them by helping them all the time."

Do any of those comments sound familiar? Many of us think that way even if we haven't made the overt statements. Adults also use an interesting criterion to establish exactly who is "poor." Ask your students what is their definition of "poor." Adults may find that those just above the poverty line are ignored or treated worse than those below it. Regardless of the social and economic circumstances of the people we encounter, the Letter of James summons us to honor them unconditionally with the kindness, compassion, and respect that Christ offers.

Introduction for Youth

Topic: *No Bench? Don't Judge!*

Have you ever tried to remove a speck of dirt or a tiny insect from your eye by yourself? It's hard because you can't see well enough to do it. Jesus said that often some things in our lives blur our spiritual vision. Without clear vision, we cannot give help to others, we cannot choose the right moral path, and we cannot discern what is true from what is false.

Jesus made it clear that blurry spiritual vision is caused by pride, self-righteousness, hypocrisy, and a failure to love others. The result can be the kind of judgmental attitude that James condemned in his letter. How important it is to have our spiritual eyes free of obstructions.

Sin clouds our judgment and keeps us from following God's ways. The first step in obtaining clearer spiritual vision is to confess our sin. When we come to Jesus in repentance and faith, we are asking Him to give us clearer vision. The moment we make this our prayer request, our relationships with others will improve.

Concepts for Children

Topic: *Don't Play Favorites*

1. Playing favorites goes against the teachings of Jesus.
2. Because God created all people, everyone deserves to be treated with kindness and fairness.
3. When we learn to love God, we will also be able to love all kinds of people.
4. Playing favorites results from evil thoughts and selfish motives.
5. God is pleased when we refuse to play favorites.

Lesson Commentary

I. THE BELIEVER AND FAVORITISM: JAMES 2:1-7

A. Favoritism Prohibited: vs. 1

My brothers, as believers in our glorious Lord Jesus Christ, don't show favoritism.

In addressing his friends in the faith, the author literally referred to the Savior as "our Lord Jesus Christ of glory" (Jas. 2:1). The focus is on Jesus having the divine attribute of glory. The latter refers to the indescribable majesty and splendor of God (Isa. 6:3), as well as His moral perfection, especially in connection with His righteousness (Rom. 3:23). Concerning the readership of James, some believers were guilty of showing favoritism and partiality toward the wealthy among them (2:1). The author made it clear that all forms of prejudice had to stop. The construction of the original Greek sentence, and the writer's accusation in verse 6, indicates that this discrimination had been an ongoing problem.

Long ago, God set the pattern for showing no prejudice. The Mosaic law charged its judges to be impartial in the decisions they made on behalf of rich and poor alike (Deut. 1:17). In the New Testament, the Jewish leaders accused Jesus of many things, but playing favorites was not one of them (Matt. 22:16; Mark 12:14; Luke 20:21). Still, the idea that God does not favor Jews over Gentiles stunned Peter at the home of Cornelius (Acts 10:34). That was a difficult concept for the members of the early church, steeped as they were in their Jewish traditions, which kept a wide gulf between Jew and Gentile. Nonetheless, the theme that God shows no favoritism is repeated throughout the New Testament (Rom. 2:11; Eph. 6:9; Col. 3:25; 1 Pet. 1:17).

B. Discrimination Illustrated: vss. 2-4

Suppose a man comes into your meeting wearing a gold ring and fine clothes, and a poor man in shabby clothes also comes in. If you show special attention to the man wearing fine clothes and say, "Here's a good seat for you," but say to the poor man, "You stand there" or "Sit on the floor by my feet," have you not discriminated among yourselves and become judges with evil thoughts?

The scene that follows James 2:1 serves as a sermon illustration to drive home a point. The author asked his readers to imagine two people who visited the Christian "meeting" (vs. 2). This term renders the Greek noun *synagogue*, which originally referred to a Jewish place of worship. In this verse, it denotes a gathering of the church, possibly in a home or even in a synagogue (which is where some early Christians may have met). One person at the assembly was wealthy, for he was well dressed and wearing gold jewelry. In those days, it was a common practice to wear gold rings as a sign of economic success (see Luke 15:22) and high social status (such as being a politician or an important official). The other person in filthy, old rags was poor.

The seating arrangement at gatherings indicated the honor and respect extended to those present. For example, imagine the hypothetical congregation giving special attention and a good seat to the rich person. Meanwhile, the impoverished beggar had only two options: either remain standing or be seated in the lowliest spot in the house, namely, out of sight on the floor (Jas. 2:3). Perhaps the author knew about such a situation taking place among his readers. In any case, James labeled this behavior as discrimination, and it showed that the judgments being made were guided by evil motives (vs. 4). In brief, it was unjust to say that some people (such as the rich) were better than others (such as the poor).

The congregants James described were not impartial judges but biased individuals motivated by an inappropriate desire for human approval or economic gain. The author taught that acceptance and fellowship among Christians should be without regard for anyone's social or economic status. We must also be careful not to discriminate on the basis of preferred clothing styles, hair length, or musical tastes. Quite often, how we relate to a person is determined by our perception of what this person can or cannot do for us. Since God is impartial to any racial, social, or economic class, those who bear the name "Christian" should also be equitable and fair. In all respects, the ground is level at the foot of the Cross.

C. God's Blessing on the Poor: vs. 5

Listen, my dear brothers: Has not God chosen those who are poor in the eyes of the world to be rich in faith and to inherit the kingdom he promised those who love him?

According to James 1:9, the poor Christian should be proud of his or her high position in Christ. This is because all believers, regardless of their material means, are joint heirs with Christ in His coming Kingdom. The believing poor understand that their self-worth is dependent upon their position in Christ, not their place on an economic ladder. Rich believers can also be glad in trials because difficult circumstances have a way of putting wealth in proper perspective (vs. 10). Social prominence and monetary affluence are compared to a wildflower in the searing heat of the sun. Every so often in Israel, a powerful hot wind called the sirocco suddenly comes out of nowhere and scorches all the vegetation in its path. Just as plants can be destroyed by this wind, so too the prominence brought by riches can be suddenly lost. Even if a person's wealth lasts a lifetime, he or she eventually dies. The rich, not necessarily their wealth, fades away in the end. Indeed, mortality has a way of leveling the spiritual playing field between rich and poor.

James 2:5-7 returns to the theme of God blessing the poor. The author asked several pointed questions to show why all forms of prejudice are morally wrong and make no sense. Against the backdrop of the first question is the faulty assumption that the presence of great wealth in one's life is evidence of God's approval. Oppositely, those who are impoverished supposedly are languishing under the searing gaze of God's disapproval. Verse 5 shatters these mistaken notions by maintaining that God has deliberately chosen the poor of the world to be rich in faith.

They also are the ones who will inherit the divine kingdom.

These truths mirror Jesus' declaration in Luke 6:20, where He revealed that God will bless the righteous poor by giving them His Kingdom. Scripture teaches that God has extended His free gift of salvation to people of all economic classes. The poor, however, tend to be more aware of their need for God. Also, the security often associated with wealth is a spiritual barrier that the poor don't have to overcome. Consider Proverbs 30:8-9, where Agur prayed that God would not make him excessively rich lest he be tempted to abandon his faith for material gain. There's also the rich young ruler, who rejected Jesus' invitation to follow Him because the young man's security was too wrapped up in his wealth. After the rich man left, Jesus said that it is easier for a camel to go through the eye of a needle than for the wealthy to enter the kingdom of God (see Matt. 19:24).

D. Excesses of the Rich: vss. 6-7

But you have insulted the poor. Is it not the rich who are exploiting you? Are they not the ones who are dragging you into court? Are they not the ones who are slandering the noble name of him to whom you belong?

In the early years of the church, the Gospel was primarily spread throughout the lower classes in the Roman Empire. Tragically, these were the very ones the self-appointed judges had dishonored and disdained. It was even more incongruous to favor the wealthy, for they had exploited and persecuted Christians (Jas. 2:6). The oppression of the rich involved using the court system to intimidate and harass believers. The wealthy had also spoken disrespectfully and irreverently of the noble name of the glorious Messiah (vs. 7). "Of him to whom you belong" is more literally rendered "which has been called upon you." Some think this phrase refers to the time when new converts were baptized and affirmed their devotion to Christ (see Matt. 28:19; Acts 2:28; 8:16, 36-38; 16:30-33). During the church ritual, participants confessed their faith in the Savior. Then, the leaders of the congregation invoked the honorable name of the Lord Jesus over these believers to signify His ownership of them as His people (see 2 Chron. 7:14; Isa. 63:19; Jer. 14:9; 15:16; Dan. 9:19; Amos 9:12; Acts 15:17).

II. THE BELIEVER AND THE LAW: JAMES 2:8-13

A. Keeping the Law: vs. 8

If you really keep the royal law found in Scripture, "Love your neighbor as yourself," you are doing right.

Within both Judaism and Christianity, the Ten Commandments (as found in Exod. 20:1-12 and Deut. 5:6-21) hold a premier status. Many consider them to be the moral law, or the basic list of God's universal ethical norms for proper human conduct. Some also think the Ten Commandments are the theological foundation for all other ordinances and directives in Scripture. During the first century A.D., specialists in Judaism debated which of these many commandments was the greatest. When an expert in the interpretation of the Mosaic law asked Jesus for His opinion, the Savior declared that loving God with all one's heart, soul, and mind was the foremost commandment (Matt. 22:39; see Deut. 6:5). The second premier directive was to love one's neighbor as oneself (Matt. 22:40; see Lev. 19:18). Jesus noted that the entire Old Testament was based on these two commands.

In a similar vein, Paul asserted that every directive recorded in Scripture was summed up in the command to love others as much as we love ourselves (Rom. 13:9). Verse 10 states that when we make every effort to treat others with the sensitivity and compassion of Christ, we do what is prescribed in the law. In short, love is the essence and fulfillment of the law. The apostle repeated the same truth in Galatians 5:14, when he wrote that believers, by loving and serving others, satisfied what the law required. Expressed differently, God's people are closest to pleasing Him when they are unconditional and unreserved in their compassion and kindness toward others.

The directive recorded Leviticus 19:18 is the supreme commandment in terms of defining how people should treat one another. This dictum is also royal, for among all the commandments given by God (who is the sovereign King of the universe), it sums up the entirety of the law. James 2:8 builds on this truth by stressing that the royal law will become the guiding principle in the future messianic kingdom. The author observed that believers are doing well when they love others as much as they love themselves. The point is that they cannot heed the most important directive in Scripture and discriminate against others at the same time.

B. Breaking the Law: vss. 9-11

But if you show favoritism, you sin and are convicted by the law as lawbreakers. For whoever keeps the whole law and yet stumbles at just one point is guilty of breaking all of it. For he who said, "Do not commit adultery," also said, "Do not murder." If you do not commit adultery but do commit murder, you have become a lawbreaker.

In the New Testament, "law" (Jas. 2:9) is often used to refer to the Lord's commands, which His people are to obey. "Law" can also denote a principle by which an individual's conduct is governed (Rom. 3:27; 7:23). Both testaments of Scripture are one unified expression, given by one Lawgiver. This means believers cannot make exceptions or subtract the commands they do not like. Against the backdrop of God's infinitely perfect moral standard (Rom. 3:23), the person who observes every divine law except for one, is still liable for violating them all (Jas. 2:10). The sobering reality is that everyone fails to heed the whole law (Rom. 3:9-18), which is why people must depend on the righteousness of the Lord Jesus in order to be saved (vs. 24).

James set up a clear contrast between treating others the way we would like to be treated and showing favoritism toward somebody for any reason (Jas. 2:9). Doing the first pleases God, while doing the second is sin. Accordingly, failing to observe the royal law—the most liberating, relationship-building command God ever gave—makes one a lawbreaker. Perhaps James thought that some among his readers would look upon showing favoritism as more a social convention than as sin. How, they might ask, could such a custom compare to sins like adultery and murder (vs. 11)? The answer James provided is clear and direct. If we transgress any part of the law, we are guilty of breaking all of it (vs. 10). To better understand this concept, imagine a balloon with all the commands of God written upon it. Next, imagine trying to cut out one of the commands with a razor blade without affecting the others. James used the weighty sins of adultery and murder to explain that selective obedience to the provisions of the law was absurd. The author would scoff at the popular notion that certain iniquities won't affect our relationship with God because they are less serious than others.

C. Respecting the Law: vss. 12-13

Speak and act as those who are going to be judged by the law that gives freedom, because judgment without mercy will be shown to anyone who has not been merciful. Mercy triumphs over judgment!

The author seems to have associated obedience to the law with fellowship with God, the one who gave the law. From this perspective, obedience to the precepts of the law is a display of faith and springs from love. Disobedience to God's law, on the other hand, is a breach of faith that disrupts fellowship with God, the Lawgiver. In James 2:12, the author placed an equally strong emphasis on talking and acting as if one is going to be judged by the liberating law of God. There is also an emphasis in the original language to make this behavior a matter of habit. Because of the wise counsel contained in God's law, James could say that it gives spiritual freedom (see 1:25)—but only if it is respected and obeyed. Disobedience results in bondage and restricted living.

According to 2:13, the believer who has been merciful will be shown mercy when his or her character flaws and weaknesses are exposed on the final day. In contrast, those who have shown little mercy to others will receive little themselves. Furthermore, the believer who has demonstrated mercy to others will have nothing to fear at the time of divine assessment, for the mercy shown to him or her will triumph over that judgment (see 1 John 4:17). As Jesus' followers strive to become more merciful, there is hope. The liberating power of Christ working within them makes it possible for them to obey God more fully and completely.

In addition to James 2:12-13, the writings of Paul teach that a future day of evaluation awaits believers. Sometime after Jesus' return, He will preside over the judgment (1 Cor. 4:5). In relation to believers, the issue at the Judgment Seat of Christ will not be our spiritual status (a determination of whether we are saved or lost), but rather the bestowal of rewards (see 2 Cor. 5:10). All that a believer has thought and done will be scrutinized at that time. Jesus' bestowal of rewards will be conducted in a fair and impartial manner. Whatever was done contrary to God's wishes will be regarded as worthless and will not be rewarded. Whatever was accomplished through the power of the Holy Spirit will be regarded as worthy of praise and will be rewarded (see 1 Cor. 3:10-15). Clearly, one of the qualities assessed in this judgment is the degree of mercy shown by the Christian.

Discussion Questions

1. What does it mean to show favoritism?
2. What example did James describe to illustrate what he meant by showing favoritism?
3. Why would God chose the poor of this world to be rich in faith?
4. Why is it illogical to favor the rich over the poor?
5. How is possible that one transgression of God's law makes one guilty of violating all of it?

Contemporary Application

The church gathering in this week's passage reflected the values of the world: economic accumulation, social status, and outward appearance. When the church reflects God's values, however, it will usually value the opposite of what our overall culture applauds. For instance, the world says that the poor in spirit, the mourners, the meek, the merciful, the pure in heart, and the peacemakers will be society's losers, but Jesus called them "blessed" (Matt. 5:3-9). The world, in general, might ignore the poor, but the Gospel seeks them out. God has always valued the poor in a way our world does not. For example, the people whom God chose to use in history were slaves in Egypt. When God became human, He came as a poor Galilean with no influence. Jesus identified so closely with the hungry, thirsty, naked, and estranged that He said that to mistreat them was to mistreat Him (Matt. 25:31-46). The early church was not populated with the elite of society (see 1 Cor. 1:26).

Of course, God also uses rich people. Abraham was rich and owned a lot of land and flocks. Moses lived in the luxury of Pharaoh's court for 40 years. Paul and Luke were well educated. But God also seems to delight in using the underdog, the unexpected person, so that His power is made visible through their weakness (2 Cor. 12:9-10). The temptations for the rich are great: enticements to become proud, to trust in what is uncertain, and so on (1 Tim. 6:7). At one point in history, the church rented favored pews to people who could pay for them. This practice was abolished, but we Christians must root out all favored treatment of people based on money.

Political parties give special privileges to generous benefactors, but this should not happen in the community of faith. Money must never be a bargaining chip or a way to gain status or leadership in the church. Within any congregation, leadership and respect are given to those who honor and obey the royal law of love: to be as compassionate and kind to others as they want others to be to them. With the Spirit's help and the encouragement of one another, it's possible for this to become a consistent reality throughout the body of Christ.

Wise Speakers

Scripture

Background Scripture: *James 3*
Scripture Lesson: *James 3:1-10, 13-18*
Key Verse: *Out of the same mouth come praise and cursing. My brothers, this should not be.* James 3:10.
Scripture Lesson for Children: *James 3:1-12*
Key Verse for Children: *With the tongue we praise our Lord and Father.* James 3:9.

Lesson Aim

To respond to others with godly wisdom and verbal self-control.

Lesson Setting

Time: *The early 60s of the first century* A.D.
Place: *Jerusalem*

Lesson Outline

Wise Speakers

   I. The Tongue Personified: James 3:1-10
      A. *The Gravity of Teaching: vs. 1*
      B. *The Importance of Controlling the Tongue: vs. 2*
      C. *The Point Illustrated: vss. 3-4*
      D. *The Power of the Tongue: vss. 5-6*
      E. *The Potential of the Tongue: vss. 7-8*
      F. *The Inconsistency of the Tongue: vss. 9-10*
  II. The True Source of Wisdom: James 3:13-18
      A. *The Truly Wise Person: vs. 13*
      B. *The Worldly Wise Person: vss. 14-15*
      C. *The Outcome of Worldly Wisdom: vs. 16*
      D. *The Harvest of Divine Wisdom: vss. 17-18*

Introduction for Adults

Topic: *Thoughtful Speech*

Our words are like boomerangs. They come back either to haunt us or bless us. In this week's lesson about speech, we find many moral boomerangs. Some of them warn us about the serious repercussions and troubles that will befall us if we do not control our tongues. Others promise us the rich blessings of proper speech, directed by the Word of God and controlled by the Holy Spirit.

Every person could probably tell stories filled with regrets of times when their "big mouth" caused them to sin, as well as deep satisfaction when the Lord gave them just the right words to say. The sins of the tongue are many, and each one warrants our study because we need to know the consequences of our failure to heed these warnings.

On the other hand, people need to be encouraged to practice blessing others with their words. We don't need instructions in how to sin with our tongues, but we do need help in guarding our lips, giving gentle answers, and ministering "pleasant words" to others. We can help each other by telling stories of how we have learned to do better.

Introduction for Youth

Topic: *Put a Sock in It!*

How many times a day do we have to watch our tongues? Perhaps it's while sitting at breakfast, or while nagging our parents, or while picking on our siblings. It could be when we meet our friends and one of them decides to spread a false rumor or denigrate someone else.

It's no wonder David asked God to set a guard over his mouth (Ps. 141:3). Each day, we have to ask God to control our tongues. When we are tempted to join the fun of running someone down, we have to ask God to help us say something positive.

God can use us to turn curses into blessings, especially if we are courageous enough to use our tongues as instruments of righteousness and truth. Our walk with Jesus will be strengthened as we trust Him for this courage.

Concepts for Children

Topic: *Speak Wisely*

1. Proper speech involves saying the right words at the right time.
2. Proper speech involves controlling our desire to say what should not be said.
3. The devil can use the mean words we say to make others feel angry or sad.
4. The Holy Spirit can help us say things that are kind and helpful to others.
5. God is pleased when we encourage others with our words.

Lesson Commentary

I. THE TONGUE PERSONIFIED: JAMES 3:1-10

A. The Gravity of Teaching: vs. 1

Not many of you should presume to be teachers, my brothers, because you know that we who teach will be judged more strictly.

Perhaps there was great eagerness among many early Christians to teach. It was a ministry that carried considerable rank and honor, like that of rabbi in Jewish circles. But as we consider James 3:1, we discover that knowing divine truth is not necessarily the same as living it. Expressed differently, it is one thing to have an intellectual grasp of the Bible, but it is quite another matter to practice what it teaches. Also, while it is noble to aspire to a teaching ministry, we should also be ready to "be judged more strictly." This means God will evaluate our lives more rigorously and stringently based on our increased awareness of the truth and influence over the lives of others.

This sobering truth is not intended to discourage teachers in the church who are gifted and called by God. Providing biblical instruction continues to be an essential part of carrying out Jesus' Great Commission to make disciples (Matt. 28:19-20). But the responsibility of teaching carries with it a degree of power and authority, and regrettably, this often attracts people who are not called by God to instruct others in Scripture, but rather who desire the esteem and influence the position seems to offer.

B. The Importance of Controlling the Tongue: vs. 2

We all stumble in many ways. If anyone is never at fault in what he says, he is a perfect man, able to keep his whole body in check.

A primary way to convey the truth of God's Word is by means of the tongue. The downside, of course, is that a slip of the tongue can create a great offense, and the recipient of our harsh words may or may not forgive us. Admittedly, the human struggle with sin plagues us all in many and varied ways. But the tongue is the part of our body that most reveals our wayward tendencies. The tongue is the gateway from the inner to the outer world. It discloses to others what is inside of us. While it is true that some people talk more than others, the issue here is not how much they say, but rather the words that come out when they speak.

James 3:2, in affirming that "we all stumble in many ways," used a verb that describes active sin, not simply human error. According to the context, much of this stumbling occurs because of harmful forms of speech (including lying, slander, and gossip, to name a few examples). The writer revealed that if people can control their tongue, they can control their entire body and are perfectly self-controlled people. The Greek adjective rendered "perfect" denotes those who are fully developed in a moral sense and meet the highest ethical standards in their conduct (see Matt. 5:48). The emphasis is on the maturity of one's behavior. The idea is that believers who do not sin with their tongues will probably show themselves mature in other areas of their lives. The simple truth is that there can be no spiritual maturity while the tongue remains untamed and out of control.

C. The Point Illustrated: vss. 3-4

When we put bits into the mouths of horses to make them obey us, we can turn the whole animal. Or take ships as an example. Although they are so large and are driven by strong winds, they are steered by a very small rudder wherever the pilot wants to go.

James 3:3-4 offers two illustrations to demonstrate how a small device can positively or negatively control the destiny of a much larger vehicle. First, an eight-ounce metal bar placed in the mouth of a 1,000-pound horse allows the rider to dictate to the large animal where it will go (vs. 3). Second, a ship's rudder (a wooden blade about the size of a person's arm) determines the course of its many-times-larger vessel. The pilot steering the 500-foot ship needs only to change the direction of the rudder and, despite harsh winds, can keep the vessel on course (vs. 4).

D. The Power of the Tongue: vss. 5-6

Likewise the tongue is a small part of the body, but it makes great boasts. Consider what a great forest is set on fire by a small spark. The tongue also is a fire, a world of evil among the parts of the body. It corrupts the whole person, sets the whole course of his life on fire, and is itself set on fire by hell.

James 3:5 says that though the tongue is a small member of the human body, it can do a great deal of good or evil. Also, despite the tongue's pretentious claims, it can wreck untold havoc in the lives of its victims. To illustrate his point, James noted how a "small spark," which by itself is extinguished in the blinking of an eye, can reduce acres of forest to a charred rubble. In a sense, the tongue is like a flame of "fire" (vs. 6), because a few ill-chosen words can do a vast amount of damage in little time. And like an incendiary device, the tongue can set a person's entire life on fire. In short, the tongue is a source of "evil." When the tongue goes unchecked, it spews forth wickedness that spiritually defiles "the whole person" as well as the entire direction of one's existence. Perhaps the writer was thinking of Jesus' teaching that a person's words reflect what is really in his or her heart (see Luke 6:45).

These blunt statements should not surprise us when we realize that the tongue is "set on fire by hell" (Jas. 3:6). The Greek word here is *Gehenna*. This is a transliteration of the Hebrew words *ge hinnom*, which mean "Valley of Hinnom." This was the lower area of land along the southwest corner of Jerusalem. This valley formed part of the dividing line between the tribes of Judah and Benjamin. It was also the place where kings Ahaz and Manasseh offered their sons in fiery sacrifice to the Ammonite god Molech (Jer. 7:31; 19:5-6; 32:35). Following the period of the Old Testament, Jewish apocalyptic writers first called the Valley of Hinnom the gateway to hell, but later referred to it as hell itself. In first-century Jerusalem, inhabitants continuously used the spot to dump and burn garbage and bodily waste, so that smoke could be seen rising virtually nonstop. For that reason, it provided an apt illustration of hell. James 3:6, in making reference to "hell," indicated that the tongue, when left uncontrolled, could become a tool for vice, rather than virtue. For instance, under the influence of the devil, people can say things that are quite destructive in nature.

E. The Potential of the Tongue: vss. 7-8

All kinds of animals, birds, reptiles and creatures of the sea are being tamed and have been tamed by man, but no man can tame the tongue. It is a restless evil, full of deadly poison.

In James 3:7-12, the writer continued his description of the tongue. He had just compared this small organ to an out-of-control fire. Next, he compared it to an untamed animal. The author pointed out that while all kinds of animals—birds, reptiles, and even sea creatures—had been tamed and were continuing to be domesticated, one entity, the tongue, was not included among them (vss. 7-8). Humankind has successfully carried out God's command to rule over virtually every aspect of creation (Gen. 1:26). But the tongue has remained beyond the control of God's crowning creation. To subdue that entity, nothing less than the power of God is required. The reason the author gave his readers for their lack of success in taming the tongue was blunt. James 3:8 says the human instrument of speech is "restless" and "evil." The Greek word translated "restless" suggests a staggering, unsteady, and uncontrollable kind of wickedness. The implication, perhaps, is that the tongue could strike anytime, without warning or even rational cause.

The phrase "full of deadly poison" brings to mind Psalm 140:3—"They make their tongues as sharp as a serpent's; the poison of vipers is on their lips." Like a poisonous snake concealed in the brush beside a hiking trail, the tongue is loaded with deadly venom and poised to strike. Though the viper is a small serpent, it has a particularly mean disposition. It strikes swiftly and holds fast to its victim with great tenacity. The fact that it hisses each time it breathes in and out gives it the appearance of being an adder with an attitude. It is no wonder James admonished in 1:19, "be quick to listen, slow to speak."

In the eastern Mediterranean area, there are some 20 poisonous snakes. Several of these are true vipers (called "adders" in some translations of the Bible). The class of vipers are poisonous snakes with curved, retracted fangs that extend forward when the serpent strikes. One snake in this class, called the horned viper, though only 12 to 18 inches long, has been known to strike at large animals like horses and bears (Gen. 49:17). This snake often buries itself in the sand. With only its eyes and the hornlike protrusions on its head visible, it lies in wait to ambush an unsuspecting victim. Viper poison attacks the central nervous system and destroys red blood cells. Jesus and John the Baptizer both made reference to the viper (Matt. 3:7; 12:34; 23:33). Luke, too, recorded an incident in which a viper struck Paul (Acts 28:3).

F. The Inconsistency of the Tongue: vss. 9-10

With the tongue we praise our Lord and Father, and with it we curse men, who have been made in God's likeness. Out of the same mouth come praise and cursing. My brothers, this should not be.

> The tongue—representing intelligent human speech—shows its deadly nature in its erratic and inconsistent behavior. It can strike at any time. One moment it blesses God; the next it curses a human, who is made in the image of God (Jas. 3:9; see Gen. 1:26-27). Even within fallen humanity, though the image of God has been defaced through sin, people still bear the divine likeness to some degree (Gen. 5:1; 9:6), and this sets them apart from the rest of earth's creatures. James despaired that the same mouth could spout blessings and cursings in almost the same breath. Such inconsistency does not occur in the natural world. A spring gives either fresh or brackish water, not one now and the other later. Also, fruit trees and vines bear their natural harvests, never unnatural ones. The tongue, by contrast, is perverse (Jas. 3:10-12).

II. The True Source of Wisdom: James 3:13-18

A. The Truly Wise Person: vs. 13

Who is wise and understanding among you? Let him show it by his good life, by deeds done in the humility that comes from wisdom.

> We can imagine some Bible teachers claiming they were wise and understood God's ways. James 3:13 admonished them to prove their moral insight and intellectual perception by living in an honorable manner. They were also to show their expert knowledge by doing good works with the humility that comes from godly wisdom. Wisdom may be defined as the ability to handle matters skillfully, to exercise sound judgment, and to apply biblical truths to one's conduct. Divine wisdom guides the believer to live in an upright, virtuous, and well-pleasing manner. The wise person is committed to God, devoted to His will, and obedient to His Word.
>
> There are numerous facets of wisdom worth considering. There is an intellectual dimension in which sublime truths are taught (Prov. 4:1) and an ethical dimension in which such virtues as righteousness, justice, and equity are commended (2:7; 8:20). Wisdom stresses the importance of revering God (1:7; 2:5) and caring for the needy (Jas. 1:26-27). Divine wisdom also reveals how one can lead a truly satisfying life (Prov. 2:10-21). The Word of God strongly urges believers to embrace the wisdom of God (3:1-2) and forsake the folly of the world (9:13-18). The wise person enjoys a productive life, peace with the Lord, and spiritual joy (3:16-18). The foolish person, however, reaps sorrow, emptiness, and death (4:14-17). The fruit of wisdom is far superior to gold and silver (8:19) and far more creative than anything humankind can produce (vss. 22-31). Those who appropriate the wisdom of Scripture are pleasing to the Lord, while those who reject it are condemned by Him (12:2).

Truly wise people are humble because they are aware of the depth of their ignorance. The more they learn, the more they realize how little they really know. In Greek thought, humility was a negative trait that suggested weakness and a lack of worth or dignity. Jesus, however, made humility the cornerstone of Christian character (Matt. 18:4; 23:12; Luke 18:14). Scriptural humility involves an absence of arrogance, and it is rooted in the understanding that all we are and have we owe to God. A humble person is secure enough to praise and lift up others without any need for self-exaltation (Phil. 2:3-4). The biblical concept of humility knows nothing of harsh self-abasement, belittling of oneself, or putting oneself down. This is a form of false humility (Col. 2:18, 23).

B. The Worldly Wise Person: vss. 14-15

But if you harbor bitter envy and selfish ambition in your hearts, do not boast about it or deny the truth. Such "wisdom" does not come down from heaven but is earthly, unspiritual, of the devil.

Against the backdrop of humility and graciousness that characterizes a truly wise person, it is easier to spot the cheap imitations. The worldly wise (the so-called "street smart") are characterized by bitterness, envy, and selfish ambition. The trail of deceit and strife they leave behind is nothing to boast about; in fact, their bragging and lying are used to cover up the truth (3:14). Verse 15 spotlights the real source of worldly wisdom. The jealousy and selfishness it spawns originate from below, not "from heaven." In this light, we can more fully appreciate the emphasis being placed here on seeking divine wisdom.

C. The Outcome of Worldly Wisdom: vs. 16

For where you have envy and selfish ambition, there you find disorder and every evil practice.

James 3:16 explains that where envy and selfish ambition are present, the natural result is confusion and a variety of immoral behaviors. These vices, of course, are in direct opposition to the unity, peace, and righteousness God intends to be at work in the relationships His people have with one another. A person focused on nothing but his or her own advancement is less likely to be concerned with the "troublesome" issue of ethics. Moral boundaries are usually perceived by such people as obstacles in the way of their success. Since the Lord is neither a God of disorder nor receptive toward evil, the worldly wisdom that produces such bitter fruit cannot come from Him (see 1 Cor. 14:33; 1 John 1:5).

D. The Harvest of Divine Wisdom: vss. 17-18

But the wisdom that comes from heaven is first of all pure; then peace-loving, considerate, submissive, full of mercy and good fruit, impartial and sincere. Peacemakers who sow in peace raise a harvest of righteousness.

After being exposed to the unwholesome images associated with earthly wisdom, it is refreshing to learn more about heavenly wisdom. First of all, divine prudence is known for its purity and compassion. Such, in turn, promotes tranquility and harmony, gentleness and humility (Jas. 3:17). The wisdom from above is furthermore characterized by sensibility and kindness, mercifulness and charity, impartiality and sincerity. None of these virtues comes about immediately; rather, the Spirit cultivates them as believers yield to God's will. The emphasis in verse 18 is on being peacemakers, rather than peace-breakers. James compares peace to seeds that the godly plant. The harvest is an abundance of righteousness, goodness, and justice. These graces are worth cultivating!

Discussion Questions

1. Why did James encourage those who taught in the church to be careful about what they said with their tongues?
2. In what ways is being able to control one's tongue, or speech, an indication of spiritual maturity?
3. In what ways can an uncontrolled tongue bring great harm and sadness to oneself and others?
4. Why is earthly wisdom so prone to brag about how much it supposedly knows?
5. What is the fruit of godly wisdom, and why is it to be preferred over that of earthly wisdom?

Contemporary Application

Godly wisdom is not just meant for life-and-death situations. It should be a part of everyday living. For instance, imagine that a neighbor storms up to your front door. He is angry because he is certain your dog is responsible for tearing up his vegetable garden last night, and he is letting you know exactly what he thinks about you and your pet.

There is one mistake, however. Only two weeks earlier, you had to take your dog to the veterinarian to be put to sleep. The dog had been like a part of the family, and you are still sad about the loss. Perhaps your first impulse would be to blast your rude, insensitive neighbor with some sharp retorts to his accusations; but should you follow your impulse? Your neighbor has finished his tirade, and now you have an opportunity to respond. What will you say?

On the surface, this situation may seem relatively insignificant; but what if this neighbor is not a Christian and knows that you are one? Our lives are filled with situations that offer opportunities to demonstrate our faith to others by what we say and do. Such opportunities can come quickly. We never know how one of our responses might impact someone. A good or bad word at a critical time in someone's life may leave an indelible impression on his or her thinking about Christians and ultimately about the Savior. As God's ambassadors, we need His wisdom daily to guide our words and actions.

People of Godly Behavior

Scripture

Background Scripture: *James 4*
Scripture Lesson: *James 4:1-12*
Key Verse: *Come near to God and [God] will come near to*
you. James 4:8.
Scripture Lesson for Children: *James 4:7-8, 11-12;*
Matthew 7:1-5
Key Verse for Children: *Do not judge, or you too will be*
judged. Matthew 7:1.

Lesson Aim

To recognize the importance of humility and proper
motives in our pursuit of righteousness.

Lesson Setting

Time: *The early 60s of the first century* A.D.
Place: *Jerusalem*

Lesson Outline

People of Godly Behavior

   I. Friendship with the World: James 4:1-6
      A. The Strife Resulting from Selfish Desires: vs. 1
      B. The Futility of Envy and Greed: vss. 2-3
      C. The Folly of Affection for the World: vs. 4
      D. The Concern and Care of God: vss. 5-6
  II. Submission to God: James 4:7-12
      A. Humbling Oneself before God: vss. 7-8
      B. Yielding Oneself to God: vss. 9-10
      C. Recognizing God as the Judge: vss. 11-12

Introduction for Adults

Topic: *Living Responsibly*

Charles Wesley, the hymn writer, captured the essence of James when he wrote, "A humble, lowly, contrite heart, believing, true and clean." The Bible consistently cautions against pride and encourages living in a humble, responsible manner. Some people say that pride is the essence of sin. If so, then humility is the essence of godliness.

We have to confess that too often our pride overrides our humility. Each day seems to bring some opportunity to exalt ourselves and our ways of thinking and doing things. We show pride not just in positions and possessions, but also in our church traditions.

At the beginning of each day we should ask God to keep us humble; and at the end of each day we should confess our pride. Then, as James affirmed, we will receive more grace.

Introduction for Youth

Topic: *Greed Is Out!*

The father remembered well when his teenaged son, John, first encountered James 4:4. "How can this be?" he asked. "I like lots of things in the world. Does that make me a greedy person? Am I God's enemy?"

The father tried to explain that being the world's "friend" means more than liking sports, music, fishing, good food, and a happy family. It means shaping your own values according to the world's standards. For example, if the world says it's okay to lie, steal, and cheat, then we part company with the world. When we cave in to the world's greedy desires, we choose to be God's enemy.

Of course, those who follow the world's way of thinking and acting hate to make such choices. As Christians, who place God's will above everything else, we choose to follow Him, even if we lose some friends who do not.

Concepts for Children

Topic: *Let God Be the Judge*

1. Believers who submit to God are empowered to resist the devil.
2. When believers yield the control of their lives to God, the Spirit helps them to live virtuously.
3. God, the only Lawgiver, is the final Judge.
4. God calls us to evaluate the way we live.
5. God calls us to help others, especially by forgiving them when they wrong us.

Lesson Commentary

I. FRIENDSHIP WITH THE WORLD: JAMES 4:1-6

A. The Strife Resulting from Selfish Desires: vs. 1

What causes fights and quarrels among you? Don't they come from your desires that battle within you?

James 4 deals with the presence of conflict among the first recipients of the letter. The author asked what was causing the discord among them (vs. 1). The question was framed in the language of military conflict. The Greek word translated "fights" actually means a state of war, while "quarrels" has reference to battles. In effect, the Christians to whom James wrote were clashing with each other. They were warring among themselves about things they wanted but could not acquire. James stated that the source of these conflicts was not circumstances or personalities, but selfish passions that battled within their own hearts. The Greek word rendered "desires" here and the word rendered "pleasures" in verse 3 are both translations of *hedonon*, the root from which our English term *hedonism* comes. Hedonism is the pursuit of pleasure merely for the sake of the sensual satisfaction it brings.

While it is easy to blame others for initiating and sustaining conflict, we must often take a hard look at our own hearts to see whether there is any harmful attitude within that is perpetuating the conflict unnecessarily. James described the frustration of this stop-at-nothing pursuit of self-serving pleasure. Contentment is always elusive. The desire for more is never satisfied. Some will even go to extreme measures to attain what can never be theirs.

B. The Futility of Envy and Greed: vss. 2-3

You want something but don't get it. You kill and covet, but you cannot have what you want. You quarrel and fight. You do not have, because you do not ask God. When you ask, you do not receive, because you ask with wrong motives, that you may spend what you get on your pleasures.

The readership of James, in their shortsightedness, strongly desired what they did not have and thus resorted to scheming and injustice to get it. The more envious they became, the more they tried to obtain what others had through worldly, underhanded means (Jas. 4:2). The writer was possibly using exaggeration when he said that Christians committed murder in the pursuit of pleasure. Since James had previously used war imagery when there was no actual physical battle, the Greek word he chose for "kill" might also be translated "hate." The Lord Jesus and the apostle John made it clear that harboring hatred toward another person was a spiritual form of murder (see Matt. 5:21-22; 1 John 3:15).

The displays of jealousy and greed among believers led only to futility and frustration. The solution was to pray to God about these and other pressing matters. James explained that his readers did not receive what they desired because they left God out of their pursuits. Perhaps these believers recognized the selfish or immoral nature of what they craved, so they felt that asking God's assistance would

417

be futile. Of course, if so, they would have been correct. Some of those who did make their requests known to God used prayer as a means of self-gratification. Their motives were impure because they sought pleasure for its own sake—not the joy and satisfaction one derives from implementing the will of God (Jas. 4:3). When someone's motives are outside the will of God, the Lord is not going to grant that person's requests.

C. The Folly of Affection for the World: vs. 4

You adulterous people, don't you know that friendship with the world is hatred toward God? Anyone who chooses to be a friend of the world becomes an enemy of God.

The envy, rivalry, and violence previously described are widespread in fallen human society. When they also appear among Christians, it is because believers have jettisoned loyalty to God for "friendship with the world" (Jas. 4:4). This means believers have embraced the outlook of the unsaved and decided to operate by their twisted logic. Put another way, Christians are guilty of drinking deeply from the cesspool of the world's way of thinking and acting.

In the New Testament, there are basically three meanings for the term "world" (which translates the Greek word *cosmos*). The first is the created universe, namely, the heavens and earth where humankind and animals live (see John 1:10). In this context, "world" essentially means the planet earth and its environment. Second, "world" often refers to all the people on earth. This is the meaning of the term in 3:16—God so loved the world, that is, those who inhabited physical earth. A third meaning for "world" is the network of godless values spearheaded by Satan. This system of thought is hostile toward God and His Word (see Eph. 2:2; Jas. 1:27; 4:4; 1 John 5:19). As we see in John 17:15, Jesus asked His Father not to take believers out of the (physical) world, but to protect them from the evil one who cultivated worldly thinking.

In James 4:4, the author used strong language when he labeled compromising believers as "adulterous people." The idea is that by embracing the values and aims of the world, they had become spiritually unfaithful to the Lord (see Jer. 3:6-10; Ezek. 16:38; 23:1-49; Hos. 2:2-5; 3:1-5; 9:1). The more believers turn their hearts away from God, the greater is their alienation from Him. In the Sermon on the Mount, Jesus declared that believers cannot serve two masters. Their devotion is either to God or money (Matt. 6:24). James reflected this teaching when he declared that those who are a friend of the world are also the enemy of God. Nothing less than enmity can exist when one's aim is to enjoy the world rather than love and serve God.

D. The Concern and Care of God: vss. 5-6

Or do you think Scripture says without reason that the spirit he caused to live in us envies intensely? But he gives us more grace. That is why Scripture says: "God opposes the proud but gives grace to the humble."

It remains unclear which specific Old Testament passage is being referenced in James 4:5. Perhaps the general teaching of a broad range of verses is in view—for instance, Exodus 20:3, 5; 34:14; Deuteronomy 6:15; 32:21; Joshua 24:19; and Nahum 1:2. In these passages, the Lord's exclusive claim on His people is being addressed. The teaching of the Old Testament is that God maintained a burning zeal and passion for the covenant community and would deal with all rivals firmly. Thus, any believer who was spiritually unfaithful to the Lord would experience His hand of discipline (see Prov. 3:11-12; Heb. 12:5-6).

There are three primary ways James 4:5 has been rendered. First, the NIV says, "the spirit he caused to live in us envies intensely." This refers to the individual human spirit that God placed within Adam at creation (Gen. 2:7). With the fall of humankind into sin (Rom. 5:12-14), the individual human spirit is filled with envy; put another way, the jealous yearning refers to the covetous desires of people. A second rendering for James 4:5 is that "God jealously longs for the spirit that he made to live in us." The idea is that when God's people become unfaithful in their commitment, He zealously desires to have them return to Him in faithfulness and love. A third rendering is that "the Spirit he caused to live in us longs jealously." In this case, the Holy Spirit, who dwells in us, cares for us deeply and wants us to be faithful to the Lord. Regardless of which rendering is preferred, the overall thrust of the verse is clear. When we opt for friendship with the world, it provokes God to anger. Indeed, He will not permit us to have divided loyalties between Himself and the world.

Sometimes when we talk about God's love, we misconstrue it to be merely static and willful in nature; but verse 5 suggests that there is also a strong affective dimension to God. He longs to be in relationship with us and is displeased when we stray from Him. Thankfully, God in His "grace" (vs. 6) does not abandon us in our spiritual waywardness; instead, He is ready to shower us with His kindness to overcome our envy and greed. In fact, we need His strength to turn from the world and back to Him. As the quote from Proverbs 3:34 teaches, God opposes all who are arrogant, but manifests His grace to the lowly. The divine remedy for conflict among believers, then, is a humble spirit energized by the grace of God. With this, harmony can be restored to the body of Christ, which in turn enables a cease-fire among warring factions.

II. SUBMISSION TO GOD: JAMES 4:7-12

A. Humbling Oneself before God: vss. 7-8

Submit yourselves, then, to God. Resist the devil, and he will flee from you. Come near to God and he will come near to you. Wash your hands, you sinners, and purify your hearts, you double-minded.

The original recipients of this letter apparently had problems with backbiting and judgmental attitudes. To challenge these sins, the writer issued a series of commands in James 4:7-10. The exhortations were given in a Greek tense that signified the urgent need to make a definite break from these sinful practices, which can quickly destroy unity in the body of Christ. The author's aim was to restore harmony among his fellow believers and to promote personal holiness. To that end, James called upon them to reject their unrighteous conduct and to draw near to God with repentant hearts. In turn, this would promote a harmonious relationship with God and one's fellow believers, both of which are essential for growth and development toward spiritual maturity. As we grow strong and mature in the faith, we will not wait for others to take the initiative in creating harmony. Because we have known the Lord for a while, we have the courage to tactfully expose relational problems so they can be addressed in a constructive manner.

The first part of the process of renewal and recommitment is like the two sides of a coin: "Submit . . . to God" (vs. 7) and "resist the devil." The initial readers were doing the opposite—they were resisting the will of God and cooperating with the powers of darkness! The word "then" refers back to Proverbs 3:34, which was quoted in James 4:6. Since the Lord gives grace to the humble, it only makes sense that an attitude of submission would be the most beneficial way to relate to God. The act of submission carried the idea of subordinating oneself to a superior. Submission is not simply obedience, but the humble attitude that makes obedience possible. The act of resisting, on the other hand, meant to take a stand against something. In this case, the stand was against the devil and his pervasive influence in the world.

As the readers of this letter drew near to God, they had the assurance that He would reciprocate by drawing near to them. But such close communion with God required divine cleansing. Expressed differently, clean hands (signifying outward conduct) and a pure heart (signifying inward thoughts and motives) were necessary prerequisites to intimacy with a holy God (vs. 8). In this verse, James made reference to concepts drawn from the Old Testament. In ancient Israel, the priests would wash their hands before approaching God (Exod. 30:19-21). This process of external cleansing symbolized the internal purification of the worshiper's thoughts, motives, and desires (Ps. 23:3-4; Jer. 4:4; 1 Tim. 1:5). The need for cleansing was highlighted by the writer's description of his readers as "sinners" (Jas. 4:8) and "double-minded." Their evil conduct warranted the label "sinners," and their double-mindedness stemmed from their attempts to be close to God while pursuing the selfish and immoral pleasures lauded by the world.

B. Yielding Oneself to God: vss. 9-10

Grieve, mourn and wail. Change your laughter to mourning and your joy to gloom. Humble yourselves before the Lord, and he will lift you up.

In light of the severity of the sins these believers were perpetually committing, the writer called for a response of grief, mourning, and wailing (Jas. 4:9). There was no room here for a lighthearted attitude. They couldn't just brush these actions off as social conventions. The author further admonished his readers to turn their empty laughter into mourning and their artificial joy into gloom. The meaning of the Greek word rendered "gloom" was to cast one's eyes down. It is a picture of a contrite heart that in shame and sorrow confesses grievous wrongdoing. James was not describing a long-term Christian disposition here, but rather an appropriate short-term emotional response to failing God. In verse 10, the writer turned once again to the theme of humility. In order to be lifted up, one must follow the path of humility before God. Humility is the key that unlocks the treasure of God's grace.

Some people indulge in worldly pleasures and use laughter to distract them from sobering issues such as life and death, sin, and judgment. The Christian, however, understands that before the joy of salvation can be fully appreciated, we must enter into the sorrow of repentance. Thus, the point of mourning and weeping is to express our grief over sin and our desire to enter into a relationship with God. He will not spurn the heart that is truly broken and contrite. In fact, He welcomes such displays of humility, for they reflect what He desires to see in the penitent. He even promises to honor those who humble themselves in this way.

C. Recognizing God as the Judge: vss. 11-12

Brothers, do not slander one another. Anyone who speaks against his brother or judges him speaks against the law and judges it. When you judge the law, you are not keeping it, but sitting in judgment on it. There is only one Lawgiver and Judge, the one who is able to save and destroy. But you—who are you to judge your neighbor?

The opposite of humility is the attitude that leads a believer to speak harshly to fellow Christians. James called upon his readers to stop their mean-spirited verbal attacks. In effect, they were being unjustly critical and judgmental toward one another. Moreover, to spread falsehoods about other believers or to censure them unfairly was equivalent to sitting in judgment over the law of God. When the self-appointed critics placed themselves above the law, they treated it with contempt and transgressed its commands (Jas. 4:11).

God's law was intended to govern people. But those who dared to assume a superior stance over this divine legal code were attempting to take a position that belongs only to God. After all, He alone is the righteous "Lawgiver and Judge" (vs. 12), and only He has the authority to overrule or change His edicts. This is true because as the "Lawgiver," God is the author of the law. Also, as the "Judge," He is the administrator of the law. In short, He is both the legislator and enforcer of His eternal decrees. Accordingly, only He has the right and power to "save and destroy." While the law given by the Lawgiver brings condemnation to transgressors, the righteous Judge is the only one with the authority to save the condemned offender. In light of this truth, James rebuked his readers for setting themselves up as judges of their neighbors.

The presence of envy and greed prompted some among the readers of this letter to defame and reprimand their fellow Christians. Those who treated others in this way had forgotten about the transitory nature of life. They were blinded by their own desires to go to a certain town, conduct business there, and make a profit (vs. 13). The point is that we are shortsighted to make the pursuit of a commercial enterprise an end in itself, rather than a means to glorify God. After all, our lives are like a "mist" (vs. 14) that appears for a short moment and then disappears.

Since we do not know what will happen in the future, we should align all our aims and desires with the will of God. James was not advocating that we discontinue living because of the uncertainties of the future; rather, his desire was for us to submit our goals and dreams to God. Thus, when we make plans, we should do so in conjunction with what the Lord wants for us (vs. 15). The opposite tendency, then, is filled with peril and characterized by folly. Ultimately, nothing eternally wholesome can come from a life characterized by arrogant self-sufficiency; instead, only "evil" (vs. 16)—such as frustration or failure—is the most that can be expected.

Discussion Questions

1. What was the origin of the conflicts and disputes to which James referred?
2. In what way does God give grace to the humble?
3. Why is it important to relate to God with an attitude of humility?
4. How can believers submit all their plans to God?
5. Why is God displeased when we go through our lives with an attitude of arrogance?

Contemporary Application

James 4 teaches the necessity of humility in the Christian life. Because pride causes us to depend on ourselves rather than God, it takes us far from the path of righteousness. Humility, however, allows us to submit to God, enables us to resist the devil, and acknowledges the Lord's role in our future.

The type of humility that accords with righteousness in our lives is one that says, "Lord, I want what You want for my life." Such submission concedes that God knows what is best for our lives and keeps us from plunging ahead without consideration of God or what He may be trying to teach us. Humility is essential for godliness because it alone gives us access to the necessary strength to resist the devil. God does not give this power to those who arrogantly rely on themselves, but only to those who acknowledge their inability to live the Christian life by themselves.

Along with pride, another stumbling block in the life of faith is improper motives. James said that the prayers of his readers were not being answered because they asked from their desire to be friends with the world. Thus, even when we pray, we should question the motives behind our requests. God wants us to pray about everything and bring our requests before Him (Phil. 4:6). But how often do we find ourselves pleading for things with no thought of God's will or consideration of all the things for which we can give thanks?

Prayerful Community

Scripture

Background Scripture: *James 5*
Scripture Lesson: *James 5:13-20*
Key Verse: *Is any one of you in trouble? He should pray. Is
anyone happy? Let him sing songs of praise.* James 5:13.
Scripture Lesson for Children: *James 5:13-18*
Key Verse for Children: *The prayer of a righteous man is
powerful and effective.* James 5:16.

Lesson Aim

To affirm the power of prayer.

Lesson Setting

Time: *The early 60s of the first century* A.D.
Place: *Jerusalem*

Lesson Outline

Prayerful Community

   I. Praying in All of Life's Circumstances:
      James 5:13-18
      A. Praying in Times of Joy and Suffering: vs. 13
      B. Praying in Times of Illness: vss. 14-15
      C. Praying Earnestly and Effectively: vss. 16-18

  II. Restoring Wandering Believers: James 5:19-20

Introduction for Adults

Topic: *Powerful and Effective Living*

During Haddon Robinson's tenure as president of Denver Seminary, lawsuits were brought against the school. Because he was named in one of the suits, Robinson had to give a deposition. For two days, prosecutors relentlessly grilled him as they questioned his motives and tried to cast everything he said in a negative light.

Robinson not only faced legal problems, but he also had to deal with attacks against his reputation. For example, a disgruntled former employee of the seminary spread false statements about Robinson throughout the community. Robinson and his wife responded to the devastating emotional pain they experienced by bathing their circumstance in prayer.

Looking back on this trying ordeal, Robinson wrote, "If anything good for me came out of this painful time, it was the overwhelming sense of my need of God. I felt completely vulnerable. Although I was not guilty of any legal negligence or failure, I felt more in need of grace than ever."

Introduction for Youth

Topic: *Knee Theology Works!*

Oswald Chambers (1874–1917) was a Scottish minister whose teachings on the life of faith have endured to this day. He observed that prayer is hard work. "There is nothing thrilling about a laboring man's work but it is the laboring man who makes the conceptions of the genius possible; and it is the laboring saint who makes the conceptions of the Master possible. You labor at prayer and results happen all the time from His standpoint. What an astonishment it will be to find, when the veil is lifted, the souls that have been reaped by you, simply because you had been in the habit of taking your orders from Jesus Christ."

As God did with Chambers, He also upholds us during joyful and sad times in our life. As we spend time with Him on our knees in prayer, He gives us the strength to remain faithful to the work He has called us to do.

Concepts for Children

Topic: *Pray Always*

1. Prayer is a proper response when we experience sad times.
2. Singing hymns of praise is a good way to express our joy.
3. God wants us to pray for those who are sick.
4. The prayers of faithful church leaders are often part of God's healing process.
5. When we have mistreated others, we need to ask God for forgiveness and ask them to forgive us.

Lesson Commentary

I. PRAYING IN ALL OF LIFE'S CIRCUMSTANCES: JAMES 5:13-18

A. Praying in Times of Joy and Suffering: vs. 13

Is any one of you in trouble? He should pray. Is anyone happy? Let him sing songs of praise.

James 5 opens with a volley of accusations aimed at wealthy people who were morally bankrupt. Though successful in their economic pursuits, they were indicted for their disregard for God's righteous principles. In the end, rather than enjoying their abundance, these rich ones would be condemned by their wealth. In the same way James addressed the boasting merchants in 4:13-16, the author called on the self-indulgent rich to listen attentively (5:1). While the rich were usually envied for their abundant wealth, James had only contempt for their status and condemnation for their failure to be good stewards of what God had given them. "Cry your eyes out," he in effect told them, because the judgment of their ill-gotten gain was going to come down upon them. This is not a call to repentance as we saw in 4:9; rather, it is an intense emotional reaction to the coming judgment. The author's comments are reminscent of the condemnation of the immorally rich by some of the Old Testament prophets (see Isa. 23; Ezek. 27).

Unlike eternal treasures that can be laid up in heaven, earthly wealth is temporal. For instance, hoarded riches rot and fancy clothes make fine meals for moths (Jas. 5:2; see Matt. 5:19-21). Gold and silver are regarded throughout the world as standards of real, tangible wealth. Technically speaking, these metals cannot rust or even corrode. Perhaps James 5:3 uses the image of corroding gold and silver as a metaphor to emphasize the eternal worthlessness of temporal wealth. Archaeologists have unearthed the tombs of fabulously rich people whose decayed bodies were literally surrounded by precious metals. Obviously, this wealth had no enduring value for the departed. The wicked rich had hoarded their wealth at a time when Jesus was expected to come back at any moment, which thus demonstrated their faithlessness. The future corrosion of seemingly indestructible metals would testify against those who placed their trust in these commodities. Indeed, the futility of their "faith" in these items would consume them like fire burns flesh. This is a graphic way to illustrate how greed devours the consumer.

Wealthy figures in the Bible, such as Abraham and Job, show that it is possible to be materially rich and still maintain a sense of dependence upon God. In the Letter of James, the condemnation of rich people was directed toward the way in which some gained their wealth and then spent it entirely on themselves. The rich whom the author addressed not only exploited the poor, but refused to pay them as well (vs. 4). The prophets were clear on the matter of timely payment of wages and treatment of the poor (see Amos 8:4-7; Mal. 3:5). The cries of these exploited workers had reached the all-powerful Lord of heaven's armies, so retribution was on its way.

In their quest for riches, the wealthy often took the poor to court on trumped-up charges in order to rob them of what little they had (see Jas. 2:6). With no influence or connections, the poor were unable to resist. James charged the rich oppressors of the poor of his day with living in ease at the expense of others. By doing this in wanton excess, the wicked were unknowingly preparing themselves like fattened animals for the slaughter (5:5). The author's initial Jewish readers would have known very well the fate of fattened animals—the altar of sacrifice. This was a fitting end for people who brought unjust condemnation and sometimes death on those too powerless to defend themselves (vs. 6).

Having dealt with the wicked rich, the author turned his attention to the persecuted poor. While he chastised the wealthy, he offered impoverished believers words of consolation. "Be patient" (vs. 7), James told them, until the Lord Jesus' return. The poor had suffered all manner of economic and social injustice. When the Savior comes back, however, these wrongs will be addressed. The righteous Judge will overturn and reverse all inequitable judgments against His followers. As an illustration of patience, James offered the example of farmers. In order to have a successful harvest, it was essential for them to patiently wait for both the autumn rains at planting time and the spring rains as crops were maturing. They had no control over these rains, but showers would come in God's good time and produce a crop.

In light of the Lord's impending return, James admonished harshly treated believers to wait patiently, strengthen their hearts, and not seek retribution when wronged (vs. 8). While revenge may seem to promise relief from the pain of injustice, it only deepens the sense of emptiness, for it is never satisfying. At the same time, these Christians were also to stop grumbling among themselves or risk facing God's judgment. When dealing with an abusive person who is more powerful than ourselves, it is easy to vent our frustration on people who have done nothing to us. Because the Judge (the Lord Jesus) can return at any moment, we should be especially careful how we speak to one another (vs. 9).

Next, James turned to the Old Testament prophets as an example of patience in times of adversity (vs. 10). As they spoke out on God's behalf, they were often persecuted and insulted. Many lost their lives. As a classic example of perseverance, the author cited Job. This is the only mention of this Old Testament luminary by name in the New Testament (though the apostle Paul quotes from the Book of Job in 1 Cor. 3:19). The point of James using Job's account as an illustration, was to remind believers that God has a purpose He wishes to accomplish in every trial and tribulation—even though His people might not understand His purpose.

The author warned his readers not to make frivolous oaths (Jas. 5:12). Not all pledges are necessarily forbidden by this verse. Only vows made lightly or in a blasphemous and profane way are forbidden. Many people invoke flippant oaths in an attempt to increase their credibility. Admittedly, there are examples of the use of oaths in Scripture to validate the truth of one's claim (see Exod. 22:11; Matt. 26:63-

64; Rom. 1:9). But the point in James 5:12 is that if a person trusts the Lord, there is no need for invoking any type of oath by making reference to heaven (the throne room of God), earth (the footstool of His feet; see Isa. 66:1), or any other aspect of creation. When a person appealed to any of these entities while making an oath, they became as binding as if the individual had invoked the name of the Lord. If a person's word is truthful and honest, then a simple yes or no (which reflects unambiguous language) should be all that is necessary. James was clearly referring to the teaching of Jesus in this matter (see Matt. 5:33-37). Ignoring this command will result in the condemnation of the flippant oath taker.

James concluded his letter with an emphasis on prayer. Prayer is the most potent action a believer can take in time of trouble. Prayer ought to be a Christian's reflexive response to all of life's problems—accompanied with praise to God for His bountiful gifts. The English word *prayer* comes from the Latin word *precarious*, which means to be in a vulnerable position. In prayer, we are acknowledging our vulnerability and deepest needs before an all-powerful and holy God. The author employed a series of questions as springboards for conveying some important principles of prayer to his readers. The Greek word rendered "trouble" (Jas. 5:13) in the first question refers to suffering that comes from any source. The author used the same word in verse 10 when describing the trials of the prophets. The matter of offering songs of praise (a type of prayer) in response to happiness is easy to understand. The difficulty, however, comes in times of illness.

B. Praying in Times of Illness: vss. 14-15

Is any one of you sick? He should call the elders of the church to pray over him and anoint him with oil in the name of the Lord. And the prayer offered in faith will make the sick person well; the Lord will raise him up. If he has sinned, he will be forgiven.

If a Christian is ill, God should be the first healer to whom he or she turns. It is also a faith action to turn to other members of the church body. The elders should be available for counsel and comfort, and willing to help the afflicted in any way possible (Jas. 5:14). Elders were leaders in the early church. They are first mentioned in Acts 11:30 as the recognized leaders of local congregations (see 1 Tim. 3:1-7; 5:17; Titus 1:6-9). Once called, the elders were to pray over the sick and anoint them with oil in the Lord's name. The oil symbolized the presence of God (see Ps. 23:5). But in Bible times, it was also thought to contain some medicinal properties (see Luke 10:34).

Since olive trees, which grew even in rocky places, produced much oil, olive oil came to be regarded as a special gift from God. This oil was also associated with the outpouring of God's Spirit. Anointing with oil customarily accompanied the consecration of individuals to God's service. It was used to set apart prophets (1 Kings 19:16), priests (Lev. 8:12), and kings (1 Sam. 16:13; 1 Kings 1:34). The use of oil for healing is seen in Jesus' parable of the Good Samaritan. While binding the wounds of the man who had been mugged, the Samaritan poured in oil and wine

(Luke 10:34). Apparently, it was for the same purpose that the 12 disciples took oil for healing when Jesus sent them out two by two on a ministry mission (Mark 6:13).

James 5:15 says that if the elders of the congregation have faith when they pray for the sick, they will get well. In fact, the Lord will restore the afflicted to health. "Faith" primarily refers to a person's belief or trust in God. The term is also used in the New Testament to refer to the body of truths held by followers of Christ. This second use became increasingly prevalent as church leaders and scholars defended the truths of the faith against the attacks of false teachers. Faith can be understood as having four recognizable elements. First is cognition, an awareness of the facts; second is comprehension, an understanding of the facts; third is conviction, an acceptance of the facts; and fourth is commitment, trust in a reliable object. As James made clear in his epistle, genuine faith is evidenced by more than mere words. It leads to a transformed life in which the believer reaches out to others in need with the Savior's love.

Some have understood James 5:15 to teach that complete physical health is always assured through prayer. Whenever illness strikes, the Christian should pray in faith as a guarantee for healing. If illness persists (in this view), then the prayer must not have been offered in genuine faith. Others see the verse as teaching cooperation between prayer and medicine (the anointing with oil), that is, between God and a physician. According to this view, just prayer or just medicine alone is less than a full prescription for renewed health. Together they are a powerful remedy for serious illness.

An important question concerns what is meant by the Greek word rendered "sick." In verse 14, the term literally means "to be weak" and is used in the New Testament for physical illness as well as for weakness of faith or conscience (see Acts 20:35; Rom. 6:19; 14:1; 1 Cor. 8:9-12). Thus, it would seem that James could have been referring to either sicknesses of the body or sicknesses of the spirit. This reminds us that there are times when physical illness might have a spiritual cause, namely, sin. The remark in James 5:15 about forgiveness of sin might be a reference to an illness brought on by personal sin in the believer's life. In this case, the writer assured the sick that the prayer of faith would result in forgiveness and spiritual restoration. Of course, the use of the word "if" in this verse implies that sometimes illness is not the result of personal sin. Irrespective of the details, God is not limited as to the methods He may employ in restoring ailing believers. Also, with regard to prayer, God answers only according to His will. Sometimes God's will does not include physical healing (see 2 Cor. 12:7-9).

C. Praying Earnestly and Effectively: vss. 16-18

Therefore confess your sins to each other and pray for each other so that you may be healed. The prayer of a righteous man is powerful and effective. Elijah was a man just like us. He prayed earnestly that it would not rain, and it did not rain on the land for three and a half years. Again he prayed, and the heavens gave rain, and the earth produced its crops.

All of us need some kind of healing, whether physical, spiritual, or emotional; and we should be able to turn to other believers for help. This includes confessing our sins to each other as well as praying for each other (Jas. 5:16). The acknowledgment of sins among believers helps to promote wellness and wholeness of individuals and relationships. In particular, believers draw their fellow Christians toward a deeper, more mature walk with the Savior. Members of the faith community also deepen their commitment to one another in the bonds of Christian love. This verse does not signify a call for indiscriminate airing of a believer's every shortcoming. The Spirit should always be given complete charge over the matter of conviction and confession of sin. He will lead the believer in the knowledge of which sins to confess in private prayer and which to confess in the company of other believers.

In every case, whether public or private, one truth is clear, namely, that prayer is a powerful and effective means of accomplishing the will of God. The Lord especially uses the earnest prayer of righteous believers (those who are characterized by virtue and integrity) to produce wonderful results in the lives of His people. As was his practice, James offered an illustration to support his point. This time it was Elijah, an Old Testament prophet with the same human frailties that we have. This man, who was just like us, prayed earnestly that no rain would fall, and none fell for three and a half years (vs. 17; see Luke 4:25). Then, when he prayed again, rain fell from the skies and made the crops grow (Jas. 5:18; see 1 Kings 17:1; 18:41-46). Because prayer is our most powerful tool, it should be our first option in responding to a crisis, not a last resort. It only makes sense to rely on God's power, which is infinitely greater than our own.

II. RESTORING WANDERING BELIEVERS: JAMES 5:19-20

My brothers, if one of you should wander from the truth and someone should bring him back, remember this: Whoever turns a sinner from the error of his way will save him from death and cover over a multitude of sins.

The author's final appeal to his readers concerned individuals who had wandered from the way of truth. Some think James 5:19 refers to those who claimed to be Christians but whose faith was spurious (see Heb. 6:4-6; 2 Pet. 2:20-22). Others think James 5:19 is dealing with genuine believers who have strayed into sinful patterns. In either case, when anyone belonging to a congregation wanders from the path of moral rectitude, it is the duty of God's people to seek out the wayward and bring them back into the fellowship—through prayer, counseling, friendship, or whatever it takes (Jas. 5:19). When sinners are turned back from their error-prone ways, it means they have been rescued from the path of destruction.

For some, the "death" (vs. 20) being averted is eternal separation from God (see Rev. 21:8). For others, James 5:20 denotes avoiding the experience of premature physical death (see 1 Cor. 11:29-32; 1 John 5:16). When the wayward are spiritually restored, it signifies the forgiveness of many sins (Jas. 5:20). Often, the process includes godly sorrow that leads to repentance and salvation (2 Cor. 7:10). Most likely, there will also be the confession of sin, which brings about divine pardon and cleansing from all unrighteousness (1 John 1:9). James provided his readers with the valuable instruction necessary for progress on the road to spiritual restoration and growth. Whether the issue was taming the tongue or persevering in persecution, all that a believer needed to grow in holiness was found in the One who answered the prayers of the faithful.

Discussion Questions

1. Why is prayer appropriate in times of trouble?
2. Why are ailing believers encouraged to summon the elders of the church?
3. What is the purpose of anointing an ailing believer with oil in the name of the Lord?
4. In what way is Elijah the prophet an example of someone who prayed humbly and earnestly?
5. How can concerned believers restore the wayward to the truth?

Contemporary Application

Prayer works. Anyone who prays regularly would agree. It is our strongest communication link with the God who created us. It is a powerful means for giving voice to our faith. Most important of all, God can use our prayers to change our world. Clearly, our petitions matter.

Hands, feet, back, and pocketbook—these are some of the means that come to mind when we think of helping our fellow Christians. They enable us to comfort, carry, accompany, and contribute. They are solid, tangible realities. Beside them, the ethereal act of prayer can seem like little more than nice words spoken more to comfort the person doing the petitioning than to actually accomplish anything tangible. But James 5:16 points out that a committed believer's prayer can produce powerful results. Powerful is hardly the way to describe nice words whose sole purpose is to offer psychological comfort to those who pray them. No, prayer changes things. Instead of being the last thing we do—when all other avenues are exhausted—it should be the first thing we do in every situation.

Prayer can be power-producing and effective in more ways than we might realize at first. For instance, while prayer may not change our circumstances, it can indeed alter our response to those circumstances. On the other hand, prayer very well may change our circumstances. As we pray, our lives will reflect our prayerful hearts. We will find ourselves more in tune with the needs of others and better able to meet them because of our deeper walk with God. Our spiritual maturity will enrich our own lives even as it extends to those to whom we minister, bearing fruit in many ways as it touches many lives.